ISBN 978-1-5280-9575-4
PIBN 11010798

English
Français
Deutsche
Italiano
Español
Português

www.forgottenbooks.com

Mythology Photography **Fiction**
Fishing Christianity **Art** Cooking
Essays Buddhism Freemasonry
Medicine **Biology** Music **Ancient
Egypt** Evolution Carpentry Physics
Dance Geology **Mathematics** Fitness
Shakespeare **Folklore** Yoga Marketing
Confidence Immortality Biographies
Poetry **Psychology** Witchcraft
Electronics Chemistry History **Law**
Accounting **Philosophy** Anthropology
Alchemy Drama Quantum Mechanics
Atheism Sexual Health **Ancient History**
Entrepreneurship Languages Sport
Paleontology Needlework Islam
Metaphysics Investment Archaeology
Parenting Statistics Criminology
Motivational

OF THE

GENERAL ASSEMBLY

OF THE

COMMONWEALTH OF KENTUCKY,

PASSED AT THE

ADJOURNED (JANUARY, 1869) SESSION OF THE GENERAL ASSEM-
BLY, WHICH WAS BEGUN AND HELD IN THE CITY
OF FRANKFORT ON MONDAY, THE SEC-
OND DAY OF DECEMBER, 1867.

PUBLISHED BY AUTHORITY.

FRANKFORT, KY.:
PRINTED AT THE KENTUCKY YEOMAN OFFICE.
S. I. M. MAJOR, PUBLIC PRINTER.
1869.

CONTENTS.

PUBLIC ACTS

PASSED AT ADJOURNED JANUARY SESSION, 1869.

CONTENTS.

CONTENTS.

CONTENTS.

CONTENTS.

CONTENTS.

RESOLUTIONS.

LOCAL AND·PRIVATE ACTS.

CONTENTS.

PAGE.

CONTENTS.

PAGE.

CONTENTS.

CONTENTS.

CONTENTS.

PUBLIC ACTS

OF

THE STATE OF KENTUCKY,

PASSED AT THE ADJOURNED SESSION OF THE
GENERAL ASSEMBLY, WHICH WAS BEGUN
AND HELD IN THE CITY OF FRANK-
FORT ON MONDAY, THE SECOND
DAY OF DECEMBER, 1867.

J. W. STEVENSON, *Governor.*

WM. JOHNSON, *Lieut. Governor and Speaker of the Senate.*

JOHN T. BUNCH, *Speaker of the House of Reps.*

S. B. CHURCHILL, *Secretary of State.*

JOHN RODMAN, *Attorney General.*

CHAPTER 1239.

AN ACT to amend an act to authorize the General Council of Louisville to increase the salary of the Judge of the Louisville Chancery Court, and of the Court of Common Pleas of Jefferson county, approved March 9, 1868.

Be it enacted by the General Assembly of the Commonwealth of Kentucky:

§ 1. That all the provisions of an act entitled "An act to authorize the general council of Louisville to increase the salary of the judge of the Louisville chancery and of the court of common pleas of Jefferson county," approved March 9, 1868, shall likewise apply to the judge of the Jefferson circuit court; and said general council are hereby authorized to appropriate the same sum to him which they are by said act authorized to appropriate to each of said other two judges.

§ 2. This act shall take effect from its passage.

1869.

City council of Louisville granted authority to increase salaries of judges.

JOHN T. BUNCH,
Speaker of the House of Representatives.
WM. JOHNSON,
Speaker of the Senate.

Approved January 12, 1869.
J. W. STEVENSON,
Governor of Kentucky.

By the Governor:
S. B. CHURCHILL, *Secretary of State.*

CHAPTER 1240.

AN ACT changing the time of holding the Quarterly Courts and Courts of Justices of the Peace for Taylor County.

Be it enacted by the General Assembly of the Commonwealth of Kentucky:

§ 1. That the times of holding the quarterly courts and courts of justices of the peace for Taylor county shall be held in the months of February, May, August, and November, instead of January, April, July, and October, as now fixed by law; said courts to be held on the respective days of said months of February, May, August, and November as heretofore fixed; and all processes returnable to the January term of said courts shall be made returnable and stand for trial at the February term.

§ 2. This act to take effect from its passage.

Approved January 14, 1869.

Time of holding quarterly and justices' courts changed in Taylor county.

CHAPTER 1241.

AN ACT to change the line dividing Simpson and Logan Counties.

Be it enacted by the General Assembly of the Commonwealth of Kentucky:

§ 1. That the line dividing Simpson and Logan county be so altered and changed as to begin and run thus, viz: Beginning at —— Turner's, the present northwest corner of Simpson county, and running thence due west to the east edge of the Memphis Branch of the Louisville and Nashville railroad, and with said edge of said road to the South Union Depot, and thence to the present corner of Logan and Simpson, in David Low's yard, but so running as to include the residence of John McCutchen in Simpson county; thence to Leland Pierce's residence, leaving the same in Logan county; thence to Benjamin Fresh's residence, leaving the same in said county; thence to a red oak at B. D. Taylor's horse-lot gate, and west of his residence; thence to the Phelps House northwest, but near Middleton; thence to John W. Baker's residence, including same in Simpson county; thence to John Rutherford's residence, and including him in same county, and thence to Jo. Pennington's well, in his yard, and thence to the Tennessee State line at the residence of Dr. Press McClenden, but leaving said residence in Logan county; and all that territory heretofore belonging to Logan county, lying east of said line, is hereby added to Simpson county.

§ 2. That the persons and property embraced within the limits of said change shall continue to remain bound, in the same way, and to the same extent, for the debt and interest thereon owing by Logan county on account of subscribing stock to the Memphis Branch of the Louisville

Dividing line of Simpson & Logan counties changed.

and Nashville railroad company; and said obligation to pay their due proportion thereof shall continue as if this act had never passed; and in the event that it shall become necessary for the county court of Logan county to levy and collect taxes to pay off said debt, or any part thereof, then the same rates of taxation which are levied and collected in Logan county for said purpose shall be collected by the sheriff of Simpson county off of the persons and property embraced in the limits of said change, and made subject to taxation for said purpose by law; and said collection in Simpson county shall be based upon the real and personal estate, including the valuation under the equalization law, as fixed by the valuation under the assessment for State revenue purposes; and the State shall pay over such taxes to the Logan county court or its authorized agent; and the bond taken of the sheriff of Simpson county for the security, collection, and payment of county and State taxes shall be deemed to embrace this special tax; and the sheriff of Simpson shall, in the collection of said special tax, have all the rights and powers which are conferred on him by law in collecting the State revenue; and he shall proceed to collect said taxes when the county court of Logan county shall furnish him with the order of levy and collection.

§ 3. That John A. Finn and Geo. B. Starks, of Simpson county, and Geo. R. Beall and Isaac G. Mason, of Logan county, be, and are hereby, appointed commissioners to run out and mark the line indicated in section first of this act; and they will proceed to perform their duty on or before the 1st day of May, 1869; and they will report their proceedings to their respective county courts, and the same shall be spread upon the records of each county; and the Simpson county court shall allow and pay said commissioners reasonable compensation.

§ 4. This act shall take effect on and after the day of its passage.

Approved January 14, 1869.

———

CHAPTER 1243.

AN ACT to provide for the payment of certain claims for work and labor done, materials furnished, and other expenses incurred on the Green and Barren and Kentucky rivers.

WHEREAS, Certain claims against the State, on account of work and labor done, and materials furnished, and expenses incurred on the Green and Barren and Kentucky river lines of navigation, have been referred to the Committee on Expenditures of the Board of Internal Improvement for an investigation of the same, and to take proof as to the justness and correctness thereof; and whereas, after a full and fair investigation of said claims, the committee reported that they were due from the Green and Barren river line of navigation the following sums: To William Brown, sr., the sum of twenty-eight hundred and four dollars and fifty-four cents ($2,804 54); to George W. Terry, the sum of fourteen hundred and eighty-two dollars and forty-eight cents ($1,482 48); to John V. Sprowle, the sum of thirty-one hundred and twenty-two dollars and ninety-one cents ($3,122 91); and from the Kentucky river line of navigation—to Samuel Steele, the sum of seventeen hundred and twenty four dollars and fifty-five cents ($1,724 55)—all of which are unpaid; and said debts were contracted and incurred prior to the year 1867; and whereas, it appears from a report of the Committee on Expenditures of the Board of Internal Improvement, that there is a large amount of claims for work and labor done, materials furnished, and expenses incurred, presented by persons against the State for the year 1867, on account of the Kentucky river line of navigation, and which are still unpaid; therefore,

Be it enacted by the General Assembly of the Commonwealth of Kentucky:

§ 1. That the Auditor be, and he is hereby, directed to draw his warrant on the Treasurer in favor of William Brown, sr., for the sum of twenty-eight hundred and four dollars and fifty-four cents ($2,804 54); and in favor of George W. Terry, for the sum of fourteen hundred and eighty-two dollars and forty-eight cents ($1,482 48); and in favor of John V. Sprowle, for the sum of thirty-one hundred and twenty-two dollars and ninety-one cents ($3,122 9:); and in favor of Samuel Steele, for the sum of seventeen hundred and twenty-four dollars and fifty-five cents ($1,724 55); and also in favor of the following persons for work and labor done, and materials furnished, and expenses incurred during the year 1867, on the Kentucky river line of navigation, viz: J. H. Dennis, for the sum of thirty-eight hundred and forty-four dollars and thirty-seven cents ($3,844 37); G. W. Cubbage, for the sum of seven hundred and ninety-five dollars and eighty-three cents ($795 83); Louisville Rolling Mill, one hundred and ninety-seven dollars and eighty-one cents ($197 81); W. S Gwinn, for the sum of three hundred and sixty-four dollars and ninety two cents ($364 92); Lewis Dedrick, for the sum of one hundred and ninety-five dollars and ninety-two cents ($195 92); Joel Payne, for the sum of three hundred and sixty-three dollars ($363); George W. Guthrie, for the sum of ten dollars and eighty-five cents ($10 85); T. J. Hardin, for the sum of eleven dollars and five cents ($11 05); William Brisbin, for the sum of four dollars and twenty-five cents ($4 25); J. M. Rowlett, for the sum of nineteen dollars ($19); J. L. Booth, for the sum of two dollars and fifty cents ($2 50); Harkins & Walston, for the sum of six hundred and fifty-six dollars and eighty cents ($656 80); Geo. Wells, for the sum of fifteen hundred and ninety-six dollars and three cents ($1,596 03); Thomas Heffner, for the sum of seven dollars and seventy cents ($7 70); Louisville and Frankfort railroad, for the sum of two dollars and five cents ($2 05); Berryman & Brothers, for the sum of thirty-six dollars and twenty cents ($36 20); William Skelton & Co, for the sum of one hundred and seventy-eight dollars and fifty-five cents ($178 55); Reuben Harkins, for the sum of thirty-seven hundred and forty-three dollars and forty-six cents ($3,743 46). J. R. Hardin, for the sum of one hundred and twenty-five dollars ($125); N. B. Carrico, for the sum of seventy-eight dollars and seventy-five cents ($78 75) The said sums to be paid out of any funds in the Treasury not otherwise appropriated.

§ 2. This act to take effect from and after its passage.

Approved January 16, 1869.

CHAPTER 1245.

AN ACT to provide for the change of cases from Courts of Common Pleas to Circuit Courts, and from Circuit Courts to Courts of Common Pleas, in certain cases.

Be it enacted by the General Assembly of the Commonwealth of Kentucky:

§ 1 That hereafter, whenever the judge of the court of common pleas shall be interested in any suit now pending, or which may hereafter be pending in his court, either at law or in equity, as attorney or otherwise, or, from any cause, cannot properly preside, it shall be the duty of the court to order the clerk of said court, in the county where the suit is pending, to transfer said case to the circuit court of said county, where it shall be docketed, and progress as other suits in circuit courts.

Suit to be removed from court of common pleas to circuit court when the judge is interested therein.

§ 2. That hereafter, whenever the judge of any circuit court shall be interested in any suit pending in his court, as attorney or otherwise, that the court shall order the clerk of said court to transfer the case to the court of common pleas for said county, provided there is a court of common pleas in said county, where it shall be docketed, and progress as other suits in said court.

When judge of circuit court interested, suit to be transferred to court common pleas.

§ 3. This act to take effect from and after its passage.

Approved January 18, 1869.

1869.   CHAPTER 1247.

AN ACT to amend chapter 61 of the Revised Statutes, title "Laws."

Be it enacted by the General Assembly of the Commonwealth of Kentucky:

Justices to file affidavit in county court when books of predecessor are lost, & court to certify to the Secretary.

§ 1. That whenever any justice of the peace shall file an affidavit in the county court that he has demanded of his predecessor in office the books now by law furnished to justices of the peace, and has failed to receive them of such predecessor, that said books are lost or destroyed without his connivance or fault, the said court shall certify the same to the Secretary of State, who, at the time the laws are distributed, shall furnish any such books, if the State has them for distribution.

§ 2. That if any justice of the peace, upon the expiration of his office, shall fail to return any law book furnished him by law, he and his securities shall be liable on his official bond for the value of the same; and the county court shall enforce such liability by rule.

§ 3. This act shall take effect from its passage.

Approved January 20, 1869.

———

CHAPTER 1252.

AN ACT to re-enact and continue in force the first and second sections of "An act to amend section 3 of article 6, chapter 27, of the Revised Statutes," approved February 22d, 1865.

Be it enacted by the General Assembly of the Commonwealth of Kentucky:

The first and second sections of an act to amend sec. 3 of art. 6, chap. 27, Rev. Stat., re-enacted.

§ 1. That the first and second sections of "An act to amend section 3 of article 6, chapter 27, of the Revised Statutes," approved February 22d, 1865 (Myers' Supplement, page 131), be, and the same is hereby, re enacted and continued in force, with the same effect in all respects as if the same had not been limited to two years, as provided in the third section of said act: *Provided,* That no volume of reports of the decisions of the Court of Appeals hereafter to be printed shall contain less than seven hundred pages.

§ 2. That this act shall take effect from and after its passage.

Approved January 20th, 1869.

CHAPTER 1275.

AN ACT for the benefit of the Common School System.

Be it enacted by the General Assembly of the Commonwealth of Kentucky:

§ 1. That it shall be the duty of the sheriffs and other officers, conducting the next annual election, to be held on the first Monday in August next, to open a poll in the various precincts in their respective counties, and take the sense of the qualified voters of this Commonwealth upon the propriety and expediency of imposing an additional tax of fifteen cents on each one hundred dollars' worth of property in the State, for the purpose of increasing the Common School Fund of Kentucky: *Provided,* That the said additional tax, and all taxes for common school purposes provided for by existing laws, shall be levied and collected only upon the property of white persons, and the fund realized under the provisions of this act, or any act supplemental hereto, or amendatory hereof, and all moneys hereafter raised for common school purposes under the laws now in force, shall be expended for the education of white children exclusively.

Tax to be collected from white persons only.

§ 2. That it shall be the duty of the proper officers conducting said election to propound distinctly to each voter the question: "Are you for or against levying an additional tax of fifteen cents on each one hundred dollars' worth of property to increase the Common School Fund?" If said voter shall answer in the affirmative, it shall be the duty of the clerk of the election to record his vote in favor of levying the tax for the purposes aforesaid. If he shall answer in the negative, it shall be the duty of said clerk to record his vote against it.

Question asked each voter,

§ 3. That it shall be the duty of the sheriffs and other returning officers to make out a correct list of the vote required to be taken under the provisions of this act; and it shall be the duty of the county judges and county clerks of the several counties to compare and certify said lists of their respective counties; and said county clerks shall cause the same to be delivered to the Secretary of State within sixty days after the date of the said election; and upon a failure of any one of them to do so, he shall be fined in the sum of two hundred dollars, to be recovered against him as other fines are recovered under existing laws regulating elections in this State.

List of vote to be made out, certified by county judges, and to be delivered to Secretary of State.

Penalty for failure to deliver lists.

§ 4. If it shall appear that a majority of the votes cast under the provisions of this act are cast in the affirmative, it shall be the duty of the Secretary of State to report to the General Assembly, within five days after its next convening after the said election, a statement of the vote directed to be taken as so cast, when it shall be the duty of

Secretary to report to General Assembly.

1869.

the Legislature to adopt such measures as may be necessary to carry out the purposes of this act.

Act to be printed, and 15 copies to be sent to each member, to county courts, &c.

§ 5. That it shall be the duty of the Public Printer to print and deliver to the Secretary of State fifteen hundred copies of this act; and it shall be the duty of said Secretary of State to forward fifteen copies of the same for each representative district of the Lower House of the Legislature, to the various clerks of the county courts, in proportion to the representation, by the first of July preceding the said election; and the said clerks are required by this act to deliver said copies to the sheriffs of their respective counties, and to take a receipt therefor; and it shall be the duty of said sheriffs to put one copy of this act at the place of holding elections in each election precinct in their respective counties, at least twenty days before the election at which the vote mentioned under this act is to be taken.

§ 6. That any person, other than a qualified voter of this State, who shall vote for or against the propositions in this act mentioned, shall be subject to all the fines and penalties now in force under the existing laws regulating elections.

Superintendent of Public Instruction to prepare new code of laws for better management of the common school system of Kentucky.

§ 7. Should it be found that a majority of the votes cast at the said election, under the provisions of this act, are in favor of levying the proposed additional tax, the Superintendent of Public Instruction, as soon as the fact is ascertained, shall proceed to prepare a revised or remodeled code of laws for the better organization and management of the Common School System of Kentucky, by the next meeting of the General Assembly; and, to aid him in this work, he may, with the counsel and advice of the other members of the Board of Education, the Attorney General, and Secretary of State, provide himself with the means and facilities for consulting the most experienced and competent men of the State, with such other authorities as may be thought necessary, in order to the highest improvement of the system.

Approved January 22, 1869.

CHAPTER 1277.

AN ACT to amend section 3, article 7, chapter 55, of the Revised Statutes.

Be it enacted by the General Assembly of the Commonwealth of Kentucky:

Trustees of jury fund allowed five per cent. of funds that come in their hands.

§ 1. That the trustees of the jury fund in the several counties of this Commonwealth shall hereafter be allowed a commission of five per centum upon all sums that come into their hands, and they shall be credited with the said commission in their settlements with the courts

§ 2. This act to take effect from its passage.

Approved January 22, 1869.

CHAPTER 1283.

AN ACT to amend article 4, chapter 55, of Revised Statutes, entitled "Mode of summoning Petit Jurors—Jury Commissioners."

Be it enacted by the General Assembly of the Commonwealth of Kentucky:

§ 1. That the jury commissioners shall draw from the box thirty names instead of twenty-four, and record the same, one by one, as drawn, which shall be certified and signed by them, directed to the circuit judge, and indorsed "a list of the standing jury;" they shall dispose of the remaining seventy names as prescribed by law.

Jury commissioners to draw 30 names instead of 24.

§ 2. The clerk shall furnish the sheriff the list of the thirty names, who shall be summoned by the sheriff as prescribed by law.

§ 3. Twenty-four shall be selected from the thirty so summoned in the order in which their names appear upon said list, who shall compose the regular pannel.

§ 4. No person shall be allowed to serve as a petit juryman more than one term in any one year, and it shall be good cause of challenge to any juror that he has so served.

§ 5. The provisions of this act shall apply to the Louisville city court, and all courts of common pleas and circuit courts in this Commonwealth.

§ 6. This act shall take effect from its passage.

Approved January 22, 1869.

CHAPTER 1284.

AN ACT to repeal so much of section 14, chapter 67, title "Mills," of Revised Statutes, as applies to the town of Salyersville, in Magoffin county.

Be it enacted by the General Assembly of the Commonwealth of Kentucky:

§ 1. That section 14, chapter 67, title "Mills," of Revised Statutes, be repealed, so far as the same applies to the town of Salyersville, Magoffin county.

Stant. Rev Stat., vol. 2, p. 183.

§ 2. This act to take effect from its passage.

Approved January 22, 1869.

1869.

CHAPTER 1286.

AN ACT to amend section 3 of article 2 of chapter 32 of Revised Statutes.

Be it enacted by the General Assembly of the Commonwealth of Kentucky:

§ 1. That section 3 of article 2 of chapter 32 of Revised Statutes be, and the same is hereby, so amended as to authorize the county court to change the districts for the election of justices of the peace and constables, and to change election precincts and places of voting at any regular term thereof, not less than sixty days next before the time of holding any regular election; but this act shall in no other particular interfere with the manner of making such changes.

§ 2. This act to be in force from and after its passage.

Approved January 22, 1869.

CHAPTER 1304.

AN ACT to repeal an act, entitled "An act to change the time of holding the Justices' of the Peace Courts in Washington County," approved 9th of March, 1868, and to fix the term of holding the same.

Be it enacted by the General Assembly of the Commonwealth of Kentucky:

Washington county.

§ 1. That an act, entitled "An act to change the time of holding the justices' of the peace courts in Washington county," approved 9th March, 1868, be, and the same is hereby, repealed; and that said courts shall hereafter be held in the months of January, April, July, and October of each year, as heretofore fixed by law.

§ 2. This act shall take effect from its passage.

Approved January 26, 1869.

CHAPTER 1317.

AN ACT to re-enact "An act to fix the fees of sheriffs," approved February 4th, 1865.

Be it enacted by the General Assembly of the Commonwealth of Kentucky:

Myers' Supplement. p. 468.

§ 1. That an act, entitled "An act to fix the fees of sheriffs," approved February 4th, 1865, be, and the same is hereby, re-enacted, and shall continue in force two years from and after its passage.

§ 2. This act to take effect from its passage.

Approved January 26, 1869.

CHAPTER 1319.

AN ACT to amend the Penal and Criminal Laws of this State.

Be it enacted by the General Assembly of the Commonwealth of Kentucky:

§ 1. That the criminal and penal laws of this State be so amended, that it shall be unlawful for any person to cut out of any book, newspaper, periodical, or any literary work or production whatever, any leaf, picture, painting, or engraving, or in any other manner mutilate, destroy, or injure any such book, newspaper, periodical, or any other literary work or production whatever, kept in any public library in this Commonwealth.

§ 2. That any person violating the provisions of this law shall be fined in any sum not less than twenty-five dollars nor no more than one hundred dollars, to be recovered by indictment in the criminal courts of this Commonwealth, or in any circuit court having penal and criminal jurisdiction; twenty per cent. of said fines to be received by the Commonwealth's Attorney, and the remainder to go into the common school fund of this State.

§ 3. This act to take effect from its passage.

Approved January 26, 1869.

Misdemeanor to injure any painting, book, &c, in an) public library in this Commonwealth.

Penalty.

CHAPTER 1324.

AN ACT for changing the days of Quarterly Court in Webster County.

Be it enacted by the General Assembly of the Commonwealth of Kentucky:

§ 1. That hereafter the quarterly court for Webster county shall be held on the first Monday in February, May, August, and November of each year, and may continue in session as many days as the business of said court may require.

§ 2. This act shall take effect from its passage.

Approved January 26, 1869.

Time of holding Webster quarterly court changed.

CHAPTER 1325.

AN ACT to amend an act, entitled "An act to amend the revenue laws of this Commonwealth," approved February 28, 1862.

Be it enacted by the General Assembly of the Commonwealth of Kentucky:

§ 1. That so much of an act, entitled "An act to amend the revenue laws of this Commonwealth," approved February 28, 1862, contained in section eight, as reads, "and that he has not aided or abetted the rebellion, and is

1869.   opposed to the overthrow of the Union," be, and the same is hereby, repealed.

§ 2. This act shall take effect from its passage.

Approved January 26, 1869.

CHAPTER 1331.

AN ACT to change the time of holding the County and Quarterly Courts of Pike County.

Be it enacted by the General Assembly of the Commonwealth of Kentucky:.

Time of holding quarterly court & county court of Pike county changed

§ 1. That from and after the passage of this act the county court of Pike county shall commence on the fourth Monday of each month, and that the quarterly court of said county shall commence on the Tuesday next succeeding the fourth Monday in the months of March, June, September, and December of each year.

§ 2. That all process on recognizances now in the hands of the officers shall be returned to the courts as fixed by the above change.

§ 3. This act shall be in force from and after its passage.

Approved January 27, 1869.

CHAPTER 1332.

AN ACT to regulate the time of holding County and Quarterly Courts in Jackson County.

Be it enacted by the General Assembly of the Commonwealth of Kentucky:

Time of holding county court of Jackson county changed.

§ 1. That hereafter the county courts of Jackson county shall begin and be holden on the first Monday in each month, and continue so long as the business may require.

Time of holding quarterly court of Jackson county changed.

§ 2. That the quarterly courts of said county shall begin and be holden on the Tuesdays after the first Monday in the months of March, June, September, and December, and shall continue from day to day so long as the business of the courts may require.

§ 3. That all acts or parts of acts coming in conflict with the provisions of this act are hereby repealed.

§ 4. This act shall take effect and be in force sixty (60) days after its passage.

Approved January 27, 1869.

CHAPTER 1334.

AN ACT to change the times of holding the Washington Quarterly Courts.

Be it enacted by the General Assembly of the Commonwealth of Kentucky:

§ 1. That the Washington quarterly court shall hereafter be held on the third Mondays in January, April, July, and October of each year, and at each time may continue as many days as the business may require.

§ 2. This act shall take effect from its passage.

Approved January 27, 1869.

Time of holding Washington quarterly court changed.

CHAPTER 1335.

AN ACT changing the time of holding the Quarterly Courts of Mason County.

Be it enacted by the General Assembly of the Commonwealth of Kentucky:

§ 1. That, from and after the passage of this act, the judge of the Mason county court shall commence the quarterly terms of said court on the Tuesday next following the second Monday of March, June, September, and December, instead of the second Monday, as now fixed by law.

§ 2. This act shall take effect from and after its passage.

Approved January 27, 1869.

Time of holding Mason quarterly court changed.

CHAPTER 1343.

AN ACT to amend an act, entitled "An act fixing the time for holding the Circuit, Criminal, and Equity Courts of this Commonwealth," approved March 9, 1868.

Be it enacted by the General Assembly of the Commonwealth of Kentucky:

§ 1. That, from and after the first day of March, 1869, the circuit courts for the county of Henderson, in the 3d judicial district, shall be held as follows: On the first Mondays in March and September of each year, each term continuing thirty (30) judicial days.

§ 2. This act shall take effect from its passage.

Approved January 27, 1869.

Henderson circuit court.

1869.

CHAPTER 1346.

AN ACT to change the time of holding the civil terms of the Police Court of Elizabethtown.

Be it enacted by the General Assembly of the Commonwealth of Kentucky:

Time of holding police court of Elizabethtown changed.

§ 1. That hereafter the judge of the police court of Elizabethtown shall hold his court for the trial of civil actions on the last Wednesday in February, May, August, and November.

§ 2. This act shall take effect from its passage.

Approved January 27, 1869.

CHAPTER 1350.

AN ACT to further provide for the collection of the Revenue Tax.

Be it enacted by the General Assembly of the Commonwealth of Kentucky:

Governor to appoint collector of revenue where there is no sheriff.

§ 1. That the Governor of Kentucky be, and he is hereby, authorized and empowered to appoint a collector of the revenue tax due the Commonwealth in each county in this State where there is no sheriff, and to pay him such compensation for his services as may be agreed upon between them: *Provided,* That the sum to be paid shall not exceed fifteen per cent. on the whole amount collected.

Collector to take oath and give bond.

§ 2. The collector provided for in the first section of this act, before entering upon the discharge of the duties of his office, shall go before the county court of the county in which he resides, and execute bond, with good and sufficient security, to be approved by the court, conditioned as sheriff's bonds now are by law; and he shall also take an oath for the faithful discharge of the duties imposed upon him by the provisions of this act.

Same power as sheriff.

§ 3. When the collector provided for by the first section of this act shall comply with the terms and conditions stipulated in the second section, he shall then be invested with all the power and authority that the sheriffs of this Commonwealth are now by law vested with in the collection of the revenue tax: *Provided, however,* That so soon as a sheriff shall be qualified and give bond in such county, after the said collector of revenue has been so appointed, the duties and powers of said collector of revenue so appointed by the Governor shall cease, and he shall at once deliver to the sheriff a list of the revenue and the persons from whom he has collected the same in such county. And it shall be the duty of said sheriff to proceed to collect the balance and account for the same in the same manner, and be responsible there-

When sheriff qualified, collector to resign.

for on his bond, as if the entire list of revenue tax-payers and property had come to his hands, and no revenue collector had been appointed: *And provided further*, That the said collector of revenue so to be appointed, and his securities on his bond, shall and may be proceeded against for any dereliction in office, or failure to comply with his duties, and shall be liable to the same pains and penalties that are provided against sheriffs for similar failures.

§ 4. This act shall take effect from its passage.

Approved January 28, 1869.

Liability of bond. *(margin note)*

CHAPTER 1351.

AN ACT to provide for the punishment of false swearing and subornation of perjury in certain cases.

Be it enacted by the General Assembly of the Commonwealth of Kentucky:

§ 1. That if any person shall, within this Commonwealth, willfully and knowingly swear or affirm, depose or give in evidence, that which is untrue and false, in any case of a contested election for the office of Senator or Representative from this State in the Congress of the United States, or before any committee appointed by the Congress of the United States, or either branch thereof, for the purpose of inquiring into the qualifications or eligibility of any person returned as elected from this State to the Senate or House of Representatives of the United States; or shall willfully and knowingly state that which is untrue and false in any affidavit or deposition used, or intended to be used, before the Congress of the United States, or either branch thereof, or any committee appointed thereby, touching or relating to the qualifications or eligibility of any person returned as elected from this State to the Senate or House of Representatives of the United States, the person so offending shall, upon conviction, be confined in the penitentiary for a period of not less than two nor more than six years, and be forever thereafter disqualified from giving evidence in any judicial proceeding, and from being a witness in any case or matter whatever.

(margin note: Perjury in contested election cases, in deposition, to be used before Congress.)

(margin note: Penalty.)

§ 2. That if any person shall unlawfully and corruptly cause or procure another, by any means whatever, to commit the offense or offenses described in the preceding section, he shall be guilty of subornation of perjury, and, upon conviction thereof, shall be subject to the same punishment and disqualifications therein provided.

§ 3. That this act shall take effect from and after its passage.

Approved January 29, 1869.

1869.

AN ACT to amend an act approved 9th of March, 1868, entitled "An act to fix the time for holding the Circuit, Criminal, and Equity Courts in this Commonwealth."

Be it enacted by the General Assembly of the Commonwealth of Kentucky:

§ 1. That an act approved 9th of March, 1868, entitled "An act fixing the time for holding the circuit, criminal, and equity courts of this Commonwealth," be amended as follows: There shall be held in the county of Clark, in the tenth (10th) judicial district, two (2) terms, of twelve (12) juridical days each, commencing on the first Mondays in May and November. In the county of Fayette the June term shall begin on the second Monday in June, and continue twelve (12) juridical days, and said term, and the June term in the county of Madison, and July term in the county of Bourbon, shall be for the trial of criminal, penal, and equitable proceedings and actions.

§ 2. This act shall take effect from its passage.

Approved January 29, 1869.

See Public Acts 1868, p. 60.

AN ACT for the benefit of the Institution for the Education of Idiots and Feeble-minded Children.

Be it enacted by the General Assembly of the Commonwealth of Kentucky:

§ 1. That the sum of forty thousand dollars ($40,000) be, and are hereby, appropriated, out of the Treasury, for the benefit of the Institution for the Education of Idiots and Feeble-minded Children, to be devoted to the following purposes, to-wit: To the building of corridors, beginning at the present building, running to a wing, and for the erection of a wing, twenty-eight thousand dollars ($28 000). To the necessary excavation under the present building, and the new building, so as to have basement room under the same, thirty-five hundred dollars ($3,500). To building a new furnace, to heat the rooms in said building, furnishing boiler, engine, washing machine, &c., five thousand dollars ($5,000). To furnish the building, erect a barn, &c., thirty-five hundred dollars ($3.500): *Provided,* That not more than one thousand dollars ($1,000) of said sum shall be applied to the erection of a barn.

§ 2. That the Commissioners of said Institution shall employ an architect to furnish a suitable plan, upon which to make said improvements, and to superintend their erection; but before the plan shall be executed, it shall be laid before the Governor by the Commissioners, and approved by him. The Commissioners shall, before they let out said work, advertise the same for sealed proposals for thirty days, in the newspapers at Frankfort, Louisville, and Lexington, as well as the payments to be made therefor, and shall make the contract with the lowest and best bidder, who shall, before he begins said work, execute a bond, with good security, in the penalty of fifty thousand dollars, to the Commonwealth of Kentucky, conditioned for the faithful performance of his contract. And six thousand dollars ($6,000) per annum are appropriated to pay officers, teachers, and attendants, instead of five thousand dollars ($5,000), as now provided by law: *Provided*, That the additional one thousand dollars ($1,000) hereby provided for shall be applied exclusively to procuring additional teachers and assistants.

§ 3. This act shall take effect from and after its passage.

Approved February 1, 1869.

1869.

CHAPTER 1368.
AN ACT to Improve the Navigation of Licking River.

Be it enacted by the General Assembly of the Commonwealth of Kentucky:

§ 1. That the sum of seventy-five thousand dollars ($75,000) be, and the same are hereby, appropriated, out of any money in the Treasury not otherwise appropriated, for the purpose of removing the mill dams and other obstructions to the navigation of the Licking river, from Salyersville, in Magoffin county, to the mouth of said river. *Amount appropriated.*

§ 2. That M. D. Martin, of Harrison county, Moses Kirk, of Fleming, and William Mynhier, of Morgan, any two of whom may act, are appointed commissioners, and are authorized to go upon said river, from its mouth to said Salyersville, and examine the obstructions which may exist to the free and safe navigation of said river between said points; and whenever, in their judgment, any dam, rock, or other obstruction, exists, and ought to be removed, they shall proceed, in the manner hereafter described, to remove said obstruction or obstructions from said river. *Commissioners*

§ 3. The said commissioners may negotiate with the owner or owners of any mill-dam or dams, whose interests are to be injuriously affected by the removal thereof, and agree upon the amount of damages, if any, to be paid therefor; but if such agreement cannot be made, the said commissioners may apply to the clerk of the county *Powers of commissioners.*

court of the county in which the mill of such dam or dams may be, and sue out a writ of *ad quod damnum* to condemn the said dam or dams, and have the damages assessed by a fair and impartial jury, as land is condemned and damages assessed for turnpike roads by the laws now in force.

§ 4. The said commissioners shall enter upon the discharge of their duties in the month of May or June next, and shall use diligence in the prosecution of the work. They shall severally receive, for each day that they are actually employed, as compensation, the sum of five dollars; but, before they enter upon their duties, each one, in the county court of the county where he resides, shall enter into bond, with sufficient security, for the faithful performance thereof.

Time when duties of commissioners to commence. Compensation.

§ 5. The Auditor of Public Accounts, upon the requisition of the commissioners, accompanied with a certified copy of their bond, is authorized to draw his warrant upon the Treasurer for such sums of money as may be necessary to pay their contracts and expenses, not exceeding the amount above appropriated; and a vacancy in the commission, from any cause, may be filled by appointment of the Governor.

Auditor to draw warrant, &c.

§ 6. They shall make a full report of all their acts and doings at the next session of the Legislature.

§ 7. This act to take effect from its passage.

Approved February 1, 1869.

CHAPTER 1376.

AN ACT to provide for the erection of Fire-proof Offices at the Seat of Government.

Be it enacted by the General Assembly of the Commonwealth of Kentucky:

§ 1. That the sum of one hundred thousand dollars, or so much thereof as may be necessary, be, and the same is hereby, appropriated, out of any moneys in the Treasury not otherwise appropriated, to be paid in current funds, for the purpose of erecting a building or buildings to contain suitable apartments and fire-proof rooms for the principal public officers of the State, required by law to reside at the Seat of Government.

Amount appropriated for the erection of public offices.

§ 2. That the Governor of this Commonwealth, *ex-officio*, G. W. Craddock, Hugh Rodman, S. I. M. Major, A. W. Dudley, John Mason Brown, Philip Swigert, G. W. Anderson, Norvin Green, and I. T. Martin, are hereby appointed commissioners, whose duty it shall be to employ a competent architect, and first cause to be made a suitable plan and specification of the improvements herein contem-

Commissioners, and their duties.

plated; and when agreed upon by a majority of the said commissioners, it shall be their duty to advertise the fact in the newspapers printed in Frankfort, those printed in Lexington, three of those printed in Louisville, and one in Cincinnati, that sealed proposals will be received for the execution of said work.

§ 3. That the contract or contracts for the work shall be given to the lowest and best bidder or bidders, at the option of the commissioners, after being first advertised, as directed, for the space of one month. The said commissioners, in deciding thereon, shall have due regard to the ability and competency of the bidder to execute the same, and shall take bond of the said bidder, with good security, for the faithful performance of his contract.

Contract for work.

§ 4. That said commissioners shall have the authority and are hereby directed to select a competent architect, whose duty it shall be to give strict and constant attention to the said improvements until complete, and who shall receive such compensation as said commissioners shall allow; and he shall be subject at any time to be removed and to have another employed in his stead.

To select architect.

§ 5. That said commissioners, before they enter upon the duties hereby imposed, shall severally take an oath, before some judge or justice of the peace, that they will faithfully discharge the duties hereby enjoined, and execute a joint bond, with security, payable to the Commonwealth, conditioned that they will faithfully appropriate and account for all money, from time to time, that may come to their hands for said purpose, which bond shall be taken and approved by the Governor, and filed in the office of the Secretary of State; but the provisions of this section shall not apply to the Governor as one of the commissioners, of whom no bond or oath shall be required.

Commissioners to take oath and give bond.

§ 6. It shall be the duty of the Auditor of Public Accounts to draw his warrant upon the Treasurer for such sums of money as the said commissioners may, from time to time, order in the prosecution of said work, not exceeding in all the sum appropriated by this act.

Auditor to draw warrant, &c.

§ 7. The said commissioners may appoint a clerk, whose duty it shall be to keep a correct record of the acts of said commissioners, and a correct account of the moneys expended by them in the prosecution of said work, and shall pay him a reasonable compensation for his services, out of the appropriation made in this act: *Provided,* That said commissioners shall receive no compensation for any services rendered under this act, except that those who reside elsewhere than at Frankfort shall be allowed the same mileage as members of the General Assembly for attendance upon the meetings of the Board, to be paid out of the aforesaid appropriation.

Commissioners to appoint clerk, and his duty.

1869.

§ 8. That should said commissioners, or either of them, refuse to act, or hereafter die or resign, it shall be the duty of the Governor to fill such vacancy.

§ 9. That said buildings shall be made of stone, and as near fire-proof as may be.

Explanation of section one.

§ 10. The appropriation made in the first section of this act shall be held and intended to mean for the erection of a building or buildings to contain suitable apartments and fire-proof rooms for the offices of the State, required by law to be kept at the Seat of Government.

§ 11. This act shall take effect from its passage.

Approved February 2, 1869.

CHAPTER 1395.

AN ACT to change and fix the times of holding the Circuit Courts in the Sixth Judicial District.

Be it enacted by the General Assembly of the Commonwealth of Kentucky:

Time of holding circuit court in Adair.

§ 1. That the regular terms of holding the circuit courts in the sixth judicial district be fixed and held as follows: In the county of Adair on the third Mondays in February and August, and continue twelve juridical days at each term, if the business thereof require it. In the county of

In Clinton.

Clinton on the first Mondays in March and September, and continue six juridical days at each term, if the busi-

In Cumberland

ness thereof require it. In the county of Cumberland on the second Monday in March and September, and continue twelve juridical days at each term, if the business

In Monroe.

thereof require it. In the county of Monroe on the fourth Monday in March and September, and continue twelve juridical days at each term, if the business re-

In Barren.

quire it. In the county of Barren on the second Monday in April and October, and continue twenty-four juridical days at each term, if the business thereof re-

In Hart.

quire it. In the county of Hart on the second Monday in May and November, and continue twelve juridical days, if the business thereof require it. In the county

In Green.

of Green on the fourth Monday in May and November, and continue nine juridical days, if the business require

In Metcalfe.

it. In the county of Metcalfe on the first Thursday in June and December, of each year, and continue nine juridical days, if the business require it; and in the

In Allen.

county of Allen on the third Mondays in June and December, and continue in session twelve juridical days.

§ 2. It shall be lawful, whenever the business of any one of the courts in said district shall require it, for the judge of said district to call a special term of said court, upon giving ten days' notice thereof, as now required by law, and shall have the same power and authority as at a regular term to make the necessary orders to prepare, hear, and determine criminal and penal prosecutions, common law and equity cases, in all respects as if made at a regular term.

§ 3. That all persons who are, or shall be, summoned, recognized, or are or may be under bonds to appear in either of said courts at any of the terms at present fixed by law, shall be bound to appear therein at the first regular term of said court, as fixed by this act, and for failing to do so shall be subject to the same penalties as if they had been summoned, recognized, or bonded to appear at that time; and it shall be the duty of the clerks of the several courts aforesaid, so soon as they are informed of the passage of this act, to issue their process, and make out their dockets accordingly.

Persons on bond to appear at the regular term, &c.

§ 4. That immediately upon the passage of this act it shall be the duty of the Secretary of State to cause to be published a certified copy thereof in the daily Frankfort Yeoman, and the daily Louisville Courier-Journal, and to transmit to the clerk of each of said courts, by mail, a certified copy of this act.

Secretary to have act printed, and send to clerks, &c.

§ 5. This act to be in force from its passage.

Approved February 5, 1869.

CHAPTER 1397.

AN ACT to amend article 2, chapter 84, of the Revised Statutes, title "Roads and Passways."

Be it enacted by the General Assembly of the Commonwealth of Kentucky:

§ 1. That whenever it shall appear to the county courts of the county in which any manufactory is situated, that it is necessary for said manufactory that water from any public spring or water course shall be carried over the lands of any person by pipes, the said county court shall have power, upon the application of the owner or managers of any such manufactory, to appoint viewers, and take such steps for condemning the right to lay pipes over said land, and to issue writs of *ad quod damnum*, as it has under article 2, chapter 84, of the Revised Statutes, title "Roads and Passways." The proceeding under this act shall conform to the said article as far as practicable.

Right of a manufactory to passway to spring, &c.

Mode of obtaining passway.

§ 2. That the said court shall direct said pipes to be so placed as to do the least injury to the proprietor's right to the use and enjoyment of said land, and shall, at all times, have full power to order the repairs and keeping of said pipes in the order prescribed in the order allowing the

1869. placing of them over said land. This act shall apply
only to the county of Woodford.

§ 3. This act shall take effect from its passage.

Approved February 5, 1869.

CHAPTER 1407.

AN ACT amending an act, entitled "An act to fix the rent of the Kentucky
Penitentiary," approved 9th of March, 1867.

WHEREAS, Harry I. Todd was elected keeper of the Kentucky Penitentiary on the 9th day of February, 1866, and,
on the 1st day of March, 1867, succeeding, did execute the
bonds required by law, conditioned for the payment of
rent for the penitentiary at the rate of six thousand dollars for the first two years, per annum, and eight thousand
for the next two years of his lease, which was in full compliance with the then existing law; and whereas, said
Todd immediately thereby entered upon the discharge of
his duties as keeper of the penitentiary aforesaid, and
afterwards, to-wit: on the 9th day of March, 1867, by an
act of the General Assembly, approved on that day, the
rent of the penitentiary was raised to the sum of sixteen
thousand dollars per annum; and the said Todd, on the
13th day of March, 1867, entered into new bonds for the
payment of said increased rent, after being warned by
the Governor of the Commonwealth that he could not be
legally required to do so, stating at the time that the returning prosperity of the South would enable him to pay
the said increased rent and leave him a fair profit for himself; and whereas, said reasonable anticipations of said
Todd have been wholly disappointed by causes entirely
beyond his control; therefore,

*Be it enacted by the General Assembly of the Commonwealth
of Kentucky:*

§ 1. That the third subdivision of the first section of an
act to fix the rent of the Kentucky Penitentiary, approved
March 9th, 1867, be so amended as to read: Harry I.
Todd, the present keeper of the penitentiary, shall be
bound to pay to the Treasury, to the credit of the Sinking
Fund, six thousand dollars per annum for the first two
years of his lease, and eight thousand dollars per annum
for the last two years of said lease, with interest on said
sums from the time the same fell due up to their payment.

§ 2. The intention of this act is simply to release the
said Harry I. Todd from the payment of ten thousand dollars per annum for the first two years, and of eight thousand dollars per annum for the last two years of his
lease, and not to alter the original obligations of said
Todd: *Provided, however,* This act shall not take effect

Marginal note: Todd to pay $6,000 per year for first 2 years of lease, and $8,000 per year for last two.

unless the said Harry I. Todd, and the sureties on his official bond, shall, within sixty days after the passage of this act, signify their acceptance of its provisions in writing, filed in the office of the Secretary of State.

§ 3. This act shall take effect from its passage.

Approved February 6, 1869.

CHAPTER 1416.

AN ACT to provide expenses to the Governor when absent from the Seat of Government on business of the State.

Be it enacted by the General Assembly of the Commonwealth of Kentucky:

§ 1. That whenever the Governor of this Commonwealth shall leave the city of Frankfort upon the business of the State of Kentucky, he shall be paid by the State all his expenses of travel and otherwise while so absent; and the Auditor of Public Accounts is directed to draw his warrant upon the Treasurer, in favor of the Governor, for such sum as he may certify as having been expended by him from time to time for the purposes aforesaid; and the same is directed to be paid to him by the Treasurer.

Governor's expenses to be paid when engaged in the business of the State.

§ 2. This act shall take effect from its passage.

Approved February 10, 1869.

CHAPTER 1427.

AN ACT to establish a Chancery Term of the Washington Circuit Court, and for the trial of motions not requiring a jury.

Be it enacted by the General Assembly of the Commonwealth of Kentucky:

That a term of the Washington circuit court shall hereafter be held, on the first Monday in each January, for the preparation and trial of causes in equity and motions not requiring a jury, and continue six juridical days, should the business require it.

Equity term in Washington county in January.

Approved February 10, 1869.

CHAPTER 1443.

AN ACT regulating proceedings against Sheriffs in the Franklin Circuit Court.

Be it enacted by the General Assembly of the Commonwealth of Kentucky:

§ 1. That motions and proceedings in the Franklin circuit court in the name of the Commonwealth against

1869.   sheriffs, clerks, and other officers, except at the January
terms of said court, may be docketed for any day of the
term, at the discretion of the clerk of said court.

§ 2. This act to take effect from its passage.

Approved February 10, 1869.

CHAPTER 1447.

AN ACT to establish the office of Interpreter for the Jefferson Circuit Court.

Be it enacted by the General Assembly of the Commonwealth of Kentucky:

§ 1. That the judge of the Jefferson circuit court shall
appoint a person, who is thoroughly competent to speak
the English and German languages, to act as interpreter
of said court, who shall hold his office for one year from
the time of his appointment; and shall, before entering
upon the duties of his office, take the oath prescribed for
other officers of this court.

§ 2. It shall be the duty of said interpreter to be in attendance during the sittings of said court, and shall be
under the orders of the judge of said court, who shall
regulate his duties therein.

§ 3. That said interpreter shall receive, as compensation
for his services, while acting as interpreter for said court,
the sum of five hundred dollars ($500) per annum, to be
paid out of the State Treasury as other officers of this
court are paid.

§ 4. This act shall take effect from and after its passage.

Approved February 10, 1869.

Margin notes: Judge of Jefferson circuit court to appoint interpreter. His duty. Compensation.

CHAPTER 1455.

AN ACT to prevent Prize-fighting and Training for Prize-fighting in this Commonwealth.

Be it enacted by the General Assembly of the Commonwealth of Kentucky:

§ 1. That if any person shall, in this State, engage in a
prize-fight, or a fight for a bet, wager, or stakes, by whatever name it may be called, he shall, on conviction thereof,
be fined not less than two hundred and fifty nor more than
one thousand dollars, and imprisoned not less than three
months nor more than twelve months.

§ 2. If any person or persons shall be a second or sec-
onds in such a fight, or bear a challenge or the acceptance
of a challenge, either verbal or written, for such fight, or
make up or aid in making up the stakes for such fight, or

Margin notes: Unlawful to engage in prize-fight. Penalty. Unlawful for any person to act as second, &c.

shall, in any capacity or in any way, aid or assist in bringing on or conducting such fight, he or they shall, on conviction thereof, be fined not less than one hundred dollars
nor more than five hundred dollars, and imprisoned not
less than two months nor more than six months. *Penalty.*

§ 3. If any person shall bet or lay any wager on any
such fight, or be present at any such fight as a voluntary
spectator thereof, he shall, on conviction thereof, be fined
not less than twenty nor more than one hundred dollars. *Voluntary spectator and person betting liable to fine.*

§ 4. If any person owning or occupying, or having control
of land, shall voluntarily permit the use of the same for
any such fight, he shall, on conviction thereof, be fined not
less than one hundred dollars nor more than five hundred
dollars. *Owner of land liable to fine.*

§ 5. If any person shall train or prepare, in this State,
or assist another in training or preparing, in this State, for
such a fight in this State, or any other State, he shall, on
conviction thereof, be fined twenty dollars for each and
every day he engages in such training or preparing, or in
assisting another in training or preparing for such fight. *Penalty for training prise-fighters.*

§ 6. If in any such fight, in this State, either of the
combatants is killed, or if he dies within three months
thereafter, from injuries received in such fight, the other
combatant, and the aids and assistants of both combatants, and all who shall have participated in any way in
conducting such fight, shall be guilty of manslaughter,
and, on conviction, shall be confined in the penitentiary
not less than two nor more than ten years. *If one of combatants is killed, the other combatant, & all others participating, guilty of manslaughter, &c.*

§ 7. It shall be the duty of all judges of courts, justices
of the peace, mayors of cities, trustees of towns, and
other conservators of the peace, all sheriffs, constables,
marshals, and other police officers, on being informed,
or having reason of their own knowledge to believe,
that such a fight is about to take place, or that there is
training or preparation, in any place within their jurisdiction, for such fight, to suppress and prevent the same;
and, for this purpose, they shall arrest the offending parties, or have them arrested, and hold them to security for
their good behavior, and also commit them to prison if
they do not give bail for their appearance at the next circuit court to answer the charge; and, in order to suppress
and prevent the same, they shall exercise all the powers
vested in them for the prevention of crimes and misde-
meanors. *Judges, justices, &c., to suppress and prevent prise-fights, &c.* *Their powers to do so.*

§ 8. This act shall be in force from its passage.

Approved February 12, 1869.

1869.   CHAPTER 1456.

AN ACT to amend an act to increase the jurisdiction of Quarterly Courts
and Courts of Justices of the Peace in Whitley County, approved 15th
of February, 1864.

Be it enacted by the General Assembly of the Commonwealth
of Kentucky:

§ 1. That an act, entitled "An act to increase the jurisdiction of the quarterly courts and courts of justices of the
peace in Whitley county," approved 15th of February,
1864, be so amended, that, in suits before justices of the
peace, under said act, in said county, the pleadings shall
be oral, and no attorney's fee shall be taxed; but the justices of the peace shall collect from each litigant, before
the issuing of any warrant, on all sums when the amount
sued for is fifty dollars ($50) or over, exclusive of interest
and costs, fifty cents tax, which they shall pay over to the
trustees of the jury fund for said county on the first day of
the circuit court for said county; and shall file with the
circuit court clerk a written report, sworn to, of the
amount of said taxes received by him.

§ 2. This act shall take effect from its passage.

Approved February 12, 1869.

Marginal note: Jurisdiction of quarterly & justices' courts of Whitley county increased.

CHAPTER 1460.

AN ACT to change the time of holding the Woodford County Court, and
providing for the holding of the Court of Claims for Woodford County.

Be it enacted by the General Assembly of the Commonwealth
of Kentucky:

§ 1. That hereafter the regular terms of the Woodford
county court shall commence on the fourth (4th) Monday
in each month, and the regular court of claims for
Woodford county on the fourth (4th) Monday in the
month of November, in each year; the said courts to
be adjourned, continued, or convened, and to remain
open as now provided by law.

§ 2. All acts and parts of acts inconsistent herewith
are hereby repealed.

§ 3. This act shall take effect from its passage.

Approved February 12, 1869.

Marginal note: Woodford county.

CHAPTER 1468.

AN ACT for the benefit of the late Clerks, late Sheriffs, late Jailers, and other Civil Officers of this Commonwealth having uncollected fee bills.

Be it enacted by the General Assembly of the Commonwealth of Kentucky:

§ 1. That late clerks of the circuit, county, and chancery courts of this Commonwealth, and the late clerks of the court of appeals, and the late sheriffs, jailers, and other civil officers of this Commonwealth, or their personal representatives, have the further time of two years, from the first day of April, 1869, to collect their uncollected fee bills; and that such fee bills are hereby made distrainable; and that the aforesaid officers be subject to all the penalties now in force by law for issuing and collecting illegal fee bills. *{Time given clerks, sheriffs, &c., to collect fee bills, &c.}*

§ 2. That all of said sheriffs and town marshals, and the personal representatives of any who may be dead, shall have the further time of two years in which to collect any uncollected taxes due them, and for which such sheriff has accounted and paid, and the same right and power of levy and distraint in the collection thereof as sheriffs now have for the collection of the public revenue; but the said sheriffs and their representatives, and the securities upon their bonds, shall be responsible to any one injured by an illegal signer or proceeding under the privileges of this act. *{Time given sheriffs, town marshals, &c., to collect taxes.}*

§ 3. This act shall take effect from and after its passage.

Approved February 12, 1869.

CHAPTER 1472.

AN ACT to amend Section 3, Article 6, Chapter 16, of the Revised Statutes.

Be it enacted by the General Assembly of the Commonwealth of Kentucky:

§ 1. That section 3, article 6, chapter 16, of the Revised Statutes, be, and the same is hereby, so amended as to apply to and embrace the clerk of the court of appeals. *{Stant. Rev. Stat., vol. 1, p. 244.}*

§ 2. This act shall take effect from its passage.

Approved February 13, 1869.

1869.

CHAPTER 1475.

AN ACT to amend the Revenue Laws of this Commonwealth.

Be it enacted by the General Assembly of the Commonwealth of Kentucky:

Sheriffs' bonds valid when executed after the time now fixed by law.

§ 1. That all bonds executed by sheriffs and collectors of revenue shall be valid and binding upon them and their sureties, whether said bonds be executed at the time now fixed by law or after that time; and the same remedies shall be had to recover thereon as are now given upon bonds executed at the January or February terms of county courts.

Remedy.

§ 2. That the same remedies shall be had upon bonds of sheriffs heretofore executed after the January or February terms of county court as though they had been executed during either of said months.

§ 3. This act shall take effect from its passage.

Approved February 13, 1869.

CHAPTER 1497.

AN ACT to establish a State House of Reform for Juvenile Delinquents.

Be it enacted by the General Assembly of the Commonwealth of Kentucky:

Governor to appoint 6 commissioners to select grounds.

§ 1. That the Governor of the State of Kentucky shall, within thirty days after the passage of this act, appoint six commissioners, for the purpose of selecting a suitable site and grounds on which to be erected the "House of Reform for Juvenile Delinquents;" and the said com-

Powers and duties of commissioners.

missioners, who are hereby given full power to contract for and purchase land, consisting of not less than one hundred and fifty, nor more than three hundred acres, for a site, shall, within four weeks from the time of their appointment, proceed to examine and determine upon the site aforesaid, and shall locate the same at some suitable place within this State. In determining such location, the said commissioners shall take into consideration any proposition which may be made to them, and of the performance of which they shall have satisfactory assurance, to give or sell to the State the land necessary for the site of said House of Reform, or any part thereof, or to give to the State any materials or money to aid in the erection thereof; and any bond or other obligation, executed to the Commonwealth of Kentucky, and delivered to said commissioners to secure any such land, money, or materials, for the purpose aforesaid, shall be valid and binding upon the parties executing the same.

If land procured by purchase, deed to be made to the Auditor.

§ 2. If the said commissioners shall procure, by purchase or voluntary cession, the land, or any part thereof, necessary for the site for said House of Reform, the deed thereof shall be duly executed to the Commonwealth of Kentucky, and delivered to the Auditor of this State, who shall cause the same to be recorded in the office of the county where the land lies. The Treasurer of this State is hereby directed, after the execution and delivery of said deed, to pay, on the warrant of said Auditor, to the grantor or grantors of whom the said land shall be purchased, such sum or sums as may be required to pay for said land, agreeable to the contract of said commissioners, not exceeding twenty thousand dollars.

Treasurer to pay for land in warrant of Auditor.

§ 3. At any time, not exceeding thirty days, after the said land shall be obtained by the commissioners, the Governor shall appoint three other commissioners to contract for the erection and inclosure of the said House of Reform, on such plan and such terms as they may deem just and proper: *Provided*, That said House of Reform shall be built in a plain and substantial manner, and shall not cost, including inclosure and improvements, more than thirty thousand dollars, unless the amount paid for the land shall be less than twenty thousand dollars, and then so much may be expended for improvements, when added to the amount paid for the land, as will make the sum of fifty thousand dollars: *And provided also*, That said commissioners shall select and designate one of their number, who shall superintend the building of said House of Reform, with a view to a due execution of the work on the part of those with whom the said commissioners shall contract for the erection and inclosure thereof.

Governor to appoint three other commissioners to contract for erection of house.

Amount to be expended for house.

§ 4. The said commissioners mentioned in the last preceding section, before they enter upon the duties of their office, shall each give his covenant to the Commonwealth of Kentucky, with two or more sufficient sureties, to be approved by the Auditor, conditioned for the faithful performance of the duties required of him by this act.

Commissioners to give bond, &c.

§ 5. The Treasurer is hereby directed to pay the said commissioners, on the warrant of the Auditor, out of any money in the Treasury not otherwise appropriated, such sum or sums of money as they may require, from time to time, for the building of said House of Reform, not exceeding such amount as will, with the sum drawn and paid for the land for said House of Reform, amount to fifty thousand dollars, at such time as the same may be wanted by said commissioners, in sums not exceeding five thousand dollars at any one time.

Treasurer to pay commissioners, &c.

§ 6. It shall be the duty of said commissioners to make a detailed report of all the moneys received and expended by them, by virtue of this act, and of the progress which shall have been made in the erection and inclosure of said buildings, to the Governor, on or before the first day of

Commissioners to report by December next, &c.

1869.

December next, and as often thereafter as he shall or may require.

§ 7. Each of said commissioners first mentioned in this act shall be allowed and paid by the Auditor his necessary expenses while actually employed in the duties of his appointment.

§ 8. Each of said commissioners to be appointed by virtue of this act, to contract for and superintend the building of said House of Reform, shall be allowed for his services, and paid by the Treasurer, out of any money not otherwise appropriated, upon the warrant of the Auditor, while necessarily employed in the duties of his office, the sum of five dollars per day.

§ 9. The said commissioners shall, for at least four weeks, advertise in a newspaper published in each of the cities of Louisville, Frankfort, Lexington, Covington, for sealed proposals for erecting and completing the said buildings and inclosures, and shall make a contract for the same with the lowest and best bidder or bidders: *Provided*, Such bidder or bidders shall, in the opinion of said commissioners, be competent in all respects to do said work, and shall give satisfactory security for the performance of his or their contract: *And provided further*, That said contract, in the opinion of said commissioners, shall be for the best interests of the State.

§ 10. The Governor shall appoint and commission five discreet men, who shall act as Managers of the House of Reform established by virtue of this act, and who shall, on the acceptance of their respective appointments, perform the duties required of them by virtue of this act without compensation.

§ 11. Whenever a vacancy occurs in the said board of managers, such vacancy shall be filled by the Governor, with the consent of the Senate; the term of office of such managers shall be four years. The managers shall have power to make all such rules, regulations, ordinances, and by-laws for the government, discipline, and management of said House of Reform, and the inmates and officers thereof, as to them may appear just and proper: *Provided*, That said rules, regulations, ordinances, and by-laws be submitted to, and approved of by, the Governor.

§ 12. The said managers shall appoint a superintendent of the said House of Reform, and such other officers as they may deem necessary for the interest of the institution, with a view to the accomplishment of the object of its establishment and the economy of its management; and the said managers shall make a detailed report to the Governor of the performance of their duties, and the con-

dition of the institution, on or before the 15th day of
November in each year.

§ 13. The said managers and superintendent shall receive and take into said House of Reform all white male
and female children under twenty years of age, who shall
be legally committed to the said House of Reform, or on
conviction of any criminal offense less than murder, by
any court having authority to make such commitments.
The said managers shall have power to place the children committed to their care, during the minority of
such children, at such employments, and cause them to
be instructed in such branches of useful knowledge, as
shall be suited to their years and capacities: *Provided*,
That the charge and power of said managers upon and
over the said children shall not extend beyond the age
of twenty-one years: *Provided further*, That all of the
courts of this State have criminal jurisdiction, upon the
conviction of a white woman of any crime less than
murder, may sentence her to the House of Reform for
any number of years not exceeding the time, by the
criminal laws of this State, she may now be sent to the
penitentiary for a like offense.

To take all males in under 20 years of age sentenced by a court for a less crime than murder.

Proviso.

§ 14. That it shall be the duty of the Governor to draw
from the Treasury such sums of money as he may deem
necessary to pay the superintendent and other officers,
and the support and maintenance of said institution, for
one year from the time it is opened to receive inmates;
not exceeding, however, the sum of ten thousand dollars.

Governor to draw money to pay superintendent, &c.

§ 15. Whenever the said House of Reform shall, in the
opinion of the commissioners authorized to be appointed
by the third section of this act, be in readiness for the reception of persons committed thereto, the said commissioners shall make duplicate certificates thereof, one of
which they shall transmit to the Governor of this State,
and the other of which they shall cause to be filed in the
office of the clerk of the county court in which such House
of Reform shall be situated. The Governor, in receiving
such certificate, shall notify the fact to the people of this
Commonwealth by official proclamation.

When house is complete, commissioners to notify Governor, & Governor to notify the people by proclamation.

§ 16. From and after making such proclamation, the
courts of criminal jurisdiction of this State shall sentence
to said House of Reform every white male and female
under twenty years of age who shall be convicted before
such court of any less felony than murder. The said
courts may, in their discretion, sentence to the said House
of Reform any such male or female who may be convicted
before them of petit larceny; and the courts and magistrates having jurisdiction of vagrancy shall send to said
House of Reform any such male or female who may be
convicted before them as a vagrant.

Kind of persons to be sent to said House of Reform.

1869.

Age of person to be inserted in order of commitment.

§ 17. It shall be the duty of the courts of criminal jurisdiction in this State to ascertain, by such proof as may be in their power, the age of every delinquent by them respectively sentenced to the said House of Reform, and to insert such age in the order of commitment; and the age thus ascertained shall be deemed and taken to be the true age of such delinquent.

Age to be ascertained & entered in book for that purpose.

§ 18. In cases where any such court shall omit to insert in the order of commitment the age of any delinquent committed to said House of Reform, the managers shall, as soon as may be after such delinquent shall be received by them, ascertain his or her age by the best means in their power, and cause the same to be entered in a book to be designated by them for the purpose; and the age of such delinquent thus ascertained shall be deemed and taken to be the true age of such delinquent.

Managers to discharge person for good conduct.

§ 19. The managers are hereby vested with power to discharge such persons, who have not been convicted of crime by the judgment of some court of competent jurisdiction, from said House of Reform, whose good conduct may warrant their discharge.

Managers to give person discharged certificate of character.

§ 20. In all cases where persons are discharged from said House of Reform, or their time expires by limitation, the managers shall give to each one entitled thereto a certificate of good character and recommendation for the particular business in which he or she has been instructed.

Sectarianism not permitted in said institution.

§ 21. No sectarian influence or teaching shall be allowed or permitted in said institution; but the ministers of all denominations may, at suitable times, be allowed to teach the inmates of said institution, of their own faith only, the doctrines of their church; and any of said ministers shall be called in at any time, in cases of sickness, to administer the rites or ordinances of their church to any inmate demanding the same.

§ 22. In selecting the commissioners to designate and fix the locality of said "House of Reform for Juvenile Delinquents," it shall be the duty of the Governor to appoint two commissioners from the section of the State south of Green river; two from the section between the Green and Kentucky rivers, and two from the section north of the Kentucky river.

§ 23. This act shall take effect from its passage.

Approved February 15, 1869.

CHAPTER 1510.

1869.

AN ACT to amend an act, entitled "An act to incorporate the Kentucky River Navigation Company."

Be it enacted by the General Assembly of the Commonwealth of Kentucky:

§ 1. That the Board of Directors of the Kentucky River Navigation Company, or their agent or president, may require the county court of any county bordering upon the Kentucky river, or interested in its navigation, to submit to the legal voters of said county a proposition for said county to subscribe stock in said navigation company, said subscription to be made upon such conditions as said company may propose in writing to said court; and it shall be the duty of said county court to submit to the legal voters of said county, at such times as said company may designate, the question whether or not said county shall subscribe the sum proposed to be subscribed, according to the conditions which may be proposed by said company. The said court shall cause public notice, at least thirty days, to be given by said company to the voters of the county, by advertisements in the Louisville Courier-Journal and the newspapers published in counties bordering on said river; and shall appoint the necessary officers to hold the elections, and said officers shall hold the same at the various election precincts in said county, and make return thereof to the county court, and they and all voters shall act and vote under the same requirements and penalties as are now prescribed by law for holding the election for members of the Legislature; and if a majority of the voters voting shall be in favor of making said subscription, it shall be the duty of the presiding judge of the county court of said county to make a subscription, upon the application of said company, in the name of said county, to the capital stock of said company, for the amount so voted to be subscribed, payable according to the propositions and orders.

§ 2. That it shall be the duty of the county court of said county, upon the application of said company or its agent or president, to levy a tax upon all the property in said county, now subject to taxation for State revenue, sufficient to pay such subscription of stock as agreed upon in said order of subscription; also a sum sufficient to pay the sheriff or collector a compensation not exceeding two per cent. for collecting said sums, and all such sums as may, in the discretion of said court, be sufficient to cover the taxes for delinquents and other contingencies incidental to the collecting of the aforesaid subscriptions. The sheriff shall have all such rights and privileges as he now has

Proposition to subscribe stock to Kentucky River Navigation Company to be submitted to counties on said river.

County court to give 30 days' notice, &c.

Manner of holding elections.

County court to levy tax.

Sheriff to collect, and his compensation. To give bond.

If sheriff refuse to act, then court to appoint collector.

in the collection of the State revenue. He shall be required by the county court to execute separate bond, with
proper sureties, conditioned for the faithful performance of
his duties in the collection of said subscriptions as levied
for, and the paying over the same to the company, or its
authorized agent to receive them, at the time the State
revenue is now required to be paid by him; and if the
sheriff shall fail or refuse to collect the same, then the
court shall appoint a collector, with like duties and privileges as required of and given to the sheriff as aforesaid.

§ 3. That the sheriffs and collectors mentioned in this

Sheriff & col-
lector to give
bond.
act, before paying over the taxes or money collected by
them to the said company, shall take a bond in the penalty
of double the amount of the sum or sums paid over by
them, from the said company, with sufficient sureties, to be
certified by the county judge, and approved by the Attorney General, with condition for the faithful application of
said moneys so paid over, according to the provisions of
this act, and for the issue of the proper certificates of stock
to the stockholders.

§ 4. That the subscription of counties which have not
yet subscribed to said navigation company shall be null
and void, unless the said subscriptions shall create a sum
or fund sufficient, according to the estimates, to complete
the work to the Three Forks of the Kentucky river.

§ 5. That the tax-payers of any such county shall be

Tax-payers
to have stock
in company.
entitled to stock in said company for the amount of the tax
which shall be paid by them. The sheriff's or collector's
receipts for tax paid may be assigned, and shall pass by
assignment to the holder free from all equities or set-off;
and whenever an amount of one hundred dollars is produced to said company, it shall issue a certificate of stock
therefor, and also for one half and one fourth shares, upon
the production of receipts for that amount of tax paid.

§ 6. That in all cases where county courts have hereto-

Rights of tax-
payers.
fore subscribed stock to the capital of said company, the
tax-payers in such counties may have all the rights and
privileges as are granted in the preceding section to the
tax-payers, upon the county court of said county entering
upon the record an order granting such rights and privileges.

§ 7. That each county court subscribing, according to
the provisions of this act, shall have power to appoint one
director of said corporation, with equal power and privileges with the present directors, who shall hold their
offices until a complete organization is effected under the
regular elections provided for by the charter of said company.

§ 8. This act is in nowise to affect the powers of the
county courts as granted in section nine of the original

act, as to any subscriptions heretofore made, but shall apply to future subscriptions.

§ 9. That the time fixed for the commencement of the contemplated works in the Kentucky river, according to the provisions of the twelfth section of the act of incorporation, approved March 1st, 1865, be, and the same is hereby, extended to the 1st day of October, 1869.

Time fixed for work.

§ 10. That the county courts that have or may hereafter subscribe stock to the capital of the said Kentucky River Navigation Company make such other arrangements with the president of the board of directors or agent of the said company for the payment of such subscriptions of stock, in such annual installments as they may agree upon : *Provided*, The time is not extended beyond five years from the time of said agreement.

Manner of paying installments.

§ 11. That no part of this act shall apply to the county of Henry or its county court.

§ 12. This act to take effect from its passage.

Approved February 16, 1869.

CHAPTER 1512.

AN ACT to repeal the Court of Common Pleas in Calloway County, in the First Judicial District.

Be it enacted by the General Assembly of the Commonwealth of Kentucky:

§ 1. That so much of an act approved 5th of February, 1867, creating the court of common pleas in the first, third, and fourteenth judicial districts, so far as relates to the county of Calloway, be, and the same is hereby, repealed.

Public Acts of 1867.

§ 2. It shall be the duty of the clerk of said court to transfer all suits on the common pleas docket to the docket of the circuit court of said county.

Clerk to transfer suits to circuit court docket.

§ 3. That the sheriff, jailer, marshal, and constables of said county, and throughout the State, shall return all precepts and process, summons and writs of execution, which to them have been directed by said court, to the circuit court of said county, and said officers shall be responsible in like manner as for process, precepts, summons, and writs of execution issued from the circuit court of this State.

Process to be returned to circuit court.

§ 4. This act to take effect from and after its passage.

Approved February 16, 1869.

1869.   **CHAPTER 1518.**

AN ACT to amend an act, entitled "An act to prevent the destruction of Fish in Green river and its tributaries and other water-courses," approved February 26th, 1868.

Be it enacted by the General Assembly of the Commonwealth of Kentucky:

§ 1. That, from and after the first day of March, 1869, it shall be unlawful for any boat having on board fishing nets, or seines, or snares used in catching fish, to land on Green river, or be moored in the stream within the limits named in the act to which this is an amendment.

Public Acts 1868 p. 26.

§ 2. When such nets, or seines, or snares are found, or such boat or boats landed or moored in the said stream, the person or persons owning or having such nets, seines, and snares in possession shall be subject to all the pains and penalties prescribed in sections 2, 3, and 4 of the act approved February 6th, 1868, to be collected in the mode and manner prescribed therein: *Provided*, That this act shall not be construed and refer to steamboats plying on the said river carrying as freight such nets, seines, or snares.

Penalty.

§ 3. This act shall take effect and be in force from and after its passage.

Approved February 18, 1869.

———

CHAPTER 1523.

AN ACT to amend an act, entitled "An act in relation to Conveyances by Commissioners," approved 31st May, 1865.

Be it enacted by the General Assembly of the Commonwealth of Kentucky:

§ 1. That the provisions of an act, entitled "An act in relation to conveyances by commissioners," approved 31st of May, 1865, shall apply to and embrace all cases in which real estate sold by the order of a court of competent jurisdiction and any of the parties to the proceedings under which the sale was ordered shall die after the confirmation of each sale.

Myers' Sup. p. 313.

§ 2. This act shall take effect from its passage.

Approved February 18, 1869.

CHAPTER 1524.

AN ACT providing for suit against certain persons for trespassing on the property of the State.

WHEREAS, The State of Kentucky was the owner of a bridge extending from bank to bank across Barren river, part of the turnpike road leading from Louisville to Nashville through Barren and Allen counties, which bridge was burned down in the year 1861 or '2, leaving there a quantity of valuable iron, the property of the State; and whereas, certain parties, without right or just claim, seized and appropriated to their own use said iron, and have not paid or offered to pay for the same; therefore,

Be it enacted by the General Assembly of the Commonwealth of Kentucky:

§ 1. That James P. Garrett, Esq., be appointed agent for the State, and he is directed to institute suit and prosecute the same in any of the courts of this Commonwealth having jurisdiction under existing laws, in the name of and for the Commonwealth of Kentucky, against any and all persons so guilty as aforesaid of taking or converting said iron, and recover judgment for the value thereof, and such damages as the jury shall deem right under the facts and circumstances. Said agent shall collect the money and pay the same into the Treasury of the State; and the Treasurer shall allow and pay him a reasonable compensation for his trouble and expenses: *Provided, however,* Said Garrett shall execute bond, with good security, before the county court of Barren county, conditioned to do and perform all the duties imposed upon him by this act. He shall execute such bond before he enters upon said duties, and a certified copy of said bond shall be sent by the clerk of said court to the Auditor of Public Accounts.

Jas. P. Garrett appointed agent to bring suit for State for loss of iron, &c.

§ 2. This act to take effect from its passage.

Approved February 18, 1869.

CHAPTER 1530.

AN ACT to amend chapter eighty-four (84) of the Revised Statutes, title "Roads and Passways."

Be it enacted by the General Assembly of the Commonwealth of Kentucky:

§ 1. That chapter eighty-four (84) of the Revised Statutes, title "Roads and Passways," be so amended [as] to authorize the opening of a public road or passway, in the manner prescribed [in] said chapter, to any depot or switch on any railroad: *And provided,* Said road or passway shall remain open only so long as the said depot on switch may be used by said railroad as such.

Right of passway given to railroads to depots, &c.

1869.   § 2. That when the railroad shall cease to use any
switch or depot, the county court of the county in which
it is situated shall have full power to order the discontinuance of any public road or passway provided for in the
first section of this act.

§ 3. This act shall take effect from its passage.

Approved February 18, 1869.

CHAPTER 1532.

AN ACT to authorize the election of a Chancellor of the Louisville Chancery Court when the Chancellor is absent or interested in a cause.

*Be it enacted by the General Assembly of the Commonwealth
of Kentucky:*

§ 1. Whenever, from any cause, the chancellor of the
Louisville chancery court shall not be in attendance at
any term day of said court, the members of the bar present may, on motion of one of their number, elect a chancellor *pro tem.*, and thereupon the clerk of said court shall
administer to him the same oath of office required to be
taken by the chancellor, and shall enter his election upon
the order book of said court; and the chancellor *pro tem.*
so elected shall serve as such, and discharge all the
duties of said office until the chancellor shall return and
resume his duties.

§ 2. Whenever the chancellor of said court, or any chancellor *pro tem.* of said court, shall be disqualified to sit in
any cause, the parties may agree upon a chancellor to try
such cause, or failing so to agree, a special chancellor shall
be elected by the bar at any term day of said court, who
shall take the oath of office, and his election be entered of
record, after which he shall discharge the duties of chancellor in such cause.

§ 3. Any causes submitted for trial to any chancellor
pro tem., and remaining in his hands undecided when the
chancellor resumes his duties, may be decided by such
chancellor *pro tem.: Provided,* That the said chancellor
pro tem. shall receive no greater compensation out of the
State Treasury than circuit judges *pro tem.* are allowed by
law, and shall only receive it when circuit judges *pro tem.*
would be entitled thereto.

§ 4. This act shall be in force from and after its passage.

Approved February 19, 1869.

[margin notes]

Members of the bar of the chancery court of Louisville to elect chancellor pro tem.

Chancellor disqualified, parties to select; otherwise bar to select.

CHAPTER 1539.

AN ACT to amend chapter eighty-four (84) of the Revised Statutes, title "Roads and Passways."

Be it enacted by the General Assembly of the Commonwealth of Kentucky:

§ 1. That so much of chapter eighty-four (84), section seventeen (17), of the Revised Statutes, entitled "Roads and Passways," as prohibits the county courts from establishing roads and passways through orchards, be, and the same is hereby, repealed as to the counties of Boyd, Lawrence, Johnson, Floyd, and Pike ; and the county court of said counties may establish roads and passways through orchards in said counties in the same manner that they are now established by law over any other lands.

Stant. Rev Stat., vol. 2, s. 289.

§ 2. That section twenty-three (23) of said chapter be so amended that every person required to work on said road in said counties, who shall fail to attend with proper tools, without legal excuse, when notified by the surveyor of his precinct, as directed in section twenty-nine (29) of chapter eighty-four (84), Revised Statutes, title "Roads and Passways," or who shall fail to labor when in attendance, or to furnish a proper substitute, shall be fined not less than two dollars ($2 50) and fifty cents nor more than five dollars ($5), at the discretion of the court, for each day he shall fail to attend, or attending and failing or refusing to labor. The surveyor shall report such delinquents to the county court clerk, who shall issue a summons, in the name of the Commonwealth, against such delinquent persons to appear on the first day of the next regular term of the county court, unless said term shall come within less than five days from the issuing of said summons, then, in that event, it shall be returnable to the next succeeding term, at which time the presiding judge of said court shall hear and determine all such cases, unless for good cause shown the same be continued ; and if, upon hearing, the delinquent can show no good and legal excuse for such failure, the presiding judge shall render judgment against him for the amount of said fine and costs, upon which judgment the clerk shall issue a *capias ad satisfaciendum* at the expiration of ten days from the rendition of said judgment, or sooner for good cause shown, and so ordered by the court, returnable as executions are now returnable by law : *Provided,* That all such fines may be replevied as other executions or judgments are now replevied.

Stant. Rev. Stat., vol. 2, p. 290.

Surveyor to report delinquent to county court and summons to issue, &c.

§ 3. That section thirty-nine (39) of said road law be so amended, that when any surveyor of a public road shall fail to perform his duty, he shall be fined not less than ten nor more than twenty five dollars for each offense, and the county court shall have jurisdiction over all such cases, and the presiding judge of said court shall, upon his own

Stant. Rev. Stat., vol. 2, p. 293.

view, or information of any failure or delinquencies of any such surveyor to comply with the order of the said court, cause a rule to be entered or a summons to issue against such surveyor, returnable on the first day of the next regular term of said court : *Provided*, Five days shall intervene between said issual and return day; and if not, then the same shall be returnable to the next succeeding term ; said summons shall be in the name of the Commonwealth, notifying said delinquent to appear, and show cause why he has not performed the order of the court, or his duty, as prescribed by law. To compel and answer, said summons shall be served on the defendant at least five days before the first day of the term. If a jury be demanded the court shall cause the same to be empanneled to try the cause, which shall be under his supervision and direction. In all cases where judgment is rendered against the defendant, the clerk of said court shall issue a "capias," as provided in section second (2d) against delinquent hands.

County judge to order out hands to open roads, &c.

§ 4. The judge of the said county court is authorized and empowered to make an order, ordering out as many companies of hands—that is, the surveyors of roads and their hands—or as many hands or persons subject to work on roads, residing in a described boundary in said county, to open and establish new roads, and to open and repair old roads, and to make changes in old roads, as he may think proper in said counties in each particular case; and when more companies than one, or hands are ordered that belong to different companies for such purposes, he shall appoint a superintendent to take charge of them, whose duty it will be to fully execute the order of court; and in case he fails to do so without a reasonable excuse, or in case the surveyors of the companies that are placed under his charge, or the hands that are placed under his charge, or the hands that may

Penalty for failure to perform duty under this act.

be allotted as aforesaid, fails to discharge their duties without reasonable excuse therefor, they, are either or all of them, shall be punished by fines as provided in sections second (2d) and third (3d) of this act; said fines, when collected, to be expended upon the road for the failure to work upon which said fine was assessed.

Penalty for county judge's failing to perform his duty.

§ 5. The presiding judge of the county court is especially empowered and directed to see that this act is enforced, and if he shall negligently or willfully fail or refuse to discharge his duties herein required, he shall be liable to indictment in the circuit court of his county for malfeasance in office, and if found guilty, shall be removed therefrom.

§ 6. It shall be the especial duty of the county attorney to attend to all prosecutions under this act. The fees for sheriff and other officers under this act shall be the same as now allowed by law for similar services.

§ 7. All fines collected under this act shall be paid over to the county treasurer by the sheriff or collector, who, together with the treasurer, shall be responsible on their official bonds for any failure they may make to comply with the provisions of this act. Said treasurer shall keep a separate account of said fund, and the same shall be payable alone upon the order of the county court as aforesaid.

Fines to be paid to county treasurer.

§ 8. The provisions of this act shall apply to the counties of Lawrence, Johnson, Floyd, and Pike.

§ 9. This act shall take effect from its passage.

Approved February 20, 1869.

CHAPTER 1572.

AN ACT to change the time of holding the Quarterly Court in Fleming County.

Be it enacted by the General Assembly of the Commonwealth of Kentucky:

§ 1. That hereafter the quarterly court of Fleming county shall be held the third Mondays in March, June, September, and December, instead of the time they are now held.

Time of holding Fleming county court changed.

§ 2. This act to take effect from and after its passage.

Approved February 24, 1869.

CHAPTER 1577.

AN ACT requiring the chartered Banks of this Commonwealth to make semi-annual reports of their condition.

Be it enacted by the General Assembly of the Commonwealth of Kentucky:

§ 1. That all banks or other institutions receiving deposits, chartered by, or doing business under, the laws of this State, shall make out a correct and sworn statement of their condition, embracing a list of depositors who may have money to their credit unclaimed for five years or more, the name of each depositor, and the sum to his credit, and time when made, at the close of each half year business; and shall, by the 10th January and July in each year, forward to the Auditor a copy, and also publish the statement at least five times in one or more newspapers published in their place of business; and if none be published there, then in those published in Frankfort or Louisville.

Banks to make semi-annual statement, & furnish Auditor copy thereof.

To publish statement.

1869.

Penalty.

§ 2. Any corporation failing to comply with this act shall be fined not less than $100 nor more than $500, recoverable by the Franklin circuit court, on motion of the Auditor, after ten days' notice.

§ 3. This act to take effect from its passage.

Approved February 24, 1869.

CHAPTER 1580.

AN ACT directing the Commissioners of the Sinking Fund to lease the Improvements of the Kentucky River.

Be it enacted by the General Assembly of the Commonwealth of Kentucky:

Commissioners of Sinking Fund to lease all locks, dams, &c., after advertisement for 30 days.

§ 1. That the Commissioners of the Sinking Fund shall, after having first advertised for thirty days in two or more newspapers published in the city of Louisville, and in one or more newspapers published in the city of Frankfort, offer for lease, for a term of fifty years, all the locks, dams, lock-houses, tools, implements, apparatus, and materials, of every kind and description, now belonging to, forming part of, or in anywise used in connection with, the slackwater improvements of the Kentucky river: *Provided*, That it shall be discretionary with the commissioners whether they accept the bid at the first leasing or not; and if rejected, they shall readvertise and lease as hereinbefore provided.

Lease to be made to highest bidder.

§ 2. That such lease shall be executed by the Commissioners of the Sinking Fund to the highest and best bidder, who shall agree to pay to the Commissioners of the Sinking Fund, for the use of the Commonwealth, a stipulated annual rental, being the amount of such bid by the lessee. The lessees shall keep the said locks and dams in good repair at their own expense.

Lease to be made at public auction at court-house door in Frankfort.

§ 3. That such lease shall be made at public auction at the court-house door, in the city of Frankfort, after advertisement first made, as provided in the first section of this act. But no person or corporation shall be entitled to demand a lease, under the terms of this act, who shall not satisfy the Commissioners of the Sinking Fund of his or its ability and intention, in good faith, to complete the slackwater navigation of the Kentucky river, by substantial and permanent locks and dams, to the Three Forks of said river; and who shall fail to satisfy the commissioners that a *bona fide* stock of at least $300,000 has been subscribed by responsible parties to the object of said improvement.

§ 4. The Commissioners of the Sinking Fund shall, in awarding said lease, and in determining the goodness and worth of bids, have regard to the franchises already conferred by law upon the Kentucky River Navigation Company, and other things being equal, shall give said corporation a preference in the bidding.

§ 5. That the lessees shall have a right to renew said lease for a term of twenty-five years on the same conditions, upon a re-valuation of the fair annual rent of the improvements leased under this act. *Renewal of lease.*

§ 6. That if the lessee shall fail, for sixty days after the award of said lease, to commence, in good faith, the extension of slackwater improvements on said river, then the lease shall be void, and the same shall be forfeited to the Commonwealth. *Forfeiture.*

§ 7. That the lease hereinbefore mentioned shall be drafted by the Attorney General, with proper covenants to secure the navigation of said river and purposes in view, and that they shall, at the end of their lease, turn the same over to the State in good repair, and shall be signed by the Governor in behalf of the Commissioners of the Sinking Fund. It may be recorded by the lessee in the office of the county court of Franklin county, and copies certified under seal of said court shall be deemed authentic, and of full force as the original. A duplicate of said lease shall be filed with the Auditor of State. *Lease to be drafted by Attorney General and recorded in Franklin county clerk's office.*

§ 8. The Governor of the State shall, at the request of the lessee, or his authorized agent, transfer and deliver all the locks, dams, lock-houses, tools, materials, implements, and apparatus of the Kentucky river slackwater improvements, to the lessee, by proclamation to that effect, according to the terms of said lease, after the same shall have been fully executed. *Duty of Governor.*

§ 9. That the lessee or lessees of said work shall not, at any time during the continuance of the lease, charge or receive a higher rate of toll than is now allowed by the charter of the Kentucky River Navigation Company: *Provided*, That said company, in adjusting its rates of toll, shall have no power to discriminate in favor of boats which may belong to said company in whole or part, but the navigation of said river shall be open to all boats on equal terms. *Rate of t"*

§ 10. The State reserves the right to reduce the rate of tolls on said improvements leased under this act whenever the dividends on the stock exceed ten per cent. free of all expenses; but no such reduction shall be made which will reduce the net dividends below ten per cent. *Reservation.*

§ 11. The lessees shall make a full report to each regular session of the Legislature, which report shall exhibit the receipts and expenditures and all other material facts showing the condition of said company. Said report shall be verified under oath. *Lessee to report to each regular session.*

1869.

Reservation.

§ 12. The State reserves the right to resume possession, at any time, of the property used in the navigation of the Kentucky river or convenient therefor, upon one year's notice first given to the lessees or owners, and after ascertaining and paying to the lessees or owners the full and fair value thereof.

§ 13. The President of the Board of Internal Improvement shall pay and discharge all debts due for contracts heretofore made by him, whether completed or yet unfinished.

§ 14. This act shall take effect from its passage.

Approved February 24, 1869.

CHAPTER 1581.

AN ACT to amend the charter of the Bank of Ashland, and to incorporate the Bank of Shelbyville.

Be it enacted by the General Assembly of the Commonwealth of Kentucky:

Stockholders to vote on separation of parent bank, at Ashland, from branch at Shelbyville.

§ 1. That at the annual meeting of the stockholders of the Bank of Ashland, to be held on the first Monday in May next, the question of separating the parent bank at Ashland from the branch at Shelbyville shall be submitted to a vote of the stockholders. Should a majority of the stock be voted in favor thereof, the same shall be entered on the minutes of the stockholders' meeting, and such vote shall be deemed an acceptance of this act.

Branch bank incorporated under name & style of Bank of Shelbyville

§ 2. That the stockholders of the branch of the Bank of Ashland, at Shelbyville, are hereby incorporated as a body politic and corporate, under the name and style of the Bank of Shelbyville, with all the powers and privileges, and subject to all the restrictions contained in the act incorporating the Bank of Ashland, approved February the 15th, 1856, and the several amendments thereto, or any general law applying thereto, except that the Bank of Shelbyville shall

Amount of capital stock.

not be authorized to establish any branch, nor shall the capital stock exceed two hundred thousand dollars.

Stockholders to elect directors, &c.

§ 3. If this act shall be accepted, as provided in the first section, then the stockholders of the branch at Shelbyville shall hold an election at their banking house in Shelbyville, on the first Monday in June, 1869, for the election of a board of directors, who shall enter upon the discharge of the duties of their offices on the first day of July, 1869, and continue in office until their successors are elected and qualified. After the first election, as above provided, an annual election of directors shall be held at Shelbyville, on the first Monday in May, as provided in section eight (except as to the place) of the act incorporating the Bank of Ashland.

§ 4. Notice of the acceptance of this act shall be given to the Governor, and notice, also, of the election of a board of directors for the Bank of Shelbyville; whereupon the Governor shall, by proclamation, published in one or more newspapers in this State, give notice that the branch of the Bank of Ashland, at Shelbyville, has been incorporated as an independent bank, under the name of the Bank of Shelbyville, and authorized to commence business on the first day of July, 1869.

§ 5. The business of the parent bank and branch shall be continued up to and including the 30th day of June, 1869, when the connection shall cease: after which the Bank of Ashland and the Bank of Shelbyville shall make a settlement, and an equitable division of the assets and property owned by the Bank of Ashland, on the 30th of June, 1869.

§ 6. That the Bank of Ashland shall retain all its chartered rights and privileges under the original charter, or any amendments thereto, or any existing law, except the right to have branches.

§ 7. This act shall take effect from its passage.

Approved February 24, 1869.

1869.

Notice to be given Governor and his duty to issue proclamation, &c.

The parent & branch bank to make settlement, &c.

CHAPTER 1596.

AN ACT creating a special term of the Bullitt Circuit Court for the trial of equity causes and motions not requiring the intervention of a jury.

Be it enacted by the General Assembly of the Commonwealth of Kentucky:

§ 1. That, in addition to the terms now prescribed by law, there shall be held a term of the Bullitt circuit court on the first Monday in June of each year, for the trial of equitable causes and motion not requiring the intervention of a jury, which term shall continue six juridical days, if the business of the court requires it.

§ 2. This act shall take effect from its passage.

Approved February 25, 1869.

Bullitt circuit court.

CHAPTER 1597.

AN ACT changing the time of holding the Bullitt Circuit Court.

Be it enacted by the General Assembly of the Commonwealth of Kentucky:

§ 1. That hereafter the Bullitt circuit court shall commence on the third Monday in October, and continue twelve juridical days, instead of the third Monday in August, as now prescribed by law.

§ 2. This act shall take effect from its passage.

Approved February 25, 1869.

Bullitt circuit court.

1869.   CHAPTER 1606.

AN ACT to amend an act, entitled "An act to protect Graves and Graveyards," approved March 9th, 1854.

*Be it enacted by the General Assembly of the Commonwealth
of Kentucky:*

§ 1. That section one (1) of an act, entitled "An act to
protect graves and graveyards," approved March 9th,
1854, be so amended as to read: Sec. 1st. That if any person shall violate the grave of a person by willfully destroy-
ing, removing, or injuring the head or foot-stone of the
tomb or monument over or the inclosure protecting such
grave, or by willfully digging into or plowing over any
grave, he shall, upon conviction thereof, be fined not less
than one hundred dollars nor more than five hundred dollars, and imprisoned in the county jail not less than six nor
more than twelve months, or both so fined and imprisoned, at the discretion of the jury; one half of said fine
to go to the Commonwealth, the other half to the informer.

Stant. Rev.
Stat., vol. 1, p
412.

§ 2. This act shall not apply to cases of the opening of
graves by relatives or friends for the removal of the remains to other places of interment.

§ 3. This act to take effect from and after its passage.

Approved February 25, 1869.

CHAPTER 1607.

AN ACT to amend an act authorizing and empowering County Courts
to create additional Justices' Districts, establish voting precincts in such
districts, and fix the boundary lines and places of voting therein, approved march 7th, 1868.

*Be it enacted by the General Assembly of the Commonwealth of
Kentucky:*

§ 1. That an act authorizing and empowering county
courts to create additional justices' districts, establish
voting precincts in such districts, and fix the boundary
lines and places of voting therein, be so amended as to
give the county courts full power to change the boundary lines of voting precincts and justices' districts, or to
change or abolish the place of voting in any voting precinct in their respective counties, as well as to exercise
the power that they now have: *Providing,* No such
change shall be made within sixty days of any regular
election.

Public Acts
of 1868, p. 47.

Power of
county court to
change voting
precincts, &c.

§ 2. This act shall take effect and be in force from and
after its passage.

Approved February 25, 1869.

CHAPTER 1612.

AN ACT to amend an act, entitled "An act to amend article 3 of chapter 48 of the Revised Statutes," approved October 3d, 1861, and to regulate the number of the Board of Managers of the Eastern Lunatic Asylum of Kentucky, and fix the mode of their appointment and their terms of office.

Be it enacted by the General Assembly of the Commonwealth of Kentucky :

§ 1. That an act, entitled "An act to amend article 3 of chapter 48 of the Revised Statutes," approved October 3d, 1861, be, an the same is hereby, repealed. *Myers' Sup., p. 35.*

§ 2. That from and after the 1st of March, 1869, there shall be seven Managers of the Eastern Lunatic Asylum of Kentucky, who shall be appointed by the Governor and confirmed by the Senate, in the room and stead of the present board of managers of said institution, and shall have all the powers and perform all the duties and be subject to all the responsibilities now prescribed by law for the board of managers of said institution. The term of their said office shall commence on the 1st day of March, 1869, and shall be for four years; but two of said managers so first appointed shall go out of office at the end of the first year after their appointment; two of them shall go out of office at the end of the second year; two of them shall go out of office at the end of the third year, and one of them shall go out of office at the end of the fourth year; and they shall, on going into office, arrange by lot which of them shall so go out of office at the end of the respective years as aforesaid; but they may be re-appointed by the Governor if he deems proper; and it shall go on in that way, so many as above going out of office at the end of every year, their places to be filled by appointment of the Governor and confirmation of the Senate; but vacancies may be filled by the Governor in the recess of the Senate until the end of its next session. Incumbents at any time shall hold their office until a successor is appointed and qualified. Five shall constitute a quorum. *Hereafter Governor to appoint seven Managers of Eastern Lunatic Asylum. Power & duty of managers. Term of their office. Vacancies filled by Governor. Quorum.*

§ 3. All acts and parts of acts inconsistent with this act are hereby repealed.

§ 4. This act shall take effect from its passage.

Approved February 26, 1869.

CHAPTER 1641.

AN ACT to appropriate money to improve the North Fork of the Kentucky River.

WHEREAS, There are divers obstructions in the North Fork of the Kentucky river which greatly endanger the navigation, and heavy losses are often sustained by persons

1869.

who transport coal and lumber down said river to market; and whereas, it is important to the citizens of this Commonwealth that said obstructions be removed; therefore,

Be it enacted by the General Assembly of the Commonwealth of Kentucky:

§ 1. That the sum of five thousand dollars be appropriated, to be expended as hereinafter provided in removing obstructions to the navigation of the North Fork of the Kentucky river from the mouth of the Middle Fork of said river to a point opposite a place known as Brashear's Salt Works.

$5,000 appropriated to remove obstructions from the North Fork of the Kentucky river.

§ 2. That J. W. Cardwell, John Wilson, Zachariah Morgan, Elijah Cornett, of Perry, James W. Lindon, of Breathitt, and William Spencer, are appointed commissioners to expend said sum of money in removing obstructions as provided in the first section of this act. They may let out the work in such parcels and on such terms as they may deem best: *Provided,* They shall always give at least ten days' public notice of the time and place and terms of such letting of contracts for improvements as aforesaid. They shall not pay any contractor more than one half of the amount agreed upon until the work is completed. They shall give each contractor a copy of the agreement, and may, upon his executing bond in the Breathitt county court, with approved security, payable to the Commonwealth, with a covenant for the faithful performance of said contract, advance to said contractor one half of the price agreed upon.

Commissioners appointed. Their duties, &c.

§ 3. That the commissioners aforesaid shall certify to the Auditor a true copy of every contract they make under this act; whereupon said Auditor of Public Accounts shall draw his warrant on the Treasurer in favor of said commissioners for half of the amount set forth in said contract.

Commissioners to certify contracts to Auditor, &c.

§ 4. When the work is completed according to contract, the said commissioners shall certify the same to the Auditor of Public Accounts, whereupon he shall draw his warrant on the Treasurer, in favor of said contractor, for the remaining half of the amount agreed upon in said contract.

§ 5. This act to take effect from its passage.

Approved March 1, 1869.

CHAPTER 1643.

AN ACT to change the times of holding the Circuit and Criminal Courts in the 12th Judicial District.

Be it enacted by the General Assembly of the Commonwealth of Kentucky:

§ 1. That the several terms of the circuit and criminal courts in the several counties composing the twelfth judicial district shall hereafter commence on the Mondays next preceding the several times now fixed by law, and continue at each term one juridical day longer.

Time of holding courts in the twelfth judicial district changed.

§ 2. That in lieu of the February terms of the Campbell circuit court, at Alexandria, there shall be held at said place, in each year, a term commencing on the second Monday in April, to continue six juridical days.

Campbell circuit court.

§ 3. This act shall take effect from its passage.

Approved March 1, 1869.

CHAPTER 1644.

AN ACT to change the time for holding the Franklin County Court.

Be it enacted by the General Assembly of the Commonwealth of Kentucky:

§ 1. That hereafter the county court of Franklin county shall be held on the first Monday in each month instead of the time now fixed by law.

Franklin.

§ 2. This act shall take effect from its passage.

Approved March 1, 1869.

CHAPTER 1646.

AN ACT changing the time of holding the Quarterly Courts of Hancock County.

Be it enacted by the General Assembly of the Commonwealth of Kentucky:

§ 1. That the terms of the Hancock county quarterly court shall hereafter commence on the second Monday in March, June, September, and December of each year, instead of the time now prescribed by law.

Time of holding Hancock quarterly court changed.

§ 2. This act shall take effect from and after the 1st day of June, 1869.

Approved March 1, 1869.

1869.

'CHAPTER 1653.

AN ACT to regulate the holding of the Circuit Courts in the 14th Judicial District.

Be it enacted by the General Assembly of the Commonwealth of Kentucky:

§ 1. That after this act shall take effect the circuit courts in the several counties composing the 14th judicial district shall be held as hereinafter directed, to-wit:

Fleming.

§ 2. In the county of Fleming the court shall commence on the second Mondays in February and August of each year, and shall be holden eighteen juridical days at each term, if the business so requires.

Greenup.

§ 3. In the county of Greenup the court shall commence on the first Mondays in March and September of each year, and shall be holden eighteen juridical days at each term, if the business so requires.

Nicholas.

§ 4. In the county of Nicholas the court shall commence on the fourth Mondays in March and September of each year, and be holden twelve juridical days at each term, if the business so requires.

Mason.

§ 5. In the county of Mason the court shall commence on the Tuesday next after the second Mondays in April and October in each year, and be held twenty-three juridical days at each term, if the business so requires.

Lewis.

§ 6. In the county of Lewis the court shall commence on the second Mondays in May and November in each year, and be held twelve juridical days at each term, if the business so requires.

Rowan.

§ 7. In the county of Rowan the court shall commence on the fourth Mondays in May and November, and be holden six juridical days at each term, if the business so requires.

§ 8. This act shall take effect on the first day of July, 1869.

Approved March 2, 1869.

———

CHAPTER 1654.

AN ACT to compensate Jurors in Justices', Police, and Quarterly Courts, in the counties of Kenton, Estill, and Fleming.

Be it enacted by the General Assembly of the Commonwealth of Kentucky:

Juror entitled to 50 cents for each day.

§ 1. That in all jury trials before justices', police, and quarterly courts of this Commonwealth, each juror shall be paid fifty cents, to be taxed as costs, for each trial in which he shall be engaged: *Provided,* The number of jurymen engaged in each trial shall exceed six.

§ 2. This act shall apply only to the counties of Kenton, Estill, and Fleming.

§ 3. This act to be in force from its passage.

Approved March 2, 1869.

CHAPTER 1655.

AN ACT to repeal section four (4) of an act to amend an act establishing the Louisville Chancery Court, and to fix the fees of the Marshal of said Court.

Be it enacted by the General Assembly of the Commonwealth of Kentucky:

§ 1. That section four of an act to amend an act estab- lishing the Louisville chancery court, approved January 22d, 1866, is hereby repealed; and the fees of the marshal of said court shall be, for making a sale of real or per- sonal estate under the order or judgment of court, five per cent. on the first three hundred dollars, and one per cent. on all sums over and above three hundred dollars, and costs for advertising and taking care and carriage of any personal estate; no fee shall be charged by or allowed to the marshal on any sale until it is approved by the court; and in cases where the sales are not ap- proved by the court, he shall be allowed for advertising the same, and reasonable charges for removing or taking care of personal property ordered to be sold by the court, or which has been attached by proceedings in said court. For all other services of said marshal required by law to be performed, or by order or judgment of said court, he shall charge and be allowed the same fees which are now allowed by law to the sheriff of Jefferson county.

Myers' Sup., p. 768.

Fees of mar- shal of Louis- ville chancery court

Sale to be approved by the court.

§ 2. This act shall take effect and be enforced from its passage.

Approved March 2, 1869.

CHAPTER 1658.

AN ACT to amend article 2, chapter 99, Revised Statutes.

Be it enacted by the General Assembly of the Commonwealth of Kentucky:

§ 1. That section 1, of article 2, chapter 99, Revised Statutes, be so amended as to leave it discretionary with the county court as to granting the license therein pro- vided.

Stant. Rev. Stat., vol. 2, p. 409.

§ 2. This act to take effect and be in force from and after its passage.

Approved March 2, 1869.

1869.   CHAPTER 1659.

AN ACT to amend section 4th, article 4th, chapter 28th, of the Revised Statutes.

Be it enacted by the General Assembly of the Commonwealth of Kentucky:

§ 1. That section 4, article 4, chapter 28, title "Crimes and Punishments," of the Revised Statutes, be so amended as to read as follows : Whoever shall unlawfully and carnally know any white woman against her will or consent, or by force, or whilst she is insensible, shall be guilty of rape, and shall be punished by confinement in the penitentiary for a period not less than ten nor more than twenty years, or by death, in the discretion of the jury.

§ 2. That section third of an act approved March the 9th, 1867, entitled "An act to amend chapter 28, article 4, title 'Crimes and Punishments,' of the Revised Statutes," be, and the same is hereby, repealed.

§ 3. This act shall be in force from its passage.

Approved March 2, 1869.

Marginal notes:
Stant. Rev. Stat., vol. 1, p. 379.
Public Acts, p. 104.

CHAPTER 1660.

AN ACT to amend the charters of the Lexington and Frankfort and Louisville and Frankfort Railroad Companies.

Be it enacted by the General Assembly of the Commonwealth of Kentucky:

§ 1. That the executive committee of the Louisville and Frankfort and Lexington and Frankfort railroad companies shall be, and they are hereby, authorized to issue and sell the preferred joint stock of said railroads to the amount of five hundred thousand dollars, in addition to the million of such stock authorized to be issued by the fifth section of an act amendatory of the charters of said companies, approved January 19th, 1867 : *Provided,* That the certificates for such additional stock, when issued, shall bear upon their face a stipulation that the entire amount of such preferred joint stock, issued and to be issued, shall at no time exceed in amount one million and a half of dollars.

§ 2. That said executive committee shall have authority to extend their road into either or both of the cities of Covington and Newport on such rates as they may agree upon with the authorities of said cities.

§ 3. That said companies may contract with each other for the consolidation of the stock of the two companies into one common stock, upon such terms and conditions as may be approved by the stockholders of the two companies at any regular or called meeting of the same; and such contract and consolidation, when so approved, shall

Marginal notes:
Executive committee of the Louisville and Frankfort and Lexington and Frankfort railroad companies authorized to sell stock, &c.

To extend road into city of Covington & Newport.

Companies to consolidate stock, &c.

be valid and binding in every respect upon the said com- 1869.
panies and the stockholders thereof.

§ 4. This act shall take effect from its passage.

Approved March 2, 1869.

CHAPTER 1670.

AN ACT to amend title 5, Civil Code of Practice.

*Be it enacted by the General Assembly of the Commonwealth
of Kentucky*:

§ 1. That where any action embraced in section 106 of Myers' Code,
the Civil Code of Practice is against several defendants, p. 33.
one or more of whom has been served with summons in
the county where the suit is brought, the subsequent discharge in bankruptcy of such defendant or defendants, or
the suspension, discontinuance, or dismissal of the action
as to any or all of them so summoned, by reason of such
discharge in bankruptcy, shall not entitle the defendants
summoned in any other county previous to the commencement of the proceedings in bankruptcy to have the action
dismissed as to them, but the same shall proceed as though
all the defendants had been summoned in the county·
where the suit is pending.

§ 2. This act shall take effect from its passage.

Approved March 3, 1869.

CHAPTER 1685.

AN ACT requiring certain actions to be brought against certain persons
indebted to the Commonwealth.

*Be it enacted by the General Assembly of the Commonwealth
of Kentucky:*

§ 1. That the Attorney General be, and he is hereby, Attorney Gen-
directed to institute proceedings, in the fiscal court—the eral directed to
Franklin circuit court—against all such persons as are against parties
shown, by the books and records of the Quarter-Master indebted to the
General's office, to be indebted to the Commonwealth for Commonw'th.
moneys advanced to them to aid in raising, equipping, or
maintaining State or other troops during the late civil
war, or for any other purpose; and said court is hereby
vested with jurisdiction to try and determine such actions
and proceedings: *Provided*, That the party may make any
equitable defense they may have to any such suit, and
may be allowed credit for any sums they may have disbursed in good faith for the purpose for which said money
was furnished: *Provided*, Such equitable and other defense, and the expenditure of money in good faith by

1869. them, or any of them, shall be shown by other satisfactory evidence, in addition to their own affidavit.

§ 2. This act shall take effect from its passage.

Approved March 3, 1869.

CHAPTER 1695.

AN ACT to prescribe penalties for illegal charges made and collected by Street Railways.

Be it enacted by the General Assembly of the Commonwealth of Kentucky:

Street railways prohibited from making exorbitant charges.

§ 1. That if any street railway corporation, or the servant or agent employed by any such corporation, shall demand or take from any person a greater sum for transportation than by law, ordinance, or contract is allowed, such street railway corporation or company shall be fined any sum not exceeding fifty dollars, to be recovered by warrant in the name of the Commonwealth, before the mayor or police judge of the city or town in which such street railway corporation is situate; and said fine, when collected, shall go into the common school fund of the city or town wherein the same may be imposed.

Penalty.

§ 2. This act to take effect from its passage.

Approved March 4, 1869.

CHAPTER 1703.

AN ACT to repeal an act, entitled "An act, to amend an act, entitled 'An act to amend section 1, article 3, chapter 32, title Elections,' of the Revised Statutes," approved February 11th, 1858, the said amendatory act hereby repealed having been approved March 15th, 1862.

Be it enacted by the General Assembly of the Commonwealth of Kentucky:

Myers' Sup., p. 197.

§ 1. That an act, entitled "An act to amend an act, entitled 'An act to amend section 1, article 3, chapter 32, title Elections,' of the Revised Statutes," approved February 11th, 1858, which amendatory act was approved March 15th, 1862, be, and the same is hereby, repealed.

§ 2. This act shall be in force from its passage.

Approved March 4, 1869.

CHAPTER 1755.

AN ACT concerning the Louisville Chancery Court.

Be it enacted by the General Assembly of the Commonwealth of Kentucky:

§ 1. That whenever a vacancy shall occur in the office of clerk or marshal of the Louisville chancery court, it shall be the duty of the chancellor of said court to issue his proclamation or writ to the proper officers for an election on the first Monday in the August ensuing after such writ or proclamation, to fill such vacancy, and to appoint some suitable person to fill such vacancy until such election can be had, and the person who may be elected shall qualify.

When vacancy, chancellor of Louisvill chancery court to appoint clerk until election held.

§ 2. This act shall be in force from its passage.

Approved March 5, 1869.

CHAPTER 1757.

AN ACT for the protection of Game in certain Counties of the State.

Be it enacted by the General Assembly of the Commonwealth of Kentucky:

§ 1. That it shall be unlawful, at any time before the first of October and after the first of February, to catch, kill, or in any manner destroy, or expose for sale, deer; or at any time before the first of October and after the first of February to catch, kill, or in any manner destroy, or pursue with such intent, any wild turkey, pheasant, partridge, quail, dove, or rabbit; or at any time before the first of June and after the first of January to kill squirrels; or at any time before the first of July and after the first of January to kill woodcock, or to have in possession, or to expose for sale, contrary to the intent and meaning of this act, any of the above mentioned game during the time that the killing of the same is prohibited.

Unlawful to kill game before first October and after first February.

Unlawful to kill squirrels before 1st June and after first January.

Woodcock between 1st January and 1st July.

§ 2. Any person violating any of the provisions of this act shall be liable to immediate arrest, under warrant issued and returnable before any county court judge, justice of the peace, or police judge, and, upon conviction, shall be subject to a fine for each and every offense of not less than five dollars nor more than twenty dollars and costs of suit, one half of the fine to be paid into the jury fund and the other half to the informant, if claimed; but, if not claimed, the whole amount to go to the jury fund.

Penalty.

§ 3. This act shall apply to the counties of Henderson, Boyle; and all acts and parts of acts, so far as the same may be inconsistent herewith, are, to that extent, hereby repealed.

§ 4. This act shall take effect from and after its passage.

Approved March 5, 1869.

CHAPTER 1762.

AN ACT to re-enact article 18, chapter 36, of the Revised Statutes.

Be it enacted by the General Assembly of the Commonwealth of Kentucky:

Stant. Rev. Stat., vol. 1, p. 88.

§ 1. That nothing in the Civil Code of Practice shall be construed to repeal any part of article 18, chapter 36, of the Revised Statutes, but that said article of said chapter shall be and remain in full force.

§ 2. This act shall take effect from its passage.

Approved March 5, 1869.

CHAPTER 1763.

AN ACT to repeal an act, entitled "An act to amend article 2, chapter 42, of the Revised Statutes, entitled 'Guardian and Ward,'" approved February 18th, 1864.

Be it enacted by the General Assembly of the Commonwealth of Kentucky:

Myers' Sup., p. 254.

§ 1. That an act, entitled "An act to amend article 2, chapter 42, of the Revised Statutes, entitled 'Guardian and Ward,'" approved February 18th, 1864, be, and the same is hereby, repealed.

§ 2. This act shall be in force from its passage.

Approved March 5, 1869.

CHAPTER 1792.

AN ACT in relation to Warehousemen and Warehouse receipts.

Be it enacted by the General Assembly of the Commonwealth of Kentucky:

Persons receiving cotton, and with or without compensation, be deemed warehousemen.

§ 1. That hereafter, in this State, all and every person or persons, firms, companies, or corporations, who shall receive cotton, tobacco, pork, grain, corn, wheat, rye, oats, hemp, whisky, coal, or any kind of produce, wares, merchandise, commodity, or any other kind or description of personal property or thing whatever, in store, or undertake to receive or take care of the same, with or without compensation or reward therefor, shall be deemed and held to be warehousemen.

Warehouseman to give receipt, &c.

§ 2. That every warehouseman receiving anything enumerated in section one of this act shall, on demand of the owner thereof, or the person from whom he receives the same, give a receipt therefor, setting forth the quality, quantity, kind, and description thereof, and which shall be designated by some mark, and which receipt shall be evidence in any action against said warehouseman.

§ 3. All receipts issued by any warehouseman, as provided by this act, shall be negotiable and transferable by indorsement in blank, or by special indorsement, and with like liability, as bills of exchange now are, and with like remedy thereon.

§ 4. That no warehouseman or other person or persons shall issue any receipt or other voucher for any goods, wares, merchandise, produce, or other thing enumerated in the first section of this act, or for any other commodity or thing, to any person or persons, company, companies, corporation or corporations, or beings, unless such goods, wares, merchandise, produce, property, commodity, or thing shall have been *bona fide* received into possession and store by such warehouseman or other person, and shall be in store and under his or their control, care, and keeping, at the time of issuing such receipt.

Receipt not to be issued until goods bona fide received into possession, &c.

§ 5. That no warehouseman or other person shall issue any receipt or voucher upon, or for any goods, wares, merchandise, produce, commodity, property, or other thing, of any description or character whatever, to any person, persons, company, companies, corporation or corporations, as security for any money loaned, or other indebtedness, unless such goods, wares, merchandise, produce, commodity, property, or other thing so receipted for, shall be, at the time of issuing such receipt or voucher, the property without encumbrance of said warehouseman; and if encumbered by prior lien, then the character and extent of that lien shall be fully set forth and explained in the receipt, and shall be actually and in fact in store and under the control of said warehouseman at the time of giving such receipt or voucher.

Warehouseman not to issue receipt as security unless goods unencumbered.

§ 6. That no warehouseman or other person shall issue any receipt or other voucher for any goods, wares, merchandise, produce, or other thing enumerated in section first of this act, whilst any former receipt for any such goods, wares, merchandise, produce, commodity, property, or thing as aforesaid, or any part thereof, shall be outstanding and uncanceled.

Receipt not to be issued if one is outstanding.

§ 7. That no warehouseman or other person shall sell or encumber, ship, transfer, or in any manner remove, beyond his immediate control, any goods, wares, merchandise, produce, commodity, property, or chattel, for which a receipt or voucher shall have been given, without the written consent of the person or persons holding such receipt, and the production of the receipt.

Property not to be removed without consent of holder of receipt.

§ 8. Any warehouseman or person who shall willfully and knowingly violate any one, or any part of the provisions of the foregoing act, shall be deemed a cheat and swindler, and subject to indictment in a court of competent jurisdiction, and, upon conviction, shall be fined in

Penalty.

1869.   any sum not exceeding five thousand dollars, which shall
             inure to the Commonwealth, and shall be imprisoned in
             the Penitentiary of this State not exceeding five years;
             and all and every person aggrieved by the violation of
             any of the provisions of this act, shall have and main-
             tain an action against the person or persons, company
             or companies, corporation or corporations, violating any
             of the provisions of this act, to recover all damages, im-
             mediate, consequent, legal, and extraordinary, which he
             or they may have sustained by reason of such violation
             as aforesaid, whether such person may have been con-
             victed before the criminal court or not.

Party to   § 9. That hereafter when any receipt or voucher shall
assign receipt   have been issued as provided by this act, and used or
when pledged.   pledged as collateral security or otherwise, for the loan
             of money, the bank or person to whom the same may
             be pledged, hypothecated, or transferred, shall have power
             and authority to sell the same, and transfer title thereto
             in such manner and on such terms as may be agreed to
             in writing by the parties at the time of making the pledge.

             § 10. This act shall take effect and be in force from its
             passage.

                                        Approved March 6, 1869.

CHAPTER 1806.

AN ACT to amend the 844th section of the Civil Code of Practice.

*Be it enacted by the General Assembly of the Commonwealth
of Kentucky:*

             That the section 844 of the Civil Code of Practice be
Myers' Civil amended so that the same shall read as follows: Where
Code, p. 276. an order for a provisional remedy has been made by a
             judge or justice in an action within the jurisdiction of
             their respective courts, and the order has been served or
             levied, the trial of the action and disposition of the order
             may take place at any time after five days' notice to the
             opposite party, without waiting for the regular term of
             such judge's or justice's court, which notice may be given
             by the officer at the time of serving the summons or
             levying the order, or by the defendant after he files a
             counter affidavit with such judge or justice; and if the
             justice before whom the trial should regularly [be] had is
             sick, absent, or unable to act, the officer may return the
             case for trial before the most convenient magistrate.

                                        Approved March 8, 1869.

CHAPTER 1810.

AN ACT to amend section 457 of the Civil Code of Practice.

Be it enacted by the General Assembly of the Commonwealth of Kentucky:

§ 1. That section 457 of the Civil Code of Practice be so amended as to read as follows: "The action for alimony or divorce shall be by equitable proceedings, and must be brought in the county where the wife usually resides, if she has a residence in this State; if not, in the county of the husband's residence." ·

§ 2. This act shall take effect fifty days after its passage.

Myers' Sup., p. 128.

Approved March 9, 1869.

CHAPTER 1812.

AN ACT to repeal an act, entitled "An act to prevent the destruction of fish in Green River and its tributaries and other water-courses," approved February 26th, 1868.

Be it enacted by the General Assembly of the Commonwealth of Kentucky:

§ 1. That an act to prevent the destruction of fish in Green river and its tributaries and other water-courses, approved February 26th, 1868, be, and the same is hereby, repealed, so far as it applies to Kentucky river and its tributaries above the mouth of Paint Lick creek.

§ 2. This act to take effect from and after its passage.

Public Acts of 1868, p. 26.

Approved March 9, 1869.

CHAPTER 1815.

AN ACT to amend an act to empower County Courts to take stock in Turnpike Roads in this Commonwealth, approved March 9th, 1868.

Be it enacted by the General Assembly of the Commonwealth of Kentucky:

§ 1. That an act to empower county courts to take stock in turnpike roads in this Commonwealth, approved March 9th, 1868, be so amended as to exempt the counties of Oldham, Lincoln, and Garrard from the provisions of the same, and that charters passed for the benefit of road companies in said counties, which are affected by the act hereby amended, are in full force as if said act had not been passed.

§ 2. This act to take effect from its passage.

Public Acts of 1868, p. 58.

Approved March 9, 1869.

1869.

CHAPTER 1818.

AN ACT regulating and changing the times of holding the Quarterly and County and Magistrates' Courts in the County of Greenup.

Be it enacted by the General Assembly of the Commonwealth of Kentucky:

Greenup quarterly and magistrate's courts. § 1. That hereafter, the quarterly and magistrates' courts of Greenup county shall be held quarterly as now; but the time of holding the same is hereby so changed that said courts shall be held in the months of February, May, August, and November of each year, and the terms of the quarterly courts in said county shall commence on the third Monday of each of said months, and continue so many days as the business may require; and the times of holding the magistrates' courts in said months shall be regulated by the presiding judge of said county, under the authority now conferred upon him by law.

County courts. § 2. The county courts of Greenup county shall hereafter be held on the first Monday of every month, except in the months in which the circuit court is held for said county, when the county court shall be adjourned to some other day in the month, not a circuit court day, by the presiding judge, or stand adjourned until the next regular county court day: *Provided*, That this act shall not be construed so as to prohibit the county courts from sitting in the morning before the circuit court sits, or in the evening after the circuit court adjourns, should the business of the county court demand such sitting, as the intention of this section is only to prevent the county court from interfering with the circuit court by holding a session at the same time.

§ 3. This act shall be in force from its passage.

Approved March 9, 1869.

CHAPTER 1819.

AN ACT to fix the time of holding the Courts of Justices of the Peace in Bourbon County.

Be it enacted by the General Assembly of the Commonwealth of Kentucky:

Bourbon. § 1. That after this act takes effect, the courts of justices of the peace in the county of Bourbon shall be held in the months of February, May, and November, and the days in said months on which the several justices' courts are to be held shall be fixed and determined as now provided by law.

§ 2. This act shall take effect upon the first day of April next.

Approved March 9, 1869.

CHAPTER 1825.

AN ACT to authorize the assignment of executions in favor of the Commonwealth against Sheriffs and their sureties.

Be it enacted by the General Assembly of the Commonwealth of Kentucky:

§ 1. That when any judgment on the revenue bond of any sheriff of any county of this Commonwealth has heretofore been, or shall hereafter be, paid, in whole or in part, by the sureties of such sheriff in such bond, such judgment, when the same shall have been fully satisfied and discharged, shall be assigned by the Auditor of Public Accounts to such sureties, or any of them, to the extent the same may have been paid by them; and that such sureties, or any of them, shall have the right to have an execution or executions issued thereon, which shall be indorsed for the benefit of the sureties so ordering it to the amount the same may have been paid by them respectively.

Judgment against sheriffs paid by the sureties to be assigned to said sureties by the Auditor to extent of payment

§ 2. This act shall take effect and be in force from its passage.

Approved March 9, 1869.

CHAPTER 1841.

AN ACT to amend sections 445 and 373, of the Civil Code of Practice.

Be it enacted by the General Assembly of the Commonwealth ,of Kentucky:

§ 1. That section 445, of the Civil Code of Practice, shall not apply to judgments granting a divorce, so far as the divorce itself is involved, nor shall section 373 apply thereto.

Myers' Sup., pp. 108 and 195.

§ 2. This act shall be in force from its passage.

Approved March 9, 1869.

CHAPTER 1856.

AN ACT to establish a Court of Common Pleas for the County of Warren.

Be it enacted by the General Assembly of the Commonwealth of Kentucky:

§ 1. There shall be established a court of justice in and for Warren county, which shall be known as the Warren court of common pleas, to be a court of record held by a single judge, who, after the election of the first judge, shall be elected in the same manner and at the same time as circuit judges of this Commonwealth, and who shall have the like qualifications, and receive a salary

Court of common pleas established in Warren county

1869.

Salary of judge

of fifteen hundred dollars, seven hundred and fifty of which shall be paid to him from the State Treasury, in the same manner as circuit judges are paid, and the remaining seven hundred and fifty dollars to be paid by the county of Warren as hereinafter provided; he shall be a conservator of the peace; be commissioned and qualified as circuit judges are, and be subject to impeachment in like manner and for like causes; have like powers as circuit judges, as a magistrate or judicial officer out of court.

Manner of election.

§ 2. The first judge shall be chosen at the regular August election, 1869, and vacancies shall be filled and special judges elected in and for the said court in like manner as in the circuit courts of this Commonwealth; the same practice and the same fees, as far as applicable, shall prevail in said court as in circuit courts, and it shall have a seal, bearing its name and˙the arms of the Commonwealth.

Sheriff and circuit court clerk officers of said court—their powers & duties.

§ 3. That the sheriff of Warren county shall perform all the duties in all cases and proceedings in said court, which would otherwise devolve upon him in the circuit court; and the clerk of the Warren circuit court shall perform the clerical duties of said court, and shall be entitled to the same fees as allowed him as clerk of the Warren circuit court for similar services; he shall be responsible on his official bond for the faithful discharge of his duties herein, and his certificate of the records of said court shall have the same force and effect as his certificate of records from the Warren circuit court; and , before the holding of the first court of common pleas, which shall be on the fourth Monday in November, 1869, he shall, without fee or reward, transfer to said court all civil common law cases depending in the Warren circuit court, except on forfeited recognizances, bail bonds, &c., which shall thereupon proceed in said court of common pleas; and said clerk shall keep a common docket and a motion docket, as is now required by law to be kept in circuit courts.

Jurisdiction.

§ 4. The said court of common pleas shall have all the civil common law jurisdiction, original and appellate, which, by the existing law, appertains to the circuit court for Warren county, except on forfeited recognizances, bail bonds, &c.; and to its clerk's office, transcripts from justices' courts on appeal, and for executions and replevin bonds for rent shall be returned; and suits may be transferred from this court to the equity docket of the circuit court, in all cases and in the same manner that suits are now authorized to be transferred from the common law to the equity docket in the circuit courts.

§ 5. The Warren court of common pleas shall hold annually two terms, beginning on the fourth Mondays in May and November in each year, and continuing each term four weeks : *Provided, however,* That the judge of said court shall have power to extend any regular term of the court, or to hold a call term at any time when, in his judgment, the business of said court may require.

§ 6. All summons, actual or constructive, in actions commenced in said court, must be served and returned in like manner as in circuit courts.

§ 7. Said court shall have full power to make all rules to facilitate its business not inconsistent with the Constitution and the laws of the State, and its judgments and final orders shall be subject to appeal to the Court of Appeals in like manner as those of circuit courts, and not otherwise.

§ 8. In the summoning and selection of juries, and in the trial by jury, and the payment of jurors in said county, the same shall be governed by the laws now in force and which are applicable to circuit courts.

§ 9. At the request of parties to common law actions now pending in the Warren circuit court, and with the consent of the present judge thereof, not exceeding fifty of the oldest litigated cases may remain upon the docket of said circuit court, and be there tried in the same manner as if this act had not passed.

§ 10. The county court for the county of Warren is hereby directed to levy an annual tax on the taxable property of said county, in addition to the taxes already provided for, sufficient to raise the sum of seven hundred and fifty dollars, which shall be collected as other taxes, and by the sheriff of said county paid over to the judge of said court of common pleas on or before the first Monday of January in each year; or, in lieu of the foregoing, said court may, in its discretion, raise said sum of money by levying a poll-tax; or, said court may, in its discretion, adopt both of the foregoing methods. The sheriff shall be responsible on his official bond for moneys so collected. The moneys hereby provided to be raised shall be for the payment of the salary of the judge of the Warren court of common pleas, and shall be applied to no other purpose whatever.

§ 11. Nothing in this act shall be taken to disqualify the judge of the Warren court of common pleas from practicing in any other court of this Commonwealth.

§ 12. All laws or parts of laws within the province of this act and conflicting therewith are repealed from and after the passage of this act.

§ 13. The office of judge of said court of common pleas shall not be incompatible with the office of judge of the

Marginal notes:

1869.

To hold two terms annually, and power to have call term, &c.

Summons returned as in circuit court.

Fines.

Cases to remain in circuit court docket.

County court to levy annual tax to pay judge.

Sheriff to collect, &c.

Said court not incompatible with county court.

1869.

county court for the county of Warren: *Provided*, That in case the same person shall be judge of the said court of common pleas and of the county court, all appeals from the county or quarterly court shall 'be taken to the circuit court for said county.

§ 14. This act shall take effect from its passage.

Approved March 10, 1869.

CHAPTER 1862.

AN ACT to amend chapter 16, article 6, section 3, of the Revised Statutes.

Be it enacted by the General Assembly of the Commonwealth of Kentucky:

Stant. Rev. Stat., vol. 1, p. 244.

§ 1. That section 3 of article 6 of chapter 16 of the Revised Statutes be so amended as to apply to and include the State Treasurer and Register of the Land Office.

§ 2. This act shall be in force from its passage.

Approved March 10, 1869.

CHAPTER 1871.

AN ACT supplemental to an act to improve the navigation of Licking River.

Be it enacted by the General Assembly of the Commonwealth of Kentucky:

Appropriation embraces the Licking river between Salyersville & Mason's branch.

§ 1. That that part of Licking river between Salyersville and the mouth of Mason's branch, in Magoffin county, be, and the same is hereby, embraced by the appropriation made at the present session of the General Assembly to remove the mill-dams and other obstructions to the navigation of said river.

Additional commissioners, & their duties.

§ 2. That Joseph Gardner, of Magoffin county, and John D. Young, of Bath, be additional commissioners on the part of the State to negotiate with mill-owners as to damages, and that their pay be the same as that fixed upon for the other commissioners; but the act of any three of the commissioners shall be lawful and binding, and not more than three shall act at one time; and said commissioners shall only be paid for the time they act.

Number of challenges to jurors.

§ 3. When a jury is being empanneled, as provided for in the law to which this is a supplement, each party may challenge ten persons without cause.

When mill in litigation to be paid according to order of court.

§ 4. That where any mill or other property which is condemned or agreed to be paid for under the act to which this is a supplement is in litigation, the payment shall only be made to the party to whom the court in which the suit is pending shall order: *Provided*, Notice thereof shall by said party be given to the commissioners, when the commissioners shall pay the money into the court wherein such litigation is pending.

§ 5. This act shall be in force from its passage.

Approved March 10, 1869.

CHAPTER 1872.

AN ACT to establish the County of Menifee.

Be it enacted by the General Assembly of the Commonwealth of Kentucky:

§ 1. That from and after the first day of May, 1869, so much of the counties of Bath, Montgomery, Morgan, Powell, and Wolfe as is included within the following boundary is hereby erected into and established a separate and distinct county, to be known and called Menifee county: Beginning at the mouth of Beaver creek; thence a straight line to the divide between Buck creek and Clear creek; thence with said divide to the gate-post on said ridge; thence with the great road to the crossing of Salt Lick; thence with the dividing ridge between main Salt Lick and Clark's Fork of Salt Lick to the divide between Clark's Fork and Mud Lick; thence with said dividing ridge to the head of Mill creek and East Fork of Slate creek, so as to include all the waters of said East Fork of Slate; thence running down the ridge on the west side of said East Fork to the farm of W. J. Rose, including said farm; thence crossing main Slate to a point between Hawkins and Cook's branches; thence running the dividing ridge between Hawkins and Cook's branches to Pointer's farm, including said Pointer's farm; thence a straight line to the mouth of Copperas creek; thence a straight line to the house of Catron, in or near the Indian Valley, including him; thence a straight line to the old farm known as the Boone Howard farm, including it; thence a straight line to Licking river, opposite the mouth of the North Fork; thence down Licking river to the beginning. [margin: Boundary.]

§ 2. For the purpose of locating and determining the most suitable and convenient place for the seat of justice for said county, William Mynhei, of Morgan county; John A. Tuneer, of Bath; Oliver Crawford, of Estill; C. M. Hanks, of Wolfe county; John Deaton, of Breathitt county, and D. D. Sublett, of Magoffin county, are hereby appointed commissioners for that purpose, any three of whom may act after having been first qualified faithfully to discharge the duty assigned them. Said commissioners shall meet at the house of Thomas N. Perry on the fourth Mon- [margin: Commissioners appointed, their duties.]

1869. day in March, 1869, and on said day shall locate said county seat of justice; and they may adjourn from place to place, and time to time, until they shall have completed the duties assigned them ; or if, from any cause, a majority do not meet on that day named, those meeting shall adjourn to another day, and so on until three or more shall attend ; and when they have located the county seat they shall draw up duplicates of the same, of which they shall transmit to the Secretary of State at Frankfort, and the other they shall lodge in the hands ot W. S. Pierce, who shall deliver the same to the clerk of the county court of said county as soon as one shall have been elected and qualified ; and said seat of justice, when located, shall be known and called Frenchburg.

§ 3. The county of Menifee shall be divided into four justices' districts, which shall also be voting precincts, in each of which there shall be elected two justices of the peace and one constable.   J. C. Lyons, R. E. Frisby, and T. N. Perry, or a majority of whom may act, are hereby appointed to lay off said districts, and to designate the places of voting therein.   Before they enter upon their duties they shall take an oath faithfully to discharge the same; they shall meet at the house of T. N. Perry on the first Monday in April, 1869, or as soon thereafter as may be, and proceed to discharge their duties imposed on them by this act, and may adjourn from time to time and place to place until they complete the same; they shall lodge in the hands of William S. Pierce, certified copies of the boundaries of said districts, who shall hold same until a county clerk is elected and qualified for said county, and then deliver the same unto the said clerk, to be recorded in his office; and said commissioners shall also transmit to the Secretary of State a certified copy of said districts, to be filed in his office.   They shall also, at the same time, designate two suitable persons to act as judges, also a clerk, and some fit person for sheriff in each of said districts, whose duty it shall be to hold the first election for officers of said county; and the persons so appointed shall take the oaths faithfully and impartially to discharge the duties of their respective offices.

County to be laid off in districts; persons appointed to lay it off; their duties, &c.

Commissioners to appoint judges of election.

§ 4. An election shall be held in said county on the first Saturday in May, 1869, for the election of circuit court clerk, a county court clerk, a presiding judge of said county court, sheriff, jailer, coroner, assessor of tax, and county attorney, and two justices of the peace and one constable in each justices' district in said county.   The person who act as sheriff of the election shall meet at T. N. Perry's on the third day after the election, and carefully compare the polls, and shall sign three certifi-

Election held in May, 1869, to elect county officers.

cates of the election of the persons elected to each office, designating the person who received the highest number of votes, and the office to which he is elected, one of which they shall transmit to the Secretary of State, one to the officers elected, and they shall lodge one in the hands of W. S. Pierce, who shall deliver it to the county court clerk of said county of Menifee, after one is elected, to be recorded in his office. It shall be the duty of the Governor of this Commonwealth to commission such of said officers so elected as are required by existing laws to be commissioned. The officers first elected under the provisions of this act shall hold their respective offices until the next regular election for like offices, and until their successors are elected and qualified. They shall take the oaths, and execute such bond or bonds as is required by the existing laws of like offices.

§ 5. The presiding judge of the county court and justices of the peace of said county, a majority of the justices concurring, are authorized and empowered to select suitable lots of ground at the seat of justice of said county upon which to erect the necessary buildings, and to purchase and make provision for the payment therefor, by levying a poll tax, not exceeding five dollars on each tithable in said county, from year to year, until the same is fully paid, or they may receive such lots of ground by donation; and when so purchased or donated, the vendor or donor shall make proper deeds therefor to the county court of said county, and the title thereto shall vest in the county court for the use of said county; and they may receive subscriptions in work or materials or for money to be paid, to be used in the erection or payment for the erection of the necessary public buildings.

§ 6. The county court of said county shall be held on the first Monday in each month, and the quarterly courts on the Tuesdays succeeding the first Mondays in March, June, September, and December.

§ 7. That nothing in this act shall be construed to release the citizens and property now subject to taxation within the boundary of the first section of this act from being held liable for the bonds and interest thereon which were issued to the Lexington and Big Sandy railroad company as though this act had never been passed. The assessor of tax of Menifee county shall annually assess and take in all taxable property within the boundaries of their counties as existing before the passage of this act for the purpose of being taxed to contribute as heretofore to the payment of said bonds and interest; and the county court of Menifee county shall levy annually on the portions of citizens and property in the parts of Menifee county which are taken from the counties of Bath and Mont-

1869.

Certificates of election to be sent to Secretary of State, one to officers elected, and one to county court clerk.

Term of office.

Judge of county court and justices empowered to select suitable lots, and levy tax to pay for public buildings, &c.

Time of holding county court.

Persons liable for the bonds issued to the Lexington and Big Sandy railroad company.

Assessor.

1869.

gomery the same rates of taxation as are levied and collected for the purpose of paying such bonds and interest thereon which are levied and collected in the counties of Bath and Montgomery for that purpose; and the sheriff of Menifee county shall collect the said railroad tax, and so on from year to year, until the bonds and interest shall have been fully paid; and when so paid or otherwise discharged, the power to assess, levy, and collect shall cease; and said sheriff shall pay over to the county judges of the counties of Bath and Montgomery the respective proportions of said counties of said tax at the time he is by law required to pay other taxes, and they shall account and be responsible therefor under existing laws.

County court to provide suitable rooms for circuit court, &c.

§ 8. The county court of Menifee county shall provide suitable rooms in which to hold the circuit and county courts and to keep the clerks' offices in until public buildings shall be provided; and while courts are held at the places provided, all advertisements, notices, &c., required to be put up at the court-house door, or sales or other acts to be done at the court-house door, shall be legal and binding if done at the places provided for holding courts as aforesaid.

Charles Glover appointed to run boundary line.

His duties.

§ 9. That Charles Glover, of Bath county, be, and he is hereby appointed a commissioner, and he, with William S. Pierce, and such other assistance as he may employ, shall run and make the boundary line of Menifee county as provided in the first section of this act. He shall make out duplicate certificates of his work, transmit one to the Secretary of State, to be filed in his office, and he shall deliver the other to the county court clerk of Menifee, to be filed in his office, after being first duly recorded.

§ 10. The county court of Menifee county shall allow to each of the commissioners named in this act and to their assistants reasonable compensation, to be paid out of the county levy.

Assessors.

§ 11. The assessors of tax of the several counties from which Menifee is formed shall, for the year 1869, proceed, as though this act had not passed, to take in the list of taxable property, except that they shall make out separate books of that portion of their respective counties that has been given to Menifee, and return the same to the county court of Menifee.

To have use of the jails of either of the counties from which Menifee is taken.

§ 12. The county court of Menifee shall have the use of the jails of either of the counties from which Menifee is taken, and the jailers shall receive all persons committed from Menifee under the same rules as if committed from either of the counties from which Menifee is taken.

Secretary to furnish books.

§ 13. The Secretary of State shall furnish the county of Menifee and its several officers with all the books now allowed by law to the several counties and officers.

§ 14. The county of Menifee is hereby attached to the 1st judicial district for the election of judge of the Court of Appeals, and to the 13th judicial district for the holding of circuit court ; and the time of holding circuit courts in said county shall be on the Mondays succeeding the Elliott circuit courts, and continue six days at each term.

1869.

Attached to 1st judicial district for election of Judge of Court of Appeals; to 13th for holding circuit courts.

§ 15. The several counties from which Menifee is taken shall have jurisdiction to these limits, before this act was passed, until Menifee shall have elected officers and they have qualified as required herein.

§ 16. The said county of Menifee, for the election of Representatives in the Legislature, shall vote with the county of Bath, and in the election of a Senator it shall vote with, and constitute a part of, the 28th Senatorial District, and for the election of members of Congress it shall vote with, and form a part of, the 9th Congressional District until the next regular apportionment.

How county to vote.

Approved March 10, 1869.

CHAPTER 1297.

AN ACT to establish the county of Elliott out of parts of Morgan, Lawrence, and Carter counties.

Be it enacted by the General Assembly of the Commonwealth of Kentucky:

§ 1. That from and after the first day of April, 1869, so much of the counties of Morgan, Carter, and Lawrence as is included within the following boundary, is hereby erected into and established a separate and distinct county, to be called the county of Elliott, viz: Beginning on the county road where it crosses the dividing ridge between the open fork of Little Sandy and the North Fork of Licking river, in Morgan county; thence due west to the county road leading from West Liberty to the head of the Chusty Fork of Triplett creek; thence with said road to the Rowan county line; thence with the Rowan county line to the Carter county line; thence around the dividing ridge with the same between the waters of Caney creek and the waters of Triplett and Tygart creeks, to opposite the head of Big Gimblett; thence around with the ridge between said Big Gimblett and Tygart waters, to the ridge or point on the north side of said Gimblett, and down said ridge or point, including all the waters of said Big Gimblett, to Little Sandy river; thence down Little Sandy river, with the meanders of the same, to a point below the farm of Travis Herton; thence a straight line so as to include said Herton's farm, running to the mouth of a branch near the house of William Stevens Huen as the "Squire Frazier" branch; thence up

Boundary of the county of Elliott.

1869.

said branch to its head, on the dividing ridge between the waters of Little Sandy river and the waters of the Little Fork; thence with said dividing ridge to the head of the Brushy Fork of Little Fork of Little Sandy; thence down the point or ridge, so as to include all the waters of said Brushy Fork, to the Little Fork; thence a straight line to the Lawrence county line, running to the top of the ridge on the southeast side of said Little Fork; thence running up said ridge, including all the waters of said Little Fork, to the head of Blain, to where the Morgan and Lawrence county lines come together at the head of Newcomb's Fork, where the county road leading from Sandy Hook to Louisa crosses the ridge; thence with the Morgan and Lawrence county lines to the top of the ridge at the head waters of Paint creek; thence around said ridge, between said Paint creek and Newcomb's Fork, including all the waters of said Newcomb's Fork, to the head waters of Elk Fork; thence running with the dividing ridge between the waters of Elk Fork and the waters of Little Sandy, to the head waters of the right hand fork of the North Fork, Licking river; thence with the dividing ridge between the waters of Little Sandy and the said right hand fork of the North Fork of Licking river to the beginning.

§ 2. For the purpose of locating and determining the most suitable and convenient place for the seat of justice in said county, Major William Mynhin, W. W. Cox, of the county of Morgan, D. D. Sublett, of the county of Magoffin, Benjamin F. Shepherd, of the county of Carter, and William Holbrook, of Lawrence, are appointed commissioners for that purpose, a majority of whom may act, after having been duly qualified faithfully to discharge the duty assigned them. Said commissioners shall. meet at the house of J. K. Hunter, on Little Sandy, on the first Monday in April, 1869, and, on said day, shall proceed to locate said seat of justice, and may adjourn from time to time and place to place until they shall have completed the duties herein assigned them ; and when they shall have located the county seat of said county, they shall sign two written certificates of the same, one of which they shall transmit to the Secretary of State, and the other they shall lodge in the hands of J. K. Hunter, who shall deliver the same to the county court clerk of said county, when one shall have been elected, who shall record the same in his office.

§ 3. The county of Elliott shall be divided into five justices' districts, which district shall also be election precincts, in each of which there shall be elected two justices of the peace and one constable. Wm. H. Vancant, G. W. Stamper, J. K. Hunter, Travis Herten, and A.

Commissioners appointed to select seat of justice, &c.

Commissioners appointed to lay off and district & designate places of voting in said county.

Divided into five precincts.

Isom, a majority of whom may act, are appointed commissioners to lay off and district and designate the places of voting therein. Before they enter upon the duties herein assigned them, they shall take an oath faithfully to discharge the same. They shall meet at the house of J. K. Hunter on the first Monday in April, 1869, or as soon thereafter as may be, and proceed to discharge the duties imposed on them by this act, and may adjourn from time to time and place to place until they complete the same. They shall lodge in the hands of P. J. Livingston certified copies of said districts, who shall hold the same until a county court clerk for said county is elected, and then deliver the same to said clerk, who shall record the same in his office; and said commissioners shall also transmit to the Secretary of State a certified copy of said districts; they shall also, at the same time, designate two suitable persons to act as judges; also a clerk, and some fit person for sheriff in each of said districts, whose duty it shall be to attend the first election of officers for said county; and the said officers thus appointed shall take an oath faithfully and impartially to discharge the duties of their respective offices.

§ 4. An election shall be held in said county on the first Saturday in May, 1869, for the election of circuit court clerk, a county court clerk, a presiding judge of the county court, sheriff, jailer, coroner, assessor of tax, and county attorney, and two justices of the peace and one constable in each justices' district in said county. The persons who act as sheriff of the election shall meet at the house of J. K. Hunter on the third day after the election, and carefully compare the polls, and shall sign three certificates of the election of the persons elected to each office, designating the person who received the highest number of votes, the office to which he is elected, one of which they shall transmit to the Secretary of State, one to the officer elected, and they shall lodge one in the hands of the clerk of the election, who shall deliver it to the hands of the county court clerk of the county of Elliott, when one shall be elected, which shall be by said clerk duly recorded in his office. It shall be the duty of the Governor of this Commonwealth to commission such of said officers so elected as are required by existing laws to be commissioned. The officers first elected under the provisions of this act shall hold their respective offices until the next regular election for like officers, and until their successors are elected and qualified; they shall take the oaths and execute such bond as required by the existing laws for like offices.

§ 5. The presiding judge of the county court and justices of the peace of said county, a majority of said justices

Time of electing county officers, &c.

County judge and justices to select ground for public buildings and purchase same, &c.

concurring, are authorized and empowered to select suitable lots of ground at the seat of justice of said county upon which to erect the necessary public buildings, and to purchase and make provision for the payment of the same by levying a poll-tax on each tithable in said county from year to year until the same is fully paid, or they may receive lots of ground by donation; and when so purchased or donated, the vendor or donor shall make deeds of conveyance to said county for said lots or lot of ground, and the title thereof shall vest in the county court for the use of said county.

Time of holding county and quarterly court § 6. The county court of said county shall he held on the third Monday in each month, and the quarterly court shall be held on the Tuesday after the third Monday in March, June, September, and December.

This act does not release bonds issued to Lexington and Big Sandy railroad company. § 7. That nothing in this act shall be constructed to release the citizens and property now subject, or which may hereafter become subject, to taxation within the boundary of Carter county, included in the first section of this act, from being held and made liable for the bonds and interest issued to the Lexington and Big Sandy railroad company, as though this act had never been passed. The commissioners of tax for Carter county shall annually assess and take in all taxable property within the aforesaid boundary; and the sheriff of Carter county shall annually collect the revenue and railroad tax within the boundary, as included and described in the first section of this act, and shall account for and pay the same as required by the existing laws: *Provided*, This section shall become inoperative whenever the county of Carter pays off the debt and interest on the bonds issued to the Lexington and Big Sandy railroad company, or becomes otherwise released or discharged from the payment thereof.

County court to provide rooms. § 8. It shall be the duty of the county court of said county to provide suitable rooms in which to hold circuit and county courts until a court-house shall be erected for said county.

J. K. Howard to make boundary line, &c. § 9. That J. K. Howard be, and he is, appointed, with such assistance as he may deem necessary to employ, to run and plainly mark the boundary line of Elliott county, as laid down in the first section of this act. He shall make out two written certificates, one of which he shall transmit to the Secretary of State, and the other he shall deliver to the county court clerk, who shall record the same in his office.

Compensation of commissioners, § 10. It shall be the duty of the county court of said county to allow each of the commissioners appointed in this act and their assistants reasonable compensation for their services, and make provision for the payment of the same out of the county levy.

1869.

§ 11. The assessors of tax of the counties [of] Lawrence, Carter, and Morgan, for the year 1869, shall proceed as though this act had not passed, except they shall make out separate books of that portion of their respective counties that has been stricken off and included within the county of Elliott, and return the same to the county court of Elliott county as the law directs the return of assessors' books.

Assessors to proceed for 1869 as if this act had not passed, except to make separate list.

§ 12. The county of Elliott shall have the use of the jail of Carter county until a jail shall be built for the said county of Elliott, and the jailer of Carter county shall receive all persons committed from the county of Elliott under the same rules and regulations as if committed from Carter county.

Jail.

§ 13. The Secretary of State is hereby directed to furnish the county of Elliott all the necessary books required by law to be furnished to county officers and clerks' offices within this Commonwealth.

Secretary of State to forward books.

§ 14. The justices of the peace stricken off of the counties of Morgan, Carter, and Lawrence by this act, and included in the county of Elliott, shall retain their books, records, and papers until their successors are elected and qualified under this act, when they shall deliver the said books, records, and papers over to their successors in office, and said books, records, and papers shall be the records of Elliott county.

Justice to keep books until successors qualified.

§ 15. The counties of Morgan, Carter, and Lawrence shall have jurisdiction in all things until this act takes effect.

§ 16. The name of the seat of justice for the county of Elliott shall be called Martinsburg.

Name of seat of justice.

§ 17. That the qualified voters of Elliott county, embraced in the territory stricken from the counties of Morgan, Carter, and Lawrence, shall vote for Senator and Representative as the apportionment now stands by law, and until the next regular apportionment for Senator and Representative.

To vote for Senator & Representative.

§ 18. That said county of Elliott shall be included in the 13th judicial district, and that the circuit courts for said county shall be holden on the Mondays succeeding each term of the Morgan circuit courts, and shall continue six judicial days.

Time of holding circuit court.

Approved January 26, 1869.

CHAPTER 1873.

AN ACT to authorize the Attorney General to bring suit against William
T. Samuels, late Auditor of the State.

*Be it enacted by the General Assembly of the Commonwealth
of Kentucky:*

Attorney General instructed to institute suit against W. T. Samuels.

§ 1. That the Attorney General be directed forthwith to
bring suit in the fiscal court of the State against William
T. Samuels, late Auditor of Public Accounts, to recover
from him the sum of five hundred and twenty dollars and
seventy cents, with interest from its receipt, the amount
he is shown by report of the committee of this House to
have received from James Brien, a member of this House
from Marshall county for 1865–67, under the resolution of
this General Assembly, approved 19th February, 1867, and
4th March, 1867, concerning the payment of the members
and officers of the said General Assembly in gold.

§ 2. This act shall take effect from its passage.

Approved March 10, 1869.

CHAPTER 1879.

AN ACT to change the time of holding the Todd Quarterly Court.

*Be it enacted by the General Assembly of the Commonwealth
of Kentucky:*

Time of holding the Todd quarterly court changed.

§ 1. That hereafter, the Todd quarterly courts shall be
held on the Tuesday after the second Monday in March,
June, September, and December of each year, and continue so long as the business of the court may require at
each term; and all acts and parts of acts fixing a different time for the holding of said court are hereby repealed.

§ 2. This act shall take effect from after the 30th day
of April, 1869.

Approved March 10, 1869.

CHAPTER 1880.

AN ACT to exempt certain Counties and Districts from tax on seals in
certain cases.

*Be it enacted by the General Assembly of the Commonwealth
of Kentucky:*

Counties and districts which have voted tax for railroads & navigation exempt from tax on seals.

§ 1. That the counties or districts where voters have or
may hereafter vote a tax upon such counties or districts to
aid in the construction of railroads or to improve the navigation of any of the rivers of this State, be, and they are
hereby, exempt from paying any tax or revenue on the
seals of such county used in the issuing of the bonds of
such county or district to aid in the construction of rail-

roads or to improve the navigation of the rivers of this
State: *Provided*, Nothing in this act shall be construed so
as to prevent the clerks from collecting the fees now
allowed them by law for the use of such seals.

§ 2. This act to take effect from its passage.

Approved March 10, 1869.

CHAPTER 1892.

AN ACT to change the time of holding the Quarterly Court in Gallatin
County.

*Be it enacted by the General Assembly of the Commonwealth
of Kentucky:*

§ 1. That hereafter, the terms of the Gallatin county
quarterly court shall be begun and held on the Tuesdays
after the third Mondays in the month of January, April,
July, and October of each year, and continued at each term
until the business of said court is disposed of.

Time of hold-
ing Gallatin
quarterly court
changed.

§ 2. This act to take effect from the first day of March,
1869.

Approved March 11, 1869.

CHAPTER 1896.

AN ACT to change the time of holding the Court of Claims in Meade
County.

*Be it enacted by the General Assembly of the Commonwealth of
Kentucky:*

§ 1. That hereafter, the court of claims in Meade county
shall be held on the fourth Monday in September in each
year, instead of the time now provided by law.

Meade county.

§ 2. This act to take effect from its passage.

Approved March 11, 1869.

CHAPTER 1930.

AN ACT to provide a Public Guardian in certain Counties.

*Be it enacted by the General Assembly of the Commonwealth
of Kentucky:*

§ 1. That the public administrator in the counties of
Barren, Monroe, Metcalfe, and Allen shall also be public
guardian, and, by virtue of his office of public administrator, he shall, whenever so ordered to do by the county
or circuit court of his county, take into his possession and
preserve the effects of every kind belonging to any ward
so committed, with its effects, to his charge and guardianship.

Public ad-
ministrator of
Barren &c., al-
so public guar-
dian.

1869.

Guardian to
bring suit, &c.

§ 2. The said public guardian shall have full power to bring suit and prosecute any proceeding, or defend the same in order to recover possession of his ward or its effects, or to defeat any unlawful withholding of its effects in any way in any of the courts of this Commonwealth; and he shall be held to account to said courts and to his wards, under the same rules, regulations, and liabilities that the law now imposes upon guardians and under chapter 43 of the Revised Statutes, the subsequent statutes upon the same subject, and decision of the courts thereunder.

To execute
bond and other
duties.

§ 3. Before any of the present public administrators, or any that shall hereafter be appointed in said counties, shall be ordered by the court to take charge of any child or its estate under this act, said public administrator shall appear in the county court of his county, with his securities, and execute the bond as now required to do before entering upon the duties of the office of public administrator, with the additional condition and obligation that he will truly and faithfully perform his duties as public guardian, and account for and pay over to each child committed to his guardianship, or to its legal representative, all moneys or other effects to such child belonging, which shall or ought to come to his hands,.and the lawful increase thereof, when so required to do by the proper authority, and shall, in all other things, discharge the duties imposed upon him by law; and it shall be the duty of each public administrator now in office in said counties, to go before the said county court and execute the bond, with security as required by this act, on or before the first day of July next, and for failing to do so may be dismissed from his office by the county court upon motion of the county attorney upon due notice.

§ 4. This act to take effect from its passage.

Approved March 11, 1869.

CHAPTER 1960.

AN ACT to amend an act to appropriate money to improve the North Fork of the Kentucky River.

Be it enacted by the General Assembly of the Commonwealth of Kentucky:

§ 1. That the second section of an act to appropriate money to improve the North Fork of the Kentucky river, be so amended as that J. W. Cardwell and John Wilson, of Breathitt county, be substituted as commissioners, in place of J. W. Cardwell and John Wilson, of Perry county.

§ 2. This act shall take effect from its passage.

Approved March 12, 1869.

CHAPTER 2022.

AN ACT appropriating two thousand dollars to remove obstructions out of the Sturgeon Fork of the Kentucky River.

Be it enacted by the General Assembly of the Commonwealth of Kentucky:

§ 1. That there is hereby appropriated the sum of two thousand dollars, out of any money in the Public Treasury not otherwise appropriated, for the purpose of removing the obstructions out of the Sturgeon Fork of the Kentucky river, in Owsley county, from the mouth of said Fork up to the forks of said Fork, near the widow Roberts' farm; and John S. Branenburg, John C. Leadford, and A. J. Herd, of Owsley county, are hereby appointed commissioners to apply said sum of money to the purpose above named, who shall, before they act in the premises, execute bond in the Owsley county court, with sufficient security for their true performance in applying said money to the purpose above named.

§ 2. The Auditor of Public Accounts, upon the receipt of a duly certified copy of the order and copy of bond showing that said John S Branenburg, John C. Leadford, and A. J. Herd, of Owsley county, have executed the bond as required in the first section of this act, accompanied with the order of said John S. Branenburg, John C. Leadford, A. J. Herd, of Owsley county, shall draw his warrant on the Treasury for the sum of two thousand dollars, payable to them.

§ 3. The said John S. Branenburg, John C. Leadford, A. J. Herd, of Owsley county, shall report to the Owsley county court every six months, and oftener if required, how they have applied said money hereby appropriated, and shall receive one dollar and fifty cents per day compensation for their services.

§ 4. That this act shall be in force from its passage.

Approved March 13, 1869.

[Margin notes: $2,000 appropriated to remove obstructions out of Sturgeon Fork of Kentucky river. Commissioners appointed to give bond, &c. Commissioners to report to county court.]

CHAPTER 2025.

AN ACT to change the county line between Taylor and Green Counties.

Be it enacted by the General Assembly of the Commonwealth of Kentucky:

§ 1. That all that part of the territory of Green county which lies between the present boundary line of Green and Taylor counties, and the line hereinafter named, be stricken from the county of Green and added to the county of Taylor, to-wit: Beginning on the north bank of Green river at Tate's old mill, where the present line crosses said river; thence down the river, with its meanders, to a large poplar tree standing on the bank at the lower end of John

[Margin note: County line between Green and Taylor changed.]

1869.   Shively's farm; thence on a direct line in the direction of
New Hope Church, in Taylor county, to the present line.

§ 2. It shall be the duty of the county surveyors of Taylor and Green counties to run and mark the line designated in the first section of this act, and to file a correct
plat of said survey and line in the county court clerk's
office of each of said counties; and in case that either of
said surveyors shall fail or refuse to act, then, in that
event, the other shall perform the duties hereby prescribed.

§ 3. It shall be the duty of the Taylor county court, at
its regular court of claims, to levy and collect a tax to pay
for said survey.

§ 4. This act to take effect from its passage.

Approved March 13, 1869.

CHAPTER 2030.

AN ACT concerning Quarter-Master General's Office, continuing salary
thereof for one year.

*Be it enacted by the General Assembly of the Commonwealth
of Kentucky:*

§ 1. That the Quarter-Master General's office be, and
is hereby, continued upon its present footing, with the
same clerical force, and at the same salaries, for the period
of one year from and after the 16th day of February,
1869.

§ 2. This act to take effect from and after its passage.

Approved March 13, 1869.

CHAPTER 2033.

AN ACT to amend an act, entitled "An act for the benefit of persons holding lands lying back of other lands in the vicinity of any of the navigable
streams in this State."

*Be it enacted by the General Assembly of the Commonwealth
of Kentucky:*

§ 1. That the said act mentioned in the title of this
act be so amended that lessees of coal banks, mines, or
iron works may acquire the right of way and establish
roads over the lands of others in the same manner prescribed in said recited act for the acquisition of such roads
by the owners of such coal banks, mines, and iron works.

Lessees of coal banks may acquire right of way.

§ 2. That the first section of said recited act be so
amended as to authorize the county courts of this Commonwealth to establish such roads, not exceeding sixty
feet wide, in the manner prescribed in said act.

§ 3. That said act be further amended so as to authorize

such roads and rights of way to be acquired and estab-   1869.
lished through orchards as well as other lands.

§ 4. This act shall apply only to Hancock county.

Approved March 13, 1869.

CHAPTER 2050.

AN ACT authorizing certain officers to reside temporarily at or in the vicinity of the Seat of Government, without changing or losing their former legal and permanent residence.

Be it enacted by the General Assembly of the Commonwealth of Kentucky:

§ 1. That officers of this Commonwealth who are, or may be required, in the discharge of the duties imposed on them by law, to remain at the seat of government more than three months in each year, may, with their families, temporarily reside at or in the vicinity of the seat of government for any space of time during the term for which they were elected, without in any manner whatever changing or losing their legal and permanent residence in the district and precinct in which they resided at the time of such temporary removal; and they shall, in all respects, and for all purposes, be held and regarded as residents of the precinct and district from which they have so removed: *Provided, however,* That in all cases it shall be necessary for the officer so intending to temporarily remove, to file and cause to be recorded in the clerk's office of the county court of the county of his residence, a written statement of such intention, which written statement he shall also cause to be recorded in the clerk's office of the county court of the county in which the seat of government is situated.

§ 2. This act shall take effect from its passage.

Persons required by law to stay at seat of government more than 3 months in each year, may temporarily reside there without losing residence, &c.

Approved March 13, 1869.

CHAPTER 2052.

AN ACT to provide for the advertisement of Sheriff's and Marshal's sales in the City of Louisville and Jefferson County.

Be it enacted by the General Assembly of the Commonwealth of Kentucky:

§ 1. That hereafter it shall be the duty of the marshal of the Louisville chancery court, and the sheriff of Jefferson county, to cause all sales of real or personal property, made by them under any order or decree of court, or under any attachment or execution, to be advertised for the length of time now required by law in two newspapers published in the city of Louisville, one of which paper

Marshal of the Louisville chancery court and sheriff to advertise sales.

1869.

shall be printed in the English language and one in the German language; and in selecting the said papers the said officers shall choose those having the largest circulation in said city.

§ 2. That the costs of said advertisements shall be taxed by the officer, and paid as other costs in the action.

§ 3. That this act shall take effect from and after its passage.

Approved March 13, 1869.

CHAPTER 2053.

AN ACT to abolish the Board of Internal Improvement.

Be it enacted by the General Assembly of the Commonwealth of Kentucky:

Myers' Sup., p. 277.

§ 1. That an act, entitled "An act in relation to the Board of Internal Improvement," approved February 20th, 1861, be, and the same is hereby, repealed.

§ 2. That the Chairman of the Board of Internal Improvement report the state of his accounts to the Commissioners of the Sinking Fund, who are hereby authorized to settle the same, and receive any balance on hand, which they will pay into the Treasury, to be placed to their credit.

§ 3. That the Chairman of the Board of Internal Improvement be allowed one hundred and twenty days, from and after the passage of this act, to settle and close up all unfinished business now in his hands relating to the Kentucky river.

§ 4. That the Auditor of Public Accounts of this Commonwealth be, and he is hereby, authorized, by proxy, to vote the stock of the State for directors in all the turnpike roads in which the State has an interest.

§ 5. This act shall take effect from and after its passage.

Approved March 15, 1869.

CHAPTER 2060.

AN ACT to amend the Revenue Laws.

Be it enacted by the General Assembly of the Commonwealth of Kentucky:

Purchases of land by agents of Auditor valid.

§ 1. That all purchases of land, made under execution in behalf of the Commonwealth against sheriffs and their sureties, for revenue, made by the Commonwealth, through agents appointed by the Auditor, be, and the same are hereby, declared valid: *Provided,* That the right of the State to make such purchase is only intended to be established by this act, and nothing herein shall be so construed as to cure any defect or irregularity in any execution, levy, or sale under which such purchase may have been made.

§ 2. That the Auditor shall proceed to sell at public sale, at the court-house door in the county where the land is situated, on the first day of a county or circuit court, having first advertised the same as lands are directed to be advertised when sold under execution, and also for two weeks in a newspaper, if one is published in the county, all lands so purchased after existing rights of redemption have expired, upon a credit of not less than one nor more than three years, in his discretion; and he shall take bonds, with good security, from the purchasers, bearing interest from the sale, and shall execute, for and on behalf of the Commonwealth, deeds of conveyance therefor, reserving a lien to the Commonwealth for the purchase money. He shall be authorized to collect all said bonds by suit in the Franklin circuit court, if not paid to him at maturity; and the lien upon the land shall be enforced in that court. When said moneys are collected they shall be paid by him into the Treasury.

Auditor authorized to sell land and to make deeds to the purchasers.

To collect money by suit in Franklin circuit court.

§ 3. That the Auditor shall be authorized to employ, in his discretion, an agent, residing near to the place of sale, in any case where land is to be sold under an execution in favor of the Commonwealth against sheriffs and collectors of the revenue, to bid for said land, if it shall be necessary so to do to insure the collection of said execution; and he shall pay said agent not exceeding eight per cent. upon the amount realized by the Commonwealth out of the land after it is sold.

Auditor to employ agent & his compensation.

§ 4. That no property or estate shall be exempt from executions in behalf of the Commonwealth.

§ 5. This act to take effect from its passage.

Approved March 15, 1869.

CHAPTER 2070.

AN ACT to authorize the Auditor to employ Counsel for the State.

Be it enacted by the General Assembly of the Commonwealth of Kentucky:

§ 1. That the Auditor of Public Accounts be, and he is hereby, authorized and instructed to employ an attorney to represent the interest of the State in the case of the First National Bank of Louisville against the Commonwealth of Kentucky, now paying upon appeal in the Supreme Court of the United States.

Auditor to employ counsel in case in the Supreme Court United States,

§ 2. This act shall take effect from and after its passage.

Approved March 15, 1869.

PUB. L.—6

1869.   CHAPTER 2093.

AN ACT to punish the malicious cutting of hose.

Be it enacted by the General Assembly of the Commonwealth of Kentucky:

Persons cutting hose at fire, guilty of felony.

§ 1. That if any person shall, within the limits of any incorporated city or town in this Commonwealth, having a fire department, and during or about the time of any fire in such city or town, and with intent to prevent or hinder the extinction thereof, maliciously cut, deface, or otherwise injure any of the hose which is used for the conveyance of water in the extinction of such fire, the person committing such offense shall be deemed guilty of felony, and

Penalty.

shall, on conviction thereof, be confined in the penitentiary not less than one nor more than five years.

§ 2. This act shall take effect from and after its passage.

Approved March 15, 1869.

_____

CHAPTER 2094.

AN ACT to provide for paying County Court Clerks for copying Delinquent Lists.

Be it enacted by the General Assembly of the Commonwealth of Kentucky:

Fees of county court clerks for copying delinquent lists.

§ 1. That county court clerks shall hereafter be allowed the same fees for copying the delinquent lists of their respective counties as they are now allowed by law for copying the assessor's books, to be paid in the same manner.

§ 2. This act shall be in force from its passage.

Approved March 15, 1869.

_____

CHAPTER 2098.

AN ACT to permit the vending or distribution of Bibles, Hymn-books, Prayer-books, and other Religious Publications, without license.

Be it enacted by the General Assembly of the Commonwealth of Kentucky:

No license necessary to sell Bibles, &c.

§ 1. That no peddler's or other license shall be required of colporteurs or other persons distributing or vending bibles, tracts, hymn-books, prayer-books, or other religious publications, in any town, city, or county in this State.

§ 2. This act shall be in force from its passage.

Approved March 15, 1869.

CHAPTER 2133.

AN ACT in relation to the accounts of the late State Geologist and his Assistant.

WHEREAS, The General Assembly, at its last session, passed an act, entitled "An act authorizing a settlement of the accounts of Sidney S. Lyon, late Assistant State Geologist," approved March 9th, 1868, whereby the Governor was authorized to cause a settlement of the accounts of said Lyon to be made, and to direct payment out of the Treasury of any balance found to be due him; and whereas, it appears by the report of James A. Dawson, commissioner appointed by the Governor to make said settlement, communicated to the House by the Governor, that there is a balance justly due to said Lyon of six hundred and eighty-two dollars ($682); and whereas, the yeas and nays not having been taken on the passage of said act, the Auditor is not authorized to issue his warrant on the Treasurer for said sum; and whereas, it appears from said report and the message of the Governor transmitting the same, that the State has claims against the estate of David D. Owen, deceased, for property of the State remaining in his hands at the time of his death; and that there are in the hands of the personal representatives of Mr. Owen, or of other persons, sundry "maps, plats, unpublished data as to the Geological Survey, with plates, &c., which justly belong to the State of Kentucky;" therefore,

Be it enacted by the General Assembly of the Commonwealth of Kentucky:

§ 1. That the Auditor of Public Accounts is hereby directed to draw his warrant on the Treasurer in favor of Sidney S. Lyon for the sum of six hundred and eighty-two dollars ($682), the balance due him as aforesaid: *Provided,* That said Lyon shall first turn over to said commissioner all memoranda, notes, maps, plats, unpublished data, plates, or other property in his hands belonging to the State, which shall be carefully preserved in such place as the Governor may direct, for future use and reference.

§ 2. That the Governor be, and he is hereby, authorized to appoint a competent commissioner to settle with the personal representative of David D. Owen, deceased, on account of property of the State in the hands of said Owen at the time of his death; and such commissioner, after ascertaining by the records of the State, and such other means as may be accessible, the amount and value of any such property of the State so in the hands of said David D. Owen at the time of his death, and not yet accounted for, or any property of the State remaining in the hands of any one of the assistants of said Owen in

[margin notes:] Auditor to draw warrant in favor of Sidney S. Lyon for $682.

Lyon to turn over to commissioner all notes, &c., of the State in his hands.

Governor to appoint a commissioner to settle with the personal representative of D. D. Owen, and the duties of said commissioner.

1869.

the matter of the Geological Survey, or in the hands of any one else, may demand, receive, receipt for the same, or the value of such part thereof as is now destroyed or dead, or worn out; and in case of the failure or refusal of any such person to surrender such property, or to pay the value thereof, said commissioner may prosecute suit therefor in the name of the Commonwealth. He shall report his acts to the Governor, and shall certify the time actually employed by him in attending to the business of his commission, and the amount of the actual expense incurred by him in so doing, whereupon the Governor shall direct the Auditor to issue his warrant on the Treasurer for the said actual expenses, and the sum of five dollars per day as compensation to said commissioner, which shall be paid by the Treasurer: *Provided*, That he shall not be paid for more than

Commission- er to execute bond, &c.

thirty days for services herein directed. Said commissioner shall execute bond to the Commonwealth, conditioned for a faithful performance of his duties, with good security, to be approved by the Governor, and any money collected by him shall be reported to the Gov-

To deposit property with State Libra- rian.

ernor and paid into the Treasury; and all property received by him shall be deposited with the State Librarian, who shall carefully preserve the same. If such property be perishable, it may, by direction of the Governor, be sold by the commissioner, and the proceeds paid into the Treasury.

§ 3. This act shall take effect from its passage.

Approved March 15, 1869.

CHAPTER 2134.

AN ACT for the benefit of Common Schools in Kentucky.

Be it enacted by the General Assembly of the Commonwealth of Kentucky:

Superintend- ent of Public Instruction to certify to Aud- itor and direct payment for teaching com- mon schools.

§ 1. That the Superintendent of Public Instruction be, and he is hereby, authorized and directed to certify to the Auditor, and direct payment on the reports of the common schools taught in the districts hereinafter named or to be named: *Provided 1st*, That payment be made for said districts out of any surplus for the school year 1868 which may remain to the credit of the counties respectively in which said districts lie, and at a rate per child not exceeding that at which payment was made out of the revenue of the School Fund proper for the years respectively for which the schools are reported to have been taught: *Pro-*

Proviso.

vided 2d, That payment shall not already have been made for said districts: *Provided 3d*, That, for such of said schools as were taught less than three months for the years specified herein, payment shall be made only for the time during which they were so taught: *Provided 4th,* That if, in the case of any county herein named, there shall not be a sufficiency of surplus for the year 1868 to pay the full claim of each of the districts reported from such county and named herein, each of the said districts shall be paid its demand, or balance in full of its demand, from the surplus fund bond, and the same shall be charged against such county in renewing the said bond on the first of July, 1869: *And provided 5th,* That the reports from said districts, duly made out, shall have been received by the Superintendent of Public Instruction on or before the 20th day of May, 1869, previous to which date he may add to the list of districts herein named such as may be reported and properly certified as coming within the provisions of this act, and, in his judgment, entitled to its benefits.

§ 2. That the 22d section of article 4th of the common school law, prohibiting county school commissioners from teaching common schools, be, and the same is hereby, repealed.

Counties.	Nos. of Districts.	Years.	Time Taught.
Owen	16	1868	3 months.
Shelby	64	1867	
Meade	4	1867	3 months.
Bracken	17	1868	2 months.
Webster	51	1868	1½ months.
Webster	39	1867	3 months.
Webster	25	1866	3 months.
Webster	33	1866	3 months.
Webster	37	1866	3 months.
Clinton	12	1866	3 months.
Harlan	19	1864	3 months.
Graves	71	1867	3 months.
Madison	9	1867	3 months.
Washington	9	1867	3 months.
Washington	33	1867	9 months.
Washington	65	1867	3 months.
Garrard	2	1863	3 months.
Graves	1	1866	3 months.
Marion	36	1864	3 months.
Butler	45	1866	3 months.
Fleming	28	1867	3 months.
Breckinridge	71	1866	3 months.
Anderson	11	1867	6 months.
Whitley	6	1863	3 months.
Wayne	4	1866	3 months.
Hopkins	57	1868	3 months.
Knox	23	1861	3 months.
Knox	43	1861	3 months.
Knox	46	1861	3 months.
Ohio	53	1868	3 months.
Calloway	35	1867	3 months.
Calloway	17	1867	3 months.
Marshall	28	1861	3 months.

Counties.	Nos. of Districts.	Years.	Time Taught.
Marshall	9	1865	3 months.
Marshall	23	1865	3 months.
Gallatin	9	1868	3 months.
Nelson	26	1867	3 months.
Hardin	1	1868	60 days.
Lincoln	37	1867	3 months.
Lincoln	58	1867	3 months.
Hopkins	22	1868	3 months.
Oldham	6	1867	
Oldham	4	1863–4–5–6	3 mos. each.
Lyon	27	1868	3 months.
Todd	49	1867	3 months.
Madison	36	1868	3 months.
Montgomery	16	1867	3 months.
Barren	5	1867–8	
Nicholas	15	1862	3 months.
Ballard	16	1862 & 1864	
Nicholas	36	1868	3 months.
Whitley	48	1864	3 months.
Harrison	44	1867	
Union	84	1865–6	3 months.
Simpson	16	1864	3 months.
Taylor	21	1868	5 months.

§ 3. This act to take effect from and after its passage.

Approved March 15, 1869.

––––

CHAPTER 2139.

AN ACT to provide for the sale of the stock of the State of Kentucky in the Louisville and Salt River Turnpike Road Company.

Be it enacted by the General Assembly of the Commonwealth of Kentucky:

Commissioners of Sinking Fund directed to sell stock of the State in the Louisville and Salt River turnpike road company.

§ 1. That the Commissioners of the Sinking Fund be, and they are hereby, directed to sell at public sale, at the court-house door in the city of Louisville, after an advertisement of at least ten days, in such manner as said commissioners shall deem most advisable, the stock of the State in the Louisville and Salt river turnpike road company; that said sale shall be for cash, and the proceeds thereof shall be, by said commissioners, paid into the Treasury of this State to the credit of the Sinking Fund :

Sales to be in lots not exceeding 25 shares.

Provided, Said sale of stock shall be in lots of not exceeding twenty-five shares to the lot, and shall be made prior to the annual election for directors of said company in the year 1869.

§ 2. This act shall take effect from and after its passage.

Approved March 15, 1869.

CHAPTER 2143.

AN ACT to authorize the sale and conveyance of certain lands and personalty belonging to the State on Licking River.

Be it enacted by the General Assembly of the Commonwealth of Kentucky:

§ 1. That Culvin Sanders be, and is hereby, appointed a commissioner, with full power and authority to sell and convey all the lands belonging to the State of Kentucky on Licking river that were formerly purchased by the State when improving Licking river, and also any personalty purchased for the same purpose.

C. Sanders authorized to sell lands of State on Licking river.

§ 2. Before he sells any of the lands or personalty he shall advertise the sale thereof for at least twenty days previous to the day of sale in the Covington Journal and the Cynthiana Democrat.

To advertise sale, &c.

§ 3. That before he proceeds to execute the duties assigned by this act, said commissioner shall execute a bond to the Commonwealth, with good security, to be approved by the Governor, conditioned for the faithful performance of his duties, and to pay into the Treasury all such sums of money as he shall receive arising from the sale of said property.

To execute bond, &c.

§ 4. This act shall be in force from and after its passage.

Approved March 15, 1869.

CHAPTER 2144.

AN ACT to change the time of holding the Lincoln County Court.

Be it enacted by the General Assembly of the Commonwealth of Kentucky:

§ 1. That the time of holding the Lincoln county court is hereby changed from the first to the second Monday in each month.

Lincoln.

§ 2. That this act to take effect from and after its passage.

Approved March 15, 1869.

CHAPTER 2145.

AN ACT to exempt Telegraph Operators, and the employees of Telegraph Offices, from sitting on Juries.

Be it enacted by the General Assembly of the Commonwealth of Kentucky:

§ 1. That telegraph operators, and the employees of telegraph offices, are hereby exempt from sitting upon juries in this Commonwealth.

Telegraph operators.

§ 2. This act to take effect from its passage.

Approved March 15, 1869.

1869.

CHAPTER 2153.

AN ACT to fix the time of holding the summer term of certain Circuit Courts in the Seventh Judicial District.

Be it enacted by the General Assembly of the Commonwealth of Kentucky:

Marion cir-cuit court.

Nelson cir-cuit court.

Mercer cir-cuit court.

§ 1. That hereafter the June term of the Marion circuit court shall commence on the third Monday of each June, and continue twelve juridical days, if the business requires it. The summer term of the Nelson circuit court shall commence on the first Monday in each July, and continue twelve juridical days, if necessary. The summer term of the Mercer circuit court shall be held on the third Monday in each July, and continue twelve juridical days, if necessary.

§ 2. This act shall take effect from its passage.

Approved March 15, 1869.

CHAPTER 2163.

AN ACT in relation to the office of Examiner and depositions heretofore taken by Examiners.

Be it enacted by the General Assembly of the Commonwealth of Kentucky:

Myers' Sup., p. 180.

§ 1. That subdivision 2d, of section 621, of the Civil Code of Practice, be, and the same is hereby, repealed; and all other sections and provisions of said Code in relation to examiners shall remain in force, and be as valid as if expressly hereby re-enacted.

Examiners to hold office 4 years.

§ 2. The examiners of this Commonwealth shall hold their offices for the term of four years from the dates of their respective appointments, subject to removal at the will of the circuit judges of their respective counties.

§ 3. All depositions heretofore taken by persons known as examiners shall be held to have been taken before officers legally qualified and authorized to take depositions.

§ 4. This act shall take effect from its passage.

Approved March 16, 1869.

CHAPTER 2166.

AN ACT for the Appropriation of Money.

Be it enacted by the General Assembly of the Commonwealth of Kentucky:

§ 1. That the following sums of money are hereby appropriated to the following persons, to be paid by the Treasurer, out of any money in the Treasury not otherwise appropriated, upon the warrant of the Auditor, viz :

§ 2. To the Speaker of the Senate and House of Representatives, ten dollars each per day, during the present session of the General Assembly.

§ 3. To the principal Clerks of the Senate and House of Representatives, ten dollars each per day, during the present session of the General Assembly, and the same for fifteen days after the adjournment, for preparing the acts for publication.

Clerks.

§ 4. To the Assistant Clerks, each, ten dollars per day, during the present session.

Assistant Clerks.

§ 5. To the Sergeant-at-Arms of the Senate and House of Representatives, each, eight dollars per day, during the present session.

Sergeant-at-Arms.

§ 6. To the Door-keepers of the Senate and House of Representatives, each, eight dollars per day, during the present session.

Door-keepers.

§ 7. To Isaac Wingate, jr., and D. D. Sublett, Clerks of the Enrolling Committees for the Senate and House of Representatives, six dollars each per day during the present session.

Enrolling Committees.

§ 8. To the Pages of the Senate and House of Representatives, two dollars and fifty cents per day, each, during the present session.

Pages.

§ 9. To the Ministers of the Gospel of Frankfort, three hundred and fifty dollars, to be distributed among them by W. N. Robb, Sergeant-at-Arms of the House.

Ministers of Gospel.

§ 10. To William N. Robb, Sergeant-at-Arms of the House of Representatives, for the benefit of Henry Morton, two dollars and fifty cents per day, and also ten dollars to buy him a coat; and for the benefit of Daniel Morton, two dollars and fifty cents per day, during the present session, for waiting on the House of Representatives.

W. N. Robb for others.

§ 11. To Howard Todd, Sergeant-at-Arms of the Senate, for the benefit of Lewis Harris, two dollars and fifty cents per day, during the present session, for waiting on the Senate, and ten dollars to buy him a coat.

H. Todd for others.

§ 12. To Gip. Morton, a man of color, two dollars per day, for waiting on the "back capitol" and clerk room during present session.

Gip Morton.

§ 13. To Courier-Journal Company, three hundred and seventy-three dollars and seventy-six cents, for —— copies Courier-Journal, furnished Senate and House of Representatives during the present session.

Courier-Journal.

§ 14. To S. I. M. Major, four hundred and sixty-four dollars and seventy cents, for daily Yeoman, furnished Senate and House of Representatives, and for advertising.

S. I. M. Major.

§ 15. To A. G. Hodges, eighty-five dollars, for —— copies of the Commonwealth, furnished Senate and House of Representatives during the present session, and for advertising proclamations.

A. G. Hodges.

§ 16. To the Editor of the Louisville Democrat, two hundred dollars, for —— copies Democrat, furnished Senate and House of Representatives during the present session.

§ 17. To John M. Helms, three thousand dollars and twenty-five cents, for sundries furnished Senate and House of Representatives.

§ 18. To Samuel C. Bull, nine hundred and eighty-eight dollars and seventy cents, for sundries furnished Senate and House of Representatives during the present session.

§ 19. To John N. Crutcher, one hundred and fifty dollars and fifty cents, for sundries furnished Senate and House of Representatives.

§ 20. To John L. Moore, thirty-seven dollars and fifty-eight cents, for sundries furnished Senate and House of Representatives during the present session.

§ 21. To James A. Hodges & Co., sixty-three dollars and forty-one cents, for sundries furnished the Senate and House of Representatives.

§ 22. To John R. Graham, one hundred and twenty-seven dollars and seventy-five cents, for sundries furnished Senate and House of Representatives during present session.

§ 23. To Rodman & Brothers, one hundred and thirty-five dollars and eighty-six cents, for sundries furnished Senate and House of Representatives.

§ 24. To George W. Miller, sixty-eight dollars and seventy cents, for sundries furnished Senate and House of Representatives.

§ 25. To A. Conery, fifty-six dollars, for sundries furnished Senate and House of Representatives.

§ 26. To Harry I. Todd, one hundred and thirty-two dollars and ninety cents, for furniture furnished Senate and House of Representatives.

§ 27. To W. H. Averill, forty-seven dollars and fifty cents, for sundries furnished Senate and House of Representatives during the present session.

§ 28. To Noel & Taylor, twenty-six dollars, for hacks for funeral occasion.

§ 29. To Kyte & Power, ten dollars and seventy-five cents, for sundries furnished House of Representatives.

§ 30. To J. M. Mills, seventeen dollars and seventy-five cents, for sundries furnished Senate and House of Representatives.

§ 31. To B. F. Meek, one dollar and seventy-five cents, for sundries furnished.

§ 32. To W. L. Jesse, three hundred and six dollars and five cents, for foreign papers furnished.

§ 33. To the Editor Kentucky Statesman, five dollars, for three copies Statesman.

Marginal notes (left column):

1869.
Editor Louisville Democrat.
J. M. Helms,
S. C. Bull.
J. N. Crutcher.
J. L. Moore.
J. A. Hodges & Co.
J. R. Graham.
Rodman & Bro.
G. W. Miller.
A. Conery.
H. I. Todd.
W. H. Averill.
Noel & Taylor.
Kyte & Power.
J. M. Mills.
B. F. Meek.
W. L. Jesse.
Editor Ky. Statesman.

§ 34. To W. Franklin, five dollars and seventy-five cents, copy record against Craig.

W. Franklin.

§ 35. To A. W. Vallandingham, for having wood sawed, fifteen dollars.

A. W. Vallandingham.

§ 36. To M. E. Jett, for repairs done to Senate Chamber and House of Representatives, one hundred and forty dollars.

M. E. Jett.

§ 37. To Editor Kentucky Gazette, forty dollars, for — copies Gazette, furnished Senate and House of Representatives during the present session.

Editor Ky. Gazette.

§ 38. To Thomas M. Green, two dollars and ninety-eight cents, for — copies Maysville Eagle, furnished Senate and House of Representatives.

T. M. Green.

§ 39. To John C. Noble, forty dollars, for twenty-five copies Paducah Herald, furnished Senate and House of Representatives during the present session.

J. C. Noble.

§ 40. To W. D. Givens, four dollars, for two copies of the Horse Cave Intelligencer, furnished House of Representatives.

W. D. Givens.

§ 41. To John Haly, three dollars and twenty-five cents, for sundries furnished Senate and House of Representatives.

John Haly.

§ 42. To the Editor Lexington Observer and Reporter, thirteen dollars, for — copies Observer and Reporter, furnished Senate and House of Representatives.

Editor Lexington Observer.

§ 43. To Bond & Meek, Editors Big Sandy Herald, thirty-five dollars, for twenty-one copies of the Big Sandy Herald, furnished Senate and House of Representatives during the present session.

Bond & Meek.

§ 44. To the Editor of the Georgetown Times, ten dollars.

Georgetown Times.

§ 45. To William N. Robb, ninety-two dollars and sixty cents, as per bill rendered.

W. N. Robb.

§ 46. To William N. Robb, forty dollars, for services in attending upon the Electoral College, and John A. Crittenden and John M. Todd, forty dollars each; to James Lobban, ten dollars, and to Henry Morton, ten dollars, for like services.

W. N. Robb and others.

§ 47. To D. C. Barrett, for preparing indexes to the Journals of the Senate and House of Representatives, two hundred dollars.

D. C. Barrett.

§ 48. To William N. Robb, one hundred and fifty dollars, for extra services as Sergeant-at-Arms of the House of Representatives.

W. N. Robb.

§ 49 To M. D. Martin, one hundred dollars; to Thompson S. Parks, one hundred dollars; to Moses Kirk, eighty dollars, and to William Mynheir, sixty dollars respectively, for their services in going and ascertaining the probable cost of the improvements on Licking river.

M. D. Martin.

1869.

J. W. Gorin.

§ 50. To J. W. Gorin, thirty-five dollars, for attending as a witness before the Senate Finance Committee.

B. J. Webb

§ 51. To Ben. J. Webb, six hundred and thirty-five dollars, for his services in writing biographies of Governors Helm and Powell, and traveling expenses, &c.

J. M. Alexander.

§ 52. To J. M. Alexander, one hundred and fifty-two dollars, for his attention to preparing lives of Governors Helm and Powell.

T. B. Gray.

§ 53. To T. B. Gray, ninety-five dollars and fifty-five cents, for sundries furnished House and Senate.

Editor Cynthiana Democrat.

§ 54. To Editor Cynthiana Democrat, ten dollars, for paper furnished during the present session.

L. Tobin.

§ 55. To L. Tobin, five dollars, for sundries.

W. N. Robb.

§ 56. To W. N. Robb, forty dollars, for contingent expenses, postage, and papers present session.

Ross & Rosser.

§ 57. To Ross & Rosser, for Maysville Bulletin, eight dollars.

Extra clerk hire.

§ 58. The Auditor is authorized to draw his warrant upon the Treasurer, in favor of the principal Clerks of the Senate and House of Representatives, for the amount of extra Clerk hire in enrolling bills and other clerical duties, to be estimated and certified by the Clerks.

T. S. Pettit.

§ 59. To Thomas S. Pettit, twelve dollars, for twelve copies of the Owensboro Monitor, during the present session.

Daniel Clark.

§ 60. To Daniel Clark, the "Ancient Governor," seventy-five dollars, for his services in waiting upon the Executive Department.

San. Goin.

§ 61. To Sandford Goin, for ice furnished the House and Senate, thirty-six dollars.

H. Todd.

§ 62. To Howard Todd, three dollars and eighteen cents for postage.

J. A. Dawson.

§ 63. To James A. Dawson, for services in settling accounts of Sidney S. Lyon, under appointment of the Governor, receiving and disposing of property at Jeffersonville, Indiana, and Louisville, Kentucky (five days), fifty dollars.

§ 64. To editor of Kentucky Times, five dollars.

Webber & Co.

§ 65. To Webber & Co., for Evening Sun, three dollars.

E. Y. Kilgore.

§ 66. To E. Y. Kilgore, for Glasgow Times, four dollars.

U. B. Sebree.

§ 67. To R. B. Sebree, for ringing bell for meeting of General Assembly, twenty dollars.

Editor Flemingsburg Democrat.

§ 68. To Editor of Flemingsburg Democrat, for four copies of same, eight dollars.

Samuel Davis & Son.

§ 69. To Samuel Davis & Son, Covington Journal, fifteen dollars.

Editor Bowling Green Democrat.

§ 70. To Editor of Bowling Green Democrat, four dollars; to Editor of Lebanon Clarion, two dollars, and editor Uniontown Appeal, six dollars, for copies of their papers furnished the General Assembly.

§ 71. To Margaret Bett, for making mail-bags, towels, and washing same during the present session, twelve dollars.

§ 72. To J. R. Marrs, four copies of Danville Advocate, fifteen dollars.

§ 73. To Editor Stanford Baffner, for copies of same, fifteen dollars.

§ 74. To Editor of Hickman Courier, for six copies of same, ten dollars.

§ 75. To James Hines, Editor Bowling Green Democrat, for papers furnished, ten dollars.

§ 76. To J. C. Adams, Editor Franklin Sentinel, for papers, ten dollars.

§ 77. Editor Clark County Democrat, six dollars.

§ 78. Strike out ten in section appropriating to editor Hickman Courier, and insert twenty-five dollars, for papers.

§ 79. To John B. Major, twenty-nine dollars and twenty-five cents, for balance due on crape furnished the last session of the General Assembly.

§ 80. This act to take effect from its passage.

Approved March 16, 1869.

CHAPTER 2168.

AN ACT to protect the owners of Wood-lands.

Be it enacted by the General Assembly of the Commonwealth of Kentucky:

§ 1. That any person who shall feloniously cut, or saw down and carry away, timber growing upon the lands of another, of the value of twenty dollars or more, without the consent of the owner or his agent, and without color of title in himself to the land upon which said timber was growing, or to said timber, upon conviction thereof, be confined in the penitentiary for a period of one year.

§ 2. That if such timber so cut and carried away shall be of less value than twenty and more than five dollars, the offense shall be deemed petit larceny, and punished by a fine of not less than fifty nor more than one hundred dollars, or by imprisonment in the county jail or workhouse for not more than six months, at the discretion of the jury, the fine imposed to be collected as other fines are collected.

§ 3. This act shall not apply to persons who may cut timber on lands of another through mistake as to the boundary thereof, believing, in good faith, that it was his own land.

1869.

§ 4. This act shall be given in charge by the circuit courts and courts having original jurisdiction in this Commonwealth.

§ 5. This act shall take effect sixty days after its passage.

Approved March 16, 1869.

CHAPTER 2177.

AN ACT to amend chapter 55 of the Revised Statutes, in reference to Jury Commissioners and the mode of selecting Grand and Petit Jurors in the Jefferson Circuit Court and the Jefferson Court of Common Pleas.

Be it enacted by the General Assembly of the Commonwealth of Kentucky:

Stant. Rev. Stat., vol. 2, p. 75.

Judges of the Jefferson circuit court and court of common pleas to appoint not less than 3 nor more than 10 commissioners to select jurors.

Duties of commissioners.

§ 1. That chapter 55 of the Revised Statutes be, and hereby is, so amended that the Jefferson circuit court and the Jefferson court of common pleas may appoint any number of jury commissioners, not less than three nor more than ten, for the selection of grand and petit jurors for said courts; and said courts may authorize said jury commissioners to draw the panel of twenty-four jurors from not exceeding five hundred names of persons, to be selected by them, and to draw the grand jury from not exceeding one hundred names of persons, to be selected by them. The present law in reference to the selection of grand and petit jurors is not interfered with in any other respect than the above.

§ 2. This act shall be in force from its passage.

Approved March 16, 1869.

CHAPTER 2185.

AN ACT authorizing Circuit and Chancery Courts to appoint Commissioners to relinquish the Dower of Married Women when confirmed lunatics or insane.

Be it enacted by the General Assembly of the Commonwealth of Kentucky:

When married woman is a lunatic or insane, chancery or circuit court of county to appoint a commissioner to make deed with husband to convey interest of wife on the petition of husband.

Husband to give bond to indemnify wife in case she recovers.

§ 1. That whenever any married woman may be a confirmed lunatic or laboring under confirmed insanity, any circuit or chancery court of the county in which the estate is situated may, on the petition of the husband, appoint a commissioner, and authorize and empower him to unite with her husband in any deed or conveyance to relinquish any right, title, or interest which she may have or might acquire as dower in his estate; and said deed shall pass all right or title which she may have or might have to the grantee: *Provided, however,* That no such deed shall be executed and approved and delivered until the husband shall execute a sufficient bond, with approved security, to the Commonwealth, for the use of such married woman, with condition to pay to her the full value of the interest or dower so relinquished, should her inchoate right to dower vest and become complete in her at any future time.

§ 2. The court in any such proceeding may order defense to be made in behalf of such married woman against such petition, whenever in its discretion it may deem the same necessary.

Court to order defense for married woman.

§ 3. This act shall be in force from its passage.

Approved March 16, 1869.

·CHAPTER 2196.

AN ACT concerning Public Books, and providing for the supply to destitute Counties.

WHEREAS, It is represented to this General Assembly that in many counties of this Commonwealth the public offices and public books have been destroyed by fire, and otherwise by force, which no reasonable care and diligence could avoid, and that some of said counties are yet without the public books allowed to their offices and officers under the law, as found in chapter 61 of the Revised Statutes—

Be it enacted by the General Assembly of the Commonwealth of Kentucky:

§ 1. That hereafter when there shall be filed in the office of the Secretary of State a copy of an order of the county court of any county in the State, certified by the clerk of said county, showing that the public books, or any of them theretofore furnished by the State, and delivered to any public officer of said county, have been destroyed by fire, or otherwise destroyed without the fault or neglect of the officer or other person having lawful custody thereof, and showing further a full list of such books so lost and destroyed, it shall be the duty of said Secretary of State to procure, at the most reasonable cost, such of said class of lost books as are included in said chapter of the Revised Statutes, and as may so be certified as aforesaid to have been lost or destroyed, and forward the same to the presiding judge of such county at the same time other public books are sent to such county, and take the receipt of said judge therefor.

When copy of order of county court filed with Secretary of State, showing that public books have been lost without fault of officer, he is to purchase books & send to officer.

§ 2. That said county judge shall deliver said books to the officers of such county entitled thereto, and take their receipts for the same, which receipt he shall cause to be entered at full length upon the records of the county court, as part of its proceedings, at the next regular term of the

County judges shall deliver books to officers and take receipts therefor. Receipts to be spread on record.

1869.

court; and the clerk of the court shall file away and carefully preserve in his office said receipts.

§ 3. It shall be the duty of each and every public officer, in each of the counties of this Commonwealth, who has possession, by virtue of his office, of any public book or books recovered and referred to in said chapter of the Revised Statutes, to make out a full and perfect list thereof, showing when he received the same, and from whom, and swear to and file the same in open court at the January term of said court of each year; and the same shall be entered as aforesaid upon the records of said court, and the original filed and preserved in the clerk's office of said court. The court of claims of such county shall allow to said clerk a just compensation for his services required by this act, to be paid out of the county levy.

Public officer to give written statement of books in his hands by virtue of the office, when received, and who from, and file same in county court.

§ 4. It shall be the duty of each one of said public officers, into whose custody said books shall be placed, or who shall now have possession of such books, to deliver the same as they respectively go out of office, to their respective successors in office, and take their receipts therefor and file the same in court, which shall be entered of record and preserved as hereinbefore required as to other receipts and reports. Any public officer failing to comply with the duties imposed on him by this act shall be fined in any sum not exceeding one hundred dollars, to be recovered by indictment of a grand jury, one half to the Commonwealth and the other to the informer; and it shall be the special duty of the circuit and criminal courts of this Commonwealth to give this act in charge to each grand jury empanneled by them.

Officers to deliver books to successors.

Penalty.

§ 5. Each public officer in this Commonwealth entitled by law to any of said public books, and who is required to give an official bond, shall, with his securities, be held and bound to the Commonwealth for the faithful preservation, care, and delivery to his successor in office of each and every public book to him delivered. It shall be the duty of the presiding judge of each county court in this Commonwealth to make out a report in writing to the trustee of the jury fund of his county, at the first term of the circuit court of his county in each year, showing how many public officers in his county, to whom said books had been delivered, have gone out of office the year preceding, and whether any of them have failed to deliver to their successors said books, and if so, what particular books, and their value; and if it shall appear thet any such retiring officer has failed to deliver over to his successor in office any or all of the public books aforesaid which have come to his hands, said trustee of the jury fund shall institute suit therefor immediately against such defaulting officer and his securities, or against the officer

Bond of officers responsible for books.

Judges of county courts to make out reports of officers going out, and condition of books, &c.

Suit to be instituted against person failing to deliver over books by trustee of jury fund.

alone, in case he has no securities, for the cost or value of the books so failing to be delivered; and it shall be the duty of the attorney for the county to prosecute and attend to the suit for the State; and the money recovered shall form a part of the jury fund in the hands of said trustee, when collected, and be so reported and accounted for.

§ 6. The Auditor of Public Accounts shall draw his warrant upon the Treasury, in favor of the Secretary of State, for such amounts, from time to time, as he shall certify is needful to pay for any books he may buy under the provisions of this act, and the same shall be paid: *Provided*, That no requisition shall be made by any county judge upon the Secretary of State for books as herein provided, until such judge shall have, by an order entered upon the records of his court, appointed some competent and suitable person to investigate and report to said court the number and character of books lost or destroyed, and, so far as can be ascertained, how the same were lost or destroyed; and said report shall be made under oath and spread at large upon the record, and a certified copy thereof shall accompany each requisition.

§ 7. This act shall not be construed so as to allow the purchase of any of the Session Acts of the General Assembly, Journals, or Public Documents.

Approved March 16, 1869.

CHAPTER 2208.

AN ACT regulating the Election of Directors and other Officers of Turnpike Road Companies in this Commonwealth.

Be it enacted by the General Assembly of the Commonwealth of Kentucky:

§ 1. That in all election for directors and other officers of turnpike road companies in this Commonwealth, each shareholder shall be authorized to cast one vote for each and every share of stock by him or her held in said company; and the State shall be authorized to vote by proxy in like manner in all the road companies wherein the State owns stock: *Provided*, This act shall not apply to Shelby county.

Stockholders in turnpike road companies entitled to vote for each share of stock.

Not to apply to Shelby county.

§ 2. This act to take effect from and after its passage.

Approved March 16, 1869.

PUB. L.—7

1869.   CHAPTER 2210.

AN ACT concerning the Revenue and Sinking Fund.

Be it enacted by the General Assembly of the Commonwealth of Kentucky:

§ 1. That the Governor of the State be, and he is hereby,

Governor authorized to borrow £500,000 from Sinking Fund, to pay appropriations. &c. authorized to borrow from the Commissioners of the Sinking Fund any amount of money, not exceeding five hundred thousand dollars, which to him shall be made appear as necessary in aid of the ordinary revenue of the State in the Treasury, to meet the appropriations and expenses

Same to be paid back to Sinking Fund. of the present General Assembly : *Provided, however,* The same shall be placed back to the credit of the Sinking Fund as soon as it shall be paid into the Treasury by those now having charge of the revenues of the State not yet paid over.

§ 2. This act to take effect from its passage.

Approved March 16, 1869.

CHAPTER 2214.

AN ACT concerning the Adjutant General.

Be it enacted by the General Assembly of the Commonwealth of Kentucky:

§ 1. That all that part of an act, entitled "An act to

Myers' Sup., p. 792. amend an act, entitled 'An act to organize and discipline the militia of Kentucky,'" approved February 16th, 1866, so far as the same applies to the office of Adjutant General, be, and the same is hereby, re-enacted.

§ 2. That the Adjutant General shall receive a salary of

Salary of Adjutant General and clerk hire. one thousand five hundred dollars for the year beginning on the 17th day of February, 1869, and for no longer, to be paid monthly as other salaries are paid. He shall also be allowed one thousand two hundred dollars for clerk hire for said year.   The clerk hire allowed said Adjutant General may be drawn from the Treasury monthly, as other clerk hire is drawn; but there shall at no time be drawn more than is actually expended for such clerk hire, and for which proper vouchers shall be shown and filed.

§ 3. This act to take effect from its passage.

Approved March 16, 1869.

CHAPTER 2217.

AN ACT to authorize the Commissioners of the Sinking Fund to lease the turnpike road leading from Bowling Green to the Simpson County line.

Be it enacted by the General Assembly of the Commonwealth of Kentucky:

§ 1. That the Commissioners of the Sinking Fund are hereby authorized to contract with any person, company, or corporation for the lease of the turnpike road leading from Bowling Green to the Simpson county line, so far as the State owns an interest in the same, upon such terms and conditions as may be agreed upon by the contracting parties, not exceeding thirty years; the person or persons, company or corporation, executing bond, with approved security, to return said road, with the property attached thereto, in as good condition as when they have received the same.

Commissioners of Sinking Fund authorized to lease interest of State in the turnpike road leading from Bowling Green to the Simpson county line. Lease not to exceed 30 years. Lessee to execute bond.

§ 2. This act to take effect from its passage.

Approved March 16, 1869.

CHAPTER 2218.

AN ACT in relation to Stationery furnished members of the General Assembly.

Be it enacted by the General Assembly of the Commonwealth of Kentucky:

§ 1. That all laws by or under which stationery of any character is furnished to any member of the General Assembly be, and they are hereby, repealed.

Stationery laws repealed.

§ 2. That in lieu of stationery heretofore furnished members of the General Assembly, there shall be allowed to each member thereof (including the Lieutenant Governor), the sums following: to each Senator the sum of thirty-five dollars, and to each Representative the sum of twenty dollars, and for which sums the Auditor shall draw his warrant on the Treasurer in favor of such Senators and Representatives, at the close of each session of the General Assembly, to be paid out of any money in the Treasury not otherwise appropriated: *Provided, however,* That five dollars additional shall be allowed, under this act, to each chairman of the several committees of the two Houses.

$35 allowed each Senator and $20 each member of the House.

$5 additional allowed each chairman of committee.

§ 3. This act shall take effect from and after the 1st day of April next.

Approved March 16, 1869.

1869.

CHAPTER 2231.

AN ACT to change the time of holding the circuit courts in Todd and Butler Counties.

Be it enacted by the General Assembly of the Commonwealth of Kentucky:

Time of holding circuit court of Todd county changed.

§ 1. That hereafter, the circuit courts of Todd county shall begin on the first Mondays in April and October, and continue each twelve juridical days.

Time of holding Butler circuit court changed.

§ 2. That the circuit courts of Butler county shall begin on the fourth Mondays in May and November, and continue each twelve juridical days.

§ 3. This act shall take effect from its passage.

Approved March 16, 1869.

CHAPTER 2251.

AN ACT to pay Military Claims audited by the Quarter-Master General.

Whereas, The General Assembly, by acts approved February 17th, 1866, and March 9th, 1867, provided for the auditing of certain military claims against the State of Kentucky, with a view to their collection from the United States; and whereas, the Quarter-Master General has made report to this Legislature, at its present winter's sitting, that there are claims now on file in his office, properly proven and authenticated, as the said enactments require, against the State of Kentucky, amounting to sixteen thousand eight hundred and thirteen dollars and ninety-two cents, which are for balances due State troops, forage, subsistence, &c.; and in order to carry out the purposes of said enactments of said General Assembly, and in order to pay said debts against the State—

Be it enacted by the General Assembly of the Commonwealth of Kentucky:

Auditor to draw warrant on Treasurer to pay certain military claims, &c.

§ 1. That the Auditor of Public Accounts be, and he is hereby, directed to draw his warrant upon the public Treasury in payment of each of said claims so reported as aforesaid by said Quarter-Master, and the same shall be paid out of the first moneys received from the United States on account of the war debt now due the State of Kentucky, or which shall become due.

Quarter-Master to present claims to general government.

§ 2. The said Quarter-Master General is hereby directed to cause the said claims, so soon as they are paid, to be made up into an installment of the war debt and presented to the General Government for payment.

Quarter-Master General to report to next General Assembly all the claims filed by the 1st day of November, 1869

§ 3. That said Quarter-Master General shall report to the next General Assembly of this State such further list and amount of claims against the State as shall be presented and filed in his office, authenticated and proven up as the said acts of 11th of February and 9th of March required, on or before the first day of November, 1869; and all claims against the State for services, subsistence, or anything else covered and referred to in said acts, shall be presented and filed with said Quarter-Master, regularly proven and made a sufficient voucher under the law, on or before that day. And all laws allowing such claims to be presented and proven before said Quarter-Master General, and requiring him to make report of them in any way, are hereby declared repealed from and after the 15th day of December, 1869, it being the purpose of this Legislature to thus give ample time to claimants, and close up this class of supposed indebtedness at that time.

§ 4. This act to take effect from its passage.

Approved March 16, 1869.

CHAPTER 2252.

AN ACT to amend chapter 15, title 10, Civil Code of Practice.

Be it enacted by the General Assembly of the Commonwealth of Kentucky:

§ 1. That in all cases wherein a judgment or decree for the sale of an infant's real estate has been rendered, or may hereafter be rendered, upon the petition of the guardian of such infant, and a sale has been made under such judgment or decree, and it shall appear that there are such errors or defects in the proceedings in which the judgment or decree was obtained as will or may vitiate the same, it shall be lawful for any purchaser of the estate, or any party interested therein, under such judgment or decree, to file his petition in the court rendering the same, making the infant and all other persons interested parties, reciting the facts of such proceeding, judgment, or decree and sale, and averring that the sale was fairly made, and at the reasonable value of the property, and that the price was paid by the purchaser, and that the price paid was expended by the guardian in the necessary support, education, and nurture of the infant, or had been invested, upon ample security, for the benefit of the infant, and that the court, through inadvertence or oversight, had failed to confirm the sale, and that the sale was at the time beneficial to the infant; which petition shall be sworn to by the purchaser.

When upon sales made by infants, on petition of guardian, it appears that there are errors fatal to proceeding, the purchaser can file his petition stating the whole transaction against the parties interested.

§ 2. Upon the filing of such petition, and the parties being regularly before the court, it shall proceed to hear proof; and if satisfied of the truth of the allegations, it shall render a judgment or decree confirming the original judgment, or decree and sale, which shall render the same

Duty of court to hear proof, and if satisfied of truth of allegations of petition, to render judgment confirming original judgment, &c.

1869.　aṣ valid and binding in all respects as if the original proceedings had been, in every particular, according to the requirements of the law.

§ 3. This act shall take effect from and after its passage.

Approved March 16, 1869.

CHAPTER 2257.

AN ACT authorizing the Auditor to sell lands for the non-payment of taxes, and regulate the conveyance, redemption, and recovery thereof.

Be it enacted by the General Assembly of the Commonwealth of Kentucky:

Auditor to direct agent to sell lands for non-payment of taxes, &c.

Duty of agent.

§ 1. It shall be the duty of the Auditor, by written direction to his agent, when lands have been forfeited to the Commonwealth for the non-payment of taxes, to cause the same to be sold by the agent of the Auditor for the county in which the lands lie, or so much thereof as shall be necessary to pay the taxes due thereon, the commissions due to the agent, and the expenses for said sale, on a credit of four months. The said agent shall advertise the time, place, and terms of the sale for fifteen days previous thereto, at the court-house door of the county. He shall take a bond from the purchaser, with good security, for the purchase money, and shall file the bond with the Auditor. If the bond shall not be paid at maturity the Auditor shall file the same, with a memorandum of the amount due thereon, in the Franklin circuit court, and judgment shall be rendered thereon without notice.

Auditor to make conveyance.

Right of redemption.

§ 2. When such land shall have been sold, and the purchase money paid as required, the Auditor shall execute to such purchaser a conveyance of the land so purchased, with a proper description thereof, by metes and bounds, and give the number, block, and the number of feet in length and depth, if a town or city lot, and its exact locality, as near as may be done: *Provided*, That the owner of said land, and all persons who have, in good faith, purchased the same from the person against whom the lands have been listed for taxation, or his heirs or devisees, shall have the right to redeem the land by paying to the purchaser, within two years next after the sale, the amount paid by him, and ten per cent. thereon: *And provided further*, That infants and married women shall have one year after they arrive at the age of twenty-one years, or the termination of the disability of coverture, to redeem said land from the purchaser, by paying to the said purchaser the money paid by him, and ten per centum per annum thereon.

§ 3. In all cases when lands shall be sold for the non-payment of taxes, and a recovery thereof is had, by due process of law, by the claimant or owner from the purchaser thereof, by reason of any informality in the proceedings to subject such land to the payment of taxes, the Auditor shall refund to such purchaser the amount paid by him to the State for such land, less twenty-five per cent.; and the land so recovered by said claimant and owner shall still be liable to the State for the said seventy-five per cent. so refunded until paid, with interest at the rate of one hundred per centum per annum on said amount until paid; and the Auditor may cause said land to be sold for the payment of the same, and interest, costs, and charges, at any time after he refunds said amount, according to the provisions of the first section of this bill; and the agent shall be allowed a commission of twenty (20) per cents on said amount, to be charged as costs, for his services in regard to the same.

§ 4. The Auditor shall not refund to the purchaser of such lands said seventy-five per centum, except on presentation to him by such purchaser, or his agent or representative, of a properly certified copy of the final judgment of the court adjudging such recovery by the claimant or owner from the purchaser or holder; but, upon the filing with him such order, judgment, or decree, he shall draw his warrant upon the Treasurer for the said seventy-five per centum, specifying for what the same is drawn, and the Treasurer shall thereupon pay the same.

§ 5. In cases of the sale and conveyance of lots or lands held in trust, all proceedings to subject the same to the payment of taxes shall be against the trustee (provided his title as trustee to such land be of record), and no beneficiary or *cestui que trust* of lots or lands so sold, as required by law, shall recover or redeem any trust lands so sold (except for some other disability now otherwise provided for by law) after the expiration of two years from the time of such sale.

§ 6. This act to take effect from and after its passage.

Approved March 16, 1869.

Marginal notes: 1869. When owner or claimant of land recovers it from purchaser Auditor to refund the money less 25 per cent.; but land still liable for tax at the rate of 100 per centum per annum until amount paid by Auditor.

Copy of judgment to be presented to Auditor before payment by him.

In cases of sale of lots held in trust, proceedings to be against trustee.

1869.

CHAPTER 2266.

AN ACT to require the Auditor to cause Sheriffs to give good and sufficient bonds for the collection of the revenue.

Be it enacted by the General Assembly of the Commonwealth of Kentucky:

§ 1. That whenever, in the judgment of the Auditor of Public Accounts, the bond for the collection of the revenue of any sheriff is insufficient, or that the sureties therein were, at the time the bond was executed, or have since become insufficient to respond to the liability of the bond as contemplated by law, it shall be his duty to cause said sheriff to be summoned before the county court of the county in which he qualified, and compel him to give a good and sufficient bond; and should said court refuse to compel the giving of another and sufficient bond, or accept another, which, in the judgment of the said Auditor, is still insufficient, he shall make application to the judge of the circuit court of said county, who shall cause said sheriff to be summoned before him and hear and determine the question of the sufficiency of said bond or bonds; and if, in his judgment, said bond or bonds are insufficient, he shall require said sheriff to execute a good and sufficient bond, as herein contemplated, which bond shall be acknowledged in said circuit court and certified by the clerk thereof, and delivered to the clerk of said county court, who shall record the same as required by law; and said bond shall be as obligatory and binding in all respects as if executed in the county court at the time now required.

§ 2. Should said sheriff fail and refuse to execute any bond required of him by said county or circuit court, he shall thereby forfeit his office, and cease to exercise the functions thereof, and the vacancy thereby created shall be filled as now provided by law.

§ 3. This act shall take effect from its passage.

Approved March 16, 1869.

Marginal notes: When sheriff's bond insufficient in judgment of Auditor, it is his duty to have sheriff summoned before county judge and give a new bond.

If the bond is not executed or insufficient, it shall be the duty of Auditor to bring the case before the circuit judge

Bond to be recorded in county clerk's office, &c.

If sheriff fails to execute bond, he forfeits his office.

CHAPTER 2268.

AN ACT to authorize the Auditor of Public Accounts to Compromise certain Demands in favor of the Commonwealth.

WHEREAS, There are many demands in favor of the Commonwealth against late sheriffs and their sureties for revenue due and unpaid; and whereas, by reason of the insolvency of many of said sheriffs and their said sureties, and of irregularities in the execution of their revenue bonds, and in the rendition of judgments against them, as well as in proceedings under executions issued on said judgments; and whereas, it is desirous, in all

cases in which the substantial rights of the Commonwealth can be secured, to avoid vexatious litigation;
therefore,

*Be it enacted by the General Assembly of the Commonwealth
of Kentucky:*

§ 1. That the Auditor of Public Accounts be, and he is
hereby, authorized and empowered, in all cases in which
the Commonwealth has demands against any late sheriff
and his sureties, on account of the non-payment of revenue, and by reason of the insolvency of said sheriff and
his sureties, or any of them, or of any irregularity in the
execution of the revenue bond of said sheriff, or in the
rendition of the judgment against said sheriff and sureties, or in any proceedings under executions issued on said
judgments, and in any and all cases where such demands
cannot, with a reasonable degree of certainty, be collected
by the remedies now provided by law, to make such compromise or other arrangement with the parties against
whom such demands are held as in his judgment is to the
best interest of the State. He shall have the right to give
such parties reasonable time to pay the amounts due from
them by law; take their notes or bonds, payable to the
Commonwealth, bearing legal interest from date, and due
at such time or times as may be agreed upon, not exceeding three years from the 1st of January, eighteen hundred
and sixty-nine (1869). The same to be secured by mortgages or deeds of trust upon unincumbered real estate, or
by personal security, or, if no such mortgage, deed of
trust, or personal security can be obtained, or when the
same is sufficient to secure the debt, he may accept the
assignment or transfer of any note, bond, bill, or other
chose in action, and the amount realized from any such
note, bond, bill, or other chose in action shall be applied
to the payment of the demand the same was intended to
secure; but no credit shall be entered on said demand,
except for such amount as may be actually realized from
said notes, bonds, bills, and other choses in action; nor
shall the Commonwealth be held or required to exercise
more than reasonable diligence in the collection of any of
the aforesaid evidences of debt; and such attorney's fees
as the Auditor may be compelled to pay in enforcing the
collection of the same, not exceeding seven and a half per
cent. on the amount collected, shall be deducted before any
credit shall be given.

§ 2. All mortgages or deeds of trust taken by said Auditor in pursuance to this act shall be recorded in the same
manner and at the same place as though executed to individuals, and all costs attending the execution, stamping,
and recording of the same shall be paid to the Auditor by
the vendors therein, before the same shall be accepted.

[margin notes:]
1869.

Auditor au-
thorized to
compromise
doubtful cases
against sheriff
and his sureties

To give par-
ties reasonable
time; to take
notes or bonds.

Same to be
secured by
mortgage.

May accept
assignment of
bonds, notes,
&c.

Mortgage to
be recorded.

1869.

Suits on mortgages, &c.; to be brought to Franklin circuit court.

§ 3. All actions and proceedings to collect any notes or bonds, or to foreclose any mortgage, or to sell any property embraced in any deed of trust executed in pursuance to this act, shall be in the same manner and under the same regulations as though the same had been executed to individuals, except that the Franklin circuit court, at either of its fiscal or regular terms, shall have jurisdiction of all such actions or proceedings. All such actions or proceedings shall be instituted and conducted by the Attorney General; and in all judgments rendered in said actions or proceedings there shall be taxed, as part of the costs therein, a fee for said Attorney General of six per cent. on the first five hundred dollars, and two per cent. on the remainder of such judgment.

Auditor to employ counsel to investigate titles, &c.

§ 4. The Auditor shall have the right to employ counsel to investigate the title to any real estate upon which any party may propose to give a mortgage or deed of trust, or the solvency of any party or parties proposed to be given as sureties; and such reasonable fees for such counsel as may be agreed upon shall be paid to the Auditor by the parties proposing to execute such mortgage or deed of trust, or give such surety, before the same shall be accepted. The Auditor shall also require such surety, before he is accepted, to file in his office a written statement of what amount he is worth in property, subject to execution after the payment of his just debts, to be sworn to before some circuit or county court clerk; and any person who shall swear falsely to any such statement shall be punished as in other cases of false swearing.

Attorney General to advise Auditor.

§ 5. It shall be the duty of the Attorney General to give the Auditor advice on all such points as he may desire, relative to all negotiations entered into and conducted by him under the provisions of this act; and the Auditor shall not accept any note, bond, mortgage, or deed of trust, until the same shall have first been submitted to the Attorney General, and approved by him.

§ 6. That an act approved March 10th, 1856, entitled "An act to prevent fraudulent assignments in trust for creditors, and other fraudulent conveyances," shall not apply to any assignment, conveyance, or deed of trust made and executed under the provisions of this act; but all such shall be valid and enforceable against all and every person except such as in good faith held liens upon the property so assigned or conveyed, at the time such assignment, conveyance, or transfer was made.

§ 7. That this act and all its provisions shall cease, and have no force or effect, from and after the first day of March, 1870.

§ 8. This act shall take effect from its passage.

Approved March 16, 1869.

CHAPTER 2279.

AN ACT to abolish the Criminal Court in Robertson County.

Be it enacted by the General Assembly of the Commonwealth of Kentucky:

§ 1. That the criminal court of Robertson county be, and the same is hereby, abolished, and that all cases now pending, and appearances, indictments, and motions pending in said court, be, and are hereby, transferred to the circuit court of said county, which shall have jurisdiction of them.

Criminal court of Robertson county abolished; cases to be transferred to circuit court.

§ 2. That there shall be five juridical days added to each term of the circuit court now required by law to be held in said county, if the business of said court shall require it.

Five juridical days added to circuit court.

Approved March 16, 1869.

CHAPTER 2288.

AN ACT authorizing the Governor to appoint an Engineer to survey and examine certain portions of Cumberland River, and make report.

Be it enacted by the General Assembly of the Commonwealth of Kentucky:

§ 1. That the Governor be, and is hereby, empowered and requested to appoint a competent engineer to survey and examine that part of Cumberland river lying between the town of Williamsburg and the mouth of Laurel river, and report to the next General Assembly what obstructions there are in the way of the navigation of said river, the probable cost of removing said obstructions, and the advantages to be derived by the 'State by said removal: *Provided, however,* Said survey shall not cost more than two hundred and fifty dollars.

Governor to appoint surveyor to examine Cumberland river between Williamsburg and mouth of Laurel river, and report condition. &c., to next General Assembly.

§ 2. This act to take effect from and after its passage.

Approved March 16, 1869.

CHAPTER 2303.

AN ACT to amend an act, entitled "An act to amend section 4, article 2, chapter 83, Revised Statutes."

Be it enacted by the General Assembly of the Commonwealth of Kentucky:

§ 1. That the city of Frankfort be, as are now the cities of Louisville and Lexington, exempt from the provisions of an act approved 17th February, 1866, entitled "An act to amend section 4, article 2, chapter 83, Revised Statutes."

Myers' Sup., p. 745.

§ 2. This act shall take effect from its passage.

Approved March 16, 1869.

1869.   The following became a law without the approval of
the Governor, he not having returned it to the House, in
which it originated, in the time required by the Constitution, viz:

CHAPTER 2306.

AN ACT to repeal the sixth (6th) section of an act approved 6th of February, 1854, entitled "An act to amend the charter of the Covington
and Lexington Railroad Company," and to alter the rates of freight
thereon charged.

*Be it enacted by the General Assembly of the Commonwealth
of Kentucky:*

Sixth section
of an act to
amend the
charter of Cov-
ington and
Lexington
railroad com-
pany repealed.
Amount com-
pany allowed
to charge for
freight.

§ 1. That the sixth section of an act approved sixth
(6th) of February, 1854, entitled "An act to amend the
charter of the Covington and Lexington Railroad Company," be, and the same is hereby, repealed; but it is
hereby provided that said company be allowed to charge
for way freight, for a distance of fifty miles and less, not
exceeding twenty-five per cent. more per mile than they
charge for through freight, and for way freight for a distance of over fifty miles, they shall be allowed to charge
not exceeding twelve and a half per cent. more per mile
than they charge for through freight.

§ 2. This act shall be in force from its passage.

RESOLUTIONS.

No. 41.

RESOLUTION in relation to Firing National Salute.

Resolved by the General Assembly of the Commonwealth of Kentucky:

That the Governor be requested to have a salute fired on the eighth (8) of January, inst., at twelve (12) o'clock, M., by round of cannon answering to the number of States, in commemoration of the victory obtained by our forces under General Andrew Jackson at New Orleans; and the like number on the twenty-second (22d) of February, ult., in honor of the Father of his Country, General George Washington.

1869.

Approved January 9, 1869.

No. 42.

RESOLUTION in regard to employment of Counsel in suit between this Commonwealth and State of Missouri.

Resolved by the General Assembly of the Commonwealth of Kentucky:

That his Excellency, the Governor of this Commonwealth, be, and he is hereby, empowered to employ such counsel as he may deem necessary to defend the interest of this State in a suit now pending in the Supreme Court of the United States against the State of Missouri, and that he draw his warrant on the Treasurer for the costs of the same.

Approved January 12, 1869.

No. 43.

RESOLUTION giving certain instructions to the Judiciary Committees of the two Houses of the General Assembly.

Resolved by the General Assembly of the Commonwealth of Kentucky:

That the Judiciary Committees of the Senate and House of Representatives be, and they are hereby, directed to inquire into the present laws relating to the organization of corporations in this Commonwealth, and to report by bill or otherwise, at the earliest practicable day.

Approved January 16, 1869.

No. 44.

RESOLUTION requesting the Governor to return certain Bills.

Resolved by the General Assembly of the Commonwealth of Kentucky:

That the Governor be requested to return to the House of Representatives, unsigned, a bill, entitled "An act to incorporate the Exchange Bank," and also return to the Senate a bill, entitled "An act to incorporate the Green River Bank," and also a bill, entitled "An act to incorporate the Eastern Kentucky Coal, Iron, and Railroad Company."

Approved January 16, 1869.

No. 45.

RESOLUTION in favor of Mrs. L. B. Helm.

WHEREAS, The Hon. John L. Helm, late Governor of this Commonwealth, departed this life within one week after his inauguration as Governor; and whereas, he spent the services of a long life in the interest and for the benefit of his native State, with comparatively little compensation therefor; and as a further acknowledgment of his invaluable services to the State, therefore, be it

Resolved by the General Assembly of the Commonwealth of Kentucky:

That there is hereby appropriated out of the Treasury, to Mrs. Lucinda B. Helm, wife of the late Hon. John L. Helm, the sum of five thousand dollars ($5,000), an amount about equal to one year's salary with the perquisites, of the office of Governor of this Commonwealth; and the Auditor is directed to draw his warrant on the Treasury in favor of Mrs. Lucinda B. Helm for the same.

Approved January 22, 1869.

No. 46.

RESOLUTION in relation to the Death of General L. H. Rousseau.

WHEREAS, It is made known to us, through the public prints, that Gen. Lovell H. Rousseau has recently departed this life, therefore,

Resolved by the General Assembly of the Commonwealth of Kentucky:

That we receive with the deepest sadness the mournful intelligence of the death of our distinguished and beloved fellow-citizen, General Lovell H. Rousseau.

Resolved, That in the death of General Rousseau, Kentucky, his motherland, has lost a gallant, patriotic, and cherished son, our common country has lost a brave soldier and able statesman, and liberty an advocate and friend.

Resolved, That Kentucky will ever cherish, with just and generous pride, the memory of his talents, virtue, and valor; and that, among our historic names, our people will point to that of General Rousseau as one of the brightest and best that gilds the pages of our country's history.

Resolved, That we tender to his bereaved family our sincere sympathy and deepest condolence for this sad dispensation of Providence.

Resolved, That these resolutions be spread upon the Journals of both Houses of this General Assembly, and that a copy of the same be forwarded to the family of the deceased.

Approved January 28, 1869.

No. 47.

RESOLUTION in relation to the remains of General Crist.

Be it resolved by the General Assembly of the Commonwealth of Kentucky:

That a committee of five upon the part of the Senate, and eight on the part of the House of Representatives, be appointed by the respective Speakers, meet the several committees in charge of the remains of General Henry Crist at the depot, in Frankfort, on the 3d day of February, and accompany his remains to the State cemetery, their place of interment.

Approved February 2, 1869.

No. 48.

RESOLUTION to pay Officers of the General Assembly their daily wages.

Resolved by the General Assembly of the Commonwealth of Kentucky:

That the Auditor shall draw his warrant on the Treasury, from time to time, for the services rendered by the officers of either House of this General Assembly: *Provided, however*, That the sum drawn for by him shall not exceed the daily wages heretofore allowed such officers, computed from the time of the meeting of this General Assembly.

Approved February 2, 1869.

No. 49.

RESOLUTION in regard to printing report of the Trustees of the Institution for the Education of the Blind.

Resolved by the General Assembly of the Commonwealth of Kentucky:

That the usual number of the report of the Trustees of the Kentucky Institution for the Education of the Blind be printed for the use of the members of the General Assembly, and one thousand copies for the Institution.

Approved February 5, 1869.

No. 50.

RESOLUTION on the death of Charles S. Morehead.

WHEREAS, His Excellency, the Governor, has announced in his message the death of Charles S. Morehead, formerly Governor of Kentucky; and the Legislature desire to manifest their respect for his private character and public services; therefore, be it

Resolved by the General Assembly of the Commonwealth of Kentucky:

1. That the people of Kentucky lament the death of Charles S. Morehead, and honor his memory for the ability and probity with which he discharged important public trusts, for his manly constancy and courage under great trials, and for the virtue, dignity, and wisdom of his private life.

2. That the Governor is hereby requested to transmit a copy of this resolution to the family of the deceased; and to proffer the removal and interment of the remains of the dead for interment in the cemetery at Frankfort, with a funeral and appropriate monument at the expense of the State.

Approved February 18, 1869.

No. 51.

RESOLUTION in regard to the Reports of the Auditor and Treasurer.

Resolved by the General Assembly of the Commonwealth of Kentucky:

That hereafter the reports of the Auditor and Treasurer shall be made as far as possible in tabulated form, similar to that in which the Abstract of the late Census of the United States was printed, so as to exhibit in the least possible space, and in a form most easy for reference and comparison, the statistics of each county in this Commonwealth.

Approved February 18, 1869.

No. 52.

RESOLUTION providing for a recess and for firing salute on the 22d of February.

WHEREAS, The time-honored custom, from the earliest period of our national existence, has ever kept the 22d inst. as a national anniversary, and a feeling sense of deep gratitude for the distinguished services of the "Father of his Country," and to commemorate his memory, and transmit to posterity our reverence for his great and noble character, and perpetuate his name as a cherished inheritance; therefore, be it

Resolved by the General Assembly of the Commonwealth of Kentucky:

That when the two Houses of the General Assembly of the Commonwealth of Kentucky adjourn at noon on Saturday, the 20th inst., that they adjourn to meet on Tuesday, the 23d inst., at 10 o'clock, A. M., and that his Excellency, the Governor, be, and is hereby, requested, at the hour of 12 meridian, on the 22d inst., to have a national salute fired of one gun for each State of the Union, and one gun extra for Old Virginia, the mother of States and Presidents.

Approved February 20, 1869.

No. 53.

RESOLUTION in relation to the Executive Mansion.

Resolved by the General Assembly of the Commonwealth of Kentucky:

That a joint committee of two from the Senate and three from the House of Representatives be appointed, whose duty it shall be to make a personal examination of the Executive Mansion, with the view to the improvement or addition thereto; and that they report by bill or otherwise.

Approved March 5, 1869.

No. 54.

RESOLUTION in relation to a Final Adjournment.

Resolved by the General Assembly of the Commonwealth of Kentucky:

That when this General Assembly adjourns on the 16th day of March, 1869, it shall adjourn *sine die*.

Approved March 8, 1869.

PUB. L.—8

No. 55.

RESOLUTION in relation to the Ordnance of the State.

WHEREAS, During the existence of the late war, it is represented that the State authorities loaned to the General Government all or a portion of the artillery belonging to the State, then in the arsenal, and there is doubt whether or not the same have been returned or otherwise accounted for; therefore, be it

Resolved by the General Assembly of the Commonwealth of Kentucky:

That the Quarter-Master General be requested and instructed to report, as far as he is able, to the General Assembly, the number of cannon, and the calibre and value of the same thus loaned to, or otherwise obtained by, the General Government, together with the amount of ammunition and value of ammunition accompanying the same; what number, if any, have been returned or otherwise accounted for, and what number of cannon are remaining in the State arsenal at the present time.

Approved March 8, 1869.

No. 56.

RESOLUTION in relation to General George Rogers Clarke.

WHEREAS, By an act, entitled "An act to provide for the removal of the remains of General George Rogers Clarke to the Frankfort Cemetery, and the erection of a monument to his memory," approved 10th of March, 1856, the Governor was authorized and directed to carry into effect said act, which has never been complied with; for remedy wherefore, be it

Resolved by the General Assembly of the Commonwealth of Kentucky:

That his Excellency, the Governor, be, and he is hereby, authorized and directed to cause said recited act to be carried into effect.

Approved March 10, 1869.

No. 57.

RESOLUTION in relation to the Cities of Hickman and Columbus.

Resolved by the General Assembly of the Commonwealth of Kentucky:

That the Governor appoint some competent civil engineer to examine Columbus and Hickman, and report to the next General Assembly if the banks can be preserved from washing, and its probable cost; and the cost of said investigation shall not exceed two hundred and fifty dollars.

Approved March 10, 1869.

No. 58.

RESOLUTION to print Report of Regent of Kentucky University.

Resolved by the General Assembly of the Commonwealth of Kentucky:

That 2,000 copies of the Report of the Regent of the Kentucky Agricultural College be printed, 500 of which shall be delivered to the Regent for distribution, and the balance shall be sent by mail to the Senators and Representatives of the present General Assembly, postage paid.

Approved March 13, 1869.

No. 59.

RESOLUTIONS on the death of Hon. James Guthrie.

WHEREAS, This General Assembly have heard, with feelings of profound regret, of the death of our distinguished fellow-citizen, Hon. James Guthrie; therefore, be it

Resolved by the General Assembly of the Commonwealth of Kentucky:

That a joint committee of three from the Senate and five from the House be appointed to prepare and submit suitable resolutions, and report same.

Approved March 16, 1869.

No. 60.

RESOLUTION for the benefit of H. Pope Hawkins.

Be it resolved by the General Assembly of the Commonwealth of Kentucky:

That the sum of one hundred dollars is hereby appropriated to H. Pope Hawkins, for extra services as Page of the Senate, to be paid out of any money in the Treasury not otherwise appropriated; this resolution to take effect from and after its passage.

Approved March 16, 1869.

No. 61.
RESOLUTION in favor of Gip Morton.

Resolved by the General Assembly of the Commonwealth of Kentucky:

That Gip Morton, colored man, be allowed fifty cents per day additional, for taking care of clothing, &c., in committee room.

Approved March 16, 1869.

No. 62.
RESOLUTIONS in regard to the death of the Hon. James Guthrie.

WHEREAS, The Legislature of Kentucky have heard with deep regret of the death of the Hon. James Guthrie, of Louisville, at an advanced age, after a life distinguished by many public trusts of importance, which were discharged with honor to himself and benefit to his country, and consider it proper to testify their respect to his memory; now, therefore, be it

Resolved by the General Assembly of the Commonwealth of Kentucky:

1. That James Guthrie, during a long and useful existence as a Representative and Senator of this body; as President of the Convention that formed the present Constitution of this State; as Secretary of the Treasury of the United States; and as Senator from this State in Congress, displayed great force of character, and a strength of intellect equal to the various duties of his active and distinguished public life.

2. That in private life Mr. Guthrie was remarkable for the fidelity of his friendship; the warmth of his affections; his manly courage; the large social influence exercised by him; and his arduous labors for the advancement of the wealth, learning, and prosperity of his city and his native State.

3. That these resolutions be spread upon the Journals of the respective Houses, and that his Excellency, the Governor of this Commonwealth, be requested to forward a copy of the same to his family.

Approved March 16, 1869.

No. 63.
PREAMBLE AND RESOLUTION in relation to the Hon. Joshua F. Bullitt.

WHEREAS, The Hon. Joshua F. Bullitt, during the progress of the late civil war, was compelled, by military despotism, to leave the State in order to save himself from illegal arrest and imprisonment; and being at the time one of the judges of the court of appeals and chief justice of the State of Kentucky; and the civil authority at the time being wholly under the domination of the military, and unable to protect any citizen in his rights of person or property; and whereas, the Governor of the State of Kentucky, upon the address of the General Assembly, during said military domination, and at a time when the said Bullitt was absent by compulsion from the State and dared not return to it, removed the said Bullitt from said office; therefore, be it

Resolved by the General Assembly of the Commonwealth of Kentucky:

That it is our deliberate opinion that there was, in fact, no legal or constitutional cause for the removal of the said Hon. Joshua F. Bullitt; and the ground alleged therefor in the said address was palpably untrue; and the proceedings of the said General Assembly against him were a violation of the spirit of the Constitution (which guarantees to every man a fair and impartial trial); a flagrant outrage upon his constitutional rights; a manifest violation of all rules of equality and justice, and an insult to the honor and dignity of the Commonwealth of Kentucky.

Approved March 16, 1869.

No. 64.

RESOLUTION for the benefit of D. D. Sublett.

Resolved by the General Assembly of the Commonwealth of Kentucky:

That the sum of one hundred dollars be, and is hereby, appropriated to D. D. Sublett, of the Committee on Enrollments of the House of Representatives, in addition to the sum provided in the general appropriation act, and that the Auditor draw his warrant for that sum in said Sublett's favor on the Treasurer, who shall pay the same.

Approved March 16, 1869.

No. 65.

RESOLUTION in favor of Isaac Wingate.

Resolved by the General Assembly of the Commonwealth of Kentucky:

That the sum of one hundred dollars be, and is hereby, appropriated to Isaac Wingate, jr., clerk of the Committee on Enrollments of the Senate, in addition to the sum

1869.   provided in the general appropriation act, and that the Auditor draw his warrant for that sum in said Wingate's favor on the Treasurer, who shall pay the same.

Approved March 16, 1869.

No. 66.

RESOLUTION to appoint Visitors to Foreign Prisons.

Be it resolved by the General Assembly of the Commonwealth of Kentucky:

That it shall be the duty of the Governor to appoint three citizens of this Commonwealth, as a committee to visit the prisons or penitentiaries of such other States as they may deem proper, and inquire into and report such reforms in prison discipline, and such reorganization of the convict labor, as the result of their investigations shall show to be desirable. Said committee shall report by bill or otherwise to the next session of the General Assembly of this Commonwealth; that the entire cost of such commission shall not exceed three hundred dollars ($300).

Approved March 16, 1869.

No. 67.

RESOLUTION in regard to the Printing, Binding, and Distribution of the Acts, Journals, and Documents.

Resolved by the General Assembly of the Commonwealth of Kentucky:

The Acts, Journals, and Documents of the present session of this General Assembly shall be printed, bound, and distributed as soon after the adjournment of the present session as can be conveniently done.

Approved March 16, 1869.

No. 68.

RESOLUTION directing Public Printer to Print Synopsis of General Acts, &c.

Resolved by the General Assembly of the Commonwealth of Kentucky:

That the Public Printer print one thousand copies of a synopsis of the general acts, and the titles of private acts of this session; and that he forward same by mail to the members of this General Assembly.

Approved March 16, 1869.

No. 69.

RESOLUTION providing for Publication of Acts in Pamphlet Form.

Resolved by the General Assembly of the Commonwealth of Kentucky:

That as soon as practicable after the adjournment of this General Assembly, the Public Printer is directed to print in pamphlet form all the general laws and joint resolutions passed at the present adjourned session; and that he send one copy thereof, post-paid, to each member of this General Assembly and the officers of the same; to each judge of the court of appeals; each circuit, common pleas, or criminal judge; to the chancellor of Louisville; to each county judge; and the clerks of each of said courts; to each Commonwealth's Attorney and county attorneys; also to the Governor, Secretary of State, Attorney General, Auditor, Treasurer, Superintendent of Common Schools, President of the Board of Internal Improvement, Register of the Land Office, Adjutant and Quarter-Master General.

Resolved, further, That the Auditor draw his warrant in favor of the Public Printer on the Treasurer for a sum sufficient to pay said postage.

Approved March 15, 1869.

No. 70.

RESOLUTIONS in regard to the proposed Amendment of the Constitution of the United States.

WHEREAS, The Congress of the United States did, at the last session of the Fortieth Congress, propose to the Legislatures of the several States, for their ratification, the following amendment to the Constitution of the United States, to-wit:

"ARTICLE XV.

"SEC. 1. The right of citizens of the United States to vote shall not be denied or abridged by the United States, or by any State, on account of race, color, or previous condition of servitude.

"SEC. 2. The Congress shall have power to enforce this article by appropriate legislation."

And whereas, the same has been officially laid before the Legislature of Kentucky for its consideration and action; therefore, be it

Resolved by the General Assembly of the Commonwealth of Kentucky:

1. That said proposed amendment to the Constitution of the United States be not ratified, and that the propo-

1869.   sition to amend the Constitution of the United States, as
aforesaid, be, and the same is hereby, rejected.

2. That the Governor be requested to forward the
foregoing preamble and resolution to the President and
Secretary of State of the United States, and also to the
President of the Senate, and the Speaker of the House
of Representatives, of the Congress of the United States.

Approved March 13, 1869.

INDEX TO PUBLIC ACTS.

PUB. L.—9

LOCAL AND PRIVATE ACTS

OF

THE STATE OF KENTUCKY,

PASSED AT THE ADJOURNED SESSION OF THE
GENERAL ASSEMBLY, WHICH WAS BEGUN
AND HELD IN THE CITY OF FRANK-
FORT ON MONDAY, THE SECOND
DAY OF DECEMBER, 1867.

J. W. STEVENSON, *Governor.*

WM. JOHNSON, *Lieut. Governor and Speaker of the Senate.*

JOHN T. BUNCH, *Speaker of the House of Reps.*

S. B. CHURCHILL, *Secretary of State.*

JOHN RODMAN, *Attorney General.*

CHAPTER 1237.

AN ACT to amend the Charter of the Town of Somerset.

Be it enacted by the General Assembly of the Commonwealth of Kentucky:

§ 1. That the charter of the town of Somerset be, and the same is hereby, so amended that the trustees of said town shall have the right to tax retail dealers in liquors, as a license fee, not less than one hundred nor more than five hundred dollars per annum, for the privilege of retailing spirituous liquors within said town.

§ 2. That the police judge of said town shall have authority to try and decide, without the intervention of a jury, all cases of alleged drunkenness, breach of the peace, or disorderly conduct committed within the limits of said town.

§ 3. That upon the finding of any person or persons guilty of either of the above offenses, he or they shall be fined in any sum not less than three nor more than fifteen

1869.

1869.   dollars, upon which judgment a *capias pro fine* may issue instanter.

§ 4. This act to be in force from its passage.

JOHN T. BUNCH,
Speaker of the House of Representatives.
WM. JOHNSON,
Speaker of the Senate.

Approved January 9, 1869.

J. W. STEVENSON,
Governor of Kentucky.

By the Governor:

S. B. CHURCHILL, *Secretary of State.*

CHAPTER 1238.

AN ACT to amend an act, entitled "An act to incorporate the Western Financial Corporation."

Be it enacted by the General Assembly of the Commonwealth of Kentucky:

§ 1. That the act, entitled "An act to incorporate the Western Financial Corporation," approved 10th February, 1865, be, and the same is hereby, amended so that the capital stock of said corporation shall not be less than eight hundred thousand dollars ($800,000), with the privilege to increase the same to five millions of dollars ($5,000,000), divided into shares of one hundred dollars ($100) each; and it shall be lawful to reduce the present capital stock of one million dollars to eight hundred thousand dollars, and to replace the present shares of stock for five hundred dollars each by issuing to the holders thereof shares for one hundred dollars each for their proportions of the reduced capital stock; and no person shall at any time be president or director in said corporation who does not own at least ten shares of said reduced capital stock.

§ 2. This act shall not take effect until it is accepted by a vote of at least three fourths in value of the present capital stock at a meeting of the stockholders.

Approved January 9, 1869.

CHAPTER 1242.

AN ACT to amend an act approved March 2, 1865, entitled "An act allowing School Districts to levy a District School Tax."

Be it enacted by the General Assembly of the Commonwealth of Kentucky:

§ 1. That an act, entitled "An act allowing common school districts to levy a district school tax," approved March 2, 1865, be, and the same is hereby, amended as to allow common school district No. 15 (Cherry Grove), in the county of Bracken, to levy and collect a tax, not exceeding twenty-five cents on the one hundred dollars' worth of taxable property in said district in any one year, for school purposes.

§ 2. The election and other proceedings under this act shall be governed by said act approved March 2, 1865.

§ 3. This act shall take effect and be in force from and after its passage.

Approved January 16, 1869.

CHAPTER 1244.

AN ACT to amend the charter of the City of Covington.

Be it enacted by the General Assembly of the Commonwealth of Kentucky:

§ 1. That the city of Covington shall be, and is hereby, authorized and empowered to borrow, from time to time, as may be deemed necessary, by the common council of said city, any sum or sums of money, not exceeding at any one time one hundred thousand dollars; and may execute and deliver promissory notes, bills of exchange, or bonds, with coupons attached, to secure the payment of any such loan.

§ 2. That this act shall take effect from and after its passage.

Approved January 16, 1869.

CHAPTER 1246.

AN ACT to incorporate the Cairo Junction Railroad Company.

Be it enacted by the General Assembly of the Commonwealth of Kentucky:

§ 1. That William J. Allen, H. Watson Webb, William H. Green, Samuel Stoats Taylor, Daniel Bodkin, Thomas H. Richardson, and William White, and their associates, successors and assigns, be, and they hereby are, created a body-politic and corporate, under the name and style of the "Cairo Junction Railroad Company;" and by that name be, and they are hereby, made capable in law and in equity to sue and be sued, plead and be impleaded, defend and be defended, in any court of law and equity in this State or elsewhere; to make, have, and use a common seal, and the same to renew and alter at pleasure; and shall be, and hereby are, vested with all powers, privileges, and immunities which are or may be necessary to construct, complete, and operate a railroad, with double or single track, from any point opposite or within two

Corporators' names, and corporate powers.

1869.

miles (2) of a point opposite the city of Cairo, in the State of Illinois, to any point on the Mobile and Ohio railroad between the city of Columbus, Kentucky, and the State line between the State of Tennessee and Kentucky; and

May enter upon lands, &c.

for that purpose, to enter upon and take possession of so much land as may be necessary to construct, complete, and operate said railroad and its appendages; and if said

How right of way may be obtained.

company cannot agree with the owner or owners of said land taken as aforesaid, application may be made to any justice of the peace of the county in which the land may be situated, who, thereupon, shall issue his warrant, directed to the sheriff of his county, requiring him to summon a jury of twenty (20) *bona fide* house-keepers, not related or in anywise interested, to meet on the land, or as near it as is practicable, to be valued, on a day named in said warrant not less than ten nor more than twenty days after the issuing of the same; and if any of the jurors shall fail to attend, said sheriff shall forthwith summon as many jurors as may be necessary, with those in attendance, to complete the panel aforesaid; and from them each party, or the attorney or agent of either party, if present—if not, then the sheriff for the party absent— may strike off four jurors each, and the remaining twelve shall act as the jury of inquest of damages, after having been sworn by the sheriff justly and impartially to fix the damages which the owner or owners shall sustain by the use and occupation of the land required by the company. In estimating the damages, the jury shall take into consideration the benefits resulting to the owner from conducting said road through the lands of said owner, but only in the extinguishment of damages. The jury shall reduce their verdict to writing, and sign the same, and it shall be returned by the sheriff to the clerk of the circuit court for said county, who shall docket the same as other suits, giving it the precedency of all civil business; and, upon the call of the docket, the court shall enter an order confirming the said inquisition, unless defense be made and sufficient cause be shown against it; and when so confirmed, the clerk shall enter it of record, at the expense of the company; but if set aside, the court may direct another inquisition to be taken in the same manner; such inquisition shall describe the bounds of the land taken, and the extent and duration of the interest in the same; and such damages, when tendered or paid to the owner or owners of said land, or his, or her, or their agent or legal representative, or to the clerk of said court for the use of any such owner, when he, she, or they may refuse to receive the same, or reside out of the county, shall, *ipso facto*, vest in the company the right to the land, or to the use of the same, to all intents and purposes, as fully as if the same had been acquired by valid conveyance.

§ 2. The capital stock of said company shall be one million of dollars, which may be increased by said company to any sum not exceeding three millions of dollars, which may be divided into shares of one hundred dollars each, which shall be deemed personal property, and may be issued and transferred in such manner as the board of directors may prescribe. *Capital stock.*

§ 3. The affairs of said company shall be managed by a board of seven directors, which may be increased to any number not exceeding thirteen; and William J. Allen, H. Watson Webb, William H. Green, Samuel Stoats Taylor, Daniel Bodkin, Thomas H. Richardson, and William White, are hereby appointed the first board, who shall hold their offices until their successors shall be elected and qualified, in such manner as may be prescribed by the by-laws of said company; said board shall have the power of electing one of their number president, and such other officers as may be prescribed by the by-laws. *Who to manage affairs of company, first board of directors, &c.*

§ 4. Said corporation shall have power to unite its railroad with any other railroad now constructed, or which may hereafter be constructed, upon such terms as may be mutually agreed upon between the companies so connecting; and, from time to time, to borrow such sums of money as may be necessary for the purposes of said company, and at any rate of interest not exceeding ten per cent. per annum, and to issue and dispose of their bonds in denominations of not less than one hundred dollars for any amount so borrowed; and to mortgage their corporate property, real or personal, and their franchise, or convey the same by deed of trust to secure the payment of any money so borrowed, or any other debt of said company. *May unite with other roads.* *May borrow money.*

§ 5. This act to take effect from and after its passage.

Approved January 18, 1869.

CHAPTER 1248.

AN ACT for the benefit of the Board of Internal Improvement for Scott County.

Be it enacted by the General Assembly of the Commonwealth of Kentucky:

§ 1. That the act passed and approved March the 9th, 1867, entitled "An act to repeal an act, entitled 'An act for the benefit of the Board of Internal Improvement for Scott county,'" approved January the 21st, 1865, is hereby repealed; and the act, entitled "An act for the benefit of the Board of Internal Improvement of Scott county," ap-

1869. proved January the 21st, 1865, is hereby revived and declared to be in full force.

§ 2. This act to take effect from its passage.

Approved January 20, 1869.

CHAPTER 1249.

AN ACT for the benefit of the Frankfort City School.

Preamble. WHEREAS, The board of councilmen of the city of Frankfort did, on the 4th day of December, 1868, adopt and pass the following ordinance, to-wit:

"*Be it ordained by the Board of Councilmen of the City of Frankfort*, That, in order to raise the money necessary to the completion of the city school building, and furnishing the same, and to meet the outstanding liabilities of the commissioners thereof, as well as to provide means for the employment of a sufficient corps of teachers, the mayor be, and he is hereby, authorized and directed to issue twenty-five bonds of the city, of the denomination of one thousand ($1,000) dollars each, with coupons attached, for the payment of interest at the rate of six per cent. per annum, payable semi-annually, to-wit: On the first day of January and July, at the Bank of America, New York, said bonds to be payable twenty years after date at said Bank of America, New York. The bonds to be signed by the mayor and countersigned by the clerk, with the corporate seal of the city attached, and the coupons to be signed by the clerk; which said bonds, so issued as aforesaid, shall be delivered by the mayor to said school trustees, who may put them upon the market, and from the sale thereof realize said funds necessary as aforesaid: *Provided*, That said bonds shall not be sold for a sum less than seven hundred and fifty dollars for each bond."

Which said ordinance was, on Saturday, the 2d day of January, instant, submitted to the qualified voters of said city of Frankfort for ratification or rejection, after due notice; and whereas, the vote thereon was two hundred and eight for and eighteen against said ordinance; and whereas, the board of councilmen of the said city, by resolution, have asked the passage of an act authorizing the issual of the bonds of the city as provided in said ordinance; therefore,

Be it enacted by the General Assembly of the Commonwealht of Kentucky:

Bonds to be issued. § 1. That the mayor of the city of Frankfort and the clerk of the board of councilmen be, and they are hereby, authorized, empowered, and directed to issue the bonds of said city for the purposes specified in said ordinance, and as provided therein, the said ordinance being hereby legalized and confirmed. 1869.

§ 2. That the board of councilmen of the said city of Frankfort shall, from year to year, levy upon the taxable property in said city and collect an additional tax sufficient to pay the interest on said bonds, and to redeem and pay off the same when they shall become due, which said taxes, as levied and collected, shall be kept separate and apart from the other revenues of said city, and shall not be expended for any other purpose than the payment of the interest and principal of said bonds. *Shall levy tax to meet interest and principal of bonds.*

§ 3. That it shall be lawful for the board of councilmen aforesaid to create a separate fund of the revenues of the city, to be denominated the "School Fund," which shall embrace all taxes and moneys collected and received for school purposes, as well as all moneys arising from levies to pay the interest or principal of the school bonds; and they may require the clerk, treasurer, and tax collectors to keep separate accounts and make separate reports and returns of all moneys which belong to the school fund, which shall not be appropriated to any other than the purposes of the city school, as provided by law: *Provided*, That the moneys of the school fund shall be divided into moneys for the support of the city school and moneys for the payment of the interest and principal of the debt of the city created for school purposes as hereinbefore provided, each division of the fund to be appropriated exclusively for the purpose specified. Any accumulation of surplus money in either division of the fund may be invested in safe and remunerative securities by the board of councilmen. *May create school fund.* *Accounts to be kept separate.* *Moneys of to be classified.*

§ 4. All taxes authorized to be levied and collected by this act, or any act heretofore passed within the city of Frankfort for school purposes, shall be assessed, levied, and collected alike upon the property and residents of North and South Frankfort. *Apply to North & S'y of Frankfort.*

§ 5. This act shall be in force from its passage.

Approved January 20, 1869.

CHAPTER 1250.

AN ACT to amend the charter of the Mayslick and Sardis Turnpike Road.

Be it enacted by the General Assembly of the Commonwealth of Kentucky:

§ 1. That the persons hereinafter named be, and they are hereby, authorized and permitted to work out the road tax imposed upon them by the road law of Mason county on the Mayslick and Sardis turnpike road, instead of on the roads to which they are now allotted, at any point on

1869.

said Mayslick and Sardis turnpike road which may be designated by the president of said road: *Provided,* They shall have reasonable notice given them by the president of said road of the time and place where and when said work is required to be done. The names of those referred to are as follows: William P. Clark, Henry Cracroft, Dil. Watson, Isaac Dye, Washington Prather, Michael Roney, Thomas Y. Johnson, H. F. and A. M. Hawkins, James M. Piper, David Raymond, the heirs of Thomas Raymond, deceased, Mrs. Virginia Triplett, Silas A. Cleft, John S. Mitchell, Benjamin Longnecker, John Longnecker, Mrs. Julia Longnecker, and all persons now living upon the lands of the above named persons, or those who may hereafter live upon them; and upon the failure of the above named persons, or any of them, to work out their tax after having been duly notified by the president of the time and place where the work is required to be done, the president of said road shall sue for and collect the same, and shall appropriate it to the completion or repairs of said turnpike road.

§ 2. This act to take effect from its passage.

Approved January 20, 1869.

CHAPTER 1251.

AN ACT to incorporate the Orangeburg and Tollsboro Turnpike Road Company, in Mason County.

Be it enacted by the General Assembly of the Commonwealth of Kentucky:

§ 1. That a body corporate be, and is hereby, created, and authorized to be formed and organized, under the name and style of the Orangeburg and Tollsboro turnpike road company, in Mason county; and under that name and style it shall have perpetual succession; may have a common seal; may contract and be contracted with, sue and be sued, in all the courts of this Commonwealth.

§ 2. The object and business of said corporation shall be to construct, keep up, and maintain a turnpike road, commencing in Orangeburg, Mason county, and running so as to intersect the Vanceburg, Tollsboro, and Maysville turnpike road at the Mason and Lewis county line, near the house of Lewis Tolle.

§ 3. The capital stock of said company shall not exceed twenty thousand dollars, to be divided into shares of fifty dollars each.

§ 4. Wm. D. Coryell, R. P. Tolle, M. B. Tolle, Marshall Stubblefield, Samuel Lyons, and Robt. L. Cooper, commissioners, having already secured a large amount of stock subscribed and made payable to them for the purpose of constructing said road, and said road being all under contract, and a large amount of work done on same, it is now declared that all subscriptions of stock to said road, and all acts, contracts, &c., of whatsoever kind, relating to said road, are hereby made valid and binding on all parties interested.

§ 5. The commissioners before named, or those of them who may act as such, shall give ten days' notice to the subscribers of stock, by written notices posted up at three or more public places in the vicinity of said road, of the time and place of holding an election for officers of said company, which shall consist of a president and five directors; no one but a stockholder being eligible to office. Each stockholder shall be entitled to one vote for each share of stock owned by him, which may be cast in person or by proxy. The first election shall be under the supervision of the commissioners, or those acting. The president and directors shall each take an oath for the faithful performance of their duties, which shall be certified by the officer administering same, and filed with the papers of the company; and said officers shall serve until their successors are elected and qualified. After the first election, the regular annual election for officers shall be on the first Saturday of January in each year. If any vacancy occur before the regular election, the remainder of the directors may fill said vacancy.

§ 6. The president and directors may continue to receive subscriptions of stock until a sufficient amount shall be raised for the completion of said road. They may, at any time, build a branch road, beginning near the house of Mrs. Lucy Dickson, and running to Phillips' creek; thence to or in the direction of Esculapia Springs. So soon as one mile of said branch road is completed, toll may be collected, at the usual rates, for that distance, on all travel which passes through the gate on the main road; and so soon as two and a half miles of said branch road shall be finished, the president and directors may erect a toll-gate house, and charge toll for all travel in proportion to distance traveled. The charges for toll on the main road and its branch shall be in conformity with the laws of this State regulating tolls on turnpike roads.

§ 7. The said company may receive releases of right of way for said road, and ground for toll-houses and rock quarries, by consent or purchase; and if they deem it necessary, may, by proceedings instituted in conformity with the laws of this State on the subject of turnpikes and plank roads, condemn land for right of way for said road, for toll-houses and rock quarries; just compensation being first paid to the owners thereof, to be assessed by a jury empanneled for such purpose, according to law as aforesaid.

§ 8. The president and directors may appoint a secretary and treasurer, and prescribe their duties, fix their compensation, and may remove them at pleasure; said secretary and treasurer shall take an oath, and give bond and good security for the faithful performance of their duties; a certificate of said oath and the bond shall be filed with the papers of said company; they may appoint a superintendent or agent to superintend the construction of said road and its maintenance afterwards; also, gatekeepers, and such other employes as they may deem necessary.

§ 9. Said president and directors shall have power to pass any by-laws, rules and regulations, for their own government, and the government and conduct of said company, its officers and affairs, not inconsistent with the Constitution of the United States or with the Constitution and laws of this State.

§ 10. The said turnpike road shall be not less than thirty feet, nor more than forty feet wide; and any person who shall unlawfully obstruct said road shall be subject to a fine of not less than five nor more than fifty dollars, recoverable as other fines are recoverable by law, and be for the use of said company when collected; said president and directors may pass by-laws fixing fines for a failure to pay toll, or for the evasion of toll on said road, which may be recovered as other fines of similar amount are recovered under the laws of this Commonwealth, and be for the use of said company.

§ 11. The president and directors shall prescribe in what installments the subscriptions of stock shall be paid; and if any stockholder shall fail to pay his amount of stock so called for, for thirty days after the same is due, the president may proceed to enforce the collection of the same by law as other debts are collected in the courts having jurisdiction under the laws of this Commonwealth; and should any stockholder fail or refuse to pay the amount called, for three successive calls, then his or her stock may be forfeited at the option of the said president and directors; and all amounts remaining unpaid shall be collected as similar amounts are collected under the laws of this State, and be for the use of said company.

§ 12. The president and directors may borrow money for the use of said company, not to exceed five thousand dollars, and give personal security therefor, or a mortgage on said road and its franchises, which may be enforced and foreclosed.

§ 13. This act shall take effect and be in force from its passage.

Approved January 20, 1869.

CHAPTER 1253.

AN ACT to authorize the Hancock County Court to appropriate the excess of County Levy, for the year 1867, to the payment of the deficiency in the Court-house Fund for the year 1868.

WHEREAS, The "Court-house Fund," levied for the year 1868, by the Hancock county court, in accordance with the provisions of "An act to authorize the county court of Hancock to impose additional taxes, and execute bonds to erect public buildings in said county," approved January 30th, 1867, is ascertained to be insufficient, by the sum of five hundred and fifty-three dollars and fifty cents, for the payment of court-house bonds issued in pursuance of said act, and payable 1st November, 1868; and whereas, The excess of five hundred and eleven dollars, county levy collected by the sheriff of Hancock for the year 1867, and appropriated by the Hancock county court for the purpose of repairing the county jail, on condition that certain commissioners, appointed for such purpose by said court, deemed it expedient, remains unappropriated and unexpended, in consequence of said commissioners having reported such expenditure inexpedient; now, therefore,

Be it enacted by the General Assembly of the Commonwealth of Kentucky:

§ 1. That the judge of the Hancock county court be, and he is hereby, authorized and directed, at any regular or special term of said court, held as soon as may be after the passage of this act, to appropriate the aforesaid sum of five hundred and eleven dollars, or any excess (over and above the payment of county indebtedness) that may or should have been collected by the sheriff of Hancock for the year 1867. to and for the payment of court-house bonds, payable 1st of November, 1868, issued under the provisions of the act aforesaid.

§ 2. That this act shall take effect from and after its passage.

Approved January 20, 1869.

CHAPTER 1254.

AN ACT to amend an act, entitled "An act to amend an act to levy a tax to aid in building Turnpike Roads in Lewis County."

Be it enacted by the General Assembly of the Commonwealth of Kentucky:

§ 1. That an act approved December the 18th, 1867 (*Session Acts of* 1867 *and* 1868, *vol.* 1, *page* 120, *chap.* 20), be, and the same is, amended as follows: the tax levied by said act, or the one to which said act is an amendment, shall no longer be levied or collected on any property above Slate creek, above Vanceburg, as said property is now made subject to a tax to build the Vanceburg, Quincy, and Springville turnpike; and said tax shall no longer be levied or collected on any land below Salt Lick creek, and between the Ohio river and the dividing ridge between said river and the waters of Salt Lick and Fly Hollow, as said lands are subject to a tax to build the Vanceburg, Quick's Run, and Concord turnpike road; the taxes accrued on said property, up to the close of 1868, shall, however, be paid and collected.

§ 2. That the tax of one dollar on the one hundred dollars' worth of property, shall hereafter be on all property and money subject to taxation for State revenue, situated, owned, or found within the prescribed distance on Salt Lick creek; and said tax shall continue to be levied and collected until said Vanceburg, Salt Lick, Tollsboro, and Maysville turnpike shall be completed to the divide between Salt Lick and Cabin creek, near Hervie's shop, and paid for; and then said local tax on Salt Lick shall cease and be no longer assessed, levied, or collected.

§ 3. That the tax of one dollar on the one hundred dollars' worth of property on each side of said road (after the same passes the head waters of Salt Lick creek), shall continue to be assessed, levied, and collected on all property within one mile of said road on each side of the same, from the head waters of Salt Lick to the Mason county line, where said road crosses said line; and on the second mile the tax shall, from the beginning of 1869, be only fifty cents on the one hundred dollars' worth of property. The tax collected on the property subject to this local tax, along the line of said road, from the head waters of Salt Lick to where said road crosses Cabin creek, shall be expended in building the road between those two points; and when said road is finished and paid for between said points, said local tax, from head of Salt Lick to Cabin creek, shall cease; in no event shall said local tax be collected on property beyond the dividing ridge, between Cabin creek and the Esculapia Fork of Salt Lick creek, as the property on the Salt Lick side of said ridge is subject to a local tax to build the pike leading up said Esculapia Fork of Salt Lick. That when the said road is finished and paid for, from the line between Mason and Lewis county to where said road crosses Cabin creek, and a bridge built across said creek, and also paid for, then the local tax on property, on each side of said road, from the Mason county line to Cabin creek, shall cease; but if any part of the money collected on property east of Cabin creek shall have been expended on that part of the road west of said creek, then the tax-payers subject to said tax shall make up said sums, it being the intention to expend the tax collected in each section aforesaid in said section, and on that part of the road; and the sheriff in collecting the taxes, and the company in expending the money, shall be governed by these principles, and collect and apply the money accordingly.

§ 4. That persons who pay, or have paid said local tax, and are stockholders in said company, by having subscribed to the capital stock of said company, shall have a credit on their stock subscriptions for the amount of their tax paid; or, if they have paid their calls on their stock and not their tax, then the tax shall not be collected from them until the taxes paid by the tax-payer, who owns no stock, or less stock in proportion to his property taxed, shall have paid an equal sum according to the value of his property, money, &c., subject to tax for State revenue, and who is taxed under this amendment, or the original act, or any amendment thereto, it being the intention of this act to equalize the tax and burthens of building said road as near as possible; and the company, in collecting said tax, shall hereafter levy and collect it upon all property and money subject to tax for State revenue, within the prescribed distance and districts, for the length of time prescribed in this act, and according to the principles set forth in this act. The taxes due up to the close of 1868 shall be collected and paid according to the law as it stood before the passage of this act.

§ 5. This act shall be in force from its passage.

Approved January 20, 1869.

CHAPTER 1255.

AN ACT to incorporate the Barren River Bridge Company.

Be it enacted by the General Assembly of the Commonwealth of Kentucky:

§ 1. That there is hereby incorporated a bridge company, by the name and style of "The Barren River Bridge Company," for the purpose of building and constructing a bridge across Barren river, on the turnpike road which leads from Bardstown to Nashville, Tennessee. The capital stock of said company shall be twenty thousand dollars, to be divided into shares of fifty dollars each. *Company incorporated, &c.*

§ 2. The books for subscription of stock shall be opened by John J. Gatewood and John H. Collins, at Scottsville, in Allen county, and by James G. Page, John T. Rogers, John F. Jewell, and Joseph H. Lewis, in Glasgow, Barren county, on the first day of March, 1869, and at such other times and places as any three of said commissioners may designate by written advertisements first posted up in *Commissioners to open books, when & where.*

1869.

Obligation of subscribers.

three public places ten days. The subscribers of stock shall sign their names to a writing in said books, as follows: "We, whose names are hereto subscribed, promise to pay to the president and directors of the Barren River Bridge Company the sum of fifty dollars for each share of stock in said company attached to our names, at such time and place as they may order and direct. Witness our hands, this —— day of ———, 18—." That said com-

May build bridge upon abutments already erected.

pany may, and they are hereby permitted to, build said bridge upon, and to use the abutments and pillars at, said crossing of said river, now owned by the State of Kentucky; and there is hereby appropriated and subscribed

$5,000 subscribed by State

by the State of Kentucky to the capital stock of said company five thousand dollars; and the Auditor of Public Accounts is directed to draw his warrant therefor upon the Treasurer in favor of the president of said company, and the same shall be paid by said Treasurer: *Provided, however,* Said warrant shall not be drawn and delivered

Not to be drawn until sufficient sum is subscribed to build bridge.

till there is a sum sufficient, in addition thereto, subscribed and paid into said company by an individual or individuals, to finish and complete said bridge, including the cost of its covering in, which fact of subscribing and paying in of said sum shall be certified to said Auditor by the judges of the Barren and Allen county courts, under their hands and seals of office; and when so certified, it shall be sufficient evidence to the Auditor to issue his warrant aforesaid.

County courts of Barren and Allen may take stock.

§ 3. That the county court of Barren county, a majority of the justices of the peace of said county concurring therein, and the county court of Allen county, a majority of the justices of the peace of said county concuring therein, may, at any time, subscribe such amount of stock in said company as either of them may deem proper, not exceeding twenty-five hundred dollars for each county, and the same shall be entered at large upon the records of said courts; and when so subscribed by either court, it shall be a debt against the county, and shall be levied and collected as other levies upon said county: *Provided, however,* Not more than one half of the sum so levied shall be collected in any one year.

When election of officers to be held.

§ 4. So soon as one thousand dollars of the stock is subscribed, the stockholders shall be convened at Glasgow, in Barren county, upon ten days' public notice, and, under the supervision of some three of said commissioners, an election shall be held—each share of stock casting one vote—for president and three directors, each of whom

Term of office, regular elections, &c.

must be a stockholder in said company. They shall hold their office till the first Saturday in April, 1870, when an election shall again be held at said town for their successors; and every first Saturday in April in each year a new election shall be held to fill said offices : *Provided, however,* Each of said officers shall take and subscribe an oath, which shall be recorded in the books of said company, that they will, to the best of their judgment and ability, faithfully perform all the duties of their said offices ; and they shall continue to act till their successors are duly qualified. They shall appoint a treasurer and clerk, who shall also take a like oath, to be recorded as aforesaid ; and the treasurer shall give bond, with good security, to be approved by the board, in a sum of at least twenty-five thousand dollars, conditioned that he will faithfully perform all the duties of his said office, and pay over all moneys which shall come to his hands as such, in obedience to the orders of said board ; and for a violation of his bond, he may be proceeded against, with his securities, by motion or suit in the circuit court of any county in this Commonwealth, as sheriffs may now be proceeded against for failing to pay over money collected on executions.

§ 5. The said company shall be a body corporate and politic, under the name of "The Barren River Bridge Company;" and in that name may sue and be sued, plead and be impleaded; and may have and use a common seal; and shall have perpetual succession.

§ 6. When said bridge is so far finished as that it is safe for wagons and other vehicles to pass and be drawn over it, it shall be the duty of said company to allow them to pass; but the company shall provide a bridge-keeper to be, and at all times to remain, there; and shall exact and collect such rates of toll for each horse, mule, head of cattle, footman, wagon, buggy, and carriage, of every description, that shall pass over said bridge, the rates following: Each footman, five cents; each horse and rider, ten cents; each led or loose horse, five cents; each head of loose cattle, sheep, hogs, or goats, two cents; each one-horse buggy and horse, thirty cents; each two-horse wagon or carriage, with two horses attached, fifty cents; each wagon, with four horses attached, sixty cents; each wagon, with three horses attached, fifty-five cents; each wagon, with five horses attached, sixty-five cents; each wagon, with six horses attached, seventy-five cents : *Provided, however,* That when a wagon or other vehicle is drawn by oxen, each ox shall be the same as a horse in this tariff; each cart, with one horse, fifteen cents; each cart, with two horses, twenty cents; but no charge shall be made for the driver or load upon any wagon, buggy, or carriage.

§ 7. The said bridge-keeper shall take an oath, to be recorded in said book, that he will truly and faithfully carry out and execute the duties of bridge-keeper under this act, and truly and honestly account for and pay over

Marginal notes:

1869.

Officers to take oath.

Treasurer and clerk to be appointed, to give bond, &c.

Name & style.

Bridge-keeper to be appointed, and rates of toll.

Bridge-keeper to take oath and give bond.

1869.

to said company all moneys received by him for toll aforesaid; and said company shall require him to give bond,
with good security, conditioned to account for and pay to
said company all moneys received by him as bridge-keeper
aforesaid, at such time and place as they shall require;
and, for a violation of his bond, he and his security shall
be liable, by motion or suit, in the circuit or quarterly
court, and may be proceeded against as sheriffs can be
proceeded against for money collected on executions, and
subject to like recoveries.

President to
render, under
oath, amount
of receipts and
expenditures to
Auditor. first
Jan. in each
year, &c..

§ 8. It shall be the duty of the president of said company to render, under oath, a true and full statement of
the receipts and disbursements of said company, to the
Auditor of Public Accounts, on or before the 10th day of
January of each year; and all the receipts of said company for tolls which shall remain after paying said bridge-
keeper and necessary repairs and costs of carrying on the
business of said company, shall be paid by said president
into the Treasury of the State, on the 10th day of January of each year, and the Treasurer shall give a receipt
therefor, which shall be recorded in the books of said company; and when said receipts to the State shall amount
to five thousand dollars, then, from and after that time, the
net incomes of the company shall be equally divided, and
paid to the stockholders in said company according to
their shares of stock, the State being one stockholder to
the amount aforesaid of five thousand dollars, and her
dividends shall be paid into the Treasury as aforesaid.

May make
rules and regu-
lations, &c.

§ 9. The said company shall have power to make such
rules and regulations, prohibiting or permitting any and
all persons traveling said road from crossing said river,
otherwise than upon said bridge, for two hundred yards
above and below the same; and when any person shall
leave said road and cross the river above or below said
bridge to avoid paying toll, within the distance aforesaid,
such person may be proceeded against by common warrant before a justice of the peace by said company, and
compelled to pay four times the toll it would have cost to
cross on the bridge; and it shall be the duty of said company and said bridge-keeper so to prosecute such person
in every instance, and collect the same; and, for the
purpose of effectuating this provision, any justice of the
peace may issue his warrant against such offender, and
the same may be served and set for trial immediately;
and the justice shall hear and adjudicate the same at
once, without waiting till his regular term : *Provided, however*, Said company may make contracts with resident citizens and families living within five miles of said bridge to

pass over said bridge at such price per year, or for six months, as the company may deem just and proper.

§ 10. This act to take effect from its passage.

Approved January 20, 1869.

CHAPTER 1256.

AN ACT for the benefit of the County Court of Nelson County.

Be it enacted by the General Assembly of the Commonwealth of Kentucky:

§ 1. That the proceedings of the county court for the county of Nelson, at the October term, 1868, of said court, in fixing the county levy at more than two dollars and fifty cents, be, and the same is hereby, legalized; and the sheriff of said county is required to collect said levy as fixed by said court at said term.

§ 2. That hereafter, said county court shall have power to fix the levy of said county at any amount necessary to pay the indebtedness of said county, although said levy may exceed two dollars and fifty cents.

§ 3. This act shall take effect from its passage.

Approved January 21, 1869.

CHAPTER 1257.

AN ACT for the benefit of Butler County.

Be it enacted by the General Assembly of the Commonwealth of Kentucky:

§ 1. That the county court of Butler county be, and is hereby, authorized to issue county bonds to the amount one thousand dollars, due in three years from date, bearing six per cent. interest, payable annually; said bonds to be of such amount or denomination as the court may see proper to issue, and shall be in substance as follows: Three years after date, the county of Butler promises to pay the bearer or holder —— dollars, with interest thereon at the rate of six per cent. per annum, payable annually, which bonds shall be signed by the county judge and attested by the clerk, and bear the seal of the court, and may be sold at not less than ninety cents on the dollar. That the county judge shall make sale of the bonds, and be responsible on his official bond for the money, and apply the same to the payment of the county claims now due, and make report to the next annual court of claims of his proceedings under this act. That it shall be the duty of the court of claims to make provision for the payment of said bonds, and to enable them to do so,

1869.   they are hereby authorized to increase the county levy to three dollars per head.

§ 2. That this act shall be in force from and after its passage.

Approved January 21, 1869.

CHAPTER 1258.

AN ACT to authorize the County Court of Wolfe County to levy a tax and increase the County levy.

Be it enacted by the General Assembly of the Commonwealth of Kentucky:

§ 1. That the county judge of Wolfe county is hereby authorized to cause the justices of the peace in said county to be summoned, to convene at the court-house thereof, for the purpose of revising the county levy for the year 1868, and to increase the same, if necessary, not to exceed three dollars and fifty cents upon each tithe, for the purpose of paying the claims allowed in 1868 to complete the public buildings in said county.

§ 2. That they are hereby authorized to levy and collect an *ad valorem* tax, not to exceed twenty cents upon each one hundred dollars' worth of property in said county, for the purposes mentioned in the first section of this act.

§ 3. This act to take effect from its passage, and to remain in force for two years.

Approved February 21, 1869.

CHAPTER 1259.

AN ACT to authorize the Trustees of the Town of Rumsey to sell the Public Grounds in said Town.

· *Be it enacted by the General Assembly of the Commonwealth of Kentucky:*

§ 1. That the trustees of the town of Rumsey, in the county of McLean, be, and they are hereby, authorized and empowered to sell and convey any of the public lands or ground belonging to said corporation, and lying within the corporate limits of said town; the proceeds to be appropriated to the improvement of said town, in such manner as the trustees may, from time to time, direct.

§ 2. This act shall take effect and be in force from and after its passage.

Approved January 21, 1869.

CHAPTER 1260.

AN ACT authorizing the Muhlenburg County Court to levy a tax, and to increase the County levy of said County.

Be it enacted by the General Assembly of the Commonwealth of Kentucky:

§ 1. That the county court of Muhlenburg county, a majority of the justices being present and concurring therein, shall have power, at any regular term of said court, to levy a tax of not exceeding ten cents on the one hundred dollars' worth of taxable property in said county, and to levy an additional poll tax of not exceeding one dollar upon each tithable in said county, for the purpose of paying and discharging the debts of the county, and for the building of bridges and such other public improvements as the said court may, from time to time, order.

§ 2. This act shall take effect from its passage, and shall continue in force for five years.

Approved January 21, 1869.

CHAPTER 1261.

AN ACT for the benefit of John W. Howard, of Ballard County.

Be it enacted by the General Assembly of the Commonwealth of Kentucky:

§ 1. That John W. Howard, of Ballard county, is hereby authorized to transact business in his own name and for his own benefit; and all his acts shall be binding, and he shall be responsible to the same extent in law as though he was of the full age of twenty-one years.

§ 2. This act shall be in force from its passage.

Approved January 21, 1869.

CHAPTER 1262.

AN ACT authorizing George C. Rogers, Judge of the 4th Judicial District, to Sign the Orders of the Muhlenburg Circuit Court at the December Term, 1867, and May Term, 1868.

WHEREAS, R. T. Petree, late judge of the Muhlenburg circuit court, failed to sign the orders at the December term, 1867, and May term, 1868; and whereas, said Petree's term of office has expired; and whereas, Muhlenburg county is now in the 4th judicial district; therefore,

Be it enacted by the General Assembly of the Commonwealth of Kentucky:

§ 1. That George C. Rogers, judge of the 4th judicial district, be, and he is hereby, authorized to sign the orders for any day, that may not have heretofore been signed, of the Muhlenburg circuit court at its December term, 1867, and the May term, 1868; and that the signing thereof shall be as legal as though they had been signed heretofore by the judge thereof.

§ 2. That this act be in force from its passage.

Approved January 21, 1869.

CHAPTER 1263.

AN ACT to amend an act incorporating the Danville and Pleasant Hill Turnpike, approved 11th February, 1854.

WHEREAS, Since the passage of said act, the said turnpike road has been made from Danville to the dividing line between the counties of Boyle and Mercer, near Wallace's shop, on said line; and whereas, a large private subscription has been made by the citizens of Mercer county in the vicinity of the place laid out from said beginning point on said line, to continue said turnpike road from said line to Pleasant Hill, in Mercer county; and whereas, the Mercer county court, at its November term, 1865, entered up an order taking stock in said road, and appointing commissioner Phil. B. Thompson to subscribe one thousand dollars per mile, to be paid on each mile on the completion of said mile; now, therefore,

Be it enacted by the General Assembly of the Commonwealth of Kentucky:

§ 1. That said act, entitled "An act to incorporate the Danville and Pleasant Hill turnpike road company," approved the eleventh day of February, 1854, be so amended, that said company shall be required to construct the said turnpike road from where the Danville turnpike road strikes the said dividing line between the said counties of Boyle and Mercer, near Wallace's shop, continuing said turnpike road, running by Curd's blacksmith shop, and near the White Oak Spring to Pleasant Hill, in Mercer county, in place and instead of from Danville.

§ 2. That the organization of said company under the act aforesaid, heretofore made, and all acts of said company, by its directors and managers and officers and agents, done in pursuance of said act, are hereby approved, confirmed, and declared to be valid and lawful.

§ 3. That the 3d section of said act of incorporation is hereby so amended, that, in lieu of the commissioners therein appointed to open books for the subscription of stock, the following persons are hereby appointed, to-wit: F. Nicholas, W. M. Shumate, W. A. Cooke, Dr. A. T. Stephenson, F. M. Bush, and A. H. Bowman, who, or any two of the above named commissioners, may act as commissioners.

§ 4. That said commissioners may or may not, at their discretion, advertise the time and place of receiving subscriptions of stock, or either of them may, at any time or place, receive subscriptions of stock, until the capital stock, or so much thereof as may be necessary, is subscribed. And all such subscriptions heretofore taken by all or either of said commissioners, and which may hereafter be by them taken, are herein and hereby declared valid and binding on the subscribers thereto.

Approved January 21, 1869.

CHAPTER 1264.

AN ACT for the benefit of Sanford M. Collins, of Mason County.

WHEREAS, The Governor of this Commonwealth, having received information on which he relied that Wm. Brookover, a felon convicted in the Mason circuit court, but who had escaped from jail after the judgment of conviction was affirmed by the court of appeals, was in the northern part of Ohio, in the town of Findlay, did commission Sanford M. Collins, of Mason county, to proceed to Ohio and demand, arrest, and receive said felon, and bring him back to Kentucky, to be confined in the Penitentiary under the said judgment of conviction ; and whereas, said Collins did, under said commission of the Governor, in good faith proceed, with a proper assistant, to the northern part of Ohio for said felon, and resorted to diligent efforts to discover and arrest him; and whereas, it turned out that the information on which the Governor relied was gotten up by the friends of the felon for purposes of deception, in order to enable said felon to escape detection and recapture; but said Collins, having acted in good faith under said commission as the agent of the State in said matter, and having necessarily expended in said business the sum of one hundred and ninety-three dollars and thirty-eight cents, it is deemed just that the State should reimburse him for said expenses; therefore,

Be it enacted by the General Assembly of the Commonwealth of Kentucky:

§ 1. That the sum of one hundred and ninety-three dollars and thirty-eight cents be, and hereby is, allowed and ordered to be paid to said Sanford M. Collins for the money so necessarily expended by him in said business; and the Auditor is hereby ordered to draw his warrant on the Treasurer in favor of said Collins for said sum of one hundred and ninety-three dollars and thirty-eight cents,

1869.   payable out of any money in the Treasury not otherwise appropriated.

§ 2. This act shall take effect and be in force from its passage.

Approved January 21, 1869.

CHAPTER 1265.

AN ACT to incorporate a Turnpike Road Company to construct a road from Pleasant Hill to the Boyle County Line.

Be it enacted by the General Assembly of the Commonwealth of Kentucky:

§ 1. That it may be lawful for the county court of Mercer county, a majority of all justices of the peace concurring, to form a company to construct a turnpike road from Pleasant Hill to the Boyle county line, in the direction of Danville.

§ 2. That said court shall appoint five commissioners to locate said turnpike road. When said company shall be fully organized, a majority of the stock subscribed by individuals and the amount by the county court shall govern in said location.

§ 3. That said commissioners shall have power to determine the width of road, also the width and depth of stone, as well as the degree of elevation of said road.

§ 4. That said commissioners shall possess all the powers granted similar companies found in the Revised Statutes, in acquiring right of way, earth, rock, timber, or other materials, out of which to build said road, also land on which to erect a toll-house and gate, not exceeding in quantity five acres. They shall have power to appoint a gate-keeper or keepers, and do all other things that a body-politic can or may lawfully do.

§ 5. That said commissioners shall continue in office one year and until others are elected by the stockholders and by the stock held by the county.

§ 6. This act to take effect from its passage.

Approved January 21, 1869.

CHAPTER 1266.

AN ACT for the benefit of Louisa P. Harris, of Catlettsburg.

Be it enacted by the General Assembly of the Commonwealth of Kentucky:

That Louisa P. Harris, of the town of Catlettsburg, Kentucky, be, and she is hereby, relieved from all the disabilities arising from coverture; she may sue and be sued

in her own name; contract and be contracted with; and
any property, either general or separate, which she may
now have, or that she may hereafter acquire, either personal or real, or choses in action, shall be liable for any
debts she may now owe or that she may hereafter incur,
which liability may be enforced as fully and in the same
manner as though she were a *feme sole.*

1869.

Approved January 21, 1869.

CHAPTER 1267.

AN ACT for the benefit of Joseph A. Foree, of Ballard County.

*Be it enacted by the General Assembly of the Commonwealth
of Kentucky:*

§ 1. That John M. Neal, guardian of Joseph A. Foree,
is hereby authorized to purchase for his said ward, Joseph
A. Foree, a piano, and that the county judge of Ballard
county allow him a credit for the same in the settlement
of his account as guardian as aforesaid.

§ 2. This act to take effect from and after its passage.

Approved January 21, 1869.

CHAPTER 1268.

AN ACT for the benefit of the United Baptist Church, at Lebanon.

*Be it enacted by the General Assembly of the Commonwealth
of Kentucky:*

That Samuel Ray, Hugh B. Phillips, William Warren,
and James M. Fogle, the trustees of the United Baptist
Church at Lebanon, Kentucky, be, and they are hereby,
authorized to sell and convey so much of the lot belonging to said church, in the town of Lebanon, Marion
county, Kentucky, to Lebanon Female College, and take
the amount of the consideration of the land so sold as so
much stock in the Lebanon Female College, said land so
conveyed never to be used for any other purpose than educational purposes, under the Baptist Church; and when
the ground is ceased to be used for educational purposes,
then the ground is to revert to the trustees of said United
Baptist Church at Lebanon, Kentucky.

Approved January 22, 1869.

1869.

CHAPTER 1269.

AN ACT to amend the Charter of the Shelbyville and Bardstown Turnpike Road Company.

Be it enacted by the General Assembly of the Commonwealth of Kentucky:

§ 1. That the road managers of said company shall have full power and authority to sell the property of said road at any time, and buy any other in lieu thereof.

§ 2. That no stockholder shall be allowed to vote for managers of said company but those who have paid all the calls on their stock.

§ 3. That no further amendment shall be made to this charter only upon the petition of a majority of stockholders therein ; but the State reserves the right to amend or repeal at any time said charter.

§ 4. This act shall take effect from and after its passage.

Approved January 22, 1869.

CHAPTER 1270.

AN ACT to incorporate the Pendleton and Washington Trace Turnpike Company.

Be it enacted by the General Assembly of the Commonwealth of Kentucky:

§ 1. That a company be, and is hereby, created, under *Company incorporated, route of road, &c.* the name and style of the " Pendleton, Washington Trace road company," which shall be a body-politic and corporate, for the purpose of constructing a turnpike road, on the McAdams plan, from the Campbell county line, on the Washington Trace ridge, to the Bracken county line, intersecting the Foster turnpike road near A. McGill's, and upon such immediate route as the president and directors shall select. They shall have the power, and it shall be their duty, to call to their aid some competent engineer in the location of said road.

§ 2. The capital stock of said company shall be thirty *Capital stock.* thousand dollars, to be divided into shares of fifty dollars each.

§ 3. Books shall be open at convenient places for the *Commissioners to open books for the subscription of stock.* subscription of stock in said company, under the direction of Anthony McGill, J. B. Pribble, Joseph H. Dickens, L. H. Ellis, and Wm. Barnard, any one of whom may procure a book or books, in which the subscribers of stock to said company shall enter into the following obligation : *Obligation of subscribers.* " We, whose names are hereto subscribed, do respectively promise to pay to the Pendleton, Washington Trace turnpike road company, the sum of fifty dollars for each and every share of stock in said company set opposite our names, in such manner and proportion, and at such times, as shall be required by the president and directors of said company,"

1869.

§ 4. The book or books shall be opened as soon as said commissioners may think proper, and remain so until the whole capital stock, or enough to complete the road, shall have been subscribed.

When books may be opened.

§ 5. As soon as eight thousand dollars of stock shall have been subscribed in good faith by responsible persons, it shall be the duty of said commissioners, or some one of them, to give notice of the meeting of the stockholders of said company at some convenient point, for the purpose of choosing officers, which shall be given by notice at three of the most public places, on or near the line of the contemplated road, for at least ten days previous to the meeting; and at said meeting at least two of said commissioners must be present to superintend the election. There shall be elected a president and five directors, who shall hold their office for one year from the day of their election, and until their successors are elected and duly qualified. The said directors shall elect a treasurer and such other officers as they may deem necessary; and said treasurer shall, before he enters upon the duties of his office, execute bond with security, approved by the directory, to the effect that he will perform the duties of his office; and whenever a demand is made upon him by the directory or their authorized agent, pay over any and all sums of money that may be in his hands as treasurer.

When officers to be chosen.

President and five directors.

Treasurer to to be elected; to give bond.

§ 6. The stockholders, at all elections, shall be entitled to one vote for each share of stock in said company, which vote or votes may be given in person or by proxy in writing.

Stock; how voted.

§ 7. It shall be lawful for the president and directors, with their superintendents, engineers, and workmen, with their tools, instruments, carts, wagons, and other carriages, and their beasts of draught and burden, to enter upon the land, in and over, contiguous, and near to which said road shall pass, having first given notice of their intention to the owners or occupiers thereof, or their agents: *Provided,* That if the president and directors shall not agree with the owners of said land, over or through which said road is to pass, as to damages the owner or owners may sustain by reason of the road passing through said lands, the president and directors shall apply to the county court of the county in which said lands are situated, for a writ of *ad quod damnum,* to assess the damages which may be sustained by the owner or owners of said land; and, upon the payment or tender of the damages assessed, it shall be lawful for the president and directors to open and make said road, and dig and carry away any stone, gravel, or

May enter upon lands.

How right of way may be obtained.

1869.

other material necessary to the construction or repairing said road, after paying the owner the full value of the same.

§ 8. The president and directors shall severally take an oath faithfully to discharge the duties of their respective offices to the best of their ability.

President and directors to take oath.

§ 9. That the president and directors may put said road under contract, or any portion of it, for construction, whenever the board shall deem it right and proper.

May contract for construction of road.

§ 10. That the county court of Pendleton, a majority of the justices of said county concurring therein, may take stock in said road, not exceeding, however, one thousand dollars per mile, and to pay for the same, may levy a tax on each one hundred dollars' worth of property in said county subject to taxation, as will be sufficient for that purpose, or issue county bonds for the payment of said stock, as in their judgment may be right and proper.

Pendleton county court may take stock.

§ 11. The grade on said road shall not exceed four degrees, and the stone on the same shall not be less than fourteen feet wide and an average of nine inches deep; the width of said road outside of the metal on the same shall be left to, and in the discretion of, the directors of said road.

Grade and width of road.

§ 12. That the president and directors of said road, when the same is completed, shall, with the aid of some competent person as engineer, view said road, and report to the county court of said county the quality and condition of said road; and said county court, upon hearing said report, if it appears that said road has been constructed according to law, the court shall make an order authorizing the erection of gates and the collection of tolls, in pursuance of the rates established by law.

When toll-gates may be erected.

§ 13. That the president and directors shall have power to let out said road to contractors, on such terms, and in such portions, as they may deem beneficial to the interests of said company.

May let out road.

§ 14. That said company may sue and be sued, plead and be impleaded, contract and be contracted with, and in all litigations shall be dealt with as a natural person.

May sue and be sued, &c.

§ 15. That any of the stockholders in said road failing to pay their calls when due, shall be subject to suit in any of the courts in this Commonwealth having jurisdiction of the matter in controversy; they shall likewise pay interest at the rate of ten per cent. per annum thereon until paid.

Stockholders may be sued for failing to pay calls.

§ 16. It shall be the duty of the president and directors to keep a record of their proceedings in a well-bound book, and the same shall be open to inspection by the stockholders in said road at all times.

To keep record of proceedings.

§ 17. This act shall take effect and be in force from its passage.

Approved January 22, 1869.

CHAPTER 1271.

AN ACT to amend the Charter of the Massie's Mill Turnpike Road Company.

Be it enacted by the General Assembly of the Commonwealth of Kentucky:

§ 1. That the corporators of the Massie's Mill turnpike road company, in Bourbon county, be, and are hereby, authorized to extend their road from its commencement, at the blacksmith-shop on the Paris and North Middletown turnpike, to the old cooper-shop on the Paris and Winchester turnpike, or near thereto, and may acquire the right of way, one acre of land for a toll-house, and quarries, by the mode required by the Revised Statutes, title "Turnpikes and Plank Roads."

§ 2. That Benjamin F. Bedford, sr., shall be one of the commissioners, for all the purposes and as fully as if named in the original act incorporating said company.

§ 3. The first annual election of officers of said company shall be on the first Saturday in January, 1870, and on the same day each year thereafter.

§ 4. This act shall take effect from its passage.

Approved January 22, 1869.

CHAPTER 1272.

AN ACT for the benefit of John M. Duke, jr., late Clerk of the Mason Circuit Court.

Be it enacted by the General Assembly of the Commonwealth of Kentucky:

§ 1. That the further time of two years, from and after the passage of this act, be, and hereby is, allowed John M. Duke, jr., late clerk of the Mason circuit court, to collect all his uncollected fee bills; and, for the time aforesaid, the same shall be distrainable, and there shall be all the rights and powers now granted by law as to the collection of fee bills for the collection of the same; but said John M. Duke, jr., shall be liable to all the penalties now imposed by law for collecting or issuing illegal fee bills.

§ 2. This act shall be in force from and after its passage.

Approved January 22, 1869.

CHAPTER 1273.

AN ACT to extend the charter of the Blandville and Cairo Gravel Road
Company to Mayfield, in Graves County.

*Be it enacted by the General Assembly of the Commonwealth
of Kentucky :*

§ 1. That the charter of the Blandville and Cairo Gravel
Road Company be extended to Mayfield, in Graves county; and said company is hereby vested with all the powers
to construct or extend the road from Blandville to Mayfield, in Graves county, that is granted or given them in
the original charter to construct and build the road from
Blandville to Cairo.

§ 2. This act to take effect from and after its passage.

Approved January 22, 1869.

CHAPTER 1274.

AN ACT for the benefit of the City of Frankfort.

Preamble.

WHEREAS, The board of councilmen of the city of
Frankfort have entered into a contract with John Haly,
in effect, that if he would construct, finish, furnish, and
complete a building on Montgomery street, in the city of
Frankfort, known and called "Major Hall," that the city,
in its corporate capacity, would, by soliciting private subscriptions, and by the city's own subscription and credit,
make a loan to the said John Haly of two thirds of the
cost of constructing said building, and of furnishing the
concert hall in said building, not exceeding in all forty
thousand dollars; and whereas, private individuals have
subscribed to said loan a part of the amount thereof, and
the city itself has subscribed to said loan the balance
not subscribed by individuals—say the sum of seventeen
thousand six hundred and sixty-seven dollars—and has
taken a mortgage upon said building and the lot of
ground on which it is erected, and all the furniture and
fixtures therein or pertaining thereto, to secure the payment of the money so subscribed by individuals and by
the city in its corporate capacity; the said mortgage
having been made to the said city council in trust for
the individual subscribers, and intended to secure the
payment of the whole sum so loaned by individuals, as
well as by the city in its corporate capacity, as will more
fully appear from said mortgage on record in the clerk's
office of the Franklin county court; and whereas, the
said city council, in order to raise the amount so agreed
to be subscribed to said loan on the part of the city, has
been compelled to borrow money, and, in some instances,
to guarantee the payment of loans made by private indi-

viduals, and will have to resort to similar expedients to raise other sums for the same purpose, and, in some instances, has agreed to pay interest at the rate of ten per centum per annum; and whereas, doubts are entertained of the authority of the board of city council aforesaid to enter into the contract with said Haly as above stated, and to borrow money, and to become guarantors to others so lending money as above stated; therefore,

Be it enacted by the General Assembly of the Commonwealth of Kentucky:

§ 1. That the proceedings of the board of council of the city of Frankfort, in the matter referred to in the preamble of this act, be, and the same are hereby, declared to be legal and of full force and effect; and that said board of city council shall have full authority and power to carry out the contract so made with John Haly, and all contracts made by the said board of council for the purpose of raising money; and such contracts as may be hereafter made for the same purpose shall be binding in law and in equity upon the said city in its corporate capacity: *Provided*, That the said city shall not be required to pay interest upon any sum or sums so borrowed or guaranteed at a greater rate than ten per centum per annum; and all certificates given by the mayor of said city, by authority of the council, as evidence of indebtedness on the part of the city for the purposes aforesaid, shall be binding on the city, and may be assigned and transferred as promissory notes are now authorized by law to be assigned; and the certificates given by said mayor to individuals on account of loans made by them respectively shall be taken and held as evidence of the amounts so loaned to said Haly by them respectively, according to the terms of said mortgage.

§ 2. That said board of councilmen shall have power to raise the money necessary to pay and discharge the said indebtedness and liability incurred under said contract with Haly, when due, by the levy and collection of a tax on the taxable property of the city sufficient for that purpose, or by the issual and sale of the bonds of the city, running for any time not exceeding twenty years, and bearing interest, payable semi-annually, at any rate not exceeding ten per centum per annum; and that said board of council may, by suit in the Franklin circuit court, enforce the performance of said contract on the part of said Haly, and foreclose said mortgage for the protection of the rights and interests of the city as well as of the individuals and corporations which have or may hereafter lend or advance money under the contract aforesaid.

§ 3. This act to take effect from its passage.

Approved January 22, 1869.

Action of council legalized and contracts may be enforced.

Interest not to exceed 10 per cent.

Certificates of mayor binding on city.

Certificates to individuals evidence.

Board may levy tax, or issue bonds to meet claims.

May enforce contract with Haly by suit

CHAPTER 1276.

AN ACT to amend an act, entitled "An act to amend the charter of the Mayslick and Helena Turnpike Road."

Be it enacted by the General Assembly of the Commonwealth of Kentucky:

§ 1. That the 5th section of an act, entitled "An act to amend the charter of the Mayslick and Helena turnpike road company," approved February 11th, 1868, be, and the same is hereby, so amended as to repeal that portion which requires the president and directors to open said road not less than thirty-two feet wide; but they shall be vested with discretion to open it any width they may deem best: *Provided, however,* It does not exceed fifty feet in width.

§ 2. This act to take effect from and after its passage.

Approved January 22, 1869.

CHAPTER 1278.

AN ACT to allow James E. Wright, late Clerk of the Logan Circuit and County Courts, further time to collect his Fee Bills.

Be it enacted by the General Assembly of the Commonwealth of Kentucky:

§ 1. That James E. Wright, late clerk of the Logan circuit and county courts, be, and he is hereby, allowed the further time of two years to collect his unpaid fee bills as clerk aforesaid: *Provided, however,* That he shall be subject to all the penalties now provided by law for illegal distraint.

§ 2. This act shall be in force from and after its passage.

Approved January 22, 1869.

CHAPTER 1279.

AN ACT to authorize the Logan County Court to increase the County Levy for the year 1869.

Be it enacted by the General Assembly of the Commonwealth of Kentucky:

§ 1. That the county court of Logan county, a majority of the justices of said county being present and concurring therein, be, and the said court is hereby, authorized to increase the poll-tax heretofore levied by said court for the year 1869, to the sum of three dollars and fifty cents on each person in said county subject by law to pay a poll-tax.

§ 2. The levy hereby authorized to be increased may be made by said court at any regular meeting thereof in the months of January, February, March, April, May, or June, 1869.

§ 3. That this act take effect from its passage.

Approved January 22, 1869.

CHAPTER 1280.

AN ACT for the benefit of the Trustees of M. E. Church, of Madisonville.

Be it enacted by the General Assembly of the Commonwealth of Kentucky:

§ 1. That the trustees of the Methodist Episcopal Church, South, of the town of Madisonville, have power and authority to sell and convey the church house and ground upon which the same is situated, and to sell and convey the parsonage property belonging to said church, and reinvest the proceeds in other property in said town.

§ 2. This act to be in force from its passage.

Approved January 22, 1869.

CHAPTER 1281.

AN ACT for the benefit of Benoni Mills, late Sheriff of Wayne County.

WHEREAS, Certain claims against the Treasury belonging to Benoni Mills, late sheriff of Wayne county, were lost in transit to the Auditor's Office or otherwise, and others not presented in proper time for the Auditor to recognize; therefore,

Be it enacted by the General Assembly of the Commonwealth of Kentucky:

§ 1. That the clerk of the Wayne circuit court have until the first day of July, 1869, to draw off and certify to the Auditor a complete list of claims against the Treasury as allowed by the circuit court of said county during the years of 1865 and 1866, and now appearing upon the records of said court; and for any and all of such claims, not heretofore presented, or omitted in the clerk's list heretofore, the Auditor is hereby directed to issue his warrant upon the Treasurer therefor, out of any money in the Treasury not otherwise appropriated.

§ 2. That the further time of two years from the first of January, 1869, is allowed said Benoni Mills to distrain for and collect any unpaid taxes or fee bills due him during his term of office as aforesaid, subject to all the penalties now prescribed by law for illegal distraint.

§ 3. That said sheriff have until the first day of June, 1869, to return his delinquent lists for the year 1866: *Provided,* Said delinquent lists shall not exceed three hundred and twenty-six dollars and fifty-six cents; and when the same are properly certified to the Auditor, he is hereby directed to issue his warrant upon the Treasurer therefor.

§ 4. That the damages recovered and collected by the Commonwealth against said sheriff, amounting to four hundred and ninety dollars and forty-two cents, be, and are hereby, remitted, except fifty dollars thereof to pay expenses of collection; and the Auditor is directed to issue his warrant upon the Treasurer therefor, payable out of any money in the Treasury not otherwise appropriated.

§ 5. This act shall take effect from its passage.

Approved January 22, 1869.

CHAPTER 1252.

AN ACT to amend an act, entitled "An act to extend the charter of the Louisville Gas Company," approved January 30, 1868.

WHEREAS, The city of Louisville and stockholders of the old Louisville Gas Company have accepted the said extended charter, and have agreed to certain amendments thereof, and desire that they may become a part of said extended charter—

Be it enacted by the General Assembly of the Commonwealth of Kentucky:

§ 1. That any person, who may be entitled to a fractional share of stock under the provisions of section second (2d) of said extended charter, may have his or her election either to take the same in cash at par, or have issued a whole share by paying the difference of par value of the fractional share and a whole one.

§ 2. That the gas company shall be bound to extend its main pipes whenever the public and private lights immediately arising from said extension will pay seven (7) per cent. profit on the cost thereof; and so much of the fifth (5th) section of said extended charter as requires a profit of eight (8) per cent. on the cost of an extension is hereby repealed.

§ 3. That the gas company shall put lamp-posts, fixtures, &c., along the street mains as they are extended, at a distance apart of about two hundred feet, or as near that distance as the dimensions of the squares may admit, so as to make an equal distribution of the same; and whenever there are street mains on both sides of the streets, the lights are to be located so as to alternate, preserving the same distance, namely, about two hundred feet for the lamps on each side of the street. The gas company are to keep the lamp in order, to furnish gas, and light and extinguish the same, giving to each light an illuminating power of about twelve sperm candles; and the time of burning shall be from the close of twilight at evening until dawn of day in the morning, except in clear moonlight nights, when the light may be dispensed with; and said public lights shall be furnished to the city at actual cost; but in no event to exceed thirty-five ($35) dollars per lamp; and the charge for gas to private consumers shall be so graded as that the company's profits shall not exceed twelve per cent. per annum on the par value of the stock; ten (10) per cent. of which may be drawn by the stockholders, in semi-annual dividends, and the other two per cent. to be laid out for extensions, and not to be capitalized, except at the end of every five years. Section seven (7) of said extended charter is hereby repealed.

§ 4. That the stock and other interest the city has, or may have, in the gas works, shall not be disposed of ; but the dividends arising therefrom shall, as far as necessary, be applied to paying for the public lights of the city; and all investments of unused dividends belonging to the city shall be made by the directors of the gas company, as trustee, with the concurrence and advice of the city council, and held as a permanent trust during the continuation of this charter.

§ 5. That said gas company shall have the exclusive privilege of erecting and establishing gas-works in the city of Louisville during the continuation of this charter, and of vending coal gas-lights and supplying the city and citizens with gas by means of public works: *Provided, however*, This shall not interfere with the right of any one to erect, or cause to be erected, gas-works on their own premises, for supplying themselves with light.

§ 6. That no alteration or amendment to the charter of the gas company shall be made without the concurrence of the city council and the directors of the gas company.

§ 7. This act shall take effect from its passage.

Approved January 22, 1869.

CHAPTER 1285.

AN ACT authorizing the Hancock County Court to grant administration on the estate of Joseph F. Wilson, deceased.

WHEREAS, It is represented that doubts are entertained as to whether the county court of Hancock or of Marshall county have jurisdiction to grant administration on the estate of Joseph F. Wilson, deceased, but that his lands and effects are situate in the former county, and are now the subject of litigation in the Hancock circuit court—

Be it enacted by the General Assembly of the Commonwealth of Kentucky:

§ 1. That full power and jurisdiction is hereby conferred upon the county court of Hancock county to grant administration on the estate of Joseph F. Wilson, deceased, pursuant to existing laws.

§ 2. This act shall take effect from its passage.

Approved January 22, 1869.

CHAPTER 1287.

AN ACT to incorporate the Bullitt County Turnpike Road Company.

Be it enacted by the General Assembly of the Commonwealth of Kentucky:

§ 1. That the organization existing in the county of Bullitt, known as the Bullitt County Plank Road Company, formed for the purpose of constructing a plank road from the Jefferson county line to the town of Shepherdsville, shall hereafter be known as the Bullitt County turnpike road company.

§ 2. That the election of Jilson P. Johnson as president and H. C. Crist and George C. Shanklin as managers of said company, at a meeting held on the 31st day of October, 1868, shall be, and is hereby declared, legal; and the officers elected as aforesaid shall be held to be, and are declared to have been, duly elected; and they are hereby created a body-politic and corporate, in fact and in law, by the name and style of the Bullitt County turnpike road company, with the privileges and franchises of a corporation; shall be capable of holding their capital stock, and the increase and profits thereof, and holding, by purchase, gift, or otherwise, all things proper and necessary for the prosecution of their work, with power and authority to condemn lands for their roadway, and for the erection of such buildings and toll-houses as are required, and such timber, stone, gravel, and earth as may be needed in building and repairing their road in accordance with and in the manner prescribed in section 18, chapter 54, of the Revised Statutes. They shall continue in office for one year from the date of their election, and until their successors are elected and qualified. They shall have power to contract and be contracted with, sue and be sued, in all courts of law and equity, and generally to do all and every act or thing lawful for a corporation to effect the object for which said corporation is created.

§ 3. That the said president and managers shall have power to run said road at any degree of elevation they may think proper, and also to fix upon the width of the

grade and the width and depth of the stone or gravel to
be used on same.

§ 4. They are authorized, upon the completion of two and one half miles of said road, to erect a toll-gate, and to collect one half tolls; and to enable them to complete said road, they are hereby empowered to establish and collect such rates of tolls as will secure to the company an income not exceeding six per cent. on the capital stock of the road, said income to be appropriated to the completion of the road and bridges; and this latter right shall not be abridged from the inability of the company to construct the bridges on said road.

§ 5. Said corporation may, by contract, provide for the building of any lateral road by additional subscriptions of stock, and admitting the subscribers thereto as original stockholders, upon such terms as may be agreed upon.

§ 6. That the provisions of the Revised Statutes under which the Bullitt County Plank Road Company organized shall apply to the Bullitt County turnpike road company, and are declared to be part of this charter, so far as the same are applicable and are not altered or changed hereby.

§ 7. This act shall take effect from and after its passage.

Approved January 22, 1869.

CHAPTER 1288.

AN ACT to incorporate the Mount Carmel Cemetery, in Fleming County.

Be it enacted by the General Assembly of the Commonwealth of Kentucky:

§ 1. That the trustees of the town of Mount Carmel, in the county of Fleming, shall have power to purchase, or, in case that they cannot purchase, then to condemn, two acres of land within one mile of the corporate limits of said town, to be used as a public cemetery. If condemned, the land to be valued by a jury of twelve disinterested housekeepers of the county, to be summoned by the sheriff upon an order from the county judge; said proceedings to be governed and regulated by the laws now in force in relation to writs of *ad quod damnum:* *Provided,* The land so condemned, shall not be within four hundred yards of any dwelling.

§ 2. The trustees shall cause said land to be laid off into lots for burial purposes, and may sell or convey titles to same, which titles shall be valid in law; and said lots shall be exempt from execution or taxation.

§ 3. The trustees shall enact such rules, regulations, and

1869.   ordinances, as they may deem necessary, not inconsistent
with the general laws of this Commonwealth.

§ 4. That an act, entitled "An act to incorporate the
Fleming County Cemetery Company," approved January
26, 1866, shall apply to and govern the trustees of this
cemetery. so far as the same is not inconsistent herewith.

§ 5. This act shall take effect from its passage.

Approved January 26, 1869.

CHAPTER 1289.

AN ACT to incorporate the Louisville and New Orleans Transportation
Company.

*Be it enacted by the General Assembly of the Commonwealth
of Kentucky:*

Corporators' names, and corporate powers.

§ 1. That L. B. Dunham, Herman Verhoff, Otto Verhoff, Frederick Leib, Jacob Peter, Henry Peter, Edwin
Moore, Frank P. Schmidt, and John R Montgomery, together with all others who may hereafter become stockholders in the company incorporated by this act, shall
be, and they are hereby, created a body-politic and corporate, by the name of the Louisville and New Orleans
Transportation Company, and by that name may have
perpetual succession; may contract and be contracted
with, sue and be sued, plead and be impleaded, answer
and defend, in all courts and places as a natural person;
and may have and use a common seal, and alter and
change the same at will; and said company shall have,
and may exercise, all other powers usual and incident to
corporations, and that may be necessary and proper for
the carrying out of the true intent and purpose of its
creation.

Rights & priv-ileges of com-pany.

§ 2. The said company shall have the right to transport
persons and property to and from any point or points,
place or places, on the Ohio and Mississippi rivers, or
any of their tributaries, for such considerations, and
upon such terms and conditions as may be stipulated,
expressed, and contained in the respective bills of lading
and contracts, made and entered into by the company
through its proper officers, agents, and employes; and
for that purpose, said company may construct, purchase,
charter, or otherwise acquire and own, hold, use, occupy,
and control; and may grant, bargain, sell, and convey, as
a natural person, all such steamboats, flatboats, keelboats,
and other water craft, with all equipments, appendages,
and other personal property that may be necessary and
desirable for the conducting of its business; and said
company may lease or purchase any wharves, landings,
or other real estate necessary for the transacting of its

business; and may grant, bargain, sell, convey, or otherwise dispose of the same as a natural person.

1869.

§ 3. The property, business, and affairs of said company shall be governed, managed, and controlled by a board of directors, to consist of such a number of the stockholders as the by-laws shall prescribe; and the persons named in the first section of this act are hereby constituted and appointed the first board of directors for said company; and they and their successors in office are hereby authorized and empowered to make and put in force such by-laws, rules and regulations, for the management and government of said company, its property, business, and affairs, as they may deem proper, and alter, amend, and repeal the same at will. They shall also have the power to elect or appoint such officers, agents, and employees as they may deem necessary for carrying on the business of the company, and may require of any or all of them bonds in such penalties as they may think necessary and proper to secure the faithful and honest performance of their respective duties; and, upon any bonds thus taken, recovery may be had for breaches of the conditions thereof.

Who to manage affairs of company.

May make by-laws.

May appoint officers, &c.

§ 4. The persons named in the first section of this act may, by resolution, fix the capital stock of said company at such an amount as they may think proper; and the same shall be divided into shares of one hundred dollars each; and said persons may open books for, and receive subscriptions to, the capital stock of said company, at such times and places, and subject to such terms and conditions, as they may think proper; and the stock of said company shall be held to be personal estate and pass as such, and shall be issued, sold, and transferred as the by-laws may direct.

Capital stock.

§ 5. The board of directors named in this act shall provide for an election of directors by the stockholders within one year from the time the said company shall be ffrst organized, and for annual elections thereafter, first giving the stockholders suitable notice of the time and place of such elections; and at all such elections each stockholder shall be entitled to one vote for each share of stock which he or she may own, and may cast the same in person or by proxy.

To provide for election of directors.

§ 6. A majority in interest of the stockholders may, at any time, by resolution, increase the capital stock of said company to such an amount, not exceeding five hundred thousand dollars, as they may deem desirable, and may prescribe the terms and conditions upon which the same may be subscribed and paid.

Capital stock may be increased.

§ 7. A majority of the board of directors shall constitute a quorum for the transaction of business; and said board

Quorum, executive, committee, &c.

may appoint an executive committee, to consist of two or more directors, as the by-laws may prescribe; and said committee may, when the board is not in session, exercise all the powers vested in the board of directors, except where it has been otherwise provided in the by-laws. All vacancies occurring in the board of directors may be filled by the remaining directors.

§ 8. This act shall take effect and be in force from and after its passage.

Approved January 26, 1869.

CHAPTER 1290.
AN ACT to incorporate the Louisville Medical College.

Be it enacted by the General Assembly of the Commonwealth of Kentucky:

§ 1. That W. N. Haldeman, John Joyes, J. W. Akin, J. J. Porter, D. Cummins, B. M. Wible, Thomas E. Wilson, and Lyttleton Cooke, be, and they are hereby, created a body corporate and politic, with perpetual succession, to be known as the trustees of the Louisville Medical College; and by this style be empowered to acquire and hold, in the city of Louisville, property, personal, real or mixed, to the amount of one hundred thousand dollars ($100,000), to be used for the benefit of said Louisville Medical College, in the said city of Louisville.

§ 2. That said trustees shall elect a president and secretary, and such other officers as may be necessary to transact the business of the corporation; and when thus organized, may make, have, and use a common seal, which they may change or alter at pleasure.

§ 3. That the property, real, personal, or mixed, which may be acquired and held by said trustees for the use and benefit of said medical college, whether held in fee or under lease, shall be entitled to all the immunities, in reference to State and local taxations, which have been heretofore extended to educational institutions by the statute laws of the Commonwealth.

§ 4. That the said trustees shall have power to appoint as many teachers, or professors of medicine, surgery, dentistry, and the collateral sciences, as they may deem necessary, and may confer the degrees or titles of Doctor of Medicine, Doctor of Dentistry, or the minor degrees of Bachelor or Master of these professions, upon such applicants as may be recommended by the faculty or corps of teachers or professors, or by any examining board of experts to whom they may commit the duty or office of examination, and grant diplomas in ordinary or *causa honoris* to such persons as they may deem worthy.

§ 5. A majority of the whole number of trustees shall constitute a quorum to transact all of the ordinary business of the corporation; but in the election or removal of professors or teachers, a majority equal to three fourths of the whole body shall be necessary to a final decision.

§ 6. Vacancies in the board of trustees, from any cause, may be filled by the acting members.

§ 7. The trustees may create and sell scholarships; provided, that all money received through the sale of such scholarships shall be invested for the benefit of said school, and that the amount realized from this source shall be limited to twenty thousand dollars ($20,000).

§ 8. That, as W. N. Haldeman and John Joyes are the only surviving corporators of the Clay School of Medicine, now residing in Kentucky, and the Louisville College is intended to take the place of said Clay School, the charter of said Clay School of Medicine be, and the same is hereby, repealed.

Approved January 26, 1869.

CHAPTER 1291.
AN ACT to amend the Charter of the Town of Clinton.

Be it enacted by the General Assembly of the Commonwealth of Kentucky:

§ 1. That all that portion of the charter of the town of Clinton making it the duty of the trustees of said town to keep the streets in repair, be, and the same is hereby, repealed; and said streets are hereby placed upon the same footing with other public highways.

§ 2. That it shall be the duty of the county court of Hickman county to appoint a surveyor of said streets, who shall hold his office for the same time, and have the same powers, and be subject to the same penalties, with surveyors of the public roads of this Commonwealth. In the order making this appointment, the court shall designate what portion of said streets shall be kept in repair; and the surveyor shall not be required to work any portion of the streets not thus designated.

§ 3. That all male citizens residing in said town, who would be subject to road duties by the general laws of this Commonwealth, shall be required to work said streets; and the names of all such persons shall be entered upon the list of hands furnished said surveyor; and such persons shall be subject to the same penalties for failing or refusing to work the streets when required as is imposed by law upon other persons subject to road duty.

§ 4. This act shall not be so construed as to deprive the trustees of said town of the power to levy and collect

1869. taxes for the purpose of constructing and keeping in repair the sidewalks.

§ 5. This act shall take effect from and after its passage.

Approved January 26, 1869.

CHAPTER 1292.

AN ACT to incorporate the Town of Morehead.

Be it enacted by the General Assembly of the Commonwealth of Kentucky:

§ 1. That the town of Morehead, in the county of Rowan, be, and the same is hereby, incorporated; and the town limits shall extend and embrace all the area included in the following boundary, viz: Beginning at the mouth of the Dry Fork of Triplett creek, at the south corner of C. Alley's farm; thence with Triplett creek, on the south side, to include Thomas J. Trumbo, to Ben. Martin's mill; thence to the foot of the hill on the west side of the creek, so as to include Ben. Martin; thence with the foot of the hill down the west side of Triplett creek to the beginning, including Cyrus Alley; which survey and boundary shall be recorded in the clerk's office of the Rowan county court.

§ 2. That John Hargis, H. G. Burns, P. G. Day, J. T. Sellards, and J. E. Clarke, are hereby appointed trustees of said town, who shall hold their office until the first Saturday in May, 1870, at which time, and annually thereafter, there shall be an election by the qualified voters of said town for five trustees, to serve for one year and until their successors are duly elected and qualified. Said trustees herein mentioned shall, before they enter upon the duties of their office, be duly qualified by some justice of the peace for said county that they will faithfully discharge the duties of their said office.

§ 3. That said trustees, and their successors in office, shall be a body-politic and corporate, and shall be known as the " Trustees of the Town of Morehead;" and by that name shall be capable of contracting and being contracted with, suing and being sued, of pleading and being impleaded, in all courts of this Commonwealth.

§ 4. That said trustees, any three of whom shall constitute a quorum, shall elect one of their number as chairman, who shall preside over the deliberations of said board when convened, and who shall have power to convene the board in session whenever he may deem it necessary.

§ 5. There shall be an election held on the first Saturday in May, 1869, and annually thereafter, for a police judge and town marshal for the town of Morehead, who shall serve until their successors are elected and qualified,

[Marginal notes:]
Town incorporated.
Boundary.
Trustees, &c.
To take oath.
Body-politic.
Chairman to be elected.
Police judge and town marshal to be elected: their powers and duties.

whose jurisdiction and powers shall be the same as justices of the peace and constables of the State of Kentucky. The police judge shall be commissioned by the
Governor. The town marshal shall give bond and be
qualified in the Rowan county court, the same as constables.

§ 6. The board of trustees created under this act shall
provide, prior to the first election, proper officers for holding the same; and they shall give at least ten days' notice
of the time and place of holding said election, by written
notices posted in at least three public places in said town.

§ 7. That said trustees shall have power over the streets,
alleys, and sidewalks, and may direct the opening, straightening, altering, or improving the same, in such manner as
they may deem most beneficial to said town. They shall
have power to make all by-laws for the regulation and
government of said town, not inconsistent with the Constitution and laws of the United States and this Commonwealth. They shall have power to levy and collect
a tax upon the property and tithes in said town, not exceeding twenty-five cents on each hundred dollars' worth
of property, and not exceeding one dollar on each tithe,
to be applied to the improvement of the streets, alleys,
sidewalks, or other improvements necessary therein; they
shall have power to purchase any lot or piece of ground
for the use of said town, necessary to straighten or extend the streets therein; to tax shows and all public exhibitions such sums as they, in their by-laws, may fix   It
shall be the duty of said board of trustees to appoint a
treasurer, clerk, and such other officers as they may deem
necessary, and to take bonds with sureties; and for a
violation of duty, or default of any officer so appointed,
suit may be brought before any tribunal having jurisdiction thereof. A majority of said trustees may, for
proper cause, remove any officer and appoint others to
fill the vacancy.

§ 8. That no street or alley shall be extended over the
land of any person, unless such land, so to extend said
street or alley, shall have been purchased as provided for
in section seventh, or unless it has been condemned as
provided in chapter 84, section 1, Revised Statutes, in
reference to public roads; and the proceedings to extend
said street or alley shall be in strict conformity to said
chapter.

§ 9. That all fines and forfeitures inflicted and collected
under the ordinances and by-laws of said town, shall be
paid to the treasurer of the town for the use and benefit
of the corporation.

§ 10. It shall be the duty of the trustees to keep the
streets and alleys in good repair; they are hereby author-

1869.

Who to con-
duct elections.

Powers and
duties of trus-
tees.

How streets
and alleys may
be extended.

Fines to go
into treasury.

Streets & al-
leys to be kept
in repair.

1869. ized to tax the citizens and owners of property a sum sufficient for that purpose : *Provided*, The taxation does not exceed the rates specified in section seven. The citizens of said town are hereby exempt from working on public roads outside of the corporate limits.

Jurisdiction of police judge. § 11. The police judge, in addition to the powers conferred upon him by section fifth, shall have exclusive jurisdiction, subject to appeal, of all violations of the town ordinances and by-laws. It shall be the duty of the town marshal to execute all processes directed to him by the police judge, and to collect the revenue of said town. Before entering upon the discharge of this duty, he shall give bond with sureties, to be approved of by the trustees. Vacancies occurring in the office of police judge or town marshal are to be filled in the same manner that vacancies in the office of justice of the peace and constables are filled.

§ 12. This act shall take effect from and after its passage; and the right to repeal, alter, or amend this act, is reserved to the General Assembly.

Approved January 26, 1869.

CHAPTER 1293.

AN ACT to incorporate the Paducah and Clark's River Railway, Lumber, and Mining and Manufacturing Company.

Be it enacted by the General Assembly of the Commonwealth of Kentucky:

§ 1. That William F. Norton, George Lanstaff, George W. Norton, and Oscar Turner, their associates, successors, and assigns, be, and are hereby, constituted a body-politic and corporate, with perpetual succession, under the name and style of the "Paducah and Clark's River Railway, Lumber, and Mining and Manufacturing Company;" and by said name may sue and be sued, contract and be contracted with, and have a common seal if they see proper, and change the same at pleasure; said corporation or company may purchase, acquire, hold, transfer, lease, sell, and convey such real and personal estate, choses in action and securities, negotiable and otherwise, as may be deemed expedient by said corporation or company for carrying on their business; may make such by-laws and ordinances for the government of its prudential and fiscal business, not inconsistent with the laws of Kentucky, which may be deemed expedient by said company for carrying on a general lumber, mining, and mercantile and manufacturing business; with power to keep open offices at its places of business.

1869.

§ 2. Said company may erect mills and manufactories, and run or operate the same; open and work any silver or other mines; construct railways, railroads, tramways, plank or ditched and raised roads; build bridges and maintain the same, and cut canals and operate the same, from its mills or manufactories to or through its lands, and from its manufactories, mills, or lands to the city of Paducah, or to any points on Clark's river; and if, for these purposes, it be necessary or convenient to pass over the lands of others, they may condemn the same for the purposes in the same manner provided by the Revised Statutes for turnpikes.

§ 3. That said company or corporation may construct boats and rafts for the transportation of lumber, minerals, and merchandise, and navigate the same, and to this end may build and keep in repair such dams as may be deemed expedient for their purposes aforesaid, in and on Clark's river, not to exceed ten feet in height, and to remove any trees or obstructions to the navigation of Clark's river.

§ 4. That if any person shall willfully or maliciously injure or destroy any of said roads, boats, rafts, or dams, or shall knowingly and willfully loose, turn adrift any such rafts, boats, logs, or lumber, or shall knowingly stop or take away, or in any way injure any logs or other property of said company, or deface any works, or any of the logs or lumber of said company, they shall pay double the damages so done, to be recovered by action of trespass, and shall be liable to the same penalties imposed by the general laws of Kentucky for such offenses.

§ 5. That books shall be opened at such times and places as shall be directed by the corporators herein mentioned for the subscription of stock in said company. The capital stock shall not exceed one million of dollars, and shall be divided into shares of one hundred dollars each. The stock shall be evidenced by certificates, and transferable on the books in such manner as the by-laws of said company may prescribe. As soon as five thousand dollars of the stock, or more, is subscribed, the said corporators shall designate a time and place for the election of president and directors of said company, and give ten days' notice to the stockholders; and the said stockholders shall elect a president and five directors, who shall hold their office for twelve months and until their successors are elected; and each successive election shall be annual; any vacancy that may occur by death or otherwise may be filled by the directors until the regular election by the stockholders, who, in all elections, shall cast one vote for each share of stock. It shall be the duty of the president to convene

1869.

the board whenever he thinks the business requires it, and shall preside at all meetings.

§ 6. That the business and affairs of said company shall be controlled by the president and directors of said company. Said board of directors shall have power to make and enforce such by-laws, rules and regulations, as they may deem expedient. not inconsistent with laws of this State, subject to be altered by said board at any of its meetings. Said directors may make such calls for payment on the stock as they may deem proper to meet liabilities or purposes of the company, and may sue any delinquent stockholder or forfeit his stock for non-payment of what he owes the company; and said directors may do all acts and things necessary or proper to be done for successfully carrying on the business of the corporation. Said board of directors may elect one of their number, or any one else, clerk and treasurer, who shall execute bond, with such security as the board may require, for the faithful performance of his duties as prescribed by the board of directors; and suit may be instituted on said bond for breach of same by the president and other directors, if the said officer should be one of the directors, or by the president and directors if any one else is elected.

§ 7. The provisions of this act shall in nowise affect the rights, powers, and privileges of the citizens of, nor apply to any part of, the county of Calloway.

§ 8. This act shall take effect from and after its passage.

Approved January 26, 1869.

———

CHAPTER 1294.

AN ACT to amend an act incorporating the Cynthiana Burial Association.

Be it enacted by the General Assembly of the Commonwealth of Kentucky:

§ 1. That an act, entitled "An act to incorporate the Cynthiana Burial Association," approved January 25th, 1868, be so amended that the name of said corporation shall be "Battle Grove Cemetery," of Cynthiana, Kentucky, and the following persons, Gen. Lucius Desha, Hon. A. H. Ward, John McKee, R. C. Wherritt, F. G. Ashbrook, Thomas V. Ashbrook, J. S. Withers, T. J. McGibben, S. J. Ashbrook, Hon. I. T. Martin, H. W. Shawhan, John W. Kimbrough, Henry Williams, Charles R. Kimbrough, J. Mac. Kimbrough, C. B. Cook, George R. Sharp, J. W. Peck, W. W. Trimble, M. Kimbrough, Judge J. S. Boyd, J. H. Dills, J. Q. Ward, James Miller, Andrew

Garnett, Wm. Winston, Hugh M. Keller, Levi Patterson, N. C. Dille, J. A. McKee, Wm. H. Roberts, J. H. Shawhan, N. B. Wilson, Joseph Howard, Spears M Smith, Noah S. Patterson, Rev. Wm. H. Forsythe, James N. Snell, G. W. Taylor, Wm. G. Vanderen, J. J. Parrish, D. C. Fergurson, William C. Cook, H. E. Shawhan, John L. Shawhan, J. B. McClintock, James Gray, Jno. C. Wilson, H. E. Eals, Joseph Shawhan, sr., H. E. McShane, Jacob Reneker, jr., Amos Ammerman, D. A. Givens, Luther Vanhook, W. L. Northcutt, C. C. Carpenter, J. W. Musselman, and John S. Day, are named as incorporators under said name of Battle Grove Cemetery, of Cynthiana, Kentucky, and are hereby invested with all the powers and privileges heretofore granted to the incorporators of the Cynthiana Burial Association.

§ 2. That section second of said act be so amended that each person owning burial lots to the value of one hundred dollars shall be regarded as holding a share.

§ 3. That all acts or parts of acts heretofore passed inconsistent with this act are hereby repealed.

Approved January 26, 1869.

***

CHAPTER 1295.

AN ACT to incorporate the Shepherdsville, Bullitt's Lick, and Pitt's Point Turnpike Road Company.

Be it enacted by the General Assembly of the Commonwealth of Kentucky:

§ 1. That a company may be formed and created a body-politic and corporate, by the name and style of the Shepherdsville, Bullitt's Lick, and Pitt's Point turnpike company, for the purpose of making and constructing a turnpike road from Shepherdsville, in Bullitt county, to Pitt's Point.

§ 2. The capital stock of said company shall be fifteen thousand dollars, with the privilege of increasing it to thirty thousand dollars, to be divided into shares of fifty dollars each.

§ 3. That A. C. Kennison, Wesley Phelps, Jno. W. Glenn, J. D. Bryan, and Jas. Shepherd, are hereby appointed and created commissioners, for the purpose of obtaining subscription to the capital stock of said road, any two of whom may open books for that purpose at such times and places as they may deem best for that end; when the sum of five thousand dollars shall have been subscribed to the capital stock of said company, it shall be the duty of the commissioners, or a majority of them, to give ten days' notice to the stockholders to meet at the court-house, in the town of Shepherdsville, for the purpose of electing a president and three directors; one vote shall be allowed for each share of stock; and such president and directors so elected shall continue in office until their successors are elected and qualified. After the first election, the president and directors shall be elected annually by the stockholders of this company, at the court-house in Shepherdsville, on the first Monday in May.

§ 4. So soon as said company is organized by the election of officers, the president and directors shall be a body-politic and corporate, in fact and in law, under the name and title of the Shepherdsville, Bullitt's Lick, and Pitt's Point turnpike road company; and by said name shall have perpetual succession, and all the privileges and franchises incident to such corporations; and shall be capable of holding their capital stock, and the increase and profits of same; and also of taking and holding, by purchase or gift, such real and personal property, and the increase of same, as may be necessary for the prosecution of the objects of this corporation; they shall also have power to contract and be contracted with, to sue and be sued, plead and be impleaded, answer and be answered, in any court of law or equity in this State; also to have and use a common seal, and generally to do all lawful acts to effectuate the objects for which this corporation was created.

§ 5. The said president and directors shall have power to fix and graduate the elevation and grade of said road, the width and the portion thereof to be covered with stone or gravel; to designate the points of beginning and termination; the points for the erection of toll-gates, and to fix the rates of toll, not going, however, beyond the rates of toll fixed by the general law of the Commonwealth. The president and directors shall have power, after three consecutive miles are completed, to erect a gate and collect toll, and shall apply the proceeds thereof to the completion of said road.

§ 6. For the purpose of locating said road, it shall be lawful for the president and directors, and they are so empowered, to enter, with their surveyor, chain-carriers, engineers, and artist, upon the lands, inclosures, and public roads in, through, and over which the intended road may pass, and to examine and survey the grounds most suitable for that purpose; and also to examine quarries, beds of stone, gravel, and all other materials necessary to the construction of said road.

§ 7. It shall be lawful for the president and directors of said company, with their agents and employes, wagons, carts, and other carriages, and beasts of draught or burden, to enter upon the lands over and near to which said road shall pass, having first given notice in writing of their intention to the owner or occupier or their agents: *Provided, however*, That if the president and directors shall not be able to agree with the owners of the land through and over which said road shall be located, as to the damages which said owner may sustain by reason of said road passing through and over their land, the president and directors shall apply to the county court of Bullitt county for a writ of *ad quod damnum*, to have the damages ascertained which the owner of the land may sustain; and the jury, in assessing the damages, shall take in consideration the advantages and disadvantages resulting to the party claiming by the establishment of said road; but the advantages shall not be used as an offset to the actual value of the land taken; and upon payment or tender of payment of the damages assessed, it shall be lawful for the president and directors of said road, together with their agents and employes, to open and make said road, and dig and carry away any stone, gravel, or other material necessary for the construction or repairing of said road.

§ 8. The president shall give notice in such manner as he may deem best of the amount of the call on each share of stock, and of the time and place of payment; and if any stockholder or subscriber to the capital stock of said company shall neglect to pay his amount of stock so called for for the space of six months after said notice, his said stock shall be forfeited to this company, together with its increase. No stockholder shall vote at any election, or be entitled to any rights of a member of said company, unless the whole amount of his stock shall have been paid agreeably to the requisitions of the president.

§ 9. The president and directors shall appoint a treasurer, gate-keepers, and such other officers as they may deem necessary, and may require bond of them for the faithful performance of their duties; to hold their offices at the pleasure of the board of directors.

§ 10. That the written or printed certificate of the secretary, countersigned by the president, shall be evidence of the ownership of stock in this company; and the same may be sold and transferred on the books of the secretary, in person or by agent or attorney, when all arrearages are paid, and not till then.

§ 11. That the president may call meetings at such times and places as he may desire, for the transaction of business, or to do any other lawful thing in effectuating the objects of this act.

§ 12. The president, directors, and other officers of this company, shall receive such compensation for their services as a majority of the stockholders may agree upon.

Approved January 26, 1869.

CHAPTER 1296.

AN ACT to amend the act, entitled "An act to enlarge the **Town of Bowling Green**."

Be it enacted by the General Assembly of the Commonwealth of Kentucky:

§ 1. That that portion of Warren county included in the following limits be, and the same is hereby, added to the corporate limits of the town of Bowling Green: Beginning at a point in the middle of the Portage railroad, where the present old line of the said town crosses said Portage railroad; thence with said Portage railroad to a point opposite the first street beyond Frank Kister's; thence in a straight line southwestwardly with said street to Brown's Lock road; thence with said road to the large pond near Whitten's; thence, excluding said pond, running so as to include the old fair ground to the southwestward corner between said fair ground and the land of Barclay; thence with the line of said fair ground towards said town, and continuing in the same direction of that line to the present old town boundary line: *Provided,* The property hereby added to the town of Bowling Green shall be subject to the payment of all town taxes as fully and in the same manner as it would have been had this act been adopted prior to 10th January, 1869.

§ 2. This act to take effect from its passage.

                                        Approved January 26, 1869.

———

                        CHAPTER 1298.

AN ACT to amend the Charter of the City of Lexington.

WHEREAS, It is represented to the General Assembly, that, on the 7th day of May, 1867, an ordinance was adopted by the mayor and council of the city of Lexington, whereby certain streets in said city were ordered to be graded, paved, or macadamized at the expense of the persons owning lots and parts of lots fronting on the same streets; and whereas, the said mayor and council did proceed, under and by virtue of said ordinance, to let to contract the work of paving, grading, or macadamizing of said streets, and the contractors were, in good faith, to do the same work, and have completed the same, in the expectation of being paid the contract price therefor by the lot-owners, as provided by said ordinance; and whereas, many of the lot-owners have paid the cost of such improvements, while others have refused to pay the same, on the ground that the ordinance under which the work was done was informally passed, and was therefore invalid, and have taken the cases into the courts, where the same are still pending; and whereas, the contractors are suffering for want of payment of their claims, which, in the event of an adverse decision, they may not be able to enforce, either against the city or the lot-owners; for remedy whereof,

Be it enacted by the General Assembly of the Commonwealth of Kentucky:

§ 1. That in the event that it shall be decided by the Court of Appeals that the said ordinance of May 7, 1867, was invalid from any cause, and that the lot-owners are not liable for the work of paving, grading, or macadamizing the streets in front of their lots, then, and in that event, it shall and may be lawful for the mayor and council of the city of Lexington to assume, on behalf of the city, the payment of all the costs and expenses of grading, paving, and macadamizing the streets aforesaid; and in that event said mayor and council shall be, and they are hereby, authorized to levy and collect a special tax, not exceeding in amount one per cent. of the assessed value of all the real and personal property situate in said city, and assessed for taxation for the present year by the city assessor; which tax, when collected, shall be applied exclusively to the payment of such of said contractor's claims as have not been discharged and paid by the lot-owners, and to the repayment of such sums as may have been paid by the lot-owners to contractors for work done in front of their lots under said ordinance of May 7, 1867.

§ 2. Said mayor and council may appoint a special collector of the tax authorized to be levied and collected by the first section. They may require of him bond, with good security, for the faithful performance of his duties; may fix the time within which his collection may be returned, and may allow him compensation for his, services at a rate not exceeding five per cent. on the amount collected by him.

§ 3. In collecting the tax herein authorized, each and every person shall be credited with the full amount of any payment which he may have made to any contractor or contractors for work done in paving, grading, or macadamizing under and by virtue of said ordinance of May 7, 1867; and if the payments so made by any person shall be found to have been greater than the amount of the tax assessed upon him under and by virtue of this act, then the excess shall be refunded to him by the said mayor and council.

§ 4. This act shall take effect from its passage.

Approved January 26, 1869.

CHAPTER 1299.

AN ACT to amend the Charter of the Louisville Cement and Water Power Company.

Be it enacted by the General Assembly of the Commonwealth of Kentucky:

§ 1. That the name of the Louisville Cement and Water Power Company be, and the same is hereby, changed to that of the Louisville Cement Company, by which name said company shall hereafter be known: *Provided*, That the change of name shall in nowise affect any obligations entered into by said company in its former name.

§ 2. That hereafter no purchases of real estate shall be made by said company without the written consent of the holders of three fourths the stock of the company.

§ 3. That said company may issue and sell, not exceeding one hundred and fifty thousand dollars in amount of the bonds of said company, having not more than twenty years to run, and bearing interest at a rate not exceeding ten per cent. per annum, payable semi-annually. The punctual payment of the principal and interest of said bonds may be secured by mortgage or deed of trust upon the whole or any part of the franchises, property, and effects of the company.

§ 4. This act shall take effect from its passage.

Approved January 26, 1869.

CHAPTER 1300.

AN ACT to amend an act incorporating the Bardstown and Bloomfield Turnpike Road Company.

Be it enacted by the General Assembly of the Commonwealth of Kentucky:

§ 1. That the act approved March 4, 1867, entitled "An act to incorporate the Bardstown and Bloomfield turnpike road company," be, and the same is hereby, amended as follows: That said turnpike road may enter the town of Bloomfield directly, or intersect the Bloomfield and Louisville turnpike road near Bloomfield.

§ 2. That the board of directors of the Bardstown and Bloomfield turnpike road company, if unable to procure stock enough to build the road, and after having used the stock subscribed in the building of same, may sell the said road with all its rights, franchises, and privileges, for a term of years, or absolutely, to any individual or company who will bind himself or themselves to complete the road within a reasonable time, and keep the same open for public use: *Provided*, That the holders of a majority of the stock shall have consented to the sale in writing, and that fact be recorded in the minutes of the board.

§ 3. It shall be the duty of said board of directors, by 1869. their president and secretary, to issue certificates of stock, making the same transferable on the books of the company.

§ 4. This act to take effect from its passage.

Approved January 26, 1869.

CHAPTER 1301.

AN ACT to amend the Charter of the Louisville Journal Company.

Be it enacted by the General Assembly of the Commonwealth of Kentucky:

§ 1. That said company shall hereafter be known and designated by the name and style of the "Louisville Courier-Journal Company."

§ 2. That said company may increase its capital stock at pleasure, from time to time, to an amount not exceeding five hundred thousand dollars.

§ 3. That said company may borrow money, but not in excess of its capital stock subscribed; and may secure the same by mortgage or deed of trust on its real or personal property, or pledge of stocks or bonds, or otherwise, and on such time, and at such rate of interest, as the president and directors thereof may deem expedient.

§ 4. This act shall take effect from its passage.

Approved January 26, 1869.

CHAPTER 1302.

AN ACT to create a Special Road Law for the County of Pendleton.

Be it enacted by the General Assembly of the Commonwealth of Kentucky:

§ 1. That the county court of Pendleton county shall, in the month of June next, and in the month of June every two years thereafter, appoint a commissioner of roads in said county, who shall, before he enters upon the duties of his office, take the following oath or affirmation, to-wit: "I, A. B., do solemnly swear, or affirm, as the case may be, that I will fairly and impartially, to the best of my skill and ability, perform the duties of road commissioner during my continuance as such, according to law." And the said commissioner shall, at the same time, enter into bond, with good security, to be approved by said court, payable to the Commonwealth of Kentucky, for the faithful performance of his duty as commissioner.

§ 2. That it shall be the duty of said commissioner to divide the county into convenient road precincts, and recommend to the county court for appointment suitable persons as overseers in each precinct, whose duty it shall be to cause the road in his precinct to be improved and kept in repair agreeable to law.

§ 3. That it shall be the duty of the clerk of the county court of said county of Pendleton to make out for the said commissioner a copy of the books of the commissioner of tax, and furnish the same to him on or before the first day of July in each year; and it shall be the duty of the road commissioner, on or before the first day of September in each year, to furnish each overseer appointed by the county court the boundaries of their respective precincts, with a transcript of so much of said commissioner's books as will embrace all the persons and property within the bounds of his precinct, showing, in an appropriate column, the amount of revenue to be paid by each individual within the bounds of his precinct, at a rate to be fixed by said commissioner, subject, however, to the revision of the county court at its court of claims, not exceeding ten cents on the one hundred dollars' worth of property subject to taxation for revenue purposes by the laws of this State, and add to that revenue a poll-tax upon each tithable within said county, not exceeding one dollar and fifty cents; and each overseer shall notify the individuals within his precinct to work upon the particular road of which he is overseer until each person liable to pay revenue or a poll-tax as aforesaid shall have worked upon said road a length of time equal to one day for every one dollar and fifty cents to which such tax shall amount, or three dollars and fifty cents per day for a yoke of oxen or two horses and plow or wagon, and seventy-five cents additional for each extra horse, including the driver; and this estimate shall determine the quantity of work due upon the road by each person liable to the same: *Provided*, That the county court of said county may exempt any person from the whole or any part of the labor which would be due by the aforesaid estimate, to be limited as to time by the court, and not retrospective in its effects. That the labor to be done may at all times be performed by able-bodied substitutes; and it shall be the duty of the overseers to dock any individual at the rate of fifteen cents per hour for every hour he shall willfully idle away; and the overseer shall, within ten days, notify said delinquent of the amount and intent of the sum docked. The county court shall have power to strike out, for good cause, any sums for which the hands may be docked. That the whole of the labor due by any individual shall be payable in one road precinct convenient to his place of residence, if he resides in the county; and when he resides out of the county, it shall not be deemed necessary for the overseer to notify him, but he shall have the privilege of working out his tax in the precinct in which his land, or a majority thereof, lies; if he does not work out said tax, then the sheriff shall collect the amount due by him as he now collects the revenue of the State: *Provided*, That nothing in this act shall effect the person or persons of those residing within the limits of any incorporated town or city in said county, who are exempt by the charters of said town or city; but the property of persons residing within said incorporated town or city, which shall be situated without the limits of such incorporations, shall be liable to such tax, and the same shall be assessed by the commissioner and placed upon some convenient road precinct in said county.

§ 4. That the road overseers shall, on or before the first Monday in July in each year, return to the commissioner the list delivered to him, with the amount of work done by each person upon said list; and for his failure to return said list, with the credits as aforesaid, he shall be fined, after ten days' notice to him, one dollar for each day he shall fail or refuse to return the same after the said first day of July, to be assessed by the county court upon the information of the commissioner. The commissioner shall, at the August term of the county court in each year, report to the county court a list of overseers in the county, together with the names of those who have failed to return their lists as aforesaid; and he shall, in each year, deliver to the sheriff of the county a list of all those who have failed to work out the amount of their taxes, and the amount which each delinquent owes; said list to be furnished the sheriff on or before the first day of September in each year, and take the sheriff's receipt therefor. The sheriff shall proceed to collect from delinquents the amount placed in his hands by the commissioner, together with fifteen per cent. and his fees allowed for such collections additional; and for his failure to collect and pay over the same, he shall be liable in the same manner that he is now liable for a failure to collect and pay over the county levy; and for his services in collecting the delinquent list, the sheriff shall have the same commission as now allowed by law for collecting the county levy. The commissioner shall report to the county court the amount received by him from the sheriff, and shall, as far as practicable, cause to be expended in each precinct the amount collected from delinquents in that precinct.

§ 5. The overseers of roads shall be liable to presentments and fines as by the general law of the State; and the commissioner shall, for a failure to discharge any of the duties required of him, be liable to presentment by the grand jury, and to be fined at the discretion of the jury.

The county court shall fill any vacancy that may occur in the office of road commissioner by death, resignation, or otherwise, and may remove said commissioner at any time for malfeasance or misfeasance, or for other good cause. The commissioner shall, for his services, receive a reasonable compensation, to be fixed by the county court at the court of claims, and paid out of the county levy.

§ 6. The commissioner may purchase, for the use of the roads, any tools or implements he thinks necessary, to be paid for out of the funds collected by the sheriff from delinquents in the precinct where the tools are to be used. The overseers shall be liable for any tools placed under his control by the commissioner, the value thereof to be recovered before any justice of the peace upon suit brought by the commissioner in the name of the Commonwealth of Kentucky. The commissioner shall not be liable for any costs in any suit brought by him as road commissioner.

§ 7. The general road law of this State is hereby adopted and made part of this act, except where it comes in conflict with the provisions of this act.

§ 8. All other road laws passed for Pendleton county are hereby repealed from and after the first day of June next.

§ 9. This act shall be submitted to the voters of Pendleton county at the next May election, and a poll shall be opened, and every person voting shall be asked by the sheriff of each voting precinct whether he votes for or against the road law, and his vote shall be recorded accordingly; and if a majority of the votes cast shall be in favor of said road law, then it shall be considered a law, and the county shall be organized under this law as soon as convenient; but if a majority of the votes cast shall be against said law, then it shall remain null and void.

Approved January 26, 1869.

———

CHAPTER 1303.

AN ACT to incorporate the Paris and Ruddle's Mills Turnpike Road Company, No. 2.

Be it enacted by the General Assembly of the Commonwealth of Kentucky:

§ 1. That there is hereby created a body corporate by the name of " The Paris and Ruddle's Mills turnpike road company, No. 2," with power to construct a turnpike road in Bourbon county, beginning where the old county dirt road enters upon the Maysville and Lexington turnpike road, opposite to the place where Alexander's old hemp factory formerly stood, extending from thence to Ruddle's Mills, or as near thereto as the company's means will enable the same to build. Said turnpike road must be built on the bed of the above named dirt road, or near thereto; and where the company, when it desires to deviate from the bed of the old dirt road, and cannot procure the right of way and quarries for material by contract, the same may be condemned as provided in the Revised Statutes, title "Turnpike and Plank Roads."

§ 2. The capital stock of said company may be sixteen thousand dollars, divided into shares of fifty dollars each. Willis D. Collins, John Redman, Joseph Redman, Robt. Horace Miller, William Sheaks, or any two of them, may obtain, as commissioners, subscriptions to the capital stock of said company; and the book or books therefor may be kept open as long as they may think proper.

§ 3. As soon as the sum of three thousand dollars shall be subscribed, said commissioners shall, by a notice published two weeks in a newspaper printed in Paris, and giving the time and place, call a meeting of the stockholders to elect five directors to manage the affairs of said company, who shall hold office for one year, and until their successors have been elected and qualified. The persons elected shall take an oath faithfully to discharge the duties of their office; and elect of their number a president, and such other officers as may be necessary, fix the time for the annual election of directors, and perform such other acts and duties as are usually performed by directors of such like companies.

§ 4. Said directors, when said road has been completed, or three miles thereof, may erect a toll-gate and charge such tolls as the Maysville and Lexington turnpike road company are allowed by law to charge.

§ 5. The county court of Bourbon county may, at any regular term of said court, a majority of the justices being present and concurring, subscribe to the capital stock of said company, not exceeding the rate of thousand dollars per mile, upon satisfactory proof of the ability to finish the road, or three miles thereof. Upon making said subscription, said court shall provide for its payment by levying a sufficient *ad valorem* tax upon the taxable property of said county of Bourbon, to be collected and accounted for and paid over as other county taxes are.

§ 6. This act shall take effect from its passage.

Approved January 26, 1869.

CHAPTER 1305.

AN ACT to incorporate Lebanon Female College.

Be it enacted by the General Assembly of the Commonwealth of Kentucky:

§ 1. That E. P. Mahon, J. M. Cardwell, R. C. Harris, T. J. Foster, John McElroy, Milton Rogers, Sam. T. Ray, H. B. Phillips, and James M. Fogle, and successors, be, and are hereby, constituted a body-politic and corporate, under the name and style of the Lebanon Female College; and by that name they shall have perpetual succession; and may adopt and use a common seal, and change the same at pleasure; to make contracts for the benefit of said female college; to sue and be sued, to plead and be impleaded, in any courts of this Commonwealth; to acquire, by gift, grant, devise, purchase, or otherwise, any real or personal estate for the use of said company, not to exceed fifty thousand dollars in value; to sell and dispose of the same at pleasure, according to the by-laws which may be hereafter established by the trustees of said institution, and reinvest the proceeds thereof in such real and personal estate, for the use and benefit of said female college, as they may deem proper.

§ 2. The capital stock of said college shall be divided into shares of one hundred dollars each, and half shares of fifty dollars each, to be subscribed and paid for according to the regulations laid down in its by-laws; it is also hereby declared that the stock which has been subscribed for the benefit of said Lebanon Female College shall be entitled to the benefits conferred by this charter. For every additional share of stock, after the first, the holder shall be entitled to one additional vote in the election of trustees; but no stockholder shall be allowed to cast more than ten votes. The said trustees shall be empowered to hold the property already acquired for the benefit of said institution, and may dispose of the same as may be determined by its by-laws.

§ 3. The trustees may open books for the subscription of stock at such time and place as they may. determine, and the stock so subscribed, together with that already taken, shall be entered in a book to be kept for that purpose by the secretary; and no stock shall be transferable from one person to another except the transfer be entered in such book.

§ 4. The trustees hereby incorporated shall be self-perpetuating, and shall hold their office until they resign or are deposed by the by-laws to be established for their regulation under this charter: *Provided, however,* That a majority of the stockholders may, upon one month's notice, published in the county paper, call for the election of new trustees; the mode and manner of said election to be conducted as in similar institutions, and which may be fixed by the by-laws of the company.

§ 5. All real and personal estate acquired under this charter shall be vested in the board of trustees and their successors in office. and shall be forever held for the purposes of education, and shall not be diverted to any other use whatever, nor shall the same be subject to taxation.

§ 6. The trustees shall have power to choose, from their own body, a president, secretary, and treasurer; and shall have power to fill all vacancies in their own body occasioned by death or otherwise; and, at all meetings of the board, a majority shall constitute a quorum to do business.

§ 7. The trustees shall have power, a majority of them concurring, to elect a president or principal to preside over said institution, on such terms as they may deem expedient, leaving him, however, to select his own teachers and tutors to instruct those committed to his charge.

§ 8. The trustees, with the advice of the president or principal of said college, shall have power to confer upon such pupils as may have taken the regular course for graduation, the honors usually conferred by similar institutions, by granting diplomas, duly signed by the principal, teachers, and trustees of said college.

§ 9. The trustees shall also have power, from time to time, to establish such by-laws, rules and ordinances, not inconsistent with this charter, the Constitution and laws of the State, or of the United States, as they shall deem necessary for the supervision and government of said Lebanon Female College.

§ 10. This act to take effect from its passage.

Approved January 26, 1869.

CHAPTER 1306.

AN ACT authorizing the County Court of Graves County to sell Poorhouse and lands, and to invest proceeds thereof.

Be it enacted by the General Assembly of the Commonwealth of Kentucky:

§ 1. That it shall be lawful for the county court of Graves county, a majority of the magistrates being present and concurring therein, to sell the poor-house and lands of said county, make a title, and receive the money for the same.

§ 2. The money derived from said sale to be expended in the purchase of other land better suited for the erection of a poor-house.

§ 3. This act to take effect from and after its passage.

Approved January 26, 1869.

CHAPTER 1307.

AN ACT authorizing the County Court of Pendleton County to close certain Alleys upon the Public Grounds.

Be it enacted by the General Assembly of the Commonwealth of Kentucky:

§ 1. That the county court of Pendleton county, a majority of all the justices in said county concurring, may have power to close up so much of the alleys situate upon either side of the present court-house yard as lies between said court-house yard and the remainder of the grounds belonging to said county, and known as the county grounds belonging to the court-house square.

§ 2. This act shall take effect from its passage.

Approved January 26, 1869.

CHAPTER 1308.

AN ACT authorizing the County Court of Crittenden County to levy an additional tax.

Be it enacted by the General Assembly of the Commonwealth of Kentucky:

§ 1. That the county court of Crittenden county, a majority of the justices in commission being present and concurring therein, be, and it is hereby, authorized, in addition to the capitation tax now allowed by law, to levy and collect an additional capitation tax not exceeding one dollar upon the tithe, the same to be used in paying for the construction of public buildings and defraying other necessary expenses of said county.

§ 2. That the presiding judge of said county court may cause the justices of the peace of said county to be summoned and assembled at such time as he may designate, for the purpose of levying the tax herein authorized.

§ 3. That the sheriff of said county shall collect the additional tax so levied in the same manner and at the same time he collects the ordinary county levy and State revenue; and he and his sureties shall be liable therefor in the same manner and way that they are liable for the county levy and State revenue.

§ 4. This act shall take effect from and after its passage.

Approved January 26, 1869.

CHAPTER 1309.

AN ACT to incorporate the Cloverport Cemetery Company.

Be it enacted by the General Assembly of the Commonwealth of Kentucky:

§ 1. That David R. Murray, sr., Wm. H. Bowmer, A. L. Simons, A. B. Skillman, R. L. Newsom, R. R. Pierce, John Walter, Wm. Vest, Wm. H. Webb, P. V. Duncan, and Jacob M. Cooper, and their associates and successors, be, and they are hereby, created a body corporate and politic, under the name and style of the "Cloverport Cemetery Company;" and by that name shall be able and capable in law to have and use a common seal; to sue and be sued, to plead and be impleaded, and do all such other things as are incident to such a corporation. The said corporation shall have power to purchase or acquire title to any quantity of land within one mile of the corporate limits of Cloverport, in Breckinridge county, not exceeding twenty-five acres, and receive a conveyance for the same, with such covenants of warranty as they may think proper. The lands and appurtenances, when conveyed to said company, shall be held solely and exclusively for a cemetery and ornamenal grounds connected therewith, and a residence for a superintendent or sexton, and shall never be alienated, sold, or used by said company for any other purposes than burial lots, as hereinafter provided. The said company may receive and take by devise or bequest any legacy or legacies that may be devised to them, to be appropriated solely and exclusively to the ornamenting and improvement of said cemetery grounds, and invest or loan out any spare funds that, from time to time, they may have, but they shall never exercise or attempt to exercise any banking powers.

§ 2. The affairs of said company shall be managed by five directors, who shall elect one of their number chairman; the said directors to be chosen annually by the lot-owners from among their number, on the first Saturday of April in each year; and if, for any cause, the election is not held at this regular annual meeting, it shall be held at the next lot-holders' meeting. The said directors shall hold their offices for one year, and until their successors are regularly elected and installed.

§ 3. The said directors shall have power to appoint a treasurer, secretary, sexton, and such other officers as they may think necessary, and take from them such bonds as may be required. The secretary shall keep a full and fair record of all the proceedings of the corporation, and shall always preserve an accurate map and survey of the grounds and lots. The funds arising from the sale of lots for burial purposes, and all other funds of the corporation, shall be held and used exclusively for keeping said grounds in repair, and ornamenting and improving the same, and paying the salaries and expenses of the necessary officers.

§ 4. The said directors shall have power to lay out and ornament said grounds, and, from time to time, alter and repair the same, and add such buildings and fixtures as may be necessary for the use or ornament of the cemetery grounds. They shall have power to lay off, sell, and convey burial lots, either at private or public sale; to make, from time to time, all such by-laws, rules and regulations, as may be necessary for the purposes of the corporation. They may levy a tax on the lot-owners in said cemetery to raise the necessary funds for keeping said grounds in repair.

§ 5. When a burial lot is purchased, the directors shall give a certificate thereof, under the seal of the company, which shall vest the purchaser with title. This may be transferred according to such rules and regulations as may be prescribed by the company, but in no other way. If not transferred by the grantee, it shall descend or pass by devise, as other real estate. Such lots shall never be used for any other purposes than burial lots; and if· applied to any other purpose, the title shall revert to the corporation.

§ 6. The said directors shall have power to forfeit any lot or lots in said cemetery grounds taken up by any person or persons who shall fail to make payment for such lot or lots; and where any interments have been made on any such lot or lots, the directors shall have the power to enter upon the same and remove, or cause to be removed, the bodies to the public grounds in said cemetery: *Provided*, That the said directors shall, before forfeiting any such lot or lots, give a written notice to the person or persons in whose name such lot or lots are entered, of at least thirty days before such action; and if such person or persons cannot be found, then said notice is to be posted on said lot or lots for sixty days before such action.

§ 7. If any person shall forcibly or unlawfully violate any of the graves of the dead, or deface or remove any of the tomb-stones, monuments, or inclosures, or injure any of the grounds or inclosures of the company, such person or persons so offending, besides being liable to an indictment for misdemeanor, and punishable according to the discretion of a jury, shall be liable to the corporation, or to the owner of a lot, in an action for whatever damage may be committed.

§ 8. This act to take effect from its passage.

Approved January 26, 1869.

CHAPTER 1310.

AN ACT to amend an act, entitled "An act to extend the civil jurisdiction of the Police Court of the City of Hickman, and for other purposes."

Be it enacted by the General Assembly of the Commonwealth of Kentucky:

§ 1. That no civil action shall be instituted or prosecuted in the court of the police judge of the city of Hickman, unless the defendants shall, at the time said action is instituted, reside within the corporate limits of said city, or out of the county of Fulton.

§ 2. This act shall take effect from and after its passage.

Approved January 26, 1869.

―――

CHAPTER 1311.

AN ACT for the benefit of John T. Thompson.

Be it enacted by the General Assembly of the Commonwealth of Kentucky:

§ 1. That the Auditor shall draw his warrant on the Treasurer for one hundred and twenty-eight dollars and thirty-five cents, in favor of John T. Thompson, the same being allowed the said Thompson, and hereby appropriated, in compensation for services and expenses in going to St. Louis, Missouri, and bringing one Dr. J. H. Jerry, a fugitive from justice, to the city of Covington.

§ 2. This act to take effect from and after its passage.

Approved January 26, 1869.

―――

CHAPTER 1312.

AN ACT for the benefit of John S. Gallagher.

Be it enacted by the General Assembly of the Commonwealth of Kentucky:

§ 1. That the Auditor shall draw his warrant on the Treasurer for two hundred and twenty-two dollars and five cents, in favor of John S. Gallagher, the same being allowed the said Gallagher, and hereby is appropriated, in compensation for services and expenses in pursuing to the State of Mississippi, detecting and capturing, John A. Minor, charged with a felonious crime against the laws of this Commonwealth.

§ 2. This act to take effect from and after its passage.

Approved January 26, 1869.

CHAPTER 1313.

AN ACT for the benefit of W. W. Hancock, Marshal of the Town of Greenville.

WHEREAS, W. W. Hancock was duly elected and qualified as marshal of the town of Greenville, in Muhlenburg county, Kentucky; and whereas, there are some doubts as to whether the said Hancock, at the time of his election, or at this time, resides within the corporation of said town, and whether his official acts are legal and binding; therefore,

Be it enacted by the General Assembly of the Commonwealth of Kentucky:

§ 1. That the residence and lot of ground owned by the said W. W. Hancock, marshal of the town of Greenville, be declared to be within the corporate limits of the town of Greenville; and that all of his past official acts, when acting within the scope of his authority as town marshal, be declared to be legal and binding.

§ 2. That this act shall take effect upon its passage.

Approved January 26, 1869.

CHAPTER 1314.

AN ACT to amend the Charter of the Harmony and Fork Turnpike Company.

Be it enacted by the General Assembly of the Commonwealth of Kentucky:

§ 1. That an act incorporating the Harmony and Fork turnpike road company, approved 12th of February, 1858, be amended so as to vest the said road company with the power of extending said road from the point where the intersection of the Bryantsville and Cane Run turnpike road may be, to any point said company may desire, on the Nicholasville and Danville turnpike road.

§ 2. That said road company be empowered to intersect or cross the Bryantsville and Cane Run turnpike road, at any point they may deem best.

§ 3. That any section or part of section in the original charter of this company, or any amendments thereof, contrary to the provisions of this amendment, be, and are hereby, repealed.

§ 4. That said road company have five years from the passage of this act in which to complete said road.

§ 5. This act to take effect from its passage.

Approved January 26, 1869.

CHAPTER 1315.

AN ACT to establish an additional District and Election Precinct in Simpson County.

Be it enacted by the General Assembly of the Commonwealth of Kentucky:

§ 1. That an additional district and election precinct be, and is hereby, established in Simpson county; and said district shall embrace all that territory and boundary which was added to Simpson county by an act of the General Assembly approved January 14th, 1869, and entitled "An act to change the line dividing Logan and Simpson counties;" and the voting place in said precinct and district shall be at Middleton.

§ 2. That Geo. B. Starks, a constable of Logan county, and W. W. Mosely, a justice of the peace for said county, who held their offices prior to the change of said county line, and who now reside in Simpson county by reason of said change, within the limits of said district hereby created, are hereby continued in their respective offices as constable and justice of the peace for Simpson county, and until the next regular election for district officers, and until their successors are qualified; and the county court may appoint a person to fill the place of the other justice until the first Saturday in May next.

§ 3. Said district is established subject to all the rules and regulations as now provided by law in regard to justices' districts: *Provided, however,* That the county court of Simpson shall have full power and authority to readjust the boundary lines of said district, and such others adjacent thereto, in Simpson county, as in his opinion may be necessary for the better convenience of the voters thereof.

§ 4. This act shall take effect from and after its passage.

Approved January 26, 1869.

CHAPTER 1316.

AN ACT to incorporate the "German Evangelical Lutheran St. Paul Church," of Paducah.

Be it enacted by the General Assembly of the Commonwealth of Kentucky:

§ 1. That Rev. B. Sickel, August Slusmeyer, Paul Mattil, Henry Mammen, Henry Diehl, and Louis Kolb, trustees of the "German Evangelical Lutheran St. Paul Church, of Paducah, Kentucky," and their successors in office, be, and they are hereby, created a body-politic and corporate, by that name and style; and shall have perpetual succession, with all powers and privileges incident to corporations; to sue and be sued, to plead and be implead-

1869.

ed, to answer and be answered, in all the courts of law and equity in this State; and said trustees may have and use a common seal, and may alter, change, modify, or break the same at pleasure.

§ 2. That whenever a vacancy in the board of trustees shall occur, from any cause, the vacancy shall be filled as the by-laws of said corporation may prescribe; and said board shall meet annually and elect one of its members as chairman, one member as secretary, and one member as treasurer, whose term of office shall be one year from the time of their election or appointment, and until their successors are elected or appointed; and said annual election to take place when prescribed by the by-laws of corporation.

§ 3. Said board of trustees shall have power to purchase. hold, and possess real estate in said city of Paducah, Kentucky, not exceeding in value forty thousand dollars; to erect a church building thereon and other necessary improvements for the benefit of the congregation; and which real estate and improvements shall be exempt from all taxation. And said board of trustees are also empowered to make sale of any real estate said corporation may, own whenever beneficial to the corporation; and a deed to the purchaser, signed and acknowledged and delivered by a majority of the trustees, shall be sufficient to pass the title.

§ 4. That all the real and personal estate of said corpotion shall be the property of, and remain with, that party who adhere to the doctrines of the Evangelical Lutheran Church, as represented by the General Council of that church and faith in the United States, whether that party be in the minority or in the majority; and no minister of the gospel shall ever officiate as pastor of this church or corporation who has not been regularly ordained by, and in cordial sympathy and connection with, an Evangelical Lutheran Synod.

§ 5. Said board may meet from time to time to enact by-laws for their government; but they are not to be in conflict with the Constitution and laws of this State or of the United States.

§ 6. This act to take effect from its passage.

Approved January 26, 1869.

CHAPTER 1318.

AN ACT to authorize the Trustees of the Baptist Church in Paris to sell and convey its Lands, and to confirm a sale thereof made by them.

Be it enacted by the General Assembly of the Commonwealth of Kentucky:

§ 1. That the trustees of the Baptist Church at Paris, in Bourbon county, are hereby empowered to sell and convey, by deed, such part of the land owned by said church as the church may direct at a regular meeting.

§ 2. The said trustees, by order of said church, having heretofore sold a piece of their land, the said sale and conveyance is hereby legalized.

§ 3. This act shall take effect from its passage.

Approved January 26, 1869.

CHAPTER 1320.

AN ACT for the benefit of E. C. Atherton and Thos. Landram, of McLean County.

Be it enacted by the General Assembly of the Commonwealth of Kentucky:

§ 1. That the Auditor of Public Accounts be directed to draw his warrants upon the Treasurer in favor of E. C. Atherton, for six dollars and twenty-five cents, and the other in favor of Thomas Landram, for five dollars and twenty-five cents. Both of said persons are of McLean county, and said sums are for State taxes improperly paid by them in 1866; said warrants to be paid out of any money in the Treasury not otherwise appropriated.

§ 2. This act shall take effect from its passage.

Approved January 26, 1869.

CHAPTER 1321.

AN ACT for the benefit of Elijah Litton, late Sheriff of Whitley County.

Be it enacted by the General Assembly of the Commonwealth of Kentucky:

§ 1. That Elijah Litton, late sheriff of Whitley county, be, and he is hereby, released from the payment of the damages assessed and adjudged against him in the fiscal court at Frankfort on his revenue for the year 1866, he having paid the full amount of said judgment, including principal, interest, and costs of suit.

§ 2. That this act shall take effect from its passage.

Approved January 26, 1869.

CHAPTER 1322.

AN ACT to repeal an act, entitled "An act to establish a Ferry across the Cumberland River at Eddyville," approved March 9th, 1868.

Be it enacted by the General Assembly of the Commonwealth of Kentucky:

§ 1. That an act, entitled "An act to establish a ferry across the Cumberland river at Eddyville," approved March 9th, 1868, be, and the same is hereby, repealed.

§ 2. This act to take effect from its passage.

Approved January 26, 1869.

CHAPTER 1323.

AN ACT for the benefit of Henry Farmer, of Ballard County.

Be it enacted by the General Assembly of the Commonwealth of Kentucky:

§ 1. That Henry Farmer, of Ballard county, is hereby released from the payment of the taxes due by him for the year 1865, including damages, interest, &c.; and that the Auditor of Public Accounts is hereby directed to give the sheriff of said county credit on his revenue for the year 1868 in his settlement.

§ 2. This act to take effect from and after its passage.

Approved January 26, 1869.

CHAPTER 1326.

AN ACT for the benefit of Jno. L. Slavin, Sheriff of Garrard County.

WHEREAS, The sheriff of Garrard county failed, at the January term, 1868, of the Garrard county court, to present the Auditor's list of taxable property for the year 1867, &c., of persons who have removed from other counties to the county of Garrard, together with such lands as have been returned without the tax being paid on the same; therefore,

Be it enacted by the General Assembly of the Commonwealth of Kentucky:

§ 1. That said sheriff have permission to present said list at the January term, 1869, and that, upon his settlement with the Auditor for revenue for the year 1868, shall be entitled to a credit for all taxes upon said list, which shall be allowed by said court, and certified to the Auditor as uncollectable, as now required by law.

§ 2. To take effect from its passage.

Approved January 26, 1869.

CHAPTER 1327.

AN ACT to amend article five of an act, entitled "An act to amend and reduce into one the several acts concerning the City of Henderson," approved February 11, 1867.

Be it enacted by the General Assembly of the Commonwealth of Kentucky:

§ 1. That when, from any cause, the judge of the Henderson city court fails to attend, or, if in attendance, cannot properly preside in a case pending in said court, the attorneys of the court who are present shall elect one of the said attorneys then in attendance to hold the court for the occasion, who shall accordingly preside and adjudicate.

§ 2. The election shall be held by the clerk of said court, and in case of tie, he shall give the casting vote.

§ 3. This act shall take effect from its passage.

Approved January 26, 1869.

CHAPTER 1328.

AN ACT to incorporate the Rich Grove Turnpike Road Company, in Christian County.

Be it enacted by the General Assembly of the Commonwealth of Kentucky:

§ 1. That a company shall be, and the same is hereby, created and established, under the name and style of the Rich Grove turnpike road company, for the purpose of making a road from Casky's Station, on Evansville, Henderson, and Nashville railroad, to the Clarksville and Hopkinsville turnpike road.

§ 2. That the capital stock of said company shall be ten thousand dollars, to be increased as the board of directors may deem necessary for the completion of said road; said stock shall be divided into shares of fifty dollars each:

§ 3. Books for the subscription of stock in said company shall be opened at any time after the passage of this act, at such times and places most convenient, under the directions of the following commissioners, to-wit: James W. Fields, W. E. Warfield, W. P. Wallace, W. T. Radford, James Clark, and Winston Henry, or any three of whom may act; and they shall open a book or books for the subscription of stock as above named; and the subscribers to the stock of said company shall enter into the following obligation in said books, to-wit: We, whose names are hereunto subscribed, do promise to pay to the president, directors, and company of the Rich Grove turnpike road company fifty dollars for each share of stock in said company which we have set opposite to our names, in such manner and proportions, and at such times, as shall

LAWS OF KENTUCKY.

be required by the president and directors of said company. Witness our hand, this —— day of.———, 18—, which amount shall be collected in the proper courts.

§ 4. When the amount of five thousand dollars shall have been subscribed, the commissioners, or a majority of them, may, if deemed expedient, proceed to finish the organization of said company by giving two weeks' notice of the time and place when an election shall be held for a president and directors of said road, which election shall be held and the voting be regulated by the rules allowing and regulating elections of president and directors held in the Lexington, Versailles, and Frankfort turnpike road company; and when the elections are held, the president and directors thus elected, who shall be five in number, shall thereafter manage and conduct the affairs of the said company, under the name and style of the Rich Grove turnpike road company, by which name they shall be a body-politic and corporate, in fact and in law; and by that name shall have perpetual succession; and shall have all the privileges and franchises incident to the Lexington, Versailles, and Frankfort turnpike road company; and they may keep open the books of subscription, and receive further subscriptions, until all their stock necessary to the completion of the road be taken.

§ 5. Said president and directors shall fix and regulate the elevation and grade of said road; the width of the part thereof to be covered with stone, not less than fifteen feet; shall have the power of erecting of toll-gates; shall have the power of erecting a toll-gate, and to charge half toll, when two and one half continuous miles of said road shall have been completed: *Provided*, That only half toll be exacted; and for every additional mile completed, proportionable toll may be taken.

§ 6. That as soon as the company is organized, the president and directors shall possess all the power. authority, rights and privileges, and shall and may do all acts and things necessary for carrying on and completing said turnpike road, as well as laying out and locating the same; shall be subject to all the duties, qualifications, restrictions, penalties, fines and forfeitures, if any, and be entitled to take toll and profits as are granted and given to the Lexington, Versailles, and Frankfort turnpike road company, by amended act approved February 14, 1835; and all the provisions of said act are hereby received and made part thereof, except so far as they are local in their application: *Provided also*, That the treasurer of said company shall only be required to execute bond in such security and penalty as the president and directors may prescribe; and that the work on said road shall commence in good faith on or before the 1st day of June, 1870.

§ 7. This act shall take effect from its passage.

Approved January 26, 1869.

CHAPTER 1329.

AN ACT Chartering the Cassady Creek Turnpike Road Company, in Nicholas and Bath Counties.

Be it enacted by the General Assembly of the Commonwealth of Kentucky:

§ 1. That a company be, and the same is hereby, created and established, under the name and style of the "Cassady Creek turnpike road company," for the purpose of constructing a turnpike road on the McAdams plan, from the Carlisle and Parks' Ferry turnpike road, at the mouth of Scrub Grass creek, up Cassady creek to Buzzard Roost; thence the most practicable route to the forks of Little Flat creek, in Bath county.

§ 2. The capital stock of said company shall be twenty thousand dollars, to be increased or diminished as the board of directors may determine, to be divided into shares of fifty dollars each.

§ 3. Books for the subscription of stock in said company shall be opened at any time after the passage of this act, at such places as may be most convenient, under the direction of John T. Craycraft, A. W. Shrout, James F. Lock, George W. Myers, Levi Kerns, Jos. B. Woods, and W. G. P. Ledford, any one or more of whom may procure a book or books, in which the subscribers to the capital stock of said turnpike road company shall enter into the following obligation: "We, whose names are hereunto subscribed, do respectively promise to pay to the Cassady Creek turnpike road company the sum of fifty dollars, for each and every share of stock in said company set opposite our names, in such manner and proportion, and at such times, as shall be required by the president and directors of said company.

§ 4. As soon as a sufficient amount of stock to build four miles of said road has been subscribed, it shall be the duty of the commissioners to call a meeting of the stockholders at some convenient point, for the purpose of choosing officers; notice of which shall be put up at three of the most public places on the contemplated road, at least ten days previous to the meeting. There shall be elected a president and five directors, who shall hold their office for one year from the time of qualifying, and until their successors are elected and qualified. The directors shall elect a treasurer and such other officers as

Marginal notes:
Company incorporated, route of road, &c.

Capital stock.

Commissioners to open books for the subscription of stock.

Obligation of subscribers.

When officers to be chosen. term of office, &c.

Treasurer to be elected; to give bond.

they may deem necessary; and said treasurer shall, before entering upon the discharge of his duties, execute bond with security, to be approved by the directory, to the effect that he will faithfully discharge the duties of his office; and whenever a demand shall be made upon him by the directory or their authorized agent, pay over any or all sums of money that he may have in his hands as treasurer.

§ 5. The president and directors, when elected and qualified, shall be a body corporate and politic, in fact and in law, by the name and style of "The Cassady Creek turnpike road company;" and by that name shall have perpetual succession, and all the privileges and franchises incident to a corporation; and shall be capable of taking and holding, to them and their successors and assigns, and of selling, transferring, conveying in fee simple, all such lands, tenements, hereditaments, and estate, real and personal, as shall be necessary to them in the prosecution of their work; and to sue and be sued, plead and be impleaded, answer and be answered, defend and be defended, in courts of record, or any other place whatever; and to do all and every other matter or thing which a body-politic or corporate may lawfully do.

Corporate powers.

§ 6. The stockholders, at all elections, shall be entitled to one vote for each share of stock in said company, which votes may be given in person or by proxy.

Stock; how voted.

§ 7. The president and directors shall take an oath before some person authorized to administer oaths, that they will faithfully discharge the duties of their respective offices.

President and directors to take oath.

§ 8. The grade and width of said road, and the quantity of metal to be put upon it, shall be fixed and determined by the president and directors of said road company.

Grade and width of road.

§ 9. It shall be lawful for the president and directors, with their superintendents, engineers, and workmen, with their tools, instruments, carts, wagons, and other carriages, and their beasts of draught or burden, to enter upon the land in and over and near to which said road shall pass, having first given notice of their intention to the owners or occupiers thereof, or to their agents: *Provided*, That if the president and directors shall not agree with the owners of said land, over or through which said road is to pass, as to the amount of damages the owner or owners may sustain by the road passing through their lands, the president and directors shall apply to the county court of the county in which said land is situated for a writ of *ad quod damnum* to assess the damages which may be sustained by the owner or owners of said land; and the jury, in assessing the damages, shall take into consideration the advantages

May enter upon lands.

How right of way may be obtained.

and disadvantages resulting to the party claiming dam-   1869.
ages by the establishment of said road ; and by the payment or tender of the damages assessed, it shall be lawful
for the president and directors to open and make said road,
and dig and carry away any stone, gravel, or other material necessary for the construction or repairing of said
road.

§ 10. That the president and directors shall be author-   When toll-
ized to erect toll-gates on said turnpike road when the   gates may be erected.
same shall be completed a distance of not less than five
miles in length, and examined by two justices of the peace
in no ways interested in the road, who shall be appointed
by the county court of the county in which that portion of
said road may lie, for the purpose, who, with the aid of
some competent person as civil engineer, shall view the
road and report its quality and condition. Upon hearing
the report, and any exceptions or proof that may be made
in relation thereto, if it appear to said court that the road
has been constructed according to law, the court shall
make an order authorizing the erection of gates, and collection of toll pursuant to rates established by law.

§ 11. That said president and directors shall have power   May let out
to let out said road to contractors, on such terms and in   road.
such portions as they may deem beneficial to the interest
of said company.

§ 12. That the stockholders in said road failing to pay   Stockholders
their call when due, shall be subject to suit in any of the   may be sued for
courts of this Commonwealth having jurisdiction of the   calls.
matter in controversy; they shall likewise pay six per
cent. per annum interest thereon until paid.

§ 13. This act to take effect from and after its passage.

Approved January 26, 1869.

CHAPTER 1330.
AN ACT for the benefit of Boyd County.

Be it enacted by the General Assembly of the Commonwealth of Kentucky:

§ 1. That the presiding judge of the Boyd county court
shall cause the justices of the peace for said county to
meet at the court-house in Catlettsburg, at the first regular term of the Boyd county court after this act becomes
in force, or some time thereafter; said judge, with a majority of said justices being in attendance, is authorized
and permitted to levy an additional tax to that which is
now permitted of fifty cents upon each one hundred dollars' worth of property in said county subject to taxation.
The money arising from the levy herein authorized shall
be applied to the payment of the debt now owing by the

county not now specially provided for, and for the purchase or the leasing of a poor-house, with the necessary
lands, for the benefit of the poor of said county; and to
make the necessary improvements on said lands for the
institution, as the court which is authorized to make levies
for said county may deem for the best interest of the
county.

§ 2. If the said court shall determine to purchase land
for a poor-house as now authorized by the provisions of
chapter 75 of the Revised Statutes, title "Poor and Poor-
houses," they are hereby authorized, and may direct the
treasurer of said county, to issue bonds of the county,
bearing interest not exceeding six per cent. per annum,
payable annually, the interest and so much of the principal of the whole cost, that the same shall be paid off
within five years from the purchase.

§ 3. If the said court in their judgment shall think best
to have lands and buildings for a term, instead of purchasing, they are authorized to do so, and, to meet the
liability, may issue bonds as directed in the second section
of this act.

§ 4. The court of claims of said county shall have the
power to make the levy directed in the first section, so
long and whenever the levy now directed by law shall be
insufficient to pay the expenses of the county.

§ 5. The collector of said county shall be liable on his
bond, together with his sureties, for the money collected
under this act, and for the faithful collection and paying
over to the order of the Boyd county court, and which shall
be due and payable as the levy is now directed to be collected and paid for said county, and the same proceeding
shall be pursued for the enforcement of the payment
thereof.

§ 6. This act shall take effect and be in force from its
passage.

Approved January 27, 1869.

CHAPTER 1333.
AN ACT for the benefit of the McCracken County Court.

*Be it enacted by the General Assembly of the Commonwealth
of Kentucky:*

§ 1. That whereas, McCracken county is now in debt,
and the ordinary revenue of said county is insufficient to
pay off the debts of said county and make the necessary
bridges, &c.; therefore, be it enacted, that it shall be lawful for the county court of said county to meet at any time
before the first day of March, 1869, a majority of all the
justices in commission being present, and levy a tax on

all the property subject to railroad tax in said county, not to exceed ten cents on the one hundred dollars' worth of property, one half of said tax to be applied to the repair of the court-house and grounds and fences, and to the furnishing of said house; the other half to be applied towards the building of a bridge at Jersey, over Island creek, on stone pillars.

§ 2. The said tax shall be collected by the same person and in the same manner that the railroad taxes of said county are collected; and said collector shall have same powers to sell property to enforce the payment of said taxes that the collector of railroad tax has or may have by law in said county.

§ 3. It shall he the duty of the county judge to appoint the same person to collect said tax that he does to collect the railroad tax for 1869, and take bond and good security from him to account for and pay over such tax in such manner as may be ordered by said county court composed of a majority of justices; and for his services as collector shall be allowed six per cent.; and on his failure to pay over said money, shall be liable to said county in the same manner, and may be proceeded against as the collectors of railroad taxes are now by law.

Approved January 27, 1869.

CHAPTER 1336.

AN ACT to amend an act, entitled "An act to authorize the County Court of Scott County to increase the County Levy, &c.," approved February 27, 1867.

Be it enacted by the General Assembly of the Commonwealth of Kentucky:

§ 1. That section two of the act, entitled "An act to authorize the county court of Scott county to increase the county levy and lay an ad valorem tax for county purposes and to pay the debts of the county," approved February 27th, 1867, be so amended as to allow said court, in the manner therein provided, to impose a tax not exceeding fifteen cents on each one hundred dollars' worth of property in the county liable to be taxed for revenue purposes; and that section four of said act be so amended as to authorize the said county court hereafter, at its regular court of claims, to impose a tax of fifteen cents on each one hundred dollars of said property in aid of the county levy.

§ 2. That the sheriff, in the collection of these taxes, if he finds it necessary, shall have power to distrain for the same by first levying upon and selling a sufficient amount of personalty to pay the tax due said county; but if he cannot find sufficient personal property for that purpose, he will then levy upon and sell a sufficient amount of real property to discharge the taxes due said county. In selling real property for the payment of county taxes as aforesaid, the sheriff will first advertise the time and place of sale at least sixty days prior thereto, by written handbills posted at six or more public places in Scott county, the court-house door in Georgetown being one.

§ 3. This act to take effect from its passage.

Approved January 27, 1869.

CHAPTER 1337.

AN ACT for the benefit of William Lykins, late Judge of the Morgan County and Quarterly Courts.

Be it enacted by the General Assembly of the Commonwealth of Kentucky:

§ 1. That William Lykins, late judge of the Morgan county and quarterly courts, have the further time of two years to collect and distrain for his uncollected fee bills.

§ 2. Said Lykins shall be under all the pains and penalties now prescribed by law against the collection of illegal fee bills.

§ 3. This act shall take effect from and after its passage.

Approved January 27, 1869.

CHAPTER 1338.

AN ACT for the benefit of the Court of Claims of Clinton County.

Be it enacted by the General Assembly of the Commonwealth of Kentucky:

§ 1. That the court of claims for Clinton county be, and the same is, authorized to levy a tax upon the citizens of said county, not exceeding ten cents upon the hundred dollars' worth of property, and not exceeding fifty cents per capita or poll, for the purpose of paying for a poorhouse and poor-house farm recently purchased by said court's commissioners, and for the purpose of completing the repairs on the court-house burnt during the late rebellion.

§ 2. That the presiding judge of said county be, and he is, authorized to call the justices of said county together at any time to make the levy for the year 1869; and, at the next regular court of claims, they may, if necessary, make a like levy, to be collected in the year 1870.

§ 3. That the sheriff of said county be responsible on his bond for the collection of the county levy for any money collected by him under this act.

§ 4. That this act take effect from its passage.

Approved January 27, 1869.

CHAPTER 1339.

AN ACT for the benefit of the Clerk of the Nicholas Circuit Court.

WHEREAS, It appearing from an order of the Nicholas circuit court authorizing books to be provided for that purpose, that it is necessary that a general cross index should be made for the use of said court and the litigants thereof; therefore,

Be it enacted by the General Assembly of the Commonwealth of Kentucky:

That the clerk of the Nicholas circuit court be, and he is hereby, required to make and complete said general cross-index, under the order of said circuit court of the county of Nicholas; and the judge of said court is authorized to make such order of allowance to said clerk for his services for said work as to him may appear, on proof, just and reasonable, and certify said allowance to the county court of Nicholas county; and said county court shall thereupon make an order to pay the same out of the county levy of said county.

Approved January 27, 1869.

CHAPTER 1340.

AN ACT for the benefit of the Shelby Circuit Clerk.

Be it enacted by the General Assembly of the Commonwealth of Kentucky:

§ 1. That the appointment and qualification of Ed. Mc-Grath as deputy clerk of the Shelby circuit court, by J. L. Caldwell, judge of the Shelby county court, out of term time, is hereby legalized; and all acts done by him as such are, and shall be, as valid as though he had been appointed and qualified by an order of said court in open court.

§ 2. This act shall take effect from its passage.

Approved January 27, 1869.

CHAPTER 1341.

AN ACT for the benefit of the Crittenden County Court.

Be it enacted by the General Assembly of the Commonwealth of Kentucky:

§ 1. That it shall be lawful for the Crittenden county court, a majority of the justices in commission being present and concurring therein, to make an order appropriating to the payment of the court-house indebtedness, or other general indebtedness of said county, any surplus funds remaining unexpended which may have been levied and collected under an act approved January 15, 1864, entitled "An act to enable the county court of Crittenden county to build a jail."

§ 2. This act shall take effect from and after its passage.

Approved January 27, 1869.

CHAPTER 1342.

AN ACT for the benefit of F. M. Allison, late Clerk of the Butler County and Circuit Courts.

Be it enacted by the General Assembly of the Commonwealth of Kentucky:

§ 1. That the further time of two years be allowed to F. M. Allison, late clerk of the Butler county and circuit courts, to collect by distraint his unpaid fees: *Provided,* That said Allison shall be liable to all the penalties prescribed by law for issuing and collecting illegal fee bills.

§ 2. This act shall take effect from and after its passage.

Approved January 27, 1869.

CHAPTER 1344.

AN ACT to regulate the election of Sinking Fund Commissioners in Hart County.

Be it enacted by the General Assembly of the Commonwealth of Kentucky:

§ 1. That hereafter the election of the sinking fund commissioners for Hart county shall be held at the regular court of claims for said county.

§ 2. That the present sinking fund commissioners shall remain in office and discharge their duties as such after the expiration of their term of office, and until their successors are elected and qualified under the provisions of this act.

§ 3. Should a vacancy occur in the board of sinking fund commissioners by death, resignation, or otherwise, said vacancy shall be filled by the presiding judge of the Hart county court until the next regular election.

§ 4. This act to take effect from and after its passage.

Approved January 27, 1869.

—

CHAPTER 1345.

AN ACT to legalize the proceedings of the Boone County Court at its October Term, 1868, and its January Term, 1869.

WHEREAS, The Boone county court, sitting as a court of claims, at its October term, 1868, fixed the county levy for said county at two dollars and fifty cents upon each tithe of said county; and whereas, the said court met again on the first Monday in January, 1869, and then rescinded the order fixing the levy at two dollars and fifty cents, and thereupon agreed to and fixed the county levy at three dollars upon each tithe of said county; and whereas, the said court, at its said January term, appointed N. E. Hawes and W. L. Norman a committee to borrow three hundred dollars, at a rate of interest not exceeding eight per cent., to be used in the support of the paupers of said county; and whereas, there are doubts as to the authority of said court to fix said levy at three dollars; and there are also doubts as to the legality of the manner of the imposing and fixing said levy; and whereas, there are also doubts as to the power and authority of said court to authorize the appointment of said committee to borrow said sum of money; all of said proceedings of said court being necessary and proper, and it is just and right they should be legalized; therefore,

Be it enacted by the General Assembly of the Commonwealth of Kentucky:

§ 1. That the orders and proceedings of the Boone county court at its January term, for 1869, fixing the levy at three dollars, be, and the same is hereby, legalized, and said levy fixed at three dollars.

§ 2. That the orders and proceedings of the said county court appointing N. E. Hawes and W. L. Norman a committee to borrow three hundred dollars, for the purpose and on the terms stated in the preamble, be, and the same are hereby, legalized; and all acts and proceedings of the said committee under said appointment shall be binding upon the county court.

§ 3. This act to take effect from and after its passage.

Approved January 27, 1869.

CHAPTER 1347.

AN ACT for the establishment of a Pauper-house in Hancock County.

Be it enacted by the General Assembly of the Commonwealth of Kentucky:

§ 1. That the county judge of Hancock county is authorized to have a poll opened in the various precincts of said county, on the first Monday in August, 1869, for the purpose of ascertaining the sense of the people of said county as to the erection of a house for paupers in said county. If a majority of the votes in the county are cast in favor of building a pauper-house, it shall be the duty of the county judge to appoint three commissioners, who shall select an eligible location and grounds for said house, and contract for the same. The county court, a majority of justices concurring, is authorized to levy an *ad valorem* tax, not exceeding ten cents per hundred dollars on the valuation of the taxable property of the county, and also a poll-tax, if necessary, not exceeding one dollar per capita, for any one year, to be continued annually until a sufficiency is made to erect the building and purchase so much land as in the discretion of the court may be necessary. The tax to be collected in the same manner, and under the same fines and penalties, as other taxes are collected.

§ 2. This act shall take effect from its passage.

Approved January 27, 1869.

CHAPTER 1348.

AN ACT to amend an act to establish the Mechanics' Institute, in the City of Paducah.

Be it enacted by the General Assembly of the Commonwealth of Kentucky:

§ 1. That an act, entitled "An act to establish a Mechanics' Institute in the town of Paducah," approved February 23, 1846, be, and the same is hereby, amended as follows: That said institute shall have power to pass by-laws regulating the amount and collection of all dues, and may pass by-laws declaring a forfeiture of all rights and interest as a stockholder in said institute, against any member or members who shall fail or refuse to pay any dues or assessments, regularly made by said institute against him or them; but it is provided, that no such forfeiture shall be had until the delinquent member shall have been tried and convicted at a regular meeting of the institute; and no trial or conviction shall be had, unless the delinquent member shall have been served with written notice by the secretary of the institute to appear and defend, at certain time and place, at least five days before the trial.

§ 2. All forfeitures accruing by virtue of this act, or by laws under it, shall inure to the benefit of this corporation in its aggregate capacity.

§ 3. This act to be in force from its passage.

Approved January 28, 1869.

CHAPTER 1349.

AN ACT to incorporate Grace Church, Louisville.

Be it enacted by the General Assembly of the Commonwealth of Kentucky:

§ 1. That Rev. Oscar B. Thayer, Ed. Wilson, Dr. J. M. Bodine, Joseph Hackett, Jno. A. Dake, Jno. Wood, Frank Maury, Wm. Grubb, T. J. Wyatt, John Duhurst, P. B. Bate, A. W. Hyde, and Richard Isaacs, and their successors in office, shall be, and they are hereby, constituted a corporation and body-politic, by the name of the Rector, Wardens, and Vestry of Grace Church, Louisville; and by that name shall have perpetual succession; and may sue and be sued, plead and be impleaded; and may purchase and hold property, whether acquired by purchase, gift, devise, or bequest, and whether real, personal, or mixed; and may make and have a corporate seal, and the same break and alter at pleasure; and shall have the power to make contracts and pass by-laws, not inconsistent with the laws of this State.

§ 2. That the entire management of the affairs and concerns of said corporation and church, and all the corporate power hereby granted, shall be, and are hereby, vested in a board of thirteen trustees, resident within this State, consisting of the rector, wardens, and vestry of said church, for the time being; the persons named in the first section of this act being the present rector, wardens, and vestry.

§ 3. That the majority of the trustees in vestry assembled shall have power, from time to time, to enact by-laws for the regulation and management of the affairs and concerns of the said corporation and church, for filling up vacancies in the board occasioned by death, resignation, removal from the State, or otherwise, as may be provided for by the by-laws; to prescribe the number and description, duties, and powers of the officers; the manner of their election, and the term of their offices; to sell the pews in said church, subject to a quarterly or annual tax, and to enforce the payments thereof, as well as of the quarterly or annual rent of pews; to confiscate or sell, at their option, for the use of said corporation and church, any and all pews on which the. quarterly tax remains unpaid for the space of six months, provided the same be consistent with the terms of lease.

§ 4. That for the purpose of carrying out the object declared in this act, or for any purpose connected therewith, the said corporation shall have power to have, hold, take by purchase, or otherwise, real and personal estate, and to sell, lease, and dispose of the same.

§ 5. That all of the real and personal estate, of whatsoever kind, at present belonging to, or held in trust for, the use and benefit of Grace Church, Louisville, or for its congregation, be, and is hereby, vested in said rector, wardens, and vestry, and their successors in office.

§ 6. That this act is subject to amendment or repeal by the Legislature at any time.

§ 7. This act shall take effect from its passage.

Approved January 28, 1869.

CHAPTER 1352.

AN ACT to incorporate Mozart Lodge, No. 149, Independent Order of Odd Fellows, at Louisville.

Be it enacted by the General Assembly of the Commonwealth of Kentucky:

§ 1. That A. Rammers, John Laufer, Frank Fensterer, Henry Hintzen, A. Reutlinger, I. C. Fink, J. J. Fisher, E. Halbleib, John B. Kramer, charter members of Mozart Lodge, No. 149, I. O. O. F., and their associates and successors, be, and they are hereby, created a body corporate, by the name and style of the Mozart Lodge, No. 149, of the Independent Order of Odd Fellows; and they and their associates and successors shall so continue and have perpetual succession; and by that name are made capable in law as natural persons to sue and to be sued, plead and be impleaded, contract and be contracted with, answer and be answered, in all courts of law and equity in this Commonwealth; to make, have, and use a common seal, and the same to break, alter, or amend at pleasure; they may make and ordain by-laws and regulations for their government, and those now in force in said Lodge to alter when deemed proper; and may change and renew the same at pleasure, provided they be not in contravention of the constitution, laws, and regulations of the Grand Lodge of the Independent Order of Odd Fellows incorporated by an act approved February 16, 1838, nor in contravention of the Constitution and laws of the United States or of this State. The said corporation shall have power and authority to acquire and hold real and personal estate not exceeding twenty thousand dollars in value; and from time to time, if deemed expedient, to sell and convey the same, or any part thereof, and to reinvest and dispose of the proceeds. The right to alter, amend, or repeal this act, is hereby reserved to the General Assembly.

§ 2. This act to take effect from and after its passage.

Approved January 29, 1869.

CHAPTER 1353.

AN ACT to incorporate the German Building Association, No. 1, of Covington.

Be it enacted by the General Assembly of the Commonwealth of Kentucky:

§ 1. That Bernard Viet, Jacob Bold, H. C. Flaute, Herman Tonnies, L. Schnorbus, George Bose, B. Gautenberg, Herman Wente, Frank Weber, John H. Blau, F. Kehler, Anton Anto, and Henry Schneider, their associates and successors, be, and they are hereby, created a body corporate, by the name and style of "The German Building Association, No. 1, of Covington, Kentucky," and they and their associates and successors shall so continue and have perpetual succession; and by that name are made capable in law as natural persons to sue and be sued, plead and be impleaded, contract and be contracted with, answer and be answered, in all courts of law and equity in this Commonwealth; to make, use, and have a common seal, and the same to break, alter, or amend at pleasure.

§ 2. They are hereby authorized, by means of weekly contributions, to raise a fund or funds to be loaned or paid out to and among the members of said association, to enable them to build a homestead or establish a business, upon such terms and conditions as they among themselves may fix and agree upon.

§ 3. The capital stock of this corporation shall consist of shares of four hundred and fifty dollars each; no member shall, however, hold more than ten shares in his own right.

§ 4. The office of said corporation shall be in the city of Covington, Kenton county, and State of Kentucky. The affairs of said association shall be managed by a president, vice president, treasurer, first and second secretaries, and nine directors, who, together, shall constitute and form the board of directors. The annual meeting for their election shall be held annually, on the first Wednesday in January of each and every year.

§ 5. The said association may make and ordain a constitution, and such regulations and by-laws for their government as they may deem proper and expedient to carry out the object of their association, and those now in force in said association to alter or amend when deemed proper, and may change and renew the same at pleasure : *Provided*, They be not in contravention of the Constitution and laws of the United States or of this State.

§ 6. The said corporation shall have power and authority to acquire and hold real and personal estate, and, from time to time, if deemed expedient, to sell and convey the same, or any part thereof, and to dispose of the proceeds according to the rules and regulations of said association.

§ 7. The right to alter, amend, or repeal this act is hereby reserved to the General Assembly.

§ 8. This act shall take effect from and after its passage.

Approved January 29, 1869.

CHAPTER 1354.

AN ACT to incorporate the Elizabethtown, Lexington, and Big Sandy Railroad Company.

Be it enacted by the General Assembly of the Commonwealth of Kentucky:

§ 1. That Samuel B. Thomas, M. H. Cofer, C. G. Wintersmith, of the county of Hardin, and State of Kentucky; Lieut. Gov. Johnson, E. W. Graves, and Isaac Stone, of the county of Nelson, in said State; Wm. McBrayer, Dr. Witherspoon, John F. Wills, and John Draffin, of the county of Anderson, in said State; Thomas Grundy and R. J. Browne, of the county of Washington, in said State; B. Magoffin, sr., S. M. McBrayer, Dr. Conner, and Dr. A. Thompson, of the county of Mercer, in said State; L. S. Trimble, S. W. Morton, and J. M. Bigger, of the county of McCracken, in said State; T. P. Porter, Hart Gibson, S. Robinson, Henry Graddy, J. P. Ford, F. P. Kinkead, D. J. Williams, James R. Stephenson, Thos. Elmore, and J. D. Helm, of the county of Woodford, in said State; I. C. Vanmeter, John R. Viley, J. B. Bowman, W. R. Estill, and Joseph S. Woolfolk, of the county of Fayette, in said State; Harrison Thompson, B. B. Groom, Benjamin Vanmeter, and Lewis Gay, of the county of Clark, in said State; Jno. Clay, Henry Howard, Rich'd Reid, and Thos. Turner, of the county of Montgomery, in said State; Geo. Hamilton, Wm. Sudduth, and A. P. Read, of the county of Bath, in said State; A. M. West and Samuel Tate, of the State of Mississippi, be, and they are hereby, appointed commissioners, under the direction of whom, or any three of whom, subscriptions may be received to the capital stock of the Elizabethtown, Lexington. and Big Sandy Railroad Company, which is hereby incorporated; and they may cause books to be opened, at such times and places as they may direct, for the purpose of receiving subscriptions to the capital stock of said company, after having given such notice as they deem proper; and if such amount of subscriptions to the capital stock of said company as is necessary to its incorporation shall not have been obtained, said commissioners, or a majority of them, may cause said books to be opened, from time to time, and may adjourn to such place as they may deem proper, until the sum necessary to its incorporation shall be subscribed: *Provided*, That any subscription, tendered at any time and place other than those advertised, that may be received by said commissioners, or any one of them, shall be as valid against the parties subscribing, as if received at the time and place advertised; and if any of said commissioners shall die or resign, or refuse to act during a continuance of the duties devolved upon them by this act, others may be appointed in their stead by a majority of those remaining.

§ 2. That the capital stock of the Elizabethtown, Lexington, and Big Sandy Railroad Company shall be five millions of dollars, in shares of one hundred dollars each, which may be subscribed by any individual, company, or corporation; and as soon as two thousand shares of said stock shall be subscribed, the subscribers, their successors and assigns, shall be, and are hereby declared to be, incorporated into a company, by the name of the Elizabethtown, Lexington, and Big Sandy Railroad Company; and by this name shall be capable of purchasing, holding, selling, leasing, and conveying real estate, not exceeding ten thousand acres, and personal estate so far as the same may be necessary for the purposes of the corporation, and shall have perpetual succession; and by said corporate name may sue and be sued, contract and be contracted with; and may have and use a common seal, and alter or renew the same at pleasure; and shall have any, and enjoy all the privileges, which other similar corporate bodies may lawfully do. *Capital stock.*

Name & style, and corporate powers.

§ 3. That there shall be paid, at the time of subscribing for stock in said company, to the person receiving the subscription, the sum of one dollar on each share, either in money, or in a note or notes, at not more than sixty days, payable to some one or more of said commissioners, and negotiable in some bank. The residue of said subscription shall be payable in installments, at such times as may be required by the board of directors of said company. But no such payment shall be demanded, until at least ten days' notice shall have been given, by publication in one or more newspapers published on the line of said road; and if any subscriber shall fail to pay any installment, or part of any *How subscriptions paid.*

1869. installment, when so demanded, the same may be recovered by an action in the name of the corporation, before any court having jurisdiction in such cases; and in all such actions it shall not be necessary to prove any other demand than the publication provided for in this section :

Stock may be forfeited. or, in case such failure to pay any installment, or part of installment, so demanded, shall continue for the space of sixty days after the time the same is required by such demand to be paid, the board of directors may, at their discretion, order the same to be forfeited to the company, and may, if they think proper, sell said share or shares for the benefit of the company, or, in the event of the highest bid being less than the unpaid balance and interest on said subscription, then the company may become the purchaser, and shall retire said subscription. But the board of directors, by a majority of the whole, may remit such forfeiture

Subscriptions may be received, payable in contracts, &c. on such terms as they may think proper : *Provided*, It shall be lawful for the commissioners, or board of directors, to receive subscriptions to said capital stock, payable in contracts, well secured, to build any parts of said road, or any bridge or bridges on the same, or to perform any work, or furnish any materials which may be accepted by the com-

Subscriptions may be made in real estate. pany : *And provided further*, That subscriptions to said capital stock may be made in real estate, situated in Kentucky, if said subscriptions shall be tendered to the board of directors after their organization ; said real estate to be taken at its cash value, to be assessed at the time by three commissioners on oath, of whom two shall be selected by the company, and one by the person proposing to subscribe. Upon their report in writing, describing the land, and assessing its cash value, the company may receive the same at its value and issue a stock certificate, and may take a deed of conveyance in fee simple ; and the real estate received for stock subscriptions, and which the company is hereby authorized to receive, shall be over and above the ten thousand acres mentioned in the second section of this act

§ 4. That at the expiration of the period for which the

When directors may be elected. books are first opened, if two thousand shares of the capital stock shall have been subscribed, and if not, as soon thereafter as the same shall be subscribed, said commissioners, or a majority of them living, shall call a meeting, at such time and place as a majority of those acting shall designate, giving at least ten days' notice of the time and place in one or more newspapers published as aforesaid;

How stock voted. and at such meeting said commissioners shall lay the subscription books before the subscribers then present, and thereupon said subscribers, or a majority of them then present, shall have power to elect, out of their own number, by ballot, nine directors to manage the affairs of said company, and these nine directors, or a majority of them, shall have power to elect a president of said company from among the directors, and to allow him such compensation for his services as they may think proper; and at such election, and on all other occasions, where a vote of the stockholders of said company is to be taken, each stockholder shall be allowed one vote for every share of stock owned by such voter; and any stockholder may, in writing, depute any other person to act as proxy for it, him, or her; and said commissioners aforesaid, or any three of them, shall be judges of said first election.

§ 5. That to continue the succession of the president and directors of said company, nine directors shall be chosen annually on the first Saturday in June of each year, at such place as the president and directors may appoint, by the stockholders of said company: *Provided*, That the president and directors may change the time and place of holding elections upon publishing such change, not less than thirty days prior to the election, in the newspapers aforesaid; and that the directors of said company, or a majority of them, shall have the power to appoint judges of all elections, and to elect a president of said company from among themselves, and to allow him such compensation for his services as they may deem proper; and if any vacancy shall occur by death, resignation, or refusal to act, of any president or director, before the year for which he was elected shall have expired, a person to fill such vacancy shall be appointed by the president and directors, or a majority of them; and that the president and directors of said company shall hold and exercise their offices until their successors are duly elected and enter upon the discharge of their duties; and all elections which are by this act, or by the by-laws of said company, to be made at a particular time, if not made at such time, may be made in ninety days thereafter, upon notice published in the newspapers aforesaid.

§ 6. That a general meeting of the stockholders of said company may be called at any time during the interval between the annual meetings by the president and the directors, or a majority of them, or by the stockholders owning one half of all the stock subscribed, upon giving thirty days' notice of the time and place of holding the same in the newspapers aforesaid; and when any such meeting is called by the stockholders, such notice shall specify the object of the call; and if, at any such called meeting, a majority of all the stockholders are not present in person or by proxy, the same shall be adjourned from day to day, without transacting any business, for any time not exceeding five days; and if, within said five days, stockholders having a majority in value of all the stock subscribed do

1869.

Annual elections.

President to be elected.

Vacancies.

Term of office.

General meetings of stockholders may be called.

not attend in person or by proxy, such meeting shall be dissolved.

Annual report of condition of company to be made.

§ 7. That the president and directors of said company in office for the preceding year shall, at the regular annual meeting of the stockholders, exhibit a clear and distinct account of the affairs of said company; that, at any called meeting of the stockholders, or a majority in value of the whole of the stock subscribed being present, may demand and require similar statements from the president and directors, whose duty it shall be to furnish such statement when so required.

President, &c., to take oath.

May elect treasurer.

§ 8. That the president and directors of said company, before he or they act as such, shall swear or affirm, as the case may be, that they will well and truly discharge the duties of their respective offices to the best of their skill and judgment; and the said president and directors, or a majority of them, shall have power to elect or appoint a treasurer of said company, and require and take of him a bond, in such penalty, and with such securities as they may prescribe, payable to said company, conditioned for the faithful keeping and disbursing of all such money as may come into his hands, and with such other conditions as may be prescribed, upon which bond recovery may be had for a breach of the conditions thereof, by suit in the name of the company, and in any court having jurisdiction.

Books may be reopened.

§ 9. That if any of the stock authorized by this act shall remain unsubscribed until after the election of president and directors, as provided for in the fourth section of this act, the said president and directors, or a majority of them, shall have power to open the books and receive subscriptions to the stock which shall remain unsubscribed, or to sell and dispose of the same for the benefit of the company, not under the par value of such stock; and the subscribers or purchasers of such stock shall have all the rights of original subscribers, and be subject to the same regulations and liabilities.

Officers, agents, &c., may be appointed; their pay.

§ 10. That said president and directors, or a majority of them, may appoint all such officers, agents, or servants, as they may deem expedient for the business of the company, and may remove the same at pleasure, or said board of directors may delegate to their president the power to appoint or remove any or all such employes, subject to their approval at their first meeting thereafter. That they, or a majority of them, may determine by contract the pay of such officers, agents, or servants, and regulate by by-laws the manner of adjusting all accounts against the company, and the extent of the liability of the company to its em-

May erect work-shops, &c.

ployes; that they shall have power to erect, carry on, conduct, and control work-shops, eating-houses, warehouses, and any buildings or edifices necessary or convenient for the use of said company; that they shall have power to direct and regulate in what manner and by what evidence stock in said company may be transferred; and to pass all by-laws they may deem necessary and proper for exercising the powers hereby vested in said company, and for carrying into effect this act, and to alter the same at pleasure, provided the same be not contrary to the Constitution and laws of the United States or of this State.

§ 11. That if the capital stock of said company shall be deemed insufficient for the purpose of this act, it shall be lawful for the president and directors to increase the same as much as they may deem necessary, not exceeding the sum of ten millions dollars, giving notice as hereinbefore required; and the said company may borrow any sum of money, not exceeding five millions of dollars, and secure the payment of the same by the issue of first mortgage bonds of their road, or in such way as may be agreed upon.

§ 12. That the president and directors of said company are hereby vested with all the powers and rights necessary to the construction of a railroad from Elizabethtown to a point on the Big Sandy, at or within twenty miles of its mouth, along such route as may be selected by the president and directors; and that they may cause to be made contracts, which shall be signed by the president, with any corporations, companies, or individuals, for making said road, or any part of it; and that they may purchase or lease any road or roads connecting with their said road, and that they, their agents, engineers, etc., or those with whom they may contract for surveying or making the same, or any part thereof, may enter upon, use, and excavate any land which may be wanted for the site of said road or the erection of warehouses or other structures or works necessary and convenient to said road, or for its use, or for any other purpose necessary or useful in the construction and repair of said road or its works and appurtenances; and they may build bridges and construct tunnels, provided such bridges shall not obstruct navigation on any navigable stream; and may fix scales and weights, take and use timber, earth, gravel, stone, and other materials necessary or useful in the construction and repair of said road.

§ 13. That the president and directors, or a majority of them, or their authorized agents, may agree with the owners of any land, earth, stone, timber, or other materials or improvements which may be wanted for the construction or repair of said road or any of their works, for the purchase in fee simple, or the use and occupation of the same; and if they cannot agree, or if the owner or

1869.   owners of any of them be a *feme covert*, under age, *non
compos mentis*, or out of the county in which the property
may lie, application may be made to any justice of the
peace of said county, who shall, thereupon, issue his warrant, directed to the sheriff or any constable of said county,
requiring him to summon twenty discreet men, not related
to the owner, nor in any way interested, to meet on the
land, or near the property or materials to be valued, on a
day named in said warrant, not less than ten nor more
than twenty days after the issuing of the same; and if, at
the time and place, any of the said jurors do not attend,
said sheriff or constable shall forthwith summon as many
jurors as may be necessary, with the jurors in attendance,
and from them each party, if present, or, if not present,
by agent or otherwise, the sheriff or constable, for the
party absent, may strike off four jurors, and the remaining
twelve shall act as the jury of inquest of damages. The
sheriff or constable may adjourn the jury from day to
day; and if they cannot agree upon a verdict, it shall be
his duty to discharge them and summon another, to meet
as soon as convenient. Before the jury acts, the sheriff
or constable shall administer to them an oath or affirmation. that they will justly and impartially fix the damages
which the owner or owners will sustain by the use and
occupation of said property required by said company;
and the jury, in estimating the damages, shall find the
owner or owners the actual value of the land or other
thing proposed to be taken; but in estimating damages
resulting incidentally to the other land, or other property
of such owners, they shall offset the advantages to such
residue to be derived from the building and operating of
said road by, through, or near such residue. The jury
shall reduce their verdict to writing, and sign the same,
and it shall be returned by the sheriff or constable to the
clerk of the circuit court of his county, and such clerk
shall receive and file it in his office; and such verdict shall
be confirmed by the circuit court at its next regular term,
if no sufficient reason is shown by either party for setting
it aside; and when so confirmed, it shall be recorded by
the clerk, at the expense of said company; but if set aside,
the court shall direct another inquisition to be held by
the sheriff of the county in the manner above prescribed:
Provided, That the company may proceed to construct
their said road as soon as the first verdict of the jury
shall be returned, whether the same be set aside and a
new jury ordered or not; and every inquisition shall describe the property or the bounds of the land condemned,
and the duration of interest in the same, valued for the
company; and such valuation, when tendered or paid to
owner or owners of said property, or to the sheriff of the

county in which said inquest is held, when the owner or owners do not reside in such county, shall entitle said company to the use or interest in the same thus valued as fully as if it had been conveyed to it by the owner or owners of the same; and the valuation of the same, if not received when tendered, may, at any time thereafter within one year, be received from the company without costs or interest by the owners, his, their, or its legal representatives: *Provided*, That land condemned for roadway shall not be more than one hundred feet wide, unless said company shall file with the justice, at the time of applying for a warrant, the affidavit of some one of its engineers, stating that a greater width is necessary, and how much more is required, when the inquision shall be for the quantity thus stated.

§ 14. That whenever it shall be necessary for said company to have, use, or occupy any land, material, or other property, in order to the construction or repairing of said road or their necessary works or buildings, the president and directors, or their agents, or those contracting with them for constructing or repairing the same, may immediately take and use the same, they having first caused the property wanted to be viewed by a jury formed as hereinbefore prescribed; and it shall not be necessary, after such view, in order to the use and occupation of the same, to wait the issue of the proceedings upon such inquest; and the inquest of the jury, after the payment or tender of such valuation, shall be a bar to all actions for taking and using such property, whether before or after such confirmation or payment of such valuation.

§ 15. That any county, town, or city, through which said proposed road shall pass, is hereby authorized to subscribe stock in said railroad company in any amount any such town, city, or county may desire; and the county court of any such county is authorized to issue the bonds of their respective counties, in such amount as the county court may direct; and the chairman and board of trustees, or mayor and aldermen of any town, or the mayor and aldermen or council of any city, are hereby authorized to issue the bonds of their respective towns or cities in like manner. All said bonds shall be payable to bearer, with coupons attached, bearing any rate of interest not exceeding six per cent. per annum, payable semi-annually in the city of New York, payable at such times as they may designate, not exceeding thirty years from date; but before any such subscription on the part of any town, city, or county shall be valid or binding on the same, the mayor and aldermen or chairman and board of trustees of any town, the mayor and aldermen or council of any city, and the county court of any county, shall submit the question of any such subscription to the qualified voters of any town, city, or county in which the proposed subscription is made, at such time or times as said chairman and board of trustees or mayor and aldermen of any town, mayor and aldermen or council of any city, or the county court of any county, may by order direct; and should a majority of the qualified voters voting at any such election vote in favor of subscribing stock in said railroad company, the mayor and aldermen or chairman and board of trustees of any town, the mayor and aldermen or council of any city, or county court of any county, to which such vote shall be presented, shall be authorized to make the subscription in the name of their respective towns, cities, or counties, and proceed to have issued the bonds to the amount of such subscription as hereinbefore directed; and the mayor and aldermen or chairman and board of trustees of any town, mayor and council of any city, or the county court of any county, that may subscribe for stock in said railroad company, are hereby authorized and required to levy annually and collect a tax upon the taxable property in their respective towns, cities, and counties, as listed and taxed under the revenue laws of this State, a sum sufficient to pay the interest on said bonds as it accrues, together with the cost of collecting the same. They are also authorized and required to make provision for paying said bonds at their maturity; and to enable them to do this, they may establish a sinking fund, and loan out the same at any rate of interest they can obtain, and, if necessary, collect the same by law, or may adopt such other means as to them may seem proper and expedient, and may levy and collect taxes annually or otherwise on the property aforesaid for this purpose. The person collecting said tax shall give tax receipts for the same; and any tax-payer paying tax to said road under the provisions of this act, shall be entitled to stock in said railroad company to the amount of taxes he may pay, and the towns, cities, and counties under whose subscription the tax is levied shall be divested of stock to the extent of stock issued on said tax receipts; and whenever such receipts to the amount of one share or more shall be presented to the company, or an officer or agent designated by it, a certificate of stock shall be issued to the holder and owner of the receipt; but no certificates shall be issued for a fractional part of a share: *Provided*, That the said towns, cities, and counties shall receive no dividends on their stock, but the holders of stock issued on said receipts as aforesaid shall be entitled to the same dividends, and to all the rights and privileges, as original and cash stockholders: *And provided further*, That said company may, in any way that may seem expedient to it, provide for pay, each or any year, to the towns, cities, and counties, or any of them, the amount of tax levied by reason of said bonds, and thus stop the collection of the tax for that year: *And provided further*, That the company may purchase said bonds and surrender them at any time to the towns, cities, and counties issuing them, and have the same canceled; and the mayor and aldermen or chairman and board of trustees of any town, or the mayor and aldermen or council of any city, or the county court of any county, may appoint collectors for said tax, or may require the sheriffs or marshals of the counties, cities, or towns to collect the same, all of whom shall have the same powers and remedies, and shall proceed in the same way for the collection of said tax, as the sheriffs in the collection of the State revenue. The mayor and aldermen or chairman and board of trustees shall require and take from the person collecting the tax a bond, with sufficient sureties, conditioned as they may think best. If the collections are made by the sheriff or marshal, they shall settle and pay over the tax at the same times that sheriffs are required to pay the State revenue; and for their services in collecting, they shall in no case be allowed more than three per cent. commission on the amount collected.

§ 16. All acts or parts of acts inconsistent with this act are hereby repealed.

§ 17. That this act shall take effect from and after its passage, the General Assembly reserving the right to alter, amend, or repeal this act.

Approved January 29, 1869.

────

CHAPTER 1355.

AN ACT to amend the Charter of the Town of Bardstown.

Be it enacted by the General Assembly of the Commonwealth of Kentucky:

§ 1. That the charter of the town of Bardstown, in the county of Nelson, be, and the same is hereby, amended as follows, to-wit: All real estate within the corporate limits of said town, upon which the taxes imposed by the authorities of said town are due, or may become due, and in arrears for six months, may be sold publicly by the marshal or other collector of taxes for said town, or so much thereof as may be necessary for the purpose of the payment of said taxes, including the costs of sale. The time and place of sale being advertised by written or printed bills at least twenty days before sale; the sale to be made upon the premises, and the officer making the sale shall convey the property thus sold to the pur-

chaser, subject to redemption within five years from the
day of sale by the owner, his heirs, assigns, or legal representatives, upon paying the purchaser the amount of
his bid, including costs of sale and twenty per cent. per
annum thereon.

§ 2. The board of trustees of said town shall have
power to tax and license all omnibuses and other vehicles
run in said town for pay or hire.

§ 3. The board of trustees of said town are hereby
authorized. to subscribe stock to the amount of three
thousand dollars, to aid in the building of a turnpike
road from Bardstown to Bloomfield, in said county; and
for the purpose of paying said stock, may levy a tax
upon the real and personal estate in said town subject
to tax for the uses and purposes of said town, not exceeding twenty-five cents on each hundred dollars of the
value of property for any one year; and may borrow the
money to pay said stock; and through their chairman or
other authorized agent, may execute their bonds therefor, bearing interest not exceeding eight per centum per
annum.

§ 4. This act to take effect from its passage.

Approved January 29, 1869.

CHAPTER 1356.

AN ACT to incorporate the Mutual Aid Society of the Employes of the
Louisville and Nashville Railroad Company, of Louisville, Kentucky.

*Be it enacted by the General Assembly of the Commonwealth
of Kentucky:*

§ 1. That the Mutual Aid Society of the Employes of
the Louisville and Nashville railroad company, be, and
the same is hereby, created a body corporate and politic;
and under this charter shall have and possess all the
powers usually granted to such corporations.

§ 2. The said society shall have the right to sue and be
sued, plead and be impleaded, in any court of competent
jurisdiction under the laws of this State; shall purchase
and hold any and all property, real, personal, and mixed,
necessary to the pursuit of the object of their business.

§ 3. The incorporators, viz.: Jeremiah Kavanach, Jos.
Shallcross, N. B. Thompson, Joel Henry, G. B. Kiteley,
and their associates and successors, shall make and ordain
all the needful rules and by-laws for the government of
the said Mutual Aid Society, and may break and alter
them at pleasure; they may have a common seal, which
they may break and alter at pleasure.

§ 4. This act shall take effect from and after its passage.

Approved January 29, 1869.

CHAPTER 1357.

AN ACT for the benefit of R. W. Wilson, Clerk of the Crittenden County Court.

Be it enacted by the General Assembly of the Commonwealth of Kentucky:

§ 1. That R. W. Wilson, clerk of the Crittenden county court, be, and he is hereby, relieved from the disabilities and penalties of an act, entitled "An act declaring it unlawful for the presiding judge and clerk of a county court to be appointed executor, administrator, or guardian in the county in which he holds office," approved February 17, 1858, so far as to make it lawful for said R. W. Wilson, clerk of said county court, to qualify in said court as administrator of the estate of his father, James W. Wilson, deceased; and also to qualify as executor of the will of his sister, Mrs. Mary E. Armstrong, deceased, and as guardian of his nieces, M. J. Armstrong, S. F. Armstrong, and J. E. Armstrong.

§ 2. That this act take effect from and after its passage.

Approved January 29, 1869.

CHAPTER 1358.

AN ACT to incorporate the German Roman Catholic St. Aloysius Benevolent Society, of Covington.

Be it enacted by the General Assembly of the Commonwealth of Kentucky:

§ 1. That Louis Schurbus, J. H. Romer, B. Willenbrink, H. Flaute, Henry Nie, and John Seiler, and their successors and associates, be, and they are hereby, created a body-corporate and politic, by the name and style of the "German Roman Catholic St. Aloysius Benevolent Society, of Covington, Kentucky;" and by that name they are hereby invested with power to sue and be sued, to answer and be answered, plead and be impleaded, defend and be defended, in all courts of law and equity in this State; to have perpetual succession; to make, alter, amend, abolish, or change their constitution, and such rules and by-laws and ordinances thereunder, as they see fit, and as they may deem necessary for the good government and management of said corporation, so that they are not incompatible with the Constitution of the United States, the laws of the United States, and the Constitution and laws of the State of Kentucky; to have and use a common seal, and change the same at pleasure; to contract and be contracted with; to purchase, hold, and acquire real and personal estate and property, not exceeding in value fifty thousand dollars; to dispose of the same as their Constitution and by-laws may direct; provide for administering oaths and taking bonds from the officers and employes of the corporation, to secure the faithful discharge of their duties.

§ 2. Within three months from the passage of this act said society shall go into operation as an incorporated body by complying with this act and the constitution and by-laws of said society. Said corporators can call meetings of said society at any time to elect members, receive membership, and do and perform all things necessary and proper to be done to carry out and effectuate the purposes of said association.

§ 3. This act shall take effect from and after its passage.

Approved January 29, 1869.

CHAPTER 1359.

AN ACT to incorporate the Stone-masons' Benevolent Society, of Covington.

Be it enacted by the General Assembly of the Commonwealth of Kentucky:

§ 1. That Henry Kuhlman, Henry Dreier, Charles Keller, Simon Wehr, and their associates and successors, be, and they are hereby, created a body-politic and corporate, by the name and style of the Stone-masons' Benevolent Society, of Covington, Kentucky, with succession for thirty years; and by their corporate name may sue and be sued, plead and be impleaded, in all courts of law and equity in this State and elsewhere; may have a common seal, and the same may alter at pleasure; shall be capable of holding personal property and real estate, by purchase, gift, or devise, not exceeding ten thousand dollars in value, and may sell, dispose of, and convey the same; and they shall have power to form and ratify a constitution; to adopt by-laws for the government of said corporation, and to carry out the ends and objects of said corporation; to sue and recover from the members all fees, dues, and moneys owing to the same; together with all powers necessary for the efficient management of its concerns.

§ 2. The Legislature retains the right to repeal, alter, or amend said act of incorporation at pleasure.

§ 3. This act to take effect from its passage.

Approved January 29, 1869.

CHAPTER 1360.

AN ACT to incorporate the General Building Association, of Covington.

Be it enacted by the General Assembly of the Commonwealth of Kentucky:

§ 1. That F. Tieke, F. Fisher, C. Winston, L. Schneider, L. Breaker, George Welling, F. Kohl, J. Rehfuss, H. Wenzel, H. Schleutker, C. Koch, J. Hempel, A. Albrecht, and C. Rosenthal, and their successors in office, be, and they are hereby, created a body-corporate and politic, by the name and style of the General Building Association, of Covington, in the county of Kenton; and by that name have perpetual succession, and be, in law, capable to sue and be sued, plead and be impleaded, in all courts; may have a common seal, the same alter, change, or renew at pleasure.

§ 2. The object of this association shall be to form a capital, for the use of the members of this association, by weekly contribution or imposts, to aid them in purchasing lots, building houses, or starting them in business; said contributions may be enlarged from time to time, but shall not, at any time, exceed, in the aggregate, one hundred thousand dollars on hand at any one time; and may purchase and hold real estate for an office and other purposes of this association not to exceed six thousand dollars.

§ 3. The officers of this association shall be a president, vice president, first and second secretary, treasurer, and nine directors, and such other officers as the association may provide for in their constitution and by-laws. The association shall have right to enact such by-laws, from time to time, for the government of this association, as they may deem proper, not inconsistent with the Constitution and laws of the United States and the Constitution and laws of the State of Kentucky; and have the right to repeal or alter them at pleasure; to require such bonds of its financial officers as may be deemed safe and prudent. The officers to be chosen in the manner, and to hold their offices for the terms and under such restrictions, as may be prescribed by the by-laws of the association.

§ 4. This act to take effect from and after its passage.

Approved January 29, 1869.

CHAPTER 1362.

AN ACT to incorporate the St. Leopold's German Roman Catholic Benevolent Society, of Louisville.

*Be it enacted by the General Assembly of the Commonwealth
of Kentucky:*

§ 1. That Urban Stengal, John Boes, T. T. Wiesemann,
and Lewis Kissel, and their associates and successors, be,
and they are hereby, created a body-corporate and politic,
and by the name and style of the St. Leopold's German
Roman Catholic Benevolent Society, of Louisville; and
by that name shall be known; and shall have the right to
contract and be contracted with, plead and be impleaded;
of purchasing and holding real estate sufficient for benevolent purposes, and dispose of the same at pleasure; to
have a common seal, and have the right to alter the same
at pleasure; to make their own constitution and by-laws,
and to alter and amend the same whenever they see proper or deem necessary for the good of their society; nothing,
however, to be in conflict with the Constitution of the
United States or the State of Kentucky.

§ 2. The above named corporators shall be the first
board of managers, select therefrom their officers, and to
remain in office until others are elected and qualified according to the rules laid down in their constitution and
by-laws.

§ 3. This society shall have the power to levy and collect such fees for membership, and such stated dues thereafter, to be paid by its members, and at such times of
payment, as may be fixed by its constitution or by-laws;
and shall also have the right to prescribe its own mode of
paying out or loaning out its surplus funds, or to invest
the same in such other manner as it may deem profitable,
but not to exercise banking privileges.

§ 4. The object of the society is that the members, by
paying an admission fee, and by paying monthly dues,
fines, &c., create a treasury for the support of sick and
unfortunate members of the society; and, in case of death,
to help their widows and children, according to the constitution of the society.

§ 5. This act to take effect and be in force from and
after its passage.

Approved January 29, 1869.

CHAPTER 1363.

AN ACT to incorporate the Henry County Agricultural and Mechanical Association.

Be it enacted by the General Assembly of the Commonwealth of Kentucky:

§ 1. That I. N. Webb, Joseph Brinker, A. B. Smith, Dr. L. E. Brown, Chilton Scott, J. P. Smith, Frank Troutman, Joseph Pryor, R. L. Ricketts, L. H. Corbin, Richard Webb, Dr. —— Wilson, James P. Ellis, their associates, successors, and assigns, be, and they are hereby, created a body-politic and corporate, with perpetual succession, under the name and style of the Henry County Agricultural and Mechanical Association; and by that name may contract and be contracted with, sue and be sued, plead and be impleaded, with all persons or corporations, and in all courts and places in this Commonwealth; may procure, own, and hold real estate, not exceeding one hundred acres in quantity, and personal estate, not exceeding in value twenty thousand dollars, and may sell, convey, or otherwise dispose of the same, or any part thereof, at pleasure.

§ 2. The capital stock of said association shall not exceed thirty thousand dollars, which shall be divided into shares of twenty-five dollars each, which shall be deemed personal property, and be transferable on the books of said company.

§ 3. The persons hereinbefore named, or any three of them, may assume the control of the books already opened for the subscription of stock, and continue the same open, for the purpose of receiving subscriptions of stock to said association, under such regulations as they may prescribe; and all subscriptions heretofore, as well as hereafter, made to this association, are hereby declared valid.

§ 4. When stock to the amount of five thousand dollars shall have been subscribed, said persons so in charge of said books for the subscription of stock shall call a meeting of the stockholders, to be held in the town of New Castle, for the election of officers and the permanent organization of the association. Notice of said meeting shall be published for at least ten days anterior to said meeting.

§ 5. At such meeting, and annually thereafter, on the first Saturday in May, the stockholders shall elect a president, vice president, and a board of nine directors, who shall hold their offices for one year, and until their successors are elected. In all such elections, each share of stock in the association shall entitle the holder to one vote.

§ 6. The fiscal, prudential, and other affairs of said association, shall be under the control and management of the president and directors. Said board may fill vacancies in their number which occur between the annual meetings; may appoint a secretary, treasurer, and such other officers, agents, and assistants as they may deem proper, and may require bond and surety from them for the faithful performance of their duties, which bonds shall be valid and binding in law as "official bonds;" may make all needful and proper by-laws, rules and regulations, for the government and management of the said association, not inconsistent with the provisions of this act or with the Constitution and laws of the State of Kentucky.

§ 7. The president or vice president, and a majority of the board of directors, shall be a quorum to do business, and shall have power to make calls for the payment of the stock subscribed, at such times and in such amounts as they may deem proper; and in default of payment, for twenty days after notice of such call, they shall have power to declare the stock so subscribed and not paid forfeited to the company.

§ 8. The president and board of directors shall keep a record of all by-laws and resolutions, as also all their proceedings, which shall be open to the inspection of all persons interested.

§ 9. No spirituous liquors shall, directly or indirectly, during the continuance of any fair of said association, be sold upon the grounds used for such fair, nor shall any such liquor, during such fair, be sold upon any field, lot, lane, street, or road adjoining to or within one mile of the same, under the penalty of fifty dollars for each and every such offense, to be recovered by warrant before any magistrate of Henry county or police judge of the town of New Castle; and each separate act of selling shall be a distinct offense; all fines so imposed shall vest in and belong to said association.

§ 10. Any person who shall wager any sum of money or other thing upon any exhibition of the association, or upon cards or other game of chance, within the inclosure of their grounds, or shall enter their grounds with any concealed deadly weapon upon his person, except for the purpose of necessary self-defense, shall, upon conviction thereof before any justice of the peace in Henry county or the police judge of the town of New Castle, be fined in any sum not exceeding twenty-five dollars, one half to go to the informer, the other to the association.

§ 11. This act to be in force from its passage.

Approved January 29, 1869.

CHAPTER 1364.

AN ACT to incorporate Pleasant Ridge Institute, in Boone County.

Be it enacted by the General Assembly of the Commonwealth of Kentucky:

§ 1. That Caleb Carpenter, Thos. Utly, Stanton Aylor, Lewis Aylor, and William Cochran, and their successors, be, and they are hereby, created a body-politic and corporate, by the name and style of the Pleasant Ridge Institute; and by that name shall have perpetual succession; may contract and be contracted with, sue and be sued, plead and be impleaded, in all courts and places; have a common seal, and alter and break the same at pleasure; may make all necessary by-laws for the transaction of the business and government of said company, not inconsistent with the laws of the State or United States.

§ 2. The capital stock of said company or institute shall be divided into shares of twenty-five dollars, subscribed and paid for in such manner as said board of directors may, by its by-laws, prescribe.

§ 3. The stockholders of said institute shall annually elect a president, secretary, treasurer, and five directors, who shall hold their offices for one year, or until their successors are duly elected. Said elections shall be held on the first Saturday in April of each year.

§ 4. Said election shall be held at the school buildings; all voting shall be by ballot, and the individual receiving the highest number of votes cast shall be declared elected to the office for which he was voted for. The secretary shall superintend and hold each election, and make known the result.

§ 5. Any vacancy that may occur in any of the offices by death, resignation, or removal, or refusal to act, shall be filled by the remaining directors for the unexpired time.

§ 6. The board of directors, when so elected, shall have power, and it is here made their duty, to open a book for the subscription of stock to said institute; said shares of stock shall be divided into twenty-five dollars each; and when seventy-five shares are so subscribed, said book shall be considered closed, and they shall receive no further subscription; which said sums so subscribed and paid, shall be used by said directors for the benefit of said institute in such manner as a majority of the directors, so elected as aforesaid, may think best.

§ 7. The board of directors may receive donations of money or property for the purpose of assisting in the erection of school buildings, for the purchase of libraries, chemical apparatus, for the employment of teachers, or for other purposes connected with said institute.

§ 8. They may purchase lands not exceeding ten acres, joining or near to the present school buildings of Pleasant Ridge, and lay out grounds to commence and carry on a school for the advancement of education.

§ 9. That the officers herein declared to be elective, shall be elected by the stockholders of said company, and none others shall be legal voters; and each stockholder shall be entitled to one vote for each share of stock.

§ 10. That said board of directors shall have full power to hold and control, for the purposes aforesaid, the land heretofore deeded, viz: 21st day of April, 1866, by William A. Tanner and M. C. Tanner, for school purposes, known as Pleasant Ridge school-house and lands, situated on the turnpike from Union to Florence, in Boone county, containing one acre and eight poles.

§ 11. Said directors shall have the full control and management of the school and all property belonging thereto.

§ 12. It shall be the duty of the president to preside at all meetings of the directory, and perform such other duties as may be assigned by the by-laws of said company. It shall be the duty of the secretary to keep a faithful record of all proceedings had, and perform such other duties as may be required of him by the by-laws. It shall be the duty of the treasurer to collect and receive all money connected with said institute, and pay same out by order of the directory.

§ 13. The said company, when fully organized, shall cause a book to be opened, subject to the inspection of any member of the board or stockholder, which shall contain the names of all the stockholders of said company, and the number of shares owned by each; and the said shares may be transferred on said books in the manner to be prescribed by the by-laws of said company.

§ 14. That nothing herein contained shall be construed into conferring banking privileges upon said company.

§ 15. This act shall take effect from and after its passage.

Approved January 29, 1869.

CHAPTER 1365.

AN ACT to amend the Charter of the Foster Turnpike Road Company.

Be it enacted by the General Assembly of the Commonwealth of Kentucky:

§ 1. That the board of directors of the Foster turnpike road company shall have the right and power to extend said road to Powersville via the Willow Meeting-house, also to the Ohio river; and, in the making of said exten-

sions, shall have all the powers, rights, and privileges that
they have relative to the original road.

§ 2. That the president and directors shall have the power and privilege to put any distance of said extension under contract, whenever they shall have enough stock taken to complete any one mile or fraction thereof, to the lowest and best bidder.

§ 3. That all persons residing within one fourth of a mile of the said original road, on either side thereof, shall be laid off by the road commissioner of Bracken county into a road district, and all persons liable under the road laws of said county to pay road taxes, or labor on the public roads or highways in said county within the bounds of said original turnpike road; shall be paid to the treasurer of, and laid out in the repairs of, said turnpike road, under the same laws governing county roads, under the direction of the president of said road: *Provided, however*, That James Hannah, C. Hannah, A. H. Hannah, W. Barnes, and P. Quinlin, shall not be included in said boundary.

§ 4. This act shall take effect from and after its passage.

Approved January 29, 1869.

CHAPTER 1367.

AN ACT for the benefit of J. C. Calhoun, Sheriff of McCracken County.

Be it enacted by the General Assembly of the Commonwealth of Kentucky:

§ 1. That J. C. Calhoun, sheriff of McCracken county, be released from the payment of the damages upon a judgment rendered against said Calhoun and sureties for the revenue due from the county of McCracken for the year 1867, said Calhoun having paid the principal, interest, and costs of said judgment.

§ 2. This act shall take effect from its passage.

Approved February 1, 1869.

CHAPTER 1369.

AN ACT to incorporate the Brick-layers' Union, No. 2, of Covington.

Be it enacted by the General Assembly of the Commonwealth of Kentucky:

§ 1. That J. B. Eblen, President, Henry Moore, Vice President, A. J. Abbott, Recording Secretary, E. L. Duelle, Financial Secretary, Henry Overnane, Treasurer, J. P. Jolly, B. Pugh, and A. Ambrose, Trustees, and their associates and successors, be, and they are hereby, constituted a body corporate, under the name and style of the Brick-layers' Union, No. 2, of Covington, Kentucky.

§ 2. That said union shall afford relief and assistance to its members in case of sickness, death, or disability, preventing them from work; and also in case of the death of any of its members in good standing, shall assist in providing for the support of the widows and orphans of such members who have not left sufficient estate for that purpose.

§ 3. That said union shall, by the name and style set forth above, have perpetual succession, and be capable of suing and being sued, of defending and being defended, of pleading and being impleaded, of having a common seal, and the same to make, break, or alter at pleasure; to acquire and hold estate real and personal or mixed, and the same to buy, sell, exchange, mortgage. transfer, pledge, or otherwise encumber or alienate, as the union may deem expedient; and the said union shall be capable in law of receiving, holding, selling, and transferring all manner of property, whether by donation, bequest, conveyance, or devise: *Provided, however,* The same does not exceed twenty-five thousand dollars in value, and can be used and enjoyed for the purpose mentioned in the second section of this act.

§ 4. That the officers of this union shall be a president, vice president, recording secretary, financial secretary, treasurer, and three trustees, and such other officers as they may deem proper to have, to be elected for such periods and at such times as said union may fix in its by-laws; and said officers are to continue in office till their successors are elected and installed.

§ 5. That said union shall regulate and conduct its affairs by its members, when in session at their regular meetings. Such a number of the members shall constitute a quorum to do business as shall be by the constitution and by-laws of this union designated.

§ 6. That the said union, by its members, shall have power to make such laws for the government of said union as shall seem best calculated to promote the ends and objects of the union. They shall have power to make such laws, from time to time, for the admission of members, for the imposing of fines and otherwise, or for any other purpose connected with the government of the association, with reference to the members thereof, or the duties of said union: *Provided, however,* That said laws shall not be repugnant to the Constitution and laws of the State of Kentucky or of the United States.

§ 7. This charter shall expire at the end of fifty years, unless renewed, and the property, if any there be belonging to said union, shall not be divided among its members while seven are dissenting therefrom.

§ 8. This act to take effect from its passage.

Approved February 1, 1869.

CHAPTER 1370.

AN ACT to charter the St. Patrick's Benevolent Society, of Newport.

Be it enacted by the General Assembly of the Commonwealth of Kentucky:

§ 1. That Wm. McNamara, Patrick Walsh, Richard Barrett, Dennis Garigan, and Thomas M. Griffiths, their associates and successors, be, and they are hereby, created a body-politic and corporate, by the name and style of the "Saint Patrick's Benevolent Society," of the city of Newport; and by that name may sue and be sued, answer and be answered, and may make and ordain such laws, rules and regulations, for the government of said society, not inconsistent with the Constitution and laws of this State, as they may see fit, and alter, amend, or change the same at pleasure: *Provided,* That the said society shall not exercise any banking privileges.

§ 2. The General Assembly reserves the right to alter, amend, or repeal this act at pleasure; and this act shall be in force from its passage.

Approved February 1, 1869.

CHAPTER 1371.

AN ACT for the benefit of the Sureties of James Bartley, late Sheriff of Monroe County.

WHEREAS, Judgment was rendered by the Franklin circuit court against James Bartley and his securities on his revenue bond for the collection of taxes in Monroe county for the year 1867, said judgment being rendered for principal, interest, damages, and cost; and whereas, said securities have paid the entire principal, interest, and cost; therefore,

Be it enacted by the General Assembly of the Commonwealth of Kentucky:

§ 1. That the said securities of James Bartley be, and they are hereby, released from the payment of all the unpaid damages in the aforesaid case

§ 2. This act shall be in force from and after its passage.

Approved February 1, 1869.

CHAPTER 1372.

AN ACT for the benefit of C. T. Cheek.

Be it enacted by the General Assembly of the Commonwealth of Kentucky:

§ 1. That the Auditor of Public Accounts draw his warrant upon the Treasury in favor of C. T. Cheek for one hundred and twenty dollars, to be paid to him out of any money therein not otherwise appropriated, the same being compensation for his services and money expended in conveying a pauper lunatic to the Eastern Lunatic Asylum under order of court, the said lunatic being rejected for want of room in the institution.

§ 2. This act to take effect from its passage.

Approved February 2, 1869.

CHAPTER 1373.

AN ACT for the benefit of Wm. A. Nisbet.

Be it enacted by the General Assembly of the Commonwealth of Kentucky:

§ 1. That the Auditor of Public Accounts be, and is hereby, directed to draw his warrant on the Treasurer of the State in favor of William A. Nisbet for the sum of two hundred and fifty dollars, compensation and expenses in conveying a lunatic to the asylum, who was rejected for want of room.

§ 2. This act to take effect from its passage.

Approved February 2, 1869.

CHAPTER 1374.

AN ACT for the benefit of Robert McAllister, late Sheriff of Greenup County.

Be it enacted by the General Assembly of the Commonwealth of Kentucky:

§ 1. That Robert McAllister, late sheriff of Greenup county, be released from the payment of the damages upon a judgment rendered against said McAllister and sureties for the revenue due from the county of Greenup for the year 1867, said McAllister having paid into the Treasury the principal, interest, and cost of said judgment.

§ 2. That any part of said damages paid by McAllister into the Treasury shall be credited by the Auditor upon the revenue due from the county of Greenup for the year 1868.

§ 3. This act shall take effect from its passage.

Approved February 2, 1869.

CHAPTER 1375.

AN ACT to incorporate the Bracken and Pendleton Turnpike Road Company.

Be it enacted by the General Assembly of the Commonwealth of Kentucky:

§ 1. That a company is hereby created a body-politic and corporate, under the name and style of the Bracken and Pendleton turnpike road company, for the purpose of constructing an artificial macadamized road from the town of Foster, in Bracken county. via Prebble's cross-roads, to the town of Butler or Boston, in Pendleton county. *(Company incorporated.)*

§ 2. The capital stock of said company shall be twenty thousand dollars, and may be increased to forty thousand dollars, divided into shares of fifty dollars each. *(Capital stock.)*

§ 3. The following commissioners, or such of them as may choose to act, are hereby appointed to receive subscriptions of stock in said company, viz: E. W. Holmes, Geo. G. Watson, Danl. McMath, J. B. Prebble, Jas. J. Bonar, and W. Hannah, who may open books at such times and places as they, or any one of them, may think proper, until all of said stock, or so much as may be necessary to construct said road, be taken. *(Commissioners to open books for the subscription of stock.)*

§ 4. The commissioners shall procure books, in which the stockholders shall enter into the following obligation, to-wit: "We, whose names are hereunto subscribed, promise to pay to the president and directors of the Bracken and Pendleton turnpike road company, the sum of fifty dollars for each and every share of stock set opposite our names, in such proportions, and at such times and places, as the president and directors may require: *Provided,* The calls shall be thirty days apart, and that interest is to be paid on the calls if not paid within thirty days after the calls are made, at the rate of one per cent. per month." *(Obligation of subscribers.)*

§ 5. That the stockholders shall be entitled to one vote for every share of stock held by them; and when any stockholder may be absent, he may vote by proxy in writing. *(Stock; how voted.)*

§ 6. That a president and three directors shall be elected by the stockholders at a public meeting, to be held in the town of Foster, at such time as said commissioners may deem proper; notice of the time of said election to be given by posting up notices at three or more public places along the route of said proposed road, for ten days previous to the election. *(President and directors to be elected.)*

§ 7. That the president, or any two of the directors, may call a meeting of the stockholders or of the directors, at any time he or they may desire or deem it necessary. The president and two directors shall form a quorum, or, *(Called meetings, quorum, &c.)*

1869.

When to com-
mence business

in the absence of the president, the three directors shall form a quorum to transact business; and so soon as fifteen thousand dollars of said stock is subscribed and the company is organized, said company may commence and proceed with the construction of the said road.

May appoint
officers.

Corporate
powers.

§ 8. The board of directors may appoint such officers as they may deem necessary to conduct the business of the company; may have the power to sue and be sued, plead and be impleaded, answer and be answered, defend and be defended, contract and be contracted with; and may make such by-laws as they may deem necessary, which do not conflict with the laws of this State.

Grade of road,
right of way,
&c.

§ 9. The said president and directors shall have the power to fix the grade, locate, build, establish, and complete said road between the points designated, or any two of them, on the most practicable route; and may acquire, by purchase, relinquishment, gift, writ of *ad quod damnum*, deed, or otherwise, the right of way for the road upon the route adopted, and also ground for the toll-houses, not exceeding one acre for each house, and such timber, rock quarries, &c., as may be necessary for the completion and keeping in repair said road, agreeing to pay and paying a reasonable compensation therefor; the road to be thirty-five feet wide, and the part of it graded and covered with rock fourteen feet wide and nine inches deep.

Bracken
and Pendleton
counties may
take stock.

§ 10. That the county courts of Bracken and Pendleton counties may subscribe and hold stock in said company, upon the same conditions as other stockholders, to the amount of one thousand dollars per mile, and in accordance with an act of the General Assembly authorizing and empowering the county courts of Bracken and Pendleton counties to subscribe, take, and hold stock in turnpike roads in said counties.

Term of office,
annual elec-
tions, &c.

§ 11. That the president and directors shall hold their office for the term of one year, excepting the ones first elected; and, after the first election, they shall be elected on the first Monday in May, annually, in the manner provided in the sixth section of this act. They shall keep, or cause to be kept, a fair and just account of all moneys which shall be received by them, and of all moneys by them expended in the prosecution of said work; and all costs, charges, and expenses of said road shall be paid and discharged, and the aggregate amount of the same shall be kept and entered on the books of said company. The

May declare
dividends.

president and directors, at the end of every year after the completion of the road, shall make a dividend of the clear profits, if any, and pay the same to the stockholders on the first Monday in May of each and every year.

When may
contract for
construction of
road.

§ 12. That the president and directors may put five miles of said road under contract for construction, beginning at Foster, whenever ten thousand dollars of capital stock shall have been taken, and the remainder whenever they shall think a sufficient amount of stock is taken to complete said road; and that they may erect a toll-gate upon the same, and charge and collect tolls as now regulated by law.

§ 13. The stock in said road to be transferable, provided said stock is all paid.

Stock transferable.

§ 14. That if any of the stockholders in said road fail to pay their calls when due, shall be liable to suit in any court having jurisdiction.

Stock may be forfeited.

§ 15. That the said corporation shall have the power to do all other acts and things that is necessary to be done to locate, establish, and complete said road.

§ 16. This act to take effect from and after its passage.

Approved February 2, 1869.

CHAPTER 1377.

AN ACT for the benefit of the sureties in the revenue bond of Thomas H. Estis, Sheriff of Hancock County, for the year 1867.

WHEREAS, At the last June term of the Franklin circuit court, a judgment was rendered against Thomas H. Estis, sheriff of Hancock county, and his sureties, for an unpaid balance of the revenue for 1867, which judgment and damages, to the amount of five hundred and seventy-five dollars and eighty-six cents, were paid by said sureties; therefore,

Be it enacted by the General Assembly of the Commonwealth of Kentucky:

§ 1. That the Auditor is hereby directed to draw his warrant upon the Treasurer in favor of J. M. Estis, W. Q. Johnson, R. A. J. Estis, George Smith, and R. C. Beauchamp, sureties of T. H. Estis, sheriff of Hancock county, in his revenue bond for 1867, for the sum of five hundred and seventy-five dollars and eighty-six cents, the amount of damages paid by them on account of the defalcation of said sheriff to the State, to be paid out of any moneys not otherwise appropriated.

§ 2. That this act take effect from its passage.

Approved February 2, 1869.

CHAPTER 1378.

AN ACT to charter the "Building or Accumulating Fund Association," of Newport.

Be it enacted by the General Assembly of the Commonwealth of Kentucky:

§ 1. That Patrick Walsh, Joseph Lowery, Thomas M. Griffiths, B. Dowling, M. C. Walsh, Richard Barrett, John Tocher, and William McNamara, together with their associates, successors, and assigns, or any three of them, be, and are hereby, declared and created a body corporate, by the name and style of "The Building or Accumulating Fund Association," of Newport, Kentucky; and by that name shall have perpetual succession; shall be capable in law to contract and be contracted with, sue and be sued, implead and be impleaded, within all courts of competent jurisdiction; and shall have full power to receive, acquire, possess, use, and hold real estate and personal property suitable to the carrying out of the objects of the association, and the same to use, sell, convey, and dispose of; may have a common seal, and alter the same at their pleasure; may make such constitution and by-laws for the management and conducting of its affairs and business, and for the government of its stockholders, and to regulate their proceedings, expenditures, and incomes, not contrary to the law of the land, and may alter the same at their pleasure.

§ 2. The object of this association shall be to accumulate a fund to be used for building and other purposes.

§ 3. The office for conducting the business of this corporation shall be in the city of Newport, Kentucky.

§ 4. The capital stock of said association shall be five thousand dollars, with power to increase the same to fifty thousand dollars by a vote of a majority of the shareholders, and shall be divided into shares of ($2 50) two dollars and fifty cents each; and the certificate of stock shall be issued in the name of the association, signed by the president, and countersigned by the secretary; but no subscriber of stock shall be deemed accepted or binding on the association until the full amount of said shares shall have been paid to the association by each subscriber to the capital stock.

§ 5. Said association may invest money in real estate, mortgages, or other securities, the rents, interest, and dividends from which shall be applied to defray the expenses of the association, and for reinvestment, unless the board of managers unanimously recommend, and four fifths of the shareholders entitled to vote, vote in favor of appropriating it to other purposes.

§ 6. The affairs of the association shall be under the control and direction of a board of managers consisting of nine members, who shall be elected at the place of business of the association in the city of Newport, by the share-owners, on the first Monday in April, 1869, and on the first Monday in April of each and every year thereafter, to continue in office one year, and until their successors shall be elected and qualified. Said board shall elect from their number a president, a vice president, a secretary, and a treasurer, whose term of office shall expire with that of the board by whom they were elected, or until their successors are duly elected and qualified. They shall fill all vacancies that may occur in their own body during the time for which they were elected; and all acts and contracts of the majority of this board shall be binding on the association; a majority of this board shall be a quorum for the transaction of business.

§ 7. The board of managers shall fix the salary of the president; they shall also elect or appoint (and dismiss at pleasure) such clerks, officers, agents, or servants, as they may deem necessary to conduct the affairs of the association; fix their salaries, prescribe their duties, and, at their option, require and receive bonds, with security, for the faithful performance of their duties. The board of managers shall hold stated meetings at least semi-monthly, and called meetings whenever deemed necessary; and shall keep a full and complete record of their proceedings; they shall have power to make and change all necessary by-laws, rules and regulations, for the government of the association.

§ 8. At every meeting of the shareholders, each shareholder shall be entitled to one vote for every share of stock held by him, and shareholders may vote by written proxy; but no shareholder shall be entitled to a vote at any meeting of the shareholders unless all his taxes, dues, &c., have been paid; and at all meetings for the election of a board of managers, a majority of the votes cast shall be necessary to elect.

§ 9. No person shall be eligible as a candidate to serve as one of the board of managers unless he hold five shares of the stock of the association, and has fulfilled all obligations imposed on him by the government of the association.

§ 10. Shareholders shall not be personally liable for the debts of the association beyond the amount which may be due and unpaid upon the shares held by them respectively.

§ 11. The shares in this association shall be liable and holden for all assessments legally made thereon; and upon the non-payment of such assessments, or any part thereof, by the owners of such shares, within the time fixed therefor, the treasurer may proceed, in the manner fixed in the by-laws of this association, to advertise and sell such delinquent shares, or so much thereof as shall be necessary to pay the sum due thereon, and incidental expenses.

§ 12. Any of the chartered members of this corporation may, at any time after the passage of this act, open books for subscription of shares of the association, at such place or places as may he deemed necessary. Said books shall remain open until two hundred shares are subscribed for and paid, when the association shall be competent to transact all kinds of business which it is established for.

§ 13. That in no case shall said corporation exercise any banking or other privileges not plainly and fairly indicated by this act.

§ 14. This act to take effect from its passage.

Approved February 2, 1869.

CHAPTER 1379.

AN ACT to amend an act, entitled "An act to incorporate the Versailles and McCracken's Mill Turnpike Road Company."

Be it enacted by the General Assembly of the Commonwealth of Kentucky:

§ 1. That so much of the act, entitled "An act to incorporate the Versailles and McCracken's Mill turnpike road company," approved March 9th, 1868, be, and the same is hereby, so amended as to authorize and permit the president, directors, and company of said road to construct the same in width not exceeding thirty-five feet, not more than twenty feet of which shall be graded for the reception of the metal.

§ 2. This act to take effect from its passage.

Approved February 2, 1869.

CHAPTER 1380.

AN ACT for the benefit of Franklin Lodge, No. 7, I. O. O. F., &c.

Be it enacted. by the General Assembly of the Commonwealth of Kentucky:

§ 1. That Wm. H. Kinnaird, Geo. E. Hackley, N. Sandifer, and James H. Yantis, be, and they are hereby, authorized to convey to their vendees the legal title to a certain house in Lancaster, Kentucky, known as the "Franklin Institute," together with the lot of ground on which it is situated, with its appurtenances, heretofore conveyed to them by Franklin Lodge, No. 7, Independent Order of Odd Fellows; and the conveyance hereby authorized shall vest the full and complete title, in fee simple, clear and free from the provisions contained in the deed from Franklin Institute to Franklin Lodge, No. 7, Independent Order of Odd Fellows, for the same property.

§ 2. That this act shall take effect from its passage.

Approved February 2, 1869.

CHAPTER 1381.

AN ACT declaring Little Sandy River a Navigable Stream.

Be it enacted by the General Assembly of the Commonwealth of Kentucky:

§ 1. That Little Sandy river be, and the same is hereby, declared a navigable stream, from its mouth to the mouth of Jno. Adkins's creek, near the Daniel Horton farm: *Provided*, That the operation of this act shall not be so construed as to warrant the removal of the Argillite mill-dam, in Greenup county; but the same shall remain as now established by law.

§ 2. This act to take effect from and after its passage.

Approved February 2, 1869.

CHAPTER 1382.

AN ACT to amend and reduce into one all the several acts in regard to the town of Foster, in Bracken County.

Be it enacted by the General Assembly of the Commonwealth of Kentucky:

§ 1. That the boundaries of the town of Foster, in Bracken county, shall be the same as now established by law.

Town established.

§ 2. The fiscal, prudential, and municipal concerns of said town, with the government and control thereof, shall be vested in four trustees; three of whom shall form a quorum to do business; all of whom shall be citizens of the town, and shall have residence in said town, and been *bona fide* housekeepers one year next preceding their election, and take an oath, before entering upon the duties of their office, faithfully to perform the same.

Who to manage affairs of town.

§ 3. That said trustees, and their successors in office, shall be a body-politic and corporate, and shall be known by the name and style of the board of Trustees of the town of Foster; and by that name shall be capable in law of contracting and being contracted with, of suing and being sued, of pleading and being impleaded, of defending and being defended, in all courts in this Com-

Corporate powers.

1869.

monwealth; and may use or not use a common seal; and shall be vested with all general power conferred by the laws of this Commonwealth on bodies corporate of like character.

Trustees to be elected, &c.

§ 4. Said trustees shall be elected annually on the third Saturday in March, by the white male inhabitants of said town over the age of twenty-one years, who have been *bona fide* residents of said town for one year next preceding the election. The said trustees shall hold their office for one year, and until their successors shall have been elected and qualified; and shall have power to fill any vacancy which may occur in their own body; but if any trustee, elected at any annual election, shall refuse to qualify, the board shall immediately order another election to supply his place. The election for trustees shall be held at some place provided by the board of trustees in said town, by judges, sheriff, and clerk, to be appointed by the board, and shall be conducted in all respects as elections under the State laws; and the penalties imposed by the election laws of the State shall apply to offenses committed at said elections. The trustees may, from time to time, fix and regulate the time of their regular meetings, and may prescribe the mode in which special meetings may be called.

Police judge and town marshal to be elected.

§ 5. A police judge and town marshal shall be elected by the qualified voters of said town of Foster, on the third Saturday in March, to hold their offices for the term of two years, and until their successors are elected and qualified. The polls of the election of police judge and town marshal shall be certified to by the clerk of the board of trustees as to the result of the election, so far as the election of police judge is concerned, to the Governor of the State, whose duty it shall be to issue a commission for the person elected to the office of police judge, who shall be a judicial officer, to be styled the police judge of the town of Foster, and shall act as chairman of the board of trustees.

Police judge to take oath; his powers, duties, &c.

§ 6. The police judge, before he enters on the duties of his office, shall take an oath before some officer authorized to administer an oath under the laws of this State, to discharge the duties of his said office faithfully and impartially to the best of his ability. The police judge shall have jurisdiction within the limits of said town in any case, civil and criminal, in which justices of the peace have, or may hereafter have jurisdiction, except as a court of inquiry in criminal cases, in which he shall have the jurisdiction now given by law to two justices of the peace, with power, in that particular, to the extent of the county; and shall proceed in like manner as said two justices are required to proceed in criminal

cases. He shall have jurisdiction of all offenses exclusively, arising under the by-laws or ordinances of
said town, and shall have power to enter judgment and
award executions accordingly. It shall be the duty of
said judge to keep a record of his proceedings, a copy
of which shall be evidence, and shall have the same
effect as records of justices of the peace. He shall have
power to issue summons for witnesses, to give evidence
in cases pending before him; and upon their failure to
attend, issue compulsory process to compel their attendance, as in cases of attachment for contempt. He shall
have power to fine and imprison for contempt, provided
said fine shall, in no case, exceed ten dollars, nor imprisonment more than twelve hours. He shall have
power to order the marshal, or other officer authorized
to execute process in his court, to summons a jury in
any case cognizable before him, when a jury would be
required before circuit court or justice of the peace,
and to compel their attendance; shall have the same
power as an examiner of said county in the taking of
depositions, and be governed by the same rules. Said
police judge shall be entitled to the following fees, to-
wit: For a peace warrant, or for a riot, rout, or unlaw- Fees of police
ful assembly or breach of the peace, one dollar; for judge.
issuing a warrant for the violation of the by-laws or
ordinances of said town, or any case where the trustees
are the plaintiffs' benificiary, fifty cents; issuing subpoenas
for witnesses in any case, twenty-five cents; for swearing a jury and presiding over a trial in any case, two
dollars; for taking a recognizance to keep the peace,
upon the application of any person, seventy-five cents,
to be charged to the applicant; all other fees of said
judge shall be the same as those allowed justices of the
peace for like services, and to be collected in the same
way.

§ 7. The police judge of the town of Foster shall have May commit
power to commit all offenders liable to commitment to the offenders to
county jail of Bracken county, and the jailer thereof shall county jail.
receive and keep the same as other prisoners are received
and kept.

§ 8. The police judge shall have power, on all judg- Additional
ments in penal prosecutions or misdemeanors, to issue a powers.
capias pro fine, or cause the same to be replevied forthwith, or commit to the jail of the county or town until
discharged, as now allowed by law for fines and penalties.

§ 9. The police judge shall hold his courts for the trial When to hold
of civil cases on the first Saturday in every month; his court.
court shall be open at all times for the trial of any breach
of the penal and criminal laws or of the ordinances of

said town, and shall hold said trial without regard to the time of service of process, but shall continue from time to time for good cause shown.

§ 10. That upon all judgments by the police judge either **Appeals.** party shall have the right to appeal from said judgment in the same manner, and upon the same terms, appeals are taken from justices of the peace in similar cases.

§ 11. If the office of police judge shall, from any cause, **Vacancy; how** become vacant, the board of trustees shall immediately **filled.** recommend a successor to the Governor of this Commonwealth, who is authorized and empowered to commission for the unexpired term of said police judge.

§ 12. The police judge shall execute bond, with good **[To execute** security, to the board of trustees, for the payment of all **bond.** fines and money that come to his hands, as is now required by law for justices of the peace.

§ 13. That it shall be the duty of the town marshal to **Powers and** attend the sittings of the courts to be held by the police **duties of mar-** judge; to serve all process and precepts, and to collect all **shal, fees, &c.** executions to him directed from the police judge or any court that is authorized to direct the same to him, and make due return thereof, in doing which he may go to any part of the county; he shall collect all taxes due to said town, executions, and other demands which may be put into his hands to collect or execute, and account for and pay over the same to whomsoever may be entitled thereto, under the same rules and regulations required by law of sheriffs in the collection of taxes, and of constables in the collection of executions and other demands; and for failure to perform any of the duties required of him, he shall be subject to the same proceedings had against sheriffs and constables in similar cases. The said marshal shall be entitled to the same fees for collecting the town taxes as the sheriff is allowed for collecting the county levy; and, in all other cases, the same allowed constables for similar services: *Provided, however,* That said police judge shall have power and authority, whenever it is made to appear that it is impracticable, for good cause shown, that the marshal cannot execute his process, to direct the same to the sheriff or any constable of Bracken county: *Provided further,* That the said marshal shall be invested with all the powers and authority which is given to constables in all cases cognizable before said police judge; and before the said town marshal shall proceed to the execution of the duties of his office, he shall take an oath before the board of trustees, to be administered by the chairman or clerk of the board, that he will faithfully and impartially execute the duties of his office, without fear, favor, or affection; and shall also give bond, with good security, to be approved of by the board, in such

penalty as the board of trustees may fix, conditioned for
the faithful discharge of the duties of his office; and upon
which may be liable to motion before the police judge, or
motion or suit in courts having jurisdiction in similar cases
on bonds of constables, for failure to discharge any duty
or to pay over any taxes or money which ought to have
been collected by him.

§ 14. All taxes shall be due and owing from the marshal
on the first day of September each and every year, at
which time, or the first regular meeting of the board of
trustees in said month, he shall make a full settlement,
and be prepared with the delinquent list to be presented
to the board for allowance.

§ 15. The board of trustees shall have power to appoint
a clerk, who shall keep, in a fair and legible hand, a true
record of all the proceedings of the board, in a book kept
for that purpose, and shall also register in a separate book
all the ordinances and by-laws which may be adopted by
the board. Said clerk may be removed at the pleasure of
the board. The board of trustees shall allow him a reasonable compensation for his service.

§ 16. It shall be the duty of the trustees, at the first
meeting after the annual election, or as soon thereafter as
possible, to appoint an assessor, who, after being first
sworn faithfully to discharge the duties of his office, shall
call upon the owners of taxable property in said town, or
their agents, and make out a true list of their taxable
property, real and personal, with the value thereof, and
this shall be made upon the oath of the tax-payer or his
agent. If there is property owned in said town by non-
residents thereof, the said assessor shall cause the same to
be valued by two respectable citizens of said town competent to affix the value, and return the valuation thereof.
If the assessor should not be satisfied with the value fixed
by the tax-payers, he may call upon two or more persons
to give their estimation of the value thereof, who shall be
sworn by the said assessor; and said assessor shall affix
the true value from all the evidence, and return the same.
Said list embraces all the real and personal estate in said
town; and if any shall refuse to give in such list, he or
she shall be also double taxed on the value of their property, to be ascertained by the assessor on information.
Said assessor shall be paid by said trustees, out of the revenues of the town, for his services, such sum as may be
deemed by them reasonable.

§ 17. The trustees shall have power to levy a poll-tax
of not exceeding two dollars and fifty cents upon each
male adult inhabitant of the town, and an ad valorem tax
of not more than fifty cents on each one hundred dollars
of taxable property in said town. The trustees shall

1869.

*When taxes
due from mar-
shal.*

*Clerk to be
appointed; and
his duties.*

*Assessor; his
duties.*

*May levy taxes,
&c.*

1869.

have power to tax all theatrical performances, shows, and exhibitions within the limits of said town, in any sum not more than ten dollars in any one day for each performance, show, or exhibition. They may collect reasonable wharfage from all crafts landing at the public landing of said town.

Duties of collector.

§ 18. That it shall be the duty of the collector to collect all taxes which may be placed in his hands, and pay the same over to the treasurer, and make out and return to the trustees, within four months after the list shall have been placed in his hands for collection, a report of the amount collected and the names of the delinquents, and the amount due from each; whereupon, the board of trustees shall have power, and it shall be their duty, to make an order commanding and requiring the collector to levy upon so much of the delinquent's property, either personal or real, or both, as may be sufficient to pay and satisfy the amount of the tax and cost that may be due; and, in pursuance of which order, the collector shall make the said levy; and after having advertised the said property for sale at three places in said town, for at least five days, shall, thereupon, proceed to sell, at some public place in said town, so much as may be necessary to pay the tax and cost due thereon to the highest and best bidder, to whom the said collector shall give a certificate of purchase, upon his paying the amount bid, which certificate shall entitle the purchaser, his heirs or assigns, to demand from and receive of the board of trustees a deed of conveyance of the property described in said certificate, warranting alone against themselves, at any time after one year from the time of sale, unless the owner or owners thereof shall have redeemed the same by paying or tendering to the purchaser and giving notice to said trustees of the payment or tender of the amount of said purchase money and cost, with one hundred per cent. thereon, and the purchaser in all cases paying the expense of making the conveyance; and the trustees shall have a lien on all property in said town, both real and personal, for the tax; and the collector shall have the power to levy and sell personal property for tax without an order from the justices prior to the time appointed for him to return his delinquent list: *Provided, however,* That non-residents of the county or State shall have two years to redeem in, under the same regulations as provided for others, with the addition of one hundred per cent. more if not redeemed the first year.

Collector may be appointed, &c.

§ 19. That if, for any reason, the board of trustees may not think proper to intrust the marshal with the collection of the taxes or other revenues of the town, or the said marshal shall be unable to perform that duty, they shall

have the power to appoint a collector, who shall have full
power and authority to perform all the duties required of
the marshal in the collection of the taxes and other revenues of the town.

§ 20. The board of trustees of said town shall require
all vendors of spirituous, vinous, or malt liquors, within
the corporate limits of said town, to pay a tax of not less
than one hundred dollars, nor more than two hundred and
fifty dollars per annum. and obtain a license, the tax to be
paid to the treasurer of said town in advance of opening their house.

May tax ven-
dors of liquors,
&c.

§ 21. That no license shall be given by the county court
of Bracken county to keep a tavern within the corporate
limits of the town of Foster, to sell spirituous, vinous, or
malt liquors, until the applicant for such license shall first
have obtained the consent of the trustees of said town,
and shall produce to the court the written permission of
the board of trustees of the town. The party or parties
obtaining a license to keep a tavern shall, in addition to
the tax paid by law, pay to the board of trustees a sum
not less than one hundred dollars nor more than one hundred and fifty dollars, to be fixed by the by-laws of the
board of trustees. Any person who shall violate the provisions of this or the preceding section shall, for every
offense, be liable to pay a fine of fifty dollars, which may
be recovered by proceedings in the name of the Commonwealth of Kentucky, for the use [of] the board of trustees
of the town of Foster.

How license
to keep tavern,
&c., to be ob-
tained.

§ 22. The board of trustees may appoint a street commissioner, who may be removed at any time and another
appointed.

Street com-
missioner.

§ 23. The police judge shall have jurisdiction as specified in section six of this act, and all fines inflicted before
him shall be for the use of the board of trustees of the
town of Foster. All warrants for the breaches of the by-
laws and ordinances shall run in the name of the board
of trustees of the town of Foster; and all other warrants
in the name of the Commonwealth of Kentucky.

Jurisdiction
of police judge,
&c.

§ 24. The marshal shall be, by virtue of his office, supervisor of the public streets and alleys of the town.

Marshal to be
supervisor of
streets.

§ 25. The board of trustees shall have power to pass or
adopt all needful by-laws and ordinances for the due and
efficient administration of right and justice in said town,
and for the good government thereof; may legislate on all
subjects which the peace, order, and comfort of said town
may require. unless restrained by the terms of this charter
or the Constitution and laws of this State. They may
affix such penalties for a violation of any of their by-laws
or ordinances, not exceeding fifty dollars in each case, as
they may deem the good government of said town shall
require. All new ordinances of said town shall be writ-

May make by-
laws, &c.

ten out in a fair legible hand, and posted at two or more public places in said town. The board of trustees shall also have power to declare what are nuisances, and abate the same; and for any willful neglect of the police judge or marshal to enforce said ordinances, or any of them, they, or either of them, may be proceeded against in the circuit court, by indictment, and fined any sum not exceeding one hundred dollars, at the discretion of the jury.

§ 26. The board of trustees shall have power to provide for the improvement of the public streets and alleys of said town, to close any they deem useless; to close up Grace street south of Third alley, and establish the Foster turnpike road as a continuation of Grace street to the corporation line; the enlargement, extension, and improvement of the public landings, and the proper drainage of said town; they may cause to be planted upon the public streets suitable shade trees; and any person or persons who shall injure or destroy any shade tree upon the public streets, shall be subject to a fine of twenty-five dollars, to be recovered by warrant before the police judge, and enforced as other fines are enforced. They shall have power to require the owner or owners of any lot to make a brick or stone sidewalk in front thereof: *Provided, however,* The corporation shall first grade and set the curbstone not less than four feet wide, and of such grade as the trustees shall direct; and if, after a written notice of not less than three months, served upon such owner, he, she, or they shall fail to have said sidewalk made in pursuance of said notice, the said trustees shall cause the same to be done at the expense of the owner, and shall have a lien upon said lot for the amount of said expense, which may be enforced by suit in the Bracken circuit court in the name of the trustees, and at the cost of the owner; and when several owners of lots are in default, they may be joined as defendants; and said trustees may, in like manner, cause the sidewalks to be repaired and improved.

§ 27. The board of trustees shall have power to appoint a treasurer, who, before entering upon the duties of his office, shall take the oath of office required of other officers, and shall give bond for such an amount, and with such security, as [the] board of trustees shall approve, conditioned to pay over all moneys that may come into his hands while in office. It shall be his duty to receive all moneys of the town derived from taxes, license, fines, or other services; but shall not pay out or expend the same in anywise, except upon the order of the board of trustees, signed by the chairman. He shall make reports of the condition of the treasury, from time to time, as the trustees may require.

May improve streets & alleys, &c.

Treasurer to be appointed, &c.

§ 28. That the board of trustees shall have power, at any time within one month after the assessor has returned his books, to hear complaints, and change or reduce or correct the tax list of any person; and in case of a reduction, if the person has paid his tax to order, the proper proportion thereof to be refunded.

§ 29. The trustees shall have power, especially, in addition to the other powers granted by this charter—1st. To establish, erect, and keep in repair culverts and sewers, and regulate the use of the same. 2d. To provide for lighting the streets. 3d. To make and repair wharves, and to regulate and fix the rates of wharfage thereat. 4th. To suppress gaming, drunkenness, gambling-houses, and disorderly houses of all kinds. 5th. To provide for the prevention of training horses or exhibiting stallions in the public streets or places of the town. 6th. The board of trustees shall have power to appoint or employ an attorney to prosecute, for and on behalf of the board of trustees, all prosecutions in which the board of trustees may be interested, and, to allow a reasonable compensation thereof.

§ 30. The trustees may cause to be improved, leased, or rented for a term of years the wharf in front of said town, on the Ohio river, in consideration of the repairs of the same.

§ 31. The wharfmaster of said town, for the party or parties leasing or renting the same, is hereby vested, at all times when the same is not promptly paid on demand, to levy and distrain for any wharfage due the town or lessee and his costs upon the boat or craft, and his costs for which wharfage is due and payable, or upon sufficiency of the tackle, furniture, and appurtenances, or any property of the person or persons from whom such wharfage is due; and to advertise and sell the same as in cases on execution; and the board of trustees shall have power, by ordinance and by-laws, to fix the charges in such cases.

§ 32. All male persons residing in said town, over sixteen years of age, are exempt from working roads outside of the corporation of said town, but shall be required to perform two days' labor on the public streets and highways of said town.

§ 33. The board of trustees shall have power, if the office of marshal shall become vacant, by removal, resignation, or any other cause, to appoint another to fill the unexpired term; or if he should fail to qualify after election, to fill the vacancy.

§ 34. All ordinances passed by the board or by-laws shall go into effect in ten days after their passage, unless declared by the board to take effect at an earlier date.

§ 35. The trustees shall have the power to levy a special tax not exceeding fifty cents on the one hundred dollars' worth of taxable property, and a poll-tax not to exceed two dollars and fifty cents on each tithe, to erect a watch-house in said town, with cells therein for the safe-keeping of offenders.

§ 36. That an act approved 9th March, 1868, entitled "An act to prohibit the sale of intoxicating liquors in the town of Foster," be, and the same is hereby, repealed.

§ 37. This act shall take effect from its passage.

Approved February 2, 1869.

CHAPTER 1383.

AN ACT to amend the Charter of the Independence and Big Bone Turn-pike Company.

Be it enacted by the General Assembly of the Commonwealth of Kentucky:

§ 1. That so much of an act, entitled "An act to amend second section of an act, entitled 'An act to incorporate the Independence and Big Bone turnpike road company,'" approved December the 20th, 1865, as requires John Burton's to be made a point on said road, be, and the same is hereby, repealed.

§ 2. This act to take effect from and after its passage.

Approved February 3, 1869.

CHAPTER 1384.

AN ACT to incorporate the "Ford's Mill and Kentucky River Turnpike Company."

Be it enacted by the General Assembly of the Commonwealth of Kentucky:

§ 1. That James P. Ford, John McDonald, Van J. Sellers, Lewis Allen, Christopher Veach, John Furr, Jesse Moore, Ezra Bowman, Fielding Davis, Zack. Ford, sr., Joseph S. Woolfolk, Benjamin Wilson, Benjamin Hawkins, H. M. Sellers, and J. G. Manuel, and their associates and successors, be, and they are hereby, created a body-politic and corporate, under the name and style of the "Ford's Mill and Kentucky River Turnpike Company;" and by this name shall have power to contract and be contracted with, sue and be sued; to have and use a common seal, and to break, renew, and alter the same at pleasure. It shall have all the powers incident to such corporations.

§ 2. That said company is authorized to construct a turnpike or macadamized road in Woodford county, from some point on the Versailles and Munday's ferry turnpike road, or on the Mortonsville and Lexington turnpike road, to either Cummins' ferry or Oregon, on the Kentucky river, and to run near or by Ford's mill.

1869.

§ 3. That the capital stock of said company shall not exceed thirty thousand dollars, to be divided into shares of fifty dollars each; and books for the subscription of stock shall be opened at such places as may be deemed best, under the direction of the persons heretofore named, all of whom are hereby appointed commissioners for the purpose of obtaining subscriptions to the capital stock of said company; and they shall provide a book or books for the subscription of stock, in which they shall cause to be written the obligations of each person subscribing for said stock; and when the president and directors shall be chosen, as hereinafter provided, they shall have full control of said books, and may cause the same to be opened, from time to time, until the entire amount of stock herein mentioned is subscribed.

§ 4. That as soon as a majority of said commissioners shall be of opinion that a sufficient amount of stock is subscribed to justify the commencement of the work on said road, they shall call a meeting of the stockholders, and hold an election for president and seven directors, who shall hold their offices for one year, and until their successors are chosen: *Provided*, That should a vacancy occur, the remaining directors shall fill the same by appointment; and should the offices of all the directors become vacant, any three stockholders may call a meeting to elect their successors. The directors shall have power to appoint a secretary and treasurer, and such other officers and agents as may be deemed necessary, and may remove the same at pleasure; and the treasurer, before he enters upon the discharge of his duties, shall execute a bond, with security, to said company, for the faithful performance of the duties of his office.

§ 5. That said corporation shall have power to acquire, hold, or sell real or personal estate, as the same may be deemed necessary, in the construction of said road, and to do all other acts and things necessary in the exercise of the power herein expressly conferred. They shall also have power to acquire and hold a sufficiency of land on which to erect toll-houses and other necessary buildings.

§ 6. The entire width of said road shall not exceed fifty feet, and the macadamized part thereof shall not exceed thirty feet. The grade-route and location of said road shall be fixed and determined by the Woodford county court (a majority of the justices of the peace of said

county being present and constituting a part of the same):
Provided, That if the persons owning a majority of the
shares of stock subscribed up to the time of the action of
the court shall petition the court to locate the road on one
of the routes mentioned hereinbefore, the court shall select
the route designated in the petition. Whenever three or
more miles of said road shall be constructed, the directors
shall call on two justices of the peace of said county, not
interested in the road, to examine the same, and if they
shall, by a written statement filed in the office of the clerk
of said court, certify that the same is done in a good and
substantial manner, then said company may erect toll-
gates on said road, and may charge and collect from persons traveling on or using said road toll at the rates fixed
in the general laws concerning turnpikes until changed as
hereinafter directed. The county court of Woodford county, composed as aforesaid, may, at any time, and as often
as in its discretion is best, fix a scale of rates of toll for
said road, and may change or alter the same at pleasure.

§ 7. The provisions of the Revised Statutes regarding
turnpike companies, and not inconsistent with the provisions of this act, shall be parts hereof.

§ 8. This act shall be in force from its passage.

Approved February 3, 1869.

CHAPTER 1385.

AN ACT to amend the charter of the Union and Richwood Turnpike
Road Company, in Boone County.

*Be it enacted by the General Assembly of the Commonwealth
of Kentucky:*

§ 1. That the charter of the Union and Richwood turnpike road company, approved March the 4th, 1856, be,
and the same is hereby, so amended as to allow the president and directors of said turnpike road company to erect
upon the line of said road a toll-house and gate before the
completion of four miles of said road, and charge and
collect toll at said gate upon the travel on said road at
the same rates, and under the same regulations, in proportion to the distance of the road fully completed and
traveled, as are now allowed by law upon the Covington
and Lexington turnpike road.

§ 2. This act to take effect from and after its passage.

Approved February 3, 1869.

CHAPTER 1386.

AN ACT to incorporate the Mercer County Agricultural and Mechanical Association.

Be it enacted by the General Assembly of the Commonwealth of Kentucky:

§ 1. That said association is hereby created a body-politic and corporate, with perpetual succession, under the name and style of the Mercer County Agricultural and Mechanical Association.

§ 2. That the provisions of an act, entitled "An act to charter the Springfield Agricultural and Mechanical Association," approved February 18, 1856, so far as applicable, shall be the law and provisions of the association hereby incorporated.

§ 3. Said association shall be capable of acquiring, by purchase or otherwise, land not exceeding fifty acres.

§ 4. The president and directors already chosen shall continue in office until the first Saturday of April, 1869, and until their successors are duly elected and qualified; and upon the first Saturday of April in each year thereafter, there shall be an election of president and directors from among the stockholders, unless the members of the association, by resolution, shall fix upon a different day.

§ 5. A majority of the directors, with their president, shall be a quorum for the transaction of business.

§ 6. That the jurisdiction of the police court of Harrodsburg is hereby extended over the lands and grounds purchased and used by said association; and said police court shall have jurisdiction to try and inflict all penalties for crimes or misdemeanors that may be committed upon said premises; and any person or persons violating any law shall be liable to the same penalties and punishments as by law they are now liable for when committed within the corporate limits of the town of Harrodsburg.

§ 7. The jurisdiction herein given to the police court of Harrodsburg shall be to the same extent that said court now has in the town of Harrodsburg.

Approved February 3, 1869.

CHAPTER 1387.

AN ACT for the benefit of Jos. P. Nuckols, Clerk of the Barren County Court.

Be it enacted by the General Assembly of the Commonwealth of Kentucky:

§ 1. That an act, entitled "An act declaring it unlawful for the presiding judge and clerk of a county court to be appointed executor, administrator, or guardian in the county in which he holds his office," approved February 17, 1858, be, and the same is hereby, so modified as to permit J. P. Nuckols, clerk of the county court of Barren county, to qualify and act as guardian for his daughter, Lulie Nuckols.

§ 2. That this act shall take effect from and after its passage.

Approved February 3, 1869.

CHAPTER 1388.

AN ACT for the benefit of the Hon. W. H. Randall, Judge of the Fifteenth Judicial District.

WHEREAS, The dwelling-house of the Hon. G. Pearl, late judge of the 15th judicial district, was consumed by fire, and with it the books allowed by law, leaving the Hon. W. H. Randall without such books; for remedy whereof,

Be it enacted by the General Assembly of the Commonwealth of Kentucky:

§ 1. That the Secretary of State furnish the Hon. Wm. H. Randall with the public books allowed by law to circuit judges, and the Auditor will draw his warrant on the Treasurer for payment of the same.

§ 2. This act to take effect from its passage.

Approved February 3, 1869.

CHAPTER 1389.

AN ACT for the benefit of the estate of A. H. Buckner, deceased, late Clerk of the Clark Circuit Court.

Be it enacted by the General Assembly of the Commonwealth of Kentucky:

§ 1. That the further time of two years, from and after the passage of this act, is hereby allowed the administrator of A. H. Buckner, deceased, late clerk of the Clark circuit court, within which he may issue and collect the uncollected fee bills of said decedent as clerk aforesaid, and the same shall be distrainable for said time; and there shall be, within said time, the same power for the collection of the same that is granted by existing laws for the collection of fee bills; but said administrator shall be liable to all the penalties imposed by existing laws for the issue and collection of illegal fee bills.

§ 2. This act shall be in force from its passage.

Approved February 3, 1869.

CHAPTER 1390.

AN ACT making the Harrison Democrat a legally authorized Newspaper.

Be it enacted by the General Assembly of the Commonwealth of Kentucky:

§ 1. That the Harrison Democrat is hereby created and made a legally authorized newspaper for the publication of all orders, judgments, or decrees of any court of this Commonwealth, and for the publication of any advertisement of whatever character, now or hereafter required to be made by law; and the said newspaper is given all the privileges which are now given by law.

§ 2. This act to take effect from its passage.

Approved February 3, 1869.

CHAPTER 1391.

AN ACT to adopt Michael Crosby as son and heir of Peter and Ann Kelly.

WHEREAS, Peter and Ann Kelly, of Bowling Green, Kentucky, have taken Michael Crosby, a young infant, to raise as their own child, with desire to adopt him as such, and to confer upon him the right to inherit their estate; therefore,

Be it enacted by the General Assembly of the Commonwealth of Kentucky:

§ 1. That the said Michael Crosby be, and he is hereby, made an heir of said Peter and Ann Kelly, at their death, with all the right of inheritance of their estate as fully and completely as if he were their natural son; and it shall be lawful for the said Peter and Ann Kelly to confer their name of Kelly upon said infant as his surname.

§ 2. This act to be in force from and after its passage.

Approved February 3, 1869.

CHAPTER 1392.

AN ACT for the benefit of George E. Stone and James F. Montgomery.

Be it enacted by the General Assembly of the Commonwealth of Kentucky:

§ 1. That George E. Stone and James F. Montgomery, of Russell county, Kentucky, who being minors, are hereby permitted and authorized to obtain license to practice law in all the courts of this Commonwealth, when they shall have been examined and found qualified according to the present provision and requirements of the Revised Statutes of Kentucky; and all contracts and agreements made by the said parties, or either of them, shall be as valid and binding in law as if they were of full age.

§ 2. That this act shall take effect from and after its passage.

Approved February 3, 1869.

CHAPTER 1393.

AN ACT to amend the Charter of the Shelbyville Railroad Company, and to authorize certain Counties to take Stock in the same.

Be it enacted by the General Assembly of the Commonwealth of Kentucky:

§ 1. That the said company are authorized and empowered to extend their road through the counties of Anderson and Mercer to or near Danville; thence along the most practicable route to the Virginia or Tennessee line, running through or near Lawrenceburg, and through or near Harrodsburg; and the further time of five years from the — day of May, 1871, is given to said company to construct their road to Danville. This amendment, and the other amendments contained in this act, are granted, with the proviso that the present stockholders in said company shall not receive interest in stock on their present stock, but shall, in all respects, be placed upon the same terms and footing with those that may hereafter take stock in said company: It is a further condition of granting these amendments, that no part of the voluntary subscriptions made to the capital stock of said company since the year 1858 shall be collected from those persons who are taxed to pay subscriptions made by the county court of Shelby county under this act. This provision shall also apply to subscriptions made by persons now deceased, whose estates may be taxed in possession of their heirs or devisees.

§ 2. It shall be lawful for that portion of Shelby county embraced in the following described boundary, viz: Beginning at a point on the Louisville and Frankfort turnpike road, at the intersection of the Bagdad and Harrisonville turnpike, at the second toll-gate east of Shelbyville; thence north with said pike to the northern boundary of Clayvillage election precinct (precinct No. 2); thence with said boundary in a western direction to the boundary of Shelbyville election precinct (precinct No. 1); thence running with the boundary of said precinct around its northern line to a stone in the Shelbyville and Eminence turnpike road, near the residence of G. Reed, called the half-way stone; thence in a western direction to a point at which the Westport road crosses Bullskin creek; thence in a straight line to Miller & Cinnamon's store; thence to the Jefferson county line, at a point on said line west of the residence of R. A. Wellman; thence south with said line to a point in the same west of the residence of William Brumley, thence to the intersection of the Shelbyville and Bardstown turnpike road with the Shelby and Spencer county line; thence in an eastern direction with said line to the intersection of Beech creek; thence up said creek, and with its meanders, to the crossing of the Shelbyville and Mt. Eden road, near Salem church; thence in an eastern direction to Beech Creek meeting-house; thence to the Hardinsville election precinct line (precinct No. 8), at or near Daniel Brumley's blacksmith shop; thence with said line in a northern direction to the Louisville and Frankfort turnpike road, and with said road to the beginning; and for the counties of Anderson, Mercer, and Boyle to subscribe to the capital stock of said company as hereafter specified.

§ 3. The portion of Shelby county embraced in the boundary aforesaid may subscribe for any amount of stock, not exceeding three hundred thousand dollars. The county of Anderson may subscribe for any amount of stock not exceeding one hundred and fifty thousand dollars. The county of Mercer may subscribe for any amount of stock not exceeding two hundred and fifty thousand dollars. The county of Boyle may subscribe for any amount of stock not exceeding one hundred and fifty thousand dollars. The subscriptions of the county of Anderson shall be made upon the condition that the said subscriptions shall be made by the said portion of Shelby. The subscriptions of the county of Mercer shall be made upon the condition that the subscriptions shall be made by the county of Anderson and said portion of Shelby. The subscriptions of the county of Boyle shall be made upon the condition that the said subscriptions shall be made by the counties of Anderson and said portion of Shelby. The same shall be subject to further conditions, as follows, viz: That the subscriptions of the county of Anderson shall be expended in the construction of said road through the county of Anderson; the subscription of the county of Mercer shall be expended in the construction of said road south of Lawrenceburg, and the subscription of the county of Boyle shall be expended in the construction of said road south of Harrodsburg. To secure compliance with said conditions, the bonds hereinafter provided for, except the bonds of said portion of Shelby, shall not be delivered until the road shall be completed as far as Shelbyville, and the company shall be ready to begin work upon the sections embraced in the several limits aforesaid. Upon the written application of the president and directors of said company, and of ten tax-payers of any of said counties, the county judge of such county shall, within thirty (30) days thereafter, cause a vote of the legal voters residing in the county, or portion of county to be taxed, to be taken at the several places of voting therein, to ascertain whether the voters of said counties, or portion of Shelby county, are in favor of said subscription; and it shall be the duty of the county judge to cause at least twenty days' notice to be given of the time at which said vote will be taken and of the proposition to be voted upon; and it shall be his duty, in due time, to appoint judges and other officers to conduct said election.   Such elections shall be held as elections for Representatives to the General Assembly, and the returns thereof shall be made within ten days after the election, to the county clerk of the county.

§ 4. At the next term of the county court after the return of said vote, the poll-books shall be examined by the county judge, county clerk, and county attorney, and the result of said vote for and against said subscription shall be entered on the record of said court.

§ 5. If a majority of the votes cast shall be in favor of said subscription, it shall be the duty of the county judge forthwith to cause the subscription to be made in the name of said county, or portion of Shelby county, as the case may be.

§ 6. That where any such subscription to the capital stock of said company shall have been ordered, and the conditions aforesaid complied with, bonds shall be executed in the name of and under the seal of or scroll of said portion of Shelby county, or said counties, as the case may be, in such form and in such amounts; the entire amount of said bonds not to exceed the sum subscribed, and payable at such places, and bearing interest, payable semi-annually, at such rates (not exceeding eight per centum per annum) as the president and directors may elect.   The bonds shall be due and payable twenty years from their date, with the privilege reserved to the said counties to pay them after three years from date.   The bonds shall be signed by the judge of the county court and countersigned by the county clerk.   When so executed, said bonds shall be delivered to the president and directors of said company in payment of said subscription, and they may be by them negotiated, hypothecated, or sold, upon such terms and at such times as may, by said president and directors, be deemed expedient, and may be transferred by indorsement.

§ 7. That when any such subscription shall have been made, it shall be the duty of the county judge and the justices of the peace of the precincts or the counties in which the vote is taken, to levy annually a direct tax upon all the property in such county, or portion of county, subject to taxation for State revenue, to pay the

interest when due, and the principal at maturity; and
they may levy a tax to pay any portion of said bonds
at any time after three years: *Provided*, That no greater
tax than one per cent. shall be levied in any one year,
except to pay the bonds at maturity. The taxes herein
provided to be collected to pay the interest and principal of said bonds, shall be collected by the sheriff, or
such other person as the county judge and justices of
· the peace may designate, who shall execute bond, conditioned that he shall faithfully discharge his duties and
pay over the money collected by him. He shall collect
the tax in pursuance with, and according to, the law for
collecting the revenue, and shall receive such compensation as shall be voted him by the county judge and justices of said counties and said portion of Shelby, not
exceeding three per centum, which amount shall be included in the levy. He shall pay over the taxes to a
treasurer to be appointed by the county judge and justices. The treasurer shall execute a similar bond to that
of the collecting officer, and the compensation allowed
him, not exceeding one per cent., shall also be included
in the levy of taxes. The collecting officer shall execute
to each person a receipt for the amount of taxes paid by
him, which shall be assignable, and when they amount
to fifty dollars or more, shall entitle the holder, upon
presentation to the proper officers of the company, to
certificates of stock at the rate of one share for fifty
dollars, and every multiple of fifty.

§ 8. The said treasurer shall make annual settlement
with the collecting officer, and report the same to the
county court, and the county court shall make annual
settlements with the treasurer.

§ 9. The several counties and portion of counties shall
not vote the stock for which certificates may be issued to
the tax-payers, but the same shall be voted by the individual stockholders.

§ 10. It shall be lawful for the two election precincts in
the county of Boyle, known as precincts Nos. 3 and 4, to
take the stock herein provided to be taken by the whole
county, or they may take less than one hundred and fifty
thousand dollars, and the deficiency may be supplied by
individual subscriptions in said county: *Provided*, That
the said subscriptions shall be expended only as provided
for the county or precinct subscriptions. If from any
cause the said portion of Shelby county should fail to
make a valid subscription, as herein provided, the election precincts known as precincts Nos. 1, 2, 5, and 6, may
make the said subscription, and precinct No. 1 may take
forty thousand dollars of the same, in addition to a pro

rata of the remaining two hundred and sixty thousand dollars.

§ 11. If the question of making the subscriptions aforesaid shall be submitted to the voters of any of said counties, or portion of counties, and they should fail to approve of said subscription, the sense of the voters thereof may be taken a second time by vote: *Provided*, That it shall not be done within less than one year after.

§ 12. No contract that the president and directors of said company may make with the Louisville, Cincinnati, and Lexington railroad company, or any other railroad, shall be valid until the same shall be ratified by the stockholders of this company.

§ 13. In taking the vote upon the question of said subscription in the county of Shelby, the polls shall be opened at the places of voting in all of the precincts in said county, except precincts Nos. 3 and 8.

§ 14. That the citizens of the fifth voting precinct, in Anderson county, shall not be allowed to vote upon the subject of this railroad, nor shall the citizens of said precinct be taxed to build the same, or any part thereof.

§ 15. This act shall take effect from and after its passage.

Approved February 3, 1869.

———

CHAPTER 1394.
AN ACT for the benefit of Joshua B. Fitch, late Sheriff of Lewis County.

Be it enacted by the General Assembly of the Commonwealth of Kentucky:

§ 1. That the further time of two years from and after the first day of June, 1869, be, and is, given to Joshua B. Fitch, late sheriff of Lewis county, to collect and distrain for his fee bills, and all uncollected taxes due him for the time he was sheriff, subject to all the penalties and restrictions now provided by law for illegally distraining and collecting fee bills and taxes, or either.

§ 2. That said Fitch may list his uncollected fee bills and taxes with the sheriff or any constable of Lewis county, or any county where the debtor may reside or be found, for collection, who are also hereby empowered to distrain for and collect said fee bills and taxes, for two years from and after the first day of June, 1869.

§ 3. This act shall take effect from its passage.

Approved February 5, 1869.

CHAPTER 1396.

AN ACT to incorporate the Kentucky Rolling Mill Company.

Be it enacted by the General Assembly of the Commonwealth of Kentucky:

§ 1. That J. Morgan Coleman, Barry Coleman, A. V. Dupont, and B. Dupont, together with their associates, successors, and assigns, be, and they are hereby, created a body-politic and corporate, under the name, style, and title of the Kentucky Rolling Mill Company; and under that name shall have perpetual succession; and may contract and be contracted with, sue and be sued, plead and be impleaded, answer and defend, as a natural person, in all courts and places; and may have and use a common seal, and change, alter, and renew the same at pleasure; and may also make such rules, by-laws, and regulations as they may think proper for the management, government, and conduct of said company, its property, business, and affairs, and alter and change them at will, but not to be in conflict with the laws of this State or of the United States.

§ 2. The business of the company shall be the manufacture and sale of iron and steel, or of either, and the making or vending, or both, of articles made thereof, or usually sold in connection therewith.

§ 3. The capital stock of said company shall not exceed five hundred thousand dollars, in shares of one hundred dollars each, which shall be deemed personal estate, and pass as such, and be transferable upon the books of the company as may be prescribed by the by-laws; and the stock shall be paid in such installments, and at such times, as the board of directors may determine; and for default of payment, the by-laws may authorize a forfeiture of the stock; and the company shall be entitled to a prior lien upon all the stock of any stockholder indebted to the company to the full extent of his indebtedness.

§ 4. The affairs of said company shall be managed by not less than three nor more than five directors, one of whom shall be president, chosen by themselves, and all of whom shall be stockholders, and shall continue in office for the term of one year, or till their successors are elected; and the persons named in the first section of this act shall constitute the first board of directors, and continue in office till their successors are elected; and may open books of subscription to the capital stock of the company, at such times and places as they may think proper, and issue certificates of stock to subscribers; and the board of directors shall have power, from time to time, to increase the capital stock as they may deem proper, so as not to exceed the limit of five hundred thousand dollars, and to issue certificates of stock therefor in accordance with the by-

laws; and shall have power to elect all of the other officers and agents of the company, and to prescribe their
qualifications, powers, and duties, and their compensation
and terms of office, and to take bonds for the faithful discharge of their duties, and to remove them at pleasure.

§ 5. The company shall have power to buy, hold, lease,
or sell such real and personal property as shall be necessary and proper in the judgment of the directors for the
conduct of its business or to secure debts due it; and its
place of business and manufacture shall be in the city of
Louisville or any other place in the State of Kentucky.

§ 6. Every stockholder shall be entitled to one vote for
each share of his stock in the company, at the election of
directors and in stockholders' meetings, for any purpose,
and may vote either in person or by written proxy, signed
by himself.

§ 7. There shall be annual meetings of the stockholders,
and oftener, if called by the directors, or by a majority in
interest of the stockholders, under such regulations as the
by-laws may prescribe; and at every such meeting, the
officers of the company shall, if required, submit a full
statement of its affairs, business, and accounts.

§ 8. No banking privileges are conferred by this charter.

§ 9. This act shall take effect from its passage.

·   Approved February 5, 1869.

CHAPTER 1398.

AN ACT to enable the Hart County Court to pay indebtedness and current expenses of Hart County.

*Be it enacted by the General Assembly of the Commonwealth
of Kentucky:*

§ 1. That it shall be lawful for the presiding judge of
the Hart county court to cause to be summoned the justices of the peace in Hart county to attend and constitute
a court for the purpose of revising the county levy made
at the regular court of claims, in the year 1868; and the
presiding judge of said court, and a majority of the justices of the peace for said county, composing said court,
shall have the power to revise the county levy made at
said court of claims in the year 1868, and may levy an
additional poll-tax of not exceeding two dollars and fifty
cents on the head, and also an *ad valorem* tax of not more
than ten cents on the one hundred dollars, or such a proportion of either or both poll and *ad valorem* tax as may
be necessary to pay the indebtedness of said county existing at the time said revision of said levy is made, and also

to pay the current expenses of said county for the years 1868 and 1869.

§ 2. That hereafter the regular court of claims for said county may levy such poll and *ad valorem* tax as may be necessary to pay the current expenses of said county: *Provided, however*, That the poll tax shall not exceed two dollars and fifty cents and the *ad valorem* tax more than ten cents on the one hundred dollars.

§ 3. This act to be in force from and after its passage.

Approved February 5, 1869.

CHAPTER 1399.

AN ACT to amend the several acts in regard to the Town of Benton.

Be it enacted by the General Assembly of the Commonwealth of Kentucky:

§ 1. That the board of trustees of the town of Benton, in the county of Marshall, have power to provide for the improvement of the public streets, alleys, and sidewalks of said town; and, to this end, they shall have power to require any owner or owners of a lot or lots to make a stone or brick sidewalk in front thereof not less than four nor more than eight feet wide, and of such grade as they shall direct, and in the manner and within such time as said trustees may require; and if, after written notice, such owner or owners shall fail, for the period of three months, to make such sidewalk, the trustees shall cause the same to be done at the expense of such owner or owners, and shall have a lien upon such lot or lots for the amount of said expense, which may be enforced by action in the Marshall circuit court in the name of the trustees and at the cost of such owner or owners; and when several owners are in default, they may be joined as defendants in one action, and a judgment rendered severally against each for the amount due from each, with the costs apportioned as the court may direct. The notice mentioned in this section may be executed on a non-resident by posting the same in writing at the court-house door in Benton for one month.

§ 2. Said board of trustees shall have power to affix and prescribe such penalties, by fine, for a violation of any of their by-laws or ordinances, not exceeding fifty dollars in each case, as they may deem the good government of the town may require; to provide for the protection, preservation, improvement, or ornamentation of any public property or grounds situated in said town; and to prevent, by proper ordinance and penalties, the vending, giving, or loaning any liquors to minors; and, generally, said board of trustees shall have power to provide, by proper ordinance, for the general convenience, welfare, comfort, health, and morals of said town.

§ 3. In addition to the powers heretofore given, said trustees may increase the poll-tax to two dollars; and all taxes assessed against any person under this or the acts to which this is amendatory shall be and remain a lien upon all the real and personal property of such person situated in said town until the same is paid.

§ 4. The police judge of said town shall have jurisdiction of all infractions of the by-laws and ordinances of said town. The fines collected for offenses committed against the by-laws or ordinances shall be paid over to the treasurer for the use of town improvements. The town marshal shall be collector of all taxes and fines, and shall have the same powers in collecting them that sheriffs have, and shall collect the taxes in the same manner, excepting that the trustees may regulate the time, that sheriffs are required to collect the State revenue taxes.

§ 5. Any vacancy in the board of trustees may be filled by the balance of the board, or by the county court of Marshall county, until the next regular election.

§ 6. This act shall be in force from its passage.

Approved February 5, 1869.

CHAPTER 1400.

AN ACT for the benefit of Mercer Circuit Clerk.

Be it enacted by the General Assembly of the Commonwealth of Kentucky:

§ 1. That the clerk of the Mercer circuit court be, and he is hereby, authorized, by and with the consent of the court aforesaid, to procure the necessary books and make out a general index and cross-index to all suits and records in his office, and arrange and number the same in alphabetical order, and for which service, upon the approval of the judge of said court, he will be allowed reasonable compensation, to be paid out of the county levy, and fixed by the justices of the county court of Mercer county, a majority being present, at their first court of claims after the finishing of the work.

§ 2. This act shall take effect from its passage.

Approved February 5, 1869.

CHAPTER 1401.

AN ACT to amend the Charter of the Town of North Middletown.

Be it enacted by the General Assembly of the Commonwealth of Kentucky:

§ 1. That the charter of the town of North Middletown, Bourbon county, be so amended as to confer upon the trustees of said town the same rights and privileges, and under the same restrictions and penalties, to grant coffee-house license to retail spirituous and vinous liquors, as that granted to the city council of the city of Paris, in said county, under its charter.

§ 2. This act to take effect from its passage.

Approved February 5, 1869.

CHAPTER 1402.

AN ACT to incorporate the Henderson German School Association.

Be it enacted by the General Assembly of the Commonwealth of Kentucky:

§ 1. That a body-politic and corporate be, and hereby is, created, under the name and style of the "Henderson German School Association," with a capital of not exceeding one hundred thousand dollars; and by that name said corporation shall have perpetual succession; and may have a common seal; and may contract and be contracted with, sue and be sued, in all the courts of this Commonwealth.

§ 2. The object and business of said corporation shall be to establish and keep and maintain a school in the city of Henderson, where children of German parentage and descent may receive a thorough English education, and at the same time be instructed in the mother tongue, at a cost so trifling as to place educational facilities within the reach of all for whom they are intended by this association. And for this purpose, said corporation shall be authorized to lease or purchase, own and hold, in the city of Henderson, so much real estate as may be necessary for the purposes of the association; erect all needed buildings; and may acquire, own, and hold such personal property as may be deemed necessary to enable said corporation to carry out fully and successfully the object of this act. Said corporation may exchange or sell any land or personal property acquired under this act, and obtain, hold, and own other real and personal property for the uses and purposes herein provided for.

§ 3. The officers of the association shall consist of a president, treasurer, secretary, and a board of trustees, who shall be elected annually on a day fixed by the by-laws of the association. The board of trustees shall consist of the president of the association, and four members thereof elected by the association. The said above officers shall discharge their respective duties without pecuniary compensation ; but should the association, at any time hereafter, deem it proper to attach a salary to any or all of the offices, it shall be done only at or before a regular annual election of officers. All the officers above named, before entering on the performance of their duties herein, shall, before the clerk of the Henderson county court, take an oath faithfully to perform them, and the clerk shall put of record in his office a minute of the fact, the names of the parties, and the offices they respectively fill.

§ 4. In order to make the accession to this association possible to every German, the association declares itself independent of any and all religious class jurisdiction, so that all sectarian religious instructions shall be excluded from the branches to be taught.

§ 5. Said corporation and its fiscal and prudential affairs shall be under the management and control of the board of trustees. It shall be the duty of the said board (a majority of whom may legally act) to conduct the outside management of the school; employ teachers, and arrange with them their compensation, and remove them if considered advisable; prescribe the system of instruction to be adopted and pursued, and fix the price of tuition; but a majority of all the members of the association may alter, amend, or annul the action of the said board, except in matters of contracts made by them with others; or may instruct the said board in relation to their duties in any given state of case. Should the said board refuse to be governed by the expressed will of the members, a majority thereof may, at any time at a meeting called for the purpose after a week's notice, depose the said board, any or all, and elect others of their members to the position so vacated.

§ 6. Every German of lawful age may become a member of the association upon the terms and conditions prescribed by the by-laws of the association hereafter adopted; and a majority of the members shall have the right, at any time, for cause, to expel any member; and the member so expelled, unless restored to membership by a vote of two thirds of all the members, shall forfeit all rights to the privileges, advantages, and franchises of the association.

§ 7. The secretary shall keep a record of all proceedings of meetings held, and keep a faithful account of all amounts received from contributions and collections by him, as also of the accounts of the association for expenditures, &c. His books shall at all times be open to the inspection of the board of trustees; and he shall, at the expiration of his term of office, deliver them to his successor.

§ 8. The treasurer shall conduct the management of the financial matters of the association, under the advice of the board of trustees, or a majority thereof; he shall pay all orders presented to him, when signed by the president and secretary; he shall deposit the cash funds of the association in some responsible bank in the city of Henderson to his credit as treasurer, and deliver the same, with all books, orders, evidences of debt, acquittances, etc., to the board of trustees, when his term of office expires. The books and business management of the treasurer of the affairs of the association may be at any time investigated by the board of trustees. The said association may require a bond, with sufficient surety, of the treasurer, for a faithful discharge of the duties of his office; but should he appropriate for his own use any of the funds belonging to the said association, he shall be subject to all the pains and penalties of felony, as prescribed by law for similar offenses.

§ 9. Parents or guardians desiring to send their children to the school, must make application to the board of trustees; but no children of German parentage or descent will be denied its privileges, except for bad conduct or character.

§ 10. Any officer elect of the association may be removed from office during the year by a vote of two thirds of all the members; and should a vacancy thus be made, it may be filled at once by a new election.

§ 11. All property of real nature acquired by the association shall be deeded to the trustees of the German School Association, of the city of Henderson, and their successors by name; but two thirds of the members of the association may at any time direct the sale of such real estate, and its reinvestment in other real property for the purposes contemplated by this act.

§ 12. The members of the said association shall have power, and they are hereby authorized, to make and establish such by-laws for the government of the association and its concerns as they may deem proper, not inconsistent with the Constitution and laws of the State of Kentucky and of the United States.

§ 13. Said corporation shall have power and be authorized by the order of a majority of all its members to borrow money, not exceeding five thousand dollars, to carry out the purposes of this act, and give bond for the same, with personal security, or secure said bond by a mortgage on the real and personal property of the said corporation;

1869.   said bond shall be signed by the president and countersigned by the secretary as officers of the association.

§ 14. If at any time, by a vote of two thirds of all the
members, the dissolution of this corporation is determined
(and a vote of two thirds of all the members shall be sufficient to dissolve it), in that event, the property, real and
personal, of the corporation, shall, in such a way as may
be fixed on by a majority of the members, be appropriated
to similar educational purposes; or, if this be deemed impracticable, it shall then be used to aid and foster the German element in this country, in such ways as the members
of the association shall decide.

§ 15. If, from any cause, the number of members of the
association should be reduced below twelve—that being
the minimum number—then this corporation shall have
ceased to exist, and all its property, real and personal,
shall be used and disposed of as set forth in section (14)
fourteen, *supra;* and for the faithful carrying out of this
section and section fourteen, above, the board of trustees,
after action has been taken by the members, as provided
for in section fourteen, or after the membership has been
reduced below twelve, as stated in section fifteen, shall be
held responsible.

§ 16. Jac. Reutlinger, Wm. Biershent, Jac. Peter, Felix
Frey, J. J. Diehl, Peter Hofman, are authorized and empowered to carry this act into effect.

§ 17. This act to take effect and be in force from its
passage.

Approved February 5, 1869.

CHAPTER 1403.

AN ACT to incorporate the Louisville Brick and Building Company.

*Be it enacted by the General Assembly of the Commonwealth
of Kentucky:*

§ 1. That J. & E. Barbaroux, S. B. Shotwell, Thomas
Slevin, W. L. McCampbell, Thomas E. Massey, W. R.
Thompson, L. T. Thustin, R. Atwood, and John B. Lewis,
their associates and assigns, be, and are hereby, created a
body-politic and corporate, under the name and style of
"The Louisville Brick and Building Company," with succession for fifty years; and by that name may contract
and be contracted with, sue and be sued, plead and be
impleaded, in all courts and places whatsoever; may have
a common seal, and alter, break, and renew the same at
pleasure; may buy, hold, sell, and convey all kinds of
estate, real, personal, or mixed, necessary or convenient
for the prosecution of its business.

§ 2. The business of said company shall be the manufacture and sale of brick, and the construction of houses, buildings, structures, and improvements of all kinds, public or private. Its principal office shall be in Louisville, Kentucky; but it may establish agencies and manufactories in any other place in this State.

§ 3. The capital stock of said company shall be not less than twenty thousand dollars nor more than five hundred thousand dollars, divided into shares of fifty dollars each, which shall be deemed personal estate, and transferable on the books of said company in such manner as may be prescribed by the by-laws.

§ 4. The said company may buy any patent right, and may pay for the same in its capital stock; and may borrow money on such terms and at such rates of interest as may be agreed upon by its board of directors; and it may sell or transfer any or all of its franchises and property to any other person, natural or corporate.

§ 5. The business of said company shall be conducted by a board of directors of not less than three nor more than seven, one of whom shall be elected president; and they shall hold their offices for one year, and until their successors are qualified, and each one of whom shall own at least five shares of said capital stock; and the said board of directors shall have power to make all necessary by-laws, and to alter the same at pleasure; to prescribe by said by-laws the manner and times of the election of officers; to employ any and all agents necessary or proper to carry on the business; to require bonds of employes and officers; and to do all things necessary and proper to the successful prosecution of the said business.

§ 6. The above named corporators, or such of them as a majority shall appoint, shall be commissioners to open books of subscription; and when twenty thousand dollars shall have been subscribed, the said company may commence business; and the first board of directors shall be composed of such of the above named corporators as they may elect.

§ 7. This act shall take effect from and after its passage.

Approved February 5, 1869.

CHAPTER 1404.

AN ACT to incorporate the Richmond Printing Company.

Be it enacted by the General Assembly of the Commonwealth of Kentucky:

§ 1. That H. M. McCarty, Geo. M. Adams, A. T. Chenault, Joseph Anderson, William Colmesnil, R. G. Burton, their associates, successors, and assigns, be, and they are hereby, created a body-politic and corporate, by the name of the "Richmond Printing Company," for the purpose of establishing a newspaper and general printing office in the city of Richmond, in Madison county; and, when organized, they shall exercise all the rights and privileges of corporations, and be governed by the laws relating thereto.

§ 2. The capital stock of said corporation shall be five thousand dollars, divided into shares of twenty-five dollars each, which may be, after the organization of the company, increased to not exceeding ten thousand dollars, and each share of stock shall entitle the holder thereof to one vote in all elections of the company.

§ 3. The corporators named in this act, or any two or more of them, may open books for the subscription of stock, and receive such subscriptions, which shall be, when the sum of one thousand dollars in stock is subscribed, binding in law upon the subscribers, and may be collected in such installments as the company, after organization, may prescribe, by suit, or the same may be forfeited by direction of the board of directors, with any amount which may have been paid thereon; and the company may organize so soon as the said sum of one thousand dollars shall be subscribed in stock.

§ 4. The company shall be organized by the election of three directors, who shall select their own chairman and such other officers, clerks, and agents, as they may see fit, and make such by-laws, rules and regulations, not inconsistent with law, as they may see fit: *Provided*, That the term of office of directors of said company shall be one year, and until their successors are chosen; and the first board of directors shall fix the time for the annual meeting of the stockholders.

§ 5. The said company may purchase and hold, and sell and convey, when necessary, such personal and real estate as they may deem fit, in the conduct of their business, not exceeding, in real estate, the amount of ten thousand dollars.

§ 6. This act shall take effect from its passage.

Approved February 5, 1869.

CHAPTER 1405.

AN ACT to incorporate the Willow Creek Navigation Company, in Ballard County.

WHEREAS, The land in Ballard county, bordering on the Ohio and Mississippi rivers, is subject to overflow in times of high water in those rivers; and in consequence of the existence of standing timber and other obstructions, the high land in said county is inaccessible to those rivers in periods of high water, and a high water landing can be obtained by clearing out and straightening Willow creek, in said county; therefore,

Be it enacted by the General Assembly of the Commonwealth of Kentucky:

§ 1. That Thos. H. Corbett, R. P. Robbins, A. W. Simonds, W. H. Morris, and A. S. Taylor, and their successors in office, be, and they are hereby, created a body politic and corporate, by the name of "The Willow Creek Navigation Company," with all the powers and authority incident to corporations, and such as are vested and created by this act.

§ 2. That the said Willow Creek Navigation Company is hereby authorized and empowered to remove from Willow creek, in Ballard county, in this State, all drift-wood, logs, stumps, and other obstructions, and to remove from the banks of the same the leaning and standing trees, and to widen and deepen said creek, and to alter and change the course of the same, and to make a new entrance into the Mississippi river, and generally to improve said creek in such a manner as to afford, by means thereof, access to the high land for steamboats or other water-craft from the Ohio and Mississippi rivers, and provide a landing place for said water-craft at the high land in said Ballard county in high water in said rivers. The said company, in and by their corporate name of the Willow Creek Navigation Company, may contract and be contracted with, sue and be sued, plead and be impleaded, in all courts; may have and use a common seal, and shall have perpetual succession of members by the name and style aforesaid; and shall have power to acquire, hold, use, and convey all such real estate and personal estate and property, and to exercise all such powers, rights, and privileges, as shall or may be necessary for the purposes of this act.

§ 3. For the purposes of this act, said Willow Creek Navigation Company may enter upon, and take possession of, so much land as may be necessary to make the improvement in the navigation of the said Willow creek herein contemplated; and if said company cannot agree with the owner or owners of said land, taken as aforesaid, application may be made to any justice of the peace in and for said Ballard county, who, thereupon, shall issue his warrant, directed to the sheriff of his county, requiring him to summon a jury of twenty *bona fide* housekeepers, not related to such owners, or in anywise interested, to meet on the land, or as near it as is practicable, to be valued, on a day named in said warrant, not less than ten nor more than twenty days after the issuing of the same; and if any of the jurors shall fail to attend, said sheriff shall summon as many jurors as may be necessary, with those in attendance, to complete the panel aforesaid; and from them each party, or the attorney or agent of either party, if present, if not, then the sheriff for the party absent, may strike off four jurors each, and the remaining twelve shall act as the jury of inquest of damages, after having been sworn by the sheriff justly and impartially to fix the damages which the owner or owners shall sustain by the use and occupation of the land required by the company. In estimating the damages the jury shall take into consideration the benefits resulting to the owner from making said improvement and straightening said creek, but only in the extinguishment of damages. The jury shall reduce their verdict to writing, and sign the same; and it shall be returned by the sheriff to the clerk of the circuit court for said county, who shall docket the same as other suits, giving it the precedency of all civil business; and, upon the call of the docket, the court shall enter an order confirming the said inquisition, unless defense be made and sufficient cause be shown against it; and, when so confirmed, the clerk shall enter it of record at the expense of the company; but if set aside, the court may direct another inquisition to be taken in the same manner. Such inquisition shall describe the bounds of the land taken, and the extent and duration of the interest in the same; and such damages, when tendered or paid to the owner or owners of said land, or his or her or their agent or legal representative, or to the clerk of said court, for the use of any such owner, when he, she, or they may refuse to receive the same, or reside out of the county, shall, *ipso facto*, vest in the company the right to the land, to all intents and purposes, as fully as if the same had been acquired by valid conveyance.

§ 4. The capital stock of said company shall be ten thousand dollars ($10,000), which may be increased by said company to any sum not exceeding one hundred thousand dollars ($100,000), which may be divided into shares of fifty dollars ($50) each, which shall be deemed personal property, and may be issued and transferred in such manner as the board of directors may prescribe.

§ 5. The affairs of said company shall be managed by a board of five directors, which may be increased to any number not exceeding nine; and Thomas H. Corbett, R.

P. Robbins, A. W. Simonds, W. H. Morris, and A. S.
Taylor, are hereby appointed the first board, who shall
hold their offices until their successors shall be elected and
qualified, in such manner as may be prescribed by the
by-laws of said company. Said board shall have the
power to select one of their number president, and to fill
such other offices as may be prescribed by the by-laws.
If any of the directors herein named shall decline, or
refuse to serve, a majority of the others may fill the
vacancy. The board of directors of said company shall
have power to make all by-laws necessary to the management of the affairs of the company, not inconsistent
with the Constitution or laws of this State or of the
United States.

§ 6. Said company shall have authority to construct
landings, wharves, embankments, houses, and other buildings and other works necessary for their purpose, and receive and keep property therein or thereon, on storage,
and collect charges therefor, and may purchase, lease,
and acquire, hold and convey, all such real or personal
estate or property as may be deemed necessary to carry
on their business. Said company shall have and enjoy
the exclusive right to the use and navigation of that
portion of said Willow creek improved by them, and
such portions as they acquire under and by virtue of this
charter, and may transport and carry persons and property over and along said Willow creek, and over and
along the Ohio and Mississippi rivers from any point on
said creek, or from any landing constructed by said company at the high land in said Ballard county, or at the
mouth of said creek, and one mile above and below said
creek; and for the purposes of such transportation and
carriage may purchase and acquire, hold and use, or
convey steamboats, barges, and other water craft, or
may contract with other persons or companies to transport and carry such persons and property; and for the
transportation, within the limits of the State of Kentucky, of such persons and property, said company may
collect and receive such reasonable compensation and
toll as the county court of Ballard county may fix and
determine, not, however, below the rates charged for
similar services by other incorporated companies in the
neighborhood.

§ 7. Said company may, from time to time, borrow such
sums of money as may be necessary for the purposes of
said company, and at any rate of interest not exceeding
ten per cent. per annum; may issue and dispose of their
bonds in sums of not less than fifty dollars each, for any
amount so borrowed, and may mortgage their corporate
property, or convey the same by deed of trust to secure

the payment of any sum so borrowed, or any other debt of said company.

§ 8. This act to take effect from and after its passage.

Approved February 6, 1869.

CHAPTER 1406.

AN ACT to amend an act, entitled "An act to incorporate the Western Insurance Company."

Be it enacted by the General Assembly of the Commonwealth of Kentucky:

§ 1. An act to incorporate "The Western Insurance Company," approved January 26, 1865, chapter 734, be, and the same is hereby, amended as follows:

§ 2. The Western Insurance Company aforesaid shall hereafter be known by the name of "The Western Insurance and Banking Company;" and shall by that name be subject to all the duties and liabilities, and entitled to all the rights heretofore conferred upon and enjoyed by the Western Insurance Company.

§ 3. This act shall take effect from its passage.

Approved February 6, 1869.

CHAPTER 1408.

AN ACT to amend the Charter of the Bank Lick Turnpike Road Company.

Be it enacted by the General Assembly of the Commonwealth of Kentucky:

§ 1. That whenever the president and directors of the Bank Lick turnpike road company shall have made and completed, in every respect, according to the requirements of their charter, that portion of the road recently changed, and for which a new location has been selected and established between the fifth and seventh mile posts, it shall be the duty of the president and directors to call on any two justices of the peace for Kenton county to go and inspect said new piece of road, and if they shall be of opinion that the said new piece of road has been completed in every respect according to the requirements of their charter, they shall certify the same to the president and directors of said company; then the said new portion of said road shall be legalized, and the same shall be taken and considered as a part of said company's road.

§ 2. That the charter of said company be so amended as to require the bridges on said road to be not less than fourteen feet wide, and the approaches thereto to be not less than sixteen feet wide: *Provided,* That nothing in this act contained shall be construed so as to affect, in any way, the contract entered into by the Bank Lick turnpike road company with the Louisville, Cincinnati, and Lexington railroad company, for the change in the location of the turnpike road.

§ 3. That the company shall have six months' time allowed them, from and after the passage of this act, to make the alterations and improvements herein required.

§ 4. That the gate-keepers are required to report, in the months of July and January of each year, to the Kenton county court, under oath, the amount of tolls collected or due said company; and whenever it is ascertained that the road pays a greater dividend than ten per cent. per annum upon the original capital stock, then the tolls are to be reduced until it nets ten per cent. only upon its stock; and that the surveyor or president of said road shall report, under oath, to the county judge, in January and July of each year, with vouchers, &c., the cost of all repairs to said road.

§ 5. That all persons going to and returning from church, on the Sabbath day, all children going to or returning from neighborhood schools, with or without driver, and all neighborhood funerals going and returning, shall be free from toll on said road.

§ 6. That the company is hereby authorized and required to sell tickets on said road at a discount of twenty per cent. upon the present rates of toll, for amounts of one dollar and over.

§ 7. That an act, entitled "An act to amend the charter of the Bank Lick turnpike company," approved February the 17th, 1866, be, and the same is hereby, repealed.

§ 8. That an act, entitled "An act to amend the charter of the Bank Lick turnpike company," approved February 27th, 1867, be, and the same is hereby, repealed.

§ 9. That if, at any time, the said road shall be out of repair for the term of ten days, it shall and may be lawful for any person to call on two adjacent justices of the peace to go and inspect said road; and if, upon inspecting the same, and receiving proof that it had been out of repair for the term of ten successive days previous thereto, the said justices shall, by their order, delivered to the treasurer of said company, and, in case of his absence, to the president, or any of the toll-gatherers, direct that no tolls or duty shall be required on said road until the same shall be repaired and put in good order; and if any toll shall be taken or demanded after the delivery of such order, the said company shall forfeit and pay the sum of five dollars for each offense, to be recovered as other debts of like amount: *Provided, however,* That said recovery shall only be had against the company for the unlawful

1869.   demand of the toll-gatherers nearest that part of the road
so declared to be out of order or repair : *And provided fur-*
ther, That there shall have been sufficient time to inform
the gate-keeper of said order having been delivered to the
president or treasurer.   Where that is the fact, and upon
said road being repaired, the president and directors shall
call any two justices of the peace of the county of Kenton, in like manner to examine the same; and if they
shall be of opinion that the said road is in repair, they
shall certify the same and direct that the toll shall be
demanded and taken at the gate or gates, agreeably to
the provisions of the original charter and amendments
thereto.

§ 10. This act to take effect from its passage.

Approved February 10, 1869.

CHAPTER 1409.

AN ACT authorizing the Trustees of the Town of Madisonville to sell
certain Burying Grounds in said Town.

*Be it enacted by the General Assembly of the Commonwealth
of Kentucky:*

§ 1. That it may be lawful for the trustees of the town
of Madisonville, Kentucky (a majority concurring), to sell
the burying grounds in said town, situated north of Cross
Main street and west of Main street.

§ 2. That the trustees of said town (or the person to
whom they may sell the grounds) mentioned in first section, have the right and privilege of removing the dead
buried upon said grounds, and reburying them at another
and more suitable place.

§ 3. This act to be in force from and after its passage.

Approved February 10, 1869.

CHAPTER 1410.

AN ACT for the benefit of Harriet N. Robinson, of Taylor County.

*Be it enacted by the General Assembly of the Commonwealth
of Kentucky:*

§ 1. That Harriet N. Robinson, of Taylor county, wife of
Palatine Robinson, is hereby made capable in law of making, contracting, and of acquiring and holding property,
real and personal, free from the control of her husband, in
the same manner as if she were a *feme sole;* and in like
manner to sell, convey, or otherwise dispose of the same;
and may sue and be sued, as a *feme sole,* in all courts of law
and equity in this Commonwealth.

§ 2. This act shall take effect from its passage.

Approved February 10, 1869.

CHAPTER 1411.

AN ACT for the benefit of the Town of Mount Carmel, in Fleming County.

Be it enacted by the General Assembly of the Commonwealth of Kentucky:

§ 1. That all fines hereafter assessed and collected for misdemeanors committed within the corporate limits of the town of Mount Carmel, in Fleming county, shall be paid to the trustees thereof, and appropriated by them for the use and benefit of said town.

§ 2. This act to take effect from and after its passage.

Approved February 10, 1869.

CHAPTER 1412.

AN ACT for the benefit of Mrs. Pamelia M. Waggener.

Be it enacted by the General Assembly of the Commonwealth of Kentucky:

§ 1. That Pamelia M. Waggener, wife of Harrison W. Waggener, of the town of Morganfield, be, and she is hereby, authorized to engage in trade, and transact business of every description whatsoever, in the same manner and to the same extent as if she were an unmarried woman; to acquire and convey property, real, personal, and mixed, and to sue and be sued in her own name; and that any property so acquired by her shall be subject to her debts and contracts, free from the debts or control of her said husband or his creditors.

§ 2. This act to take effect from its passage.

Approved February 10, 1869.

CHAPTER 1413.

AN ACT for the benefit of James H. Hall, late Sheriff of Powell county.

Whereas, There was a judgment in the Franklin circuit court in 1868, against James H. Hall, sheriff of Powell county, and Thomas B. Hall, Malon Hall, and Joab Morton, his sureties, for one thousand and fifty-two dollars and eighty-four cents, for the revenue of said county for the year 1867, and damages thereon; and whereas, the said James H. Hall, as sheriff aforesaid, has fully paid into the Treasury of the State all of said judgment, with its cost and damages; therefore,

Be it enacted by the General Assembly of the Commonwealth of Kentucky:

§.1. That the two hundred and ten dollars in damages, paid into the Treasury by the sheriff aforesaid, be refunded, and the Auditor is hereby authorized to draw his warrant on the Treasury in favor of the said James H. Hall for said amount.

§ 2. This act to take effect from its passage.

Approved February 10, 1869.

CHAPTER 1414.

AN ACT for the benefit of the sureties of J. H. Butler, late Sheriff of Allen County.

Be it enacted by the General Assembly of the Commonwealth of Kentucky:

§ 1. That whereas, judgment was obtained in the Franklin circuit court against J. H. Butler, late sheriff of Allen county, and against Uriah Porter and others, as his sureties, for the sum of $7,193 39, and damages, $1,438 67 ; and whereas, said sureties have paid off and discharged the whole of said judgment and interest and cost thereon, except the damages aforesaid ; and whereas, they have also paid $100 of said damages as attorney's fee in the case, leaving yet $1.338 67 of said damages yet unpaid ; therefore, be it enacted, that the said sureties be, and they are hereby, released from the payment of the remainder of said damages.

§ 2. This act to take effect from its passage.

Approved February 10, 1869.

CHAPTER 1415.

AN ACT for the benefit of Leslie Johnson, late Sheriff of Letcher County.

Be it enacted by the General Assembly of the Commonwealth of Kentucky:

§ 1. That when Leslie Johnson, or any person for him, shall pay into the Treasury the amount of the revenue, together with the interest and cost due thereon, and all expenses to which the State is subject in trying to collect it, for the years 1862 and 1863, the same shall discharge said Johnson and his sureties from further liability to the Commonwealth therefor, provided said payment shall be made on or before the 1st of May, 1869.

§ 2. This act to take effect from and after its passage.

Approved February 10, 1869.

CHAPTER 1417.

AN ACT for the benefit of A. J. Lanesdowne.

WHEREAS, A. J. Lanesdowne, of the county of Carter, paid taxes both in the county of Carter and Boyd county, on certain property in the town of Catlettsburg, on three several years, the amount overpaid amounting to thirty-six dollars and sixty cents; and for remedy therefor,

Be it enacted by the General Assembly of the Commonwealth of Kentucky:

§ 1. That the Auditor of Public Accounts be, and he is hereby, directed to issue his warrant upon the Treasurer in favor of A. J. Lanesdowne, for the sum of thirty-six dollars and sixty cents, and the Treasurer shall pay the same.

§ 2. This act to take effect from its passage.

Approved February 10, 1869.

CHAPTER 1418.

AN ACT to carry into effect certain Surveys made by Robert P. Davis, deceased, late Surveyor of Breathitt County.

WHEREAS, Robert P. Davis, late surveyor for the county of Breathitt, having made sundry surveys on orders of the Breathitt county court appropriating vacant lands in said county, which surveys are now in the form of field-notes, and were not made out in form, recorded in his office, and forwarded to the Land Office for grant, because of the troubled condition of the country, and said Davis being now dead, and his memoranda and field-notes being in the possession of his widow, Mrs. Polly Davis; and whereas, it is necessary to the interest of all parties concerned that said surveys should be made out in form and carried into grant; therefore,

Be it enacted by the General Assembly of the Commonwealth of Kentucky:

§ 1. That J. Fallen, of the county of Wolfe, who is entirely disinterested, be, and he is hereby, authorized and empowered to make up in due form the certificates of surveys made by said Davis in his lifetime, and preserved in the form of memoranda and field-notes, as before recited, and to enter the same of record in the surveyor's book of the county of Breathitt, and forward the plats and certificates, accompanied by the orders of court on which they are based, to the Register of the Land Office, who shall receive and register the same, and issue grants thereon, as in case of other surveys.

§ 2. Before proceeding to carry out the authority conferred on him by this act, said Fallen shall appear in the county court of Breathitt county, and in open court make oath that he will faithfully and impartially execute the same.

§ 3. Said Fallen may make out and certify the fee bills of said Davis for said surveys, according to the fees fixed by law, and deliver the same to said Polly Davis, widow and administratrix of said Robert P. Davis, deceased, who may collect the same, or list the same for collection with any authorized collecting officer, who may distrain for them as in case of other fee bills. Said administratrix shall pay to said Fallen such compensation for his services as may be agreed upon between them.

§ 4. This act shall take effect from its passage.

Approved February 10, 1869.

CHAPTER 1419.

AN ACT for the benefit of M. B. Goble, of Lawrence County.

Be it enacted by the General Assembly of the Commonwealth of Kentucky:

§ 1. That there is hereby allowed to M. B. Goble, late sheriff of Lawrence county, the sum of one hundred and seventy-five dollars and twenty-five cents, out of any moneys in the Treasury not otherwise appropriated, being amount expended by him in procuring the arrest and delivery to the proper authorities in Kentucky of one Allen Harrison (colored), charged with felony; and the Auditor will draw his warrant upon the Treasurer in favor of said Goble for the amount aforesaid.

§ 2. This act shall take effect from its passage.

Approved February 10, 1869.

CHAPTER 1420.

AN ACT to amend the Charter of the Town of Elkton.

Be it enacted by the General Assembly of the Commonwealth of Kentucky:

§ 1. That the charter of said town be, and it is hereby, so amended as to authorize the trustees thereof to fill by appointment the office of town marshal when a vacancy shall occur by death, resignation, or otherwise, until the next general or regular election.

§ 2. That this act shall take effect from its passage.

Approved February 10, 1869.

CHAPTER 1421.

AN ACT to incorporate "The Bourbon Library Association."

Be it enacted by the General Assembly of the Commonwealth of Kentucky:

§ 1. That G. C. Kniffin, president; W. P. Chambers, vice president; Wilson Ingals, recording secretary; L. T. Fisher, corresponding secretary; James Stuart, treasurer; Wm. H. Wainright, librarian; C. K. Marshall, R. Peckover, W. F. Taylor, W. A. Bacon, W. A. Buckner, and J. K. Ford, directors, their successors and associates, be, and are hereby, created a body-politic and corporate, under the name and style of "The Bourbon Library Association," and as such shall have perpetual succession; may sue and be sued, contract and be contracted with; and have, and at pleasure break and alter, a common seal.

§ 2. The [object] of said association shall be the intellectual, moral, and social improvement of its members, and for that purpose shall have power to adopt a constitution and by-laws, not inconsistent with the laws of the State, and alter and amend the same in such manner as its officers may prescribe; and may acquire by purchase, gift, or otherwise, books, money, and other property, not exceeding twenty-five thousand dollars in value, and the same may sell and dispose of at pleasure; may institute a library in the city of Paris for the use of its members, and do such other acts, not inconsistent with law, necessary to effectuate its objects.

§ 3. That the number, name, and duties of its officers may be regulated by the constitution and by-laws, and also the time and manner of their election; and the constitution and by-laws heretofore adopted by said association shall be binding on its members until otherwise altered and amended.

§ 4. This act shall take effect from its passage.

Approved February 10, 1869.

CHAPTER 1422.

AN ACT for the benefit of James N. Frazer, of Harrison County.

Be it enacted by the General Assembly of the Commonwealth of Kentucky:

§ 1. That the Auditor of Public Accounts be, and he is hereby, required to draw his warrant upon the Treasurer for the sum of forty-two dollars, in favor of James N. Frazer, sheriff of Harrison county, in order to reimburse

1869.

him in that sum paid to the trustee of the jury fund by mistake.

§ 2. This act shall have effect from its passage.

Approved February 10, 1869.

CHAPTER 1423.

AN ACT for the benefit of School District No. 18, in Casey county.

WHEREAS, It appears from the report of the trustees of common school district No. 18, in Casey county, that there was a common school taught in said district by a competent teacher for the period of three months, in the year 1867, and that the number of children entitled to the benefit of said school being residents was fifty-three; and no money having been drawn out of the Treasury for said district for said year, by reason of the report not reaching the county commissioner's office; therefore,

Be it enacted by the General Assembly of the Commonwealth of Kentucky:

§ 1. That the Auditor of Public Accounts draw his warrant on the Treasurer in favor of G. I. Penn, one of the trustees for common school district No. 18, in Casey county, for the year 1867, for the sum of forty-two dollars and fifty cents, to be paid out of any part of the Common School Fund not otherwise appropriated, to be applied to the payment of the teacher who taught said school.

§ 2. This act shall be in force from and after its passage.

Approved February 10, 1869.

CHAPTER 1424.

AN ACT declaring the Woodford Weekly, a paper published at Versailles, Kentucky, an authorized newspaper in this Commonwealth.

Be it enacted by the General Assembly of the Commonwealth of Kentucky:

§ 1. That the Woodford Weekly, a newspaper published at Versailles, in the State of Kentucky, be, and the same is hereby, declared a duly authorized newspaper.

§ 2. That this act shall take effect from and after its passage.

Approved February 10, 1869.

CHAPTER 1425.

AN ACT to repeal an act, entitled "An act to incorporate the Stony Point Academy Boarding-house," approved February 5, 1866.

Be it enacted by the General Assembly of the Commonwealth of Kentucky:

§ 1. That an act approved the 5th February, 1866, entitled "An act to incorporate the Stony Point Academy Boarding-house," be, and the same is hereby, repealed.

§ 2. This act shall take effect from its passage.

Approved February 10, 1869.

CHAPTER 1426.

AN ACT for the benefit of Allen Walker, a Justice of the Peace in Crittenden County.

WHEREAS, The house of James H. Travis, former justice of the peace in Crittenden county, was destroyed by fire, together with all the books and papers belonging to his office; and Allen Walker having been elected as his successor in office, therefore,

Be it enacted by the General Assembly of the Commonwealth of Kentucky:

§ 1. That the Secretary of State be, and he is hereby, required to furnish to said Allen Walker, a justice of the peace for Crittenden county, all the books and laws to which justices of the peace are by law entitled.

§ 2. This act shall take effect from its passage.

Approved February 10, 1869.

CHAPTER 1428.

AN ACT conferring concurrent jurisdiction on the Fayette Circuit Court with that of the Lexington City Court in cases of misdemeanors.

Be it enacted by the General Assembly of the Commonwealth of Kentucky:

That from and after the passage of this act the Fayette circuit court shall have concurrent jurisdiction with the Lexington city court in all misdemeanors arising within the corporate limits of said city, except offenses against the ordinances and by-laws of said city.

Approved February 10, 1869.

CHAPTER 1429.

AN ACT for the benefit of the Trustees of the Class of the Methodist Church, South, in Springfield.

Be it enacted by the General Assembly of the Commonwealth of Kentucky:

§ 1. That the trustees, or a majority of them, of the Class of the Methodist Episcopal Church, South, at Springfield, be, and are hereby, authorized to sell and convey the lot of ground and buildings, or either or any part of them, on which their church building is situate, in the town aforesaid ; and shall reinvest the proceeds of the same in the building or purchase of another house for the worship of said Class; and until that, shall keep the money arising from said sale at interest on good security.

§ 2. This act shall take effect from its passage.

Approved February 10, 1869.

CHAPTER 1430.

AN ACT for the benefit of H. S. Hale, Sheriff of Graves County.

Be it enacted by the General Assembly of the Commonwealth of Kentucky:

§ 1. That Henry S. Hale, sheriff of Graves county, be, and is hereby, relieved from the payment of damages included against him in a judgment in favor of the Commonwealth for a part of the revenue for 1867, said Hale having paid the principal, interest, and costs of said judgment.

§ 2. This act shall take effect from its passage.

Approved February 10, 1869.

CHAPTER 1431.

AN ACT for the benefit of Albert G. Moore, of the County of Christian.

WHEREAS, Albert G. Moore, of Christian county, an acting magistrate in said county, has never received the books to which he is entitled by law ; therefore,

Be it enacted by the General Assembly of the Commonwealth of Kentucky:

§ 1. That the Secretary of State be, and he is hereby, directed to furnish said Albert G. Moore such books as are furnished other magistrates in this Commonwealth.

§ 2. This act to take effect from its passage.

Approved February 10, 1869.

CHAPTER 1432.

AN ACT for the benefit of John W. Duncan, late Sheriff of Wayne County.

Be it enacted by the General Assembly of the Commonwealth of Kentucky:

§ 1. That the damages, amounting to two hundred and eighty-three dollars and fourteen cents, included in a judgment rendered against Jno. W. Duncan, late sheriff of Wayne county, for the revenue of 1867, and his sureties, be, and is hereby, remitted; said Duncan having paid all of the principal, interest, cost, and Attorney General's fees embraced in said judgment.

§ 2. This act shall take effect from its passage.

Approved February 10, 1869.

CHAPTER 1433.

AN ACT for the benefit of James H. Reed, late Sheriff of Metcalfe County.

Be it enacted by the General Assembly of the Commonwealth of Kentucky:

§ 1. That James H. Reed, late sheriff of Metcalfe county, be, and he is hereby, released from the damages against him, contained in the judgment of the fiscal court against him and sureties, for the revenue for the year 1867; he having paid off and discharged the principal, interest, and costs of said judgment, and all that remains unpaid is the damages hereby released.

§ 2. This act to be in effect from its passage.

Approved February 10, 1869.

CHAPTER 1434.

AN ACT for the benefit of the Clerk of the Mercer Circuit Court.

Be it enacted by the General Assembly of the Commonwealth of Kentucky:

§ 1. That the further time of two years be, and the same is hereby, given to Ben. C. Allen, late clerk of the Mercer circuit court, in which to list and collect his uncollected fee bills, due him as clerk of the Mercer circuit court, under the existing laws of this Commonwealth, and pains and penalties for issuing or collecting illegal fee bills.

§ 3. This act to take effect from and after its passage.

Approved February 10, 1869.

CHAPTER 1435.

AN ACT for the benefit of John W. Harrell.

Be it enacted by the General Assembly of the Commonwealth of Kentucky:

§ 1. That the Auditor of Public Accounts be. and he is hereby, directed to draw his warrant on the Treasurer in favor of John W. Harrell, of Floyd county, for the sum of fourteen dollars, for common school taught in said county in 1861: *Provided*, Said sum be deducted from the amount due said county upon its school bonds.

§ 2. This act shall take effect from its passage.

Approved February 10, 1869.

CHAPTER 1436.

AN ACT for the benefit of Mary E. Hutton.

Be it enacted by the General Assembly of the Commonwealth of Kentucky:

§ 1. That the Auditor of Public Accounts be, and he is hereby, directed to draw his warrant on the Treasurer in favor of Mary E. Hutton, of Floyd county, for the sum of thirteen dollars and thirty cents, for common school taught in said county in 1861: *Provided*, Said sum be deducted from the amount due said county upon its school bonds.

§ 2. This act shall take effect from its passage.

Approved February 10, 1869.

CHAPTER 1437.

AN ACT for the benefit of R. H. Earnest, former Sheriff of Simpson County.

Be it enacted by the General Assembly of the Commonwealth of Kentucky :

§ 1. That the damages assessed against R. H. Earnest, former sheriff of Simpson county, and his sureties, amounting to the sum of ninety ($90) dollars, for failure to pay over the revenue for the year 1866, be, and the same is hereby, remitted, and the same is hereby directed to be refunded back to him; and to that end, the Auditor of Public Accounts is directed to draw his warrant upon the Treasury in favor of said Earnest for said sum, and which shall be paid out of any money in the Treasury not otherwise appropriated.

§ 2. This act shall take effect from and after the date of its passage.

Approved February 10, 1869.

CHAPTER 1438.

AN ACT to regulate the tolls on the Lexington and Newtown Turnpike Road.

Be it enacted by the General Assembly of the Commonwealth of Kentucky:

§ 1. That the Lexington and Newtown turnpike road company is hereby authorized and empowered to establish and collect such rates of toll as other turnpike roads leading into Lexington are empowered to establish and collect.

§ 2. That all laws conflicting with the provisions of this act are hereby repealed to the extent of such conflict.

§ 3. That this act shall be in force from its passage.

Approved February 10, 1869.

CHAPTER 1439.

AN ACT to abolish Civil District No. 5, Metcalfe County.

Be it enacted by the General Assembly of the Commonwealth of Kentucky:

§ 1. That civil district No. 5, known as the Walnut Grove district, Metcalfe county, be, and the same is hereby, abolished.

§ 2. That portion of the county out of which said district was formed is hereby divided and connected to the adjoining districts as follows, to-wit: All that portion of said district south of the following line, beginning at the county line at the mouth of Faris' Fork ; thence up said creek to its forks ; thence up Lafferty's Fork to its head ; thence to the Stephen Franklin old place; thence to Wilson Ferkin's, at the district line, be, and the same is hereby, connected to the Sartin district, No. 6. And all between the said described line and the following, to-wit: Beginning at the district line on South Fork, at the widow Moran's ; thence up said creek to the widow Johnson's ; thence to Moor's Spring meeting-house, is hereby connected to the Edmonton district, No. 1; and all north of the last named line is hereby connected to the Flat Rock district, No. 4.

§ 3. This act to take effect from its passage.

Approved February 10, 1869.

CHAPTER 1440.

AN ACT for the benefit of J. C. Calhoun, Sheriff of McCracken County.

Be it enacted by the General Assembly of the Commonwealth of Kentucky:

§ 1. That J. C. Calhoun, sheriff of McCracken county, be allowed the further time until the 1st day of April next, to return his delinquent list for 1867, and that the same, when allowed, be credited by the Auditor upon the revenue due from the county of McCracken for the year 1868.

§ 2. This act shall take effect from its passage.

Approved February 10, 1869.

CHAPTER 1441.

AN ACT for the benefit of Evan E. Settle.

Be it enacted by the General Assembly of the Commonwealth of Kentucky:

§ 1. That any two of the circuit judges in this State shall have full power and authority to license said Evan E. Settle, he being under twenty-one years of age, to practice law in all courts of this Commonwealth; and when so licensed, he, the said Settle, to be, in all things, entitled to the same privileges, and to be under the same responsibilities, as if he were of full age; and all contracts and agreements made by him shall be as valid and binding in law as if he were of full age.

§ 2. This act to take effect from its passage.

Approved February 10, 1869.

CHAPTER 1442.

AN ACT for the benefit of John Boyd, late Sheriff of Lyon County.

WHEREAS, John Boyd, late sheriff of Lyon county, failed, from unavoidable causes, to pay up his revenue for 1867; and whereas, a judgment was issued against him, and damages assessed to the amount of one hundred and eighty-one dollars and eighty-two cents; therefore,

Be it enacted by the General Assembly of the Commonwealth of Kentucky:

§ 1. That the said amount of damages, one hundred and eighty-one dollars and eighty-two cents, be, and the same is hereby, remitted, the said Boyd having paid the costs and fees on suit.

§ 2. This act to take effect from its passage.

Approved February 10, 1869.

CHAPTER 1444.

AN ACT for the benefit of Thomas G. Slater.

Be it enacted by the General Assembly of the Commonwealth of Kentucky:

§ 1. That the Auditor shall draw his warrant on the Treasurer for one hundred dollars, in favor of Thomas G. Slater, the same being allowed the said Slater and hereby so appropriated in compensation for services and expenses in going to Chicago, Illinois, and capturing Jaques Straus, charged with a felonious crime against this Commonwealth.

§ 2. This act to take effect from and after its passage.

Approved February 10, 1869.

CHAPTER 1445.

AN ACT to incorporate Horton Division, No. 8, Sons of Temperance.

Be it enacted by the General Assembly of the Commonwealth of Kentucky:

§ 1. That A. D. Smalley, R. D. Hayman, Henry J. Redfield, James Covert, and T. M. Rigg, and their successors, be, and they are hereby, constituted a body corporate and politic, by the name and style of Horton Division, No. 8, Sons of Temperance, and by that name and style shall have perpetual succession, and be capable of contracting and being contracted with, to sue and be sued, to plead and be impleaded, in all courts of law and equity in this Commonwealth; of purchasing and holding such real and personal property as may be required for the use of said Horton Division, No. 8; to receive all necessary conveyances; to sell, convey, or dispose of all such real or personal estate as they may now have or may hereafter acquire; that the amount invested in real estate shall not at any time exceed fifty thousand dollars.

§ 2. That the management of the concerns of said corporation shall be, and is hereby, confided to A. D. Smalley, R. D. Hayman, Henry J. Redfield, James Covert, and T. M. Rigg, and their successors in office, as trustees thereof, who, or a majority of them, shall have power to make all contracts pertaining to the real or personal property or estate of said Division.

§ 3. The said trustees shall have power to pass such by-laws, rules and regulations, not inconsistent with the Constitution and laws of the United States or of this State, as may be necessary for the safe-keeping of the property and other interests of the said Division; and may use a common seal, and change the same at pleasure; and in conveying real estate the whole board of trustees shall unite in such conveyance; and all by-laws and regulations adopted or passed by said trustees shall be approved by the action of the Division at a regular meeting of the same.

§ 4. The trustees shall be chosen annually by the Division, which election shall be had at a regular meeting when an election for officers of the Division shall be held.

§ 5. This act shall be in force from and after its passage.

Approved February 10, 1869.

CHAPTER 1446.

AN ACT for the benefit of the Representatives and Heirs of Wm. J. Fields, deceased, late Sheriff of Carter County, and his Securities.

WHEREAS, It is represented to this General Assembly that William J. Fields was qualified as sheriff of Carter county in January, 1861, and executed his bond to the Commonwealth of Kentucky for the collection of the revenue tax of said county, with J. F. Horton, C. S. Counts, Jas. Flawha, E. H. Elliott, L. H. Elliott, Sam'l McDavid, John Armstrong, James M. Fields, John Jordan, David Rice, Jacob Rice, and A. Ruckner, as his securities; and whereas, it appears from satisfactory proof, that, in September, in said year, and before he, the said William J. Fields, had collected any portion of said revenue tax, he was driven from his home and county by an organized military band, called "Home Guards," and prevented from exercising the functions of his office, and that, during his absence, died; and whereas, it is also represented and made known to this General Assembly, that, after said William J. Fields had thus been driven from his home, his securities undertook the collection of said revenue tax by a portion of them qualifying as his deputies; and that they were likewise prevented from collecting said tax by the same military force; and whereas, at the April, 1862, term of the Carter county court, John Armstrong, one of said securities, was appointed sheriff of said county by said court, in obedience to the provisions of act approved March 11th, 1862, and executed bond, as required by law, for the collection of said revenue tax, and entered upon the duties of his office, and proceeded to collect said revenue tax due the State by said Wm. J. Fields for the year 1861, but failed to do so in consequence of the disturbed condition of the country, except a small portion of it, which has been paid into the State Treasury; and whereas, at the February term, 1862, of the Franklin circuit court, a judgment was rendered against said William J. Fields and his securities for the amount of revenue tax

charged against him as the sheriff of Carter county for 1869.
the year 1861, together with interest, costs, and damages
thereon; and whereas, the State of Kentucky being un-
willing to deal unjustly with one of her officials, or exact
unreasonable and impossible duties from them; therefore,

*Be it enacted by the General Assembly of the Commonwealth
of Kentucky:*

§ 1. That the representatives and heirs of William J.
Fields, late sheriff of Carter county, and J. F. Horton, C.
S. Counts, James Flawha, E. R. Elliott, L. H. Elliott,
Samuel McDavid, John Armstrong, James M. Fields, John
Jordan, Daniel Rice, Jacob Rice, and A. Rucker, his securities, be, and they are hereby, released from the balance
of the judgment due the State, including interest, costs,
and damages rendered against them at the February term,
1862, of the Franklin circuit court, for the revenue tax of
1861.

§ 2. This act shall take effect from its passage.

Approved February 10, 1869.

––––

CHAPTER 1448.

AN ACT to legalize certain acts of the Oldham County Court, and to
authorize the enforcement of the same.

WHEREAS, A majority of the justices of the peace in and
for the county of Oldham did, at the May term, 1868, of
the Oldham county court. levy a tax, by which the sum of
two thousand dollars was raised, which said court appropriated in aid of building certain bridges in said county
upon certain turnpike road projects, one of which was, at
the time, in progress of construction, and the other is now
being rapidly built; and whereas, it was doubtful in the
minds of said court whether the local act of this General
Assembly, approved February 6th, 1867, entitled "An act
to empower the county court of Oldham county to make
subscription to the capital stock of turnpike roads in said
county," or the act of this General Assembly, approved
March 9th, 1868, entitled "An act to empower county
courts to take stock in turnpike roads in this Commonwealth," was binding on said court; and whereas, one
thousand dollars was appropriated by said court towards
the building of a bridge on the Henry, Oldham, and Jefferson turnpike road, to be held as stock in said road by
said county; and whereas, the money is now collected and
in the hands of the late sheriff of said county; and said
court, still doubting its power to order the payment of the
one thousand dollars over to the said president, directors,
and company; for remedy whereof,

1869.

Be it enacted by the General Assembly of the Commonwealth of Kentucky:

§ 1. That the levy of said tax is hereby legalized, and the county court for Oldham is hereby authorized and empowered to order the payment of the said sum of one thousand dollars, named in the preamble hereof, to the turnpike road company for whose benefit it was levied, upon the demand of the same by the president of said turnpike company; and in the event of the said sheriff not paying over said tax, the said county court or said company may proceed against him and his securities on his official bond for the same.

§ 2. This act shall take effect from its passage.

Approved February 11, 1869.-

CHAPTER 1449.

AN ACT to amend the act incorporating and chartering the City of Owensboro, approved February 16th, 1866.

Be it enacted by the General Assembly of the Commonwealth of Kentucky:

Officers of city.
§ 1. That the act chartering and incorporating the city of Owensboro, approved February 16th, 1866, be, and the same is hereby, amended as follows : That the officers of the city of Owensboro shall consist of a mayor, three councilmen from each ward, a city judge, assessor, collector, marshal, treasurer, clerk, and city attorney ; and the mayor and council are hereby authorized to create, by ordinance, such additional office or offices, from time to time, as in their judgment may be necessary for the proper government of said city.

Mayor. councilmen, and city judge to be elected, & when
§ 2. The mayor, councilmen, and city judge shall be elected by the qualified voters of said city, the next elections for which shall be as follows: For mayor, city judge, and marshal on the first Monday in April, 1870, and every two years thereafter ; and said mayor, judge, and marshal shall hold their offices, under such elections, for two years, and until their successors are elected and qualified ; and the next election for councilmen shall be held on the first Monday in April, 1869, and every one year thereafter; and said councilmen, thus elected, shall hold their offices for one year, and until their successors are elected and qualified.

Other officers to be elected by council, and when.
§ 3. All other officers herein provided for, and all such as the mayor and council may, by ordinance, provide for, shall be elected by the vote of the council ; and in case of a tie the same shall be decided by the vote of the mayor ; and the election for all such officers shall be held at the first regular meeting after the new board shall have been

elected and qualified, or, in case of a new office being created by ordinance, the first election to fill said office shall be held at the first regular meeting after the ordinance creating such office has taken effect: *Provided*, That the vote of a majority of all the councilmen elected (or one half thereof with the vote of the mayor), shall be necessary to elect: *And provided further*, That if no quorum is present at the times provided for such elections, or after balloting no election can be had, the mayor and council may adjourn the said election over to the next regular meeting, and may so adjourn same from time to time if such like necessity occurs; and the councilmen not present at such adjournments shall be summoned by the mayor or clerk, by written summons to be served by the marshal, commanding their presence at the next meeting. And all officers elected or appointed by the mayor and council shall hold their offices until the next regular election for such officers, and until their successors are elected or appointed and qualified.

Term of office.

§ 4. All officers of said city shall take an oath (or affirmation) for the faithful discharge of their respective duties, which may be administered by the mayor, city judge, or any officer of the city, county, or Commonwealth, authorized by law to administer oaths.

Officers to take oath.

§ 5. No person shall be eligible to the office of mayor who is not, at the time of his election, twenty-five years of age, a qualified voter under the laws of the State of Kentucky, and the charter and laws of the city of Owensboro, and have resided within the limits of said city for two years next preceding his election or appointment. Nor shall any person be eligible to any other office created by this charter or its amendments, or provided for by same, who has not been a resident citizen within the limits of said city for one year next preceding his election or appointment, and a qualified voter under the Constitution and laws of the State of Kentucky, and the charter and laws of the city of Owensboro: *Provided*, That no person shall be eligible to the offices of mayor or councilman who is not, at the time of his election or appointment, the owner of real estate situate in said city: *And provided further*, That no officer, into whose hands the money of the city may pass, shall be eligible to re-election or appointment until he has met and discharged said liability to the extent the same is due from him.

Eligibility of mayor & other officers.

§ 6. Every white male citizen over the age of twenty-one years, who is sane, and has paid all taxes and fines due from him to the city of Owensboro, who shall be a legal voter under the Constitution and laws of the State of Kentucky, and who shall have been a citizen of said

Qualification of voters.

1869.

city, residing therein for sixty days next preceding the day of election for officers of said city, shall be a qualified voter at all such city elections; but no other persons shall be allowed to vote for any officer of said city.

§ 7. All officers heretofore elected or appointed in or for said city, shall hold their offices until the expiration of the terms for which they may have been elected or appointed, and until their successors shall have been elected or appointed and qualified, as provided for in this act and the charter as thus amended.

Present officers to continue until expiration of term for which elected.

§ 8. The three councilmen from each ward, together with the mayor, shall constitute the board of common council. The new board shall meet on the second Thursday after their election, at which time they shall be qualified and the board organized; at which time they shall, by ordinance, fix the times and place for their regular meetings, which shall be at least once a month, and may be as much oftener as the public interest may require; and they may at any time change the time or place of meeting by an order of the council.

Quorum of council. When new board to meet, &c.

§ 9. Said board shall, at their first meeting, elect one of their members mayor *pro tem.* for the year; and such member shall, in the absence of the mayor, preside at the meetings of the council; and in case of the death or resignation of the mayor, his absence from the city, or inability to perform the duties of his office, said mayor *pro tem.* shall, during such absence of the mayor, or the existence of such disability, or vacancy in the office, perform all the duties of mayor, and shall have and exercise all the powers that are vested in the mayor.

Mayor pro tem. to be elected by council; his powers and duties.

§ 10. The clerk of the board shall keep a full and complete record of the proceedings of every meeting of the board, in plain and legible writing, in a book kept for that purpose; and the proceedings of each meeting shall be signed by the officer presiding at that meeting.

Clerk to keep record of proceedings.

§ 11. The mayor (or the mayor *pro tem.*, when authorized to exercise the duties of mayor) may, by summons or otherwise, call the board together in extra session, whenever the interest of the city or the public good requires it. A majority of the councilmen elected shall be necessary to transact business; and in the event of a meeting of the council when the mayor and mayor *pro tem.* are both absent, then the council may elect a chairman, who shall then preside over the meeting.

Called meetings, quorum, &c.

§ 12. The records of the proceedings of the council, and all orders and ordinances passed by them, shall be securely kept, but shall be subject to the inspection of any and all persons during the business hours of the day; and the meetings of the council shall be open to the public: *Provided,* That the board of council may, at any meeting, by

Records to be securely kept, & open to inspection. Meetings of council to be open, but secret sessions may be had.

a vote of the council, resolve themselves into secret session for such time during that meeting as they may think proper; and during such time shall have power to exclude from the council chamber all persons except the mayor and members of the council; and it shall be the duty of the marshal and each policeman of the city, under the direction of the officer then presiding over the board, to enforce all such orders of the council.

§ 13. It shall be the duty of the marshal, and each policeman of the city, to attend the meetings of the council whenever required to do so by the mayor or mayor *pro tem.;* and it shall be their duty, under the direction of the officer then presiding, to keep order and protect the council from interruption during their sessions; and for that purpose may arrest and imprison any and all persons who are guilty of disturbing the proceedings of the council.

Marshal and policemen to attend meetings of council when required, and keep order, &c.

§ 14. The mayor and council shall have power to pass all ordinances and by-laws necessary to prevent obstructions or interferences with any of the streets, alleys, sidewalks, wharves, and public thoroughfares of the city; to remove, abate, and prevent any and all nuisances; and for that purpose may impose fines and penalties, not, however, exceeding in amount, for any one offense, the jurisdiction of the city court of Owensboro.

Mayor & council pass ordinances in relation to streets, alleys, &c.

§ 15. It shall be the province of the mayor and council to declare what are nuisances; and they shall have power, by the passage and enforcement of all necessary ordinances as provided in the preceding section, to prevent the exercise of all noxious or offensive trades; and suppress all trades, manufactories, or other business or practices that may be dangerous to the health of the city, or any part thereof; and for the purposes named in this and the preceding section, and to pass and enforce the by-laws and ordinances therein named, the jurisdiction of the mayor and council and all other officers of the city of Owensboro shall extend for one half mile beyond the limits of the city.

In relation to nuisances, &c.

§ 16. The mayor and council shall have the exclusive control of the retail, by quantities less than one quart, of all spirituous, malt, or vinous liquors within the limits of the city of Owensboro; and they shall have the exclusive power to license for the purposes of the retail of all liquors or drinks by such quantities as aforesaid, all taverns, inns, ale, porter, or coffee-houses or shops, or any other house of public entertainment or convenience not prohibited by law; and they may, by ordinances or by-laws, prescribe rules and regulations for the sale of same; may prohibit the sale of such articles upon the Sabbath day; they shall have power to fix, by ordinance, the amount of tax which shall be paid to the city for the

Mayor and council to have exclusive control of the retail of liquors in said city, &c.

1869.

privilege of retailing as aforesaid : *Provided*, The **State** tax, as now provided, shall be paid in all cases.

§ 17. No person shall retail within the limits of the **city** of Owensboro any spirituous, malt, or vinous liquors **by** quantities less than one quart, without first procuring **a** license from the mayor and council of said city, and **they** shall have power to grant or refuse said license as to **them** may seem best for the welfare of said city; but any person who has obtained their license may sell without any additional license from State or county; but the mayor **and** council may revoke or suspend said license at pleasure **for** a violation of their ordinances. And the mayor and council may, by ordinance, prescribe such additional fines **and** penalties, not exceeding fifty dollars for each offense, **for** violations of the charter and ordinances upon this subject, as to them may seem proper; and they may further require of such dealers such bonds and securities, and prescribe such oaths as they, the mayor and council, may deem necessary to insure a faithful compliance with the laws governing said city.

§ 18. The mayor and council shall have power to license any circus or menagerie, and grant permits for the exhibition of any animal, wax figure, any natural or artificial curiosity, any feats of horsemanship, riding, leaping, tumbling. dancing, vaulting, legerdemain, ventriloquism, and all other exhibitions or performances that may be exhibited or performed for gain within the city of Owensboro, or within one mile of the boundary thereof; and the mayor and council may, by ordinance, fix upon each of said shows, exhibitions, or performances such tax as they may deem proper, and by all necessary ordinances prohibit the same within the boundary aforesaid, under penalties of such fines as they may fix, until the tax aforesaid has been paid and the license obtained ; and they may also prescribe such rules and regulations, touching such show, exhibition, or performance, as to them may seem proper; and to enforce all such ordinances and by-laws, the officers of the city shall have jurisdiction and authority for one mile beyond the limits of said city.

§ 19. The mayor and council shall have power (and they may exercise it or not, at their discretion) to license within said city billiard tables, Jenny Lind tables, ten-pin alleys, and other houses of amusement or profit, including all theatrical performances, concerts, and panoramas; and may, by ordinances and by-laws, impose such taxes for same as they may deem proper, and in like manner provide for the collection of same, and prescribe and enforce fines and penalties for a violation of any of said ordinances or laws; and no person shall exercise any of the above named privileges within said city, or within one

No one to retail less than quart without first obtaining license from council.

May prescribe additional penalties for violation of ordinances in relation to license.

In relation to circuses, &c.

In relation to billiard and Jenny Lind tables, theaters, &c.

mile thereof, without a license therefrom; and the city officials shall have jurisdiction to enforce this section, and all ordinances and laws passed by the mayor and council touching the same.

§ 20. The treasurer, collector, and marshal shall each, before he enters upon the duties of his office, execute a bond to the city of Owensboro, with good security, to be approved by the mayor and council, conditioned for the faithful discharge of all their official duties, and with such additional covenants as are now by law required in bonds of sheriffs or constables; which bond shall be attested by the clerk of the board, recorded in the record books of the council, and filed in the office of the mayor; and each of said officers, together with their securities, shall be liable to the said city for any and all money received by them, and for all neglect or violation of duties, in the same manner that sheriffs and constables, with their sureties, are now made liable; and the mayor and council shall fix, by ordinance, the penalties for all breaches of said bonds: *Provided*, That all actions for breaches of the covenants of said bonds shall be brought and prosecuted in the name of the city of Owensboro, and in either the circuit or quarterly court of Daviess county; which courts are hereby invested with jurisdiction in said cases to the extent that the amounts in controversy may be within the jurisdiction of those courts; and in such cases the right of appeal shall lie from the quarterly to the circuit court, and from the circuit court to the court of appeals of Kentucky, in the same manner that other appeals may be taken.

Treasurer, collector, and marshal to give bond, &c.

§ 21. The mayor and council may at any time require of either of said officers additional security upon said bond, by giving him ten days' notice in writing; and upon the failure of such officer to give such additional security, the mayor and council may remove him, and declare the office vacant. The mayor and council may at any time, by a like proceeding, remove all or either of said officers, or any others provided for in this charter, for drunkenness, gross misconduct, or neglect of duty; and the securities in the bonds of any such officer may, by a similar proceeding before the mayor and council, obtain relief or indemnity, in the same mode and to the same extent that sureties of constables may by law.

Additional security may be required.

Officers may be removed.

§ 22. That section fourteen of the act chartering the city of Owensboro, to which this act is an amendment, be so amended that the mayor and council shall have power to pass and enforce ordinances providing for the taking up and sale of all hogs, horses, cattle, and all other animals found running at large within said city.

May sell hogs, &c. found running at large in city.

§ 23. That section twenty-four of the act approved February 16, 1866, to which this is an amendment, be so

When by-laws and ordinances to take effect.

1869.

amended that all by-laws and ordinances of said city shall take effect and be in force from and after ten days from the date of their publication in any newspaper of said city; and in the event there should be no newspaper published in said city, then the mayor shall cause printed copies of such by-laws and ordinances to be posted at five conspicuous places in said city, and the same shall take effect ten days after such posting.

§ 24. That section twenty-five of same act be so amended, that the city judge provided for in said section shall be the judge of the city court of Owensboro, which court is hereby created. That said court shall have the exclusive jurisdiction of actions and prosecutions for violations of the charter, ordinances, and by-laws of said city (except cases otherwise provided for in this act), whether the offender be summoned or arrested in the city of Owensboro or elsewhere in Daviess county; and said court shall be opened every morning (Sundays excepted), at 9 o'clock; and all cases shall be tried before the court without the intervention of a jury. Said city judge shall be the clerk of said court, keep a docket, enter judgments, and issue executions and other process, as now provided by law for justices' courts. He is hereby authorized to issue, as judge of said court, all warrants, subpœnas, writs, and other process necessary to enforce the laws of the said city, as provided by the ordinances of same. He is authorized to issue *capias pro fines* upon fines, mittimus, &c., and may fine for contempt of court while court is in session, and is invested with all the powers for preserving order and protecting the court that justices of the peace are by law. In case of a vacancy in the office of city judge, or the absence or disability of said judge, it shall be the duty of the mayor to hold the city court, and at such times he shall have and exercise all the powers, of every description, that are herein granted to the city judge. From all judgments of the city court either party may appeal to the Daviess quarterly court, where the amount sought to be recovered exceeds ten dollars, or may appeal to the circuit court of Daviess county where the amount sought to be recovered is twenty dollars or more. In all cases of breaches of the ordinances of the city the fees of the city judge shall be regulated by ordinances and by-laws of the mayor and council. Said judge shall also have power to issue warrants in the name of the Commonwealth in cases of felonies and misdemeanors, and in such cases may sit as a court of inquiry, try, acquit, commit, or bail prisoners in conformity with the laws of the State of Kentucky, and shall be governed by the same rules, exercise the same powers, and receive the same fees, that two justices of the peace might in such cases; and he shall, where the de-

City judge to be judge of city court.

Jurisdiction of city court.

When court to be open.

Judge to be clerk of his court; his powers and duties.

Vacancies, how filled.

Appeals may be had.

Fees in certain cases to be regulated by ordinance.

Additional powers of judge

fendants in civil cases reside within the city of Owensboro, have the same jurisdiction that a justice of the peace has, and shall be entitled to the same fees in such cases. He is authorized to administer oaths; and all copies and transcripts from his office, when certified by him, shall be evidence in the courts of this Commonwealth. The civil terms of the city judge shall be fixed by the Daviess county court, in same manner as justices' courts, and from his judgments at such terms either party may appeal in the same manner as from a justices' court.

§ 25. The marshal of the city of Owensboro shall be a peace officer authorized to arrest and commit to jail any and all persons; and it shall be his duty to do so whenever he finds them violating any of the criminal or penal laws of the State or city; and it shall be the duty of the jailer of Daviess county to receive from the marshal and policemen all prisoners arrested by them; and if the city court is not then in session, he shall keep them safely in said jail until ordered out by the city court. All warrants and process of every description issuing from the city court shall be directed to and executed by the marshal, except when he may be absent, sick, or under some disability, when they may be directed to and executed by the sheriff, constable, or policemen. It shall be the duty of the marshal to attend punctually upon the meetings of the city court, and touching the business of said court, and all business of the city; he shall perform all the duties that would otherwise devolve upon constables or sheriffs; and for such services he shall be allowed the same fees that are now allowed to constables and sheriffs by law. He shall have power to execute warrants and collect debts, &c., in civil matters, as constables are now allowed to do; may execute all notices of every description and subpœnas issuing from any court in Daviess county; and his jurisdiction shall be co-extensive with Daviess county, and in all such matters he shall be allowed the same fees that sheriffs or constables are allowed for similar services, which shall be paid in like manner; and the marshal shall, furthermore, perform all duties that may be required of him by the ordinances of the mayor and council; and said mayor and council shall, for all such services, by ordinance, fix the fees of the marshal, and provide for the payment of same; and said marshal may appoint one or more deputies, in the same manner, and under the same responsibilities, that sheriffs may; and he shall also execute, in the county court, a bond, with the same covenants, and to be taken and approved in the same manner as constables' bonds are now by law; and said marshal shall have power to arrest, under warrants or other process, all persons charged with felonies or breaches of the penal laws of the

1869.

Marshal, his powers and duties.

1869.

State or city; and may, by himself or deputies, execute said power anywhere in Daviess county; and, upon his county court bond, he shall be liable to the same extent, and in like manner, as constables are now liable by law on their bonds, to same penalties, and to be recovered in same manner, and before same courts.

Sale of real estate for taxes, how conducted.

§ 26. That section twenty-seven of said act be, and the same is hereby, so amended that the sale of real estate for taxes, therein provided for, may be made on the first day of any county or circuit court, after having first advertised the same for three weeks, as therein provided, or by printed notices, posted at five public places in said city, one of which must be at the court-house door.

Proceedings in case no real estate can be found to pay taxes.

§ 27. That section sixteen of said act be so amended that when no real or personal property be found from which to make the taxes owing by any person, or is insufficient to pay the same, it shall be the duty of the city collector to make out a statement of the taxes owing by such person, accompanied by his statement that he can find no property to make same, and file said statement at the office of the city court; and the city judge shall then issue, in the name of the city, a warrant directed to the marshal or collector, commanding such officer to attach any property or interest belonging to such delinquent, and to garnishee, to the extent of such taxes and costs, any and all debts due to such person; and the service of that warrant upon any person owing or employing such delinquent person, shall operate as an attachment, and render such employer or person owing said tax-payer responsible to the city for the amount claimed in said warrant, with the costs, to the extent they may be owing debts or wages to said delinquent; and said employer shall be liable to the city for all wages that may accrue to said delinquent thereafter, until said demands to the city are paid; and to enforce this, the marshal or collector may summon said employer to appear before the city court, where he may be examined on oath (if the counsel for the city desire it) as to the amount he owes such delinquent, and how much he has paid him, if any, since the service of such warrant; and witnesses may also be summoned and examined; and the city judge shall have power to render judgment against said employer, and enforce same by execution; and the city judge shall have power, and it shall be his duty, to enforce the attendance of all said parties by attachments and fines.

Persons may be committed to jail for non-payment of fines.

§ 28. That in all cases of fines imposed by judgments of the city court, the defendant shall, until said fine and costs be paid, be committed to jail by said court, as provided by law in other cases of fines recovered before other officers; and the mayor and council are hereby authorized to provide by ordinance for the employment of such prisoner upon any work being done by order of the city during the time of his said commitment; and may, during such time, compel his service as aforesaid; and said service shall, when rendered, liquidate said fine.

§ 29. That the mayor and council shall have power, when they shall deem it necessary, to pass all ordinances necessary to prevent the erection of buildings of wood or other combustible material within a named boundary in said city; and they may at any time change or extend said boundary.

May prevent the erection of wooden buildings.

§ 30. That, section nine of the act to which this is an amendment be so amended that all property, real, personal, and mixed, money, bonds, notes, rights, and credits, shall be subject to taxation to the city: *Provided, however,* That the mayor and council shall have power, by ordinance, to declare what shall be exempt from taxation.

What may be subject to taxation.

§ 31. That the mayor and council shall have power to provide by ordinance for the filling of all vacancies that may occur in the offices of the city until the next general election for such officers.

Vacancy, how filled.

§ 32. That sections four, five, six, seven, that portion of section nine ending, in the eighteenth line of said section, with the words "to preside over their meetings," section thirteen, section eighteen, section twenty-three, and section twenty-six, of the act to which this is an amendment, be, and the same are hereby, repealed.

Certain portions of city charter repealed.

§ 33. That this act shall take effect from and after its passage.

Approved February 12, 1869.

CHAPTER 1450.
AN ACT for the benefit of James Archie Davis, a Pauper Idiot.

WHEREAS, It is represented to this General Assembly, that, in consequence of some mistake or oversight of the committee for James Archie Davis, a pauper idiot, of Nelson county, there was no inquest held in his case after the expiration of the previous inquest, which was on the 17th day of June, 1866, until the October term, 1868, of the Nelson circuit court; and whereas, the existing laws regulating the payment of allowances to pauper idiots do not authorize the Auditor of Public Accounts to audit and pay an allowance for said Davis from the 17th day of June, 1866, to the date of last inquest; and for remedy whereof,

Be it enacted by the General Assembly of the Commonwealth of Kentucky:

§ 1. That the Auditor of Public Accounts be, and he is hereby, authorized to draw his warrant on the Treasurer in favor of the committee of James Archie Davis, for an allowance, at the rate of fifty dollars per annum, from the 17th day of June, 1866, to the date of inquest held in his case, at the October term, 1868, of the Nelson circuit court: *Provided, however,* That an order of allowance shall be first made, under the authority of this act, by said court, and a copy thereof filed with the Auditor.

§ 2. This act shall take effect from its passage.

Approved February 12, 1869.

CHAPTER 1451.

AN ACT for the benefit of the Schollsville Branch of the Winchester and Red River Iron Works Turnpike Road Company.

WHEREAS, The Clark county court, at its August term, 1867, in accordance with the provisions of chapter 103 of the Revised Statutes, incorporated "The Schollsville Branch of the Winchester and Red River Iron Works Turnpike Road Company," and constituted the subscribers thereto a body corporate, by the aforesaid name; and whereas, it is feared that there exists some defect in the aforesaid proceedings of the Clark county court; and that, as a result of said defective proceedings, that the aforesaid company does not have and possess the powers intended to be conferred to the Clark county court and authorized by the statute; therefore, in remedy whereof,

Be it enacted by the General Assembly of the Commonwealth of Kentucky:

§ 1. That the proceedings of the Clark county court, had prior to and on the 25th day of August, 1867, whereby William H. Cunningham, John H. Quisenberry, and others, were incorporated and constituted a body-politic and corporate, and the name of "The Schollsville Branch of the Winchester and Red River Iron Works Turnpike Road Company," are hereby declared to be valid and regular; and said company is hereby declared to have thereby been invested with and to possess all the corporate powers enumerated in the aforesaid order of the Clark county court, made on the 25th day of August, 1867, and authorized to be exercised by the provisions of chapter 103 of the Revised Statutes; and its organization on that day is also hereby declared valid.

§ 2. Whenever the president of said road shall file with the clerk of the Clark county court his affidavit, together with the certificate of two civil engineers of competent skill, to the effect that the aforesaid road has been completed, and is, in all respects, constructed as required by chapter 103 of the Revised Statutes, it shall be the duty of the presiding judge of the Clark county court to issue an order authorizing said company to erect a gate and collect toll thereat: *Provided*, That said company shall be governed by the now existing laws of this Commonwealth in regard to the amount and rates of toll to be collected at the said gate.

§ 3. This act shall take effect from its passage.

Approved February 12, 1869.

CHAPTER 1452.

AN ACT to incorporate the Paducah, Blandville, and Columbus Gravel Road Company.

Be it enacted by the General Assembly of the Commonwealth of Kentucky:

§ 1. That a company shall be, and the same is hereby, established and incorporated, with a capital of one hundred and fifty thousand dollars, to be divided into shares of twenty-five dollars each, for the purpose of constructing a gravel road from Paducah to Blandville and Columbus, in this State, under the corporate name and style of the Paducah, Blandville, and Columbus gravel road company; and as such shall be a body-politic; and by that name and style shall have power, and be competent to contract and be contracted with, sue and be sued, plead and be impleaded, in all courts of this Commonwealth; and with power to acquire, hold, possess, use, and occupy all such real and personal property as may be necessary and convenient for the site or route of said road; for timbers, piers, and abutments; for all necessary bridges and culverts on said road, and lots for toll-houses and residences of toll-gate keepers; also the necessary stone, gravel, sand, and earth, for the construction and repairs of said road, and any and every other material necessary for the construction or repairs of said road; and to have and use a common seal, and the same to alter and renew at pleasure; to make and ordain all such by-laws as may be deemed by the company necessary for the construction, promotion, welfare, and repairs of said road, and the management of its prudential and financial concerns, not contrary to the Constitution and laws of this Commonwealth.

Company incorporated, capital stock, and corporate powers.

§ 2. That the width of said road shall not, where it will admit of it, be less than thirty nor more than sixty feet, and the artificial or metaled part shall not be less than

Width of road.

1869.

eighteen feet wide, and the graded part not less than twenty-four wide, and that the stream shall be bridged.

§ 3. That J. M. Bigger, L. D. Husbands, George W. Morrow, William G. Bullitt, Thomas Steiger, Z. W. Bugg, J. D. White, Wiley Dicus, William White, Daniel Bodkin, Richard Cook, William Taylor, Geo. W. Martin, William Weston, Dr. N. C. Thomas, G. G. Brown, and William Webb, be, and they are hereby, appointed commissioners, any three or more of whom may act, to open books for the subscription of stock or capital aforesaid. at such times and places as may be deemed necessary; and whenever fifteen thousand dollars of said stock shall have been subscribed, said commissioners shall call a meeting of the stockholders, at such time and place as they may think proper, having first advertised, for ten days, the time and place of meeting by publication in the newspaper or newspapers having the largest circulation in the counties of McCracken, Ballard, and Hickman, and by written or printed notices posted up at some conspicuous place in Blandville, Columbus, Joseph McClure's, Paducah, and Lovelaceville; and the stockholders, meeting in pursuance of said call, or by written proxy, shall choose a president and eight directors, in whom shall be vested all the powers of the corporation for the construction of said road, and the management and direction of its prudential and financial concerns; that each share of stock shall entitle the owner to one vote; and after the board is thus organized, an annual election shall be held on the first Saturday in May in each year thereafter for president and directors, who shall hold their offices for one year, and until their successors are duly elected and qualified; and no person shall be eligible to the office of president or director without being a stockholder, and shall vacate his office on ceasing to be one. Any vacancy occurring in the board may be filled by those remaining in office. If, from any cause, an annual election shall not be held at the time appointed, the president and directors may order an election to be held on any other day.

§ 4. The said Paducah, Blandville, and Columbus Gravel Road Company, or the said president and directors, shall be vested with all the power, authority, immunities, tolls, privileges, and advantages, in all and every respect, that are now vested by law in the Bardstown and Louisville turnpike company, subject to like limitations and restrictions as if they were here repeated, except as otherwise provided for or modified in this act.

§ 5. That the president and directors, at any time after the organization of the company, may again open books for subscriptions, or sell the residue of their stock, or so much thereof as they may deem proper, but at not less than par.

Commissioners to receive subscription of stock.

When meeting of subscribers to be called.

President and directors to be chosen.

Stock, how voted.

Eligibility of directors, vacancies, annual elections, &c.

Additional powers.

Books may be reopened.

§ 6. That whenever said company shall have completed twelve miles or more of road consecutively, they shall be entitled to erect gates and receive tolls on said road at distances of not less than five miles, one from the other: *Provided*, That no gate shall be erected for toll nearer than one half mile to Paducah, Blandville, or Columbus.

§ 7. This act to take effect from its passage.

Approved February 12, 1869.

1869.

When gates may be erected.

CHAPTER 1453.

AN ACT to amend the Charter of the Russellville District Turnpike Company.

Be it enacted by the General Assembly of the Commonwealth of Kentucky:

§ 1. That the act incorporating the Russellville District turnpike company, approved February 24, 1868, be, and is hereby, amended as follows: That the State Assessor shall make a separate assessment for the "Russellville District," of Logan county, which he shall return to the county clerk by the first Monday of May of each year; and the county court shall, on that day (first Monday of May of each year), levy the tax provided for in the original act to pay the interest, and provide sinking fund for the turnpike bonds of said district.

§ 2. The trusts of the payment of interest and application of the sinking fund of said district bonds, shall be performed by the treasurer of said company, subject to the government and control of the board of directors thereof, and an annual settlement shall be made by said treasurer with the county court, and all coupons paid, and bonds redeemed, shall be canceled and returned by him to said court as vouchers on said settlements.

§ 3. That on the 27th day of February, 1869, or on the same day upon which the vote of Logan county is taken on a subscription to the Owensboro and Russellville railroad, the vote of the said "Russellville District" of said county shall be taken on the question, shall the macadamized or turnpike roads built, or to be built by said "Russellville District turnpike company" be free; and an annual tax not over ten cents on the one hundred dollars' [worth of] property in said district, subject to State revenue, be collected to keep said roads in repair? and if a majority of the votes cast shall be for said free roads and tax, the court shall cause record to be made thereof, and levy such rate of tax, not exceeding ten cents, as the board of directors of said company shall stipulate as necessary.

§ 4. The sheriff or other collector of the tax of said district for said turnpike bonds shall be allowed compensation at the discretion of the county court, not over seven per cent. on the amount paid the Treasurer.

Approved February 12, 1869.

CHAPTER 1454.

AN ACT for the benefit of Wm. Grisham.

WHEREAS, It appears that William Grisham, a citizen of Rockcastle county, Kentucky, did, upon the 5th of January, 1848, procure, according to law, a Rockcastle county land warrant, upon which was made a survey of one hundred acres of unappropriated land lying in said county, bearing date February 2d, 1848, which survey was properly made by the county surveyor, and recorded and signed by him in the appropriate surveyor's book of the county aforesaid; and whereas, it appears that said survey has not been put to record in the Land Office of this State; therefore, in order that justice may be done the aforesaid Wm. Grisham by the issuing of a patent upon the survey aforesaid,

Be it enacted by the General Assembly of the Commonwealth of Kentucky:

§ 1. That the Register of the Land Office of the State of Kentucky is hereby directed to put to record a properly certified copy of the survey described in the foregoing preamble, and to issue to the aforesaid William Grisham a patent for same, as though it had been filed in due time: *Provided*, That this act shall not be so construed as to interfere with the vested rights of any other person, or any survey previously made.

§ 2. This act shall take effect from its passage.

Approved February 12, 1869.

CHAPTER 1457.

AN ACT to incorporate the Cloverport and Panther Creek Turnpike Road Company.

Be it enacted by the General Assembly of the Commonwealth of Kentucky:

§ 1. That W. H. Webb, William Vest, Frederick Walter, and R. R. Pierce, of the town of Cloverport, and James Willis, John Haynes, and Charles Cobb, of the county of Ohio, be, and they are hereby, created a body-politic and corporate, with perpetual succession, under the name of "The Cloverport and Panther Creek turnpike road company;" they shall have power to sue and be sued, in all the courts of the Commonwealth; may have and use a common seal, which they may alter at pleasure; and are hereby invested with all the powers usually granted by law to corporations to construct turnpike roads.

§ 2. The capital stock of said company shall be whatever the company may deem necessary to construct a turnpike road from Cloverport to some point on Panther Creek, in Ohio county, and shall be divided into shares of fifty dollars each.

§ 3. The corporators above named shall cause to be opened books for the subscription of stock, at such times, and at such places, as they shall deem expedient.

§ 4. When sufficient stock shall have been subscribed to make it proper, the corporators shall proceed to the organization of the company, and the subscribers shall elect a president, five directors, a secretary, and a treasurer, who shall hold their offices for one year, or until their successors shall have been duly elected and installed.

§ 5. The secretary and treasurer of said company may be removed at pleasure by the board of directors if they deem it necessary.

§ 6. The said company may construct a road of any material, width, and depth of same, as they may think best.

§ 7. This act shall take effect from its passage.

Approved February 12, 1869.

CHAPTER 1458.

AN ACT to change the place of voting in District No. 5, in McCracken County.

Be it enacted by the General Assembly of the Commonwealth of Kentucky:

§ 2. That the place of voting in district No. 5, in Mc-Cracken county, be, and the same is hereby, changed from Spring Bayou to the town of Woodville, in said district.

§ 2. This act to take effect from its passage.

Approved February 12, 1869.

CHAPTER 1459.

AN ACT to authorize the Boyd County Court to make a Road from Catlettsburg to the Lawrence County Line.

*Be it enacted by the General Assembly of the Commonwealth
of Kentucky:*

§ 1. That the presiding judge of the Boyd county court, together with a majority of the justices of said county, at any regular term of said court, are hereby authorized and empowered to levy an ad valorem tax of not exceeding twenty cents on the one hundred dollars on all property subject to taxation for revenue purposes, within the following boundary, to-wit: Commencing at the line of the corporation of the town of Catlettsburg, next to Hampton City, at the road leading up Sandy river; with said road, which passes Jesse Cyrus's, George R. Burgess's, to near Turman's ferry; thence with the county road up said river to the Lawrence county line—that is, all the property within three miles of said road, and all like property in the town of Catlettsburg, shall be subject to the tax provided for in this act—for the purpose of making a good road from said corporation line to the Lawrence county line, upon the road as now located, or any change that may be necessary to make the same a good eighteen feet wide road; any such change shall be under the direction of the Boyd county court, under the laws now in force for changing roads; and the right of way to be condemned shall be thirty feet in width; and the lands taken for the change, or to extend the width, shall be paid for by the county court as now directed by law.

§ 2. That the money arising from this levy shall be collected by the sheriff or collector of said county, and paid over to the treasurer of said county as other levies are now directed to be collected and paid; and said sheriff or collector shall be liable upon his bond as such for any defalcation of his duties herein required. The treasurer shall keep a separate account of said fund. Said fund shall be expended on the road described in the first section of this act, upon the order of the county court, in such places and in such manner as may be directed by said court.

§ 3. The levy and appropriation herein directed shall not dispense with the power of the county court to have said road worked by the hands that are now or may hereafter be liable to work on the same.

§ 4. The county court making the levy may authorize and direct the treasurer of said county to issue the bonds of the county, payable in annual installments, not exceeding in amount the yearly proceeds of said levy: *Provided,* Said bonds shall not exceed in amount eight thousand dollars, and may bear interest at the rate of six per cent. per annum.

§ 5. This act shall be in force from and after its passage, and continue in force until said road shall be completed.

Approved February 12, 1869.

CHAPTER 1461.

AN ACT to change the time of holding the Marion Quarterly Court.

Be it enacted by the General Assembly of the Commonwealth of Kentucky:

§ 1. That the time now fixed by law for holding the different terms of the Marion quarterly court be, and the same are hereby, changed from the second Mondays in February, May, August, and November, to the fourth Mondays in March, June, September, and December.

§ 2. This act shall take effect from and after March 1st, 1869.

Approved February 12, 1869.

CHAPTER 1462.

AN ACT making the amended Road Law, approved February 17th, 1866, apply to Breckinridge County.

Be it enacted by the General Assembly of the Commonwealth of Kentucky:

§ 1. That the provisions of the act approved February 17th, 1866, entitled "An act amending the law in relation to roads," shall apply to, and be in force in, the county of Breckinridge, if a majority of the citizens voting thereon at the general election in August, 1869, shall be in favor thereof.

§ 2. That the persons appointed to compare the polls for Representative of said county shall ascertain the state of the polls for and against the road law, and report the same to the next county court of Breckinridge county thereafter.

§ 3. It shall be the duty of the sheriff of said county to post notices in three public places in each precinct, informing the people that the question embraced in this act is to be submitted for their vote.

§ 4. This act to take effect from its passage.

Approved February 12, 1869.

1869.   CHAPTER 1463.

AN ACT to incorporate the Burlington and Hebron Turnpike Road Company.

Be it enacted by the General Assembly of the Commonwealth of Kentucky:

§ 1. That a company shall be formed under the name, style, and title of the Burlington and Hebron Turnpike Road Company, for the sole purpose of forming and maintaining an artificial turnpike road from Burlington, in Boone county, to Hebron, so as to intersect at that place the turnpike road leading from Petersburg to the city of Covington, by way of Ludlow.

Company formed, name and style, &c.

§ 2. The capital stock of said company shall be twelve thousand dollars; and the company aforesaid is hereby authorized to raise, by subscription, the sum aforesaid, to be divided into shares of twenty-five dollars each.

Capital stock.

§ 3. That the books for the subscription of stock in said company shall be opened on the first Monday in April, 1869, at the town of Burlington, under the direction of N. E. Hawes, E. E. Uitz, and Wm. Collins, and at Hebron under the direction of Wilson Harper, Stephen Gaines, and William Foster, or some one or more of them at each place; that such of the two classes of commissioners, appointed by this act to open books for the subscription of the capital stock of said company, or such of them as may act, shall procure one or more books, and the subscribers to the stock of said company shall enter into the following obligation in said book or books, to-wit: "We, whose names are hereunto subscribed, do promise to pay to the president, directors, and company, of the Burlington and Hebron Turnpike Road Company, the sum of twenty-five dollars for each and every share of stock in said company set opposite to our names, in such manner and proportions, and at such times, as shall be required by the president and directors of said company."

Commissioners to open books for the subscription of stock.

Obligation of subscribers.

§ 4. The books for subscription of said stock shall remain open until the whole of the capital stock shall have been taken, or enough to complete the road; and persons may subscribe at any time until the books are closed.

How long books to remain open.

§ 5. That so soon as one hundred shares in said company are subscribed, it shall be the duty of said commissioners, or such of them as may act, to give notice of a meeting of the stockholders of said company to meet in the town of Burlington for the purpose of choosing officers; said notices to be put up at Burlington and Hebron at least ten days previous to said meeting; at which election at least three of the commissioners above named shall be present, one of whom shall be president, who shall proceed to take the votes, by ballot, of said stockholders, who shall have the right to vote in person or by

When officers to be chosen.

proxy under power of attorney, satisfactorily authenticated, each shareholder having one vote for every share
so held, for a president and four directors, who shall hold
their offices for one year and until others shall be duly
qualified under this act.

§ 6. That the said president and directors shall, before *President and directors to take oath.*
they enter upon the duties of their appointments, take an
oath before some justice of the peace, that they will faithfully discharge the duties of president or directors, as the
case may be, without fear, favor, or affection, according to
law and the best of their judgments, a certificate of which
oath shall be returned to the county court and recorded on
their order book. That, upon the qualification of the pres- *Treasurer and other officers to*
ident and directors, they shall appoint a treasurer and such *be appointed.*
other officers as they shall deem necessary, who shall hold
their offices for one year and until others shall be appoint- *Treasurer to give bond.*
ed and qualified. The treasurer of said company shall,
before he enters upon the duties of his office, give bond,
with two or more good securities, in the penalty of twelve
thousand dollars, payable to the president and directors of
said company. conditioned that he will faithfully discharge
the duties of treasurer of said company, and that he will
well and truly perform the duties required of him by the
by-laws of said company.

§ 7. That, upon the election and qualification of the *Body corporate, and corporate powers.*
president and directors as aforesaid, they shall be a body-
politic and corporate, in deed and in law, by the name,
style, and title of the Burlington and Hebron Turnpike
Road Company; and by the same name the said company
shall have perpetual succession and all the privileges and
franchises incident to a corporation; and shall be capable
of taking and holding their said capital stock, and the
interest and profits thereof; and of purchasing, taking,
and holding, to them and their successors and assigns, and
of selling, transferring, and conveying, in fee simple, all
such lands, tenements, hereditaments, and estate, real and
personal, as shall be deemed necessary to them in the
prosecution of their work; and to sue and be sued, implead and be impleaded, answer and be answered, defend
and be defended, in all the courts of this Commonwealth,
or in any other place whatever; and also to have a common seal; and to do all and every other matter and thing
which a body-politic or corporate may do.

§ 8. That the president and directors, upon their enter- *Calls on stock.*
ing upon the duties of their offices, may call upon the
stockholders for the payment of five dollars on each share
subscribed by him or her in said stock; and may, if deemed necessary, call for five dollars on each share every
forty days until the whole amount subscribed shall be
paid.

1869.

Annual elec-
tions.

§ 9. The annual election for president and directors shall be held on the first Saturday in June in each year, at such places as the president and directors may direct; and the number of votes to which each stockholder shall be entitled shall be in the proportion named in the fifth section of this act; and, after the first election, no share or shares shall confer the right of voting which shall not have been holden three months previous to the election; and at each annual election the president shall lay before the stockholders an expose of the situation of said company, and also the record of their proceedings for the preceding year.

Certificates
of stock to be
given, & trans-
ferable.

§ 10. That the president and directors chosen as aforesaid shall deliver a certificate, signed by the president and countersigned by the treasurer, sealed with the seal of the corporation, to each shareholder, for each share by him or her subscribed and held, which certificate shall be transferable on the books of said corporation in person or by attorney; but no share shall be transferred until all the calls and arrearages are paid thereon; the original certificate of the share or shares transferred shall be surrendered, and a new certificate shall issue to the purchaser, who shall be a member of said corporation, and entitled to all the benefits and privileges that the original owner was entitled to.

Called meet-
ings.

To keep re-
cord, president
pro tem . &c.

§ 11. That the president may call meetings of the directors at such times and places as he may think proper; two of said directors and the president shall be necessary for the transaction of business. They shall keep a record of all their proceedings, to be entered in a book provided for that purpose, and they shall be signed by the president, and in case of the death or absence of the president, the directors shall elect a president *pro tem.;* and they may adjourn, from time to time, as they may think proper.

May appoint
surveyors, &c.

§ 12. That the president and directors shall have power and authority to agree with and appoint all such surveyors, engineers, superintendents, artists, and officers as they may judge necessary to carry on the contemplated work, and to fix their salaries and wages; to prescribe the time, manner, and proportions in which the stockholders shall make payments on their respective shares to carry on said work; to draw orders on the treasurer for all moneys necessary to pay the salaries or wages of persons employed, and for the labor and materials furnished; and to do all such other matters and things as by this charter and the by-laws of the corporation they are or shall be required to do.

Notice of calls
on stock to be
given, &c.

§ 13. That the president shall give notice, by putting such notice up at Burlington, at least fifteen days beforehand, of the amount of the call on each share of stock, and of the time of payment; and if any stockholder shall neglect or refuse to pay his proportion of the amount of stock so subscribed for and held by him or her on the books of said company, for the term of thirty days after the time appointed for the payment thereof, every such stockholder shall, in addition to the installment so called for, pay, at the rate of one per cent. per month, for every delay of such payment; and if he or she shall fail to pay the amount of such call and the penalty aforesaid for the term of sixty days after the time of such payment is required, he or she shall forfeit such share or shares to the corporation, and the amounts which shall have been paid thereon; and the president, by order of the directors, shall sell the said shares at public sale, having advertised the same for ten days, provided the same will bring the amount of the balance due on said share or shares; or the president may sue and recover of such stockholder, in the name of the company, such unpaid call and penalty: *Provided,* That no stockholder shall vote at any election, or be entitled to any one of the rights of a member of said corporation, unless the whole amount due and payable aforesaid on the share or shares by him or her held shall have been paid agreeable to the requisition of said president and directors.

§ 14. That the president and directors shall employ such surveyors, engineers, artists, and chain-carriers as they may think necessary; and they are hereby authorized to enter in and upon the land and inclosures, and public roads and highways, in, through, and over which the said intended road may be thought proper to pass, and to examine and survey the grounds most proper for the purpose, and to examine the quarries, beds of stone and gravel, and other materials necessary for the completion of said road; and they shall locate the said road on the line on which it can be constructed with the least expense to the company, and which shall be the most direct that the ground over which it may pass will admit, from a point in the eastern portion of the town of Burlington to Davis & Foster's store, in Hebron, on the Petersburg and Covington turnpike road; and they shall cause a plat of said road, as located, to be made out, and deposit the same with the treasurer of said company.

§ 15. That the said president and directors shall have the right to survey, lay out, and make their road through any improved or unimproved lands between the points aforesaid, and procure the right of way by agreement with the owner or owners, or by condemnation as now provided by law, and take from the lands occupied by said road, when surveyed and located as aforesaid, any stone, gravel, timber, or other materials necessary to con-

1869.

struct a good, secure, and substantial road, as contemplated by this act: *Provided*, The stone, gravel, or other materials have not been previously quarried, dug, or otherwise appropriated by the owner thereof; and if any difference shall arise between the owner or owners of any ground, or their agents, from which said materials are sought to be taken as aforesaid, and the agents of said company, respecting the value thereof or damages therefor, the same shall be determined in the manner directed by the Revised Statutes of this Commonwealth, chapter 103.

When & how to commence road, &c.

§ 16. That so soon as the location of said road shall have been made, the said president and directors shall proceed to commence the construction thereof at any point, or at as many points as they shall elect; and they shall cause the said road to be opened forty feet in width, of which not less than fourteen feet shall be made an artificial road, composed of stone or gravel, well compacted and put together, in a proper and suitable manner, so that the same shall measure nine inches in thickness, and shall maintain and keep the same in good repair; and in no case shall the ascent in the road be of a greater elevation than four degrees.

When toll-gates may be erected.

§ 17. That so soon as the president, directors, and company shall have completed said road, they shall call on three disinterested housekeepers in the county of Boone, who are in nowise interested in the stock of said company, to examine the same; and if they shall certify (having been previously duly sworn for that purpose) that said road is made in conformity to the provisions of this act, which certificate shall be recorded in the office of the clerk of said county, the president and directors may cause a gate, or two gates, if deemed necessary, to be erected across said road, and may collect the tolls and duties hereinafter granted to the said company, from all persons traveling the same with horses, cattle, or any other animals, and with carriages, sleds, or other vehicles of conveyance: *Provided*, That no gate shall be erected within less than one quarter of a mile of the town of Burlington.

May obtain land for the erection of toll-houses.

§ 18. That when said road shall be completed, the said president, directors, and company may contract for, purchase, and hold, to them and their successors forever, any quantity of land, not less than one nor more than two acres, at the site of each toll-gate erected upon the said road, agreeably to the provisions of this act; and if they cannot agree for such quantity of land at their respective gates with the owners thereof, they may sue out, from the county court of Boone, a writ of *ad quod damnum;* and like proceedings shall be had as directed in relation to stone, &c., in the fifteenth section of this act: *Provided, however,* That in the selection and appraisement of lands under this section, the president and directors shall not include the dwelling-houses, out-houses, orchards, or gardens of any persons without their consent, and shall not locate the said land so as to prevent the owner or owners of the adjoining lands from access to the said road on either side of any gate, to which they would have had access if such location had not been made.

§ 19. That so soon as the gates shall be erected as aforesaid, it shall and may be lawful for the president and directors to appoint such and so many toll-gatherers as they may think proper, to collect and receive of and from every person or persons using the said road the tolls and rates hereinafter mentioned, and to stop any person riding, leading, or driving any horse or other animal, sulky, chaise, phæton, cart, wagon, or any other carriage of pleasure or burthen, from passing through said gates, till they shall have paid toll agreeable to the following rates, to-wit: For every twenty head of sheep, hogs, or other small stock, two cents per mile; for every ten head of neat cattle, four cents per mile; for every horse, mule, ass, or other four-footed animal of a larger kind, one cent each per mile; for every two-wheeled pleasure carriage, one cent a mile, exclusive of the beast by which it is drawn, and the person or persons transported by it; for every four-wheeled pleasure carriage, two cents a mile, exclusive as above; for every cart, wagon, or other carriage of burthen, whose wheels shall not exceed four inches in width, four cents a mile; for a less number of cattle, sheep, or hogs, or for a less distance than a mile, the toll to be in proportion to the rates above.

Rates of toll.

§ 20. That if any person or persons, liable to pay the tolls aforesaid at either of the toll-gates erected in conformity herewith, shall, with an intent to defraud the company aforesaid, pass through any private gate or bars, or along or over any grounds or lands near to or adjoining any part of said road or gate, or with intent aforesaid, or shall take off, or cause to be taken off, any horse or other beast or cattle, or wheel carriage of draught, burthen, or pleasure, or shall practice any other fraudulent device, with intent to evade the payment of any such toll or duty, such person so offending shall, for every such offense respectively, forfeit and pay to the president and directors the sum of ten dollars, recoverable before any justice of the peace in like manner as other debts of equal amounts, in the name of the president, directors, and company aforesaid.

Penalty for avoiding payment of toll.

Proceedings
when road is
out of repair.

§ 21. That if at any time the said road shall be out of repair for the term of ten days, it shall and may be lawful for any person to call on two adjacent justices of the peace for Boone county to go and inspect said road; and if, upon inspecting the same and receiving proof that it had been out of repair for the term of ten successive days previous thereto, the said justices shall, by their order delivered to the treasurer of said company, and, in case of his absence, to the president or any of the toll-gatherers, directing that no toll or duty shall be required on said road until the same shall be repaired and put in good order; and if any toll shall be taken or demanded, after the delivering of such order, the said company shall forfeit and pay the sum of five dollars for each and every offense, to be recovered as other debts of like amount, and upon service of process upon the acting president of said company or any toll-gatherer: *Provided, however,* That there shall have been sufficient time to inform the gate-keepers of said order having been delivered to the president or treasurer, where that is the fact; and upon said road being repaired, the president and directors shall call two justices of the peace in like manner to examine the same; and if they shall be of opinion that the said road is in repair, they shall certify the same and direct that the toll shall be demanded and taken at the gate or gates agreeably to the provisions of this act.

Account of
receipts and
expenditures to
be kept.

Dividends.

§ 22. That the president and directors shall keep a fair and just account of all moneys which shall be received by them from the subscribers of stock of said company, also of all moneys expended by them in the prosecution of said work, and all costs, charges, and expenses of said road, or any section thereof, which shall be paid and discharged; and the aggregate amount, when ascertained, shall be entered on the books of the treasurer. The president and directors shall, at the end of every six months after the said road shall have been completed, make a dividend to the stockholders whose stock has been paid in and expended on said road: *Provided,* That no dividend shall be paid over to such of the stockholders as may have failed to pay over, in pursuance to the order of said president and directors, the amount of stock which they may have subscribed on the books of said company; the same shall be retained by the treasurer of said company, subject to the orders of the president and directors thereof, to be by them employed for the benefit of said road.

Printed list
of rates of toll
to be stuck up,
and penalty for
overcharge.

§ 23. That the president and directors shall cause printed lists of the rates of toll which they may lawfully demand to be fixed on or near the gates across said road; and if any toll-gatherer on said road shall demand or receive from any person or persons using said road any greater rate of toll than is allowed or authorized by this act, such toll-gatherer shall forfeit and pay, for every such offense, the sum of five dollars, recoverable by any one suing for the same before any justice of the peace, as other debts of like amount: *Provided*, That no suit to recover the penalties under this act shall be maintained or prosecuted unless the same shall have been commenced or prosecuted within six months after the offense was committed.

§ 24. That the president shall take bonds, with good security, from the gate-keepers and other persons employed by them, for the faithful discharge of the duties to them assigned respectively; which bonds they may cause to be renewed whenever they may deem it necessary, and shall be made payable to the president, directors, and company aforesaid.

§ 25. That the aforesaid company shall commence the prosecution of their work on or before the first day of October, 1869, and complete the same within six years thereafter.

§ 26. That if any person shall purposely and maliciously break, deface, or otherwise injure any of the mile-stones, parapet walls, culverts, or bridges, or any of the masonry whatever, of, and belonging to, said Burlington and Hebron turnpike road company, every person so offending shall, on conviction, be fined in a sum not more than five hundred dollars, or be imprisoned in the jail of the county not exceeding twenty days, or both, at the discretion of the jury.

§ 27. That if any person or persons shall purposely fill or choke, or otherwise obstruct any of the side drains, valleys, gutters, or culverts of said road, without conducting the same over a stone culvert, on a paved valley or other good and sufficient fixture, so as to secure a fair passage for the water along such sideway where such private road or cartway connects with the aforesaid road; or if any person shall purposely travel upon such parts of said road as may be unfinished, against the warning and consent of the superintendent of said road, or his agent, or shall remove any of the beacons placed upon said road, so in an unfinished state as aforesaid, for the diverting the traveler on or from said road, every person so offending shall, upon conviction thereof, be, for every such offense, fined in a sum not less than one nor more than. ten dollars.

§ 28. That if any person shall stand his wagon and team, or either of them, over night, upon the pavement of said road, for the purpose of feeding; or if he shall in any other manner purposely and willfully obstruct the traveler upon said road, every person so offending shall, upon con-

Gate-keepers to give bond.

When to commence & complete road.

Penalty for injury to mile-stones, &c.

Penalty for injury to side-drains, &c.

Penalty for standing or feeding teams on road,

viction thereof, for every such offense, be fined in a sum
not less than one nor more than fifty dollars.

§ 29. That if any person shall fast-lock or rough-lock
Penalty for locking wheels on road. either of the wheels of his wagon, coach, chaise, gig, sulky,
carriage, or other two or four-wheeled vehicle, while trav-
eling on the pavement of said road (excepting, however,
such parts of the said pavement as may be at the time
covered with ice, so as to render such locking necessary),
every person so offending shall, upon conviction thereof,
be fined in a sum not less than one nor more than five dollars.

§ 30. That all prosecutions under the twenty-sixth sec-
Prosecutions, how & by whom conducted. tion of this charter shall be by indictment before the circuit
court, in the county of Boone; and all fines accruing under
the same shall be collected and paid over by the prosecuting
attorney of said county, the one-half to the informer, the
other to the treasurer of said company for its use and
benefit.

§ 31. That the proceedings directed by the fifteenth section of this act shall be had and prosecuted according to
the provisions of chapter 103 of the Revised Statutes of
Kentucky; and all proper authority and jurisdiction for
the purpose is conferred upon the officers and courts specified in said chapter to effect the purpose.

§ 32. That all ordained ministers of the gospel, all per-
Who exempt from paying toll. sons summoned to attend court as jurors, while going to or
returning from court in obedience of said summons; all
qualified voters, when going to or returning from elections;
all persons going to or returning from church on the Sabbath day; and all persons while going to or returning from
burials, are exempt from tolls at any of the gates across
said road; and all persons, while going to or returning
from one part of his or her farm to another, and necessarily
passing said gate or gates, are also exempt from the payment of toll.

§ 33. That no person shall be eligible or elected to any
Eligibility of officer. office provided for in this act, who is not at the time of his
election a stockholder in said company, and a resident of
Boone county; and when any officer provided for by this
act removes from the county of Boone, or ceases to be a
stockholder in said company, his office shall thereby be
forfeited.

§ 34. This act to take effect from its passage.

                                        Approved February 12, 1869.

CHAPTER 1464.

AN ACT to incorporate the Hartford Railroad and Mining Company.

Be it enacted by the General Assembly of the Commonwealth of Kentucky:

§ 1. That William C. Chapman, A. B. Bennett, William H. Miller, Thomas Bell, Virgil D. D. Stevens, W. F. Gregory, James A. Thomas, Alfred T. Hines, Dr. William J. Berry, Dr. John E. Pendleton, R. Seth Moseley, and Frank Sullenger, be, and are hereby, appointed commissioners, under the direction of a majority of whom subscriptions may be received to the capital stock of the Hartford Railroad and Mining Company, which is hereby incorporated; and they may open books, as a majority of said commissioners may direct, to receive subscriptions to the capital stock of said company; and if any of said commissioners shall die, resign, or refuse to act, others may be appointed in their stead by a majority of those acting as such.

§ 2. That the capital stock of said Hartford Railroad and Mining Company shall be two hundred thousand dollars, in shares of one hundred dollars each, which may be subscribed by any individual or corporation; and as soon as one hundred shares of said stock shall be subscribed, the subscribers, their successors and assigns, shall be, and they are hereby declared, incorporated into a company, by the name of the Hartford Railroad and Mining Company; and by this name shall be capable of purchasing, holding, selling, leasing, and conveying, not exceeding five thousand acres of land, and personal estate so far as may be necessary for the purpose of the corporation, and no more; and shall have perpetual succession, and by said corporate name may sue and be sued, contract and be contracted with; and may have and use a common seal, and alter and renew the same at pleasure; and shall have all the rights and privileges which other corporate bodies may lawfully do.

§ 3. That there shall be paid at the time of subscribing for stock in said company, to the commissioner or commissioners receiving the same, the sum of one dollar on each share, to be paid in money, and the residue thereof shall be paid in money or real estate, to be received at a valuation to be determined by the stockholder and the board of directors; said residue shall be paid in installments as may be directed by the board of directors of said company: *Provided*, No payment shall be demanded until thirty days' notice shall be given by notices posted at the court-house in Hartford and three other public places in Ohio county; nor shall more than fifty per cent. be demanded in any one year; but if the exigencies of the company should require more money than can be de-

Commissioners to receive subscriptions of stock.

Capital stock and corporate powers.

Payment of stock, may borrow money, &c.

manded of the stockholders as provided herein, it shall
be lawful, a majority of the directors elected concurring
therein, to borrow on the credit of said company a sum
not exceeding twenty thousand dollars; and if any subscriber shall fail to pay any installment, or part of an
installment, of said subscription, when demanded according to the provisions of this section, the same may be recovered by an action, in the name of said corporation,
against such delinquent subscriber, before any court having jurisdiction of such cases; and in all such actions, it
shall not be necessary to prove any other demand than
the publication provided for in this section; or, in case
such failure to pay any installment, or part of installment,
of said subscription demanded according to the provisions
of this section, shall continue for the space of sixty days
after the time the same is required by such demand to be
paid, the board of directors may, in their discretion, order
the same to be forfeited to the company, and may, if they
think proper, sell it for the benefit of the company; but
said board of directors, by a majority of the whole, may
remit any such forfeiture, on such terms as they may think
proper; and it is further provided, that stock may be taken
in said company to the extent of fifteen per cent. of all
the real estate owned by the individual so taking stock, by
the subscription of the same in accordance with the then
present valuation thereof, as shown by the county assess-
or's books, by and with the consent of the board of directors of said company, and the same to be secured by a
lien on the said real estate so subscribed.

§ 4. That, at the expiration of the period for which the
books are first opened, if one hundred shares of the capital stock shall have been subscribed, and, if not, as soon
thereafter as the same shall be subscribed, said commissioners, or a majority of them, shall call a meeting, at
such time and place as a majority of them shall designate,
giving at least twenty days' notice of the time and place,
as provided in section three of this charter of giving such
notices; and at such meeting, said commissioners shall lay
the subscription books before the subscribers then present;
and, thereupon, said subscribers, or a majority of them
then present, shall have power to elect, by ballot, a president, secretary, and seven directors; and said directors
may allow such compensation for the services of the president and secretary as they may think proper; and on
such elections, and all other occasions when a vote of the
stockholders of said company is to be taken, each stockholder shall be allowed one vote for every share of stock
owned by such voter; and any stockholder may, in writing,
depute any other person to act as proxy for it, him, or her;

When presi-
dent, secretary,
and directors
may be elected.

and said commissioners aforesaid, or any three of them, shall be judges of said first election.

§ 5. That, to continue the succession of the president and directors of said company, a president, secretary, and seven directors shall be chosen annually on the first Monday in March, in each year, at the court-house in the town of Hartford, and that the directors of said company, or a majority of them, shall have the power to appoint judges of all elections; and if any vacancy shall occur by death, resignation, or refusal to act, of any president, director, or secretary, before the year for which he was elected shall have expired, a person to fill such vacancy shall be appointed by the president and directors, or a majority of them; and that the president, directors, and secretary of said company shall hold and exercise their offices until a new election of president, directors, and secretary; and all elections which are by this act, or by the by-laws of said company, to be made at a particular time, if not made at such time, may be made in thirty days thereafter, upon notice published in the manner aforesaid.

Annual elections; where & how held. vacancies, term of office.

§ 6. That a general meeting of the stockholders of said company may be called at any time during the interval between the annual meetings by the president and directors, or a majority of them, or by the stockholders owning one fourth of all the stock subscribed, upon giving twenty days' notice of the time and place of holding the same in the manner before stated; and when any such meeting is called by the stockholders, such notice shall specify the object of the call; and if, at any such called meeting, a majority in value of all the stockholders are not present in person or by proxy, the same shall be adjourned from day to day, without transacting any business, for any time not exceeding five days; and if, within said five days, stockholders having a majority in value of all the stock subscribed do not attend in person or by proxy, such meeting shall be dissolved.

General meetings, &c.

§ 7. That the president and directors of said company in office for the preceding year shall, at the regular annual meeting of the stockholders, exhibit a clear and distinct account of the affairs of said company; that, at any called meeting of the stockholders, a majority in value of the holders of the stock subscribed being present, may demand and require similar statements from the president and directors, whose duty it shall be to furnish said statements when so required; and that at all general meetings of the stockholders, a majority of them in value may remove from office the president, or any or all of the directors, secretary, or treasurer, and fill up

Annual statement of condition of company to be made.

the vacancies thus made in the same manner they could do at their annual meeting.

§ 8. That the president and directors of said company,

President & directors to take oath. before he or they act as such, shall swear or affirm, as the case may be, that they will well and truly discharge the duties of their respective offices to the best of their skill

Treasurer to be appointed & give bond. and judgment; and the said president and directors, or a majority of them, or a majority in value of the stockholders in said company, at any stated or called meetings of said stockholders, shall have power to elect a treasurer of said company, and to require and take from him a bond, in such penalty and with such security as they may prescribe, payable to the company, conditioned for the faithful keeping and disbursing all such money as may come to his hands, and with such other conditions as may be prescribed; upon which bond recovery may be had for a breach of the conditions thereof by suit in the name of the company in any court having jurisdiction.

§ 9. That if any of the stock authorized by this act shall

Books may be re-opened. remain unsubscribed until after the election of president and directors, as provided for in this act, the said president and directors, or a majority of them, shall have power to open the books and receive subscriptions to the stock which shall remain unsubscribed for, or to sell and dispose of the same for the benefit of the company not under the par value of such stock; and the subscribers or purchasers of such stock shall have all the rights of original subscribers, and be subject to the same regulations and liabilities.

§ 10. That if the capital stock of said company shall be

Capital stock may be increased. deemed insufficient for the purposes of this act, it shall be lawful for the stockholders, at any stated or called meetings, to increase the same as much as they may deem necessary, not exceeding the sum of three hundred thousand dollars, giving notice as hereinbefore required.

§ 11. The president and directors of said company are

May contract with other roads. hereby vested with all rights and powers necessary to contract with and aid the Elizabethtown and Paducah railroad company, and the Owensboro and Russellville railroad company, or either of them, in the construction of their respective roads: *Provided,* Said companies, or either of them, locate and construct their roads through Hartford, in Ohio county.

§ 12. That if the Elizabethtown and Paducah railroad

May make branch road. company do not construct their road through the town of Hartford, then the Hartford Railroad and Mining Company be granted the exclusive privilege of constructing a branch road to it at the most practicable point of intersection, and to extend the same to the Iron Mountains, three miles to north and east of Hartford, on Rough river.

§ 13. That the president and directors of said company are hereby vested with all powers and rights necessary to the construction of said road mentioned in the preceding section; and that they may cause to be made contracts with others for making said road, or any part of it; and that they, their agents, engineers, &c., or those with whom they may contract for surveying or making the same, or any part thereof, may enter upon, use, and excavate, any land which may be wanted for the site of said road, or the erection of warehouses or any structure or works necessary and convenient to said road, or for its use, or for any other purpose necessary or useful in the construction or repair of said road, or its works and appurtenances; and they may build bridges and construct tunnels, and may fix scales and weights; take and use timber, earth, gravel, stone, and other material necessary or useful in the construction and repair of said road.

§ 14. That the president and directors, or a majority of them, or their authorized agents, may agree with the owners of any land, earth, stone, timber, or other materials or improvements, which may be wanted for the construction or repair of said road, or any of their works, for the purchase, or the use and occupation of the same; and if they cannot agree, and the owner or owners of any of them be a *feme covert*, under age, *non compos mentis*, or out of the county in which the property wanted may lie, application may be made to any justice of the peace of said county, who shall thereupon issue his warrant, directed to the sheriff or any constable of said county, requiring him to summon twenty discreet men, not related to the owners, nor in any way interested, to meet on the land or near the property or materials to be valued, on a day named in said warrant, not less than ten nor more than twenty days after the issuing of the same; and if, at the time and place, any of said jurors do not attend, said sheriff or constable shall forthwith summon as many jurors as may be necessary, with the jurors in attendance, and from them each party, if present, or if not present, by agent or otherwise, the sheriff or constable for the party absent, may strike off four jurors, and the remaining twelve shall act as the jury of inquest of damages; before the jury acts, the sheriff or constable shall administer to them an oath of affirmation that they will justly and impartially fix the damage which the owner or owners will sustain by the use and occupation of said property required by said company, and the jury, in estimating the damages, shall find for the owner or owners the actual value of the land or other thing proposed to be taken; but in estimating damages resulting incidentally to the other land or other

Margin notes:

1869.
Corporate powers. &c.

How may obtain materials, right of way, &c.

1869. property of such owners, shall offset the advantages to such residue to be derived from the building and operating of said road, by, through, or near such residue; the jury shall reduce their verdict to writing, and sign the same, and it shall be returned by the sheriff or constable to the clerk of the county court of his county, and such clerk shall receive and file it in his office; and such verdict shall be confirmed by the county court at its next regular term, if no sufficient reason is shown by either party for setting it aside, and when so confirmed, it shall be recorded by the clerk at the expense of said company; but if set aside, the court shall direct another inquisition to be held by the sheriff of the county, in the manner above prescribed, and every inquisition shall describe the property taken or the bounds of the land condemned, and the duration of interest in the same valued for the company; and such valuation, when tendered or paid to the owner or owners of said property, or to the sheriff of the county in which said inquest is held, when such owner or owners do not reside in such county, shall entitle said company to the use or interest in the same thus valued as fully as if it had been conveyed to it by the owner or owners of the same; and the valuation of the same, if not received when tendered, may, at any time thereafter. within one year, be received from the company without costs or interest by the owners, his, their, or its legal representatives.

§ 15. That whenever it shall be necessary for said company to have, use, or occupy any lands, material, or other property, in order to the construction or repairing of said road, or their necessary works or buildings, the president and directors, or their agents, or those contracting with them for constructing or repairing the same, may immediately take and use the same, they having first caused the property wanted to be viewed by a jury formed as hereinbefore prescribed; and it shall not be necessary, after such view, in order to the use and occupation of the same, to wait the issue of the proceedings upon such inquest; and the inquest of the jury, after the payment or tender of such valuation, shall be a bar to all actions for taking and using such property, whether begun before or after such confirmation or payment of said valuation.

May take and use lands, materials, &c., after having same valued.

§ 16. That the president and directors shall have power to purchase, with the funds of said company, and place on the railroad constructed by them under this act, all machinery and necessary appurtenances of any kind which they may deem proper for the purpose of transportation of persons and property of any kind over said railroad. And the board of directors shall have power

May purchase machinery, &c.

to fix all rates of toll and transportation of persons and property of any kind over said railroad. That it shall not be lawful for any other company, person or persons, to travel upon or use the road of said company in the transportation of persons or property, without permission of the board thereof; and that the said road, with all its works and improvements for transportation used thereon, and all other species of property thereunto belonging, are hereby vested in said company incorporated by this act, and their successors forever, and shall be exempt from taxation until completed; and that it shall never be taxed at a valuation beyond the rate at which said roads are now taxed, nor exceeding its actual value.

§ 17. That the president and directors be granted the power to create a sinking fund by dividends arising from the proceeds of the road, after defraying the current expenses of said road, or otherwise by taxation, if necessary to meet the coming exigencies of the company; that the board of directors shall appoint from amongst the stockholders three persons, who shall be styled the board of commissioners of the sinking fund of the company. The commissioners so appointed shall, before they proceed to discharge their duties, be sworn faithfully to perform the same according to the best of their skill and judgment. They shall immediately appoint of their number treasurer, who shall execute bond, payable to the company, with such surety as shall be approved by the board of directors of said company, conditioned for the faithful keeping and disbursing of all money coming to his hands as treasurer aforesaid, on which bond suit may be brought, from time to time, by and in the name of said corporation, or any other person injured by any breach of his bond, in any court having jurisdiction of the sum claimed in such suit. Such treasurer may be required at any time to give a new bond, and any surety in such bond shall be entitled to the same remedies for procuring additional or counter security as are now given to the sureties of guardians, administrators, etc. Said treasurer shall be allowed for his services such compensation, not exceeding one (1) per cent. on the money received and paid out by him, as may be allowed by the board of directors of said company. In case a vacancy shall occur in said board of commissioners, such vacancy shall be filled by the board of directors by whom such board was appointed.

§ 18. That the Legislature of this Commonwealth will not, for the space of twenty years, authorize any railroad to be laid on a parallel line with the one located by this company, approaching nearer than five miles: *Provided,* Full power is hereby reserved to this State to incorporate

margin: 1869.

margin: Create sinking fund.

hereafter a company or companies to build a railroad; and that any such railroad or roads hereafter constructed may connect and join with the road hereby contemplated; and full right and privilege is hereby reserved to the State or individuals, or any company heretofore or hereafter incorporated by law of this State, to cross this road.

§ 19. That nothing in this charter be so construed as to conflict with the charter of the Elizabethtown and Paducah railroad company in their enacted rights.

§ 20. This act to be in force from and after its passage.

Approved February 12, 1869.

————

CHAPTER 1465.

AN ACT for the benefit of the Ryder Cemetery Company.

WHEREAS, It is represented to the General Assembly that Augustus Ryder, a foreigner by birth, died a citizen of Lebanon, Marion county, in this State, and by his will devised all his estate for the establishment of a cemetery at or near said place, except three thousand dollars and a gold watch, which he devised to his sister, Julia Ryder, a resident of Germany; and that more than five years have elapsed since the probate of said will, and diligent search has been made for said Julia Ryder, but unsuccessfully; and that said devise has not been claimed, and now by law vests in this Commonwealth, now, to enable a company organized to carry out the purposes of said devise, and to complete the purchase and adornment of the cemetery grounds,

Be it enacted by the General Assembly of the Commonwealth of Kentucky :

§ 1. That the Ryder Cemetery Company is hereby invested with all the title of, and right to sue for and demand said devises to Julia Ryder, that this Commonwealth has by the thirty-fourth chapter of the Revised Statutes, title "Escheats and Escheators:" Provided, Before said company shall receive said devises, it shall execute bond in the Marion county court, payable to the Commonwealth, with good security, conditioned to refund to said Julia Ryder, or her heirs or devisees, said devises, in case they shall appear and manifest their right to have received them within five years from the passage of this act.

§ 2. That the escheator for Marion county shall be paid for his services five per cent. on the amount that may be collected on said devise of three thousand dollars.

§ 3. This act shall take effect from its passage.

Approved February 12, 1869.

CHAPTER 1466.

AN ACT for the benefit of Julia Owens, widow of Samuel W. Owens, former Clerk of the Mason Circuit Court.

WHEREAS, It is represented to the General Assembly that there is no administrator of the estate of Samuel W. Owens, former clerk of the Mason circuit court, and that the creditors of his estate have generously relinquished all right to any interest in his fee bills to his widow, for the benefit of herself and children; therefore,

Be it enacted by the General Assembly of the Commonwealth of Kentucky:

§ 1. That the further time of two years, from and after the passage of this act, be, and hereby is, allowed Julia Owens, widow of Samuel W. Owens, former clerk of the Mason circuit court, to issue and collect all his unpaid fee bills; and she is authorized, within said time, to issue and collect the same, and the same shall be distrainable for said time; but she shall be liable to all the penalties now imposed by law for the collection or issue of illegal fee bills.

§ 2. This act shall be in force from its passage.

Approved February 12, 1869.

CHAPTER 1467.

AN ACT authorizing the County Court of Fayette County to subscribe Stock in Turnpike Roads.

Be it enacted by the General Assembly of the Commonwealth of Kentucky:

§ 1. That the county court of Fayette county, a majority of the justices of the peace of said county being present and concurring therein, and so appearing of record, be, and is hereby, authorized and empowered, in their discretion, to subscribe stock for and in behalf of said county, to all or any turnpike roads now in progress, or hereafter to be made, in said county: *Provided*, That the amounts of said subscription paid to any such turnpike road, corporation, or company, shall not exceed seven hundred and fifty dollars per mile; and shall not be paid over to any such turnpike company or corporation except upon and after the completion of each mile of such road or roads so subscribed for by said court.

§ 2. Said county court, a majority of the justices of the peace of said county being present and concurring therein, shall have power to levy a tax upon all the property in said county sufficient for the purpose of paying said subscription of stock; said tax to be collected in the same manner, and by the same officers, and under the same

1869.   regulations and penalties, that the revenue tax is now collected.

§ 3. The officers collecting such taxes shall give proper receipts to the persons paying the same, which shall pass by assignment; and, when presented in sums equal to the amount of one or more shares of stock in any company or companies in which subscriptions are made as hereinbefore provided, shall entitle the holders to corresponding amounts of said stock.

§ 4. This act shall be in force from its passage.

Approved February 12, 1869.

CHAPTER 1469.

AN ACT to amend the Charter of the Town of Bardstown.

Be it enacted by the General Assembly of the Commonwealth of Kentucky:

§ 1. That the charter of the town of Bardstown be amended as follows: That all taxes assessed by the board of trustees of said town shall remain a lien upon the property upon which the taxes are assessed for the term of three years.

§ 2. That in all cases where taxes may be due upon real estate situated within said town's boundaries for more than one year, the board of trustees may, by suit in equity in the Nelson circuit court, subject to public sale so much of said estate as may be necessary to pay the taxes aforesaid and the costs of such legal proceedings.

§ 3. Non-residents, owners of any estate thus sold, shall have three years from and after date of such sale in which they may redeem said property by paying to the purchaser, his heirs, executor, or administrator, the amount of the taxes for which such property may have been sold and the costs incurred in the sale, with twenty per cent. per annum thereon. Infants and married women may redeem any estates of theirs thus sold within three years after the removal of their respective disabilities.

§ 4. The provisions of this act shall apply to taxes already due said town, as well to taxes hereafter to be assessed.

§ 5. That the board of trustees of Bardstown shall have power to subscribe to the capital stock of the Bardstown and Bloomfield turnpike road company (incorporated March 4th, 1867) any amounts said board may deem fit, and may borrow money or issue bonds for the payment of said subscription; may levy and collect a tax upon the real and personal property within said town subject to taxation to the extent of twenty cents per annum upon each one hundred dollars' worth of property for the payment of said subscriptions or bonds given in payment of same.

§ 6. The police court of Bardstown shall have power over vagrants.

§ 7. This act to take effect from and after its passage.

Approved February 12, 1869.

CHAPTER 1470.

AN ACT for the benefit of Montgomery Howard, jr.

WHEREAS, Montgomery Howard, jr., was convicted for felony in the Morgan circuit court, and was sentenced to the penitentiary for two years, and said sentence has expired; and whereas, the said Howard has, ever since the expiration of the sentence, conducted himself as a good citizen of this Commonwealth, and has fully regained the confidence of his neighbors—

Be it enacted by the General Assembly of the Commonwealth of Kentucky:

§ 1. That Montgomery Howard, jr., be, and he is hereby, restored to all the rights of citizenship in this Commonwealth.

§ 2. This act shall take effect from its passage.

Approved February 12, 1869.

CHAPTER 1471.

AN ACT to amend the charter of the Owensborro and Russellville Railroad.

Be it enacted by the General Assembly of the Commonwealth of Kentucky:

§ 1. That an act, entitled "An act to charter the Owensborro and Russellville railroad company," approved February 27th, 1867, be, and it is hereby, so amended as to allow said company to build a branch road from Greenville, in Muhlenburg county, Kentucky, or from some point on the line of said road in said county through Todd county, by way of the town of Elkton, to Guthrie City, situated in Todd county, Kentucky, at the junction of the Memphis Branch of the Louisville and Nashville railroad, and the Evansville, Henderson, and Nashville railroad. *May build branch road to Guthrie city, in Todd county.*

§ 2. That all the provisions of said act, and all the provisions of an act, entitled "An act to amend an act to incorporate the Owensborro and Russellville railroad company," approved February 5th, 1868, shall apply to the *Provisions of amended act to apply to branch road.*

1869.

building of said branch road, and to Todd county, and **any**
stock that may be subscribed by it, in the same manner,
and to the same extent, they now apply to the other coun-
Todd county
may take stock,
levy a tax, and
provide for its
collection.
ties mentioned therein; and Todd county is hereby authorized and permitted to subscribe to the capital stock of said
company, for the benefit of said branch, such an amount
as may be determined by a majority of the legal voters **of**
said county. either by vote or by petition, as provided in
the aforesaid acts: *Provided,* That if a majority of the
legal voters of said county shall petition the county
judge thereof, by written petition, to subscribe to the capital stock of said company such a sum as they may fix in
their said petition, the county judge, before making such
subscription, shall give printed notice to the voters of the
county that such petition has been made, and the terms
and amount thereof, for at least thirty days; and if, at the
expiration of thirty days, a remonstrance, signed by one
half of the legal voters of said county, and who have not
before signed the petition, shall be presented to said county
judge, he shall refuse to make said subscription; but upon
no such remonstrance being filed with said judge within
the time above mentioned, he shall, immediately after the
expiration of the thirty days, make said subscription, and
levy a tax sufficient to meet the interest on said subscription
and any portion of the principal. The county court may
determine and order its collection by the sheriff or tax
collector, who shall collect the same and pay it over to a
treasurer to be appointed by the county judge of Todd
county, to be expended under the direction of the county
court thereof, and file his receipt for the same with the
county judge, who is required to keep a record of the proceedings in such case.

Tax to be
levied upon
real & personal
property.
§ 3. That the tax herein provided shall be levied upon
the taxable property of the county of Todd, real and personal, which may be subject to taxation by the general
revenue laws of the State, and collected in pursuance with,
and according to, the laws in force for the collection of the
revenue: *Provided,* That if there is not sufficient personal
property to meet the tax due by any property-holder, the
sheriff or tax collector shall sell a sufficient [quantity] of
land to pay the taxes due from the owner; which sale shall
be made on the same terms as is required by law for the
sale of real estate under execution, and subject to redemption as lands sold under execution.

When sub-
scription order-
ed bonds to be
issued.
§ 4. That when any such subscription to the capital
stock to said company shall have been ordered, bonds
shall be executed in the name of, and under the seal of,
said county, in such form and such amounts (not exceeding the amount of such subscription), and payable at
such places and times, and bearing interest, payable semi-

annually, at such rates (not exceeding seven per centum per annum) as the president and directors of said company and the county judge may elect; and when such subscription shall have been made in the name of the county, said bonds shall be signed by the judge of the county court of said county, and countersigned by the clerk thereof.

§ 5. That when so executed and signed, said bonds shall be delivered to the president and directors of said company, and they may be by them indorsed, negotiated, and hypothecated, or sold upon such terms, at such rates of discount, and at such times and places, as may be by said president and directors deemed expedient.

President and directors to dispose of bonds.

§ 6. That the following named persons, or any three of them, to-wit: H. G. Petree, Ben. T. Perkins, sr., O. Brockman, R. F. Bass, E. T. Porter, Thornton McLean, and J. D. Christain, citizens of Todd county, are hereby appointed commissioners to open books and receive subscriptions of stock for said branch road, in the same manner as provided in section first of the act approved February 27th, 1867.

Commissioners to open books in Todd county for subscription of stock.

§ 7. That the work on said branch road shall be begun at Guthrie City, and prosecuted continuously in sections of five miles, northward by way of Elkton, to such point in the northern boundary line of Todd county as may be determined by the president and board of directors: *Provided*, That any part of said branch road which shall be built outside of Todd county, may be begun and made at the option of the railroad company.

To commence work at Guthrie city.

§ 8. That the amount of stock subscribed by the county of Todd, shall be expended on said road within the limits thereof, unless otherwise directed by the county court thereof.

Amount subscribed in Todd to be expended in said county.

§ 9. That no greater amount of bonds subscribed by the county of Todd for the benefit of said branch road, shall be delivered by the county judge at one time to the railroad company, than may be sufficient to complete one half of said road within the limits of said county.

How bonds to be delivered to company.

§ 10. That no tax shall be required to be paid on said road to the State or county, until the same is completed from Guthrie through to the northern boundary line of Todd county.

When road to be taxed.

§ 11. That any of the counties mentioned in the act approved February 27th, 1867, to which this is an amendment, are hereby permitted to subscribe to the capital stock of said company, for the benefit of said branch road, upon the same footing, and in the same way, as is here permitted to the county of Todd.

Other counties may take stock.

§ 12. That this act shall take effect from and after its passage.

Approved February 13, 1869.

CHAPTER 1473.

AN ACT to incorporate the Town of Lusby, in Owen County.

Be it enacted by the General Assembly of the Commonwealth of Kentucky:

§ 1. That the inhabitants of the town of Lusby, in Owen county, be, and the same are hereby, incorporated and made a body-politic and corporate, under the name and style of the town of Lusby, with full power to contract and be contracted with, to sue and be sued, plead and be impleaded, answer and be answered, and to do and perform all such other acts and things, either in law or equity, as bodies-politic and corporate, having perpetual succession, may rightfully and lawfully do and perform.

Town incorporated, and corporate powers.

§ 2. That, on the first Monday in April next, and on the first Monday in April thereof annually thereafter, an election shall be held in said town for the choice of a chairman and three trustees for said town, to serve for the ensuing twelve months, and until their successors are elected; and at said elections, all free white male inhabitants of said town of the age of twenty-one years and upwards, and all free white persons holding real estate, either by a legal or equitable title, within the limits of said town, shall be entitled to vote; and said elections shall be held at some suitable place in said town; and, at the first election, the officers thereof shall be appointed by such voters as may be present at the time of opening the poll, and annually thereafter by the board of trustees: *Provided*, That should any officer appointed fail or refuse to act at an election, the others may fill the vacancy.

Trustees to be elected, & their qualifications, & qualification of voters.

§ 3. The chairman and board of trustees of said town shall be chosen from among the free white male voters of said town, and before entering upon the performance of the duties of their stations, shall exhibit a certificate of their election from the judges holding the election, and shall each take an oath honestly and faithfully to perform their duties as such; and the board of trustees shall have power, from time to time, to make by-laws for the government of the town; for the preservation of good order, decency, and decorum within the limits of said town; for preservation of the peace, health, lives, and property of the inhabitants and others within said town; for the preservation, repair, and improvement of the streets and alleys of said town; and for all such other matters as come properly within the police of an incorporated town; and shall have power to provide punishments for all violations of their by-laws by fine or imprisonment, or both. They shall, from year to year, lay and provide for the collection of a tax on the inhabitants and property within said town, not exceeding fifty cents per annum on the one hundred dollars' worth

Trustees to be white male citizens, take oath, &c.

May make by-laws, &c.

May levy and collect taxes.

of taxable property, and two dollars per annum on each
tithable in said town, to be expended by them in the
necessary outlays attending the good government of said
town and the repair, improvements, and preservation of
the streets and alleys of said town: *Provided*, That no by-
laws be passed which in anywise conflict with the Constitution and laws of this Commonwealth or of the United
States. They shall, at their first meeting, regulate the
time and place of their meetings, and shall have power
to change the same, from time to time; to fill all vacancies that may occur in their own body, and may enact
laws to compel the attendance of absent members. They
shall annually appoint such persons as shall be recommended by a majority of the voters at the annual town
election to fill the office of town clerk, town treasurer,
and town marshal, and regulate the amount of the penalties of their several bonds, payable to the corporation,
and fill all vacancies that may occur in either of said
offices. The chairman shall preside at the several meetings of the board, but shall have no vote except in cases
of a tie; he shall take care that all the town laws be
faithfully executed; call extra meetings of the board,
when necessary; and, in case of his absence, death, or
resignation, the board shall appoint one of its own members to fill his place *pro tempore;* and the board of trustees
shall define the duties of the town clerk and treasurer,
and, from time to time, shall fix their emoluments and
fees, as well as the emoluments of the chairman.

§ 4. The town marshal shall perform such duties as may
be required of him by the board of trustees, and execute
all process which may be requisite for the enforcement of
the by-laws of said town.

§ 5. That a majority of the board of trustees shall be a
quorum to transact business; but a less number may adjourn from day to day, fill vacancies in their own body,
and compel the attendance of absent members.

§ 6. That there is hereby established in said town of
Lusby the office of police judge; and a police judge for
said town shall be elected and commissioned as any other
justice of the peace. Said police judge shall hold his
office for two years or until his successor be appointed
and qualified; and shall, before he enters upon the duties
of his office, take an oath before some justice of the peace
for Owen county faithfully and impartially, to the best of
his ability, to discharge the duties of his office.

§ 7. That the said police judge shall have jurisdiction
within said town of civil causes to the same extent that
justices of the peace now have in this Commonwealth;
and shall have the same jurisdiction of crimes and misde-

1869.

Meetings of
trustees, fill va-
cancies, &c.

May appoint
clerk, treas-
urer, and mar-
shal.

Duties of
chairman.

Duties of
marshal.

Quorum.

Police judge
to be elected,
&c.

Powers and
jurisdiction of
police judge,
&c.

meanors committed within said county of Owen that
justices of the peace now have; and shall have full jurisdiction within said town of all offenses against the by-
laws and ordinances of said town; and shall have power
to enter judgments and issue executions for all fines and
penalties for such offenses; and his executions may be
collected by the marshal of said town in any part of said
county, or by the proper officers in any part of this Commonwealth. He shall keep a record of his proceedings,
copies of which shall be evidence to the same extent that
copies of the records of justices of the peace now are.
He shall have power to issue original process in all cases
before him, subpœnas for witnesses, and attachments to
compel the attendance of witnesses before him, to the
same extent that justices of the peace now have; and to
punish all contempts against his authority by fines, not
exceeding twenty dollars in each case, and imprisonment
not exceeding one day. He shall have power to order
the marshal to summon a jury in cases cognizable before
him, when a jury is required by law. He shall have the
same power to issue attachments for debt within the
county of Owen that justices of the peace now have; to
take and certify depositions, which shall be allowed to be
read as depositions are now allowed to be read, taken before, and certified by, justices of the peace; administer
oaths, and certify the same when necessary, in all cases
where an oath is provided for by law; and shall be entitled to the same fees now allowed justices of the peace
in this Commonwealth; and shall have the same power to
issue fee bills as justices of the peace now have, and they
shall be collectable in the same way. He shall have
jurisdiction of motions and suits against the treasurer,
marshal, clerk, and other officers of said town, for all delinquencies of said officers: *Provided*, That all process
issued by said police judge shall run in the name of the
Commonwealth.

§ 8. That appeals from all judgments rendered by said
police judge in civil cases shall be allowed to any party
under the same rules and regulations, and to the same
tribunals, as appeals are now allowed from judgments of
justices of the peace.

Appeals may be had.

§ 9. That the marshal of the said town shall be entitled
to a fee of fifty cents for each defendant for executing a
warrant for a violation of any of the by-laws or ordinances of the said town; and, in all other cases, his fees
and commissions shall be the same as those of constables
for similar services, and he shall collect them in the same
manner; and shall execute all the processes of the police
judge within the county of Owen.

Fees of mar-
shal.

§ 10. The boundary of said town shall be as follows: To be run one half mile in each direction from the mill in said town of Lusby; to run so as to include John Webb, Martin Holbrook, Hugh Stamper, Allen Holbrook, and Catherine Cobb.

§ 11. This act to take effect from and after its passage.

Approved February 13, 1869.

CHAPTER 1474.

AN ACT to repeal section 3 of an act, entitled "An act to rebuild the Bridges on the Bardstown and Louisville Turnpike Road."

Be it enacted by the General Assembly of the Commonwealth of Kentucky:

That section 3 of an act, entitled "An act to rebuild the bridges on the Bardstown and Louisville turnpike road," approved December 20th, 1865, be, and the same is hereby, repealed.

Approved February 13, 1869.

CHAPTER 1476.

AN ACT to incorporate the Allensville Turnpike Road Company.

Be it enacted by the General Assembly of the Commonwealth of Kentucky:

§ 1. That F. S. Allen, Simpson W. Brock, John W. Tuttle, Martin Brock, William Epperson, James Noland, John Martin, and their successors and associates, be, and they are hereby, created a body-politic and corporate, under the name and style of the "Allensville turnpike road company;" and by said name and style shall have power to contract and be contracted with, sue and be sued, answer and be answered, plead and be impleaded, in all the courts and places in this Commonwealth; to have and use a common seal, and break, alter, or change the same at pleasure; and do all acts which such bodies corporate may do, not inconsistent with the general laws of the State or forbidden thereby, and which may be necessary or fit to enable said corporation to execute the powers hereinafter granted.

§ 2. That said corporation is hereby authorized to construct a turnpike or macadamized road from such point on the Muddy Creek turnpike road, in Clark county, not far distant from the mouth of "Long Branch," as may be determined on by the board of directors after their election and organization, to some point at or near the mouth of Red river, in said county.

§ 3. The capital stock of said company shall not exceed twenty-five thousand dollars, and shall be divided into shares of one hundred dollars each.

§ 4. The books of said company may be opened for the subscription of stock by any of the corporators above named; and as soon as two thousand dollars of stock is subscribed, the stockholders may proceed to organize by electing a president and six directors; but the said election shall be advertised at least ten days by printed or written notices of the time and place of holding said election. Said officers shall hold their offices for one year, or until their successors are duly elected and qualified; and an election shall be held annually of officers of the said company, at such time and place as may be fixed by the board of directors; the president shall have power to appoint a treasurer, and may remove him at pleasure; and shall require of him a bond with good security, conditioned for the faithful discharge of all his duties.

§ 5. Said company may charge upon their road such tolls as the directors may determine upon, not exceeding, however, the rates allowed by the Revised Statutes; and may erect a gate and take tolls as soon as five miles of said road is completed.

§ 6. The width of metal on said road shall not be less than twelve feet in any part, and it shall be built in other respects according to the provisions of the laws of this Commonwealth, with a grade not exceeding five degrees.

§ 7. The Clark county court shall have power, a majority of the justices thereof concurring, to subscribe as much stock in said company as will suffice, when added to the amount of stock subscribed by individuals or corporations, to complete said road: *Provided*, Said subscription does not exceed one thousand dollars per mile; and for the purpose of paying said subscription, said court is authorized and empowered to levy and assess a tax on all the property and estate in said county subject to taxation for State revenue.

§ 8. That sections 7, 8, 9, and 10, of an act, entitled "An act to incorporate the Bedford and Milton turnpike road company," approved February 7th, 1866, be, and the same are hereby, enacted as a part of this act, so far as they are applicable and not inconsistent with its provisions.

§ 9. This act shall take effect from its passage.

Approved February 13, 1869.

CHAPTER 1477.

AN ACT incorporating the Claysville, Kentontown, and Mt. Olivet Turnpike Road Company.

*Be it enacted by the General Assembly of the Commonwealth
of Kentucky:*

§ 1. That a company shall be, and the same is hereby, incorporated to construct a road, on the macadamized plan, from Claysville to Mt. Olivet, by way of Kentontown, in Robertson county, under the name and style of the "Claysville, Kentontown, and Mt Olivet turnpike road company;" and by that name and style to sue and be sued, contract and be contracted with, plead and be impleaded, and use and have a common seal, and alter or amend the same at pleasure.

§ 2. The capital stock of said company shall be twenty-five thousand dollars, to be increased or diminished at the pleasure of the company, and to be divided into shares of fifty dollars each.

§ 3. That Judge Duncan Harding, William Paul, Charles French, Stark Whaly, S. W. Craycraft, Charles Bramal, A. J. Ashcraft, Archibald Hitch, A. W. Stevens, W. W. Burns, are hereby appointed commissioners, whose duty it shall be to open books of subscription of stock, at such places as said commissioners may designate; and as soon as five thousand dollars is subscribed they shall give ten days' notice at the most public places in the vicinity of the line of the road, of a meeting of the stockholders, for the purpose of electing a president and five directors for said company, a majority of whom shall be competent to do business; and to do all things authorized by this act to be done by the president and directors of said company, and the management of the fiscal and prudential affairs of said company shall be confided to said president and directors, and their successors in office, to be chosen annually at such time and places as the said president and directors, from time to time, may appoint, and who shall continue in office for one year, and until their successors are elected and qualified.

§ 4. That no person shall be eligible as president or director, who is not the owner in his name of one or more shares of stock in said road.

§ 5. The president and directors shall have the power of appointing a treasurer, gate-keeper, and all other officers or agents deemed necessary to effect the purpose of this act, and to remove the same at pleasure. They shall have power to require of the treasurer, and all other officers or agents appointed by them, bond and security, in such penalties as they may require, conditioned for the faithful performance of the duties incumbent on them as such.

§ 6. The commissioners herein appointed shall procure a book or books, and the subscribers to the stock of said company shall enter into the following obligation in said book, viz: "We, whose names are hereto subscribed, do promise to pay the president and directors of the Claysville, Kentontown, and Mt. Olivet turnpike road company, the sum of fifty dollars for each and every share of stock in said company set opposite our names, in such manner and proportion, and at such times, as shall be by them required under the law incorporating said company, to be collected as other debts. Witness our hands this — day of ——, 18—."

§ 7. That said road shall not be less than thirty feet wide, and the metal not less than twelve feet wide, and shall be graded to an elevation not exceeding five degrees in any part thereof; that whenever five continuous miles of said road are completed, the company may erect a tollgate, and charge tolls thereat, at a rate of toll not exceeding that now authorized by law on roads made under the general turnpike laws of this State.

§ 8. That the president and directors of said road shall have the right and power to acquire the right of way for said road, and of earth, stone, or gravel or timber for its construction, by voluntary concession and release, or by private contract with the land-holders: *Provided, however,* If the right of way, and if the material cannot be had as here indicated, it shall be obtained in the manner and mode prescribed by an act of the General Assembly of the Commonwealth of Kentucky, 22d February, 1836, for condemning lands and materials for the construction of turnpike roads, bridges, &c., and which act of the Assembly is hereby adopted as part of this charter, and to be as effectual as if the same was here inserted at full length.

§ 9. When the stockholder shall have made full payment of his stock, it shall be the duty of the president, over his signature, to issue certificates of stock to all persons entitled to the same, attested by the secretary of said company.

§ 10. This act to take effect from its passage.

Approved February 13, 1869.

CHAPTER 1478.

AN ACT to incorporate the Shepherdsville and Mt. Washington Turnpike Road Company.

Be it enacted by the General Assembly of the Commonwealth of Kentucky:

§ 1. That a company be, and the same is hereby, formed, by the name of the Shepherdsville and Mt. Washington turnpike road company; and by that name and style shall have corporate existence, and be a body-politic, and as such, and in that name, may sue and be sued, plead and be impleaded, have and. use a common seal. Said company is created for the purpose of constructing a turnpike or gravel road from Shepherdsville, in Bullitt county, to Mt. Washington, in said county, and from Mt. Washington to intersect with the Shelbyville pike.

§ 2. The capital stock of said company shall not exceed sixty thousand dollars, to be divided into shares of fifty dollars each; and the persons hereinafter named, or any two of them, shall have power to open books for the subscription of stock, and keep them open until a sufficient amount of stock shall have been taken to construct said road.

§ 3. The following persons are appointed commissioners to receive subscriptions, to-wit: Westly Phelps, Dr. S. H. McKay, John T. Bridges, Janus W. Stallings, Thomas J. Hall, Wm. W. Hall, Austin Hough, and Dr. S. M. Hobbs; and so soon as one hundred shares shall have been subscribed, it shall be the duty of said commissioners, or such of them as may choose to act, to give notice, by written or printed posters, at two or more public places in Mt. Washington and Shepherdsville, at least ten days, and call a meeting of the stockholders at such time and place as they may elect; at which time said stockholders, or a majority of them having convened, shall proceed to the election of a president and three managers of said road; at which election each stockholder shall have one vote for each share of stock subscribed or owned by him in said road; and when said company shall be thus organized they may appoint such officers as they may deem necessary, prescribe their duties, and require them to execute bond, with good security, conditioned as may be required, and commence the work.

§ 4. The president and directors shall have power to locate and lay out said road, receive releases for the right of way in writing, and may take the steps authorized by the general law of the State to condemn the land over which said road is to run, and material from adjacent lands.

§ 5. The company shall have power and authority, in the construction of said road, and the repairs on same, to fix the width and the manner of construction, its grade, and whatever else may appertain to such construction.

§ 6. When five continuous miles of said road are completed, it shall be lawful for said company to put up a gate and exact toll; but no such gate shall be erected within one mile of the corporate limits of the said towns of Shepherdsville and Mt. Washington.

§ 7. The rates of toll on said road shall be governed and regulated by the general law of the State with regard thereto.

§ 8. This act shall take effect and be in force from its passage.

Approved February 13, 1869.

CHAPTER 1479.

AN ACT for the benefit of W. M. Rhea.

Be it enacted by the General Assembly of the Commonwealth of Kentucky:

§ 1. That the Auditor of Public Accounts be, and is hereby, directed to draw his warrant upon the Treasurer of the State, in favor of W. M. Rhea, for the sum of eight dollars.

§ 2. This act to take effect from its passage.

Approved February 13, 1869.

CHAPTER 1480.

AN ACT authorizing Wm. A. Cardin, James A. Sims, and John Dawson, to erect a Mill-dam across the Rolling Fork of Salt River.

Be it enacted by the General Assembly of the Commonwealth of Kentucky:

§ 1. That William A. Cardin, James A. Sims, and John Dawson, be, and they are hereby, authorized to erect a mill-dam across the Rolling Fork of Salt River, at the head of the falls of said river, known as "Knob Creek Falls;" said dam shall not exceed five feet in height. They shall, in the erection of said dam, proceed and be governed by chapter 67, title "Mills," of the Revised Statutes.

§ 2. This act shall be in force from its passage.

Approved February 15, 1869.

CHAPTER 1481.

AN ACT to amend an act, entitled "An act for the benefit of the Maysville and Lexington Railroad Company, Northern Division," approved January 21, 1868.

Be it enacted by the General Assembly of the Commonwealth of Kentucky:

§ 1. That the Maysville and Lexington railroad company, Northern Division, may take, receive, and hold any and all subscriptions of stock which may be made by individuals, or any city or town, corporations or counties, for building branches of the said railroad from the town of Carlisle, in Nicholas county, to the town of Cynthiana, in Harrison county, and from the said town of Carlisle to the town of Mount Sterling, in Montgomery county; and the said Maysville and Lexington railroad company, Northern Division, may construct and build with the proceeds of said subscriptions, or with their own means, or both, branches of their said railroad from the said town of Carlisle to the said town of Cynthiana and to the said town of Mount Sterling, over such routes as said company may select; and shall have power to acquire the right of way over such routes, by purchase, or condemnation, or gift, in the manner now provided in the original charter of the Maysville and Lexington railroad company.

§ 2. That the counties of Harrison, Nicholas, and Montgomery may severally, by the presiding judges of their respective county courts, levy and collect a tax upon all the real and personal estate within said counties subject to taxation, not exceeding one per cent. of the value thereof each year, for three years, as provided in "An act to authorize the counties of Bourbon, Nicholas, and Fleming to subscribe stock in the Maysville and Lexington railroad company, Northern Division," approved February 1st, 1868, and subscribe the amount thereof to the capital stock of said railroad company, for the building of said branches; and all the provisions of the said act last above referred to are hereby made applicable to the levy, collection, and subscription of the said money to the said capital stock.

§ 3. That the subscriptions of stock made by individuals, corporations, or counties, under the authority of this act, to the Maysville and Lexington railroad company, Northern Division, for the building of either of said branches of said railroad, shall be held and sacredly applied to the purpose for which they may be subscribed, and no other; and the individuals, corporations, or counties which may become stockholders in said company by the subscription of stock for the building of said branches, or either of them, shall have all the rights, privileges, and powers, in the branch to which they subscribe, that the original

1869. stockholders have in the Maysville and Lexington rail-road company, Northern Division.

§ 4. This act to take effect from and after the passage thereof.

Approved February 13, 1869.

CHAPTER 1482.

AN ACT to amend and reduce into one all acts in regard to the Town of Concord, in Lewis County.

Be it enacted by the General Assembly of the Commonwealth of Kentucky:

Boundary of town.

§ 1. That the boundary of the town of Concord, in Lewis county, shall be the same as established by law and the original town plat.

Trustees, quorum, &c.

§ 2. That the fiscal, prudential, and municipal concerns of said town, with the government and control thereof, shall be vested in five trustees, three of whom shall form a quorum for the transaction of business, all of whom shall be citizens of the State, and shall have resided in said town and been *bona fide* housekeepers one year next preceding their election, and take an oath, before entering upon the duties of their office, faithfully to perform the same.

Corporate powers.

§ 3. That said trustees and their successors in office shall be a body-politic and corporate, and shall be known by the name and style of the Board of Trustees of the Town of Concord; and by that name shall be capable in law of contracting and being contracted with, of suing and being sued, of pleading and being impleaded, of defending and being defended, in all courts of this Commonwealth; and may use or not use a common seal; and shall be vested with all the general powers conferred by the laws of this Commonwealth on bodies-corporate of like character.

When & how trustees elected.

§ 4. Said trustees shall be elected annually on the first Saturday in May, by the white male inhabitants of said town over the age of twenty-one years, who shall have been *bona fide* residents in said town for one year preceding the election, and who shall have paid the poll-tax for the preceding year and all taxes by them due said town.

Term of office, vacancy, &c.

The said trustees shall hold their offices for one year and until their successors shall have been elected and qualified, and shall have power to fill any vacancies that may occur in their own body; but if any trustee elected at any annual election shall refuse to qualify and serve, the board shall immediately order an election to supply his place. It shall be the duty of the board to appoint one of their own body chairman, who shall preside at all their meetings, and, in case of his absence, may appoint a chairman *pro tempore;* and in case of his death, removal from town, or vacation of his seat, the trustees may appoint another in his stead. The election for trustees shall be held at some place provided by the board of trustees in said town, by judges, sheriff, and clerk, to be appointed by the board, and shall be conducted in all respects as elections under the State laws; and the penalties imposed by the election laws of the State shall apply to offenses committed at said elections. The trustees may, from time to time, fix and regulate the time of their regular meeting, and may prescribe the mode in which special meetings may be called; and may inflict a penalty, not exceeding one dollar, on any member for non-attendance at any meeting, to be applied to the purchase of stationery, lights, and fuel for said board.

§ 5. A police judge and town marshal shall. be elected by the qualified voters of said town of Concord. The marshal is to hold his office one year, and the police judge two years, and until their successors are elected and qualified. The polls of the election of trustees, police judge, and town marshal, shall be returned to the county court of Lewis county at the first term after said election; and said county court shall certify the result of the election, so far as the election of police judge is concerned, to the Governor of the State, whose duty it shall be to issue a commission for the person elected to the office of police judge, who shall be a judicial officer, to be styled the police judge of the town of Concord.

§ 6. The police judge, before he enters on the duties of his office, shall take an oath before some officer authorized to administer an oath under the laws of this State, to discharge the duties of his said office faithfully and impartially, to the best of his ability, without favor or affection, together with such other oaths as other public officers may be required by law and the Constitution to take. The police judge shall have jurisdiction, within the limits of the said town, in any case, civil and criminal, in which a justice of the peace has jurisdiction. He shall have .jurisdiction of all offenses arising under the by-laws or ordinances of said town, and shall have power to enter judgment and award execution accordingly; and it shall be the duty of said judge to keep a record of his proceedings, a copy of which shall be evidence, and shall have the same effect as records of justices of the peace. He shall have power to issue summons for witnesses to give evidence in cases pending before him; and, upon their failure to attend, issue compulsory process to compel their attendance, as in cases of attachment for contempt. He

Margin notes:

1869.

Chairman to be appointed.

When election is to be held.

Police judge and marshal to be elected.

To take oath, powers, jurisdiction, &c.

1869.

shall have power to fine and imprison for contempt: *Provided*, Said fine shall in no case exceed ten dollars, or imprisonment more than twelve hours. He shall have power to order the marshal, or other officer authorized to execute process in his court, to summons a jury in any case cognizable before him when a jury should be required before a circuit court or a justice of the peace, and to compel their attendance. He shall be a conservator of the peace, and shall, *ex-officio*, proceed against violators of the by-laws and ordinances of the board of trustees, without the need of an informer. The police judge shall have jurisdiction as specified in this act; and all fines for violations of town ordinances, inflicted before him, shall be for the use of the board of trustees. All warrants for breaches of the by-laws and other ordinances shall run in the name of the board of trustees of the town of Concord, and all other warrants in the name of the Commonwealth of Kentucky: *Provided*, That fines for violation of the laws of the State shall be paid over as now provided by law. Said police judge shall be entitled to the following fees, to-wit: For a peace warrant, or for a riot, rout, or unlawful assembly, or breach of the peace, one dollar; for issuing a warrant for the violation of the by-laws or ordinances of said town, or any case in which the trustees are the plaintiffs, fifty cents; issuing subpœna for a witness in any case, twenty-five cents; for swearing a jury and presiding over a trial in any case, one dollar; for taking a recognizance to keep the peace, upon the application of any person, seventy-five cents, to be charged to the applicant. All other fees of said judge shall be the same as those allowed justices of the peace for like services, and to be collected in the same way.

§ 7. The police judge of Concord shall have power to commit all offenders liable to commitment to the county jail of Lewis county, and the jailer thereof shall receive and keep the same as other persons are kept.

May commit offenders to county jail.

§ 8. The police judge shall have power, on all prosecutions for misdemeanors, to issue a *capias pro fine*, or cause the same to be replevied forthwith, or commit to the jail of the county until discharged, as now allowed by law for fines and penalties.

May issue capias pro fine.

§ 9. The police judge shall hold his courts for the trial of civil cases on the first Saturday in every month; he shall have a right to continue his court till all the business before him is disposed of. His court shall be open at all times for the trial of the breach of the penal [laws] or of the ordinances of said town; and shall hold said trials without regard to the time of service of process; but shall continue from time to time, for good cause shown.

When to hold courts.

§ 10. That upon all judgments by the police judge, either party shall have the right to appeal from said judgment in the same manner, and upon the same terms, appeals are taken from justices of the peace in similar cases.

§ 11. In the absence of the police judge, or his inability to attend and hold his courts, or when his office is vacant, the chairman of the board of trustees is authorized and empowered to hold his courts, and with the same authority as the police judge.

§ 12. If the office of police judge from any cause becomes vacant, the board of trustees shall immediately recommend a successor to the Governor of this Commonwealth, who is authorized to empower and commission him for the unexpired term of said police judge.

§ 13. The police judge shall execute bond with good security to the board of trustees for the payment of all fines and moneys that come to his hands, as is now required by law for justices of the peace and other officers.

§ 14. That it shall be the duty of the town marshal to attend the sitting of the courts to be held by the police judge; to serve all process and precepts, and to collect all executions to him directed from .the police judge, or any court that is authorized to direct the same to him, and make due return thereof, in doing which, he may go to any part of the county. He shall collect all taxes due the said town, executions and other demands which may be put ihto his hands to collect or execute, and account for and pay over the same to whosoever may be entitled thereto, under the same rules and regulations required by law of sheriffs in the collection of taxes, and of constables in the collecting of executions and other demands; and for failure to perform any of the duties required of him, he shall be subject to the same proceedings had against sheriffs and constables in similar cases. The marshal shall be entitled to the same fees for collecting the town tax that sheriffs are entitled to for collecting the county levy, and in all other cases the same allowed constables for similar services: *Provided, however,* That said police judge shall have power and authority, whenever it is made to appear by affidavit that it is impracticable, or, for some good cause, that the marshal cannot execute the process, to direct the same to the sheriff or any constable of Lewis county: *Provided further,* That the said marshal shall .be invested with all the power and authority which is given to constables in all cases cognizable before said police judge; and before the said town marshal shall proceed to the execution of his office, he shall take an oath before the board of trustees, to be administered by the chairman or clerk of the board, that

1839.

he will faithfully and impartially execute the duties of his office without fear, favor, or affection, and shall also give bond with good security, to be approved by the board, in such penalties as the board of trustees may fix, conditioned for the faithful discharge of the duties of said office; and upon which he may be liable to motion before the police judge, or motion or suit in courts having jurisdiction in similar cases on bonds of constables for failure to discharge any duty, or to pay over any taxes or money which ought to have been collected by him.

§ 15. The marshal shall be, by virtue of his office, supervisor of the public streets and alleys of the town; but the trustees may, at their pleasure, appoint a street commissioner to act in his place and stead.

Marshal to be inspector of streets & alleys.

§ 16 All taxes shall be due and owing from the marshal on the first day of August, each and every year, at which time, or at the first regular meeting of the board of trustees in said month, he shall make a full settlement, and be prepared with his delinquent list to be presented to the board for allowance.

When taxes due from marshal.

§ 17. The board of trustees shall have power to appoint a clerk, who shall keep a true record of all the proceedings of the board in a book kept for that purpose; and shall also register, in a separate book, all the ordinances and by-laws which may be adopted by the board. Said clerk may be removed at the pleasure of the board. The board of trustees shall allow him a reasonable compensation for his services.

Clerk: his duties.

§ 18. It shall be the duty of the trustees, at the first meeting after the annual election, or as soon thereafter as possible, to appoint an assessor, who, after being first sworn faithfully to discharge the duties of his office, shall call upon the owners of taxable property in said town, or their agents, and make out a true list of their taxable property, real and personal, with the value thereof; and this shall be made upon oath of the tax-payer or his agent; in the absence of either. the said assessor, if a resident of the town, [shall] have a notice, as now required by law for assessors of this Commonwealth, and be subject to like penalties, if, after notice, shall fail to appear and give his taxable list. If there is property owned in said town by non-residents thereof, the said assessor shall cause the same to be valued by two respectable citizens of said town, competent to affix the value, and return the valuation thereof. If the assessor should not be satisfied with the value fixed by the tax-payer, he may call upon two or more persons to give their estimate of the value thereof, who shall be sworn by said assessor, and the said assessor shall fix the true value from all the evidence, and return the

Assessor; his duties, &c.

same. Said list shall embrace all the real estate in said town, all males over twenty-one years old, with all other species of property, money, notes, and choses in action, exclusive of household furniture; and if any one shall refuse to give in such a list, he or she shall be also double taxed on the value of their property, to be ascertained by the oaths of any two respectable housekeepers of said town, to be recovered, with costs, by warrant before the police judge of the town in the name of the trustees, without regard to the amount claimed. The said assessor shall return his list within one month after his appointment, and may be fined for failure to do so upon motion of the trustees, upon five days' notice, before the police judge, in a sum not less than ten or more than twenty-five dollars. Said assessor shall be paid by the trustees out of the revenues of the town for his services such a sum as shall be deemed by them reasonable.

§ 19. The trustees shall have power to levy a poll-tax of not exceeding two dollars upon each male adult inhabitant of the town, and an ad valorem tax of not more than one dollar upon each one hundred dollars of taxable property in said town. No other tax shall be levied until, at an election to be held for that purpose under the order of the trustees, and after three weeks' notice, posted in three or more public places in said town of Concord, or published for that length of time in a newspaper issued in the town, specifying the object of the tax, and a majority of the qualified voters in said town who may vote shall vote in favor of the levy, it shall be enforced as other levies. The trustees shall have power to tax all theatrical performances, shows, and exhibitions within the limits of the said town in any sum not more than twenty dollars in any one day for each performance, show, or exhibition. The trustees of the town of Concord may collect reasonable wharfage from all crafts landing at the public landing, and within the corporation limits; and may license drays, wagons, carts, hacks, and coaches, plying in said town for hire; and may appoint extra police officers when the emergency requires it. *Trustees may levy taxes, tax shows, charge wharfage, license hacks, &c.*

§ 20. The trustees shall have a lien on all the real and personal estate in said town liable for taxes until the taxes due by the owners thereof shall be paid. The taxes shall be collected by the marshal; and the marshal shall have power to levy and distrain for taxes which the sheriffs of the Commonwealth now have, and may levy upon and sell for taxes and cost of sale the personal property within said town of any person whose taxes remain unpaid, in the same manner that personal property is sold under execution; and if, on the first day of January in any year, there may be due and unpaid any tax or taxes on any lot *To have lien on property for taxes.* *Marshal to collect taxes; proceedings in relation thereto.*

or fraction of a lot in said town, and the owner thereof has no personal property in said town out of which said taxes can be made, it shall be the duty of said trustees to cause to be posted or published in a newspaper issued in said town of Concord, a list of all the lots and fractions of lots on which the tax or taxes are unpaid, and also the amount due upon each lot and fraction of a lot, respectively, for one month, and announce upon what day the lot or fractions of lots will be sold, or so much of the lots or fractions of lots as will be necessary to pay the tax or taxes due thereon respectively, and a copy of said lists, as published, accompanied by the affidavit of the marshal, and shall be recorded in the clerk's office of Lewis county court, and, when so recorded, shall be *prima facie* evidence that said publication was made; and an attest copy thereof shall be used on the trial of any cause, and shall have the same force and effect of other attested copies as now authorized by law. If the tax or taxes, thus due and advertised, are not paid on or before the day appointed for the sale of said lots or fractions of lots on which taxes are due, it shall be the duty of the marshal to expose them for sale on the day appointed, or so much of the same as may be necessary to pay the taxes and cost due on them respectively, to the highest bidder for cash. The sale shall take place at such time in the day, and at such place in the town, as he may appoint; and the marshal shall convey by deed, duly acknowledged, to the purchaser, so much of any lot or fraction of a lot as he may sell; which deed shall pass the title to the purchaser: *Provided, however,* That all real estate thus sold for taxes may be redeemed at any time within seven years by the original owner or owners, or their assignees, by paying the purchaser, or his heirs or assigns, his purchase money, with interest at the rate of fifty per cent. per annum on the sum paid by him, and all costs of said sale: *And provided also,* That infants, *femes covert,* and persons of unsound mind, shall have two years after their several disabilities are removed to redeem their property.

§ 21. That if, for any reason, the board of trustees may not think proper to intrust the town marshal with the collection of the taxes or other revenues of the town, or the said marshal shall be unable or refuse to perform that duty, they shall have power to appoint a collector, who, after taking the oath and executing a bond, as required of the marshal, shall have full power and authority to perform all the duties required of the marshal in the collection of the taxes and other revenues of the town; and his acts so performed shall have the same validity and effect as if performed by the marshal; and he shall receive such compensation for his services as the trustees may deem

May appoint
collector, &c.

reasonable. The board of trustees of said town of Concord may require all vendors of spirituous, vinous, or malt liquors within the corporate limits to pay a tax, not to exceed fifty dollars per annum, and to obtain a license; the tax to be paid as the board of trustees may direct.

1869.

Vendors of spirituous liquors, &c., to pay tax.

§ 22. That no license shall be granted by the county court of Lewis county to keep a tavern within the corporated limits of the town of Concord to sell spirituous, vinous, or malt liquors, until the applicant for such a license shall have first obtained the consent of the board of trustees of said town. This shall not be construed to abridge the power of the county court in the exercise of its discretion in refusing a license to keep a tavern. The party obtaining license to keep a tavern shall, in addition to the tax now required by law, pay to the board of trustees, or to such officer of the town as they may direct, and to form a part of the general revenue of the town, a sum not less than ten dollars or more than fifty dollars per year, to be fixed by the by-laws of the board of trustees. Any person who shall violate the provisions of this or the preceding section shall, for every offense, be liable to pay a fine of thirty dollars, which may be recovered by proceedings in the name of the Commonwealth of Kentucky, for the use of the board of trustees of the town of Concord.

County court not to grant license without consent of trustees, &c.

Additional tax to be paid to town.

Penalty for violating this or preceding section.

§ 23. The board of trustees may appoint a street commissioner, who may be removed by said trustees at any time and another appointed.

May appoint street commissioner.

§ 24. The board of trustees shall have power to pass all needful by-laws and ordinances for the due and effectual administration of right and justice in said town, and for the good government thereof; may legislate on all subjects which the peace, order, and welfare of said town may require, unless restrained by the terms of this charter or the Constitution and laws of the State. They may fix such penalties for a violation of any of their by-laws or ordinances, not exceeding fifty dollars in each case, as they may deem for the good government of the town. All new ordinances of said town shall be written in a fair and legible hand, and posted at two or more public places in said town. The board of trustees shall also have power to provide by ordinances for the purpose and for the suppression of all houses of ill-fame, bawdy-houses, gambling-houses, houses which are a common resort for idle and dissolute and disorderly persons, and other nuisances within the limits of said town; and for any willful neglect of the police judge or marshal to enforce said ordinances, or any of them, they, or either of them, may be proceeded against in the circuit court by indictment, and fined any

May pass by-laws, ordinances, &c.

May suppress houses of ill-fame, &c.

sum not exceeding one hundred dollars, at the discretion of the jury.

§ 25. The board of trustees shall have power to provide for improvements of the public streets and alleys of said town; to close any that they may deem useless; the enlargement, extension, and improvement of the public landings, and the proper drainage of the said town. They shall have power to provide by ordinance for the protection and preservation of the public property, and may impose proper penalties for the injury thereof. They may improve or ornament any of the public grounds belonging to said town, and cause to be planted upon the same, or upon the public streets, suitable shade trees; and any person who shall injure or destroy any shade tree or shrubbery upon the public grounds or public streets, whether planted by the authority of the trustees or private citizens, shall be subject to a fine of twenty-five dollars, to be recovered by warrant before the police judge, and enforced as other fines are enforced. The trustees shall have power to require the owner of any lot to make a brick or stone sidewalk in front thereof, not less than four feet wide, and of such a grade as they shall direct; and if, after a written notice of not less than three months, served on such owner, he or she shall fail to have said sidewalk made, in pursuance of said notice, the town trustees shall cause the same to be done at the expense of the owner, and shall have a lien on said lot for the amount of said expense, which may be enforced by suit in the Lewis circuit court, in the name of the trustees, and at the cost of the owner; and when several owners of lots are in default, they may be joined as defendants in one suit. Said trustees may, in like manner, cause the sidewalks to be repaired and improved. The notice referred to in this section may be executed on a non-resident of said town, upon his agent, or by publicly posting the same for three weeks in the town of Concord.

§ 26. The board of trustees shall have power to appoint a treasurer, who shall be a resident of the town and a qualified voter, who, before entering upon the duties of his office, shall take an oath faithfully to perform the same, and also the oath required by other officers by the Constitution and laws of the State, and shall give bond for such an amount, with such securities as the board of trustees may approve, conditioned to pay over and account for all moneys which shall come into his hands while in office, and for the prompt and faithful discharge of all duties imposed upon him as treasurer of the town of Concord. It shall be his duty to receive all moneys of the town derived from taxes, licenses, wharfage, fines, or other sources; but shall not pay out or expend the same

May provide for improvement of streets, alleys, &c.

May require side-walks to be made, &c.

May appoint treasurer; his powers and duties.

in anywise, except upon the order of the board of trustees, signed by the chairman, or a certified copy of the order allowing the same, attested by the clerk, which order shall specify for what purpose the same is to be paid. He shall keep a careful and correct account of all receipts and expenditures of the trustees, which account shall always be open for their inspection or their proper committee; he shall make reports of the condition of the treasury, from time to time, as the trustees may require, and at each regular meeting in December, of each year, shall report to the trustees a full statement of the receipts and expenditures for the year. He shall receive for his services a reasonable compensation, to be allowed by the board of trustees, and may be removed at any time, upon proper notice, for good cause shown. If, for any cause, the office of treasurer shall become vacant by removal, resignation, or otherwise, the trustees may appoint another.

§ 27. The board of trustees shall have power at any time, within two months after the assessor has returned his books, to hear complaints, and change, reduce, or correct the tax list of any person; and in case of reduction, if the person has paid his tax, to order the proper proportion thereof to be refunded. *May correct tax list.*

§ 28. The trustees shall have power specially, in addition to the other powers granted by this charter—

First. To borrow money on the credit of the town, and pledge the revenues for the payment thereof, and to execute bonds of the town therefor. *May borrow money.*

Second. To prevent, abate, and remove nuisances at the cost and expense of the owners or occupiers, or of the parties whose ground they exist, and to define and declare by ordinance what shall be a nuisance within the limits of the town, and to punish by fine any person for keeping, causing, erecting, or committing a nuisance. *Abate nuisances.*

Third. To establish, erect, and keep in repair bridges, culverts, and sewers, and regulate the use of the same, and cover them over when the interest of the public requires it. *Erect bridges, &c.*

Fourth. To provide for lighting the streets, market-house, and public buildings, rooms, and offices. *Light streets.*

Fifth. To establish, support, and regulate policemen, night-watches, and prescribe their duties and compensation. *Appoint policemen, &c.*

Sixth. To erect a market-house, establish market places, and provide for the government and regulation thereof, and to appoint inspectors of the articles sold therein, and to provide for the condemnation and destruction of stale and unwholesome meats and vegetables sold within the corporated limits. *Erect market-house.*

Seventh. To erect, make, and repair wharves and docks and river landings, and to fix the rate of wharfage.

Eighth. To regulate the stationing or anchoring of vessels and boats or rafts within the town limits, and the depositing of freight and lumber on the public wharves.

Ninth. To license, tax, and regulate auctioneers, coffee-houses, peddlers, brokers, butchers, coal and wood yards, &c.

Tenth. To license, tax, regulate, restrain, and prohibit billiard-tables, tippling-houses, bowling saloons, and ten-pin alleys.

Eleventh. To suppress gaming, drunkenness, gambling-houses, and disorderly houses of all kinds.

Twelfth To regulate the sweeping and cleaning of chimneys, and fix the fees thereof, and prescribe the manner of this collection.

Thirteenth. To regulate the storage of gunpowder, coal-oils, tar, pitch, rosin, hemp, cotton, and all other combustible materials, and to appoint some person or persons, at seasonable times, to enter and examine such houses as they may designate, in order to ascertain whether any of such houses are in a dangerous condition with reference to fires, and power and authority to put the same in secure order and condition.

Fourteenth. To erect and keep in repair accurate public scales, and to appoint a public weigher to attend to the same, and fix fees and compensation for his services.

Fifteenth. To provide for the training and breaking of horses, or exhibiting stallions in the public streets and places in the town.

Sixteenth. To provide for the removal from the limits of the town, or killing of mischievous animals, and for the disposing of vicious dogs, and for the punishment, by fine and penalties, of the owner and keeper of such animals.

Seventeenth. The board of trustees shall have power to appoint or employ an attorney to prosecute, for and on behalf of the board of trustees, all prosecutions in which the board of trustees may be interested, and to allow him a reasonable compensation therefor.

Eighteenth. The board of trustees shall have power to purchase lands for and locate cemeteries, either within the town limits or elsewhere in Lewis county, and exercise full and complete control over the same, and enforce the proper regulations and management thereof by adequate fines and penalties.

§ 29. The trustees shall, by ordinance, whenever the public necessity requires it, cause any new street or alley to be opened, or an old street or alley extended, widened, and improved; or establish a market place; to build, improve, extend, grade, or pave the wharves in the said

town, on the Ohio river, and to procure the condemnation
of any real estate for such purposes: *Provided*, That in no
case shall private property be taken for any such purpose
without the written consent of the claimant, or a just and
full compensation therefor be first paid in money to said
claimant. If the amount of such compensation cannot be
fixed by agreement, the trustees shall cause a petition to
be filed in the Lewis circuit court, stating the street or
alley they wish opened, widened, or extended, or improved, or the lands they desire condemned, to build, extend, or improve the wharf or wharves, and the name of
the owners, if known, of the lots and lands through or
over which they desire to have said street or alley opened,
widened, or extended, and the width thereof, or the land
or lands they desire for the purpose of building, extending,
or improving the wharf or wharves; and thereupon the
said court shall order a summons to issue for such owner
or owners to appear on some day of that, or some subsequent terms of said court, to show cause why such street or
alley should not be opened, widened, or extended, or such
land condemned, or such wharf or wharves should not be
made, extended, or improved; which summons shall be
executed on such owners if in the county of Lewis, if not,
on his, her, or their agent, if one is known; and on the
return of the summons executed, or the return of no inhabitant or known agent, and no one appearing, after
warning order, the said court shall order the street, alley,
or land condemned to be opened, widened, or extended,
made, or improved; and if any one or more of such owners of lots or lands appear and demand it, the court shall
award a writ of *ad quod damnum*, to be directed to the
proper county officer, to be executed and returned as provided by law for writs of that nature for opening public
roads; and on the return of the writ duly executed, the
court shall order the trustees of the town of Concord to
pay the damages assessed to the party or parties entitled
thereto, and shall order the street, alley, or ground for
wharf or wharves to be opened, widened, extended,
made, or improved, upon the payment of said damages.

§ 30. Appeals may be taken to circuit court and Court
of Appeals, as now provided by law in cases of opening
public roads, as referred to in last section.

Appeals may be taken.

§ 31. The trustees shall have power to appoint a wharf-
master, and may, for good cause, remove him, and to prescribe his powers and duties, require oath, and take bond
for the faithful performance of his duties.

May appoint wharf-master.

§ 32. The wharf-master of said town is hereby vested
with full power at all times, when the same is not promptly
paid on demand, to levy and distrain for any wharfage
due the said town, and his costs upon the boat or craft

His powers and duties.

1869.

for which wharfage is due, and to advertise and sell the same as in case of an execution; and the board of trustees shall have power, by ordinances and by-laws, to fix the cost chargeable in such cases.

May prevent sale of liquor to minors.

§ 33. The board of trustees shall have power to pass an ordinance against the vending by tavern-keepers, coffee-houses, and all vendors of spirituous liquors in the town of Concord, to a minor of any spirituous, vinous, or malt liquors, without the written consent of the parent or guardian, or those having the custody of said minor. The trustees may fix a fine therefor, not exceeding fifty dollars, to be collected as other fines before the police judge of said town; but all fines for violation of the laws of the State shall be paid as now provided by law.

Citizens of town exempt from working on roads.

§ 34. All persons residing in the town of Concord are exempt from working roads outside of the corporation of said town.

Vacancy in office of marshal.

§ 35. The board of trustees shall have power, if the office of marshal shall become vacant by removal, resignation, or any other cause, to appoint another to fill the unexpired term, or if he should fail to qualify after the election, to fill the vacancy.

When ordinances to take effect.

§ 36. All ordinances passed by the board, or by-laws, shall go into effect in ten days after their passage. unless declared by an order of the board to go into effect at an earlier day.

Fines may be worked out.

§ 37. The trustees of the town of Concord shall have power to pass ordinances to permit persons fined for violation of any ordinances to work the same fine out on the public streets or alleys of said town.

Laws in conflict repealed.

§ 38. That all laws and parts of laws, or acts heretofore passed, in relation to the town of Concord, in conflict with this act. be, and the same are hereby, repealed.

§ 39. This charter and acts shall take effect from its passage.

Approved February 13, 1869.

CHAPTER 1483.

AN ACT to authorize the County Court of Franklin County to subscribe for Stock in the Kentucky River Navigation Company, to issue County Bonds, and create a Sinking Fund to pay the same.

WHEREAS, The county court of the county of Franklin has ordered the presiding judge of the said court to subscribe to the stock of the Kentucky River Navigation Company the sum of seventy-five thousand dollars, to be raised by the sale of the bonds of the said county; and whereas, the said county court has authorized and directed the sale of the bonds of the said county to raise an additional sum of ten thousand dollars, for the purpose of raising a fund for the erection of bridges in said county, and have imposed a tax of twenty cents on the one hundred dollars of value upon the taxable property of said county; and some doubts being entertained in regard to the power of the said court lawfully to make such subscription, and issue said bonds and impose said tax, now, therefore,

Be it enacted by the General Assembly of the Commonwealth of Kentucky:

§ 1. That the action of the county court in the matter referred to in the preamble of this act be, and the same is hereby, declared to be legal and binding to all intents and purposes; and it is hereby declared to be lawful for the presiding judge of said county to subscribe, for and on behalf of the said county of Franklin, for seven hundred and fifty shares to the stock of the Kentucky River Navigation Company, each share being one hundred dollars; and, in order to raise said sum, it shall be lawful for the presiding judge of said county to issue the bonds of the county to the sum of seventy-five thousand dollars, bearing interest at the rate of six per cent. per annum, payable semi-annually, and the principal sum of said bonds to be paid at the expiration of twenty years from the date thereof, reserving the right of the said county to pay said bonds, or so many of them as the said court may see proper, at any time or times after the lapse of five years next after the date thereof; and the said presiding judge is hereby authorized and empowered, in addition to the bonds above named, to issue like bonds to raise a fund of ten thousand dollars to build bridges in said county, all of which bonds, when so issued, shall be a binding and valid debt against the county of Franklin, according to the tenor and effect of said bonds.

§ 2. The said county court shall have the power and authority to levy upon the inhabitants and the taxable property in said county, from time to time, and collect a tax or taxes sufficient to pay the interest upon said bonds and to pay the principal when the same falls due.

§ 3. That it shall be lawful for the county court of said county to create and establish a sinking fund for the payment of the interest and principal of the bonds hereby authorized to be issued.

§ 4. That if the said county court, a majority of all the justices concurring, shall deem it proper to raise said sum of seventy-five thousand dollars and said sum of ten thousand dollars, or either, or any part of either, by a direct tax upon the persons and the taxable property in said county, without issuing bonds as aforesaid, it shall be

1869.

lawful for said court so to do: *Provided*, That as to the said sum of seventy-five thousand dollars, the said court and the Kentucky River Navigation Company shall agree upon the amounts of the installments and the times within which they are to be paid; and it shall be competent for the said court and the president of the said Kentucky River Navigation Company to enter into any agreement upon the subject they may see proper.

§ 5. This act shall take effect from its passage.

Approved February 13, 1869.

CHAPTER 1484.

AN ACT for the benefit of Elizabeth Haden.

Be it enacted by the General Assembly of the Commonwealth of Kentucky:

§ 1. That the Auditor of Public Accounts draw his warrant upon the Treasurer for one hundred dollars, in favor of Elizabeth Haden, which shall be paid out of such moneys as are not otherwise appropriated by law, the said one hundred dollars being compensation to her for taking care of and providing for James Gates, a pauper idiot, from April, 1866, to April, 1868.

§ 2. This act to take effect from its passage.

Approved February 13, 1869.

CHAPTER 1485.

AN ACT to incorporate the Cowan Turnpike Road Company, in Boyle and Mercer Counties.

Be it enacted by the General Assembly of the Commonwealth of Kentucky:

§ 1. That a body-corporate and politic be, and hereby is, created and authorized to be formed and organized, under the name and style of the "Cowan Turnpike Road Company;" and under that name and style shall have perpetual succession; may have a common seal; may contract and be contracted with, sue and be sued, in all the courts of this Commonwealth.

Company incorporated, and corporate powers.

§ 2. The object and business of said corporation shall be to construct, keep up, and maintain a turnpike road from the turnpike road leading from Harrodsburg, in Mercer county, to Danville, in Boyle county, to leave the last named road at a point near McLane's gate; and from there the most practicable route, to be selected and decided on by the commissioners hereinafter named, to or

Objects of company.

near a hickory tree in the county road and corner to the
Nourse farm, in Mercer county, or as near said points as
may be found most practicable by said commissioners or
those that act.

§ 3. The capital stock of said company shall not exceed Capital stock.
ten thousand dollars, to be divided into shares of fifty dollars each.

§ 4. That books for the subscription of stock in said Commission-
ers to receive
subscription of
stock.
company may be opened at any time or place after the
passage of this act, under the supervision of Peter T.
Gentry, Wm Davis, Jacob Funk, W. H. Robinson, and C.
T. Worthington, or any one or more of said persons, who
are hereby constituted commissioners for that purpose.
The subscribers for stock in said company shall sign the
following obligation, to-wit: " We, whose names are here- Obligation of
subscribers.
unto subscribed, hereby obligate ourselves to pay to the
president and directors of the Cowan Turnpike Road
Company fifty dollars for each share of stock in said
company hereby subscribed by us." The number of
shares so subscribed by each person shall be designated
opposite each subscriber's name; and said subscription
shall be made in a book in which said obligation shall
be written. And said commissioners, or those acting, or
the president and directors of said company, after the
same is organized, may receive subscriptions of stock to
said company in real estate, rock. lumber, or other personal property, which shall be valid and binding, and the
amount in value of such subscription shall be expressed in
the respective subscriptions; and if the property is not
surrendered or delivered on the demand of the said company, the value thereof in money, as expressed in the subscription, may be collected of the subscriber.

§ 5. As soon as three thousand dollars is subscribed to President and
directors to be
elected.
the stock of said company, it may be organized; and to
this end, the said commissioners, or those acting, shall
give notice to the subscribers of stock of the time and
place of electing officers for said company, which shall
be a president and five directors; the time and place of
such election shall be stated in said notice, and said
notice must be given at least two weeks before the day
of election; after the first election of said officers, the
time and place of election of said officers shall be fixed
by the said president and directors; each stockholder How stock
voted.
shall be entitled to one vote for each share of stock
owned by him or her, which may be cast in person or
by proxy. No one but a stockholder shall be an officer
in said company. The president and directors shall each President
and directors to
take oath, term
of office, &c.
take an oath faithfully to perform their duties as such,
which shall be certified by the officer administering it,
and filed with the papers of the company; and said

1869.

officers shall serve for one year, and until their successors are elected and qualified. If any vacancy occurs during the year by death, resignation, removal from the State, or in any other manner, the remainder of the directors may, if they deem it necessary, fill the vacancy.

Books may be kept open after organization of company, and Boyle county may take stock, levy tax to pay same, &c.

§ 6. The said company, after it is organized, may keep open the books for additional subscriptions of stock in said company. The Boyle county court may subscribe stock in said company to any amount not less than five hundred dollars per mile of said road, as the same may be completed, payable on the completion of each mile; and to pay said subscription made by said county court, said court is hereby authorized to levy and collect an *ad valorem* tax on all the property in said county, subject to tax for State revenue, sufficient in each year to pay the amount of the county's subscription for that year; said tax shall be collected and accounted for by the sheriff of Boyle county, in the same manner, and at the same time, he is now required by law to account for and pay over the county levy for Boyle county, except said turnpike tax shall be paid to said company or its authorized agent. For any default or failure of said sheriff to collect and pay over said tax as aforesaid, he shall be liable to a suit or suits in the Boyle circuit court on his official bond as sheriff; and upon the trial of said suit or suits, said company shall recover against said sheriff and his sureties all taxes which he has collected, or which he might have collected by due diligence, with the damages, interest, and costs allowed by law against defaulting sheriffs for the county levy; said suits shall be in the name of the president and directors of said company.

Officers to be appointed, to give bond, &c.

§ 7. The president and directors may appoint a treasurer and clerk, and prescribe their duties, fix their compensation, and may remove them at pleasure. Said treasurer and clerk shall give bond, with good security, honestly to account for all moneys that may come into their hands, and for the faithful performance of their duties, which bond, and the certificate of such oath, shall be filed and kept with the papers of said company. The said president and directors may appoint a superintendent, agent, or engineer, to superintend the construction of said road, and its maintenance afterwards; and may appoint gatekeepers and such other employes as they may deem necessary.

May make by-laws.

§ 8. The said president and directors shall have power to pass any by-laws, rules and regulations, for their own government, and the government and conduct of said company, its officers and affairs, that they may deem necessary, not inconsistent with this act or with the Constitution of this State [or] of the United States.

§ 9. The said president and directors may let out for construction any portion of said road as soon as three thousand dollars is subscribed, and may continue to let out for construction other portions of said road as soon as they have sufficient subscriptions of stock to build the portions let out, and may thus continue until said road is finished; and as soon as two and a half miles of said road are finished, they may erect a toll-gate, and collect toll for that portion of said road completed. The charges for toll on said road shall be in conformity with the general law of this State regulating tolls on turnpikes; and they shall only be authorized to charge toll on said road in proportion to the distance traveled, and only for so much of said road as shall be completed and in good repair for traveling.

May let out portion of road.

When may erect gates, collect toll, &c.

§ 10. The said company may receive releases of right of way for said road, and ground for rock quarries and toll-houses, by consent or purchase; and if they deem it necessary, they may, by proceeding instituted in conformity with the existing laws of this State on the subject of turnpike and plank roads (Revised Statutes, chapter 103, and amendments thereto), condemn land for right of way over which said road may be located and ground for toll-gates and toll-houses and rock quarries, just compensation being paid to the owners thereof, to be assessed by a jury empanneled for such purpose, according to law as aforesaid.

Right of way.

§ 11. The width and grade of said road shall be determined by said president and directors, as also that portion to be covered with metal or stone, and the thickness thereof. Any person who shall unlawfully obstruct said road shall be subject to a fine of not less than five nor more than fifty dollars therefor, which shall, when collected, be for the use of said company, and shall be recoverable as other fines are recoverable by law. Said president and directors may pass by-laws fixing the fines for a failure to pay toll, or for the evasion of toll on said road, which may be recovered as other fines of similar amount are recovered under the laws of this Commonwealth, and be for the use of said company.

Grade and width of road.

§ 12. The president and directors of said company shall prescribe in what installments the subscriptions of stock shall be paid; and the rules adopted by them shall be binding on the subscribers of stock.

§ 13. This act shall take effect from its passage.

Approved February 13, 1869.

CHAPTER 1486.

AN ACT for the benefit of T. W. Samuels, late Sheriff of Nelson County, and his sureties.

Be it enacted by the General Assembly of the Commonwealth of Kentucky:

§ 1. That the damages, amounting to five hundred and seventy-two dollars and twenty-two cents, rendered by the Franklin circuit court, in the name of the Commonwealth of Kentucky, against T. W. Samuels, late sheriff of Nelson county, and the sureties in his official bond, for failure to pay into the State Treasury the revenue for the year 1867, the said Samuels and his sureties are hereby released from the payment of said damages, the said Samuels having paid the principal, interest, and costs of said judgment.

§ 2. This act shall take effect from and after its passage.

Approved February 13, 1869. ·

————

CHAPTER 1487.

AN ACT incorporating the Berry's Station, Raven's Creek, and Dry Ridge Turnpike Road Company.

Be it enacted by the General Assembly of the Commonwealth of Kentucky:

§ 1. That the Berry's Station, Raven's Creek, and Dry Ridge Turnpike Road Company is hereby incorporated, with authority to make a turnpike road from Berry's Station, in Harrison county, through Raven's Creek, so as to intersect the Covington and Lexington turnpike in Scott county. The capital stock of said company shall be divided into shares of fifty dollars each; and subscriptions may be taken up by each of the commissioners hereinafter named for five years after the passage of this act, unless sooner taken up.

§ 2. The following persons are hereby appointed commissioners to perform the duties of this act: N. L. Hume, Dr. T. W. Hedges, S. J. Dunaway, Dr. Wm. Collend, J. R. Johnson, J. B. Crouch, Esq. Hinton, and William Webber.

§ 3. When one hundred shares of said stock shall have been subscribed, the holders thereof, upon ten days' notice posted in Berry's Station and at Colemansville, may meet at Berry's Station, according to said notice, and elect five directors, to have perpetual succession; each stockholder to have one vote, by proxy or otherwise, for each share of stock owned by him or her in all elections of officers.

§ 4. The directors elect shall elect from their body a president, secretary, and treasurer; and all officers shall hold their offices until the first Monday in January next succeeding their election or appointment, and until their successors shall be duly elected and installed; and an election shall be held on each succeeding first Monday in January, as heretofore provided.

§ 5. The directors, or a majority of them, shall constitute a board and quorum to do all legal things in the management of the road and business of the company, and may make by-laws for that purpose; may use a common seal, changeable at pleasure. The company may contract, sue and be sued in their corporate name; and do all legal acts for their well-being.

§ 6. All officers of the company shall take an oath to discharge their official duties; and, in addition thereto, the treasurer shall execute bond, with good security, binding him to collect and disburse all money as it may become his duty to do according to this charter and the by-laws, subject to the orders of the board.

§ 7. After organization of the company they may view, locate, and build said road, or so much thereof as they may deem expedient. They may obtain the right of way by contract with the owners, getting their written consent, or may have writs of *ad quod damnum*, as in cases of common roads; and they shall pay such damages as may be assessed under said writ, or according to agreement, subject to appeal. The construction of the road shall not be delayed on account of the pendency of the writ of *ad quod damnum;* but the company may proceed with the work during its pendency: *Provided, however,* That in no case shall a warning order of over thirty days be necessary in any proceeding against non-residents in the locating or construction of the road.

§ 8. The company may collect all subscriptions and all money, in such installments as they may desire, for the construction of said road; and shall keep a record of all its proceedings, and cause a report to be made and spread upon its records annually, in condensed form, showing the condition of the road and company, and all things connected with its interest. Said company and stockholders shall only be bound to the amount of their stock.

§ 9. After four consecutive miles of said road shall have been finished, a toll-gate may be erected across it, and tolls collected; but the rates of toll shall not exceed that fixed by general law, and may be regulated by said law.

§ 10. This act to take effect from its passage.

Approved February 15, 1869.

          CHAPTER 1488.

AN ACT to incorporate the Frankfort and Flat Creek Turnpike Road Company.

Be it enacted by the General Assembly of the Commonwealth of Kentucky:

§ 1. That Lewis E. Harvie, John N. Crutcher, S. V. Pence, Philip Swigert, Dennis Onan, R. E. Collins, John Rodman, W. B. Onan, and Jas. M. Lewis, be, and they are hereby, incorporated, under the name and style of the Frankfort and Flat Creek turnpike road company; and shall have and exercise by that name all the powers and privileges usual, necessary, and proper to their existence and operations as a body corporate and politic, and all the rights and powers usually granted turnpike road companies, and necessary to obtain or condemn right of way, take and use earth, stone, or timber, and such other rights, powers, and privileges, as shall authorize and enable such corporation to lay out, construct, repair, and maintain a turnpike road and necessary bridges or ferries on such route, and over such land, as said company may elect, from the town of Frankfort, in said county of Franklin, to the mouth of Marshall's Branch, on Flat Creek, in said county.

§ 2. The persons named in this act shall constitute the board of directors for said company for at least one year after the organization of said company shall have been completed, by subscription to its capital stock of at least five thousand dollars, which capital stock may be increased at the discretion of said board to a sum not exceeding fifty thousand dollars; and for any part thereof so subscribed, and the subscription being fully paid, certificates, signed by the proper officer or officers of the company, shall be issued in shares of fifty dollars each.

§ 3. The stockholders of said company shall meet annually on the first Wednesday in May, in the town of Frankfort, and may hold such other meetings as may be called by the board of directors, or a majority in interest of the stockholders; and at such meetings the stockholders may, by themselves or by written proxies, cast one vote for each share of stock held; and a majority of stock must be represented in any such meeting to constitute a quorum to transact business; and said company shall have power to elect or appoint such officers and agents, and to make such rules and by-laws for its government, as they may deem proper, not in conflict with the provisions of this act or the laws of this Commonwealth.

§ 4. Upon the expiration of the term of the board of directors appointed by this act, a new board shall be elected annually by the stockholders. Each board of

directors shall elect a president and secretary, and shall
fill by election all vacancies occurring in the board itself,
by death or otherwise, until the next annual election of
directors is held.

§ 5. The company shall keep a full record of all its
proceedings, which shall be at all reasonable times subject to examinations by the stockholders, and cause a
report to be made and spread upon its records annually,
in condensed form, showing the condition of the road
and company, and all things connected with its interest.

§ 6. The company may collect all subscriptions and
money in such installments as they may desire, for the
construction of said road ; and any stockholders in said
road failing to pay their calls when due, shall be subject
to suit in any of the courts in this Commonwealth having
jurisdiction of the matter in controversy, and shall pay
interest thereon at the rate of six per cent. per annum
until paid; said company and stockholders shall only be
bound to the amount of their stock.

§ 7. All officers of the company shall take an oath to
discharge faithfully their official duties ; and, in addition
thereto, the treasurer shall execute bond with good security, binding him to collect and disburse all money as it
may become his duty to do according to this charter and
the by-laws of the company, subject to the orders of the
board.

§ 8. The president and directors shall have power to let
out said road to contractors, on such terms, and in such
portions, as they may deem beneficial to the interests of
the company ; the said company may sue and be sued,
plead and be impleaded, contract and be contracted with,
and in all litigations shall be dealt with as a natural person.

§ 9. After two consecutive miles of said road have been
built, one toll-gate may be erected across it, and for every
additional five miles of road finished by the company, they
may erect an additional toll-gate across said road; but the
rate of toll shall not exceed that fixed by general law, and
may be regulated by law.

§ 10. Should the company conclude to establish a ferry
over the Kentucky river at or near Frankfort, they shall
have power to charge such reasonable additional tolls
over such ferry as are allowed by law and customary
with similar ferries in this Commonwealth.

§ 11. This act to take effect from its passage.

Approved February 15, 1869.

      CHAPTER 1489.

AN ACT for the benefit of the sureties of Wm. Herrin, late Sheriff of Fulton County.

WHEREAS, A judgment was rendered in the Franklin circuit court, at its fiscal term, 1869, in favor of the Commonwealth of Kentucky and against Wm. Herrin, sheriff of Fulton county, and Henry Campbell, Allan Campbell, R. A. Herrin, R. S. Kimbro, A. J. Everett, J. A. Craig, H. L. Wall, R. E. Finch, and Charles Campbell, his sureties, for the sum of $3,965 56, with interest from June 1st, 1867, and $3 05 costs, and $793 10 damages, which judgment was on account of the revenue tax due from said county for the year 1867; and whereas, it appears that, after the proper credits were entered on said judgment, that the whole of the principal, interest, and costs of the same, and that part of the damages to which the Attorney General is by law entitled, except $9 27, has been paid by said sureties; therefore,

Be it enacted by the General Assembly of the Commonwealth of Kentucky:

§ 1. That William Herrin, late sheriff of Fulton county, and his sureties, be released from the damages adjudged against them, amounting to seven hundred and ninety-three dollars and ten cents ($793 10), for the non-payment of the revenue for the year 1867: *Provided*, Said Herrin and his sureties shall pay into the Treasury all of the principal, interest, costs, and attorney's fees of the judgment on or before the first day of June, 1869.

§ 2. This act to take effect from and after its passage.

Approved February 15, 1869.

CHAPTER 1490.

AN ACT to amend an act, entitled "An act to incorporate the Cincinnati, Covington, and Cumberland Gap Railroad Company."

Be it enacted by the General Assembly of the Commonwealth of Kentucky:

§ 1. That the third section of the amendment to the act named in the title be, and is hereby, amended so as to insert the words "twenty per cent." in the last line of the third section of said amendment, in lieu of the words "ten per cent." in said line.

§ 2. This act shall take effect from and after its passage.

Approved February 15, 1869.

CHAPTER 1491.

AN ACT for the benefit of the Flemingsburg and Mt. Carmel Turnpike Road Company.

Be it enacted by the General Assembly of the Commonwealth of Kentucky:

§ 1. That the Flemingsburg and Mt. Carmel Turnpike Road Company are hereby empowered and authorized to extend their turnpike road to the three forks of the road, in the direction of, and in the vicinity of, William Foxworthy's; and that all of the provisions of the charter of said company are hereby made applicable in the construction and extension of said road.

§ 2. This act to take effect from its passage.

Approved February 15, 1869.

CHAPTER 1492.

AN ACT to incorporate the Shepherdsville and Cedar Grove Church turnpike road company.

Be it enacted by the General Assembly of the Commonwealth of Kentucky:

§ 1. That a company is hereby created, with corporate powers and corporate succession, under the name of the "Shepherdsville and Cedar Grove Church Company," for the purpose of building a turnpike or gravel road from the town of Shepherdsville, in Bullitt county, to the Cedar Grove Church, in said county.

§ 2. That the capital stock of said company shall be fifteen thousand dollars, and may be increased at any time, at the pleasure of the president and directors of said company, and shall be divided into shares of fifty dollars each.

§ 3. That books for the subscription of stock may be opened at such times and places as may be deemed best by the following named commissioners, under whose direction the stock may be subscribed, viz: Charles Lee, Wilhite Carpenter, H. O. Maraman, Jas. Y. Pope, W. P. Simmons, Myron S. Combs, D. J. Weller, Noell Simmons, and Richard H. O. Simmons: *Provided, however,* Any three or more of the foregoing named commissioners, who may first organize under this charter, shall have the same authority as if all should act

§ 4. That such of the commissioners appointed by this act to open books for the subscription to the capital stock of said company shall procure one or more books, and the subscribers to the stock of said company shall enter into the following obligation, written in said book or

books, viz: "We, whose names are hereunto subscribed,
do promise to pay to the president, directors, and company of the Shepherdsville and Cedar Grove Church
turnpike road company, the sum of fifty dollars for each
share of stock in said company, in such manner and in
such proportion, and at such times as shall be required
by the president and directors of the company.

§ 5. The books for the subscription of stock shall remain
open until the whole of the capital stock, or enough to
complete the road, shall have been subscribed, and persons
may subscribe at any time until the books are closed.

§ 6. So soon as one hundred shares in said company is
subscribed, it shall be the duty of some one or more of
the commissioners to give notice, by written or printed
notice, posted up at Shepherdsville, Weller's Mill, and
Cedar Grove Church, that a meeting of the stockholders
of said company will be held at such time and place as
may be named by the commissioner or commissioners
who may give the notice, for the purpose of choosing a
president and board of directors for said company, at
least ten days before the day of such meeting, at which
meeting such of said commissioners as may be present
shall proceed to hold an election, by taking the votes by
ballot of the stockholders, in person or by proxy; and
each stockholder shall be entitled to one vote for every
share of stock subscribed by him or her for each of the
officers of the company; at which meeting the person
securing the largest number of votes shall be duly declared elected president of the company, and each of
three directors shall be chosen in like manner. The
president and three directors shall constitute all the officers of the road except a treasurer, who shall be chosen
in the same manner as the president. All of said officers
shall hold their office for the term of one year, and until
their successors are elected and qualified. The treasurer
shall be required, before entering upon the discharge of
his duties, to execute, with sufficient surety, a bond to the
company, stipulating a faithful discharge of his duties.

§ 7. That the Shepherdsville and Cedar Grove Church
turnpike company shall by that name have perpetual succession, and shall be capable of taking and holding, and
of purchasing, selling, and conveying, in fee simple, all
such real, personal, or mixed estate as may be necessary
to carry out the object of this enactment; and may sue
and be sued in all the courts of this Commonwealth as
natural persons may do; and do all and every thing which
a body politic and corporate may do.

§ 8. That said company may erect a toll-gate and toll-
house on their said road whenever two and one half continuous miles of said road are completed, and may collect

any rate of toll fixed by the president and directors.: *Provided*, That the toll charged shall not exceed that allowed by the general law of the State.

§ 9. The president and directors may locate said road, fix and regulate the elevation and grade of said road, the width and depth of stone or gravel on said road; and may proceed by writ of *ad quod damnum* to condemn such land, stone, or earth, as may be necessary for the location and construction of said road.

§ 10. All elections of officers after the first shall be at such. time and place, and after such notice, as may be agreed upon by the president and directors.

§ 11. That the president and directors of said company shall have power to pass all by-laws necessary to promote the interest of the stockholders; and to superintend the construction of said road, and to carry out the object of this enactment.

§ 12. The president may call meetings of said board of directors at such times and places as he may think best. A majority of the directors shall constitute a quorum; and, in the absence of the president, a majority of the directors may elect a president *pro tem*.

§ 13. The written or printed certificate of the president, countersigned by the treasurer, shall be evidence of ownership of stock, and the same shall be transferable on the books of the company in person or by attorney.

§ 14. The president and directors may fill all vacancies occurring in their board, or in the office of treasurer of the company, until the next regular election.

§ 15. This act shall take effect from its passage.

Approved February 15, 1869.

CHAPTER 1493.

AN ACT to incorporate the Flemingsburg and Dobynsburg Turnpike Road Company.

Be it enacted by the General Assembly of the Commonwealth of Kentucky:

§ 1. That a company may be formed under the style and name of the Flemingsburg and Dobynsburg turnpike road company, for the construction of a macadamized turnpike road from Flemingsburg, by way of Dobynsburg, to intersect the Mt. Carmel and Maysville turnpike road, near the house of J. H. Colter, in the county of Fleming. The capital stock of said road shall not exceed forty thousand dollars, divided into shares of fifty dollars each.

§ 2. The books for the subscription of stock shall be opened, at such times and places as may be deemed convenient, in said county of Fleming, under the supervision of Dr. John Waugh, Jerome Weire, Gerand Weire, Luther Weire, James Bateman, Wm. Bateman, Reese Davis, Benjamin Ham, and R. C. Colter, or any one or more of them, who are hereby appointed and constituted commissioners for that purpose. That the subscription for stock in said company shall be made by the persons taking stock in said company subscribing the following obligation, which shall be written in a book procured for that purpose, to-wit: "We, whose names are hereunto subscribed, obligate and bind ourselves to pay to the president, directors, and company of the Flemingsburg and Dobynsburg turnpike road company, the sum of fifty dollars for each share of stock in said company set opposite our names, agreeable to an act of the General Assembly of the Commonwealth of Kentucky incorporating said company.

§ 3. That as soon as four thousand dollars is subscribed, said commissioners, or such as may act, shall, at such time and place as they may appoint, call a meeting of the stockholders of said company, who shall elect a president and five directors for said company, who shall hold their office for one year and until their successors are elected. That said president and directors, before they enter on the discharge of their duties, shall, before some justice of the peace or other officer authorized to administer an oath, take an oath that they will faithfully, without favor or affection, discharge the duties of president or director, as the case may be, according to their best judgment. A certificate of said oath shall be filed with the records of said company.

§ 4. The president and directors of said company shall appoint a clerk and treasurer for said company, who shall hold their offices for one year and until their successors are appointed and qualified, by taking the same oath prescribed to be taken by the president and directors. The treasurer of said company, before he enters on the discharge of his duties, shall execute bond, payable to the president and directors of said company, conditioned that he will faithfully discharge the duties of treasurer, and that he will, when called on, pay the amount of money in his hands to the order of the president and directors of said company.

§ 5. That the president and directors of said company may sue and be sued; shall keep a record of their proceedings in a book kept for such purpose; may let out any portion of said road on such terms as may appear advisable to them, taking an obligation in writing from each contractor, specifying the terms of his said contract. They shall have power to receive a release of right of way from any person over whose land the road may pass, or to condemn for right of way, rock quarries, or land for toll-gates and houses, according to the provisions of the general law on the subject, a writ of *ad quod damnum* having been first obtained, in the name of the president and directors of said company; to erect gates and collect tolls according to the general law of this State on such subjects.

§ 6. That the provisions of the act, entitled "An act to incorporate the Poplar Plains and Flemingsburg turnpike road company," and any act therein referred to, shall apply to this company, and shall regulate the proceedings of the president and directors and other officers of this company, their duties, powers, and authority, so far as the provisions of said act or acts may not be inconsistent with this act

§ 7. This act shall take effect and be in force from and after its passage.

Approved February 15, 1869.

CHAPTER 1494.

AN ACT to incorporate Confidence Lodge, No. 204, of the Independent Order of Good Templars, of Augusta.

Be it enacted by the General Assembly of the Commonwealth of Kentucky:

§ 1. That R. T. Weldon, N. J. Stroube, Geo. H. McKibben, T. R. Vandyke, A. J. Jones, and M. Troutman, and their associates and successors, be, and they are hereby, created a body-corporate, by the name and style of Confidence Lodge, No. 204, of the Independent Order of Good Templars, of Augusta, Kentucky; and they and their associates and successors shall so continue and have perpetual succession; and by that name are made capable in law, as natural persons, of suing and being sued, of pleading and being impleaded, of contracting and being contracted with, of answering and being answered, in all courts of law and equity in this Commonwealth; to make, have, and use a common seal, and the same to break, alter, or amend at pleasure; they may make and ordain regulations and by-laws for their government, and those now in force in said lodge to alter and amend at their pleasure, and may change and renew the same at pleasure: *Provided,* They do not conflict with the Constitution and laws of the United States and the laws of the State of Kentucky. The said corporation shall have power and authority to acquire and hold real and personal estate, not exceeding twenty thousand dollars in value; and, from time to time, if deemed expedient, sell and convey the same, or any part thereof, and to reinvest and dispose of

1869.   the proceeds; the Legislature reserving the right to repeal, alter, or amend this at pleasure.

§ 2. This act to take effect from its passage.

Approved February 15, 1869.

CHAPTER 1495.

AN ACT to incorporate Ashland Cumberland Presbyterian Church, in Crittenden County.

Be it enacted by the General Assembly of the Commonwealth of Kentucky:

§ 1. That Joseph Newcome, W. H. Walker, and E. M. Lemon, and their successors in office, are hereby created a body-politic, by the name and style of the " Trustees of Ashland Cumberland Presbyterian Church," in Crittenden county; and by said name to have perpetual succession; and may purchase, take by devise, bequest, gift, or deed, any real or personal estate or property, and the same to hold for the only use of said church, according to the discipline and economy of said church, and to sell or dispose of the same; to have and exercise all the powers necessary for, and incident to, religious corporations, not inconsistent with the Constitution and laws of this State or the United States; and by that name may contract and be contracted with, sue and be sued, plead and be impleaded.

§ 2. That said trustees hereby appointed shall continue in office for the period of one year from the date of their appointment by the church, and until their successors are elected or appointed, which shall be done according to the discipline and usage of the Cumberland Presbyterian Church now worshiping at said Ashland Church; and vacancies may be filled, from time to time, as they may occur; that a majority of the trustees shall constitute a quorum to do business; they shall appoint from their number a chairman and secretary; all contracts and conveyances shall be signed by the chairman and secretary only; and such conveyances shall pass the title of the property so conveyed out of the church; and they shall keep a record of their proceedings, which shall at all times be open to the inspection of the members of said church.

§ 3. This act shall take effect from its passage.

Approved February 15, 1869.

CHAPTER 1496.

AN ACT to enlarge the Voting Precinct of Mt. Sterling.

Be it enacted by the General Assembly of the Commonwealth of Kentucky:

§ 1. That the boundary line of the Mt. Sterling voting precinct, in Montgomery county, be so enlarged and changed as to embrace and include the old "Ribelin Brick House" and farm; and all persons residing in said house and on said farm are hereby allowed to vote in the town of Mt. Sterling.

§ 2. This act shall take effect from and after its passage.

Approved February 15, 1869.

CHAPTER 1498.

AN ACT to regulate and create the Office of Treasurer for Carroll County.

Be it enacted by the General Assembly of the Commonwealth of Kentucky:

§ 1. That there is hereby created for the county of Carroll the office of county treasurer; said officer shall be elected by the court of claims for said county in the year 1869, and by the same court, every two years thereafter, a successor to said office shall be elected: *Provided*, That the judge of the Carroll county court may appoint a treasurer to serve from the approval of this act until the first Monday in December, 1869. The person elected under the provisions of this act shall hold his office until his successor has been duly elected and qualified.

§ 2. Said treasurer shall execute bond, with sufficient sureties, to be approved by the county judge, a bond similar to that required by law to be given by collectors of the county revenue, to be sued upon in the same manner.

§ 3. It shall be the duty of said treasurer to collect, receive, and receipt for all money due or to become due to said county from the several collecting officers thereof, to be held subject to the order of the county court of said county. He shall safely keep the bonds of the county, pay the interest on them as it accrues, and issue them by the direction of the county court, or the judge thereof. He shall have power, and it shall be his duty, to institute actions against all delinquent sheriffs or collectors of said county. In the month of November of each year, such sheriffs and collectors shall settle their accounts with said treasurer, and pay over any balance due by them; and, at the court of claims held in the following month, said treasurer shall report said settlements. He shall keep a book, in which he shall keep a correct account of all moneys and bonds received by him for the county, showing when and on what account received, and when and on what account disbursed by him.

§ 4. It shall not be lawful for any one except said treasurer to receive any money due or to become due to said county: *Provided, however*, That the sheriff or collector may, as heretofore, pay off claims against the county, and receive credit therefor in his settlement with the treasurer.

§ 5. It shall be the duty of the county judge of said county, in the month of January of each year, to settle the county treasurer's accounts, and report the same to the next county court, which shall lie over to the succeeding term for exception; and if no exceptions are then taken, or those taken are overruled, said settlements shall be confirmed and recorded. Said judge shall receive five dollars for making said settlement.

§ 6. The county court clerk shall record all the settlements herein provided for, and shall receive for his services fees, as allowed by law for similar services.

§ 7. The court of claims shall annually allow the treasurer a reasonable compensation for his services.

§ 8. This act shall take effect from its passage.

Approved February 15, 1869.

CHAPTER 1499.

AN ACT to require the County Clerk of Meade County to have certain Books rebound.

Be it enacted by the General Assembly of the Commonwealth of Kentucky:

§ 1. That John G. Walker, clerk of the county court of Meade county, is hereby authorized and required to have the deed books, A, B, and C, in his office, rebound; and when they have been rebound, as herein required, the county court of Meade county shall allow him a reasonable compensation therefor, to be paid out of the county levy of said county.

§ 2. This act to take effect from its passage.

Approved February 16, 1869.

CHAPTER 1500.

AN ACT to incorporate the Vanceburg, Dry Run, and Kinniconick Creek
Turnpike Road Company.

*Be it enacted by the General Assembly of the Commonwealth
of Kentucky:*

§ 1. That a company is hereby formed and created a
body-politic and corporate, by the name and style of the
Vanceburg, Dry Run, and Kinniconick Creek turnpike
road company, to consist of a president and five directors, with the other stockholders and officers hereinafter
authorized by this act, for the purpose of building a turnpike road from a point on the Vanceburg, Salt Lick,
Tollsboro, and Maysville turnpike, near Dry Run, to
Kinniconick creek, near the present residence of J. W.
Rand; said company, by said name, shall have perpetual
existence and succession, and all the rights, privileges, and
franchises incident to such a corporation; and shall be
capable of taking and holding their capital stock, and
the increase and profits thereof; and of purchasing,
taking, and holding, to them and their successors and
assigns, and of selling, transferring, and conveying, in
fee simple, all such lands, tenements, and hereditaments
and estates, real, personal, and mixed, as shall be necessary to them in the prosecution of their work, completion,
and use of their road; and to sue and be sued, plead and
be impleaded, answer and be answered, defend and be
defended, in all courts of record, or any other proper
place or places whatever; to contract for, buy, and own
the right of way for said road; to have a common seal;
and to do all and every other act whatever within the
object and scope of their incorporation, which a body-
politic or corporate may lawfully do.

§ 2. The capital stock of said company shall be fifty
thousand dollars, and may be increased to any sum necessary to build said road, and any branch roads said company may choose to build, authorized under this act;
said stock shall be divided into shares of twenty-five
dollars each; books for the subscription of stock shall
be opened on the third Monday in March, 1869, or as
soon thereafter as the commissioners hereafter named
in this act may direct; said books shall be opened at
the clerk's office of the Lewis circuit court, in Vanceburg, at the house of Jacob W. Rand, on Kinniconick
creek, and at such other places as said commissioners
shall direct; said books shall continue open for the subscription of stock until sufficient stock shall be subscribed
to build said road, or until the commissioners named in
this act, or the board of directors, when elected, of said
company, shall see proper to and do close said books.

Marginal notes:

Company in-
corporated, &
corporate pow-
ers.

Capital stock.

Books for
subscription of
stock to be
opened.

1869.

Commissioners to receive subscription of stock.

The books shall be opened under the direction of the following persons, who are hereby appointed commissioners for that purpose, viz: Thomas W. W. Mitchell, Thomas B. Harrison, F. H. Rice, and Wm. S. Pell, at Vanceburg; Jacob W. Rand, Samuel Bate, and Thomas Bate, at the house of J. W. Rand; any one or more of said persons may act at said places and open books for and receive any and all subscriptions of stock; said commissioners shall procure the necessary books, and the subscribers for stock shall enter into the following obligation:

Obligation of subscribers.

"We, whose names are hereunto subscribed, do respectively promise to pay the president and directors of the Vanceburg, Dry Run, and Kinniconick Creek turnpike road company the sum of twenty-five dollars for each share of stock set opposite our names, to be paid in such proportions, and at such times and places, as the president and directors may or shall direct or require.

When president and directors to be elected.

§ 3 As soon as three thousand dollars have been subscribed to the capital stock of said company it shall be the duty of said commissioners, or such as act, to give notice to the stockholders for a meeting of said stockholders, at such time and place as they may designate in said notice, for the purpose of electing a president and five directors, said officers to be elected from among the stockholders, and one vote shall be allowed for each share of stock; the officers thus elected shall continue in office for one year, and until their successors are in like manner duly elected. A majority of the directors shall be competent to transact business.

Portions of another charter adopted as part of this.

§ 4. That the 4th, 5th, 6th, 7th, 8th, 9th, 11th, 12th, 14th, 15th, 17th, 18th, 19th, 20th, 21st, 24th, 25th, and 26th sections of an act, entitled "An act to incorporate the Vanceburg, Salt Lick, Tollsboro, and Maysville turnpike road company," approved February 13th, 1867, are hereby adopted and re-enacted as part of this act.

Lewis county may take stock, &c.

§ 5. That in order to encourage and assist in building said road, it is hereby made the duty of the Lewis county court, whenever a sufficient sum shall have been subscribed, by good and responsible persons, to the capital stock of said company, to build six miles of said road by the aid of one thousand dollars to the mile from the county, and said six miles shall have been let out to a responsible contractor, or contractors, who have executed a bond or bonds for the speedy building and completion of said six miles, and proof of these facts shall be made to said county court, to subscribe to the capital stock of said company one thousand dollars per mile for said six miles. Said subscription shall be made by the judge of said county court in the name of Lewis county; and upon such subscription thus being made, the county shall become a stockholder in said

1869.

company to the amount of one thousand dollars per mile. The stock of Lewis county shall be represented and voted at all elections of officers of said company by the presiding judge of the county court, and the clerk of said court, each voting one half of the stock of said county. That to pay the stock thus subscribed by said county court judge to the capital stock of said company of one thousand dollars per mile, said county judge is hereby authorized and required to issue the bonds of Lewis county, payable at not a longer date than twenty years, to bear interest at six per cent. per annum, which bonds may be in such amounts, and principal and interest payable at such place or places, as said county judge may direct. Said bonds shall be delivered to the president of said company, who shall execute a receipt for said bonds in the name of said company; and upon the delivery of said bonds to said president, the county of Lewis shall become a stockholder in said company to amount of one thousand dollars per mile.

§ 6. That to further aid in building said road, and equalize the burthens of building the same as nearly as possible, there is hereby levied, and shall be collected, an *ad valorem* tax of one dollar upon each one hundred dollars' worth of property, subject to taxation for State revenue, situated on each side of the turnpike road proposed to be built under this act; the property subject to said tax of one dollar on the one hundred dollars, shall be all the property owned and situated within two miles of each side of said road as the same shall be located, commencing one mile from where said road taps the Vanceburg, Salt Lick, Tollsboro, and Maysville turnpike, and continuing to Kinniconick creek, all property beyond said creek at Rand's, within two miles, and as much further as said company shall extend their road, as said company are hereby empowered to build their road down said creek, and over to Olive Hill or Grayson, in Carter county, and up said creek to the mouth of Indian Fork; and thence to some point in Rowan county. The taxes thus collected shall be expended in building said road, and the tax-payers shall be stockholders in said road to the amount of taxes they pay under this act; said tax shall be levied and collected until said road shall be completed and paid for; the tax collected on property between Vanceburg and Kinniconick creek. and two miles up and down said creek, shall be expended in building said road said distance; and when thus built and paid for, the tax on said part of said road shall cease.

Tax may be levied.

§ 7. That the second and third sections of an act, entitled "An act to levy a tax to aid in building turnpike

1869. roads in Lewis county," approved March 5th, 1867, are hereby adopted and re-enacted as part of this act.

§ 8. That said road shall be covered with stone at least twelve inches deep, and not less than twenty-one feet wide, and shall, in all respects, be well built.

§ 9. This act shall be in force from and after its passage.

Approved February 18, 1869.

CHAPTER 1501.

AN ACT for the benefit of the City of Dayton, in Campbell County.

WHEREAS, The city council of the city of Dayton, Campbell county, has represented to the General Assembly that they did, in their official capacity, on the 18th day of September, 1868, pass an ordinance to the effect that the city of Dayton should subscribe for and take stock in the Dayton and Four Mile turnpike road company to the amount of fifteen hundred dollars, subject to the approval of the voters of said city; and that they, the said city council, did, at the same time, order a special election to be held in the several wards of said city, on the third day of November, 1868, to take the voice of the people on the said question; and that said election was duly held as ordered, and that the same resulted in a two thirds majority of the votes cast being given in favor of the city taking said stock; now, therefore,

Be it enacted by the General Assembly of the Commonwealth of Kentucky:

§ 1. That the city council of the city of Dayton, in Campbell county, be, and the same is hereby, authorized and empowered to subscribe, in the name of the city of Dayton, any amount not exceeding fifteen hundred dollars, to the capital stock of the Dayton and Four Mile turnpike road company.

§ 2. That the said council is hereby authorized to levy a special tax, by ordinance, on all of the real estate in said city, of fifteen cents on each one hundred dollars in valuation of the property so taxed, which tax shall be levied and collected for the year 1869 only, in the same manner and at the same time the general revenue tax of said city is now authorized by law to be collected, and the revenue arising from such levy shall be set apart and used for the purpose only of paying the subscription herein authorized; and in case such revenue shall be insufficient to pay the full amount of stock subscribed, then the deficiency may be appropriated by the city council from the general revenue fund.

§ 3. That this act shall take effect from and after its
passage.

Approved February 18, 1869.

CHAPTER 1502.

AN ACT to amend an act, entitled "An act to incorporate the Concord and
Tollsboro Turnpike Road Company."

*Be it enacted by the General Assembly of the Commonwealth
of Kentucky:*

§ 1. That the eighth section of an act, entitled "An act
to incorporate the Concord and Tollsboro turnpike road
company," approved March the 3d, 1868, is hereby amended as follows: The tax levied by said eighth section of one
dollar on real estate within one mile of said road is hereby
levied on all property, real, personal, and mixed, subject
to taxation for State revenue.

§ 2. That, in like manner, there is hereby levied on all
property subject to taxation for State revenue, owned and
situated within one and a half miles of said road, on each
side of same, fifty cents on each one hundred dollars'
worth of property—that is to say, the one dollar on the
one hundred dollars' worth of property shall be levied
and collected on the first mile on each side of said road,
running parallel to said road from the Ohio river, at Concord, to the intersection of said road with the Vanceburg,
Salt Lick, Tollsboro, and Maysville turnpike road, and
the fifty cents on the one hundred dollars' worth of property shall be levied and collected on all property subject
to tax for State revenue, owned and located within one
half mile of said two miles in width, said half mile to
commence on the Ohio river, at the points where the mile
on each side of said road terminates, and then to run a
line parallel to said mile lines, on each side of the same,
to the end of said road; said half mile on each side of
said two miles in width shall be surveyed separate and
taxed as a separate section, and shall be called and designated as the second division of property subject to taxation, to help build said road. Said taxes shall continue
to be levied and collected until said Concord and Tollsboro turnpike road shall be finished and paid for. That
said company are hereby authorized and empowered to
unite their road with the said Vanceburg, Salt Lick, Tollsboro, and Maysville turnpike road, at any point from the
head waters of Salt Lick creek to Tollsboro. That the
twenty-second and twenty-third and twenty-fourth sections of an act, entitled "An act to incorporate the Vanceburg, Salt Lick, Tollsboro, and Maysville turnpike road
company, of Lewis county, and to establish a sinking

1869.

fund board for said county," approved February 13th, 1867, shall apply to the Concord and Tollsboro turnpike road company, as here modified; and it is hereby made the duty of the county judge of Lewis county, whenever one half the stock of this company shall be subscribed by responsible individual shareholders, to build this road five miles of its length, and proof of such subscription shall be made to said county judge, to subscribe to said turnpike road company one thousand dollars per mile for and in behalf and in the name of Lewis county; and said county shall, upon such subscription by the county judge aforesaid on behalf of said county, become a stockholder in said company to the amount of one thousand dollars to the mile; and to pay said subscription thus made, said county judge is hereby authorized and directed to issue the bonds of said county, payable at not a longer date than twenty years, to bear interest at a rate not exceeding six per cent. per annum, which bonds may be in such amounts, and principal and interest payable at such place or places, as said county judge may direct. Said bonds, when thus issued, shall be delivered to the president of said Concord and Tollsboro turnpike road company ; and when thus delivered, said county of Lewis shall become a stockholder in said company for the amounts called for in said bonds. It is further made the duty of said county judge, whenever said company shall finish and pay for the first five miles, by the aid of said bonds of one thousand dollars per mile, and shall have raised a sufficient sum to finish two additional miles of said road, aided by one thousand dollars per mile, and shall have let the building of said two miles to a responsible contractor or contractors, to again issue the bonds of said county to the amount of one thousand dollars per mile, and deliver said bonds to the president of said company, it being the intention to require the county of Lewis to aid said company in building their road at the rate of one thousand dollars per mile, and that the county shall be a stockholder to that amount.

§ 3. The provisions of this act shall apply to the Vanceburg, Quick's Run, and Concord turnpike road, and said county court shall aid said company to the amount of one thousand dollars per mile in building their road; and for that purpose, shall issue the bonds of Lewis county and deliver them to the president of said company as soon as four miles of said last named road is put under contract.

§ 4. This act shall take effect from its passage.

Approved February 18, 1869.

CHAPTER 1503.

AN ACT to incorporate the Vanceburg, Quincy, and Springville Turnpike Road Company.

Be it enacted by the General Assembly of the Commonwealth of Kentucky:

§ 1. That a company is hereby formed and created a body politic and corporate, by the name and style of the Vanceburg, Quincy, and Springville turnpike road company, to consist of a president and five directors, with the other stockholders and officers hereinafter authorized by this act, for the purpose of building a turnpike road from alley No. 3, in Vanceburg, Lewis county, to the public landing on the Ohio river, at Springville, in Greenup county, Kentucky. Said company, by said name, shall have perpetual existence and succession, and all the rights, privileges, and franchises incident to such a corporation; and shall be capable of taking and holding their capital stock, and the increase and profits thereof; and of purchasing, taking, and holding, to them and their successors and assigns, and of selling, transferring, and conveying, in fee simple, all such lands, tenements, and hereditaments and estate, real, personal, and mixed, as shall be necessary to them in the prosecution of their work, completion and use of their road; and to sue and be sued, plead and be impleaded, answer and be answered, defend and be defended, in all courts of record, or any other proper place or places whatever; to contract for, buy, and own the right of way for said road; to have a common seal, and to do all and every other act and thing whatsoever, within the object and scope of their incorporation, which a body-politic or corporate may lawfully do.

Company incorporated, and corporate powers.

§ 2. The capital stock of said company shall be one hundred thousand dollars, and may be increased to any sum necessary to build said road, and any branch roads said company may choose to build, authorized under this act. Said stock shall be divided into shares of twenty-five dollars each. Books for the subscription of stock shall be opened on the third Monday in March, 1869, or as soon thereafter as the commissioners hereafter appointed for that purpose may direct. Said books shall be opened at the clerk's office of the Lewis circuit court, in Vanceburg, at the store-house of Samuel Kibby, in Quincy, and at the store-house of Osbern, in Springville, and at such other places as said commissioners shall direct. Said books shall continue open for the subscription of stock until sufficient stock shall be subscribed to build said road, or until the commissioners named in this act, or the board of directors, when elected, of said company, shall see proper to close said books. The books shall be opened under the direction of the following persons, who are hereby ap-

Capital stock.

Books may be opened for subscription of stock.

Commissioners to receive subscription of stock.

1869.

pointed commissioners for that purpose, viz: Thomas W. Mitchell, James McDermitt, and J. K. Garland, at Vanceburg; Samuel Kibby, Benjamin F. Branham, and N. G. Morse, at Quincy; and Samuel Yeager, Champ Osbern, and Dr. Fulton, at Springville. Any one or more of said persons may act at said places, and open books for and receive any and all subscriptions of stock. Said commissioners shall procure the necessary books, and the subscribers for stock shall enter into the following obligation:

Obligation of subscribers.

"We, whose names are hereunto subscribed, do respectively promise to pay the president and directors of the Vanceburg, Quincy, and Springville turnpike road company the sum of twenty-five dollars for each share of stock set opposite to our names, to be paid in such proportions, and at such times and place, as the president and directors may or shall direct or require.

When president and directors may be elected.

§ 3. So soon as five thousand dollars have been subscribed to the capital stock of said company, it shall be the duty of said commissioners to give notice to the stockholders for a meeting of said stockholders, at such time and place as they may designate in said notice, for the purpose of electing a president and five directors, said officers to be elected from among the stockholders, and one vote shall be allowed for each share of stock. The officers thus elected shall continue in office for one year, and until their successors are in like manner duly elected. A majority of the directors shall be competent to transact business.

Certain sections of another act made part of this.

§ 4. That the 4th, 5th, 6th, 7th, 8th, 9th, 11th, 12th, 14th, 15th, 17th, 18th, 19th, 20th, 21st, 24th, 25th, and 26th sections of an act, entitled "An act to incorporate the Vanceburg, Salt Lick, Tollsboro, and Maysville turnpike road company, &c.," approved February 13th, 1867, are hereby adopted and re enacted as part of this act.

Lewis county may take stock. &c.

§ 5. That in order to encourage and assist in building said road, it is hereby made the duty of the Lewis county court, whenever a sufficient sum shall have been subscribed by good and responsible persons to the capital stock of said company to build five miles of said road at the beginning thereof, and said five miles shall have been let out to a responsible contractor or contractors, who have executed a bond or bonds for the speedy building and completion of said five miles, and proof of these facts shall be made to said county court, to subscribe to the capital stock of said company one thousand dollars per mile for said five miles; said subscription shall be made by the judge of said county court in the name of Lewis county; and upon such subscription thus being made, the county shall become a stockholder in said company to the amount thus subscribed; and whenever said company shall raise, by subscription, a sufficient sum to build five miles more of said road, and said five miles shall have been let out to contractors, who have given bond with good security to build a continuous distance of five miles of said road, it shall be the duty of the said county court of Lewis county to again subscribe for and on behalf of Lewis county one thousand dollars to the mile for said five miles, and to so continue to do until said road is finished. The stock of Lewis county shall be represented and voted, at any and all elections of officers of said company, by the presiding judge of the county court and the clerk of said court, each voting one half of the stock of said county. That to pay the subscriptions thus made by said county judge to the capital stock of said company of one thousand dollars per mile, said county judge is hereby authorized and required to issue the bonds of Lewis county, payable at not a longer date than twenty years, to bear interest at six per cent. per annum, which bonds may be in such amounts, and principal and interest payable at such place or places, as the county judge may direct; said bonds shall be delivered to the president of said company, who shall execute a receipt for said bonds in the name of the company; and upon the delivery of said bonds to said president, the county of Lewis shall become a stockholder in said company to the amount of one thousand dollars per mile.

§ 6. That to further aid in building said road, and equalize the burthens of building the same as nearly as possible, there is hereby levied and shall be collected an ad valorem tax of one dollar upon each one hundred dollars' worth of property subject to taxation for State revenue, situated on each side of the turnpike road proposed to be built under this act; the property subject to said tax of one dollar on the one hundred dollars shall be all the property owned and situated between the Ohio river, and running from said river where the line between Lewis and Greenup counties leaves said river; thence with said line to the dividing ridge and line between said counties, and with said ridge and line to the ridge dividing the waters of Montgomery and McDowell's creeks; thence with said ridge to Kinniconick creek, and from Kinniconick creek to Slate branch; the property subject to said tax shall be all the property held, located, or owned in a belt of two miles in width from the Ohio river back in the county, from said Kinniconick creek to Slate branch, and thence back to the place of beginning; the taxes thus levied and collected shall be expended in building said road, and the tax-payers shall be stockholders in

May levy and collect tax to pay same.

said road to the amount of tax they pay under this act; said tax shall be levied and collected until said road is completed and paid for; the tax collected on property below Kinniconick shall be expended on that part of the road below said creek, and the tax collected on property above said creek, shall be expended on that part of the road above said creek.

§ 7. That the second and third sections of an act, entitled "An act to levy a tax to aid in building turnpike roads in Lewis county," approved March 5th. 1867, are hereby adopted and re-enacted as part of this act.

§ 8. The provisions of this act shall apply to any and all branch road or roads that said company shall build, and the said company is hereby empowered to branch their road to any point or place they may choose to do; but the tax hereby levied to build the main road shall not be applied to build any branch road; nor shall any tax levied on property in Lewis county be appropriated to building that part of the road located in Greenup county; nor shall the county court of Lewis sign or subscribe for any stock in that part of said road in Greenup county, or issue any bonds for said part of said road; the taxes hereby levied, and the bonds provided for in this act, are hereby dedicated to building said road and paying for the same, and shall never be diverted from that object.

Provisions of act to apply to branch roads.

§ 9. This act shall take effect from its passage.

Approved February 18, 1869.

CHAPTER 1504.

AN ACT to Fix the Tolls on the Green and Taylor Turnpike Road.

Be it enacted by the General Assembly of the Commonwealth of Kentucky:

§ 1. That it shall be lawful for the Green and Taylor County Turnpike Road Company, in Taylor county, to charge and collect, at their toll-gate on said road near Campbellsville, the following rates of toll: For one horse and rider, and for every led horse, five cents; for one-horse sulky or sleigh, ten cents; for one-horse buggy, fifteen cents; for one-horse cart or spring wagon, twenty cents; for two-horse buggy, one seat, twenty cents; for two-horse buggy, two seats, twenty-five cents; for two-horse stage or coach, twenty-five cents; for three-horse stage or coach, thirty-five cents; for four-horse stage or coach, fifty cents; for two-horse wagon, loaded, twenty-five cents; for two-horse wagon, empty, fifteen cents; for three-horse wagon, loaded, thirty-five cents; for three-horse wagon, empty, twenty cents; for four-horse wagon, loaded, fifty cents; for four-horse wagon, empty, thirty-five cents; for five-horse wagon, loaded, sixty-five cents; for five-horse wagon, empty, forty-five cents; for six-horse wagon, loaded, seventy-five cents; for six-horse wagon, empty, fifty cents; for drove of mules òr horses, over ten in number, three cents each; under that number, five cents each; horned cattle, two cents each; hogs, one cent each; sheep, half cent each; vehicles drawn by oxen or mules, the. same as by horses.

§ 2. That said company shall have the right, and are hereby given the authority, to charge the same tariff of freights as above allowed, according to distance traveled on their road, for traveling on or using any part of their road between gates.

§ 3. Any person or persons who shall refuse to pay the tolls authorized in this act, or who shall go around a toll-gate or gates to avoid the payment of said tolls, shall be liable to a fine of not less than five nor more than fifty dollars, to be recovered before any justice of the peace of the county where the offender resides or may be found, which fines, when collected, shall be for the use of said turnpike company; and suits shall be in the name of said company.

§ 4. This act to take effect from its passage.

Approved February 18, 1869.

CHAPTER 1505.

AN ACT to amend an act, entitled "An act to incorporate the Mount Sterling and Spencer Creek Turnpike Road Company."

WHEREAS, It is represented to this General Assembly that the amount of stock has been subscribed, and the company properly organized, as required by the act to which this is an amendment; and that said company has completed said road to the distance of about seven miles from its commencement, in the town of Mount Sterling, crossing Slate creek, over which it has erected a superior bridge, at a cost of over $5,000; and said company now contemplates extending said ·road to the Bath line, in the direction of the Olympian Springs; therefore,

Be it enacted by the General Assembly of the Commonwealth of Kentucky:

§ 1. That the capital stock of said company may be increased to $40,000, to be divided into shares of twenty-five dollars.

§ 2. That books of subscription for additional stock shall be opened at such time and ·place as may be determined by the president and directors of said company;.

and shall insert an obligation in the subscription books in substance the same as that prescribed in section three of the original act; and said president and directors have all the corporate powers and privileges for extending said road from its present terminus which are granted in the original, as far as the same are applicable and necessary for the purposes herein contemplated and designed.

§ 3. That as said president and directors have constructed and completed the bridge over Slate creek, at the cost aforesaid, which is of very great public convenience and advantage, and have thereby incurred a considerable debt, in order to aid them in the speedy liquidation of the indebtedness of said road, they are hereby authorized and empowered to erect two gates on said road at any points or places they may designate: *Provided*, They shall not be authorized to erect more than two gates on said road until they shall have completed more than ten miles of said road: *And provided further*, That the second gate, there being one already up about one mile from Mount Sterling, shall be erected at some point east of the bridge over Spencer's creek, at or near to a school-house near to said Spencer bridge.

§ 4. That the president and directors of said company may fix the rates of toll, and regulate and change the same from time to time; but the rates of toll to be paid at each gate shall not exceed, though may be fixed at, the rates fixed by the general law, just as if the gates were five miles apart, each to be a full gate, and the company authorized to charge full toll at each.

§ 5. This act to take effect from and after its passage.

Approved February 18, 1869.

CHAPTER 1506.

AN ACT to amend an act, entitled "An act to amend the Bardstown and Louisville Railroad Company," approved March 6th, 1856.

Be it enacted by the General Assembly of the Commonwealth of Kentucky:

§ 1. That the county court for Nelson county shall appoint a treasurer, to whom the sheriff or other collecting officer of the public revenue for said county shall pay all taxes collected in districts numbers one, five, and nine, in said county, levied for the purpose of paying the one hundred thousand dollars capital stock subscribed by said county court, for and on behalf of said districts, to the Bardstown and Louisville railroad company. Before said treasurer shall proceed to act, he shall execute bond in said court, with good security, for the faithful discharge of the duties as treasurer aforesaid. Said court shall have power to remove said treasurer at pleasure.

§ 2. The county judge, county attorney, county clerk, and said treasurer, shall, *ex-officio*, constitute a board of commissioners of the sinking fund, whose duty it shall be to manage the fund-derived from said tax for the payment of the interest on the bonds, and final payment of the principal thereof. Said board of commissioners shall, at the annual court of claims of said county, report, in writing, the amount of money received by the said treasurer, and how the same has been applied, giving the number of the bonds on which the coupons have been paid, and the number and amount of the bonds paid off, and when due; and they shall return all of said coupons and bonds with said report, and said report shall be entered at length on the order book of said court; and said coupons and bonds so paid off shall be burned in the presence of said court, which fact shall also be entered on the order book of said court. It shall also be the duty of said board to collect all coupons and bonds heretofore paid off, and report the same to said court, which shall also be burned as aforesaid.

§ 3. The clerk of said county court shall be entitled to the same fees for services rendered under this act as for similar services, as now allowed by law, to be paid by the said treasurer out of said tax.

§ 4. Said board shall, in the months of September and February, in each year, make settlements with the sheriff or other collecting officer of said tax, and shall allow him the same commission for collecting the same as is allowed for collecting the public revenue.

§ 5. The county court for said county may, for any breach of the bond of said treasurer, maintain an action in the name of the Commonwealth.

§ 6. All acts amending the charter of said railroad company, which are inconsistent with this act, are hereby repealed.

§ 7. This act shall take effect from and after its passage.

Approved February 18, 1869.

CHAPTER 1507.

AN ACT to incorporate the Farmers and Drovers' Bank.

Be it enacted by the General Assembly of the Commonwealth of Kentucky:

§ 1. That there is hereby created and established in the

Bank estab-
lished, and cor-
porate powers.
city of Louisville a deposit bank, which shall be a body-politic and corporate, by the name of the Farmers and Drovers' Bank; and shall have power and authority in that name to contract and be contracted with, sue and be sued, plead and be impleaded, answer and defend, in all courts and places as a natural person, and may have and use a common seal, and alter and change the same at will, and may do such acts and things as may be desirable and convenient, provided the same be not contrary to laws of this Commonwealth.

§ 2. The property, business, and affairs of said bank

Board of di-
rectors, vacan-
cies, elections,
&c.
shall be under the management, government, and control of a board of seven directors, which number may be increased to thirteen, one of whom shall be elected president of the board; and J. B. O'Bannon, W. S. Pryor, Jas. P. Beard, Archibald C. Wilson, J. S. Crutchfield, E. D. Standeford, and P. D. S. Barbour, are hereby constituted and appointed a board of directors for said bank, to serve as such until others are duly elected and qualified; and should any of the persons above named fail or refuse to qualify and serve as directors, his or their place or places may be declared and treated as vacant, and the vacancy or vacancies may be filled by the remainder; and all vacancies occurring in the board of directors may be filled by the other directors, who shall provide for an election of directors by the stockholders within one year from the organization of the company, and every year thereafter, at the office of said bank, in the city of Louisville, notice of which shall be given in one or more of the city papers, for at least ten days next preceding said election; and said election shall be held by three stockholders, appointed by the board of directors, who shall certify the result for record on the books of the bank. Those having the highest number of votes shall be declared duly elected, each stockholder to have one vote for each share of stock he or she may own, and may cast the same in person or by proxy. The board may regulate the form of proxy in casting the vote.

§ 3. The capital stock of said bank shall consist of one

Capital stock.
When may pro-
ceed to busi-
ness, &c.
thousand shares, of the par value of one hundred dollars each; but may be increased, from time to time, as the board of directors may deem advisable and proper, to any number not exceeding five thousand shares of like par value; and the directors may open books of subscription for such increase of stock as they may deem proper, from

time to time, and at such places within the Commonwealth as they may deem best to promote the interest of
said bank; and whenever as many as five hundred shares
of said stock shall have been subscribed and paid in, or
secured to be paid in, in accordance with the terms and
conditions upon which the same were subscribed, and an
affidavit to that effect has been made by the president
before the clerk of the Jefferson county court, said bank
may proceed to transact a general banking and financial
business, and may loan money, discount promissory notes,
buy and sell exchange, stocks, bonds, and other securities
and things; and the promissory and negotiable notes made
payable at its banking-house, which may be discounted by
said bank, and inland bills of exchange which may be discounted or purchased by it, shall be, and they are hereby,
put upon the footing of foreign bills of exchange, and like
remedy may be had thereon, jointly and severally, against
the makers, drawers, indorsers, or other parties thereto.

§ 4. The said bank may acquire and hold, possess and *May acquire personal estate, &c.*
use, occupy and enjoy, all such real and personal property,
goods, chattels, or other things, as may be convenient for
the transaction of its business, or which may be pledged
or conveyed to it as security for any debt or purchase in
satisfaction of any debts, judgments, or decree, and sell
and convey, or otherwise dispose of the same, as a nat-
ural person; and it shall be the duty of the president or *To pay State tax.*
cashier of said bank, during the first week in each year,
to pay into the Treasury of this Commonwealth fifty cents
on each hundred dollars of capital stock held and paid for
in said bank, which shall be in full for all tax or bonus,
and be a part of the Common School Fund of this Commonwealth.

§ 5. The said bank shall have power to make advances *Make advances on approved se- curities, &c.*
on approved securities of any kind, and it may receive
stocks, bonds, and other things in pledge for the security of money loaned, or debts owing, and sell the same,
except real estate, on the non-payment of the debt or demand at the stipulated time of payment, on ten days'
notice to the party, according to any agreement made
between the parties, in writing, at the time of loan, or
renewal thereof, and pass a good title to the purchaser;
and any power given for that purpose shall be irrevocable
until the debt or demand is paid or duly tendered; said *May receive deposits of gold, &c.*
bank may receive deposits of gold, silver, bank notes,
United States Treasury notes, or other currency, and pay
the same in kind, or as may be agreed upon by special or
general contract, and may allow interest on deposits, not
to exceed the rates allowed by the laws of this Com-
monwealth. It may issue certificates of credit, payable *Issue certifi- cates of credit.*
throughout the United States, and elsewhere, for the con-

1869.

venience of merchants and travelers, but shall not issue any notes or bills to circulate as money.

§ 6. The board of directors of said bank are hereby authorized and empowered to enact and put in force such rules, by-laws and regulations, for the management. government, and control of its property, business and affairs, as they may deem expedient, and alter, amend, and repeal the same at will; and shall specify therein the number of directors necessary to constitute a quorum for the transaction of business. They may appoint such officers, agents, and servants as they may deem necessary to conduct the business of the bank, and pay them such sums for their services, and take from them bonds in such penalties to secure the faithful performance of their duties, as they may think reasonable and proper; and upon any bonds, thus taken, recovery may be had for breaches of the conditions thereof. If any officer of the bank shall appropriate any funds of said bank to his own use, or shall willfully fail to make correct entries, or knowingly make false ones, on the books of said bank, with intent to cheat or defraud the corporation or other person, such officer shall be deemed guilty of felony, and shall, upon conviction thereof, be sentenced to confinement in the jail or penitentiary of this Commonwealth for a period of not less than two nor more than ten years.

§ 7. The stock of said bank shall be deemed personal property, and shall only be assignable in accordance with such rules as the board of directors shall, from time to time, prescribe; and said bank shall hold a lien on the shares of any stockholder who may be indebted to it, and such shares shall not be assignable nor transferred until the debt shall be paid or discharged.

§ 8. This act shall take effect from its passage, and remain in force for twenty-one years from the first organization of the said institution, provided it is organized within three years from its passage.

§ 9. The General Assembly shall have the right to examine into the affairs of said corporation by any committee they may appoint for that purpose.

Approved February 18, 1869.

Sidenotes:
May make rules, by-laws, &c.
May appoint officers, agents, &c.
Penalty for misappropriation of funds.
Stock deemed personal property.

CHAPTER 1508.

AN ACT to amend an act, entitled "An act to incorporate the Paducah, Benton, and Murray Gravel Road Company."

Be it enacted by the General Assembly of the Commonwealth of Kentucky:

§ 1. That section two of said act be amended as follows: That the width of said road, where it will admit of it, shall not be less than twenty-four nor more than sixty feet, and the artificial or metaled part shall not be less than sixteen feet wide, and the graded part not less than twenty feet wide.

§ 2. That the words "twenty-five thousand dollars," where they occur in section three, be stricken out, and "fifteen thousand dollars" be inserted in lieu thereof.

§ 3. That section six be amended by striking out the words "twelve miles," and inserting "five miles" in lieu thereof; and by inserting as a part thereof the following, immediately after the word "consecutively," "or from Paducah to Clark's river."

§ 4. Section 20, chapter 103, shall not apply to this company.

§ 5. The rights and privileges granted said company by this act, and by the act to which this is an amendment, shall not be impaired or taken from said company.

§ 6. This act shall take effect from its passage.

Approved February 16, 1869.

CHAPTER 1509.

AN ACT to incorporate Christ Episcopal Church, at Bowling Green.

Be it enacted by the General Assembly of the Commonwealth of Kentucky:

§ 1. That Rev. Judson M. Curtis, Levi L. Bacon, Thos. W, Baird, Walter C. Brashear, Wm. J. Walters, Theophilus St. V. Hutchinson, and their successors in office, be incorporated, by the name of "Christ Episcopal Church, Bowling Green;" and by that name shall have perpetual succession; may sue and be sued, plead and be impleaded; may purchase, receive, and otherwise acquire and hold property, real, personal, and mixed; and may sell, lease, or otherwise dispose of the same at pleasure; and may make contracts and pass by-laws not inconsistent with the laws of the land.

§ 2. That the entire management of the affairs of said church are vested in said rector, wardens, and vestry, and their successors as such, to be, from time to time, chosen by the congregation, who shall be trustees under this act; and they, when assembled in vestry meeting, shall have power to fill vacancies, to regulate the appointment and duties of officers, to lease or sell pews belonging to the church, and enforce payments of the rents thereof, as may be stipulated in the lease or allowed by law.

§ 3. That all the real and personal estate at present belonging to, or held in trust for the use and benefit of, said church, or its congregation, be vested in the corporation created by this act; and this act shall be subject to amendment or repeal at the discretion of the Legislature, and shall go into effect from its passage.

Approved February 16, 1869.

CHAPTER 1511.
AN ACT to incorporate the Richmond Hotel Company.

Be it enacted by the General Assembly of the Commonwealth of Kentucky:

§ 1. That there shall be, and is hereby, established, in the town of Richmond, and county of Madison, on the lot or lots of E. W. Powell, recently conveyed to him by Henry M. Wyeth, of Licking county, Ohio, a company with a capital stock of thirty-five thousand dollars ($35,-000), divided into shares of one hundred dollars ($100) each, to be subscribed and paid for in the manner hereinafter specified; which subscribers and stockholders, their successors and assigns, shall be, and they are hereby, created a body-politic and corporate forever, by the name and style of the president and directors of the "Richmond Hotel Company;" and by that name shall be competent to contract and be contracted with; to have, possess, enjoy, and retain such lands, tenements, hereditaments, goods, chattels, and effects, as may be necessary and convenient for the erection and furnishing a hotel on the lands or lots aforesaid; to rent and demise said hotel, furniture, and fixtures, and all such rooms, storehouses, stables, sheds, and lots as they may construct in the erection of the said hotel; to sue and be sued, plead and be impleaded, answer and be answered, defend and be defended, in all courts and places, as natural persons; to have and use a common seal, and change, alter, or remove the same at pleasure; to ordain and put into execution all such by-laws, rules and regulations, as shall seem necessary for the government and carrying out the objects of this corportion : *Provided,* That there shall be nothing in such by-laws, rules or regulations, contrary to the Constitution and laws of this State or of the United States.

§ 2. That books for the subscription of stock in said company may be opened at such times and places as may be deemed best, under the direction of William M. Irvine, Charles S. Turner, E. W. Powell, C. R. Estill, Wm. J. Walker, James T. Shackelford, Jas. W. Caperton, and Wm. M. Ballard, or some one or more of them, all of whom are hereby appointed commissioners, or such of them as shall act, to procure a book or books, which shall contain the following obligation, and shall be signed by each and every person who takes stock in said company: "We, whose names are hereunto subscribed, do severally bind ourselves to pay to the president, directors, and company, of the Richmond Hotel Company, for each and every share of stock set opposite our names, the sum of one hundred dollars, in such manner and proportions, and at such times, as shall be required by the president and directors of said company.

§ 3. That so soon as one half of the capital stock of said company shall have been subscribed, it shall be the duty of the commissioners aforesaid, or such of them as may act, to give notice of a meeting of the stockholders of said company, to meet in the town of Richmond, for the purpose of choosing officers, said notice to be published in the Richmond Register, or Lexington Observer and Reporter, at least twenty days before said meeting, at which election at least two of the commissioners before named shall be present to take the votes, *viva voce* or by ballot, of the stockholders in said company for a president and six directors, who shall hold their offices until the last Saturday in December, 1869, and until their successors shall have been duly elected and qualified.

§ 4. That upon the election of the president and directors as aforesaid, they shall appoint a treasurer and secretary, and such other officers as they may deem necessary, who shall hold their offices during the pleasure of said president and directors. The treasurer, before he enters upon the discharge of his duties, shall execute a bond, with two or more good and sufficient sureties, in the penalty of ten thousand dollars, payable to the president and directors of said company, conditioned that he will faithfully discharge the duties of his office, as required by this charter, and the by-laws, rules and regulations, of said company, and pay over to the persons entitled thereto any money that may come into his hands as treasurer of said company.

§ 5. That, upon the election of the president and directors as aforesaid, they shall be a body-politic and corporate, by the name, style, and title of the Richmond Hotel Company; and by said name the said company shall have all the privileges and franchises incident to a corporation, and shall be capable of taking and holding their said capital stock, and the increase and profits thereof, and of taking and purchasing, taking and holding, to them and their successors and assigns, and of selling, transferring, and conveying, in fee simple, all such lands, lots, tenements, hereditaments, and such estate, real and personal, as shall be deemed necessary to them in the prosecution of the object of this charter.

§ 6. That the president and directors, upon entering upon the duties of their office, may call upon the stockholders for the payment of forty dollars (\$40) on each share subscribed in said stock; and may, if deemed necessary, call for twenty dollars on each share every twenty days thereafter, until the whole amount subscribed shall have been paid.

§ 7. That the stock in said company shall be personal estate, for which the president and directors shall issue certificates to the owners, which shall be transferable in such manner as may be prescribed by the by-laws of said company.

§ 8. The president and directors of said company shall have the right to declare when a stockholder has forfeited his stock, and the payments made; but no such forfeiture shall be made without due notice to the delinquent stockholder, at least twenty days before the record of such forfeiture shall be made on the books of the corporation; such forfeiture shall not release said stockholder from any sum which may at that time be still unpaid.

§ 9. That at all meetings of stockholders, and at all elections, each share in stock of said company shall entitle the holder to one vote.

§ 10. That said company may, at any time, sell and convey, or dispose of the whole, or any part of its property, real or personal, by the assent of two thirds of its directors.

§ 11. That the president and directors may fix the name of the hotel hereby incorporated, and may change the same whenever it may be deemed advisable.

§ 12. The annual election of officers of said company shall take place on the last Saturday in December, every year.

§ 13. This act shall take effect and be in force from its passage.

Approved February 16, 1869.

CHAPTER 1513.

AN ACT for the benefit of Thos. B. Vinson, of Grayson County.

WHEREAS, Thomas B. Vinson has paid to the Commonwealth a judgment of fifty dollars and costs, and said judgment was remitted, fees and costs excepted, by the Governor; therefore,

Be it enacted by the General Assembly of the Commonwealth of Kentucky:

§ 1. That the Auditor be directed to draw his warrant on the Treasurer for thirty-two dollars, that being the amount of said judgment remitted by the Governor.

§ 2. This act shall take effect from its passage.

Approved February 16, 1869.

CHAPTER 1514.

AN ACT for the benefit of Jno. L. Slavin, Sheriff of Garrard County.

WHEREAS, It appears that J. L. Slavin, sheriff of Garrard county, has paid off the interest and cost adjudged against him in the Franklin circuit court for the non-payment of the State revenue for the year 1867, and other public dues—

Be it enacted by the General Assembly of the Commonwealth of Kentucky:

§ 1. That J. L. Slavin, sheriff of Garrard county, be released from the damages, amounting to three hundred and thirty-eight dollars and eleven cents, adjudged against him in the Franklin circuit court for the non-payment of the State revenue and other public dues by him as sheriff aforesaid.

§ 2. This act to take effect from its passage.

Approved February 16, 1869.

CHAPTER 1515.

AN ACT to amend the Charter of Allensville.

Be it enacted by the General Assembly of the Commonwealth of Kentucky:

§ 1. That immediately after the eighth clause of section three of an act to incorporate the town of Allensville Station, in Todd county, approved January 30, 1867, the following clauses be inserted : They shall elect one of their number keeper of the lock-up, hereinafter provided for, whose duty it shall be to keep the same, together with all other public buildings in said town, in the manner the law now does, or may hereafter require county jails and other public buildings to be kept ; said keeper of the lock-up shall execute bond with good security before the board of trustees, to be approved by them, conditioned in all respects as the bond of a jailer, and shall be subject to the same penalties imposed on jailers for violations of duty, which bond shall be attested by the secretary and delivered to the clerk of the Todd county court, who shall carefully preserve and file it in his office, and shall give attested copies, when requested so to do by any person, which shall have the same force and credit in all courts of justice as other records from said office are entitled to under existing laws; said clerk shall receive therefor such fees as are allowed by law for similar services. It shall be lawful for said keeper of the lock-up to execute any process as directed in section ten, article two, chapter ninety-one, of the Revised Statutes. He shall be entitled to the same fees of a jailer for similar services.

§ 2. That immediately after the second clause in section four, the following clauses be inserted: They shall have the right to build a lock-up or house in which drunken or disorderly persons may be confined; and authority is hereby expressly given to confine drunken or disorderly persons therein, until they become sober or give bond for their good behavior; and it shall be lawful to confine persons therein who shall fail or refuse to pay or satisfy any judgment upon which a *capias ad satisfaciendum* or *capias pro fine*, shall issue for a violation of any of the ordinances and by-laws of said town, as in the county jail; said house, by consent of the board of trustees of said town, may be used for the confinement of other persons, in the same manner, and for the same purpose, of a county jail.

§ 3. This act to take effect from and after its passage.

Approved February 16, 1869.

CHAPTER 1516.

AN ACT to incorporate the Odd Fellows' Temple Association.

Be it enacted by the General Assembly of the Commonwealth of Kentucky:

§ 1. That Joseph D. Trapp, Thomas W. Foster, Isaiah King, James Chrystal, David King, Z. Gibbons, and Andrew Gilmore, and the other stockholders of the joint stock company called the Odd Fellows' Temple Association, shall be, and are hereby, declared a body-politic and corporate, by the name and style of the Odd Fellows' Temple Association; and by that name and style shall have perpetual succession; and may contract and be contracted with, sue and be sued, and have all the powers and privileges of local corporations; but shall have no power of dealing in exchange or exercise any banking powers.

§ 2. The business, purpose, and object of said corporation shall be the erection, furnishing, building, and keeping in repair an Odd Fellows' Temple, in Lexington, and the renting out, using, and managing said Temple and its appurtenances.

§ 3. The capital stock of said corporation shall be thirty thousand dollars, divided into shares of twenty-five dollars each.

§ 4. All the property and rights held by the said association shall vest in the corporation hereby created, subject to all the liens and liabilities now existing upon said property; and all liabilities now existing against said association shall devolve on said corporation; but noth-

ing in this section shall operate to release the individual
liability of the members of said company now existing.

§ 5. The management of said association shall devolve
upon directors chosen as designated by the charter under
which said association is now acting, adopted by the
stockholders, subject to repeal or alteration as therein
set out, which, with the by-laws said association may
adopt, not being contrary to the laws of this Common-.
wealth or the Constitutions of this State or of the United
States, subject to such amendments therein as said association may make, shall govern said association; and the
officers thereof shall be elected as therein set out, and the
meetings of stockholders held as therein provided.

§ 6. The stock of said association shall only be transferable on the books of the company, in such manner as
the president and directors shall determine.

§ 7. That this act may be repealed at any time.

§ 8. That this act shall take effect from its passage.

Approved February 16, 1869.

CHAPTER 1517.

AN ACT to charter the Marion School Association, in Crittenden County.

*Be it enacted by the General Assembly of the Commonwealth
of Kentucky:*

§ 1. That D. N. Stinson, J. W. Blue, S. Hodge, T. L.
Dean, and R. F. Haynes, their associates and successors,
be, and they are hereby, constituted and created a body-
politic and corporate, by the name and style of the "Trustees of the Marion School Association;" and as such shall
have perpetual succession, with full power to acquire,
hold, and transfer real and personal estate, make contracts, sue and be sued, plead and be impleaded, in their
corporate capacity; to make such rules, by-laws and ordinances, as they may deem necessary, consistent with the
Constitution and laws of this State or of the United
States.

§ 2. That said trustees shall have power over all the
business concerns of said association. They may appoint
a president, treasurer, clerk, and such other officers as they
may think necessary, and shall hold their offices until their
successors are elected and qualified.

§ 3. That a majority of said trustees, meeting in pursuance to their own rules, shall constitute a quorum for
the transaction of business. The said trustees shall have
power to employ a principal and such assistant teachers,
male or female, as they may deem necessary.

§ 4. They shall have power to increase the number of
trustees, from time to time, as they may think the interests

of the institution may require; they shall have power also to fill vacancies that may happen in said corporation, and have power to remove from office any member of the board of trustees, a majority of all the board concurring.

§ 5. That all the estate, money, or property now belonging to, or which may hereafter be acquired by, said corporation, by devise, gift, or otherwise, shall be used in such manner as the trustees, by their corporate action, may determine for the best interest of the association.

§ 6. That said trustees shall not be required to procure a common seal; but all their corporate acts may be performed and evidenced by the official signature of the president; and said president shall be chosen from their own body annually.

§ 7. That the trustees of the Marion School Association shall have power to confer upon the pupils of said association any or all the diplomas or degrees conferred by other corporate institutions of learning in this State; and the private seal of the president of the board and principal of said association may stand in lieu of a corporate seal, and until one is procured, should said board determine to use a common seal.

§ 8. That when the association hereby made corporate shall afford facilities for teaching all the children and youths in the district in which it is situated, and for the period during which each of said pupils is or hereafter may be entitled to tuition under the general laws in relation to common schools, then the school trustees may, if they see proper, report the same as the common school of said district, and it shall be entitled to all moneys coming to such district from the Common School Fund: *Provided always*, That when said association shall cease to furnish facilities for teaching as above required, then the benefits conferred on it in this section shall cease and determine, and common schools are to be taught in said district as heretofore required by law.

§ 9. That each person subscribing money or property to this association shall be entitled to one vote for each five dollars so subscribed by them in all elections for trustees and directors of said association.

§ 10. That the first annual election of trustees for said association shall be held on the fourth Monday in June, 1869, and on the fourth Monday of June annually thereafter; but if, from any cause, said election shall not be held at the time herein specified, an election of trustees of said association, until the ensuing fourth Monday in June, and until their successors are elected and qualified, may be held at any time upon ten days' notice of the time and place having been given by the president, by written notice posted at three public places in the town of Marion. At all elections for trustees, the president of the board shall act as judge of said election, and may appoint a clerk of said election; and shall give a certificate of election to the parties receiving a majority of the votes cast.

§ 11. This act shall take effect from and after its passage.

Approved February 18, 1869.

CHAPTER 1519.

AN ACT to repeal an act, entitled "An act to increase the Jurisdiction of the Quarterly Court of Henry County in Criminal and Penal Causes," approved 7th March, 1868.

Be it enacted by the General Assembly of the Commonwealth of Kentucky:

§ 1. That an act, entitled "An act to increase the jurisdiction of the quarterly court of Henry county in criminal and penal causes," approved 7th March, 1868, be, and the same is hereby, repealed: *Provided, however,* That said court shall have jurisdiction and power, and it shall be its duty, to try and adjudicate all causes of every kind and description now pending in said court, or which have been commenced therein under said act, as though this act had not been passed.

§ 2. This act to take effect from its passage.

Approved February 18, 1869.

CHAPTER 1520.

AN ACT to amend the charter of the Town of Catlettsburg.

Be it enacted by the General Assembly of the Commonwealth of Kentucky:

§ 1. That hereafter the police judge of the town of Catlettsburg shall be elected by the qualified voters of said town on the first Monday of January, 1870, and every two years thereafter; and shall hold his office for and during the two years next after his election, and until his successor in office shall be qualified.

§ 2. That if any vacancy shall occur in the office of police judge of Catlettsburg, by death, resignation, removal, or otherwise, the board of trustees shall fill said vacancy by appointment, and the person appointed by said board, if commissioned by the Governor of Kentucky, shall hold his office until the next regular election for trustees of said town in January thereafter. The certificate of the chairman of the board of trustees shall be sufficient evidence of the appointment for the Governor to issue a commission to the appointee as police judge of said town.

§ 3. The police judge of Catlettsburg, in addition to the jurisdiction heretofore conferred upon him, shall have concurrent jurisdiction with the quarterly court of Boyd county in civil cases where the amount in controversy does not exceed one hundred dollars; and the Civil Code of Practice regulating proceedings in the quarterly courts shall govern the said police judge in cases arising under this section; and the police judge shall have the same fees as are given to judges of the quarterly courts in similar cases.

§ 4. That the police court of the town of Catlettsburg shall be, and is hereby, declared a court of record, and copies of its proceedings, certified by the judge thereof, shall be competent evidence in any court in this Commonwealth.

§ 5. That, upon all judgments by the police judge, rendered under section third of this act, either party shall have the right to appeal from said judgment to the circuit court of Boyd county in the same manner, and upon same terms, as appeals are taken from quarterly courts in similar cases.

§ 6. That the tax upon coffee-house license within the town of Catlettsburg, hereafter granted, shall be one hundred dollars.

§ 7. That all persons against whom fines have been, or may hereafter be assessed by the police judge of Catlettsburg, who shall fail to pay or replevy the same, may, by order of the police judge, be compelled to work on the streets of said town, or be confined to labor in a workhouse which the trustees of said town may erect for that purpose; but persons so compelled to labor shall be allowed at the rate of two dollars per day upon the payment of their fine.

§ 8. That whatever per centage may be allowed the town attorney of the town of Catlettsburg, on the fines imposed by the police judge of said town or may be allowed him by the board of trustees as compensation for his services, shall be his fees for such services within the meaning of the tenth section of the third article of the new Constitution of Kentucky, and not subject to be remitted.

§ 9. That the marshal of the said town of Catlettsburg shall have the power and authority to summons any person or persons to assist him in the execution of any writ that may come to his hand, or in the arrest of any person or persons for the violation of any of the by-laws or ordinances of said town, or for a breach of the peace, affray, riot, rout, or to disperse any unlawful assembly; and any person or persons failing to render the necessary assistance, and obey the summons of the marshal, shall be reported to the police judge of the said town, who shall thereupon enter a judgment against each person so disobeying the order or summons for the sum of not less than five or more than ten dollars, upon which judgment he may issue a *capias pro fine*, which shall be collected according to law: *Provided*, That no such judgment shall be rendered until five days' notice, by warrant or summons, has been given to the person or persons so reported.

§ 10. This act shall take effect from its passage.

Approved February 18, 1869.

––––––

CHAPTER 1521.

AN ACT for the benefit of W. S. Hicks, late Sheriff of Henderson county, and his sureties.

WHEREAS, A judgment was rendered in favor of the Commonwealth of Kentucky, and against William S. Hicks, late sheriff of Henderson county, and others, his sureties in his revenue bond as such sheriff, at the —— term, 1867, of the Franklin circuit court, for the sum of eighteen thousand four hundred and eighty-two dollars and thirty-one cents, being the unpaid balance of the revenue from said county of Henderson for the year 1866, the whole of which judgment has been paid; and whereas, it appears from the records and papers on file in the office of the Auditor of Public Accounts, that there was included in said judgment the sum of two thousand four hundred and ninety-two dollars ($2,492), being the amount of the negro tax list for said county of Henderson, levied under the act of Assembly, entitled "An act for the benefit of the negroes and mulattoes in this Commonwealth," approved February 16th, 1866, and at the January term, 1868, of the Henderson county county, the said Hicks tendered in court his negro delinquent list for the year 1866, which was examined, corrected, approved, and ordered to be filed; and whereas, it appears from the said list, as approved by said court, that said Hicks is entitled to a credit on the said negro list for the sum of seventeen hundred and ninety-seven dollars and eighty-three cents ($1,797 83); and whereas, it further appears, that, at the —— term, 1868, of the Franklin circuit court, a judgment was rendered against the said Hicks, as such sheriff, and others, his sureties in his revenue bond, for the sum of twenty thousand eight hundred and twenty-one dollars and thirty-five cents

1869.

($20,821 35), being the unpaid balance of the revenue for Henderson county for the year 1867, and for the further sum of four thousand one hundred and sixty-four dollars and twenty-seven cents ($4,164 27) damages; and whereas, it appears from his deli, quent list, returned to and filed in the Auditor's office after the rendition of said judgment, that, upon the Auditor's list, No. 2, 1866, he is entitled to a credit of four hundred and ninety-four dollars and twenty-four cents ($494 24), and upon the Auditor's list, No. 5, 1867, to a credit of eleven hundred and thirty-five dollars and eight cents ($1,135 08); therefore,

Be it enacted by the General Assembly of the Commonwealth of Kentucky:

§ 1. That the said sum of four thousand one hundred and sixty-four dollars and twenty-seven cents ($4,164 27), being the amount of the damages in the said last mentioned judgment, be, and it is, remitted; and the said Hicks and his sureties are forever released from the payment thereof.

§ 2. That the Auditor of Public Accounts be, and he is, authorized and directed to allow the said Hicks credit on the said judgment for the sum of four hundred and ninety-four dollars and twenty-four cents ($494 24), being the amount uncollected on the Auditor's list, No. 2, for 1866, and for the further sum of eleven hundred and thirty-five dollars and eight cents ($1,135 08), being the amount uncollected on the Auditor's list, No. 5, for 1867; and that any balance thereof in favor of the said Hicks, after satisfying the said judgment, be paid over to the county court of Henderson county for the benefit of the said Hicks and his sureties: Provided, That should it hereafter appear that any part of the amounts herein directed to be credited have been collected by said Hicks, then, as to such sums so collected, the credit given shall be of no effect either as to said Hicks or his sureties.

§ 3. This act shall take effect from its passage.

Approved February 18, 1869.

CHAPTER 1522.

AN ACT to amend the charter of Estill Station and Speedwell Turnpike Road Company.

Be it enacted by the General Assembly of the Commonwealth of Kentucky:

§ 1. That so much of the seventh section of the act to which this is an amendment, as provides for the filing of a petition to the circuit court of Madison county for the purposes therein set forth, be so amended and changed as to authorize the filing of said petition in the Madison county court, and the same powers are hereby conferred on the Madison county court as by said section are conferred on the circuit court.

§ 2. This act to be of force from its passage.

Approved February 18, 1869.

CHAPTER 1525.

AN ACT for the benefit of Elijah Litton, late sheriff of Whitley County.

WHEREAS, It appears from satisfactory evidence that Elijah Litton, late sheriff of Whitley county, was charged with a delinquent list, sent him by the Auditor of Public Accounts in the year 1866, and said Litton having paid the amount thereof into the Treasury, the delinquent list so sent having been properly returned to the Auditor not collected; wherefore,

Be it enacted by the General Assembly of the Commonwealth of Kentucky:

§ 1. That the Auditor of Public Accounts draw his warrant upon the Treasurer for one hundred and sixty-five dollars and ninety cents in favor of Elijah Litton, late sheriff of Whitley county, being the amount improperly collected off of him.

§ 2. This act shall take effect from its passage.

Approved February 18, 1869.

CHAPTER 1526.

AN ACT to incorporate the Two Mile Turnpike Road Company, in Clark County.

Be it enacted by the General Assembly of the Commonwealth of Kentucky:

§ 1. That Jesse G. Hart, James Rutledge, Lewis Adams, Claiborne Lisle, James A. Bybee, Peyton Adams, and their associates and successors, be, and they are hereby, created a body-politic and corporate, under the name and style of the Two Mile turnpike road company; and by said name and style shall have power to contract and be contracted with, sue and be sued, answer and be answered, plead and be impleaded, in all the courts and places in this Commonwealth; to have and use a common seal, and break, alter, or change the same at pleasure; and do all acts which such bodies corporate may do, not inconsistent with the general law of the State or forbidden thereby, and which may be necessary or fit to enable said corporation to execute the powers hereinafter granted.

§ 2. That said corporation is hereby authorized to construct a turnpike or macadamized road from Winchester, in Clark county, Kentucky, to the mouth of Four Mile creek, in said county, or such point near thereto as may be determined on by the president and directors of said company after its organization.

§ 3. The capital stock of said company shall not exceed forty thousand dollars, and shall be divided into shares of one hundred dollars each.

§ 4. The books of said company may be opened for the subscription of stock by any of the corporators above named; and as soon as two thousand dollars of stock are subscribed, the stockholders may proceed to organize said company by electing a president and six directors; but said election shall be advertised at least ten days by printed or written notices of the time and place of holding said election. Said officers shall hold their offices for one year, or until their successors are duly elected and qualified. An election shall be held annually for officers of said company, at such time as may be fixed by the board of directors. The president shall have power to appoint a treasurer, and may remove him at pleasure, and shall require of him a bond with good security, conditioned for the faithful discharge of his duties.

§ 5. Said company may charge, upon their road, such tolls as the directors may determine upon, not exceeding, however, the rates allowed by the Revised Statutes; and may erect a gate, and collect tolls at the rate per mile agreed on, as soon as two miles and a half of said road are completed.

§ 6. The Clark county court shall have power, a majority of the justices thereof concurring, to subscribe for as much stock in said company as will suffice, when added to the amount of stock subscribed by individuals, to complete said road: *Provided*, Said subscription does not exceed ten hundred dollars per mile; and for the purpose of paying such subscription, said court is authorized and empowered to levy and assess a tax on all the property and estate in said county subject to taxation for State revenue.

§ 7. That sections seven, eight, nine, and ten of an act, entitled "An act to incorporate the Bedford and Milton turnpike road company," approved February 7, 1866, be, and the same are hereby, [made] a part of this act, so far as they are applicable and not inconsistent with its provisions.

§ 8. This act shall take effect from its passage.

Approved February 18, 1869.

CHAPTER 1527.

AN ACT to repeal an act for the benefit of E. J. Shipman.

Be it enacted by the General Assembly of the Commonwealth of Kentucky:

§ 1. That an act, entitled "An act for the benefit of Eliza Jane Shipman," approved January 20, 1860, be, and the same is hereby, repealed; and the said Eliza Jane Shipman is again placed under all the disabilities of coverture as a married woman.

§ 2. This act shall take effect from its passage.

Approved February 18, 1869.

CHAPTER 1528.

AN ACT to amend still further an act, entitled "An act to incorporate the Polish House of Israel."

Be it enacted by the General Assembly of the Commonwealth of Kentucky:

That the act approved December 13, 1851, entitled "An act to incorporate the Polish House of Israel," having heretofore, at the request of the corporate body, been amended by changing its name to " Betts Israel of Louisville," be now, upon the request of said body, still further amended by striking out these words in the first section, " for the purpose of improving each other in a knowledge of the religion of the Polish Israelites according to their peculiar customs, and in the practice of the same," &c., and inserting in place thereof the following : "As a religious society of Jews in said city."

Approved February 18, 1869.

CHAPTER 1529.

AN ACT to change the place of voting in District No. 7, Floyd County.

Be it enacted by the General Assembly of the Commonwealth of Kentucky:

§ 1. That hereafter, the voting place in district No. 7, Floyd county, shall be at the house of Benj. P. Porter, sr.

§ 2. This act shall take effect from its passage.

Approved February 18, 1869.

CHAPTER 1531.

AN ACT for the benefit W. A. Ronald, late Sheriff of Jefferson County.

Be it enacted by the General Assembly of the Commonwealth of Kentucky:

§ 1. That so much of a judgment in favor of the Commonwealth against W. A. Ronald, late sheriff of Jefferson county, for the revenue, as was for damages, amounting to eleven hundred and forty-six dollars and eighty-nine cents, be, and the same is hereby, remitted, said Ronald having paid all of the principal, interest, and costs of said judgment.

§ 2. This act shall take effect from its passage.

Approved February 18, 1869.

CHAPTER 1533.

AN ACT for the benefit of the Trustees of Providence Church, in the County of Mercer.

WHEREAS, On the first day of April, 1865, C. C. Shewmaker and Luna Shewmaker, his wife, executed a deed of conveyance to John P. Lapsley, Lambert D. Brewer, Harvey A. Woods, William E. Cleland, and Andrew Forsythe, trustees of New Providence (Presbyterian) Church, conveying to said trustees, in consideration of nineteen hundred dollars by them in hand paid, a lot or parcel of ground in the county of Mercer and State of Kentucky, on the Harrodsburg and Salvisa turnpike, near McAfee post-office, and more particularly described in said deed, which is recorded in the Mercer county clerk's office, in deed-book No. 36, pages 204 and 205; and whereas, said property was conveyed for the use and benefit of said church, and was intended to be used as a parsonage; and whereas, said property is not suitable nor convenient for the purpose for which it was purchased by said trustees; therefore,

Be it enacted by the General Assembly of the Commonwealth of Kentucky:

§ 1. That said trustees, or their successors in office, be, and are hereby, empowered to sell, alien, and convey said land and its appurtenances, a majority of the members of said church consenting thereto; and they are hereby empowered to execute and deliver a deed of conveyance to the purchaser, and the proceeds of said sale to be reinvested in other property, to be held by said trustees and their successors in office for the use and benefit of said church and for the purposes that the property sold was held for.

§ 2. This act to take effect from and after the day of its passage.

Approved February 20, 1869.

CHAPTER 1534.

AN ACT for the benefit of Benjamin F. Jameson, former Sheriff of Hart County.

WHEREAS, At the —— term, 1868, of the Franklin circuit court, there was rendered in said court a judgment against Benjamin F. Jameson, the then sheriff of Hart county, and his sureties, for the sum of two thousand and eighty dollars and thirty-four cents, with interest at the rate of six per cent. per annum from the first day of June, 1867, till paid, and also for the sum of four hundred and sixteen dollars and six cents damages and three dollars and ten cents costs; and whereas, it appears from the records on file in the Auditor's Office that the whole of said judgment, including principal, interest, and costs, and Attorney General's fee, have been paid, and the only part of said judgment yet unpaid is the sum of four hundred and sixteen dollars and six cents, adjudged as damages; now, therefore,

Be it enacted by the General Assembly of the Commonwealth of Kentucky:

§ 1. That the said Benjamin F. Jameson and his sureties be, and they are hereby, forever released from the payment of said sum of four hundred and sixteen dollars and ten cents, and the said sum as damages is hereby remitted; and the amount already paid is, and shall be, a full and complete satisfaction for the whole of said judgment.

§ 2. This act to take effect from its passage.

Approved February 20, 1869.

CHAPTER 1535.

AN ACT for the benefit of Isom Johnson, Sheriff of Henderson County.

Be it enacted by the General Assembly of the Commonwealth of Kentucky:

§ 1. That Isom Johnson, sheriff of Henderson county, be, and he is hereby, allowed one hundred and twenty-one dollars and ten cents for conveying Augustus Jewell to the penitentiary, said Jewell having been convicted of a felony at the April term, 1868, of the Henderson circuit court, said sum to be paid out of any money in the Treasury not otherwise appropriated.

§ 2. This act to be in force from its passage.

Approved February 20, 1869.

CHAPTER 1536.

AN ACT applying the General Mechanics' Lien Law to Taylor and Green Counties.

Be it enacted by the General Assembly of the Commonwealth of Kentucky:

§ 1. That an act, entitled "An act providing a general mechanics' lien law for certain cities and counties," approved February 17, 1858, and an act amendatory thereof, approved June 3, 1865, be so amended as to apply the provisions of said act and amended act to the counties of Taylor and Green.

§ 2. This act to take effect from its passage.

Approved February 20, 1869.

CHAPTER 1537.

AN ACT to amend an act, entitled "An act to incorporate the Louisville Bridge Company," approved February 19, 1861.

Be it enacted by the General Assembly of the Commonwealth of Kentucky:

§ 1. That the act incorporating the Louisville Bridge Company be so amended as that the election of directors and regular reports of the president and other officers shall take place on the first Mondays of March, of each year, instead of the first of January; and that said company shall have power and authority to purchase or condemn, by writ of *ad quod damnum*, and hold as much real estate within the limits of the city of Louisville as may be necessary for the purpose of a depot for freight or passengers, and all other buildings necessary for the operation of the said bridge company.

§ 2. Authority is hereby conferred on the Jefferson court of common pleas [to] award, try, and determine all writs of *ad quod damnum* provided for in first section of this act.

§ 3. This act to take effect from its passage.

Approved February 20, 1869.

CHAPTER 1538.

AN ACT to incorporate the Big Sandy Lumber and Improvement Company.

Be it enacted by the General Assembly of the Commonwealth of Kentucky:

§ 1. That G. W. Gallup, L. T. Moore, John M. Rice, O. C. Bowles, and A. L. Martin, John Lawshe, G. F. Hoop, D. S. Bush, J. J. Miller, G. M. Yocum, Allison White, and their associates and successors, be, and they are hereby, constituted a body-politic and corporate, by the name and

Corporators' names, and corporate powers.

style of the "Big Sandy Lumber and Improvement Company;" and by that name may sue and be sued, plead and be impleaded, in all courts of record or elsewhere; have a common seal to be altered by them at pleasure; make by-laws not repugnant to the laws of this State or of the United States, for the management of their corporate concerns, and to have and enjoy all the rights and powers of a corporation.

§ 2. That the said corporation are authorized and empowered to erect and maintain, on the Ohio river, between the mouth of the Big Sandy river and the town of Ashland, such boom or booms, with piers, as may be necessary for the purpose of stopping and securing logs, masts, spars, and other lumber floating upon said river, and erect such piers, side branch or shear booms, as may be necessary for that purpose: *Provided*, That said booms be so constructed as to admit the safe passage of rafts and boats, and not impede the navigation of said river: *And provided also*, That the said corporation shall construct, and at all times keep and maintain, their piers and booms sufficiently strong to secure all the lumber contained therein; and no person shall be allowed, at any time, to encumber said booms with rafts, either of logs or other lumber.

§ 3. That if any person or persons shall willfully or maliciously injure or destroy any of such booms or piers, or other works connected therewith, or any other buildings or improvements hereinafter mentioned and provided for, he or they shall pay treble the amount of damages to the corporation, to be recovered by action of trespass, and further be liable to indictment and prosecution before the proper criminal court for a misdemeanor; and on conviction shall be sentenced to pay a fine for the use of the county not exceeding five hundred dollars, and to suffer imprisonment in the county jail not exceeding two years.

§ 4. That it shall be the duty of the corporation to cause the passage ways or open spans in said booms on the Ohio and Sandy river to be so arranged that no lumber be permitted to escape; to secure all lumber in said booms carefully and faithfully with suitable warps and wedges for rafting and securing the same below said booms; and after three days' notice shall have been given by the corporation to the owner or agent having charge of such logs, if the owner, at the expiration of the time aforesaid, has not removed the same, the corporation may remove the same to some convenient place at the shore of the stream below, and fasten the float of logs to the shore by rope and stakes, as is usual by lumbermen in such cases, and the owners thereof shall pay such expenses as may arise in the removal and securing or fastening of the same to the shore

1869.

May erect booms, piers, &c.

Penalty for injury to same.

How booms to be erected.

Notice to owners of logs to be given, &c.

in the manner aforesaid; and if the owners of said logs shall not, within thirty days thereafter, take charge of the same, they shall be manufactured and disposed of by said corporation, as provided for in the seventh section of this act.

May collect toll or boomage, &c.

§ 5. That said corporation shall have the right to charge and collect toll or boomage upon the lumber thus boomed, rafted, and secured in the Ohio river, including warps and wedges by which they are rafted, to-wit: One dollar per thousand feet, board measure, for board logs, and fifty cents per one thousand feet, board measure, for the lumber boomed in the Big Sandy and Tug and Louisa forks of the Big Sandy river, and a reasonable sum for finding warps, rafting, and booming; all square timber, spars, clapboard, bolts, and other lumber, in proportion to other board logs. The corporation shall have a lien on all logs or other lumber thus boomed, for the payment of all boomage and other expenses, until such times as the same shall be paid to the corporation: *Provided*, That in any cases when spars, square or timber, may-have been rafted to run to market, and such rafts may be staved, or broken to pieces in any other way, and said logs should go into said boom by accident, or be taken in by the agents of said corporation, the said company shall deliver the same to the owner, on the production by him of reasonable evidence of his right thereto, for which they shall be entitled to fifty cents per log, and a reasonable sum for finding warp, rafting, and booming, and all square timber and other lumber in proportion to board logs, the same to be recovered as debts of a like amount are recoverable.

Proceedings in case persons do not wish to pay boomage.

§ 6. That should any person or persons have lumber upon said river which they are desirous of driving below the limits of said booms, and do not wish the same to be rafted at said booms, they shall give notice, in writing, to said corporation of their intentions on or before the first day of February in each year, describing the kind of lumber, and its quality, as near as may be, together with the marks thereon; and the corporation shall, upon the receipt of such notice, turn all such lumber through their booms as fast as may be conveniently done without interfering with the usual method of rafting out of said booms; and said corporation shall be entitled to receive as a toll or boomage fifty cents for each and every board log turned through said booms, and a reasonable compensation for all other kinds of lumber in proportion to board logs, to be paid on delivery of said logs through said booms as aforesaid, the corporation to retain a lien on all such logs or lumber until the toll or boomage shall have been paid.

Proceedings in case owners do not appear.

§ 7. That if any logs shall be boomed, rafted, and secured as aforesaid, and no person should appear to

claim the same and pay the tolls thereon, it shall be
lawful for the corporation, after advertising the same
for thirty days in the boroughs of Catlettsburg and Ashland, with the marks thereon, if any there be, to manufacture and dispose of the same to the best advantage
if no owner appear to claim the same; and the owner,
at any time within one year from the expiration of said
thirty days, shall be entitled to receive the avails thereof after deducting the tolls, expenses of manufacturing,
and other necessary charges; but if not claimed within
said one year, the proceeds shall be vested in the corporation for their own use.

§ 8. That it shall and may be lawful for the said corporation to build, construct, and erect such saw-mills, plan-
ing-mills, and other buildings, as they may deem necessary
for the convenient manufacture of lumber, and to fit the
same for market.

May erect saw-mills, &c.

§ 9. That for the purposes aforesaid, and for the further
purpose of supplying said mills with logs and timber, the
said corporation be, and hereby are, authorized and empowered to purchase, hold, and possess real estate adjacent to said booms or convenient thereto, or on the waters
of the Big Sandy river and its tributaries, to clear out said
tributaries and widen and deepen and improve the same,
and erect therein such booms and dams as may be necessary to conveniently hold and secure logs or drive them
out of the same: *Provided*, That said booms and dams
be so constructed as not to impede the navigation of the
Big Sandy river or its two branches, the Tug and Louisa
forks: *And provided also*, That said corporation shall pay
all such damages as may arise from said improvements of
the tributaries of the said Big Sandy river.

May purchase and hold real estate.

§ 10. That in all cases in which the said corporation
may clear out and improve the several tributaries of the
said Big Sandy river, for the purpose of driving logs or
holding and securing them therein as aforesaid, it shall
and may be lawful for the said corporation to charge
and collect from all other persons driving or floating logs
or timber therein, tolls at the rate of fifty cents per log,
and in the same proportion for all other kinds of timber;
the said tolls to be a lien on said logs or timber until paid.

May collect toll after clearing out obstructions.

§ 11. That for the purposes, the said corporation, their
agents, and those in their employ, may use and occupy
the lands on the shore of the Ohio river, and on the
shores of the Big Sandy river and its tributaries, in the
State of Kentucky, so far as may be necessary at the
place or places where said booms, dams, and piers are
erected, and at such other place or places as may be
necessary for floating, driving, rafting, and securing logs
and other timber or lumber, and to pass and repass on

May use and occupy lands on shores of Ohio and Big Sandy rivers.

foot to and from said boom or booms, and other improvements for the purpose of making repairs, from time to time, and generally for doing all matters and things necessary for the full accomplishment of the objects of this incorporation, subject, however, to pay such damages as may arise to land-owners in the prosecution of such objects or purposes.

§ 12. That if any land-owners shall suffer damage by the exercise of powers herein granted to said corporation, and the amount thereof cannot be agreed upon by the parties, nor suitable person or persons agreed upon to estimate the same, the circuit court having jurisdiction where the boom or booms or other improvements are situated shall, upon application of the party aggrieved, cause said damages to be ascertained by three disinterested freeholders of the same county, to be appointed by said court, and who shall make report to the said court on or before the first day of the next term after the award shall have been made, and which being confirmed by the court, shall have the effect of a judgment from time of such confirmation: *Provided, however,* That if either party be dissatisfied with the award of said commissions, and shall, at the term when award is presented for confirmation, apply to said court for a trial by jury, in the manner as other like cases are determined, the court shall by jury determine the amount of such damage accordingly; and if the verdict shall not be more favorable to the party applying for the jury than was awarded by the commissioners, judgment for costs shall be rendered against the applicants; and if the verdict be more favorable to the party applying for a jury than the award of the commissioners, the applicant shall receive costs, and execution shall in either case issue upon the judgment. Said corporation shall not take any private property until compensation be made or adequate security be given therefor before such property shall be taken.

§ 13. That all logs or other timber rafted out of said booms, or any of their branches, or floated or driven out of said improved tributaries of the Big Sandy river, shall be counted or measured, and their quantity ascertained by some competent person or persons, to be sworn by the county court judge, having jurisdiction in the county where the same are located, and whose duty it shall be to keep an account of all such logs, timber, or lumber as may be turned through said boom or booms or floated or driven out of said tributaries, agreeable to the sixth and tenth sections of this act.

§ 14. That the principal office of said corporation shall be located in the State of Kentucky, and in said office shall be kept a suitable book or books for the recording of such marks as may be selected by the owners of logs, timber, or lumber to be floated or driven on the said Big Sandy river and its tributaries; and said marks shall be recorded therein by said corporation on presentation, free of charge; but no person shall be permitted to record any mark already selected and recorded by some other person.

§ 15. That the capital stock of said corporation shall consist of two hundred and fifty thousand dollars, with the right to increase the same to one million dollars, in shares of one hundred dollars each; and the said corporation shall have the right to receive lands, tenements, buildings, machinery, fixtures, and materials in payment of said stock, at their real value; and the said corporation shall have the right to barter, sell, exchange, lease, mortgage, or otherwise dispose of, at their pleasure, any lands which they may acquire by purchase or otherwise, in accordance with the provisions of this act.

Capital stock.

May receive lands, &c.

§ 16. For conducting the affairs of said company, a president and three directors may be chosen, if the stockholders so desire, who shall serve until superseded by another choice; and the president and directors shall have power to appoint all agents, officers, and servants under them, and to remove them at pleasure. In all elections each share of stock shall entitle the holder to one vote, and stockholders may vote in person or by proxy.

President and directors to be elected.

§ 17. The stock of said company shall be deemed personal estate, and may be transferred on the books of the company after such share shall have been fully paid up, and under such rules and regulations as said company may prescribe.

Stock deemed personal estate.

§ 18. The first meeting of the stockholders for the election of the president and directors shall be advertised in some newspaper printed in this Commonwealth; and the president and directors shall be authorized to take and require bond with security, in an adequate penalty, from their treasurer, or any other agent or officer of said company; and for a failure to pay up the stock by any stockholder, the share or shares of such stockholder may be forfeited by the president and directors, after thirty days' notice to said stockholder requiring payment of the same, or they may sue and recover the same.

First meeting of stockholders; may take bond from treasurer, &c.

§ 19. Books for the subscription of stock may be opened at any time and place, and closed again at pleasure, by the president and one of the directors, or by the order of a majority of the board of directors: *Provided, however,* That the stock at no time shall exceed the maximum amount herein named.

Books may be opened for subscription of stock.

§ 20. It shall be lawful for the president and board of directors, from time to time, to borrow or obtain on loans

May borrow money.

1869.

such sums of money, and on such terms, as they may deem expedient and necessary for the good of the company, and to pledge or mortgage all or any part of the estate, improvements, privileges, assets, and effects whatsoever of said company, for the repayment of such loans or of any indebtedness.

§ 21. In all suits established against this corporation, the service of process may be on the president; and it shall not be necessary to show a contract under the seal of the corporation to maintain a suit against it or for it; but said corporation, by its duly authorized agent or agents, may make parol contracts, which shall be binding; and on such parol contracts suits may be maintained: *Provided*, Such contracts shall be within the fair meaning of the power or authority granted or delegated to such agent or agents.

In case of suits, service of process on president.

§ 22. An election for president, directors, and other officers of said corporation, shall be holden at such time and place as a majority of the above named corporators may prescribe, and in the manner provided for in section (16) sixteen: *Provided*, That nothing contained in this act shall be so construed as to authorize the exercise of any lottery privileges under any of its provisions, or in any manner whatever to dispose of any property or other thing of value by chance.

Election of president and directors.

§ 23. This act shall take effect and be in force from and after its passage.

Approved February 20, 1869.

CHAPTER 1540.

AN ACT to amend the Charter of the Town of Lebanon, in Marion County.

Be it enacted by the General Assembly of the Commonwealth of Kentucky:

§ 1. That an act, entitled "An act to amend the charter of the town of Lebanon, in Marion county," approved 11th January, 1868, be amended so as to require the trustees of said town to be elected by the voters of said town, and not by wards, as required by said act.

§ 2. This act shall take effect from its passage.

Approved February 20, 1869.

CHAPTER 1541.

AN ACT for the benefit of School District No. 13, in Franklin County.

WHEREAS, Common school district No. 13, in Franklin county, having recently lost their school-house by fire, and the trustees thereof being desirous to rebuild the same—

Be it enacted by the General Assembly of the Commonwealth of Kentucky:

§ 1. That the trustees of said school district be authorized to appropriate any funds now on hand, and to which said district will be entitled to draw during the present year, towards the erection of a new school-house, which is to be built upon the lot upon which the former house stood.

§ 2. This act to take effect from its passage.

Approved February 20, 1869.

CHAPTER 1542.

AN ACT to incorporate the Lexington and Virginia Railroad Company.

Be it enacted by the General Assembly of the Commonwealth of Kentucky:

§ 1. That Jacob Hughes, R. A. Buckner, Asa McConna-thy, sr., William B. Kinkead, Gwinn Gunn, J. F. Robinson, Thompson Worley, William Cassius Goodloe, Isaac Vanmeter, J. J. Miller, Wm. Preston, of Fayette county; W. M. Beckner, B. F. Buckner, Thomas H. Roberson, James D. Gay, Benj. B. Groom, James Simpson, Harrison Thompson, James French, C. S. French, J. H. Goff, J. Prewett, William C. Simpson, and John Conkwright, of Clark county; W. B. Tipton, Wm. H. Nelson, William Mitchell, M. Cassity, J. F. McGowan, R. Apperson, jr., J. J. Anderson, Josiah Anderson, R. Reed, Jno. A. Thompson, A. J. Wyatt, and William Howe, of Montgomery county; B. F. Crawford, E. P. Davis, N. Lewis, W. Bolling, James Botts, J. Hord, Dr. Jones, of Carter county; Laban Moore, Judge Rice, George Brown, W. C. Ireland, J. Lampton, George Heron, of Boyd county; Guthrie Coke, John T. Bunch, L. Cooke, E. D. Standeford, Philip Deorn, C. Henry Finck, R. A. Robinson, M. A. Downing, John S. Cain, B. F. Guthrie, G. W. Anderson, and A. J. Mussel man, of the city of Louisville; George Hamilton, A. J. Ewing, Judge Elliott, James Lee, Mat. McDaniel, Sanford Allen, Van. Young, A. J. Reed, Dr. Roe, James Hamilton, Jeff. Rice, William Riddle, and H. S. Stone, of the county of Bath; H. G. Burns, Jonathan Lewis, and John Hargis, of Rowan county; Judge Menhier and J. W. Kendall, of

Corporators' names.

1869. Morgan county, or such of them as shall act, are hereby appointed commissioners, and they and their associates and successors are created a body-politic and corporate, for the purpose of constructing a railroad from Lexington to a point at or near the mouth of the Big Sandy river.

Name & style. § 2. The style and name of the corporation hereby created shall be the Lexington and Virginia Railroad Company.

§ 3. The capital stock of said company shall be five million of dollars, to be divided into shares of fifty dollars each; and individuals, railroad companies, and other corporations, either in or out of the State, are authorized to subscribe for and hold stock in said company.

Commissioners to open books for the subscription of stock. § 4. The commissioners aforesaid, or such of them as may act, shall have power to open books and receive subscriptions of stock in said company at any place or places, either in or out of this State, and at any time they may appoint, and upon such notice as they may deem proper; said stock to be paid in money, property, work. and materials, or in such other manner and in such installments as may be agreed upon between them and the subscribers.

When president and directors may be elected. § 5. When *bona fide* subscriptions of stock to the amount or value of fifty thousand dollars shall have been made, the said commissioners shall give notice thereof and assemble the stockholders at some convenient point; and said stockholders, from their body, shall elect eleven directors, one of whom, to be elected by the directors, shall be president of the company. They shall remain in office for one year, or until their successors shall be elected, and which election shall be annually made by the stockholders at some convenient place, of which reasonable notice shall be given. The stockholders may provide that the president and four directors may constitute a quorum of the board of directors. Each stockholder shall have one vote for each share of stock, and may cast the same in person or by proxy.

After organization, directors may continue to receive subscriptions of stock. § 6. After the organization of the company as directed by the foregoing section, the management and control of the affairs of the company shall be committed to said board of directors; they may continue to receive subscriptions of stock; they may acquire and hold such real and personal estate as may be necessary and convenient for the objects of the company; may sell and convey the same, and do all and every thing else which may be necessary and proper for the building, equipping, and operating said road; to fix the rates to be paid for travel and the conveyance of freight over said road, not exceeding the rates charged by other similar roads in this State.

May purchase railways already finished. § 7. Said company shall have power to purchase, acquire, and hold any line of railway, finished or unfinished,

lying along its line, and between its termini, and all the
chartered rights and privileges granted to the same, and
all its property, right of way, &c.; and may proceed to
construct and operate their road upon and along the line
of any such finished or unfinished railway, or may construct an independent line of railroad between Lexington
and Big Sandy river.

§ 8. Said company, through its board of directors, shall
have and may exercise all the powers, and shall have all
the rights and privileges usual and incident and necessary
to the purposes of such corporations. It may contract and
be contracted with, sue and be sued, plead and be impleaded, answer and defend, in all courts and places as a
natural person; and may have and use a common seal,
and change or alter the same at will.

§ 9. That whenever the said Lexington and Virginia
railroad company shall request the county court of any
county, through or adjacent to which it is proposed to construct said road, to subscribe, either absolutely or upon
specified conditions, a specified amount to the capital
stock of said company, the county court so requested shall
forthwith order an election to be held at the several voting
places in said county, on a day to be fixed by the court, not
later than thirty (30) days after the making of such order,
and shall appoint judges and other officers necessary to
hold said election.

§ 10. That it shall be the duty of the sheriff of such
county to give notice to the officers appointed to hold said
election in the same manner as is now provided by law in
regard to other elections; and in case any of the officers
appointed shall fail to attend, or refuse to act, others may
be appointed in the same manner as at general elections.

§ 11. That the person acting as sheriff at the several
precincts shall return to the clerk of the county court,
within three (3) days after the day of such election, the
poll-books of their respective precincts, and on the next
day thereafter the county judge and county clerk shall
count the vote; and if it shall appear that the majority of
those voting voted in favor of the subscription of stock as
proposed, the county judge shall order the vote to be
entered on the record, and the subscription to be made by
the clerk, on behalf of the county, on the terms specified
in the order submitting the question to a vote.

§ 12. That whenever the city council of any city, or the
board of trustees of any town, into or near to which it is
proposed to construct said Lexington and Virginia railroad,
or the general council of the city of Louisville shall be requested to do so, it shall be the duty of such city council or
town trustees to submit to a vote of the qualified voters
of such city or town, on a day to be designated by such

Margin notes:

1869.

Corporate powers.

Elections to be held when counties requested to take stock.

Sheriff to notify officers of election.

Sheriff to return poll-books to county clerk.

Proceedings in case cities or towns are requested to take stock.

1869.

council or trustees, not later than thirty (30) days after the application is made to them by said company, the question of subscribing, for and on behalf of such city or town, the amount of stock proposed by said company on the terms proposed; and if a majority of those voting shall vote in favor of making such subscription, it shall be the duty of such city council or board of trustees to enter the vote on its records, and the mayor of such city, or president of the board of trustees of such town, shall make the subscription in accordance with the vote.

Bonds to be issued in case of subscription.

§ 13. That if any county, city, or town shall subscribe to the capital stock of said Lexington and Virginia railroad company under the provisions of this act, it shall be the duty of the county court of such county, the mayor and council of such city, and the board of trustees of such town, to issue the bonds of such county, city, or town, in denominations of not less than one hundred nor more than one thousand dollars, in payment thereof, with coupons attached, under the seal of such county, city, or town; the bonds of the counties to be signed by the county judge and countersigned by the clerk, and the coupons to be signed by the clerk alone; the bonds of cities subscribing shall be signed by the mayor and countersigned by the city clerk or auditor, and the coupons shall be signed by the clerk or auditor alone; the bonds of towns subscribing shall be signed by the president of the board of trustees and countersigned by the town clerk, and the coupons shall be signed by the clerk alone. Such bonds shall be negotiable and payable to bearer in the city of New York or city of Louisville, at not more than thirty (30) years from their date, and shall bear interest at a rate not greater than eight (8) per cent, payable semi-annually in the city of New York or the city of Louisville.

How signed, &c.

§ 14. That in case any county, city, or town shall subscribe to the capital stock of said Lexington and Virginia railroad company under the provisions of this act, and issue bonds for the payment of such subscription, it shall be the duty of the county court of such county, the city council of such city, and the trustees of such town, to cause to be levied and collected a tax sufficient to pay the semi-annual interest on the bonds issued, and the cost of collecting such tax and paying the interest on all the real estate and personal property in said county, city, or town subject to taxation under the revenue laws of the State, including the amounts owned by residents of such county, city, or town which ought to be given in under the equalization laws.

May levy tax to pay same.

Counties, cities, &c., to appoint commissioners of sinking fund; their powers & duties.

§ 15. That on levying a tax as provided for in this act to pay the interest on bonds issued by the county court of

any county, or of any city or town, it shall be the duty of
the county court, city council, or town trustees making
such levy, to appoint three (3) resident tax-payers of such
county, city, or town, who shall be styled the board of
commissioners of the sinking fund of such county, city,
or town. The commissioners so appointed shall, before
they proceed to discharge their duties, be sworn in the
presence of the court, council, or trustees appointing
them, faithfully to discharge their duties according to the
best of their skill and judgment; they shall hold their
office at the pleasure of the court, council, or trustees
by whom they are appointed. They shall immediately *Shall appoint a treasurer; his duties.*
appoint one of their number treasurer, who shall exe-
cute bond, payable to the Commonwealth, with such
security as shall be approved by the court, council, or
trustees appointing the commissioners, conditioned for
the faithful keeping and disbursing of all money coming
to his hands as treasurer of such board, on which bond
suit may be brought, from time to time, by and in the
name of such county, city, or town, or by any other
person injured by any breach of his bond in any court
having jurisdiction of the sum claimed in such suit.
Such treasurer may be required, at any time, to give
a new bond, and any surety in such bond shall be entitled to the same remedies for procuring additional or
counter security as are now given to the sureties of
guardians, administrators, &c. Said treasurer shall be
allowed for his services such compensation, not exceeding one (1) per cent. on the money received and paid
out by him, as may be allowed by the court, council, or
trustees appointing such commissioners, respectively. In
case a vacancy shall occur in said board of commissioners, such vacancy shall be filled by the court, council,
or trustees by whom such board was appointed.

§ 16. The taxes levied under the authority of this act in *Who to collect taxes.*
any county shall be collected by the sheriff of such county;
and taxes levied in any city or town shall be collected by
the officer of such city or town who is by law the collect-
or of taxes levied for the ordinary purposes of such city or
town; but before any sheriff or other officer shall be authorized to collect any such tax he shall execute bond, if
a sheriff, with such sureties as may be approved by the
county court, and if a city or town officer, with such surety as may be approved by the council or trustees of such
city or town, conditioned that such officer will promptly
and faithfully collect and pay over to the proper person,
within the time prescribed by law, all taxes levied under
this act which may be placed in his hands for collection.

§ 17. That sheriffs and other officers having in their *Powers of collectors.*
hands for collection taxes levied under this act shall have

all the powers of distraining and selling personal property which sheriffs have in the collection of the State revenue; and when such officer shall be unable to find personal property liable to sale for the unpaid tax of any individual, he may levy the same on any real estate of such person situated in the county, and sell the same under the regulations prescribed by law for selling real estate under execution; and all taxes levied under this act shall be a lien on the real estate of the person taxed which shall lie in the county in which such tax is levied; but the owner of any real estate sold may redeem the same at any time within five (5) years after such sale by paying the purchase money and (10) ten per cent. per annum thereon, with all taxes of every description paid by the purchaser after his purchase, and ten (10) per cent. per annum thereon.

Certificates of sale for non-payment of tax to be given.

§ 18. That sheriffs or other officers selling real estate for taxes levied under this act shall give to the purchaser a certificate of his purchase, which shall describe the real estate sold, and state the amount for which it was sold and the date of sale, which certificate shall be lodged by the purchaser with the clerk of the county court within sixty days, who shall record the same in a book to be kept for the purpose, and for which such clerk shall be entitled to charge a fee of fifty (50) cents; and if such certificate is not recorded as herein provided, the land may be redeemed at any time within fifteen (15) years, on paying the purchase money and six (6) per cent. per annum thereon, and other taxes paid by the purchaser, and six (6) per

Compensation of collectors.

cent. per annum thereon. That sheriffs and other officers collecting taxes levied under this act shall receive the same compensation as is allowed by law for the time being for collecting the State revenue.

When & how taxes small be collected and paid over.

§ 19. That one half of the tax levied in any one year shall be collected by the sheriff or other officer in whose hands the same is placed for collection, and paid over to the treasurer of the board of commissioners of the sinking fund within one hundred and twenty (120) days after the same is placed in his hands, and the residue within six (6) months after the first ought to have been paid; and if any sheriff or other officer, whose duty it is to collect taxes under this act, shall fail or refuse to execute bond as required by this act for thirty (30) days after the tax is levied, the court, city council, or board of trustees levying such tax may appoint a collector, who shall execute bond, with sureties, and have all the powers, and be subject to all the duties and liabilities, of sheriffs and other officers

Proceedings in case of failure of duty of collector.

in collecting taxes under this act. That if any sheriff or collector, or other officer having in his hands for collection taxes levied under this act, shall fail to collect and pay over the same within the time prescribed, such sheriff, collector, or other officer shall, with his sureties, be liable for the amount not paid as required, and ten (10) per cent. thereon, to be recovered on motion on ten (10) days' notice in any court having jurisdiction; and any execution issued on such judgment shall not be replevied, and shall be indorsed by the clerk issuing the same that no security of any kind is to be taken.

§ 20. It shall be the duty of the commissioners of the sinking fund to see that the sheriff or other officer collects and pays over taxes placed in their hands according to law, and to institute legal proceeding against them on their failure to do so. They shall appropriate such moneys, when collected, to the payment of the interest on the bonds of their county, city, or town.

§ 21. They shall, whenever a dividend is declared by said Lexington and Virginia railroad company, cause their treasurer to receive the same and pay the interest on their bonds out of it, and when a surplus shall remain after paying the interest due, they shall apply such surplus to the purchase of their bonds, if they can be purchased at par, or less than par; and if they cannot be purchased at par, they shall invest such surplus in some safe and profitable manner, and in such way, that the money may be readily realized when needed to buy or pay off bonds.

§ 22. That all dividends which shall be received upon the stock held and owned by any county, city, or town, under this act, shall be, and are hereby, set apart to be held sacred as a sinking fund, to be only used as provided in this act for the payment of the principal and interest of the bonds issued under the authority of this act.

§ 23. That in case the dividends upon the stock held and owned under this act by any county, city, or town, and for which bonds shall have been issued, shall not be sufficient to enable such county, city, or town to pay its bonds at maturity, it shall be the duty of the commissioners of the sinking fund to report such fact to the county court, city council, or town trustees, at least five (5) years before the maturity of said bonds; and if any county court, city council, or the trustees of any town owing such bonds shall deem it proper to do so, they may issue new bonds having not more than twenty (20) years to run, payable at such place as may be designated on the face of such bonds, bearing the same interest, and secured in all respects, as the bonds first issued are secured, and sell such bonds or exchange them for the old ones: *Provided, however,* That if any county court, city council, or town trustees shall deem it inexpedient to issue and sell such new bonds, or shall be unable to raise

1869.

Commissioners to see that taxes are collected, &c.

Dividends to be paid to treasurer, and how used.

Dividends to county, city, &c., how used.

Proceedings in case dividends are not sufficient to pay interest, &c.

money necessary to pay off its bonds at maturity by a sale of new bonds, it shall be the duty of such county court, city council, or town trustees to cause a tax to be levied and collected on all the property in such county, city, or town, which, by the provisions of this act, is subject to taxation to pay interest, sufficient, when added to any sum raised by sale of new bonds, to discharge the old bonds at maturity : *Provided also,* That any tax levied under the provisions of this section, shall be collected by the same officers, under the same powers, and subject to the same responsibilities in every respect, as provided in the act in relation to the collection of taxes levied to pay interest.

§ 24. That in case a direct tax shall be levied to pay all **Stock may be transferable in certain cases.** or any part of the bonds of any county, city, or town, issued under this act, at or before maturity, it shall be the duty of the commissioners of the sinking fund to cause to be transferred to the tax-payers or their assignees stock held by said county, city, or town, to the amount of the tax paid, upon the delivery to said commissioners of tax receipts by the holders thereof; such receipts shall be negotiable by indorsement, and no stock shall be transferred for a less amount than fifty dollars.

§ 25. That it shall be the duty of the treasurers of the **Certificates of stock to be issued.** several boards of commissioners of the sinking fund appointed under this act, upon the surrender to them at their respective offices of receipts given for taxes paid to defray the interest on the bonds of their respective counties, cities, and towns, prior to the time of declaring the first cash dividend by said railroad company to the amount of fifty dollars or more, to issue to the holders thereof certificates setting forth the number of shares of stock to which the holder is entitled, and to give a separate receipt for any fractional part of a share, which receipt shall be negotiable by indorsement, and may be added to other like receipts or tax receipts to make up a full share. The treasurer shall write or stamp the word canceled across the face of each tax receipt taken up by him, and file it away in his office; and he may charge and collect fifty cents per share for each certificate issued by him. He shall keep a list of the names of those to whom he issues certificates, with the number of the certificate and the number of shares for which each was given; and shall, on the last day of each month, make out and forward to the secretary of the company a copy of the list of certificates issued during that month.

§ 26. That it shall be the duty of the said Lexington and Virginia railroad company, after the first cash dividend shall be declared, on presentation at its office of the stock certificates issued under the provisions of the last preceding section, to issue stock therefor to those to whom such certificates were issued, or their representatives or assigns.

§ 27. That the commissioners of the sinking fund shall keep an exact record of all their actings and doings as such; and their treasurer shall keep a strict account of all moneys received or paid out by him, and shall settle his accounts annually, or oftener if required, which settlement shall state fully his accounts since his last settlement. *Commissioners sinking fund to keep record.*

§ 28. That all the real estate lying in any county, city, or town, issuing bonds under this act, shall be taxed for the purpose of defraying the interest on such bonds, and for the payment of the principal, if that shall be paid by taxation; and when a part only of the land of any taxpayer shall lie in such county, city, or town, the assessor of tax shall designate in his books what part lies within such county, city, or town, and its value, and only such part shall be assessed for the purposes of this act. *Real estate to be taxed for purpose of paying bonds.*

§ 29. That the commissioners of the sinking fund, or one of them, shall cast the vote to which their respective counties, cities, and towns may be entitled in any meeting of the stockholders of said Lexington and Virginia railroad company: *Provided,* That if neither of them shall attend, then any person duly authorized by any two of said commissioners may cast the vote as proxy for said commissioners. *Commissioners of sinking fund to cast vote.*

§ 30. That the president and directors of said Lexington and Virginia railroad company may, if it shall seem advisable to them, increase the capital stock of said company to a sum equal to the total cost of the road and its equipments, depots, water-stations, &c. *Capital stock may be increased.*

§ 31. That said company may acquire a right of way sixty-six (66) feet wide; but this shall not be construed as a limitation on the right to acquire any width that may be shown to be necessary by the affidavit of an engineer filed with the justice at the time of suing out the warrant for condemning such lands. *Right of way.*

§ 32. That the said Lexington and Virginia railroad company shall be exempt from taxation until completed, and that it shall never be taxed at a valuation beyond the rate at which said roads are now taxed, nor exceeding its actual value. *Exempt from taxation until road completed.*

§ 33. That the president and directors of said company may, with the assent of the holders of a majority in value of the stock of said company, purchase and hold any other railroad in this or in any other State, and may subscribe stock in or guarantee the bonds of or aid in the building of any other road in or out of this State, whenever, in their judgment, it may be to the interest of the Lexing- *May purchase other railroads.*

1869.

ton and Virginia railroad company to do so; they may sell the said Lexington and Virginia railroad, or lease the same, and may build branches from said road, and branches from such branches.

May receive donations.

§ 34. That said Lexington and Virginia railroad company may receive donations of land to be used for any of the purposes of said road, or to be sold to raise money to build the same. and may receive subscriptions, to be paid in lands at a valuation to be fixed by such means as may be agreed upon between said company or its authorized agents and the subscriber, and may lease or sell. and convey any land so given or subscribed.

Company may be consolidated with other companies.

§ 35. That said Lexington and Virginia railroad company may, the holders of a majority in value of all the stock therein concurring, agree on terms for consolidating said company with any other railroad company, on such terms as may be agreed upon; but no such consolidation shall in anywise affect the holders of mortgage bonds issued by said Lexington and Virginia railroad company.

Company may issue and sell bonds.

§ 36. That the Lexington and Virginia railroad company may issue and sell the bonds of said company of the denomination of one thousand dollars and five hundred dollars, to be signed by the president and countersigned by the secretary, with the seal of the corporation affixed, to an amount not exceeding five millions of dollars, bearing not exceeding eight per cent. interest, payable semi-annually, with coupons attached, signed by the secretary of the company, to be made payable as said company may direct, within thirty years from their date.

May mortgage road.

§ 37. To secure the prompt payment of the interest and principal of bonds issued by authority of this act, said company may execute a mortgage or deed of trust conveying said railroad and its property and franchises to a trustee or trustees, and, from time to time, fill vacancies that may occur, for the use and to secure the holders of such bonds, with such covenants and stipulations as may be necessary to effect the purpose and objects of its execution.

Proceedings in case mortgage is foreclosed.

§ 38. That if the mortgage or deed of trust authorized by the last preceding section shall be foreclosed by legal proceedings, such foreclosure shall be for the benefit of all the holders of bonds secured by its provisions. Upon such foreclosure the president shall make a correct list of all bonds secured by such mortgage or deed of trust, which have been sold, and verify it by his affidavit, which affidavit and list shall be filed in the Fayette circuit court, where only such proceedings is authorized to be had. Such foreclosure shall not take place until ninety days after publication of notice of the commencement of proceedings to that end shall have been made in one or more newspapers published in the cities of New York, Louisville, and Lexington. The person or corporation becoming the purchaser or lessee of said road, by reason of any sale or leasing to satisfy the demands of bondholders, shall be vested with all the rights, privileges, franchises, and immunities of the corporation.

§ 39. That to create and to secure a fund for the final redemption of mortgage bonds issued under authority of this act, a sinking fund shall be created by said company; and in order to create such sinking fund, said company shall, at the time of declaring the first cash dividend, ascertain what sum ought to be set aside annually in order to create a fund sufficient to redeem its bonds at maturity, and then set apart and pass into the sinking fund that sum; and thereafter, annually, there shall be set aside and pass into said fund a like sum until a fund is created sufficient to pay the outstanding bonds of the company; which fund shall be held sacred for the redemption of said bonds, and shall be used for no other purpose. That the company may loan and reloan the sums thus set apart at any rate of interest not greater than that paid on its bonds, or may invest the same in any safe and profitable manner deemed advisable, which is not inconsistent with the purposes and objects of creating said fund: *Provided*, That said company may use any or all of said funds in retiring its bonds before maturity, if deemed advisable; but no bond purchased with the proceeds of the sinking fund shall be resold, but the same shall be canceled.

Company may create sinking fund.

§ 40. The bonds of the company, nor the bonds of the counties, cities, or towns, issued under authority of this act, whether sold and delivered in this State or elsewhere, shall not be avoided, in whole or in part, by reason of the rate of interest agreed to be paid, or of the place at which they may be sold or delivered, nor by reason of their having been sold at less than their par value.

Bonds not to be avoided.

§ 41. That upon application by said company to the county court of any county into or through which it is proposed to construct said Lexington and Virginia railroad, such court shall appoint three (3) commissioners, two of whom shall be resident of said county, and one an engineer of said company, who shall be sworn faithfully to discharge their duties under this act to the best of their skill and judgment; and whenever said company shall be unable to agree with the owner of any land, earth, stone, gravel, timber, or other material or thing required for the site or construction of said road, or whenever the land or material required shall be owned by any person not a resident of said county, or who is a *feme covert*, infant, or *non compos mentis*, it shall be the duty of

How right of way, land, material, &c., obtained.

1869.   said commissioners to view the land or material required,
and fix the amount of compensation to which the owner
or owners of such land or material shall be entitled, and
make out and return to the office of the cle.k of the
county court a report in writing, particularly describing
the land or other material valued, and the interest and
duration of the interest valued, and the amount of damages assessed. The report of the commissioners shall
give the name of the owner, and state whether such
owner is a resident of the county, and whether a *feme
covert*, infant, or non-sane person. The clerk shall receive such report and file the same, indorsing thereon
the time of its being filed; and if the owner resides in
the county, he shall forthwith issue a summons commanding the owner or owners of such land to appear and show
cause why the report should not be confirmed, which summons shall be forthwith executed by the sheriff or other
officer in whose hands it may be placed. The report shall
be docketed in the county court, and stand for trial at any
term of said court, commencing not less than ten (10) days
after service of the summons. If the owner is not a resident of the county. the court shall, at the first term after
the report is filed, appoint an attorney to defend for such
owner, who may file exceptions at any time not later than
the next term; and upon exceptions being filed by the
owner, or by an attorney appointed to defend for him, or
by the company, the court shall forthwith order a jury to
be empanneled to try the question of damages, unless for
good cause shown time is given for preparation.

Further pro-
ceedings for
condemnation
of lands, &o.

§ 42. If no exceptions are filed, the report shall be confirmed. The jury and commissioners shall, in estimating
the damages to any proprietor of land or material sought
to be condemned for said road, be governed by the same
rule as prescribed in section thirteen of an act incorporating the Elizabethtown and Paducah railroad company,
approved March 5, 1867; and the mode of valuation provided for herein shall have the same effect, and confer
upon the company all the rights and privileges which
would be conferred if the proceedings had been had in
accordance with the provisions of the original charter of
said Elizabethtown and Paducah railroad company; and
whenever a verdict shall be had, the court may give judgment condemning such land or other material for the use
of said company, and against the company for the amount
of damages assessed, and also to the owner for his costs,
if the verdict shall be for more than was assessed by the
commissioners.

§ 43. The mayor and council, or general council of any
city, and the board of directors of any railroad company,
may, on behalf of their city or company, guarantee the

payment of the principal and interest of the bonds of the said Lexington and Virginia railroad company; and any railroad company or other corporation may subscribe to the capital stock of the said Lexington and Virginia railroad company.

§ 44. That the construction of this road shall be commenced within two years, and be completed within five years from the passage of this act.

§ 45. All acts and parts of acts inconsistent with the rights and privileges conferred by this act are hereby repealed.

§ 46. This act shall be in force from and after its passage.

Approved February 20, 1869.

1869.

When road to be commenced and completed.

CHAPTER 1543.

AN ACT to organize Urania School District, in Barren County.

Be it enacted by the General Assembly of the Commonwealth of Kentucky:

§ 1. That the town of Glasgow, in Barren county, Kentucky, and all the territory adjacent thereto, lying within one and a half miles in every direction from the courthouse in said town, be, and the same is hereby, incorporated into one common school district, and shall be called and known by the name Urania district, and all persons residing therein, qualified under the laws of the State to vote for trustees of common schools, shall be permitted to vote for trustees of said district.

§ 2. That on the first Saturday in May, 1869, the persons qualified to vote as aforesaid, residing in said district, may attend at the court-house in Glasgow, and there vote for three trustees of said school district, which election shall be then and there held for that purpose, and on the same day of the month of May every year thereafter. The three persons voted for having the greatest number of votes shall be certified by the clerk and judges of the election, in writing, to be so elected and chosen as the trustees for said district for one year from and after that day. The poll-book and certificate of election, signed by the officers holding it, shall be delivered to said trustees. They shall each take an oath that they will honestly and faithfully discharge all the duties imposed upon them as such trustees by law. The said poll-book, certificate of their election, and certificate of their qualification, shall be carefully filed away and preserved by them as a part of the records of said school district, and shall, with the other papers and records of the school district, be handed over by them to their successors in office, and to no one else. If a vacancy shall occur in the office of trustee for said district, it shall be filled by appointment from the two or one remaining in office. The said trustees shall hold and exercise the functions of their office until their successors are duly qualified; and said trustees are hereby declared to be vested with all the power and rights and privileges of trustees of common school districts, as accorded to them under the general laws of the State. The said trustees shall elect one of themselves chairman of the board, and he, as such, shall sign all their orders and records.

§ 3. That said trustees shall carefully ascertain the number of children within said district between the ages of six and twenty years, and make report thereof to the common school commissioner of Barren county at the same time and under the same restrictions that is required of the trustees of common school districts by the common school law of this State, and said commissioner shall report the same to the Superintendent of Public Instruction for the State; and in the disbursement of the public school money, from time to time, said district shall be entitled to receive its due proportion with others in the State, and the same shall be paid to said trustees as such moneys are by law to be paid to other trustees.

§ 4. That at any time after the first day of August, 1869, the said trustees of said district may submit to the voters of said district a proposition to levy a tax of any sum not exceeding twenty-five cents on the one hundred dollars' worth of taxable estate within said district—that is to say, such estate of every kind as is taxable for common school purposes under the laws of State—for the benefit of common schools in said district. The vote upon such proposition shall be polled as is now done under the laws for the election of trustees; but, before it is taken, there shall be at least twenty days' public notice thereof by printed advertisements posted on said courthouse door and at six other public places in said district, signed by the trustees. The election or poll upon the question shall be conducted in all respects as other elections for county or State officers. The trustees shall appoint a clerk of the election, who shall take an oath that he will truly and faithfully perform the duties of clerk of such election as required by law. Two of said trustees shall preside as judges at the election, and one of them shall act as sheriff or crying officer. There shall be a regular poll-book made out, in which the clerk, under the supervision of the judges and acting sheriff, shall record the name of each voter, showing who voted for, and who voted against, the levying of the tax. The poll shall be

1869.

opened at eight o'clock in the morning and closed at four in the evening. The poll-book shall be certified in writing, signed by the clerk and said judges and acting sheriff, showing the result of the election, and shall be filed away amongst the papers and books of said district. A record of said election and its result shall be made by said trustees on their record; the notice of said election shall also be recorded. In taking said election the clerk shall ask each voter the question "Are you for or against levying the tax now being voted upon for common school purposes in this district?" and the vote shall be recorded as the answer suggests.

§ 5. That if a majority of the qualified voters of said district shall vote for the tax, the said trustees are hereby empowered, and it shall be their duty, to levy the same upon the taxable estate aforesaid within said district as shall appear from the commissioners' books of said county, showing the last assessment, prior to said election, of the taxables in said district. The said trustees shall make out said assessment and levy from said commissioners' books, showing a list of the persons and the amount to be collected from each, and record the same, from time to time, in their record book. They shall deliver said list and assessment to the town constable or marshal of Glasgow and take his receipt therefor; and it shall be his duty to collect the same and pay it over to the chairman of said board of trustees, one half on or before the first day of February, and the other half on or before the first day of June of each year. Said officers—constable and marshal—are hereby vested with the same powers to levy and distrain and sell property for the collection of said taxes that sheriffs have in collecting the State revenue, and said power of levy and distraint shall continue till the taxes are paid; and if any one owing said taxes shall be or reside or remove outside of said district or the county of Barren, his or her property shall be subject to levy and sale for said taxes by said constable or marshal, if in Barren county, or any sheriff or constable of the Commonwealth in the county where such defaulter may be found in the State.

§ 6. That if said constable or marshal, to whom said list and assessment of taxes shall be delivered for collection, shall fail or neglect to pay over the same to said chairman of said board of trustees at the times as fixed in this act, such defaulting officer, and the securities in his official bond, shall be responsible for such amount as he fails to pay over on or before that day, and twenty-five per cent. damages thereon, recoverable by motion on his bond in the Barren circuit court, or any other court having jurisdiction of the same: *Provided, however,*

Ten days' notice of such motion shall first be given : *And provided further*, That if said officer shall, on said day, when under this act he is required to pay in said tax, produce, and file a delinquent list, sworn to in all respects as sheriffs are required to swear to their delinquent lists to get credit for them under the law, he shall not be liable to such recovery; but a certified copy of such delinquent list shall be placed back in said officer's hands, and a receipt taken therefor; and he shall be held thereafter, from time [to time], to account for the same under the same rules and regulations as to the original list. The said constable or marshal shall have as compensation for collecting said taxes — per cent. upon each dollar thereof; and whenever he shall levy upon property to sell the same, he shall have thirty cents for each levy, and such expenses as he shall incur in preserving the property before sale, and the power to levy and distrain for collection of said taxes shall continue to be in said constable, sheriff, and marshal for five years from and after each assessment.

§ 7. That said taxes, when collected and paid over to said chairman of said board of trustees, shall be by said trustees, with all sums received by them from the common school fund of the State, as hereinbefore provided, applied and used in having taught two common schools in said district, one a male school and the other a female school, ten months of each year or for such length of time as the funds will justify, taking care that each school shall be taught the same length of time each year. If said trustees can secure the tuition of said schools, one in Urania College and the other in Allen Lodge Female School, now located and carried on in Glasgow, upon terms equitable and just in the opinion of said trustees, they shall do so from time to time: *Provided, however*, Said trustees shall make out and return their annual reports as other common school trustees are required to do.

§ 8. That in submitting the question of taxation to the voters of said district as provided in this act, the trustees shall designate in the notice the length of time or number of years it is proposed the tax shall continue ; and if it is voted upon the district as hereinbefore provided, it shall then be the duty of the trustees to cause its collection each year of the time it is so voted, and apply it as aforesaid : *Provided, however*, The trustees may, at any time, reduce the per cent. of tax equally upon each list upon the pro rata principle, if, in their judgment, the wants of the district will justify it; and when the time for which it is voted shall expire, the trustees may again submit another proposition for taxation to the district for the same purposes, under the same rules and regulations, restrictions and authorities, of this act; and if it is carried, proceed to collect and apply it for the same purposes and under like restrictions.

§ 9. That at the same time or times the vote is taken in said district upon the question of taxing the property of the district for the purposes aforesaid, the question shall also be submitted as a part of the same proposition, whether each white male citizen of the district, twenty-one years old, shall be taxed and assessed one dollar capitation tax for the purposes aforesaid; and in the event of the question being carried as aforesaid, it shall be the duty of said trustees, in making out the said list of assessment of taxes as directed in a former part of this act, to include in that assessment one dollar capitation tax against each of the male white citizens of said district, to be ascertained as aforesaid from said commissioners' books, and cause the same to be collected as aforesaid; and when collected, the same shall be part and parcel of the school fund of said district, and used as aforesaid.

§ 10. That before any chairman of the said board of trustees shall be allowed to receive any of the moneys aforesaid, he shall execute bond, with approved security, in the county court of Barren county, to the Commonwealth of Kentucky, conditioned that he will faithfully perform all the duties of trustee of said district and pay over and account for all moneys which shall come to his hands under this act. The bond shall be approved by the county court and entered in full upon the records of said court, and filed away and preserved among the records of said court by the clerk thereof. The clerk shall receive a fee of fifty cents for his services in taking the bond and performing the other duties assigned him under this act, to be paid by said chairman. Any person injured by the failures or neglects of said chairman in the discharge of his duties under the law, may sue upon the bond as relator, and have judgment according to the justice of the case.

§ 11. That said trustees shall have, and be allowed to retain out of said moneys, one dollar per day each for each day he or they are engaged in the performance of their duties under this act. The clerk provided for in the elections aforesaid shall be allowed one dollar per day for his services, and one dollar for furnishing and making each book, to be paid by the chairman of said board of trustees out of said funds; and the said chairman, for his services as chairman, in assuming the responsibilities of receiving and disbursing said money, shall be allowed to retain two

1869.   and a half per cent. on all sums that may come to his
hands as such.

§ 12. That said trustees shall keep a full record of all
their proceedings, which shall be signed by their chairman; and upon their going out of office, they shall deliver
the same, with all papers pertaining to their office, to
their successors; and the said chairman shall deliver over
to his successor all money or other effects in his hands as
such. The records of the district shall show a full exposi-
tion of his accounts, the money received, how, and to
whom, and when paid out, and correct vouchers on file
for each item paid out. The said record shall at all and
any time be open to the inspection of any and every
person of said district; and when asked to do so, said
chairman shall deliver to any one a certified copy of
any order-minute thereof, the person calling for it paying
twenty-five cents for such copy. Any trustee elected and
qualified under this act, who shall willfully violate the
provisions of this act, shall be subject to indictment, and
fined in any sum not exceeding five hundred dollars.
Any person voting at any of said elections, who shall not
be entitled to vote under the law, shall be subject to like
indictment, and fined fifty dollars. Any person [who]
shall mutilate, destroy, or steal said record books of said
trustees for said district shall be subject to indictment, and
sentenced to the penitentiary for at least one year, and
longer if a jury so finds.

§ 13. That the election provided for in this act to come
off for trustees—first Saturday in May, 1869—and every
election thereafter for trustees under this act, shall be held
and conducted by the presiding judge of the Barren county
court and jailer of Barren county, who shall be judges
thereof; the clerk of the Barren county court, who shall
be clerk, and the marshal of Glasgow, who shall act as
sheriff of the election.

§ 14. This act to take effect from its passage.

Approved February 20, 1869.

CHAPTER 1544.

AN ACT to amend the Charter of the Green River Female College.

WHEREAS, Rev. Thos. H. Storts, principal of the Green
River Female College, is now conducting that institution
at his residence, in Bowling Green, Kentucky; and whereas, the charter of said institution does not authorize it to
be conducted at that place; therefore,

Be it enacted by the General Assembly of the Commonwealth of Kentucky:

§ 1. That all the rights conferred by said charter upon the principal of said institution be, and they are hereby, conferred upon said Rev. Thomas H. Storts, with the right on his part, and on the part of the board of trustees of said institution, to have its location at the residence of said Storts, or any other place in the city of Bowling Green, subject to be located and relocated by said board at their pleasure, with all the rights and privileges given by said charter to said board and said principal and his and their successors, subject in all cases to the action of said board as to the rights of said principal and his successors.

§ 2. This act to be in force from and after its passage.

Approved February 20, 1869.

CHAPTER 1545.

AN ACT for the benefit of the Clark County Institute.

Be it enacted by the General Assembly of the Commonwealth of Kentucky:

§ 1. That the president and secretary of the board of trustees of the Clark County Institute be, and they are hereby, invested with the power to make and execute such mortgages or other conveyances of the real estate of said institute as may, from time to time, be directed by an order of said board of trustees, entered on their record book.

§ 2. All such mortgages or other conveyances shall recite the date, and also the substance of the order of the board of trustees directing the same to be made.

§ 3. The board of trustees shall have and use a common seal.

§ 4. All mortgages or other conveyances shall be acknowledged by the president and secretary of the board of trustees, or proved in the manner required by law for conveyances of real estate; and when so acknowledged or proved, shall be admitted to record in the same manner as other deeds. All mortgages or other conveyances made in pursuance of the authority of this act, shall be executed under the seal of the corporation. All such mortgages and deeds executed and recorded in pursuance of this act shall be received as evidence in the courts of this Commonwealth in the same manner, and with the same effect, as other conveyances of real estate.

§ 5. For the purpose of paying off the indebtedness of the institute, the board of trustees are authorized to borrow any sum of money not exceeding ten thousand dollars, at any rate of interest that may be agreed upon, not exceeding ten per centum per annum; and the president and secretary may, in obedience to an order of the board of trustees, execute the note of the corporation, under the corporate seal, for any such sum as may be thus borrowed; and the board of trustees may secure the payment of said loan, or indemnify any surety of the board against loss by reason thereof, by a mortgage or other conveyance of its real estate, executed as herein provided.

§ 6. This act shall take effect from and after its passage.

Approved February 20, 1869.

CHAPTER 1546.

AN ACT to amend the Charter of the Maysville and Mt. Sterling Turnpike Road Company.

Be it enacted by the General Assembly of the Commonwealth of Kentucky:

§ 1. That the Maysville and Mount Sterling turnpike road company shall have power and authority, in lieu of the present rates of toll upon wagons traveling upon their road, to charge the following (if said company shall see proper), viz: For each and every heavy wagon, drawn by four horses, weighing with its load ten thousand pounds and under, at each and every gate through which said wagon shall pass, fifty cents: *Provided*, That the distance traveled shall be five miles, and if less than five miles, then they shall be charged in proportion to the distance traveled; and for each and every hundred pounds above ten thousand contained in any wagon, two and one half cents in addition upon every hundred pounds shall be charged at each gate up to twelve thousand pounds; and for every hundred pounds above twelve thousand pounds contained in any wagon, five cents per hundred pounds shall be charged at each gate in addition.

§ 2. That said company may erect scales at such convenient place or places along the route of their road as they may designate, for the purpose of determining the weight of wagons and their contents; and may, at their pleasure, require wagons using their road to be weighed (together with their loads) upon such scales; and upon the failure or refusal of any such wagon to weigh as aforesaid when required by said company, its officers or agents, the same or owners thereof shall forfeit and pay to said company the sum of ten dollars for each and every failure or refusal, to be recovered as now provided by the charter of said company in other cases: *Provided however,* That the wagoner shall be at no expense for weighing.

§ 3. That said company shall have power and authority, whenever they deem it advisable, to abandon or change the location of any part of their road, and relocate the same upon new or different ground, with all the powers, rights, remedies, and privileges in this respect provided and conferred in their charter, and subject to the same restrictions and liabilities.

§ 4. This act shall take effect thirty days after its passage; and the General Assembly of the Commonwealth shall have power to repeal or alter this act.

Approved February 20, 1869.

CHAPTER 1547.

AN ACT for the benefit of James A. Ward, late Sheriff of Johnson County.

WHEREAS, At the June term, 1862, of the fiscal court, judgment was rendered against James A. Ward, sheriff of Johnson county, for the revenue due from said county for the year 1861; and whereas, said Ward, in the years 1862-3, paid into the Treasury of the State the principal and cost of said judgment; and whereas, the failure of said Ward to pay the revenue due from said county for said year, before judgment was rendered thereon, was owing to his being prevented from collecting the same by reason of threats against his life, and the disturbed condition of the country; and whereas, the greater part of the revenue due for said year is yet outstanding and unpaid, and the judgment and costs aforesaid were paid by said Ward from his undividual funds; therefore,

Be it enacted by the General Assembly of the Commonwealth of Kentucky:

§ 1. That the interest upon said judgment be, and the same is hereby, remitted.

§ 2. This act shall take effect from its passage.

Approved February 20, 1869.

CHAPTER 1548.

AN ACT to amend the Charter of the Deposit Bank of Frankfort.

Be it enacted by the General Assembly of the Commonwealth of Kentucky:

§ 1. That said bank shall hereafter be authorized at all annual elections to elect eight directors in lieu of the number now allowed by their charter, who shall hereafter elect out of their number annually a president.

§ 2. That the present board of directors be authorized to elect two directors to serve until their next annual election.

§ 3. That said bank be authorized to declare semiannually dividends of the profits arising from their business.

§ 4. That this act take effect from its passage.

Approved February 23, 1869.

CHAPTER 1549.

AN ACT to amend the Charter of the Covington and Cincinnati Bridge Company.

Be it enacted by the General Assembly of the Commonwealth of Kentucky:

§ 1. That the said company, after the election in 1869, shall hold its annual elections for officers, and have its regular meetings of stockholders, on the second Wednesday in January, and then the annual report of the affairs of the company shall be made. All stockholders who have paid up stock shall be entitled to vote, in person or by proxy, one vote for each share of stock so held; and the authority to the proxy need not be recorded.

§ 2. That said company may construct or purchase and use such manufacturing establishments, machine shops, tools, machinery, and apparatus connected therewith, as may be considered necessary in making repairs, improvements, and conveniences to and about said bridge or the approaches thereto, or for the use thereof, to promote the facilities of travel and transportation, or to the advantage of the company; and may purchase, hold, or rent property for these purposes; and may purchase, hold, and run ferries from and to the city of Covington, and do and perform all the necessary acts in relation thereto; but the rates of ferriage shall be subject to the control of the courts as in the case of ferries owned by individuals; and such ferry or ferries shall be established by the county court as other ferries, upon the application of said Covington and Cincinnati Bridge Company; and, when so established, shall, in every respect, be regulated, controlled, and governed by the laws of this Commonwealth in relation to ferries, and shall be required to give the same bond, and shall in all respects be held to the same responsibilities as other ferries; and the right of said bridge company to run a ferry or ferries shall be forfeited in the same manner and for the same causes as other ferries are forfeited: *Provided*, That nothing herein contained shall be so construed as to in any manner abridge or interfere with the rights or privileges of the present or any future owner or proprietor of any ferry or ferries. between the cities of Covington and Cincinnati to use and run the same as is now, or may hereafter be, provided by law; nor to interfere with the establishment of any other ferries to run to and from the city of Covington.

§ 3. That this act shall take effect from and after its passage.

Approved February 23, 1869.

———

CHAPTER 1550.

AN ACT to incorporate the Clark and Montgomery Turnpike Road Company.

Be it enacted by the General Assembly of the Commonwealth of Kentucky:

§ 1. That a corporation be, and the same is hereby, created, under the name and style of the Clark and Montgomery turnpike road company, which shall have perpetual succession; have power to sue and be sued, contract and be contracted with; have and use a common seal, and to do all acts necessary and proper to the execution of the powers herein granted.

§ 2. The purpose of said corporation is to construct a turnpike road from a convenient point on the Winchester and Red River Iron Works turnpike road, near the house of John G. Wills, to some convenient point on the Montgomery county line, on or near the lands of Asa C. Barrow.

§ 3. The capital stock of said company shall not exceed fifty thousand dollars, and shall be divided into shares of one hundred dollars each, and Burgess Ecton, Asa C. Barrow, Andrew H. Hart, Columbus Thompson, Dudley Flyn, and Harrison Thompson, are appointed commissioners to receive subscriptions to the capital stock of said company, and to organize the same.

§ 4. Whenever, in the opinion of said commissioners, or such of them as shall act under the authority of this act, a sum sufficient to make it prudent to commence the construction of said road, said commissioners shall appoint a time and place for a meeting of the stockholders (and shall advertise the same for ten days previously thereto, by written or printed notices), who shall elect six of their number directors. Said directors shall have supervision, management, and control of the said company and its affairs, and shall elect one of their number president, and another secretary and treasurer. Said president and the secretary and treasurer shall give bond to the company, with good security, bound therein for the faithful discharge of their respective duties. Any

1869.

person aggrieved may, as relator, maintain an action on said bonds, which may be the subject of action, from time to time, as any misfeasance or malfeasance may occur on the part of said officers. The directors shall hold their offices for one year, and until their successors are duly elected. At all elections by the stockholders they shall be entitled to one vote for every share of stock owned, and they may vote in person or by proxy.

§ 5. The directors shall have power to regulate the width and grade of said road, the width and depth of the metal to be placed thereon; but in all other respects the said road shall be constructed as required by the act incorporating the Winchester and Mount Sterling turnpike road company.

§ 6. When five continuous miles of said road are completed, and the president shall file an affidavit with the county judge, to the effect that the road thus far completed has been constructed in all respects as required by this charter, together with the affidavit of a civil engineer of ability and experience to the same effect, it shall be the duty of the county judge of Clark county to make an order authorizing the erection of a gate, at which the company may take tolls as authorized by the Revised Statutes; and whenever an additional five miles are completed, and the affidavits above mentioned are filed, it shall be the duty of the county judge to authorize the erection of an additional gate.

§ 7. The company may acquire the right of way, and land for toll-houses and quarries, in the mode provided by the Revised Statutes.

§ 8. The Legislature reserves the right to amend, alter, and repeal this act at pleasure.

§ 9. This act shall take effect from its passage.

Approved February 23, 1869.

———

CHAPTER 1551.

AN ACT for the benefit of the Richmond and Big Hill Turnpike Road Company.

Be it enacted by the General Assembly of the Commonwealth of Kentucky:

§ 1. That the Richmond and Big Hill turnpike road company are hereby empowered to remove the first tollgate on their road, nearest to the town of Richmond, to a point without the present town limits, three fourths of a mile or more from the court-house.

§ 2. They may acquire title to one acre of land at any place they may select for such toll-gate site, by purchase

or legal proceedings, for said toll-gate purposes, and use
and occupy the same.

§ 3. This act to take effect from its passage.

Approved February 23, 1869.

CHAPTER 1552.

AN ACT to amend the Richmond and Barnes' Mill Turnpike Road Company.

Be it enacted by the General Assembly of the Commonwealth of Kentucky:

§ 1. That the charter of the Richmond and Barnes' Mill turnpike road company be, and is hereby, so amended as to allow the company to erect or remove a toll-gate within one mile of the court-house in the town of Richmond.

§ 2. This act to take effect from its passage.

Approved February 23, 1869.

CHAPTER 1553.

AN ACT for the benefit of the Cincinnati, Lexington, and East Tennessee Railroad Company.

Be it enacted by the General Assembly of the Commonwealth of Kentucky:

§ 1. That the time within which the Cincinnati, Lexington, and East Tennessee Railroad Company shall begin work upon their road, as prescribed in the act incorporating said company, approved March 9th, 1867, be, and the same is hereby, extended one year, viz: until March 9th, 1870.

§ 2. This act to take effect from its passage.

Approved February 23, 1869.

CHAPTER 1554.

AN ACT for the benefit of the Clark and Bourbon Turnpike Road Company.

Be it enacted by the General Assembly of the Commonwealth of Kentucky:

§ 1. That the Clark and Bourbon Turnpike Road Company may erect one gate upon that part of the road now completed, on the end next the Lexington and Winchester pike; and said company may charge and collect upon their said road at said gate such tolls as the directors may determine upon, not exceeding, however, the rates now allowed by the Revised Statutes.

1869. § 2. This act shall take effect from and after its passage.

Approved February 23, 1869.

CHAPTER 1555.

AN ACT to amend the Charter of the Shelbyville and Louisville Turnpike Road Company.

Be it enacted by the General Assembly of the Commonwealth of Kentucky:

§ 1. That the board of internal improvement for Shelby county shall have full power to remove their third toll-gate on said road, provided they do not locate it within less than three fourths of a mile of the court-house for Shelby county.

§ 2. That it shall not be lawful for any person riding on horseback, or driving any sort of vehicle, to pass over any of the "lattice bridges" on said road faster than a walk; and he or they so offending shall be fined not less than two nor more than five dollars for each offense, one half of such fine to go to the informer, the other half to go to said company, recoverable before any justice of the peace for the county.

§ 3. This act to take effect from and after its passage.

Approved February 23, 1869.

CHAPTER 1556.

AN ACT to repeal section nine of an act, entitled "An act to incorporate the Mount Carmel and Fox Springs Turnpike Road Company, and to levy a tax to aid in building said road."

Be it enacted by the General Assembly of the Commonwealth of Kentucky:

§ 1. That section nine (9) of an act, entitled "An act to incorporate the Mount Carmel and Fox Springs turnpike road company, and to levy a tax to aid in building said road," approved February 13th, 1868, is hereby repealed.

§ 2. This act shall take effect from and after its passage.

Approved February 23, 1869.

CHAPTER 1557.

AN ACT for the benefit of the Mount Sterling and Owingsville Turnpike Road Company.

Be it enacted by the General Assembly of the Commonwealth of Kentucky:

§ 1. That the president and directors of the Mount Sterling and Owingsville turnpike road company shall have power and authority to locate a toll-gate near the town of Owingsville, at any point on their road not nearer than three-quarters of a mile from the limits of said town, as they existed prior to the passage of an act approved 9th March, 1868, entitled "An act to extend the corporate limits of the town of Owingsville, Bath county."

§ 2. This act shall take effect from its passage.

Approved February 23, 1869.

CHAPTER 1558.

AN ACT declaring Clark's River navigable.

Be it enacted by the General Assembly of the Commonwealth of Kentucky:

§ 1. That the east fork of Clark's river be, and the same is hereby, declared a navigable stream from its mouth to the bridge on the road leading from Benton to Aurora; but this act shall not operate so as to interfere with the right of any county court or gravel road company to erect bridges across said river, or with the bridges now on said river.

§ 2. This act shall take effect from its passage.

Approved February 23, 1869.

CHAPTER 1559.

AN ACT for the benefit of the Sureties of B. W. Cleaver, late Sheriff of Grayson County, in his Revenue Bond for 1866.

Be it enacted by the General Assembly of the Commonwealth of Kentucky:

§ 1. That the Auditor is hereby directed and required to draw his warrant on the Treasury for the sum of one hundred and five dollars and forty-two cents, in favor of the sureties of B. W. Cleaver, late sheriff of Grayson county, in his revenue bond for 1866, said sum being the amount of damages paid by said sureties on account of the defalcation of said sheriff on his revenue for 1866.

§ 2. That this act take effect from its passage.

Approved February 23, 1869.

CHAPTER 1560.

AN ACT authorizing the County Judge of Green County to levy a Tax to
repair the Court-house of Green County.

*Be it enacted by the General Assembly of the Commonwealth
of Kentucky:*

§ 1. That the county judge of Green county shall levy a
tax of fifty cents upon each male citizen of Green county,
whose names were listed for taxation by the assessor of
said county in the year 1868, and is a citizen of said county
at the time of the levy, the fund arising from said levy to
be collected and applied to the repairing and refitting of
the court-house in Greensburg; and it shall be the duty of
the sheriff of said county to collect the same, in the same
manner as the county levy is now collectable by law, and
shall have the same compensation therefor, and be liable ·
upon his official bond therefor in the same way; and he
shall pay over the same when collected to such person as
the county judge may direct.

§ 2. It shall be the duty of the county judge to appoint
some suitable person to superintend the repairing and
refitting said court-house, and may allow him reasonable
compensation for so doing, to be paid out of said fund.

§ 3. The county judge shall make said levy at the first
regular county court after the passage of this act, or as
soon thereafter as can be done; and said levy shall be collected in the year 1869.

§ 4. This act to take effect from its passage.

Approved February 23, 1869.

CHAPTER 1561.

AN ACT to repeal an act, entitled "An act to establish two additional Justices' Districts in Mason County," approved February 13th, 1868, and the
act amendatory thereof, approved March 5th, 1868.

*Be it enacted by the General Assembly of the Commonwealth
of Kentucky:*

§ 1. That the act, entitled "An act to establish two additional justices' districts in Mason county," approved February 13th, 1868, and the act amendatory thereof, approved
March 5th, 1868, be, and the same are hereby, repealed.

§ 2. This act shall be in force thirty days after its passage.

Approved February 23, 1869.

CHAPTER 1562.

AN ACT to incorporate the Olympian Springs and Slate Bridge Turnpike Road Company.

*Be it enacted by the General Assembly of the Commonwealth
of Kentucky:*

§ 1. That a company is hereby formed and created a
body-politic and corporate, by the name and style of the
Olympian Springs and Slate Bridge turnpike road company, to consist of a president and five directors, with
the stockholders, for the purpose of making a road from
the Olympian Springs to the Slate bridge, near the mouth
of Spencer creek, on the Mt. Sterling and Spencer turnpike, on the McAdam plan.

§ 2. The capital stock of said company shall be four
thousand dollars, and may be increased to ten thousand
dollars, at the option of the directors, to be divided into
shares of fifty dollars each; and books for the subscription of stock shall be opened on the 1st day of May,
1869, or as soon thereafter as the commissioners may
direct, at Owingsville, Ficklin's tan-yard, and Mt. Sterling, and continue open until the stock shall be subscribed, under the direction of A. N. Crooks, Jno. Ficklin,
Jno. Botts, James Anderson Putnam, and James Ewing,
at Ficklin's tan-yard; J. A. J. Lee, Joseph H. Richart,
James Ficklin, James M. Nesbitt, and B. F. Perry, at
Owingsville; Hon. B. J. Peters, J. M. McCormack, Jas.
Gatewood, and Wm. Hoffman, at Mt. Sterling, or any
two or more of said commissioners, at each of the foregoing places, shall be empowered to act. The commissioners shall procure books, and the subscribers shall
enter into the following obligation: "We, whose names
are hereto subscribed, do respectively promise to pay to
the president and directors of Olympian Springs and
Slate Bridge turnpike road company, the sum of fifty
dollars for each share of stock set opposite to our respective names, in such proportions, and at such times,
as the said president and directors may require."

§ 3. So soon as forty shares are subscribed to the capital stock of said company, it shall be the duty of said
commissioners to give notice, in such manner as they
may think proper, for a meeting of the stockholders, at
such time and place as they may designate, for the purpose of electing a president and five directors, and one
vote shall be allowed for each share of stock; and the
said officers shall continue in office for one year, and
until their successors are, in like manner, duly elected.
A majority of the board shall be competent to transact
business.

§ 4. So soon as said company is organized by the election of officers, the president and directors shall possess

1869.   all the powers, rights, and privileges, and shall and may
do all acts and things necessary for laying out and causing a survey of the most practicable route for said road,
and for carrying on and completing said road; and may
have and enjoy all the rights and privileges, and be subject to all the duties, qualifications and restrictions, that
are given and granted to the Carlisle and Sharpsburg
turnpike road company by an act approved 26th February, 1847.

§ 5. The president and directors shall fix and regulate
the elevation and grade of said road; the width and the
part thereof to be covered with stone; shall designate the
place for the erection of gates, and may fix the rates of
tolls, and regulate and change the same; the width of the
road shall not exceed thirty feet, and the part covered
with stone shall not be less than twelve feet.

§ 6. The Legislature reserves the right to alter or amend
this charter at any time after its passage.

§ 7. That said company may, and is hereby, authorized
to take subscriptions to the capital stock of said road
company, in lands on and near to the line of said road;
the land to be valued by two disinterested persons, to
be agreed upon by the subscriber of such stock, and the
president and directors of said road and their umpire,
in case of disagreement, or the owner of the land and
subscriber of such stock and the board of directors, may
agree upon the price.

§ 8. That this act shall take effect from and after its
passage.

Approved February 23, 1869.

CHAPTER 1563.

AN ACT to incorporate the Richmond, Union, and Kentucky River Turnpike Road Company.

*Be it enacted by the General Assembly of the Commonwealth
of Kentucky:*

§ 1. That a company is hereby created a body-politic
and corporate, under the name and style of the Richmond, Union, and Kentucky River turnpike company,
for the purpose of constructing a turnpike road from
Richmond to or near Union Meeting-house, on to the
Kentucky river at or near the mouth of Muddy creek,
in Madison county, Kentucky.

§ 2. That the capital stock of said company shall be
twenty thousand dollars.

§ 3. That Wm. J. Walker, Danl. White, Josiah Gentry,
David Noble, Butler Dunn, Robt. Chenault, Thomas B.
Reem, John Brock, Joel P. Powell, Louis Hish, Milo Bax-

ter, and S. Parish, be appointed commissioners, who shall have the same rights, powers, and duties, as are conferred on the commissioners or corporators of the Richmond and Barnes' Mill turnpike company, approved ———.

§ 4. That all the provisions of said act shall apply to the company hereby incorporated, except as to the names of commissioners.

§ 5. This act to take effect from its passage.

Approved February 23, 1869.

CHAPTER 1564.

AN ACT to incorporate the Fox Run and Bullskin Turnpike Road, in Shelby County.

Be it enacted by the General Assembly of the Commonwealth of Kentucky:

§ 1. There is hereby formed a corporation, under the name of the Fox Run and Bullskin Creek turnpike road company, in Shelby county, with power to construct a turnpike road from the Eminence and Fox Run turnpike road, at or near the house of Ellen Hopkins, so as to intersect the Smithfield and Shelbyville turnpike road at or near the northeast corner of John F. Hopkins' land, on any route the president and directors thereof may determine. Newton Bright, Albert G. Drane, Thos. G. Dunlap, James W. Crawford, and ——— ———, or any two of them as commissioners, may open books at any time or place, and receive subscriptions to the capital stock thereof until enough has been subscribed to complete the same. The shares of stock shall be fifty dollars, and each share shall entitle the holder thereof at all elections to cast one vote for each share held by him, either in person or by proxy; and when a sufficient amount of stock has been subscribed to complete the road, the commissioners acting shall, by written notice posted conspicuously in the vicinity of the road at three places, call a meeting of the stockholders, at a time and place therein fixed, to elect five directors to manage the affairs of the company, who shall continue in office one year, and until their successors are elected and qualified.

§ 2. Said road shall be constructed twelve feet wide of macadamized stone, or of part stone and part gravel, as the board of managers may determine; and where the road enters upon and passes out of the land of Jilson Yates, the said Yates may demand the company to erect two good and substantial gates across the same, and it is hereby made lawful for the same to be kept there at the pleasure of said Yates.

§ 3. That they shall have all the rights, privileges, and profits arising from tolls or otherwise, and be subject to the same penalties and forfeitures as are allowed by chapter 103 of the Revised Statutes relating to turnpike and plank roads, from section one to section thirty-seven inclusive, so far as they are applicable, and not herein otherwise provided for.

Approved February 23, 1869.

CHAPTER 1565.

AN ACT to amend the Charter and supplemental and amended Charter of the Harrodsburg and Cornishville Turnpike.

Be it enacted by the General Assembly of the Commonwealth of Kentucky:

§ 1. That the charter and supplemental and amended charters of the Harrodsburg and Cornishville turnpike road be so amended that said company may, and they are hereby, authorized and empowered, with the consent of a majority of the justices of the peace for Mercer county, to build and construct said road as follows, to-wit: The road-bed of said road shall be eighteen feet in width, and the rock or metal thereon shall be fourteen feet in width, instead of twenty feet for the bed, and sixteen feet for the metal, as the charters aforesaid now require.

§ 2. The action of the president and directors of said road, heretofore taken, in letting out contracts for the construction of said road, in accordance to the provisions of this amendment, are hereby legalized.

§ 3. That the corporate name of the said company is hereby changed to the Harrodsburg and Duncansville turnpike road company.

§ 4. This act to be a law from its passage.

Approved February 23, 1869.

CHAPTER 1566.

AN ACT to amend the Charter of the Burlington and Florence Turnpike Road Company.

Be it enacted by the General Assembly of the Commonwealth of Kentucky:

§ 1. That it shall and may be lawful for the president and directors of said turnpike road company to sell and convey the house and lot formerly occupied by the gate-keeper on said road, for such price, and to such person, as they may deem proper, and to make a deed of conveyance therefor, to be signed and acknowledged by the president of said company, which shall pass the title to said property.

§ 2. It shall and may be lawful for said president and directors to contract for, purchase, and hold, to them and to their successors forever, any quantity of land, not exceeding five acres, at the site of each toll-gate to be erected across said road, and the same may be erected at any point or points outside of said towns of Burlington and Florence: *Provided*, That not more than two gates shall be erected on said road.

§ 2. That from and after the passage of this act the following rates of toll may be collected at the gate or gates on said road, to-wit : For each horse, mule, jack, or jennet, per mile, one cent; for each head of cattle, per mile, one half cent; for each hog, sheep, or goat, per mile, one third cent; for each buggy, sulky, or gig, exclusive of the team by which it is drawn, per mile, one and a half cents; for each pleasure carriage, exclusive of the team by which it is drawn, per mile, two cents; for every spring wagon, exclusive of the team by which it is drawn, per mile, two cents; for every road or jolt wagon, or cart, exclusive of the team by which it is drawn, per mile, three cents; for each omnibus, stage, or other public vehicle for the transportation of passengers, exclusive of the team by which it is drawn, per mile, five cents; for each sled or sleigh, same as a buggy.

§ 4. That it shall be lawful for guardians to vote the stock of their wards at the annual elections. In case the president or any one of the directors shall die, resign, or vacate his or their office or offices, in any manner, those remaining in office shall have power to appoint a successor or successors to serve until the next regular election; and elections may be held at any place in the town of Burlington.

§ 5. That so much of the act and amendments thereto, to which this is an amendment, as may be in conflict herewith, are hereby repealed.

§ 6. This act to take effect from its passage.

Approved February 23, 1869.

CHAPTER 1567.

AN ACT to incorporate the Doyle's Lane and Wilsonville Turnpike Road Company.

Be it enacted by the General Assembly of the Commonwealth of Kentucky:

§ 1. That Jack Allen, William Beckham, Jonathan Vandyke, Ed. Shouse, Blanton Baker, Lewis Long, and Abraham Whitaker, of Shelby county; Nathaniel Russell, Mike

Huffman, and Sol. Norman, of Spencer county; Ambrose
Carpenter, Dr. Taylor, and James Lancaster, of Jefferson
county, be, and they are hereby, constituted a board of
managers, for the purpose of constructing ·a turnpike road
from Doyle's Lane, on the Shelbyville and Taylorsville
turnpike, so as to cross Buck creek at Buck Creek Church;
thence to Fields' saw-mill; thence to the Louisville and
Taylorsville pike, between Wilsonville and Fisherville;
and, that they may be the better enabled to effect the said
object, the said managers are hereby constituted a body-
politic and corporate, in deed and in law, under the style
and name of "The Board of Managers of the Doyle's
Lane and Wilsonville Turnpike Road;" and under that
style and name shall have perpetual succession, and all
the privileges, immunities, and franchises of a body-politic and corporate; and as such shall be capable of purchasing, taking, and holding, to them and their successors
and assigns, and of selling and conveying, in fee simple,
all such lands, tenements, and estates, real, personal, or
mixed, as shall be necessary to them in the prosecution of
their work; and to sue and be sued, plead and be impleaded, answer and be answered, defend and be defended, before any or all courts of record or other judicial tribunals
whatsoever; and also to make, have, and use a common
seal, and the same to break, alter, and renew at pleasure;
and to do each and every act which a body-politic and
corporate as such may lawfully do.

§ 2. That a majority of the said managers shall constitute a quorum to do business; may appoint a secretary,
treasurer, and all other necessary officers, and prescribe
their duties: *Provided*, The treasurer shall be required to
execute bond, with good security, conditioned faithfully to
perform the duties of his office.

§ 3. That it shall be the duty of the said managers to
keep a book in which to register their transactions. The
said managers shall have power to employ engineers and
fix their salaries; to regulate the terms of subscription of
stock; make calls for proportions of the stock subscribed;
to draw orders on the treasurer for any sums of money
necessary to pay contractors, damages, and other necessary expenses incurred in the prosecution of said work;
such orders shall be signed by their chairman, and be
entered in their book of minutes.

§ 4. That it shall be lawful for said managers, together
with their surveyor, engineer, and chain-carriers, to enter
upon the lands or inclosures through or over which said
turnpike road, or any part thereof, may pass; and examine any quarries in the vicinity that may be necessary for
constructing or repairing said road.

§ 5. That when the said managers shall have decided upon the location of said road, or any part thereof, it shall be lawful for them to enter thereon with tools, wagons, carts, and workmen, in order to prosecute said work; they shall have power to go upon or over any lands, with wagons or other vehicles, for the purpose of hauling stone or other material necessary for the construction of said road, having first given notice to the owners or occupants of said lands, and having first made proper compensation for such materials; and in event of a disagreement as to the value of said materials or damages arising from their removal, with the owners of such land, then it shall be lawful for said managers to apply to some justice of the peace for the county in which said property may lie for a writ of *ad quod damnum;* and said justice shall be, and he is hereby, authorized and required to issue said writ, directed to any constable of such county, to summon twelve discreet housekeepers of the vicinage to meet at some convenient place on the line of said road at the time and place mentioned in said writ.

§ 6. That it shall be the duty of said justice of the peace to attend at the time and place mentioned in the writ and conduct said inquest; the defendants in said writ shall have at least five days' notice in writing previous to the holding said inquest; either party shall have the right to object to any of the said jurymen for cause shown, of which the justice will determine.

§ 7. That it may be lawful for said managers to buy or condemn any quantity of land, not exceeding five acres, at the site of each toll-gate, for the purpose of erecting thereon a toll-house and gate for the use of said road.

§ 8. That said managers shall remain in office one year; and at the expiration of their term of office, an election for a new board, or the same may be elected by the stockholders: *Provided,* No stock shall be voted that has not been fully paid up upon all its calls.

§ 9. That said board of managers shall have power to determine the width of said road, the width and depth of stone, and the degree of elevation of the grade: *Provided,* It shall not be greater than four degrees elevation. Said managers shall have power to fix the rates of toll from time to time: *Provided,* Said rates are no greater, in proportion to the distance traveled on said road, than is now allowed by law on the turnpike roads in Shelby county.

§ 10. This act to take effect from and after its passage.

Approved February 23, 1869.

CHAPTER 1568.

AN ACT to incorporate the Flemingsburg and Mouth of Fox Turnpike Road Company.

Be it enacted by the General Assembly of the Commonwealth of Kentucky:

§ 1. That a company be, and is hereby, created, under the name and style of "The Flemingsburg and Mouth of Fox Turnpike Road Company," for the purpose of constructing an artificial road, on the McAdam's plan, from a point near the toll-gate on the Flemingsburg and Poplar Plains turnpike road to intersect the proposed Poplar Plains and Tilton turnpike, with the privilege of extending it to intersect the Hillsboro and Mouth of Fox turnpike road, the route to be selected by the directors.

§ 2. The capital stock of said company shall be twenty-five thousand dollars, which may be increased to an amount that may be necessary to complete the road, if the above named sum be insufficient, to be divided into shares of fifty dollars each.

§ 3. Books shall be opened for the subscription of stock at any time after the passage of this act, at such place as may be most convenient, under the direction of William Fleming, Theodore Hart, William B. Hendrix, and James E. Smith. That said commissioners, or any one or more of them appointed by this act to open a book or books for the subscription of the capital stock of said company, shall procure a book or books, and the subscribers to the stock of said company shall enter into the following obligation in said book or books, to-wit: We, whose names are hereunto subscribed, do respectively promise to pay to the president, directors, and company of the Flemingsburg and Mouth of Fox turnpike road company the sum of fifty dollars for each and every share of stock in said company set opposite to our names, in such manner and proportions, and at such times, as shall be required by the president and directors of said company, which amount shall be collectable in the proper courts.

§ 4. The book or books of subscription of said stock shall remain open until the whole of the capital stock shall have been taken, or enough to complete the road, and persons may subscribe at any time until the book or books are closed.

§ 5. So soon as one hundred shares in said company be subscribed, it shall be the duty of said commissioners, or some one of them, to give notice of a meeting of the stockholders of said company, to meet in Flemingsburg, for the purpose of choosing officers; said notices to be put up at three of the most public places on the contemplated road ten days previous to said meeting; at which election at least two of said commissioners shall be present, who shall proceed to take the votes by ballot, in person or by proxy, of said stockholders. each stockholder having one vote for every share so held, for a president and five directors, who shall hold their offices for one year, and until their successors are duly elected and qualified. The time and place for all elections after the first shall be fixed by the president and directors of said company for the time being. A majority of the commissioners shall be competent to transact all business. The president and directors shall, before they enter upon the duties of their offices, take an oath before some justice of the peace that they will faithfully discharge the duties of their respective offices, without favor or affection, according to the best of their judgment. After being qualified, they shall appoint a treasurer and such other officers as they may deem necessary, who shall hold his or their offices for one year, and until others are appointed, but removable at the discretion of the president and directors. The treasurer of said company shall, before entering into the duties of his office, give such bond and security and penalty as the president and directors may desire, and the obligation made payable to them, conditioned that he will faithfully discharge the duties of treasurer of said company, and that he will, when called on, pay the amount of money in his hands to the order of the president and directors, and that he will perform the duties required of him by the by-laws of said company.

§ 6. The president and directors, when elected and qualified as aforesaid, shall be a body corporate and politic, in fact and in law, by the name and style of the Flemingsburg and Mouth of Fox Turnpike Road Company; and by the same name shall have perpetual succession, and all the privileges and franchises incident to a corporation; and shall be capable of taking and holding their capital stock, and the increase and profits thereof, and of purchasing, taking, and holding. to them and their successors and assigns, and of selling, transferring, and conveying in fee simple, all such lands, tenements, hereditaments, and estate, real and personal, as shall be necessary to them in the prosecution of their work; and to sue and be sued, plead and be impleaded, answer and be answered, defend and be defended, in courts of record or any other place whatever; and also to have a common seal, and to do all and every other matter or thing which a body-politic or corporate may lawfully do.

§ 7. The president and directors, upon entering upon the duties of their offices, may call upon the stockholders for the payment of such sums on each share, and at such times, as they, in their discretion, may deem expedient.

1869.   § 8. That sections 8th, 9th, 10th, 11th, 12th, 13th, 14th, 15th, 16th, 17th, 18th, 19th, 20th, and 21st of an act, entitled "An act to incorporate the Elizaville and Fairview turnpike road company," approved February 15th, 1858, be, and is hereby, made a part of, and applicable to, this company as a part of its charter.

§ 9. This act shall take effect from and after its passage.

Approved February 23, 1869.

CHAPTER 1569.

AN ACT to amend the Charter of the Female Literary and Benevolent Institution, of Loretto, Marion County.

WHEREAS, It appears to the satisfaction of the General Assembly that the above named literary institution has been in successful operation for many years, imparting to its scholars the benefit of a liberal education, and is still in a condition, with well qualified teachers and professors, to teach all the branches of a literary and ornamental education usually taught in our best female colleges; therefore,

Be it enacted by the General Assembly of the Commonwealth of Kentucky:

§ 1. That the said institution of Loretto be, and is hereby, invested with full power and authority to confer diplomas or other literary honors upon such of her meritorious students as have finished their education in said institution, and who may be deserving of that honor in the judgment of its faculty.

§ 2. This act to take effect from and after its passage.

Approved February 24, 1869.

CHAPTER 1570.

AN ACT to amend an act approved 5th February, 1868, entitled "An act to amend an act approved 18th February, 1860, to empower the County Court of Bath County to make Subscription to the Capital Stock of Turnpike Roads."

Be it enacted by the General Assembly of the Commonwealth of Kentucky:

§ 1. That an act approved 5th February, 1868, entitled "An act to amend an act approved 18th February, 1860, to empower the county court of Bath county to make subscriptions to the capital stock of turnpike roads," be so amended that said county court may make subscriptions

as therein provided to the capital stock of any turnpike 1869.
road in said county, the length of which is not less than
two miles.

§ 2. This act shall take effect from its passage.

Approved February 24, 1869.

CHAPTER 1571.

AN ACT for the benefit of Madison County.

*Be it enacted by the General Assembly of the Commonwealth
of Kentucky:*

§ 1. That so much of section three of an act approved
March 9th, eighteen hundred and sixty-eight, as exempts
Madison county from the provisions of an act, entitled
"An act to empower county courts to take stock in turn-
pike roads in this Commonwealth," is hereby repealed.

§ 2. This act shall take effect from its passage.

Approved February 24, 1869.

CHAPTER 1573.

AN ACT for the benefit of Frank S. Hill, late sheriff of Washington County.

*Be it enacted by the General Assembly of the Commonwealth
of Kentucky:*

§ 1. That Frank S. Hill, late sheriff of Washington, is
released from the payment of four hundred and eighty-
eight dollars and seventy-three cents, the damages adjudged against him and his securities by the fiscal court,
for the non-payment of the revenue for said county for
1867, he having paid the full amount of said judgment,
including costs and Attorney General's fees, except said
damages.

§ 2. This act shall take effect from its passage.

Approved February 24, 1869.

CHAPTER 1574.

AN ACT for the benefit of A. W. Nickell, late sheriff of Johnson County, and his sureties.

WHEREAS, Judgment was rendered by the Franklin circuit court against A. W. Nickell and his securities, for the
revenue of 1866, besides cost and damages due from him
as sheriff of Johnson county; and whereas, execution
issued upon said judgment, which was levied upon certain lands of said Nickell and his securities, situated in

said county, which were afterwards sold by the sheriff of Floyd county, and were bid in for the State of Kentucky by her agent, but at prices less than two thirds of their value. The sales, however, amounted to a sufficiency to finish paying off said execution; and it is now represented that the defendants, whose said lands were sold, contemplated redeeming them before the one year expires from the day of sale; therefore,

Be it enacted by the General Assembly of the Commonwealth of Kentucky:

§ 1. That in the event said sheriff, Nickell, or any of his securities, shall pay into the Treasury the principal, interest, cost, Attorney General's fees, and all other costs and charges to which the State has or may be subjected on account of said failure to pay said revenue on or before the first day of October, 1869, then all the balance of the damages in said execution is to stand released and forever remitted, and the Auditor is directed to settle with said parties accordingly.

§ 2. This act to take effect from its passage.

Approved February 24, 1869.

CHAPTER 1575.
AN ACT for the benefit of Nancy Hodges, of Hart County.

WHEREAS, In the year 1863, there was assessed and collected from Nancy Hodges by mistake the sum of twenty-one dollars and sixty cents ($21 60) as taxes, and paid into the revenue of the State; and whereas, the same was wrongfully assessed, collected, and paid over as revenue; and whereas, the term of two years, the time in which said error could have been certified to the Auditor and by him corrected, and said sum paid back by him, having expired, therefore,

Be it enacted by the General Assembly of the Commonwealth of Kentucky:

§ 1. That the Auditor be, and he is hereby, directed to draw his warrant on the Treasurer in favor of said Nancy Hodges for the sum of twenty-one dollars and sixty cents, and the same shall be paid out of any moneys not otherwise appropriated.

§ 2. This act to take effect from its passage.

Approved February 24, 1869:

CHAPTER 1576.

AN ACT to amend an act, entitled "An act to consolidate the Towns of Jamestown and Brooklyn, in Campbell County, and incorporate the City of Dayton," approved March 9, 1867.

Be it enacted by the General Assembly of the Commonwealth of Kentucky:

§ 1. That the legislative power of the city of Dayton is, and shall hereafter be, vested in a board to be styled "The City Council of the City of Dayton," composed of a president, to be elected by all the qualified voters of said city; and four members from each ward having the qualifications of voters of the city for one year next before their election, who shall be chosen annually by the qualified voters of the several wards, on the second Monday in March, each year.

§ 2. The city council of the city of Dayton is hereby authorized and empowered to pass all by-laws and ordinances necessary for the good government and general police of the city, and to carry into effect the provisions of this or any other act relating to the city; to levy and collect a general ad valorem tax on all the taxable property of the city, not exceeding one dollar on each one hundred dollars in valuation of the property so taxed, and a tax on each tithable in the city not exceeding two dollars, which tax shall be levied for general purposes, and to meet all contingent expenses of the city; but no ordinance levying a tax for general purposes shall continue in force, except for the collection of the tax levied under it, for a longer term than one year, unless repassed, but may be amended or repealed at any time; and the general tax ordinance shall be revised annually: and in all revisions of the tax ordinances, the city council is limited to raising a sum sufficient, as shown by the annual estimates, to meet the ordinary expenditures of the city, together with any deficit for a preceding year, and five hundred dollars for contingencies.

§ 3. That said council be, and is hereby, authorized to levy and collect, at the same time, and in the same manner, that the general revenue is now authorized by law to be collected, a special tax not exceeding twenty-five cents on each one hundred dollars in valuation of all the taxable property in the city, for any term of years not exceeding five, including the year 1869, which special tax shall be collected in par funds only, and the revenue arising therefrom shall be set apart as a "sinking fund," and shall be used only for the purpose of paying the interest on the bonds and other debts of the city, and the principal of said bonds and debts as the same may become due.

Legislative power of city in whom vested.

When city council to be elected.

May pass by-laws.

May levy and collect taxes, &c.

May levy and collect special tax.

1869.

May open, grade, and pave streets, &c.

§ 4. That said council be, and is hereby, authorized and empowered to direct the opening and grading and paving, or bowldering or macadamizing, of all or any part of any street, alley, or square in the city, upon petition of a majority of the owners in quantity of the real estate abutting on the part to be improved, or without such petition, if two thirds of all the members of the city council concur, where a portion of the street, alley, or square has been already improved, or where the unimproved portion lies between two improved streets, and to levy and collect a special tax, at a rate per lineal foot, on all the real estate abutting on the part to be improved, sufficient to pay for the paving, bowldering, or macadamizing; and to direct the owners of real estate, upon any street or part of street or square in the city, to pave or otherwise improve the sidewalks in front of their real estate, in such manner as to the council shall seem best; and after notice in person or by publication of not less than sixty days, any such real estate owner shall fail, refuse, or neglect to make such pavement or improvement, to cause the same to be done, and to levy a special tax on the real estate sufficient to pay the expenses thereof and costs of levy.

May have sidewalks paved.

§ 5. That the assessor of the city of Dayton shall have the same qualifications as members of the city council; and shall, before entering on the duties of his office, execute a bond, with good security, to be approved by the city council, payable to the city of Dayton, for the faithful performance of his duties according to law and the ordinances of the city; and he shall have a compensation for his services, payable out of the city treasury, which shall be fixed at a rate per list by the city council; and he shall proceed, in each year, as soon after he is qualified as may be, to assess all the taxable property of the city, affixing a fair actual cash valuation on the same, and also to assess the tithes of the city for taxation, and report his assessment to the city clerk before or during the first week in the month of May succeeding, and shall make an affidavit to the correctness of the same; and all vacancies in the office of assessor shall be filled by appointment of the city council.

In relation to assessor.

§ 6. That as soon as the assessor shall have returned his assessment, as provided in the last preceding section, the clerk of the city shall call a meeting of the city council to convene at their usual place of meeting, for the purpose of sitting as a "board of equalization," of which meeting the clerk shall give at least ten days' notice by posting up notices in at least five public places in the city; at which meeting any tax-payer of the city, feeling himself aggrieved and believing the assessment of his property to be too high, may appear and make motion to the council to

Board of equalization.

have the same reduced; and the president, clerk, or any member of council, may, at the same time, make motion to have the assessment of the property of any tax-payer increased; which motion shall be considered by the council, and the increase or reduction shall be made, a majority of the council concurring; but, after such meeting of the council as a board of equalization, no reduction or increase shall be made, nor shall any money paid as city taxes after that time be refunded, unless paid through error.

§ 7. That it shall be the duty of the assessor to visit personally every tax-payer of the city—if not, their agents, if any in the city—and to see and inspect all real estate assessed by him, and to examine all tax-payers on oath touching the lists of such; and should any tax-payer or agent refuse to furnish or disclose his list of taxable property, or to make oath touching the same, the assessor shall report such tax-payer or agent to the mayor's court, and the court shall forthwith summon such tax-payer or agent to appear before him, and may order him to furnish his list to the assessor, under oath, and enforce such order by proceedings as in cases of contempt, and may fine such tax-payer or agent in any sum not exceeding twenty dollars and the costs of the proceeding; and in case the assessor shall be unable to see any tax-payer or agent, he shall make out his list by the best means in his power from actual survey. Should any assessor knowingly refuse or neglect to assess any taxable property or tithe in the city as required by law, he, with his surety, shall be liable on his official bond by motion or action in the mayor's court, to pay the amount of the taxes properly assessable thereon, and fifty per centum damages; and the president of council and the city clerk may, after the assessor has made his return, require him to assess any taxable property which may have been omitted by him, and make return thereof.

Futher duties of assessor.

§ 8. That the assessor's books shall remain in the city clerk's office open to the inspection of any one concerned; and the clerk shall at once, on their being reported to him, cause a duplicate thereof to be made and filed with the city treasurer, together with the tax bills; and, until the fifteenth day of August next succeeding, all tax-payers shall have the privilege of paying their taxes and tithes to the city treasurer; and, upon their doing so, the city treasurer shall deliver to them their tax bill receipted by him.

Assessor's book subject to inspection.

§ 9. That all tax bills remaining unpaid on the fifteenth of August in each year shall be charged with a penalty of twenty per centum thereon, and shall be listed by the city clerk in a book to be kept for that purpose, and deliv-

20 p—cent. to be added on unpaid taxes, &c. And who to collect same.

1869.

ered to the city marshal or such tax collector as may be appointed by the city council, he receipting to the city clerk for the same, for collection, having first executed a bond, with good security, payable to the city of Dayton, to be approved by the city council, for the faithful performance of his duty, and to account for and pay over to the city treasurer all money collected by him on such delinquent tax bills as fast as collected; and the city marshal or collector shall at once proceed to collect the delinquent tax bills and penalties by visiting the delinquent tax-payers or their agents, if in the city, and distraining and selling, if necessary, according to law; and the city marshal or collector shall be allowed a per centum on all sums collected by him, to be fixed by the city council, out of the penalties added, and fifty cents for each distress, and one dollar for each sale, to be paid as costs by the tax-payers, for which additional property may be distrained and sold at the same time; and the city marshal or collector must, by the first day of November in each year, make a return to the city clerk of delinquent tax bills in his hands unpaid, with his affidavit on each, stating what he has done with such bill; and the same shall then be charged with a further penalty of twenty per centum; and the marshal or collector, with his surety, shall be liable upon his bond, by motion or action in the mayor's court, to pay the amount of taxes and penalty charged on any delinquent tax bill in his hands, and ten per centum damages thereon, where he may have failed or refused to discharge any of the duties enjoined upon him in the collection thereof, or failing to return such delinquent tax b.ll as herein required.

§ 10. That special taxes may be levied at any time
When special taxes may be collected. when necessary for the purposes herein specified; and when levied, the assessor shall at once proceed to assess the property for the same; and such assessment shall be returned within one month of the time the taxes are levied. The taxes shall be payable to the city treasurer within two months after the time the assessments are severally made; and collected by distress by the city marshal or collector within three months after the time for payment to the city treasurer shall expire, and subject to like costs, penalties, and proceedings that general taxes are; and officers collecting the same are required to perform like duties, under like liabilities, as in cases of collecting general taxes.

§ 11. No collecting or disbursing officer of the city shall
How collecting & disbursing officers to be paid. be allowed to retain out of the moneys coming into his hands any amount for services, or for claims, which he may have or assert against the city; but all claims of such officers, for services or otherwise, shall be paid out the

city treasury when appropriated by the city council, and all applications of the money of the city, otherwise than as directed by law, shall be deemed an embezzlement; and any officer or other person who shall embezzle or fraudulently convert to his own use bullion, money, bank notes, or other security for money, or evidences of debt, or claim, or any effects or property of the city of Dayton, shall be confined in the penitentiary not less than one nor more than ten years.

§ 12. The city council may make further regulations by ordinance or resolutions for the collection, safe-keeping, and disbursement of the public money and taxes of the city, not in conflict with the provisions of this act.

§ 13. Every officer of the city of Dayton, before enter-- ing upon the discharge of the duties of the office to which he has been elected or appointed, shall take an oath before the mayor or other person authorized to administer oaths, that he will support the Constitution of the United States, and the Constitution and laws of the Commonwealth of Kentucky, and the by-laws and ordinances of the city of Dayton, and that he will faithfully perform the duties of the office to which he is elected to the best of his ability. *Officers to take oath.*

§ 14. The city clerk shall perform the duties of city auditor, and shall keep the accounts of the city, and of the officers of the city. He must, at least once every three months, and once in each month, if the city council, by resolution, require it, lay before the city council a general statement of the finances of the city, and all collecting and disbursing officers shall report monthly to him; and at the end of each fiscal year he shall lay before the city council a detailed statement of the receipts and disbursements of the city for the preceding, and a detailed estimate for the succeeding year. *City clerk to be city auditor; his duties.*

§ 15. That the records of the city council of the city of Dayton, and all bonds, deeds, contracts, and other instruments of writing, executed to said city, or on file among the papers of the city, shall be, and are hereby declared to be, public records, and copies thereof, certified by the clerk of said city, under his hand and the seal of the city, shall be evidence in all courts, and between all parties, in the same manner that the originals would, and the clerk shall be entitled to the same fees for copies of any record, or bond, or other paper on file as aforesaid, that the clerks of county courts are entitled to for like services, except that he shall charge no fee for the copy of any record, bond, or paper on file, when the same shall be required by the mayor or other officer of the city in aid and furtherance of their duties as such officer. *Records, &c., of city declared public records.* *Certified copies of same to be evidence. &c. fees of clerk.*

§ 16. That if the clerk of said city shall willfully make any false entry on the record books of the council with *Penalty if clerk makes false entries, &c.*

1869.   intent to cheat or defraud any person or persons, or company or corporation, or shall knowingly certify any copy
of a record or paper as true, when it is not true, with the
like intent to cheat or defraud, or if he shall willfully destroy, alter, or obliterate any paper on file, with like intent
to cheat or defraud, he shall be deemed guilty of felony,
and shall be confined in the penitentiary not less than one
nor more than ten years, at the discretion of a jury.

§ 17. That the salary of the city clerk may be increased
Salary of city or diminished at any time by order of the city council; and
clerk.   the council shall make to the city clerk an allowance
equivalent to the services required of, and performed by,
him.

§ 18. That all that portion of the second section of the
Street com- act of which this is amendatory, which requires that the
missioner to be street commissioner shall be elected by the people, and
appointed by
council instead that he shall act as *ex-officio* wharfmaster, be, and the same
of elected by is hereby, repealed; and that hereafter the city council
citizens, term
of office, pay, shall, at their first meeting in each year, appoint a street
&c.   commissioner, who shall continue in office and act as such
during the current year, unless sooner discharged by the
city council for misconduct in office; and the city council
may make an allowance to the street commissioner, not to
exceed three dollars a day for every day the said commissioner may be actually engaged in work on the streets of
the city; and the said street commissioner shall, at all
times, and in all things pertaining to his duties on the
streets, be governed by the orders from time to time issued
by the council, or the street committee thereof.

§ 19. That hereafter the city marshal shall act as wharf-
City marshal master, and shall collect and promptly pay over to the city
to act as wharf-
master.   treasurer all money collected by him for wharfage due the
city; and when the same is not promptly paid on demand,
may levy and distrain upon any boats, flats, floats, rafts,
or other water crafts, for which wharfage is due and payable, or upon a sufficiency of the tackle, furniture, and
appurtenances to the same belonging, to satisfy any such
bill and costs of sale and levy, and sell the same as under
an ordinary execution of *fi. fa.*

§ 20. That section seventh of the act of which this act
Conflicting is amendatory, be, and the same, and all other acts here-
portions of act
to which this is tofore passed, and now in force for the government of the
an amendment city of Dayton in conflict with this act, be, and the same
repealed. are hereby, repealed.

§ 21. This act shall take effect from its passage: *Pro-
When act to vided*, The second, ninth, and nineteenth sections shall not
take effect, &c. take effect until the same shall have been submitted to the
legal voters of said city and approved of by a majority of
those voting, which submission shall be made at the next
municipal election; and all persons who shall vote illegal-

ly at such election shall be liable to the same pains and penalties as are imposed for illegal voting at other elections held in said city. The proper officer of said election shall propound to each qualified voter the following questions: 1. Are you for or against the second section of the amended charter? 2. Are you for or against the ninth section of the amended charter? 3. Are you for or against the nineteenth section of the amended charter? And the vote of each voter shall be recorded for or against each section as indicated by the answer. Within three days after the holding of said election the mayor of said city shall make proclamation of the vote; and such sections as shall have received a majority of the votes cast shall be adopted, and be in full force from the time of such proclamation; and such as shall not have received a majority as aforesaid shall be rejected and constitute no part of the law.

§ 22. That this act shall take effect from and after its passage.

Approved February 24, 1869.

CHAPTER 1578.

AN ACT to incorporate the Cumberland and Ohio Railroad Company.

Be it enacted by the General Assembly of the Commonwealth of Kentucky:

§ 1. That William S. Pryor, Luther Ricketts, Joseph Brinker, William B. Wilson, and Z. F. Smith, of Henry county; William C. Bullock, J. T. Veach, W. S. Caruthers, Quinn Morton, John A. Middleton, G. W. Stewart, Wm. S. Helm, and James H. Drane, of Shelby county; Stephen Beard, S. R. Noman, and Jonathan Davis, of Spencer county; N. G. Thomas, W. A. Beckham, Silvester Johnson, David P. Stout, William Johnson, I. D. Stone, L. McKay, and A. C. Wilson and J. P. Hinkle, of Nelson county; Richard J. Browne, J. P. Barbour, William J. Robinson, and Thomas S. Grundy, of Washington county; R. M. Spalding, E. A. Graves, R. H. Rountree, Thomas Jackson, Samuel Spalding, and I. G. Phillips, of Marion county; Joseph H. Chandler, Wm. Howell, A. F. Gowdy, and J. W. Lively, of Taylor county; W. H. Chelf, D. T. Towles, W. S. Hodges, and B. W. Penick, of Green county; P. H. Leslie, William H. Winlock, J. G. Garnett, M. H. Dickinson, D. M. Ashby, and Wm. H. Botts, of Barren county; B. W. Stone, S. Mannion, J. J. Gatewood, and W. T. Anthony, of Allen county; Joseph F. Ray and Samuel Shannon, of Metcalfe county; and Wm. B. Read, of Larue county, be, and they are hereby, appointed commissioners, under direction of whom, or any three of

Name of company incorporated.

Subscriptions to stock.

Vacancies in board of commissioners.

Capital stock.

Stock, how paid, &c.

whom, subscriptions may be received to the capital stock of the Cumberland and Ohio railroad company. which is hereby incorporated; and they may cause books to be opened, at such times and places as they may direct, for the purpose of receiving subscriptions to the capital stock of said company, after having given such notice as. they may deem proper; and if such amount of subscriptions to the capital stock of said company as is necessary to its incorporation shall not have been obtained, said commissioners, or a majority of them, may cause books to be opened, from time to time, and may adjourn to such place as they may deem proper, until the sum necessary to its incorporation shall be subscribed: *Provided*, That any subscription, tendered at any time and place other than those advertised, that may be received by said commissioners, or any one of them, shall be as valid against the parties subscribing as if received at the time and place advertised; and if any of said commissioners shall die or resign, or refuse to act during a continuance of the duties devolved upon them by this act, others may be appointed in their stead by a majority of those remaining.

§ 2. That the capital stock of the Cumberland and Ohio railroad company shall be five millions of dollars, in shares of one hundred dollars each, which may be subscribed by any individual, company, or corporation; and as soon as two thousand shares of said stock shall be subscribed, the subscribers, their successors and assigns, shall be, and are hereby declared to be, incorporated into a company, by the name of the Cumberland and Ohio railroad company; and by this name shall be capable of purchasing, holding, selling, leasing, and conveying real estate, not exceeding ten thousand acres, and personal estate, so far as the same may be necessary for the purposes of the corporation; and shall have perpetual succession; and by said corporate name may sue and be sued, contract and be contracted with; and may have and use a common seal, and alter and renew the same at pleasure; and shall have any and enjoy and use all the privileges which other similar corporate bodies lawfully have and use.

§ 3. That there shall be paid, at the time of subscribing for stock in said company, to the person receiving the subscription, the sum of one dollar on each share, either in money or in a note or notes, at not more than sixty days' time, payable to some one or more of said commissioners, and negotiable in some bank. The residue of said subscription shall be payable in installments, at such times as may be required by the board of directors of said company; but no such payment shall be demanded until at least ten days' notice shall have been given, by publication in one or more newspapers published on the line of said road; and if any subscriber shall fail to pay any installment, or part of any installment, when so demanded, the same may be recovered by an action, in the name of the corporation, before, any court having jurisdiction in such cases; and in all such actions, it shall not be necessary to prove any other demand than the publication provided for in this section; or, in case such failure to pay any installment, or part of installment so demanded, shall continue for the space of sixty days after the time the same is required by such demand to be paid, the board of directors may, at their discretion, order the same to be forfeited to the company, and may, if they think proper, sell such share or shares for the benefit of the company, or, in the event of the highest bid being less than the unpaid balance and interest on said subscription, then the company may become the purchaser, and shall retire said subscription; but the board of directors, by a majority of the whole, may remit such forfeiture, on such terms as they may think proper: *Provided*, It shall be lawful for the commissioners or board of directors to receive subscriptions to said capital stock, payable in contracts, well secured, to build any parts of said road, or any bridge or bridges on same, or to perform any work or furnish any materials which may be accepted by the company: *And provided further*, That subscriptions to said capital stock may be made in real estate, situated in Kentucky, if said subscriptions shall be tendered to the board of directors after their organization; said real estate to be taken at its cash value, to be assessed at the time by three commissioners on oath, of whom two shall be selected by the company, and one by the person proposing to subscribe. Upon their report in writing, describing the land and assessing its cash value, the company may receive the same at its value, and issue a stock certificate, and may take a deed of conveyance in fee simple; and the real estate received for stock subscriptions, and which the company is hereby authorized to receive, shall be over and above the ten thousand acres mentioned in the second section of this act.

§ 4. That at the expiration of the period for which the books are first opened, if two thousand shares of the capital stock shall have been subscribed, and if not, as soon thereafter as the same shall be subscribed; and said commissioners, or a majority of them living, shall call a meeting at such time and place as a majority of those acting shall designate, giving at least ten days' notice of the time and place in one or more of the newspapers published as aforesaid; and that at such meeting said commissioners shall lay the subscription books before the

1869.

Contracts may be paid in stock.

Real estate may be taken and paid for in stock.

When president and directors to be elected.

subscribers then present, and thereupon said subscribers,
or a majority of them there present, shall have power
to elect, out of their number, by ballot, nine directors to
manage the affairs of said company; and these nine
directors, or a majority of them, shall have power to
elect a president of said company from among the directors, and to allow him such compensation for his services
as they may think proper; and at such election, and on
all other occasions where a vote of the stockholders of
said company is to be taken, each stockholder shall be
allowed one vote for every share of stock owned by such
voter; and any stockholder may, in writing, depute any
other person to act as proxy for it, him, or her; and said
commissioners aforesaid, or any three of them, shall be
judges of said first election.

§ 5. That to continue the succession of the president

*Annual elec-
tions, when &
how held.* and directors of said company, nine directors shall be
chosen annually on the first Saturday in June, of each
year, at such place as the president and directors may
appoint, by the stockholders of said company: *Provided*,
That the president and directors may change the time
and place of holding elections, upon publishing such
change not less than thirty days prior to the election, in
the newspapers aforesaid; and that the directors of said
company, or a majority of them, shall have the power
to appoint judges of all elections, and to elect a president of said company from among themselves, and to
allow him such compensation for his services as they
*Vacancy, how
filled.* may deem proper; and if any vacancy shall occur by
death, resignation, or refusal to act, of any president or
director, before the year for which he was elected shall
have expired, a person to fill such vacancy shall be appointed by the board of directors, or a majority of them;
Term of office. and that the president and directors of said company
shall hold and exercise their offices until their successors in office are duly elected and enter upon the discharge of their duties; and all elections which are by
this act, or by the by-laws of said company, to be made
at a particular time, if not made at such time, may be
made in ninety days thereafter, upon notice published
in the newspapers aforesaid.

§ 6. That a general meeting of the stockholders of said
*General meet-
ings.* company may be called at any time during the interval
between the annual meetings, by the president and the
directors, or a majority of them, or by stockholders owning one half of all the stock subscribed, upon thirty days'
notice of the time and place of holding the same, in the
newspapers aforesaid; and when any such meeting is
called by the stockholders, such notice shall specify the
object of the call; and if, at any such called meeting, a

majority of all the stockholders are not present in person or by proxy, the same shall be adjourned from day to day, without transacting any business, for any time not exceeding five days; and if, within said five days, stockholders having a majority in value of all the stock subscribed do not attend in person or by proxy, such meeting shall be dissolved

§ 7. That the president and directors of said company in office for the preceding year, shall, at the regular annual meeting of the stockholders, exhibit a distinct and clear account of the affairs of said company; that, at any called meeting of the stockholders, or a majority in value of the whole of the stock subscribed being present, they may demand and require similar statements from the president and directors, whose duty it shall be to furnish such statement when so required. *Annual report to be made*

§ 8. That the president and directors of said company, before he or they act as such, shall swear or affirm, as the case may be, that they will well and truly discharge the duties of their respective offices to the best of their skill and judgment; and the said president and directors, or a majority of them, shall have power to elect or appoint a treasurer of said company, and require and take of him a bond in such penalty, and with sureties as they may prescribe, payable to said company, conditioned for the faithful keeping and disbursing of all such money as may come into his hands, and with such other conditions as may be prescribed; upon every bond recovery may be had for a breach of the conditions thereof, by suit in the name of the company, and in any court having jurisdiction. *President & directors to take oath.* *Treasurer to to be elected; to give bond, &c.*

§ 9. That if any of the stock authorized by this act shall remain unsubscribed until after the election of president and directors, as provided for in the fourth section of this act, the said president and directors, or a majority of them, shall have power to open the books and receive subscriptions to the stock which shall remain unsubscribed, or to sell and dispose of the same for the benefit of the company, not under the par value of such stock; and the subscribers or purchasers of such stock shall have all rights of original subscribers, and be subject to the same regulations and liabilities. *Books may be re-open'd.*

§ 10. That said president and directors, or a majority of them, may appoint all such officers, agents, or servants, as they may deem expedient for the business of the company, and may remove the same at pleasure; or said board of directors may delegate to their president the power to appoint or remove any or all such employes, subject to their approval at their first meeting thereafter; that they, or a majority of them, may determine by con- *Officers, agents, &c., to be appointed, may be removed, &c.*

tract the pay of such officers, agents, or servants, and regulate by by-laws the manner of adjusting all accounts against the company, and the extent of the liability of the company to its employes; that they shall have power to erect, carry on, conduct, and control workshops, eating-houses, warehouses, and buildings or edifices necessary to or convenient for the uses of said company; that they shall have power to direct and regulate in what manner, and by what evidence, stock in said company may be transferred; and to pass all by-laws they may deem necessary and proper for exercising the powers hereby vested in said company, and for carrying into effect this act, and to alter the same at pleasure: *Provided*, The same be not contrary to the Constitution and laws of Kentucky or of the United States.

Capital stock may be increased.

§ 11. That if the capital stock of said company shall be deemed insufficient for the purpose of this act, it shall be lawful for the president and directors to increase the same as much as they may deem necessary, not exceeding the sum of eight millions of dollars, giving notice as herein-before required; and the said company may borrow any sum of money not exceeding four millions of dollars, and secure the payment of the same by the issue of first mortgage bonds of their road, or in such way as may be agreed upon.

Further powers of company.

§ 12. That the president and directors of said company are hereby vested with all the powers and rights neces-sary to the construction of a railroad from the Ohio river through Henry county, Shelby county, Washington coun-ty, Nelson county, Marion county, Taylor county, Green county, Barren county, and Allen county, to a point on the boundary line between the States of Kentucky and Tennessee, to be selected by the president and directors, about due north from the town of Murfreesboro, Ten-nessee, with the view of connecting with the southern system of railways, converging at Nashville, Tennessee. They may connect with the Ohio river by intersecting the Covington extension of the Louisville, Lexington, and Cincinnati railroad, at some convenient point in Henry county, Kentucky, on such terms as may be mutually and lawfully agreed upon between the com-pany hereby incorporated and the said Louisville, Lex-ington, and Cincinnati railroad company. The president and directors may cause to be made contracts, which shall be signed by the president, with any corporations, companies, or individuals, for making said road, or any part of it; and they may purchase or lease any road or roads connecting with their said road; and they, their agents, engineers, etc., or those with whom they may contract for surveying or making the same, or any part thereof, may enter upon, use, and excavate any land which may be wanted for the site of said road, or the erection of warehouses or other structures or works necessary and convenient to said road, or for its use, or for any other purpose necessary in the construction or repair of said road, or its works and appurtenances; and they may build bridges and construct tunnels: *Provided,* Such bridges shall not obstruct navigation on any navigable stream; and may fix scales and weights, and use timber, earth, gravel, stone, and other materials necessary or useful in the construction and repair of said road.

§ 13. That the president and directors, or a majority of them, or their authorized agents, may agree with the owners of any land, earth, stone, timber, or other materials or improvements which may be wanted for the construction or repair of said road or any of their works, for the purchase, in fee simple, or the use and occupation of the same; and if they cannot agree, or if the owner or owners, or any of them, be a *feme covert,* under age, *non compos mentis,* or out of the county in which the property may lie, application may be made to any justice of the peace of said county, who shall thereupon issue his warrant, directed to the sheriff or any constable of said county, requiring him to summon twenty discreet men not related to the owner, nor in any way interested, to meet on the land, or near the property or materials to be valued, on a day named in said warrant, not less than ten nor more than twenty days after the issuing of the same; and if at the time and place any of the said jurors do not attend, said sheriff or constable shall forthwith summons as many jurors as may be necessary, with the jurors in attendance, and from them each party, if present, or, if not present, by agent or otherwise, the sheriff or constable for the party absent, may strike off four jurors, and the remaining twelve shall act as the jury of inquest of damages. The sheriff or constable may adjourn the jury from day to day; and if they cannot agree upon a verdict, it shall be his duty to discharge them and summon another, to meet as soon as convenient. Before the jury acts, the sheriff or constable shall administer to them an oath or affirmation that they will justly and impartially fix the damages which the owner or owners will sustain by the use and occupation of said property required by said company; and the jury, in estimating the damages, shall find the owner or owners the actual value of the land or other thing proposed to be taken; but in estimating damages resulting incidentally to the other land or other property of such owners, they shall offset the advantages to such residue, to be derived from the building and operating of said road

How to obtain stone, &c.

Jury may offset advantages of road.

1869.

by, through, or near such residue. The jury shall reduce their verdict to writing, and sign the same, and it shall be returned by the sheriff or constable to the clerk of the circuit court of his county, and such clerk shall receive and file it in his office; and such verdict shall be confirmed by the circuit court at its next regular term, if no sufficient reason is shown by either party for setting it aside; and when so confirmed, it shall be recorded by the clerk at the expense of said company; but if set aside, the court shall direct another inquisition to be held by the sheriff of the county in the manner above prescribed: *Provided*, That the company may proceed to construct their said road as soon as the first verdict of the jury shall be returned, whether the same be set aside and a new jury ordered or not; and every inquisition shall describe the property or the bounds of the land condemned, and the duration of interest in the same, valued for the company; and such valuation, when tendered or paid to owner or owners of said property, or to the sheriff of the county in which said inquest is held, when the owner or owners do not reside in such county, shall entitle said company to the use or interest in the same thus valued, as fully as if it had been conveyed to it by the owner or owners of same; and the valuation of same, if not received when tendered, may, at any time thereafter within one year, be received from the company, without costs or interests, by the owners, his, their, or its legal representative: *Provided*, That land condemned for roadway shall not be more than one hundred feet wide, unless said company shall file with the justice, at the time of applying for a warrant, the affidavit of some one of its engineers, stating that a greater width is necessary, and how much more is required, when the inquisition shall be for the quantity thus stated.

May proceed to construct road when verdict returned.

Width of land condemned.

§ 14. That whenever it shall be necessary for said company to have, use, or occupy any land, material, or other property, in order to the construction or repairing of said road or their necessary works or buildings, the president and directors, or their agents, or those contracting with them for constructing or repairing the same, may immediately take and use the same, they having caused the property wanted to be viewed by a jury formed as hereinbefore prescribed; and it shall not be necessary, after such view, in order to the use and occupation of the same, to wait the issue of proceedings upon such inquest; and the inquest of the jury, after the payment or tender of such valuation, shall be a bar to all actions for taking and using such property, whether before or after such confirmation or payment of such valuation.

When may take and use lands, &c.

§ 15. That any city, town, or county, through which said proposed road shall pass, is hereby authorized to subscribe

Cities, towns, and counties may take stock, and issue bonds

stock in said railroad company in any amount as the city, town, or county may desire; and the county any such county is authorized to issue the bonds respective counties in such amount as the county may direct; and the chairman and board of trustees, mayor and aldermen of any town, and the mayor and aldermen or council of any city, are hereby authorized to issue the bonds of their respective towns or cities in like manner. All said bonds shall be payable to bearer, with coupons attached, bearing any rate of interest not exceeding six per cent. per annum, payable semi-annually in the city of New York, payable at such times as they may designate, not exceeding thirty years from date; but before any such subscription on the part of any city, town, or county shall be valid or binding on the same, the mayor and aldermen, or chairman and board of trustees of any town, the mayor and aldermen or council of any city, and the county court of any county, having jurisdiction, shall submit the question of any such subscription to the qualified voters of such city, town, county, in which the proposed subscription is made, at such time or times as said chairman and board of trustees, or mayor and aldermen of any town, mayor and aldermen or council of any city, or the county court of any county, as aforesaid, may, by order, direct; and should a majority of the qualified voters voting at any such election vote in favor of subscribing said stock in said railroad company, it shall be the duty of such county court, trustees, or other authorities aforesaid, to make the subscription in the name of their respective cities, towns, or counties, as the case may be, and proceed to have issued the bonds to the amount of such subscription as hereinbefore directed; and the mayor and aldermen, or chairman and board of trustees of any town, mayor and council or aldermen of any city, or the county court having jurisdiction in any such county that may subscribe for stock in said railroad company, are hereby authorized and required to levy, annually, and collect a tax upon the taxable property in their respective cities, towns, or counties, as listed and taxed under the revenue laws of this State, a sum sufficient to pay the interest on said bonds as it accrues, together with the cost of collecting the same. They are also authorized and required to make provision for paying said bonds at their maturity; and to enable them to do this, they may establish a sinking fund, and loan out the same at any rate of interest they can obtain, and, if necessary, collect the same by law, or may adopt such other means as to them may seem proper and expedient; and may levy and collect taxes annually or otherwise on the property aforesaid for this purpose. The person collecting said tax shall give tax

taxes paid, deducted proxies; each of

Company may unite with other roads.

How subscriptions to be made.

Provision to be made for paying bonds.

471

any tax-payer paying tax **to**
ns of this act, shall be entitled
pany to the amount of taxes
s, towns, or counties, under
is levied, shall be divested **of**
issued on said tax receipts;
to the amount of one share
to the company, or an officer
certificate of stock shall be
a share: *Provided*, That the
s shall receive no dividends
s of stock issued on said re-
titled to the same dividends,
ivileges as the original and
ed further, That said com-
may seem expedient to it,
... . and pay, each or any year, to the cities, towns,
or counties, or any of them, the amount of tax levied by
reason of said bonds, and thus stop the collection of tax

Company may purchase bonds
for that year: *And provided further*, That the company
may purchase said bonds and surrender them at any time
to the cities, towns, or counties issuing them, and have the
same canceled; and the mayor and council or aldermen of
any city, or the mayor and aldermen or chairman and
board of trustees of any town, or the county court of any
county having jurisdiction, may appoint collectors for said
tax, or may require the sheriffs or marshals of the respective cities, towns, or counties, within the jurisdiction of
same, to collect the said tax, all of whom shall have the
same powers and remedies, and shall proceed in the same
way, for the collection of said tax, as the sheriffs in the
collection of the State revenue. The mayor and aldermen, or chairman and board of trustees, shall require and
take from the person collecting the tax a bond, with sufficient sureties, conditioned as they may think best. If the
collections are made by the sheriff or marshal, they shall
settle and pay over the tax at the same times that sheriffs
are required to pay the State revenue; and for their services in collecting, they shall in no case be allowed more
than three per cent. commission on the amount collected.
That if preferred, the application herein authorized to be
made to the county court, may be made to the presiding
judge of the county court; and all the powers herein given
to the county court are hereby vested in the presiding

Towns, cities, and counties may vote at elections.
judge of the county court. At all meetings of the stockholders for the purpose of electing officers or any other
purpose, the said town, cities, and counties may, by proxies duly authorized by the authorities thereof, cast a vote
for each share of stock so subscribed by said town, city,
or county: *Provided*, That whenever certificates of stock

shall be issued to persons residing therein for taxes paid, the stock represented by such certificate shall be deducted from the stock represented and voted for by said proxies; and said tax-payers shall be entitled to one vote for each certificate so issued to them representing one share of stock.

§ 16. It shall be lawful for this company to unite their road, branch, or branches (which it is authorized hereby to make, and to use and apply all the powers and privileges herein granted for the construction and operation of the main road for the construction and operation of the same), with any other railroad or railroads, and to acquire interests in other roads or parts of roads, and use the same as parts of their main line, branch, or branches, with the consent of the directors of such companies. The said railroad company shall have the same rights and privileges of prosecution, and any person or persons shall be liable to the same penalties and forfeitures for injuries done and committed upon the property of said company, or otherwise to the prejudice of said company; and shall be entitled to collect such tolls and rates for travel and transportation over their road and its branches, as are provided for in the laws incorporating the Louisville and Nashville railroad company, and acts amendatory thereto; and shall have all the powers and privileges conferred upon said Louisville and Nashville railroad company by the laws of Kentucky, for constructing and operating their said proposed railroad, not herein specified and granted, and not in conflict with the terms of this charter.

Company may unite with other roads.

Have all powers, &c., of Lou. and Nash. railroad company.

§ 17. The property of the company hereby incorporated shall be exempt from taxation under the revenue laws of this State until the said road shall have been completed, or for three years from the date of the enactment of this law and its approval by the Governor. Said railroad company may construct or purchase a telegraph line near their road and branches, or may become owners of stock in any company which may construct such line of telegraph; and may establish an express company over their line of railroad, branches, and connections, and become owners of stock in such a company, with the usual privileges of such companies, and subject to the usual restrictions upon them.

How long road exempt from taxation.

§ 18. The said company may acquire any corporate rights, franchises, and privileges in other States, and use the same, which they may receive from the Legislatures thereof, or which they may acquire therein, not inconsistent with this charter or the laws of Kentucky. They shall begin work on their road, in good faith, within three years, and complete the same within ten years from the passage

May acquire corporate rights in other States.

of this act, or forfeit the powers and franchises herein conferred.

Approved February 24, 1869.

CHAPTER 1579.

AN ACT to incorporate the Blue Lick Turnpike Road Company.

Be it enacted by the General Assembly of the Commonwealth of Kentucky:

§ 1. That a company is hereby formed for the purpose of building a turnpike road leading from the Louisville and Shepherdsville turnpike road, at or near the point where the New Cut road leading from Shepherdsville to Louisville intersects it, and running thence with or near the New Cut road to the old coal bank, in Bullitt county; thence to the school-house near H. B. North's; thence with or near the old county road to the gap in the knob, in Bullitt county, to be styled the " Blue Lick Turnpike Road Company."

§ 2. The capital stock of said company shall be sixteen thousand dollars, to be increased or diminished at the pleasure of the company, to be divided into shares of fifty dollars each.

§ 3. That books of subscription shall be opened by W. B. M. Brooks, J. H. Huber, George N. Saunders, Dr. B. F. McCauley, James McCauley, and Jordan Gilmore, who are hereby appointed commissioners for that purpose, at such times and places as they may deem proper; they shall insert in a book an obligation as follows: " We, whose names are hereto subscribed, severally promise to pay to the president and directors of the Blue Lick turnpike road company the sum of fifty dollars for each and every share of stock set opposite our names, in such manner and at such times as shall be by them required under the law incorporating said company, to be collected as other debts. Witness our hand, this — day of ———."

§ 4. That when ten thousand dollars shall have been subscribed to the capital stock of said company, it shall be the duty of the commissioners named to give notice thereof, and call a meeting of the stockholders, at such time and place as they may think proper, for the purpose of electing a president and four directors; one vote shall be allowed for each share of stock; and the president and directors chosen shall continue in office for one year, and until their successors are elected and qualified. The time and place of each election thereafter shall be fixed by the president and directors, a majority of whom shall be competent to do business.

§ 5. So soon as said company is organized by election of the officers, the president and directors shall be a body-politic and corporate, in fact and in law, by the name and style of the Blue Lick turnpike road company, with the privileges and franchises of a corporation; shall be capable of holding their capital stock, and the increase and profits thereof; and holding, by purchase, gift, or otherwise, all things necessary or proper for the prosecution of their work; they shall have power to contract and be contracted with, to sue and be sued, in all courts of law and equity, and generally to do all and every thing lawful for a corporation to effect the object for which said corporation was created.

§ 6. Said corporation shall fix and regulate the grade and width of said road, and its covering with stone or gravel; may designate the place for the toll-gates, fix the rates of toll, not, however, exceeding the rate fixed by the general laws; they may erect a gate on said road when two and one half miles of said road is completed.

§ 7. Said company is authorized and permitted by this charter to build a branch road to Brook's Station, Huber's Station, and to Hebron Church.

§ 8. It shall be lawful for the officers and employes of the company, with their tools and appliances, to enter upon the lands over and contiguous to which the road shall pass, for the purpose of procuring gravel, stone, or timber for said road, having first given notice to the owners or occupiers three days. They shall have the right to take and receive the right of way over and through the land where said road shall be located, and the release of timber, stone, or gravel; and if they cannot agree with the owners, then the president shall apply to the county court of the county in which the land lies for a writ of *ad quod damnum* to assess the damages for the right of way, or for timber, stone, or gravel; and upon the payment or tender of the damages assessed, it shall be lawful for the company to open said road, and enter upon said land, and take the stone, timber, or gravel necessary to do the work pertaining thereto.

§ 9. The commissioners and board of directors may receive subscriptions to be paid in work on said road, subject to such regulations as the board of directors may deem proper.

§ 10. The president and directors shall give notice, as they may deem proper, of the amount of call on each share of stock, and the time and place of payment.

§ 11. The president and directors may appoint such officers as they may deem necessary, and prescribe their duties.

§ 12. This act shall take effect from its passage.

Approved February 24, 1869.

1869.

CHAPTER 1582.

AN ACT to extend the limits of the Town of Warsaw, and to amend, consolidate, and reduce into one all laws pertaining to said Town.

Be it enacted by the General Assembly of the Commonwealth of Kentucky:

§ 1. That the limits of the town of Warsaw shall be

Boundary of town. extended and established as follows: Beginning at the west corner of the present town limits, running thence south 54 west, binding on the river, 32½ poles, to a stake; thence south 36, east 151¼ poles, to a stake; thence north 54, east 225¼ poles, to a stake; thence north 36, west 151¼ poles, to a stake on the Ohio river; thence down the Ohio river, binding on the same, south 54, west 193 poles, to the beginning; and the boundary aforesaid shall be, and the same is hereby declared to be, the town of Warsaw; and as such, by that name shall be capable in law of contracting and being contracted with, of suing and being sued, of answering and being answered, in all matters whatever, and in all courts and places.

§ 2. That the fiscal, prudential, and municipal concerns

Trustees to be elected. term of office, &c. of said town, with the government and control thereof, shall be vested in five trustees, who shall be elected on the first Monday in March, annually; said trustees shall hold their offices for one year, or until their successors shall have been qualified; and in case of any vacancy by death, resignation, or otherwise, it may be filled by the board at any regular meeting thereof: *Provided,* A majority of all the qualified trustees concur therein. Be-

To take oath. fore entering upon the duties of his office, each member of the board shall appear before some justice of the peace of the county, and make oath that he will perform the duties of his office to the best of his skill, and a certificate to that effect must appear on the record

Qualification of trustees and voters. book of the board. No one shall be capable of holding the office of trustee (or be considered a legal voter, unless satisfactory evidence be produced to the conductors of the election that he has paid the town tax collectable in the preceding year), and shall, at the time of their election and voting, actually reside in said town: *Provided also,* All elections for trustees shall be *viva voce.*

§ 3. That said trustees may appoint one of their body

Chairman of board to be appointed. as chairman, who shall preside over the meetings, and may call a meeting of the board at any time, and shall continue in office at the discretion of the trustees. They

Clerk. may appoint a clerk, who shall perform the duties imposed by the board, and remain in office at their discre-

Regular meetings. tion. Said trustees may have regular meetings as often as they may deem necessary, and a majority must be present and concur in all business.

§ 4. Said trustees shall have power to assess, annually, a poll-tax on the legal tithables of said town, not exceeding one dollar a head, and levy an ad valorem tax on the real and personal estate within said town that is taxed by the revenue laws of this Commonwealth, not to exceed fifty cents on each one hundred dollars' worth of property; they shall have power to contract for the grading, paving, and improvement of the streets and alleys, and the paving of the sidewalks of the same; to levy and collect from the owner or manager of all exhibitions of animals or shows of all and every description, that shall be exhibited within the limits of said town, a tax not to exceed twenty dollars for each exhibition; they shall have power to pass by-laws and ordinances for the enforcement of the powers granted by this act, by inflicting adequate penalties for the enforcement of the same, and to fix the fees of officers under their appointment.

1869.

May assess taxes.

May contract for improvement of streets, &c.

Tax shows.

§ 5. Said trustees shall have power to appoint a suitable person as a commissioner, to take in a list of taxable property in said town, who shall, before he enters upon the duties of his office, make oath before the chairman of the board (who is duly authorized to administer the proper oath) that he will faithfully and truly discharge the duties of his said office according to the best of his knowledge and ability, who shall proceed to the performance of his duty, and make return under direction of the board; and if any person or persons shall fail or refuse to give in a list of his or her property to said commissioner, together with the valuation thereon, under oath, it shall be the duty of said commissioner to report the fact to the trustees, together with the amount of property (as near as he can ascertain), owned by such individual or individuals in said town; and thereupon the said trustees shall proceed, upon the report of said commissioner, and such other information as they can obtain, to fix the amount with which such individual may be properly chargeable, and collect the same, in the same manner as if the list had been regularly given in to said commissioner.

Commissioner of tax to be appointed; his powers and duties.

§ 6. That said trustees shall, as soon as practicable, after the said commissioner's list shall be returned as aforesaid, appoint a collector to collect said tax, who shall give bond and surety, payable to the trustees and their successors in office, in a penalty of double the amount of taxes to be collected, conditioned for the prompt collection and payment of said tax to the said trustees; and that all taxes due the trustees of said town shall be due within two months after the same is levied by said board; and the collector of said tax shall have the same powers of distraining for the collection of the same that the sheriffs of the Commonwealth now have by law for collecting the State revenue and county

Collector to be appointed, give bond, and when taxes due.

Powers of collector.

1869. levy, and may proceed in the same manner: *Provided further*, That the collector may notify, by posting up at least three notices in the said town, when the tax is due; and if not paid by the tax-payers within four months after the same is levied, he may add ten per cent. thereon as a compensation for the collection thereof, to be collected by him from the delinquent tax-payers as other taxes are collected: *Provided further*, That the trustees of said town may make out a list of persons who have been assessed and failed to pay tax any year or years preceding their levy, and place the same in the hands of said collector for collection; and he shall have the same power and authority to distrain for such delinquent tax as for any other tax, and shall be responsible on his bond for collection and payment of the same: *Provided further*, That the trustees shall have a lien on all real and personal property assessed in said town for tax, until said tax is paid by the owners thereof.

Real estate may be sold for taxes; proceedings.

§ 7. That when any person or persons owning real estate within said town shall fail to pay the tax levied as aforesaid on or before the same becomes due, it shall be the duty of the collector appointed by the board to advertise the said real estate, by the number of the lot or lots on which said tax may be due, together with the sum due on each lot, for six weeks successively previous to the day of sale, at the court-house door within said town, and also for six weeks in any newspaper that may be published in said town; the said sale to be at the court-house door within said town; and should the owner or owners of such lot or lots fail to pay the said tax before the day of sale, together with all costs and expenses attending the advertising the same, then it shall and may be lawful for such collector, then and there, agreeable to such advertisement, to proceed to sell, under the direction of the trustees of said town, such lot or lots so advertised, to pay the tax thereon due, together with the costs attending such advertisement; and it shall be the duty of the said trustees and their successors, at any time after the expiration of the time limited for redemption, to convey the same to the purchaser or purchasers, by good and sufficient deed or deeds of indenture, with special warranty; that all real property sold by virtue of this act shall be redeemable within two years from the day of sale thereof, upon the payment of the tax and cost due at the time of sale and an interest of twenty-five per cent. per annum thereon, and all taxes that may have become due

Infants and femes covert may redeem.

after the sale thereof: *Provided always*, That all infants and *femes covert* whose real estate may be sold by virtue of this act shall be allowed two years after their several disabilities are removed to redeem the same, on the payment of the tax and costs due at the time of sale, and all the taxes that may be due or paid until such redemption, together with interest thereon, at the rate of six per cent. per annum from the time such tax or taxes became due until such redemption: *And provided also,* That the redemption money as aforesaid may be paid to the clerk of the board of trustees, and his certificate shall be good for the same.

§ 8. That it shall be the duty of the collector of the taxes aforesaid, within ten days after the sale of any lot or lots sold in pursuance of this act, to make out a true and faithful list of such lot or lots so sold, with the name of the purchaser, and return the same to the clerk of the board of trustees; and it shall be the duty of said clerk to record the same in a book to be kept for that purpose, for the information of all persons concerned.

§ 9. That said trustees shall have full power and authority to have the sidewalks in said town paved or streets macadamized, or any portion thereof paved or macadamized, and may levy a tax (in addition to the ad valorem and capitation) of not exceeding one dollar per foot upon the lots fronting upon the sidewalks and streets to be thus paved or macadamized, and may compel the owners thereof to pay said tax, or may sell the said lot for said tax, in the same manner that they may be sold to pay other taxes under the provisions of this act: *Provided further,* That it shall be lawful for the said trustees, whenever two thirds of the owners of lots fronting upon any street or square, or any portion of a street or square, where four lots compose a square, and whenever one half of the owners of lots fronting upon any street or square, where two lots compose such street or square, shall petition therefor, to cause the street or sidewalk of such portion of streets to be paved, at the cost and expense of the owners of the ground fronting such street or portion of a street; and the said trustees shall possess ample power to sell and convey any lot or lots, the owner or owners of which shall refuse, when required, to defray the expense of paving the sidewalks binding thereon; and whenever two thirds of the owners of lots fronting upon any street or square, or any portion of a street or square, shall petition for paving such street, or any portion of a street, to cause said street to be paved: *Provided, however,* That the owner or owners of such lot or lots so sold shall be allowed the term of one year after such sale to redeem the same, by refunding the amount for which the same may sell, with twelve per cent. per annum interest thereon till refunded.

§ 10. That said trustees and their successors shall, in addition to the powers heretofore granted them, have full power and authority to grant wharf privileges on the

Margin notes:

1869.

Lists of sales to be returned to trustees.

To be recorded.

Have sidewalks, &c., and levy tax for that purpose, &c.

Powers of trustees when owners refuse to improve.

May grant wharf privileges, fix rates of wharfage, &c.

1869.

Ohio river, at the foot of or opposite the cross streets leading to the river; to fix the rates of wharfage, and to impose upon the grantees or grantee the performance of such duties as they may think proper for the benefit of the commercial and other interests of the said town, and for such period or periods of time as they may think proper, under such rules and regulations as they may, from time to time, stipulate with the grantee or grantees of such privileges.

§ 11. That it shall and may be lawful for the trustees of said town to receive and hold any real or personal estate, not exceeding in amount ten thousand dollars, derived by purchase or otherwise, for school or other purposes; and also to purchase or receive by donation, devise, or bequest, and hold, any quantity of ground contiguous to said town, not exceeding five acres, for a burial ground; also, have power and authority, whenever the same may be deemed necessary, to purchase and hold, for the use of said town, a suitable site or sites, and erect, or cause to be erected thereon, a market-house, and make all rules for the regulation and protection thereof. They shall have power to pass by-laws and ordinances for the protection of the public property in said town, including the public square, and impose adequate penalties for the violation of the same.

May hold real or personal estate for school purposes, cemetery, market-house, &c.

May protect public property

§ 12. Said trustees shall, annually, publish an account of all the moneys received and paid out by their order during the year they are in office.

Annual report

§ 13. That no trustee of said town shall, by himself, contract for, or procure any other person to contract for him, for any public work let out or disposed of by the board during his continuance in office.

Trustee not to be contractor.

§ 14. That no person shall be eligible as a trustee unless he is a free white male citizen, of twenty-one years of age or upwards, and has been a resident of said town for one year next preceding his election.

Eligibility of trustee.

§ 15. Said trustees are hereby vested with full power to pass any and all laws or ordinances (not hereby granted) for the purpose of carrying fully into effect and executing the foregoing enumerated powers: *Provided, however*, That the said trustees shall pass no ordinances repugnant to the Constitution and laws of the United States or of this State.

May pass ordinances, &c.

§ 16. That it shall and may be lawful for the board of trustees to elect a town treasurer, who shall hold his office for the term of one year, and who shall give bond, in adequate penalty, for the faithful performance of such duties as may be assigned by the board, and the faithful and prompt payment of all orders that may be drawn on him when in funds, and deliver to his successor in office all moneys and papers that may be in his possession belonging to the town at the time he leaves his office: *Provided,*

Treasurer to be appointed; powers and duties.

Said treasurer shall not be a member of the board of trustees during the time he holds said office of treasurer.

1869.

§ 17. The trustees shall meet and transact the business of said town as often as the chairman of the board may think it necessary; and should any of them fail to attend said meetings when notified, without a good and sufficient cause, they may be fined by the chairman of the board in a sum not exceeding five dollars, to be collected by the marshal on a *capias pro fine* issued by the chairman, as other fines are collected by law. Said delinquent trustee must first be summoned to show cause for his non-attendance at least five days before his trial.

Trustees to meet, & absent members may be fined.

§ 18. Should the trustees of said town desire to establish new streets or alleys, or extend those already established, they shall petition the county court of Gallatin, setting forth in their petition specifically the location, length, and width of the street or alley that they desire to establish or extend, and the name of the owner or owners of the land over which the same is to pass, and the distance it will pass over each owner, if more than one; and upon the filing of said petition, it shall be the duty of the county judge to order process to issue against said owner or owners, to show cause why said street shall not be established or extended; and after the filing of said petition, the county court shall proceed to establish said streets or alleys, or extend the same, in the same manner as public roads are now established by law in this Commonwealth, except that the order establishing and opening the same shall be directed to the trustees of the town of Warsaw, who may proceed to open said street or extend the same, as the case may be, after paying the owner of the land the damage assessed therefor.

In relation to opening new streets, alleys, &c.

§ 19. If any person should fence up any of the public streets of said town, or obstruct the same, without the consent of the trustees of said town, it shall be considered a misdemeanor, and he may be fined not exceeding two dollars for every twenty-four hours that said street may be fenced up or obstructed; and should any street remain fenced up or obstructed after the passage of this act, without the consent of said trustees, the person who has fenced up or obstructed the same shall be guilty as aforesaid; and the parties aforesaid, or either of them, may be prosecuted before the police judge for said offense, in the same manner as other misdemeanors are now prosecuted before him by law.

In relation to fencing up public streets, &c.

§ 20. The said trustees shall have full power and authority to borrow money, and execute bonds for the payment of the same, at such rate of interest as they may deem proper, not exceeding twelve per cent. per annum, the sum

May borrow money.

1869.   borrowed not to exceed twenty-five hundred dollars; **and**
said bonds, when executed by said trustees, shall be binding upon the citizens of said town; and it shall be the duty
of said trustees to levy and collect taxes sufficient to discharge said bonds, principal and interest, within five years
from the time of the execution of the same. All money
thus borrowed shall be expended for the use, improvement,
and benefit of said town.

§ 21. The record of the proceedings of the board shall be
taken and received as record evidence in any court of this
State, when a copy thereof is signed by the chairman and
attested by the clerk.

Proceedings to be taken as evidence.

§ 22. That the qualified voters of the town of Warsaw,
in Gallatin county, shall, and they are hereby authorized
to, elect a police judge in said town on the first Monday
in March, 1869, and on the first Monday in the same
month every two years thereafter. Said judge, so elected,
before he enters upon the duties of his office, shall take an
oath, before some one duly authorized to administer the
same, to discharge the duties of said office faithfully and
impartially, to the best of his ability. Said judge shall
have jurisdiction of all misdemeanors, and of all causes,
civil, criminal, or penal, in which justices of the peace
have jurisdiction, within the limits of the town of Warsaw; and in criminal or penal cases he shall have jurisdiction conferred by law upon two justices of the peace; and
shall proceed in the same manner that justices of the
peace are required to proceed in such cases; he shall have
full authority to require bail, and receive the acknowledgment and execution of recognizance of bail in all cases
originating before him in which bail is or may by law be
hereafter required. He shall be a conservator of the peace,
and have jurisdiction over affrays, assaults and batteries,
riots, routs, breaches of the peace, and unlawful assemblies; all cases of indecent or immoral behavior or conduct
calculated to disturb the peace and dignity of said town;
of all cases of drunkenness, profane swearing, running
horses, firing guns, pistols, making reports by burning
powder or crackers, blowing horns, ringing bells, crying
aloud by day or by night, and all other riotous or illegal
and improper conduct whatever, committed within the
corporate limits of the town of Warsaw, all of which
are hereby declared to be misdemeanors. He shall have
jurisdiction of all offenses or causes arising out of the by-
laws and ordinances passed by the board of trustees of
said town for enforcement of the powers granted to them
by law. He shall have power to order the marshal to
summon a jury in any case cognizable before him when a
jury would be required before the circuit court or a justice
of the peace; and in all cases where the amount of fine

Police judge to be elected.

To take oath.

Jurisdiction and powers.

is over sixteen dollars and sixty-six and two thirds cents, and is not fixed by law, the sum shall be ascertained by the verdict of a jury. In all cases and charges arising out of, and for a violation or infraction of, any of the ordinances of said town, when the penalty therefor is sixteen dollars and fifty cents or less, he shall hear and try the same without the intervention of a jury; and in all cases in which a fine is imposed by said judge, he shall issue *capias pro fine* or *fieri facias* as in his judgment the case may warrant; but nothing herein shall deprive a defendant from the right of replevying any judgment rendered against him for fine and cost: *Provided*, He offers ample security for the same. Upon a drunken person being brought before the judge, he shall have power to order him to be confined in jail until he becomes duly sober; and upon a disorderly person being brought before him, he may require of him security for his good behavior and for keeping the peace for a period not exceeding one year; and on his failure to give such security, may commit such person until he gives security; but in no event is the confinement to exceed thirty days. He shall have power to issue summons for witnesses in cases pending before him; and upon their failure to attend, may award compulsory process to compel their attendance. He shall have power, without the intervention of a jury, to fine and imprison for contempt: *Provided*, The fine does not exceed ten dollars, nor the imprisonment twelve hours. Said judge shall have the same authority to take depositions that justices of the peace now have in this Commonwealth. He shall have full power to grant injunctions, restraining orders, attachments, and writs of *habeas corpus*, and administer oaths in all cases wherein, by existing laws, justices of the peace are required or authorized so to do. He shall keep a record of his proceedings, a certified copy of which shall be evidence in all courts of justice, and have the same force and effect as records of a justice of the peace. He shall, in all other matters not herein mentioned, have concurrent jurisdiction with justices of the peace, and be governed by the same laws and regulations. All trials before said judge shall be had and held in the town of Warsaw.

§ 23. The police judge shall issue process in the name of the Commonwealth as other warrants or arrest, except otherwise provided for in this act, and make them returnable before himself as police judge of Warsaw; the same shall be directed to the marshal, sheriff, or any constable of Gallatin county, and shall be executed and returned by the officer in whose hands the same is placed, under the same penalties as other process from justices of the peace: *Provided, however*, That when any prosecution is instituted

Further powers.

1869.

His fees.

for a breach of any of the ordinances of said town, the process shall issue in the name of the town of Warsaw, and said town shall be entitled to all the fines and penalties recovered under the provisions of this act. The police judge shall be entitled to a fee of one dollar for a peace warrant or a warrant for a riot, rout, or breach of the peace, unlawful assembly, affray, or misdemeanor, or any breach of the laws or ordinances of the town of Warsaw; and in all other cases, and for all other service, he shall be allowed the same fees as justices of the peace are allowed for similar services.

Appeals may be had.

§ 24. Appeals from all judgments rendered by said police judge in civil cases shall be allowed to any party, under the same rules and regulations, and to the same tribunals, as appeals are now allowed to be taken from judgments of justices of the peace in like cases.

Who to act when police judge is absent.

§ 25. In the absence of said police judge, or his inability to perform the duties of his office, any justice of the peace who holds his office in the magistrates' district in which the town of Warsaw is situated, may act and perform any official duty which pertains to the office of said police judge, and shall be entitled to the same fees therefor.

Marshal to be elected.

To take oath.

Jurisdiction and powers.

§ 26. There shall be a marshal elected by the qualified voters of said town at the same time and place the police judge is elected, under the same rules and regulations, and shall hold his office the same length of time that the police judge is entitled to hold his office under this act. Before he enters upon the duties of his office, he shall take an oath faithfully and impartially to discharge the duties of said office, and give bond and good security, in a sum not exceeding twenty-five hundred dollars, to the trustees and their successors in office, conditioned faithfully to discharge the duties of said office, and may contain any other condition that the board of trustees of said town may think proper to require. He shall have full power, within the county of Gallatin, to serve all process and precepts directed to him by the police judge, and, in the absence of the sheriff, all process and precepts directed to him by any officer of the Commonwealth, and make due return thereof. The marshal shall be a conservator of the peace, and may and shall, on his own view, or on reliable information of others, arrest any and all rioters and persons guilty of drunkenness or disorderly conduct, and shall safely keep said persons by confinement in the jail of the county, or otherwise, until such person can be conveniently brought before the police judge or justice for examination and trial; and for this purpose, the jailer of said county of Gallatin shall safely keep all persons placed in his care by the marshal. Said marshal shall be entitled to the same fees and per cent. for collecting the tax of said town, penalties and forfeitures, as sheriffs and constables are entitled to in like cases, and to the same fees from the State, to be paid out of the treasury and county levy, for serving warrants for felony, and warrants for misdemeanors, as constables and sheriffs are entitled to for like services. He shall collect all executions and final process placed in his hands for collection, in the same manner constables are required by law to do. He shall be subject to the same proceedings, and liable to the same penalties, that sheriffs and constables are in like cases for the non-performance of any duty imposed by this act.

1869.

His fees.

§ 27. Both the police judge and marshal shall be residents of the town of Warsaw, and removal therefrom shall vacate their respective offices.

§ 28. That whenever a vacancy shall occur in the office of police judge or marshal in the town aforesaid, either by death or otherwise, it shall be the duty of the trustees of said town to, within five days thereafter, or as soon as practicable, convene their said board, and hold an election to fill such vacancy; and the person receiving a majority vote of the whole number of trustees elected, shall be declared the police judge or marshal, as the case may be, and shall be fully empowered, after taking the oath and executing bond as now required by law, to discharge all the duties of police judge or marshal as if they, or either of them, had been duly elected at the regular election for police judge and town marshal: *Provided further*, That the police judge or town marshal thus chosen shall only hold their offices until the first Monday in March succeeding their election by said trustees, at which time an election shall take place to fill said vacancy.

Vacancies in offices of police judge and marshal, how filled

§ 29. The police judge and town marshal shall be liable to all the pains and penalties for misconduct in office, and may be tried in the same manner and before the same authorities, and punished by fine, imprisonment, and removal from office, as is now provided by law for the punishment of county judge, sheriff, or constables for similar offenses.

Liabilities of judge and marshal.

§ 30. It shall be the duty of the judge of the county court of Gallatin county, in the months of either January or February preceding said election, to appoint two judges and a sheriff to conduct said election, who shall have the same qualifications as electors of said town now have under the charter thereof, and be subject to all the pains and penalties for any misconduct that officers of elections now are under the election laws of this Commonwealth.

Judges to conduct elections to be appointed by county court.

§ 31. It shall be the duty of the trustees of said town to require the assessor appointed under the provisions of this

Assessor to give bond.

1869.

act, before he enters upon the discharge of his duty, to
execute a bond to said trustees and their successors in
office, with security approved by them in the sum of fifteen hundred dollars, conditioned that he will faithfully
and impartially discharge his duties in assessing the property of the citizens of said town; and for any breach of
the conditions of said bond, they may institute suit in any
court of jurisdiction in said county, in the name of the
town of Warsaw, and recover from him and his securities
the damage sustained by said town in consequence of the
misconduct or breach of said bond by said assessor.

Additional
powers of mar-
shal.

§ 32. It shall be the duty of the marshal of said town to
arrest all offenders and violators of the laws and ordinances of said town, and bring them before the proper
tribunals for trial; and for this purpose he may summons
a *posse comitatus*, composed of the citizens of said town;
and any citizen refusing to assist when thus summoned,
may be fined by the police judge, not exceeding ten dollars, which may be collected as other fines are collected.
It shall be the duty of said marshal to report all nuisances
or obstructions of the streets and sidewalks to the trustees
of said town for their action.

'§ 33. All acts and parts of acts pertaining to the corporate limits of said town, and all laws for the government,
organization, and control of the same, shall be, and the
same is hereby, repealed.

§ 34. This act shall take effect from its passage.

Approved February 25, 1869.

CHAPTER 1583.

AN ACT to Charter the Metropolis and Union City Railroad Company.

*Be it enacted by the General Assembly of the Commonwealth
of Kentucky :*

§ 1. That the formation of a company is hereby authorized for the purpose of establishing a communication, by
railroad, between the city of Metropolis, Illinois, to Union
City, Tennessee, through the States of Kentucky and Tennessee, the northern terminus to be on the southern bank
of the Ohio river, at some point convenient to the city of
Metropolis, until said company shall have power and authority to make immediate connection there by the erection of a bridge across said river, which company shall
consist of the stockholders; and when formed, shall, and
they are hereby, constituted a body-corporate, by the
name and style of the "Metropolis and Union City Railroad Company;" and by such name shall have and enjoy,
possess and exercise, all the rights, powers, privileges, and

franchises, so far as the same are applicable, which the Henderson and Nashville railroad company have, by the terms of an act passed November 15th, 1849, entitled "An act to amend and re-enact an act, entitled 'An act to incorporate the Henderson and Nashville railroad company,' passed by the Kentucky Legislature, and approved February 8th, 1837," and be subject to the same liabilities and restrictions therein imposed: *Provided*, That the lands and right of way for the construction of said road required by the company, shall not exceed fifty feet from the center of the road on each side: *And provided further*, That each share shall entitle the owner thereof to one vote.

§ 2. That the capital stock of said company shall be sixty thousand shares, of twenty-five dollars each; and books for subscription of stock in said road shall be opened at such times and places, and kept open for such length of time, in the States of Illinois, Kentucky, and Tennessee, as may be designated by the following named commissioners, or a majority of them: G. S. Miles, G. H. Cary, F. M. English, Thos. H. Corbett, G. W. Ratcliffe, Ben. Davis, B. Barr, and Mason Johnson, who shall have power to appoint three or more persons, in any of the towns or neighborhoods within the said States of Tennessee, Kentucky, and Illinois, to open books and receive subscriptions.

§ 3. That any three of the above-named commissioners, or such persons as may be appointed by them for that purpose, shall, at each place named and designated, open books and receive subscriptions during the time the said books are directed to be kept open; and on each share subscribed shall demand and receive the sum of fifty cents, without which the subscription shall be void.

§ 4. That said commissioners, or any three of them, appointed as above named, shall have power to secure the payment of each share by taking, as collateral security, a mortgage upon real estate, executed to them, or any three of them, as trustees, for the benefit of said railroad company, by each subscriber to the capital stock of said company.

§ 5. That G. S. Miles, G. H. Cary, F. M. English, Thos. H. Corbett, G. W. Ratcliffe, Ben. Davis, B. Barr, and Mason Johnson, or a majority of them, be, and they are hereby, constituted a board of commissioners to superintend and manage all the affairs of said company, until it shall be fully organized by the election of a board of directors, as prescribed by the charter of the Henderson and Nashville railroad company, so far as it may be applicable and not inconsistent with the provisions embraced in the several sections of this act.

1869.   § 6. That so soon as the above-named commissioners, or
a majority of them, shall ascertain that four thousand
shares of the capital stock of said company have been subscribed, on each of which there shall have been paid the
sum of fifty cents, the said commissioners shall advertise
the facts in some newspaper in the towns of Metropolis,
Union City, and Dyersburg, and shall call the subscribers
together at such time and place as may be designated by
said commissioners, or a majority of them, at which time
and place the said subscribers shall organize the company
by the election of a president and directors thereof, as provided in the charter of the Henderson and Nashville railroad company and the provisions of this act, and thenceforth the said subscribers of the stock shall form one body-
politic and corporate, in deed and in law; and the Metropolis and Union City railroad company be fully organized
in the States of Kentucky, Illinois, and Tennessee, for the
purpose aforesaid.

§ 7. That this act, whereby all the rights, powers, privileges, and franchises which the Henderson and Nashville
railroad company have by the terms of the act passed as
aforesaid, and extended to the Metropolis and Union City
railroad company, when it shall have been formed in accordance with the provisions above mentioned, shall become a
law whenever the State of Tennessee may enact the same
for the same purpose, with such modifications and amendments as they may deem right, not inconsistent with the provisions hereof: *Provided, however*, If the said State of Tennessee should not enact or co-operate in this charter during
the present year when the same shall be enacted, the time
shall be allowed thereafter, as is now allowed to do and
perform certain things required by the provisions of this
act: *Provided further*, That the people of no county, part
of county, city, or town, through which said proposed road
may be built, shall have the right to vote upon themselves
a tax for the purpose of subscribing stock to the capital
stock of the company hereby created. Nor shall the county
court of any county, or the corporate authorities of any
city or town, have the right to issue the bonds of such
county, part of county, city, or town, to assist in any manner in the construction of said road, upon the petition of
any number of voters however numerous: *Provided further*,
That this act shall not take effect until the charter is granted to the Paducah company to construct and make a railroad from Vincennes to Paducah, with powers, rights, and
privileges as liberal as are the powers granted by the Legislature of Kentucky in this charter.

Approved February 25, 1869.

CHAPTER 1584.

AN ACT to amend the Charter of the City Banking Company, of.Campbell County.

Be it enacted by the General Assembly of the Commonwealth of Kentucky:

§ 1. That the time in which the corporators named in said charter should open books for the subscription of stock, as prescribed in the act incorporating said company, approved March 6th, 1868, be, and the same is hereby, extended for one year, viz: to the 6th day of March, 1870.

§ 2. This act to take effect from its passage.

Approved February 25, 1869.

CHAPTER 1585.

AN ACT to amend an act approved March 2d, 1865, entitled "An act allowing School Districts to levy a District School Tax."

Be it enacted by the General Assembly of the Commonwealth of Kentucky:

§ 1. That an act, entitled "An act allowing common school districts to levy a district school tax," approved March 2d, 1865, be, and the same is hereby, amended as to allow common school district No. 15, in the county of Grant, to levy and collect a tax of not exceeding twenty cents in any one year on the one hundred dollars' worth of takable property in said district, for the purpose of building a school-house.

§ 2. The election and other proceedings under this act shall be governed by said act approved March 2d, 1865.

§ 3. This act to take effect from and after its passage.

Approved February 25, 1869.

CHAPTER 1586.

AN ACT to incorporate the Western Military Academy, at New Castle, Henry County.

Be it enacted by the General Assembly of the Commonwealth of Kentucky:

§ 1. That an institution of learning, located by E. Kirby Smith at New Castle, Henry county, Kentucky, is hereby styled and known as the Western Military Academy.

§ 2. That the president of the academy shall have power to confer upon the pupils thereof any or all the diplomas or degrees conferred by any other college of learning in the State.

§ 3. That in order to preserve good order and obedience among the scholars, and to protect the property thereunto

1869.

belonging from the trespasses of others, power is hereby conferred upon the president of said college, or those acting under him, to arrest, without warrant, all persons who are found trespassing upon the premises of said school, or engaged in inducing the scholars, or any of them, to leave the grounds of said institution: *Provided*, That when any such arrest is made, it shall be the duty of the president, or those acting under him, to carry the person so arrested before the police judge of the town of New Castle, or any magistrate of said district, for trial; and for a violation of this act, the persons so offending shall be fined not less than five nor more than ten dollars for each and every offense.

§ 4. That any person who shall sell, give, or loan to the students of said college, or any of them, within the county of Henry, spirituous liquors in any quantity, without the written authority of the president or one of the professors, shall be fined not less than fifty dollars nor exceeding two hundred dollars, in the circuit court of the county, upon an indictment by the grand jury thereof, as in other cases for a violation of the penal laws.

§ 5. This act to be in force from and after its passage.

Approved February 25, 1869.

CHAPTER 1587.

AN ACT to Charter the Horse Cave High School, in Hart County.

Be it enacted by the General Assembly of the Commonwealth of Kentucky:

§ 1. That the Horse Cave High School, established by J. P. Bagby, at Horse Cave, Hart county, Kentucky, shall hereafter be known under the name and style of " Horse Cave Male and Female Seminary."

§ 2. That A. Anderson, Wm. B. Young, Aaron Lawson, Thos. S. Walton, Thomas Mustain, Wade Veluzet, M. N. Lasley, and J. P. Bagby, and their successors in office, be, and they are hereby, created a body-politic and corporate, by the name and style of the " Trustees of Horse Cave Male and Female Seminary;" and as such, they and their successors may acquire, by purchase or otherwise, and hold, real estate and personal property, and dispose of the same by sale or otherwise; may make contracts, sue and be sued, plead and be impleaded; have and use a common seal, and change the same at pleasure; and also make such rules, by-laws, and ordinances, as may be necessary for the good government of said corporation, not incompatible with the Constitution and laws of this State and of the United States; they may open books for subscriptions for stock in said seminary, and issue certificates therefor in shares of fifty dollars each, at such times as they may think proper: *Provided*, That the aforenamed trustees shall appoint one of their number treasurer of the board, who shall give bond with ample security for the proper application of the moneys accruing to said company from sale of shares in the building or buildings proposed to be built for educational purposes. The moneys received by subscriptions for stock and donations made to said corporate company, shall be used and employed in founding and building and maintaining an institution of learning, in the town of Horse Cave, county of Hart, State of Kentucky, to be called and styled "Horse Cave Male and Female Seminary."

§ 3. Shares of stock held in this enterprise may be transferred by parties holding the same, in the same manner as any other species of real estate may be.

§ 4. The trustees named in this act may appoint one of their number president of the board of trustees; and the president and a two-thirds majority of the stockholders may make and change the by-laws, and appoint such agents and teachers as they may choose, from time to time: *Provided, however*, That each stockholder may count as many (and no more) votes as he may hold shares in said stock, in person or by proxy.

§ 5. The stockholders may annually elect trustees, teachers, and other officers necessary to carry on the enterprise.

§ 6. This act shall take effect from its passage.

Approved February 25, 1869.

CHAPTER 1588.

AN ACT to change the boundary of School District No. 47, in Washington County, and 48, in Marion County.

Be it enacted by the General Assembly of the Commonwealth of Kentucky:

§ 1. That the line between common school district No. 47, in Washington, and common school district No. 48, in Marion county, be so changed as to include Josephus Adams, R. Y. McElroy, Jackson Vanarsdall, and F. Spalding, within said school district No. 48.

§ 2. This act shall take effect from its passage.

Approved February 25, 1869.

CHAPTER 1589.

AN ACT to amend an act, entitled "An act to amend an act to reduce into one the several acts concerning the Town of Lagrange," approved 3d of March, 1868.

Be it enacted by the General Assembly of the Commonwealth of Kentucky:

§ 1. That an act, entitled "An act to amend an act to reduce into one the several acts concerning the town of Lagrange," approved March the 3d, 1868, be amended as follows, viz: That the police judge of said town, in addition to the powers now vested in him by law, shall have power, without the intervention of a jury, to hear and determine all cases arising in said town of any and all infractions of the criminal or penal laws of this State or the ordinances and by-laws of said town, where the punishment thereof does not exceed a fine of thirty dollars or fifteen days' imprisonment, or both such fine and imprisonment: *Provided, however*, In all cases where the fine shall exceed sixteen dollars, or the punishment imprisonment, the accused, if he demand it, shall have the right of trial by jury.

§ 2. The judge of said court shall have power to issue warrants of arrest, and executions or *capias pro fine* to enforce his judgments, which may be directed to the sheriff or any constable of Oldham county; and, when so directed, said officers shall be bound to receive and execute the same; or the same may be directed to the marshal of said town, who shall have power to execute the same anywhere in the county of Oldham.

§ 3. The trustees of said town shall have the power to impose a tax, not exceeding twenty dollars for one year, on any billiard table, ten-pin alley, or pigeon-hole table erected or kept within said town; which tax shall be collected and accounted for as other taxes levied on the inhabitants of said town.

§ 4. That all persons who shall be convicted of drunkenness or other disorderly conduct in said town, shall be fined in any sum not exceeding five dollars for each offense; and upon failure to pay the said fine assessed and costs, shall stand committed to the jail of said county at the rate of two dollars per day till said fine and costs are paid.

§ 5. That upon information to the police judge, or on his own view, that any one has been guilty of any of the offenses aforesaid, he shall issue his warrant for the apprehension of such persons, and forthwith proceed to trial, and if convicted, to enforce the penalty aforesaid.

§ 6. The police judge and town marshal shall have the

same fees for services under this act as are allowed in cases of breaches of the peace.

§ 7. This act to take effect from and after its passage.

. Approved February 25, 1869.

CHAPTER 1590.

AN ACT to Charter the Crittenden Seminary.

Be it enacted by the General Assembly of the Commonwealth of Kentucky:

§ 1. That Littleton Finley, B. M. Ratcliff, F. T. Mansfield, A. F. Hogsett, J. Poor, Thomas Rouse, and John Finley, and their successors, be, and they are hereby, created a body corporate and politic, with perpetual succession, to be styled the trustees of Crittenden Seminary, with full powers to transfer, hold, and acquire property, real and personal, make contracts, sue and be sued, plead and be impleaded, in their corporate capacity, in all the courts of this Commonwealth, both at law and in equity; to make, have, and to use a common seal, and the same to alter or change at pleasure, and to do any other act which like corporations may of right do.

§ 2. That said seminary shall be located in the town of Crittenden.

§ 3. That all funds and estate which may now belong to said Crittenden Seminary, or which may hereafter be acquired by it, are, and shall be, vested in said trustees, to be held by them and their successors, in their corporate capacity, for the sole use and benefit of said seminary, and for the purpose of promoting learning therein: *Provided,* That the whole of the moneys and estate so held shall never exceed twenty-five thousand dollars.

§ 4. That said trustees shall have power to appoint or employ such professors and teachers in the various departments of said school as they may think proper, and may remove the same at pleasure.

§ 5. That said trustees shall have power and authority to make all such by-laws, rules and regulations, for the government of said seminary and the management of its concerns, as they may deem expedient, and to alter, amend, or annul the same at pleasure: *Provided, however,* That said by-laws, rules and regulations, shall not be repugnant to the Constitution and laws of the United States, the Constitution and laws of this Commonwealth, nor inconsistent with any of the provisions of this charter.

§ 6. That a majority of the board of trustees of said school shall constitute a quorum competent to transact all the business belonging or appertaining to said school, except the appointment or removal of teachers, for which the vote of a majority of the whole board of trustees shall be requisite.

§ 7. The board of trustees shall be composed of seven members, who shall be annually elected by the stockholders of the institution on the first Saturday in July, and shall continue in office for one year, or until their successors are duly elected and qualified. The present board appointed by this charter shall continue in office until the first Saturday in July, 1869, or until their successors have been duly elected and qualified. They shall appoint a president, treasurer, and secretary; shall hold at least two stated meetings in each year; and when deemed necessary, the president may call a meeting of the board for the transaction of business at any time during the interval between the regular semi-annual meetings.

§ 8. That the president, treasurer, and secretary shall constitute the judges and clerk of the election for trustees; and in the event of either of them being absent or being a candidate, then the stockholders present may choose from their number judges and clerk, or either of them, to hold the election, and an election so held shall be valid.

§ 9. That the said trustees, before entering upon the duties of their office, shall take an oath before a magistrate that they will, to the best of their ability, discharge the duties imposed upon them.

§ 10. The board shall have power to fill vacancies occasioned in their own body by death, resignation, or removal, and to require bond and security of any officer for the faithful discharge of his duty.

§ 11. No person shall be eligible to the office of trustee unless he shall be the owner of one share of stock at least six months before the regular election. Stockholders shall be entitled to one vote for each share of stock owned by them, and may vote in person or by proxy duly appointed in writing. The stock may be negotiated and assigned on the books of the trustees, and the assignees be entitled to all the privileges of stockholders.

§ 12. The trustees shall annually declare and pay such dividends as may be earned, and shall have power to confer all the honors and degrees usually conferred by such institutions on deserving students.

§ 13. It shall not be necessary for said corporation to procure a common seal, but it may authenticate its acts by the signature and seal of the president.

§ 14. This act shall take effect from its passage.

Approved February 25, 1869.

CHAPTER 1591.

AN ACT to authorize the Greenup County Court to levy an ad valorem tax for the payment of certain Bonds therein mentioned.

Be it enacted by the General Assembly of the Commonwealth of Kentucky:

§ 1. That the magistrates of Greenup county may assemble at the county seat, and, by a majority vote of all the magistrates of said county, levy an annual ad valorem tax, which shall not exceed twenty cents on each one hundred dollars' worth of taxable property in said county, for the purpose of paying off the bonds of the county, which have been issued, and are now outstanding against the county, for the purchase of a poor-house and farm for the support of the paupers of said county.

§ 2. That it shall be the duty of the sheriff or other collecting officer to collect said taxes at the same time and in the same manner, and under the same responsibility, as is now prescribed by law for the collection of the county levy, and he shall pay the same on the order of the court of claims, which order shall be a proper voucher in the hands of the sheriff or other officer when receipted.

§ 3. It shall be the duty of the officer who collects said taxes to pay the same over to the proper authorities within the limits now prescribed by law for the paying over the county levy.

§ 4. No part of the proceeds of the taxes levied and collected under the provisions of this act shall be appropriated for any other purpose than that which is indicated in this act.

§ 5. This act shall take effect from and after its passage.

Approved February 25, 1869.

———

CHAPTER 1592.

AN ACT to incorporate the Jones' Mill and Barnes' Mill Turnpike Road Company.

Be it enacted by the General Assembly of the Commonwealth of Kentucky:

§ 1. That a company is hereby created a body-politic and corporate, under the name and style of the Jones' Mill and Barnes' Mill Turnpike Road Company, for the purpose of constructing a turnpike road from or near Jones' Mill, on Silver creek, in Madison, to Barnes' Mill or near same.

§ 2. That the capital stock of said company shall be ten thousand dollars, to be divided into shares of fifty dollars each. The books for subscription shall be opened at such times and places as may suit the convenience of any three of the commissioners, and continue open until the stock is taken.

§ 3. That the following persons are appointed commissioners or corporators to open the books, viz: Thos. Jones, Richard Clark, Irvine Roberts, Turner Davis, Dr. F. J. Dickerson, and Robert Rice and Benjamin Bogie; and each commissioner who will act shall open a book, and the subscribers therein shall sign an obligation in the following form: "We, whose names are hereunto subscribed, respectively promise to pay to the Jones' Mill and Barnes' Mill turnpike road company the sum of fifty dollars for each share of stock set opposite our names, in such proportions and at such times as shall be determined on by the president and directors of said company.

§ 4. When two thousand dollars of said capital stock is subscribed, it shall be the duty of said commissioners, or any of them, to give a notice of a meeting of the stockholders on the proposed route, for the purpose of organizing said company by choosing officers, to consist of a president and four directors, a treasurer and secretary, notice to be given at least ten days previous to the meeting. Each stockholder shall be entitled to one vote for every share of stock subscribed or owned by him or her.

§ 5. That the grade and thickness of the metal shall be determined by the president and directors of said company; one toll-gate to be erected as soon as two miles and one half of said road is completed: *Provided*, That said company shall charge the same tolls as are charged on the Richmond and Lexington turnpike road.

§ 6. That said company shall charge only half toll at said gate until more than two and one half miles are finished, and then at the same rates per mile; the amount collected to be applied for the purpose of completing said road.

§ 7. That as soon as said company shall be organized, the president and directors shall possess all powers, authority, rights, and privileges; may do and perform all acts necessary for carrying on and completing said turnpike road, as well as laying out and locating the same, and shall be subject to all the duties, qualifications, restrictions, penalties, fines, and forfeitures, and shall be entitled to the tolls as above.

§ 8. That the president and directors shall be elected annually on the second Saturday in April, and hold their office until their successors are duly elected and sworn.

§ 9. This act shall take effect from its passage.

Approved February 25, 1869.

CHAPTER 1593.

AN ACT for the benefit of Fleming Salmons, of Carter County.

WHEREAS, Fleming Salmons, of Carter county, has built a mill-dam across Little Sandy river at the site of the old Lyons mill, in Carter county; now, therefore,

Be it enacted by the General Assembly of the Commonwealth of Kentucky:

§ 1. That the said Fleming Salmons be, and he is hereby, authorized to continue said dam across the said river at said point, not exceeding four feet high, so long as he will keep a good and sufficient slope to the same ten feet long for ever foot the dam shall be in height.

§ 2. That said Salmons shall be forever absolved from all pains and penalties which he may have laid himself liable to by reason of the erection of said dam.

§ 3. This act to take effect from and after its passage.

Approved February 25, 1869.

CHAPTER 1594.

AN ACT to incorporate the Deposit and Savings Bank of Lexington.

Be it enacted by the General Assembly of the Commonwealth of Kentucky:

§ 1. That there is hereby established the Deposit and Savings Bank of Lexington, the capital stock of which shall not be less than thirty thousand dollars nor more than seventy-five thousand dollars, divided into shares of one hundred dollars each; which shall be personal estate, and transferable on the books of said bank in such manner as the board of directors may prescribe.

§ 2. That Willard Davis, George E. Billingsly, John A. Prall, Wm. F. White, Thos. Outen, and Hugh W. Adams, are appointed commissioners, any of whom, after giving notice to the others, may open books in the city of Lexington for the subscription of stock in said bank; which subscriptions shall be binding upon the subscribers thereto. At any time when a sum not less than thirty thousand dollars shall have been subscribed, said commissioners, or a majority of them, may close the books and call a meeting of the stockholders, at which a board of five directors shall be chosen, who shall elect one of their number president; and to said board shall be committed the management of the affairs of the bank. Five dollars on each share shall be paid by each stockholder at the time of subscribing, and the remainder in such calls as the board may direct; and said bank may commence business

1869.

as soon as ten thousand dollars shall be actually paid in. At all elections each stockholder shall cast one vote for each share of stock he may hold, and upon which all calls have been paid; but, after the first election, no vote shall be cast for stock which the owner has not actually owned for at least six months. The votes aforesaid may be cast either in person or by written proxy. The board thus chosen shall serve for one year and until their successors shall be chosen; but, during the year, the board may fill any vacancies occurring in their number by death, resignation, or otherwise; and a regular election of directors shall be held each year.

§ 3. That the stockholders and their successors and assigns shall be a body-politic and corporate, under the name and style aforesaid, and shall so continue for thirty years; and shall have all the rights and privileges of a natural person in contracting and being contracted with, and in suing and being sued; and may have and use a common seal, and alter the same at pleasure.

§ 4. Said board may declare, from time to time, dividends out of the profits and earnings of the bank; may appoint such officers, agents, and employees as they may deem necessary for the transaction of their business, and pay them reasonable compensation therefor; may take from the president, cashier, and other officers and employes, bonds, with good security, for the faithful performance of their duties; which bonds shall be binding upon said officers, employes, and their sureties; and may make such by-laws for the regulation of the affairs of the bank as they may think proper, and alter and amend the same at pleasure: *Provided*, That the same shall not be in conflict with this act or with the Constitution or laws of Kentucky or the United States.

§ 5. Said bank may receive on deposit gold and silver coin, bank notes, and other notes which may be lawfully circulated as money, and repay the same in such manner, at such times, and at such rates of interest, as may be agreed upon with the depositors by special or general contract, but not exceeding legal interest; may deal in the loaning of money; may buy and sell bills of exchange, promissory notes, uncurrent money, stocks, bonds, mortgages, and other evidences of debt, take personal and other security for the payment of the same, and dispose of the latter, except real estate, as may be agreed upon between the parties, and pass a valid title to the same. All promissory notes and inland bills of exchange, which may be discounted and owned by said bank, shall be. and are hereby, put upon the same footing of foreign bills of exchange, and like remedy may be had thereon, jointly and severally, against the drawers and indorsers.

§ 6. Said bank may acquire, and hold and use, all such real and personal estate as may be necessary and convenient for the transaction of its business, or which may be conveyed to it as surety for any debt, or purchased in satisfaction of any judgment or decree in its favor; and may sell and convey the same.

§ 7. It shall be the duty of said bank, on the 1st of January in each year, to pay into the Treasury of the State fifty cents on each one hundred dollars of stock paid for in said bank, which shall be in full of all tax on said stock, and shall form part of the Common School Fund.

§ 8. It shall not be lawful for said bank to issue any note or bill to circulate as money.

§ 9. If the president, cashier, teller, clerks, or other officers of said bank, shall appropriate any of the funds thereof to his own use, or shall wilfully fail to make correct entries, or knowingly make false entries on the books of said bank, with intent to cheat or defraud the bank or any person, or conceal any improper appropriations of the funds of said bank, the person or persons so offending shall be deemed guilty of felony, and, upon conviction thereof, be sentenced to confinement in the jail and penitentiary of this Commonwealth for a period of not less than two nor more than twenty years.

§ 10. The president, directors, and other officers of said bank, before entering on the discharge of their duties, shall each take an oath faithfully and honestly, and to the best of their skill and judgment, to discharge all the duties of their respective offices under this charter, or which may be required of them by the by-laws and regulations of this corporation; and that they will not, during their continuance in office, sanction, or knowingly permit, any of the provisions thereof to be violated.

§ 11. The president and directors are hereby authorized and empowered to wind up the affairs of said bank whenever a majority in interest of the stockholders shall determine that the wants of the community and the interests of the stockholders do not require its continuance.

§ 12. The bank shall have a lien on the stock to secure the payment of the unpaid calls and assessments thereon.

§ 13. This act shall take effect from and after its passage.

Approved February 25, 1869.

CHAPTER 1595.

AN ACT for the benefit of John D. Secrest, of Fleming County.

WHEREAS, An application has been made to this General Assembly by John D. Secrest, of Fleming, to have Sarah Jane Cogswell and John Davis Cogswell, two infant children, declared to be his lawful heirs; therefore,

Be it enacted by the General Assembly of the Commonwealth of Kentucky:

§ 1. That the said Sarah Jane Cogswell and John Davis Cogswell be, and they are hereby, declared to be the heirs-at-law of the said John D. Secrest.

§ 2. This act to take effect from its passage.

Approved February 25, 1869.

CHAPTER 1598.

AN ACT to authorize the County Court of Butler County to issue bonds to build a Jail and repair Court-house.

Be it enacted by the General Assembly of the Commonwealth of Kentucky:

§ 1. That the county court of Butler county, a majority of the justices of the peace being present and concurring, be, and it is hereby, authorized to issue county bonds to the amount of twenty-five thousand dollars, for the purpose of erecting a sufficient jail for said county, and for repairing the court-house.

§ 2. Said bonds shall bear interest at the rate of six per cent. per annum, to be paid annually, and shall have six years to run, but redeemable at the pleasure of the county after five years.

§ 3. That the bonds may be issued in such sums as the court may direct, not less than one hundred dollars.

§ 4. That the court shall prescribe the form of the bonds; they shall be signed by the judge, attested by the clerk, and stamped with the seal of the court.

§ 5. The court may appoint a commissioner to sell said bonds, and direct the price to be taken therefor, and the time, manner, and place where they shall be offered.

§ 6. That it shall be the duty of said court to make the necessary arrangements for the payment of the interest on said bonds, and for their final payment when due.

§ 7. That to enable the court to comply with this act, it is hereby authorized to increase the county levy of said county to three dollars per tithe, and to levy an ad valorem tax of not exceeding twenty cents on the hundred dollars' worth of property in said county.

§ 8. That the tax levied under this act shall be collected in the same manner, and under the same liability, that the other county levy and taxes are collected,

§ 9. That the court shall have power to make all orders necessary for carrying into execution the provisions of this act; and the county judge may, at any time, convene the justices of the peace for action under this act.

§ 10. That this act shall take effect from and after its passage.

Approved February 25, 1869.

CHAPTER 1599.

AN ACT to amend the Road Laws so far as the Counties of Hickman and Ballard are concerned.

Be it enacted by the General Assembly of the Commonwealth of Kentucky:

§ 1. That the county courts of Hickman and Ballard counties shall divide said counties respectively into road precincts, the boundaries of which shall be distinctly defined; and as often as may be necessary, appoint a surveyor in each precinct, whose duty it shall be to superintend all the roads therein, and see that the same are cleared and kept in good repair, and ditched and kept ditched, on one or both sides, when so ordered by the said courts. No surveyor shall be allowed to resign his place under such appointment under two years, if he continues to reside in the precinct so long; said surveyors shall have the same powers, and be subject to the same penalties, as surveyors under the general laws of the Commonwealth. The clerks of said county courts shall, within ten days after the appointment of such surveyors, deliver a copy of the order to the sheriffs of their said counties respectively, containing a full and complete description of the precinct, and take their receipts therefor; and the sheriffs, in delivering said orders, shall, in all things, be governed by existing laws.

§ 2. All persons subject under existing laws to work on public roads, who reside within limits of each of said road precincts, shall be required to work on all the roads in said precinct; and it shall be no defense in an action against such persons for failing or refusing to work, after having been notified by the surveyor, that their names are not on the list of hands furnished said surveyor by the county court.

§ 3. This act shall take effect from and after its passage.

Approved February 25, 1869.

CHAPTER 1600.

AN ACT enlarging the Powers of the Metcalfe County Court.

Be it enacted by the General Assembly of the Commonwealth of Kentucky:

§ 1. That the county court of Metcalfe county, a majority of the justices being present and concurring therein, shall have the power to raise the ad valorem tax for said county to an amount not exceeding thirty cents on the one hundred dollars of taxable property in said county, and to raise the poll-tax of said county to an amount not exceeding three dollars to each poll, for the purpose of providing means to build and pay for a court-house and clerks' offices in said county.

§ 2. That section one of an act heretofore passed, empowering the county court of Metcalfe county to borrow money and execute the bonds of the county therefor, approved January 21, 1865, be, and the same is hereby, so amended as to authorize said court to issue bonds to the amount of fifteen thousand dollars, payable at any date prior to 31st December, 1875.

§ 3. This act to take effect from its passage.

Approved February 25, 1869.

CHAPTER 1601.

AN ACT to amend the Charter of the Glasgow Railroad Company.

Be it enacted by the General Assembly of the Commonwealth of Kentucky:

§ 1. That C. L. Hill, D. M. Ashby, Joseph R. Garnett, **Corporators' names, &c.** Woodford Shobe, W. H. Botts, Joseph H. Lewis, C. C. Forbes, S. H. Boles, Thomas Jones, C. W. Terry, R. H. Porter, R. B. Evans, and A. Crenshaw, their successors and associates, or any five of them, heretofore created a body-politic and corporate, under the name and style of the Glasgow railroad company, by an act of this General Assembly approved March 6, 1868, shall have full power and authority, in addition to the power of electing a president of said company, to elect a board of directory for said company out of their own number, or out of others who may become members of said company by a subscription of stock to the capital stock of said company, to consist of seven members.

§ 2. That any election of a directory for said company **Other elections legalised.** that may have heretofore taken place, is hereby legalized and confirmed.

§ 3. That to continue the succession of the president and **Annual election of directors.** directors of said company, seven directors shall be chosen annually, on the first Saturday in May of each year, at such place as the president and directors may appoint, by the stockholders of said company: *Provided*, That the president and directors may change the time and place of holding elections, upon publishing such change not less than thirty days in some newspaper having a circulation in Barren county; and that the directors of said company, or a majority of them, shall have the power to appoint judges of all elections, and to elect a president of said company either from among themselves or other stockholders, and to allow him such compensation for his services as they may deem proper; and if any vacancy shall occur by death, resignation, or refusal to act, of any president or director before the end of the year for which he was elected, a person from among the stockholders shall be appointed to fill such vacancy by the directory, or a majority of them; that the president and directory shall hold their offices until a new election of president and directors shall take place, and until their successors are qualified. All elections which are by this act, or by the by-laws of said company, to be held at a particular time, if not held at such time, may be held in thirty days thereafter, upon publication of notice to that effect, as required above, for twenty days. At all elections held under and in pursuance of this act and the by-laws of said company, each stockholder shall be entitled to one vote for every share of stock held and owned by him in the capital stock of said company.

§ 4. That a general meeting of the stockholders of said company may be called at any time during the interval between the annual meetings, by order of the directors, or by the stockholders owning one fourth of all the stock subscribed, upon giving twenty days' notice of the same, with its time and place, in a newspaper having circulation in Barren county; and when any such meeting is called by the stockholders, such notice shall specify the object of the call; and if at any such called meeting a majority in value of all the stockholders are not present, either in person or by proxy, the same shall be adjourned from day to day, without transacting any business, for not exceeding five days; and if within said five days stockholders owning a majority in value of all the stock subscribed do not attend in person or by proxy, such meeting shall be adjourned *sine die*.

§ 5. That the president and directors of said company in office for the preceding year shall, at the regular annual meeting of the stockholders, exhibit a clear and distinct account of the affairs of said company; that at any called meeting of the stockholders, as herein provided for, a majority in value of the stockholders of said company being present, they may demand similar statements from the president and directors of said company, whose duty it

Vacancies.

Term of office.

Elections.

How stock voted.

General meetings, &c.

Annual statement to be made.

1869.

*Officers may
be removed.*

shall be to forthwith furnish such statements; and at all such meetings of the stockholders, a majority in value of all the stock subscribed being present, a majority in value of those present may remove from office the president and any and all of the directors, and fill up the vacancies thus created until the next regular annual election, in the same manner they could do at the regular annual election.

*Treasurer &
secretary to be
appointed, and
treasurer to
give bond.*

§ 6. That the president and directors of said company shall have full power to appoint a treasurer and secretary of said company, and to require and take from the treasurer bond, with approved security, in such penalty as they may prescribe, payable to said company, conditioned for the faithful keeping and disbursing, under and by order of the president and directors of said company, of all such money as may come to his hands, and with such other conditions as may be prescribed; upon which bond recovery may be had for a breach of the conditions thereof by suit in the name of the company in any court having jurisdiction.

*Vested pow-
ers of company.*

§ 7. That the president and directors of said company are hereby vested with all the powers and rights necessary and needful for the construction and operating a railroad from Glasgow to some point on the Louisville and Nashville railroad, and all the powers and rights heretofore conferred by the General Assembly of the Commonwealth of Kentucky upon the Barren County railroad company, for the purpose of building and operating a railroad from Glasgow to some point on the Louisville and Nashville railroad, are hereby, and in as full and ample manner, conferred upon the Glasgow railroad company.

*In relation to
town of Glas-
gow taking
stock.*

§ 8. That whenever the president and directors of said company and ten tax-payers and voters of the town of Glasgow shall request the board of trustees of the town of Glasgow to do so, it shall be the duty of said trustees to submit to a vote of the qualified voters of said town, on a day to be designated by said trustees, not later than thirty days after said application is made to them, the question of subscribing for and on behalf of the voters and tax-payers of said town, one thousand shares to the capital stock of said company; and if a majority of those voting shall vote in favor of making such subscription, it shall be the duty of the president or chairman of the board of trustees for said town to make such subscription in accordance with the vote, such vote being entered on the record of the trustees of said town.

*Vote to be
taken.*

§ 9. It shall be the duty of the trustees of said town to enter the request of the president and directors of said company and ten tax-payers of said town, which must be in writing, upon their record, and thereupon to make an order commanding the marshal of the town of Glasgow,

on a day to be named in the order, to open the polls at
the court-house in Glasgow, and to take the vote of the
qualified voters in said town upon the question: Shall the
trustees of the town of Glasgow subscribe, for and on behalf of the tax-payers in Glasgow, one thousand shares
to the capital stock of the Glasgow railroad company.
It shall be the duty of the trustees for said town to appoint two judges, one clerk, and the marshal of the town
of Glasgow, to hold said election, as is now required by
law in cases of elections for State officers. On the failure
of any person appointed to hold and conduct said election to attend and perform the duties herein required,
those who do attend shall appoint and qualify others in
the place of those non-attending. In the event of the
failure of all those appointed to attend and hold said
election, the board of trustees may appoint a new set of
officers to conduct said election. At least twenty days'
notice posted on the court-house door shall be given of
said election by order of said trustees.

§ 10. The poll-books shall be kept open as is now required by law and the Constitution of this State; and the
book of the election shall be certified by the officers of the
election, and returned to the trustees of said town on the
third day after the election.

§ 11. It shall be the duty of the secretary of the board
of trustees and marshal of the town of Glasgow, and
chairman of the board of trustees for said town, on the
day of the return of said book of election as is herein
required, to count the vote for and against said subscription; and if a majority of all the votes cast shall be in
favor of said subscription, they shall make out a written
certificate to that effect, which shall be entered upon the
record book of said trustees; and in the absence of either
of the foregoing persons in this section mentioned, the
duties herein enjoined may be discharged by the other
two; and thereupon, if a majority of the votes so cast
shall be in favor of said subscription, the president and
chairman of the board of trustees shall subscribe, for and
on behalf of the tax-payers and voters of said town, said
sum of twenty-five thousand dollars, or one thousand
shares, to the capital stock of said company.

§ 12. It shall be the duty of the trustees of said town to
issue the bonds of said town, payable in twenty years,
and drawing interest at seven per cent. per annum, payable semi-annually, for the amount of said subscription,
which said bonds are to be made payable to the president
and directors of said company, and are to be taken and
received by the president and directors of said company
in payment of said subscription. They shall be signed by
the chairman of the trustees of said town and counter-

1869.

By whom
taken.

How long
polls to be kept
open, &c.

Who to count
vote, &c.

Trustees to
issue bonds.

signed by the secretary of the board; shall have coupons attached for the payment of the interest, which shall be signed by the secretary of the board, and shall be of such denominations and made payable at such places as the president and directors of said company may designate; and said bonds may be negotiated by the president and directers of said company by their written indorsement thereon.

§ 13. It shall be the duty of the trustees of the town of Glasgow, from time to time, to provide for the payment of the interest on said bonds by the imposition of an ad valorem tax upon all the real and personal estate (including the amount of each tax-payer's worth under the equalization law) within said town subject to taxation for revenue purppses; and for the purpose of ascertaining the property subject to taxation, recourse may be had to the assessor's tax-book for Barren county, or the trustees may appoint an assessor and provide for his compensation; said tax may be collected by the sheriff of Barren county, or other collector of the State revenue, under the same responsibilities upon his official bond as for collecting the State revenue; or the trustees may appoint the marshal of the town of Glasgow, or any other person, their collector of said taxes; but if the marshal, or any one, shall be appointed collector thereof, he shall enter into bond, with good, sufficient, and approved security, before said trustees, and payable to said trustees, with an adequate penalty, conditioned for the faithful discharge of his duties herein, which said bond may be put in suit and recovery had thereon for a breach of its stipulations, in any court having jurisdiction of the cause; said moneys shall be paid over, under the orders of said trustees, to the treasurer of said company, to be held by him, under the responsibility created by his bond, and paid over by him by order of said trustees.

And provide for payment of same.

Who to collect tax.

Money to be paid over to treasurer of company.

§ 14. It shall be the duty of the collector of said taxes to give the persons from whom he may collect said tax a receipt therefor, specifying the amount paid, and the time of its payment.

Collector to give receipts.

§ 15. Said receipts shall be transferable; and whenever the amount of said receipts shall equal in the aggregate the sum of twenty-five dollars, and shall be presented to the president and directors of said company, it shall be their duty to take in the same and to issue to the holders thereof a certificate of stock equal to the amount of receipts surrendered; the person receiving said certificate of stock shall thenceforth be a stockholder in said company to the extent of his certificate, and entitled to all the privileges and immunities of stockholders.

Receipts transferable, &c.

§ 16. Said trustees must, so soon as it shall become necessary, impose a tax upon the real and personal estate in said town, not exceeding ten cents on the one hundred dollars' worth of property in any one year, to create a sinking fund for the extinguishment of the principal of said bonds, and may make all needful orders, rules and regulations, for that purpose; and to accomplish that object, the amount so paid shall, in like manner, be treated and converted into stock in said company, as is provided in section fifteen.

§ 17. Said trustees shall have full power and authority to appoint three commissioners for the management of the sinking fund hereby created, with power to take from them bonds, payable to themselves in adequate penalties, with good and sufficient security, to be by them approved, conditioned for the faithful discharge of their duties under this section, and under the order and direction of the board of trustees. For a breach of said bond, recovery may be had in any courts of this Commonwealth having jurisdiction.

§ 18. That said subscription shall not be made for and on behalf of the tax-payers of said town, as herein required and directed, unless the tax-payers and voters in precinct No. 1, in Barren county, commonly called the Glasgow precinct, including the town of Glasgow as a part of said precinct, shall, in like manner, as hereinafter required by a majority of all the votes cast at an election hereinafter provided to be held, determine to subscribe for the tax-payers and voters of said precinct the sum of one hundred thousand dollars to the capital stock of said Glasgow railroad company.

§ 19. That the county court of Barren county may subscribe for stock in the Glasgow railroad company upon the following terms and conditions: upon the written application of the president and directors of the Glasgow railroad company and twenty housekeepers and tax-payers, residing in election precinct No. 1, in said county, commonly known and called the Glasgow precinct, setting forth their desire that the said subscription shall be made, and the number of shares to be subscribed, not exceeding four thousand in number, and requesting the question to be submitted to the qualified voters of said election precinct.

§ 20. It shall be the duty of the county court, the judge thereof alone presiding, to enter said written application at length upon the records of his court, and thereupon to make an order commanding the sheriff of the county, on a day to be named in said order, to open the polls at the place of voting in said precinct for State officers, and to take the vote of the qualified voters in said precinct upon

1869.

May create sinking fund.

May appoint commissioners of sinking fund.

In relation to district No. 1 taking stock.

Barren county court may take stock upon certain conditions.

Proceedings in relation thereto.

the question, "Shall the county court subscribe for and on behalf of the tax-payers in said election precinct the number of shares proposed in said written application?" It shall be the duty of the county court to appoint the judges and clerk of said election, as is now required by law in cases of elections for State officers: and it shall be the duty of the sheriff of the county, either in person or by deputy, as he may prefer, to superintend and hold said election as is required by law in cases of elections for State officers. On the failure of any officer appointed to hold and conduct said election to attend and perform the duties herein required, those who do attend shall appoint and qualify others in the place of those non-attending. At least thirty days' previous notice in writing, posted at the place of voting and three other public places in said district, shall be given by the sheriff of the time and place of holding said election: *Provided*, The voters in precinct No. 1 shall not be called on to vote on the proposition to tax themselves one hundred thousand dollars as named in this act until the voters in the corporate limits of the town of Glasgow have voted to tax themselves twenty-five thousand dollars as named in this act.

§ 21. The poll-books shall be kept open as is now required by the Constitution and laws of the State; and the books shall be certified by the officers of the election and returned to the office of the clerk of the Barren county court on the third day after the election.

How long poll-books to be kept open, &c.,

§ 22. It shall be the duty of the county judge, county court clerk, and sheriff of said county, on the day of the return of said books to the office of the county court clerk, as is herein required, to count the vote for and against said subscription; and if a majority of all the votes cast shall be in favor of the subscription of the stock, they shall make out a written certificate to that effect, which shall be entered upon the records of said county court. In the absence of either of the foregoing officers, the duties enjoined in this section may be performed by the other two.

Who to compare vote.

§ 23. It shall be the duty of the presiding judge of the Barren county court, in the event that a majority of all the votes cast at said election shall be in favor of said subscription of stock, either at the next regular term of the Barren county court, or at a called and special term, if the president and directors shall desire it, to subscribe for and on behalf of the voters and tax-payers in election precinct No. 1, in Barren county, the number of shares of stock recited in the written application mentioned in section nineteen of this act to the capital stock of the Glasgow railroad company.

Presiding judge to subscribe stock, &c.

1869.

§ 24. It shall be the duty of the presiding judge of the Barren county court to issue the bonds of said election precinct, payable to the president and directors of the Glasgow railroad company in twenty years, bearing interest at the rate of seven per cent. per annum and payable semi-annually, for the amount of said subscription; which said bonds are to be taken and received by the president and directors of said company in satisfaction of said subscription. They shall be signed by said judge and countersigned by the clerk of the Barren county court, shall have coupons attached for the payment of the interest, which shall also be signed by the clerk of said court. They shall be made payable at such place within the United States as the president and directors may designate, and may be negotiated by the president and directors by their written indorsement thereon: *Provided,* The bonds of precinct No. 1 shall not be issued or sold before the bonds of the town of Glasgow are issued and sold.

Presiding judge to issue bonds.

§ 25. It shall be the duty of said Barren county court, through its presiding judge, from time to time, to provide for the payment of the interest on said bonds, by the imposition of an ad valorem tax upon all the real and personal estate (including the amount of each tax-payer's worth under the equalization law) within said election precinct, subject to taxation for revenue purposes; and for the purpose of ascertaining the property subject to taxation recourse may be had to the assessor's tax-book of Barren county; said tax shall be collected by the sheriff of Barren county, or other collector of the public revenue, as other public dues, under the same responsibilities as for collecting other public dues, and shall be paid over by him to the treasurer of said company, to be by him applied to the payment of the interest on said bonds: *Provided,* That, in the assessment of the property of the precincts named in this act, regard shall be had to the books and assessments made by the county assessor.

And provide for payment of same.

§ 26. It shall be the duty of the collecting officer to give to the persons from whom he may collect said tax a receipt, specifying the amount paid and the time of payment.

To give tax receipts.

§ 27. Whenever the amount of said receipt shall equal in the aggregate the amount of twenty-five dollars, and shall be presented to the president and directors of said company, it shall be their duty to issue to the holder thereof a certificate of stock equal to the amount of receipts surrendered; and said receipts are, and shall be, assignable. The person receiving said certificate shall thenceforth be a stockholder in said company, and entitled to all the privileges of other stockholders.

Certificates of stock to be issued.

1869.

Sinking fund may be created.

§ 28. Said county court, upon the demand of the president and directors of said company, shall impose a tax upon the real and personal estate in said election precinct, not exceeding ten cents on the hundred dollars' worth of property assessed for taxation in any one year, to create a sinking fund for the extinguishment of the principal of said bonds, and may make all needful orders, rules and regulations, for that purpose, and to accomplish that object; the amount so paid shall, in like manner, be treated as stock, as provided in section fifteen hereof.

Commissioners of sinking fund

§ 29. The county judge, county court clerk, and treasurer of the said company, shall, *ex-officio*, constitute a board of commissioners of the sinking fund, whose duty it shall be to manage the fund for the payment of the principal of said bonds.

Precincts may take stock.

§ 30. That whenever the president and directors of said railroad company, and ten resident voters and tax-payers of any other designated election precinct in Barren, shall request the county court of Barren county to do so, it shall be the duty of said county court, the presiding judge thereof alone presiding, forthwith to submit to the vote of the qualified voters of such designated precinct the question whether said court shall subscribe, on behalf of such designated election precinct, the amount of stock or number of shares specified in said written request of the president and directors of said company, and the ten resident voters and tax-payers of said precinct, to the capital stock of said Glasgow railroad company; said election shall be ordered and held on a day to be fixed by the court, after causing the sheriff to give twenty days' written notice thereof, posted at three public places in said precinct, within thirty days after making the order therefor, and on a day to be named in said order; and shall in every particular be conducted and determined as is herein provided in case of the similar election herein provided for election precinct No. 1, in Barren county, except as it may be modified or changed by this section.

Proceedings in case precincts take stock.

§ 31. That if any election precinct in said county shall, by its vote as aforesaid, determine, by a majority of all the votes cast at said election, to subscribe to the capital stock of said company, it shall be the duty of the presiding judge of said county of Barren to make said subscription for and on behalf of the voters and tax-payers of said precinct, and to issue the bonds of such election precinct in payment thereof, which shall be issued as provided in this act for election precinct No. 1, of Barren county; and the same powers are conferred upon the presiding judge of Barren county to levy a tax to pay the interest on said bonds, and to create a sinking fund to pay off the principal of said bonds, as is provided in the case of election precinct No. 1, in Barren county.

§ 32. That for the purpose of effectuating and carrying into execution any vote herein provided for other election precincts in Barren county, all the foregoing sections of this act passed to carry into effect the vote of precinct No. 1, in Barren county, subscribing shares or stock to the capital stock of the Glasgow railroad company, are hereby declared to apply to and be made applicable to such other election precincts, so far as they may apply, as if such other precincts had been mentioned in said preceding sections.

§ 33. This act shall take effect from its passage.

Approved February 25, 1869.

1869.

How vote carried into effect.

CHAPTER 1602.

AN ACT to authorize the Marshall County Court to change the State Road leading from Columbus to Hopkinsville.

Be it enacted by the General Assembly of the Commonwealth of Kentucky:

§ 1. That the county court of Marshall county be, and the same is hereby, authorized to change that part of the State road leading from Columbus to Hopkinsville that passes over the lands of D. F. Pace, in Marshall county.

§ 2. That said county court, in making said change and alteration, shall be governed by the general laws regulating alterations in roads which the county courts of this State are authorized to change.

§ 3. That this act shall take effect from its passage.

Approved February 25, 1869.

CHAPTER 1603.

AN ACT to amend an act, entitled "An act for the benefit of the Towns of Marion and Birmingham."

Be it enacted by the General Assembly of the Commonwealth of Kentucky:

§ 1. That the trustees of the town of Birmingham, in Marshall county, shall have the same power to impose a tax upon hotel-keepers for license to retail spirituous liquors that said act gives them in cases of coffee-houses; said trustees to be governed in this case in every respect by the act that this is an amendment to.

§ 2. That the time for the regular election for town officers shall hereafter be on the first Saturday in May in each year.

§ 3. This act shall take effect from its passage.

Approved February 25, 1869.

CHAPTER 1604.

AN ACT to amend the Charter of the Town of Carrollton.

Be it enacted by the General Assembly of the Commonwealth of Kentucky:

§ 1. That the charter of the town of Carrollton be, and the same is hereby, so amended as to empower the trustees of said town to take stock in the proposed turnpike roads leading out of said town, to connect with the Louisville, Cincinnati, and Lexington railroad, and to appropriate a sufficient amount of revenue to pay for said stock: *Provided*, That no stock shall be taken until the question is submitted to the legal voters of said town, and is approved by a majority of those voting on the proposition.

§ 2. That said trustees shall have authority to pass and enforce an ordinance to prevent hogs and cattle from running at large in the streets and alleys of said town.

§ 3. That all fines recovered in the police court of said town for breaches of the peace, or other violations of the penal laws, when collected, shall be paid into the treasury of said town.

§ 4. That the board of trustees of said town shall have power to levy and collect a reasonable tax upon all steamboats, and other water crafts, for the use of the public landings belonging to said town, and shall regulate the amount to be collected by ordinance.

§ 5. That said trustees shall have power to fill vacancies occurring in the offices of police judge or town marshal; the appointee to hold his office until the next regular election, and until his successor is elected and qualified.

§ 6. That, after the passage of this act, the trustees of said town shall be elected annually on the first Thursday in May.

§ 7. That this act shall take effect and be in force from its passage.

Approved February 25, 1869.

CHAPTER 1605.

AN ACT empowering the County Court of Carter County to levy a tax for the purpose of rebuilding the Clerks' Offices of the County and Circuit Courts in said County, and to build fire-proof vaults for the safe-keeping of the public records of said county.

Be it enacted by the General Assembly of the Commonwealth of Kentucky:

§ 1. That it shall be lawful for the county court of Carter county, a majority of the justices concurring therein, to levy upon the property of said county, listed for taxation for revenue purposes, an ad valorem tax of not exceeding ten cents upon each one hundred dollars of property so listed, and to provide for the collection of the same; and the proceeds of such levy, when collected, shall be applied exclusively to the rebuilding and remodeling of the county and circuit court clerks' offices of said county, so as to make them fire-proof, or for the erection of fire-proof vaults for the safe keeping of the public records of said county, as in the discretion of said county court may seem most expedient.

§ 2. That the sheriff of Carter county shall collect such tax as said county court may levy under the provisions of this act, and shall pay over the same, when so collected, to such person or persons as the county court may order; and for the faithful discharge of his duties in collecting and paying over said tax, said sheriff and his sureties shall be liable upon the bond given by them for the collection of the county levy and public dues of said county. The sheriff shall receive, for collecting said tax, the same compensation as allowed by law for collecting the revenue.

§ 3. The sheriff shall pay over said tax on or before the 15th day of December in each year, to such person or persons, as the court may order; and upon failure to do so, he and his sureties shall be liable for the amount of said tax, and ten per cent. damages upon the whole amount, to be recovered upon suit or motion in said county court.

§ 4. This act to take effect from its passage; but not more than three levies shall be made under this act, and such levies shall be in consecutive years; the first levy under this act may be made by said county court for the year 1869, at any regular term of said county court not later than the June term.

Approved February 25, 1869.

CHAPTER 1608.

AN ACT to amend the act authorizing the Counties of Bourbon, Nicholas, and Fleming, to take stock in the Maysville and Lexington Railroad Company, Northern Division.

Be it enacted by the General Assembly of the Commonwealth of Kentucky:

§ 1. That an act, entitled "An act to authorize the counties of Bourbon, Nicholas, and Fleming, to subscribe stock in the Maysville and Lexington railroad company, northern division," approved February 1, 1868, be so amended that, so far as it relates to the county of Fleming, the question of subscription to the capital stock of said company shall be submitted to any one, two, or more justices' districts in said county, separately.

§ 2. Upon a petition of twenty freeholders of any election district, it shall be the duty of the county judge to order an election to be held in that district within thirty days after the reception of such petition. If a majority of the votes cast in any district are in favor of said subscription, a tax not exceeding one per cent. per annum for three years shall be levied upon the assessed valuation of taxable property in that district; but if a majority of the votes cast are against such subscription, no tax shall be levied.

§ 3. Any election district in said county that takes subscription in said railroad, shall not be taxed to aid in constructing any branch, or any railroad to intersect said railroad, unless a majority of the votes cast in the same precinct at an election held for the purpose of ascertaining the sense of the qualified voters upon the question, are cast in favor of such taxation.

§ 4. The county judge shall appoint a treasurer or receiver, whose duty it shall be to receive the money from the tax payers of the district or districts for the railroad, and he shall give bond and approved security to the county judge for the faithful performance of his duties, and shall receive a compensation not exceeding one per cent. of the amount received by him.

§ 5. It shall be the duty of the tax-payers of the district or districts to pay to the treasurer, at his office, or other place designated by him, the railroad taxes on or before the first day of December of each year; but the place of collection shall be in one of the taxed districts, or at Flemingsburg.

§ 6. If any tax-payer refuse or fail to pay to the treasurer the amount of tax due from him by the first day of December of each year, he shall be liable for such delinquency to ten per cent. damages on the sum unpaid.

§ 7. It shall be the duty of the treasurer to make out a list of the tax uncollected by him upon the first day of

December of each year, within ten days thereafter, and deliver the same to the sheriff, who shall collect the unpaid tax, with ten per cent. thereon, which ten per cent. he shall receive as compensation for collection.

§ 8. That section thirteen of the act herein amended, be so amended that its provisions apply only to the districts that vote in favor of the tax.

§ 9. That any part or parts of the act referred to in the first section of this act, contrary to the provisions of this act, is hereby repealed, so far as the same relates to Fleming county; but in all other respects remains in full force and applicable to the county of Fleming equally with the other counties.

§ 10. This act to take effect from its passage.

Approved February 25, 1869.

CHAPTER 1609.

AN ACT to amend an act, entitled "An act to amend an act, entitled 'An act to incorporate the Owensboro and Russellville Railroad Company,'" approved February 27, 1867.

Be it enacted by the General Assembly of the Commonwealth of Kentucky:

§ 1. That section nine of an act, entitled "An act to amend an act, entitled 'An act to incorporate the Owensboro and Russellville railroad company,'" be, and the same is hereby, so amended as to read as follows, viz: That whenever a majority of the votes cast at any election held for that purpose, shall instruct the county judge of the county or precinct voting to take stock in the Owensboro and Russellville railroad, it shall be the duty of the county judge of said county to subscribe the amount so voted for, and issue bonds therefor: *Provided, however,* That this act shall not interfere with subscriptions by petition as authorized in the act to which this is an amendment, and the original act of incorporation of said company.

§ 2. This act shall take effect from its passage.

Approved February 25, 1869.

CHAPTER 1010.

AN ACT to incorporate the Paducah and Gulf Railroad Company.

Be it enacted by the General Assembly of the Commonwealth of Kentucky:

§ 1. That Ex Norton, S. B. Thomas, G. W. Norton, L. S. Trimble, and W. F. Norton, be, and they are hereby, appointed commissioners, under the direction of whom, or any three of whom, subscriptions may be received to the capital stock of the Paducah and Gulf railroad company, which is hereby incorporated; and they may cause books to be opened at such times and places as they may direct, for the purpose of receiving subscriptions to the capital stock of said company, after having given such notice of the times and places of opening the same as they may deem proper; and if such subscriptions to the capital stock of said company as is necessary to its incorporation shall not have been obtained, commissioners, or a majority of them, may cause said books to be opened, from time to time, and may adjourn to such place or places as they may deem expedient, until the sum necessary for its incorporation shall be subscribed, and may then, if they see proper, close the books: *Provided,* That any subscription tendered at any time or place other than that advertised, may be received by said commissioners, or any one of them, and, if accepted by them prior to closing the books, shall be as valid and binding on the party subscribing as if received at the time and place advertised; and if any of said commissioners shall die, resign, or refuse to act, during the continuance of the duties devolved on them by this act, others may be appointed in his or their room and stead by the remaining commissioners, or a majority of those acting as such.

§ 2. That the capital stock of the Paducah and Gulf railroad shall be three hundred and fifty thousand dollars, in shares of one hundred dollars each, which may be subscribed by any individual, corporation, or association of individuals, in or out of this State; and as soon as said sum of three hundred and fifty thousand dollars of said stock shall be subscribed, the subscribers, their successors and assigns, shall be, and they are hereby declared to be, incorporated into a company, by the name of the Paducah and Gulf Railroad Company; and by that name shall be capable of purchasing, holding, selling, leasing, and conveying real estate, not exceeding ten thousand acres, and personal estate so far as the same may be necessary for the purposes of the corporation, and no further; and shall have perpetual succession; and by said corporate name may sue and be sued, contract and be contracted with; and may have and use a common seal, and alter or renew

the same at pleasure; and shall have and enjoy all the
privileges which other corporate bodies may lawfully do.

§ 3. That there shall be paid, at the time of subscribing How stock paid, &c.
for stock in said company, to the commissioner or commissioners receiving such subscription, the sum of one dollar
on each share, to be paid in money or in a note or notes,
negotiable and payable to some one or more of said commissioners, at not more than sixty days, at some bank in
this State or within the United States; and the residue
thereof shall be paid in installments, at such time and in
such manner as may be required by the board of directors
of said company: *Provided*, No payment shall be demanded until ten days' notice of such demand shall have been
given by said board of directors, by publication in some
one or more papers published in Paducah; and if any
subscriber shall fail to pay any installment, or any part of
an installment of said subscription, when demanded according to the provisions of this section, the same may
be recovered by an action, in the name of said corporation, against such delinquent subscriber, before any court
having jurisdiction of such cases; and in all such actions,
it shall not be necessary to prove any other demand than
the publication provided for in this section; or, in case
such failure to pay any such installment, or part of an installment of said subscription, demanded according to the
provisions of the section, shall continue for the space of
sixty days after the time the same is required by such de-
mand to be paid, the board of directors may, in their dis- Stock may be forfeited.
cretion, order the same to be forfeited to the company,
and may, if they think proper, sink it for the benefit of
the company; but said board of directors, by a majority
of the whole, may remit any such forfeiture, on such terms
as they may think proper: *And provided further*, That it Stock may be paid in con-tracts.
may be lawful to receive subscriptions to the capital stock
of said company, payable in contracts, well secured, to
build such parts of the road or to perform such work or
furnish such material as may be accepted by the company.

§ 4. That so soon as three hundred and fifty thousand When di-rectors may be elected.
dollars shall have been subscribed, said commissioners, or
a majority of them, shall call a meeting, at such time and
place as a majority of them shall designate, giving at
least ten days' notice of the time and place in one or
more papers published in Paducah; and at such meeting
said commissioners shall lay the subscription books before
the subscribers then present, and thereupon said subscribers, or a majority of them then present, shall have
power to elect by ballot not exceeding eight directors to
manage the affairs of said company; and these directors,
or a majority of them, shall have power to elect a presi-

dent of said company either from among the directors or any other person, and to allow such compensation for his services as they may think proper; and in such elections, and on all other occasions when a vote of the stockholders of said company is to be taken, each stockholder shall be allowed one vote for every share of stock owned by such voter; and any stockholder may, in writing, depute any other person to act as proxy for it, him, or her; and said commissioners aforesaid, or any three of them, shall be the judges of said first election.

§ 5. That to continue the succession of the president and directors, not exceeding eight directors shall be chosen annually on the first Saturdays in June of each year, at such place as the president and directors may appoint by the stockholders of said company: *Provided*, That the president and directors may change the time and place of holding elections upon publishing such change, not less than thirty days prior to the elections, in the papers aforesaid; and that the directors of said company, or a majority of them, shall have the power to appoint judges of all elections, and to elect a president of said company either from among themselves or other persons, and to allow him such compensation for his services as they may deem proper; and if any vacancy shall occur by death, resignation, or refusal to act, of any president or director, before the year for which he was elected shall have expired, a person to fill such vacancy shall be appointed by the president and directors, or a majority of them; and that the president and directors of said company shall hold and exercise their offices until a new election of president and directors; and all elections which are by this act, or by the by-laws of said company, to be made at a particular time, if not made at such time, may be made at thirty days thereafter, upon notice published in the papers aforesaid.

§ 6. That a general meeting of the stockholders of said company may be called, any time during the interval between the annual meetings, by the president and directors, or a majority of them, or by the stockholders owning one fourth of all the stock subscribed, upon giving thirty days' notice of the time and place of holding the same in the newspapers aforesaid; and when any such meeting is called by the stockholders, such notice shall specify the object of the call; and if, at any such called meeting, a majority in value of all the stockholders are not present, in person or by proxy, the same shall be adjourned from day to day, without transacting any business, for any time not exceeding five days; and if within said five days stockholders having a majority in value of all the stock

Margin notes:
Annual elections, &c.

General meetings.

subscribed do not attend, in person or by proxy, such
meetings shall be dissolved.

§ 7. That the president and directors of said company *Annual state-ment to be made, &c.*
in office for the preceding year shall, at the regular an-
nual meeting of the stockholders, exhibit a clear and distinct account of the affairs of said company. That at
any called meeting of the stockholders, a majority in
value of the holders of the stock subscribed being present, may demand and require similar statements from the
president and directors, whose duty it shall be to furnish
such statements when so required; and that at all general
meetings of the stockholders, a majority of them in value
may remove from office the president or any or all of the
directors, and fill up the vacancies thus made in the same
manner they could do at their annual meetings.

§ 8. That the president and directors of said company, *President and directors to take oath.*
before he or they act as such, shall swear or affirm, as the
case may be, that they will well and truly discharge the
duties of their respective offices to the best of their skill
and judgment; and the said president and directors, or a *May appoint treasurer, &c.*
majority of them, or a majority in value of the stockhold-
ers in said company, at any of the stated or called meetings of said stockholders, shall have power to appoint or
elect a treasurer of said company, and to require and take
of him a bond in such penalty, and with such securities,
as they may prescribe, payable to said company, conditioned for the faithful keeping and disbursing of all such
money as may come to his hand, and with such other conditions as may be prescribed, upon which bond recovery
may be had for a breach of the conditions thereof, by suit
in the name of the company in any court having jurisdiction.

§ 9. That if any of the stock authorized by this act shall *Books may be reopened.*
remain unsubscribed until after the election of president
and directors, as provided for in the fourth section of this
act, the said president and directors, or a majority of them,
shall have power to open the books and receive subscriptions to the stock which shall remain unsubscribed for, or
to sell and dispose of the same, for the benefit of the company, not under the par value of such stock; and the subscribers or purchasers of such stock shall have all the rights
of original subscribers, and be subject to the same regulations and liabilities.

§ 10. That said president and directors, or a majority of *Officers, agents, &c. to be ap-pointed, their pay. &c.*
them, may appoint all such officers, agents, or servants, as
they may deem expedient for the business of the company,
and may remove them at pleasure; that they, or a majority
of them, may determine, by contract, the pay of such officers, agents, or servants, and regulate, by by-laws, the manner of adjusting all accounts against the company, and the

May erect warehouses, &c.

extent of the liability of the company to its employes; that they shall have power to erect warehouses, workshops, and other buildings or edifices necessary or convenient for the use of said company; that they shall have power to direct and regulate in what manner and by what evidence stock in said company may be transferred, and to pass all by-laws they may deem necessary or proper for exercising the powers hereby vested in said company, and for carrying into effect this act, and to alter the same at pleasure: *Provided*, The same shall not be contrary to the Constitution and laws of the United States or of this State.

Capital stock may be increased.

§ 11. That if the capital stock of said company shall be deemed insufficient for the purposes of this act, it shall be lawful for the president and directors to increase the same as much as they may deem necessary, not exceeding the sum required to fully complete and equip with rolling stock the said railroad, with all its branches, and every other road or roads that may be purchased or leased by said company, or any road or roads with which said company may make running arrangements, including the entire costs of the same.

Vested power of company.

§ 12. That the president and directors of said company are hereby vested with all powers and rights necessary to the construction of a railroad from Paducah to the Tennessee State line, along such route as may be selected by the president and directors; and that they may cause to be made contracts with others for making said road, or any part of it; and that they, their agents, engineers, &c., or those with whom they may contract for surveying or making the same, or any part thereof, may enter upon, use, and excavate any land which may be wanted for the site of said road, or the erection of warehouses, or other structures or works, necessary and convenient to said road, or for its use, or for any other purpose necessary or useful in the construction or repair of said road, or its works or appurtenances; and they may build bridges or construct tunnels, provided such bridges shall not obstruct navigation on any navigable stream; and may fix scales and weights, take and use timber, earth, gravel, stone, and other material necessary or useful in the construction and repair of said road.

How land, earth, stone, right of way, &c., may be obtained.

§ 13. That the president and directors, or a majority of them, or their authorized agents, may agree with the owners of any land, earth, stone, timber, or other materials or improvements which may be wanted for the construction or repair of said road or any of their works, for the purchase or the use and occupation of the same; and if they cannot agree, or if the owner or owners of any of them be a *feme covert*, under age, *non compos mentis*, or out of the county in which the property wanted may lie, that, upon application by said company to the county court of any county into or through which it is proposed to construct said Paducah and Gulf railroad, such court shall appoint three commissioners, two of whom shall be residents of said county, and one an engineer of said company, who shall be sworn faithfully to discharge their duties under this act to the best of their skill and judgment; and whenever said company shall be unable to agree with the owner of any land, earth, stone, gravel, timber, or other material or thing required for the site or construction of said road, or whenever the land or material required shall be owned by any person not a resident of said county. or who is a *feme covert*, infant, or *non compos mentis*, it shall be the duty of said commissioners to view the land or material required, and fix the amount of compensation to which the owner or owners of such land or material shall be entitled, and to make out and return to the office of the clerk of the county court a report, in writing, particularly describing the land or other material valued, and the interest and duration of the interest valued, and the amount of damages assessed. The report of the commissioners shall give the name of the owner, and state whether such owner is a resident of the county. and whether a *feme covert*, infant, or non-sane person. The clerk shall receive such report and file the same, indorsing thereon the time of its being filed; and if the owner resides in the county, he shall forthwith issue a summons, commanding the owner or owners of such land to appear and show cause why the report should not be confirmed, which summons shall be forthwith executed by the sheriff or other officer in whose hands it may be placed. The report shall be docketed in the county court, and stand for trial at any term of said court, commencing not less than ten days after service of the summons. If the owner is not a resident of the county, the court shall, at the first term after the report is filed, appoint an attorney to defend for such owner, who may file exceptions at any time not later than the next term; and upon exceptions being filed by the owner, or by an attorney appointed to defend for him or her, or by the company, the court shall forthwith order a jury to be empanneled to try the question of damages, unless for good cause shown time is given for preparation. If no exceptions are filed, the report shall be confirmed. The jury and commissioners shall, in estimating the damages to any proprietor of land, or material sought to be condemned for said road, find for the owners the actual value of the land or other material proposed to be taken; but in estimating damages resulting incidentally to other lands or property of such owners, shall offset the

1869.

advantages to such residue to be derived from the building and operating said road by, through, or near such
residue; and whenever a verdict shall be had, the court
may give judgment condemning such land or other material
for the use of said company for the amount of damages
assessed, and also to the owner for his costs, if the
verdict shall be for more than was assessed by the commissioners; and such valuation, when tendered or paid to
the owner or owners of said property, or to the sheriff of
the county in which said report is made or inquest held,
when such owner or owners do not reside in said county,
shall entitle said company to the land or interest in the
same thus valued, as fully as if it had been conveyed to
it by the owner or owners of the same; and the valuation
of the same, if not received when tendered may, at any
time thereafter within one year, be received from the company without cost or interest by the owner or owners, his,
their, or its legal representatives: *Provided,* That the land
condemned for road-way shall not be more than one hundred feet wide, unless said company shall file with the
judge of the county court, or a justice of the peace, the
affidavit of some one of its engineers stating that a
greater width is necessary, and how much more is required, when the question shall be for the quantity thus
stated; that whenever it shall be necessary for said company to have, use, or occupy any lands, material, or other
property, in order to the construction or repairing of said
road or their necessary works or buildings, the president
and directors, or their agents, or those contracting with
them for constructing or repairing the same, may immediately take and use the same, they having first caused
the property wanted to be valued by three commissioners,
as hereinbefore prescribed; and it shall not be necessary,
after the report of the commissioners, in order to the use
and occupation of the same, to await the issue of the proceedings in case exceptions are filed to the report; and the
report of the commissioners, after the payment or tender
of the amount assessed, shall be a bar to all actions for
taking and using such property.

§ 14. That said Paducah and Gulf railroad company

How long road
exempt from
taxation.

shall be exempt from taxation until completed, and that
it shall never be taxed at a valuation beyond the rate at
which said roads are now taxed or may hereafter be
taxed, nor exceeding its actual value.

§ 15. That the president and directors of said company

May purchase
and hold other
roads.

may, with the assent of the holders of a majority in value
of the stock of said company, purchase and hold any other
railroad in this or any other State, and may subscribe
stock in or aid in the building of any other road in or out
of this State, whenever in their judgment it may be to

LAWS OF KENTUCKY. 523

the interest of the Paducah and Gulf railroad company to do so. They may sell the Paducah and Gulf railroad, or lease the same, and may build branches from said road and branches from such branches.

§ 16. That the said Paducah and Gulf railroad company may receive donations of land, to be used for any of the purposes of said road, or to be sold to raise money to build the same; and may receive subscriptions to be paid in land, at a valuation to be fixed by such means as may be agreed upon between said company or its authorized agents and the subscribers, and may lease or sell and convey any land so given or subscribed.

§ 17. That said Paducah and Gulf railroad company may, the holders of a majority in value of all the stock therein concurring, agree on terms for consolidating said company with any other railroad company, on such terms as may be agreed upon; but no such consolidation shall in anywise affect the holders of any mortgage bonds issued by the Paducah and Gulf railroad company prior to the time of such consolidation.

§ 18. That the Paducah and Gulf railroad company may issue and sell the bonds of said company, of the denomination of one thousand dollars, to be signed by the president and countersigned by the secretary, with the seal of the corporation affixed, to an amount not exceeding two millions of dollars, bearing not exceeding eight per cent. interest, payable semi-annually, with coupons attached, signed by the secretary of the company, to be made payable as said company may direct within thirty years from date.

§ 19. To secure the prompt payment of the interest and principal of bonds issued by authority of this act, said company may execute a mortgage or deed of trust, conveying said railroad and its property and franchises to a trustee, and, from time to time, fill vacancies that may occur for the use, and to secure the holders of such bonds, with such covenants and stipulations as may be necessary to effect the purpose and objects of its execution.

§ 20. That if the mortgage or deed of trust authorized by the last preceding section shall be foreclosed by legal proceedings, such foreclosure shall be for the benefit of all the holders of bonds secured by its provisions. Upon such foreclosure, the president shall make a correct list of all bonds secured by such mortgage or deed of trust which have been sold, and verify it by his affidavit, which affidavit and list shall be filed in the McCracken circuit court, where only such proceeding is authorized to be had. Such foreclosure shall not take place until ninety days after publication of notice of the commencement of proceedings to that end shall have been made in one or more

1869.

May receive donations, &c.

May consolidate with other companies.

May issue bonds.

May mortgage road to secure payment of bonds, &c.

Mortgage may be foreclosed.

1869.   newspapers published in the cities of New York or Paducah. The person or corporation becoming the purchaser or lessee of said road, by reason of any sale or leasing to satisfy the demands of bondholders, shall be vested with all the rights, privileges, franchises, and immunities of the corporation.

§ 21. That to create and secure a fund for the final redemption of mortgage bonds issued under authority of

Sinking fund may be created.

this act, a sinking fund shall be created by said company; and in order to create such sinking fund, said company shall, at the time of declaring the first cash dividend, ascertain what sum ought to be set aside annually in order to create a fund sufficient to redeem its bonds at maturity, and then set apart and pass into the sinking fund that sum; and thereafter, annually, there shall be set aside and pass into said fund a like sum, until a fund is created sufficient to pay the outstanding bonds of the company; which fund shall be held sacred for the redemption of said bonds, and shall be used for no other purpose. That the company may loan and reloan the sums thus set apart at any rate of interest not greater than that paid on its bonds, or may invest the same in any safe and profitable manner deemed advisable, which is not inconsistent with the purposes and objects of creating said fund.

§ 22. That the corporators named in this act are hereby

First board of directors, &c.

constituted the first board of directors of said company, and are authorized to organize at once without pursuing the formalties required by this act, and shall hold their office and manage and control the affairs of said company until their successors are elected and qualified, with power to elect a president and appoint all such officers, agents, and servants of said company authorized by this act, and to do and perform all acts conferred by this act upon the directors of said company; and that this act of incorporation is granted to authorize the corporation therein created to run and operate a railroad upon the present track of the New Orleans and Ohio railroad, purchased by Ex. Norton, under a decree of the United States circuit court, at Paducah, in the case of the United States and W. P. Mellen, trustee, against the New Orleans and Ohio railroad company; and the said railroad may be put in as stock in said company under this act of incorporation: *Provided, however,* That nothing in this act, or authorized by it, shall be construed to alter the equities and legal rights of the stockholders in the New Orleans and Ohio railroad company, or any of them; but the same shall exist as though this charter had not been enacted: *And provided,* That should any branch of said. road be constructed within five miles of the town of Mayfield, the same shall run through or

within one half mile of said town, and a freight and
passenger depot shall be kept at said town, or within
one half mile of it; nor is this charter to authorize the
company to take up the iron or track of the New
Orleans and Ohio railroad, nor to authorize the company to cease to run and operate the same.

§ 23. That this act shall be liberally and beneficially
construed by all courts, with the view of carrying out
the rights, privileges, and franchises herein granted, and
shall be in force from its passage.

*How act to be
construed.*

Approved February 26, 1869.

CHAPTER 1611.

AN ACT to incorporate the Pleasant Spring High School, in Daviess
County.

*Be it enacted by the General Assembly of the Commonwealth
of Kentucky:*

§ 1. That R. L. Gett, Dudley Lancaster, and P. P. Kirk,
and their successors in office, who shall be duly elected as
already provided by the common school law of this State,
be, and the same are hereby, created a body corporate,
by the name and style of "The Trustees of the Pleasant
Spring High School;" and as such, they and their successors may acquire, by purchase or otherwise, and hold
real estate and personal property, and dispose of the
same by sale or otherwise; may make contracts, sue
and be sued, plead and be impleaded; and make such
rules and by-laws as may be necessary for the good
government of the same, not inconsistent with the laws
and Constitution of the United States or of this State.

§ 2. That all money and property received by donations
or otherwise by said corporation, to be employed and used
in founding, building, and maintaining this institution of
learning in the county of Daviess, in this State, to be
known as the "Pleasant Spring High School."

§ 3. The trustees named in this act and their successors,
or a majority of them, shall have power, from time to
time, to make and change the by-laws, and employ such
agents and teachers as they may think proper.

§ 4. This act to take effect from and after its passage.

Approved February 26, 1869.

CHAPTER 1613.

AN ACT to consolidate School Districts Nos. 18 and 19, in Kenton County, and for the benefit of the consolidated District.

Be it enacted by the General Assembly of the Commonwealth of Kentucky:

§ 1. That common school districts No. 18 and No. 19, of Kenton county, are hereby consolidated, under the name of Beech Grove Seminary District.

§ 2. That the said district is authorized to draw from the Common School Fund the amount due said districts for 1867 and 1868; and if any of said fund has been bonded, then the amount of the interest on the Kenton county bond that would be going to said districts.

§ 3. That this act shall take effect from its passage.

Approved February 26, 1869.

CHAPTER 1614.

AN ACT to incorporate the "Vaughn Female Academy," at Owensboro.

Be it enacted by the General Assembly of the Commonwealth of Kentucky:

§ 1. That Joseph C. Maple, Burr H. Hobbs, Wm. T. Owen, John H. McHenry, jr., and Joseph Otis, and their successors in office, be, and they are hereby, created a body-politic and corporate, by the name and style of the trustees of the Vaughn Female Academy, which said school is now under the management of Mrs. E. Sue Phillips, at Owensboro, Kentucky; and as such may sue and be sued, plead and be impleaded, make contracts, and may make such rules, by-laws, regulations, and ordinances as may be necessary for the government of said corporation, not inconsistent with the laws of the United States or the State of Kentucky.

§ 2. That the trustees named in this act, and their successors in office, shall appoint one of their number president of the board of trustees, and such other officers as they may deem necessary, and may fill any vacancy that may occur in said board, or in its officers, by death, resignation, or otherwise.

§ 3. The board of trustees shall have power to hold annual commencements and public examinations of its pupils, and may confer such honorary degrees and diplomas as is usual in other colleges and high schools in this Commonwealth.

§ 4. That so long as the property referred to in this act is used for school purposes, it shall be exempt from such taxes as public seminaries and colleges in this Commonwealth are by law exempt from.

§ 5. This act to take effect from its passage.

Approved February 26, 1869.

CHAPTER 1615.

AN ACT to incorporate the Stanford Female Seminary.

Be it enacted by the General Assembly of the Commonwealth of Kentucky:

§ 1. That Thomas B. Montgomery, James A. Harris, James Paxton, Horace S. Withers, Joseph McAllister, J. N. Craig, Thomas W. Varnon, and Henry T. Harris, trustees of the Stanford Male and Female Seminary, be, and they are hereby, constituted a body-politic and corporate, to be known by the name of the trustees of the Stanford Female Seminary; and by that name shall have perpetual succession, may sue and be sued in any court of law or equity, and shall be capable in law of purchasing, acquiring, and holding, to them and their successors, any lands, tenements, goods and chattels, of any kind, and money, which shall be purchased, given, granted, or devised for the use of said seminary, or which they may now have; and they may sell, dispose of, and convey the same, according to the by-laws which may be hereafter established by a majority of the aforesaid trustees; which by-laws they may, from time to time, establish for the good government of the school, and the management of its funds and property, provided the same are consistent with the Constitution and laws of this State. A majority of all the trustees shall be necessary for the election of a president, treasurer, and secretary, and of principal to said institution; and upon the disqualification, death, resignation, or other vacancy in the office of trustee, principal, or officer of said seminary, the board of trustees, by majority, shall fill the vacancy by appointment. A majority of the trustees shall constitute a quorum for the transaction of business, and may decide any question, resolution, or appointment, not otherwise provided in this act; and a majority must concur in any contract for the purchase or alienation of property, or as to any question of design, location, &c., of the buildings to be erected under this act.

§ 2. The trustees shall have power to confer upon the pupils of said seminary any or all the diplomas or degrees conferred by the best colleges in this State, and the private seals or scrolls of the president and secretary of said board of trustees may stand in lieu of a corporate seal: *Provided,* That such honors shall be conferred only on the recommendation of the principal of the school.

§ 3. A majority of the board of trustees, including the president, shall have power to fix tuition fees, and to do and perform all the acts necessary and expedient for the conduct and management of said institution and the promotion of its object; and the trustees, by a majority, may determine what amount is necessary to be raised before the building is begun.

1869.   § 4. The Legislature reserves the power to alter, amend, or repeal this charter.
          § 5. This act to take effect from and after its passage.
Approved February 26, 1869.

CHAPTER 1616.
AN ACT for School District No. 10, in Clinton County.

Be it enacted by the General Assembly of the Commonwealth of Kentucky:

§ 1. That the limits of school district No. 10, Clinton county, in which the town of Albany is situated, be, and the same is, extended so as to include in said district all persons residing in one mile and a quarter of the court-house in said town.

§ 2. That the trustees of said district be, and they are hereby, authorized to levy an *ad valorem* tax, not exceeding twenty cents on the hundred dollars' worth of property, on all property in said district, and a *per capita* tax not exceeding two dollars on each white male person over the age of twenty-one years, for the purpose of purchasing ground and building a school-house in said district, and furnishing it with all suitable and necessary apparatus.

§ 3. That said tax may be levied for two years and no longer.

§ 4. That the assessment of the assessor of said county shall govern in the collection of the taxes.

§ 5. That the sheriff of Clinton county is hereby authorized and directed to collect said taxes and pay the same over to the treasurer of said district, who shall be appointed by the trustees of said district; who must, before commencing the discharge of his duties, take an oath to faithfully discharge the duties of his office, and execute a bond, with good security, in the Clinton county court, for a faithful performance of his duties.

§ 6. That this act take effect from its passage.
Approved February 26, 1869.

CHAPTER 1617.
AN ACT for the benefit of School District No. 13, in Lawrence County.

Be it enacted by the General Assembly of the Commonwealth of Kentucky:

§ 1. That the commissioner of common schools for Lawrence county be, and he is hereby, allowed to make his report for school district No. 13, in Lawrence county, for the year 1867, on or before the first day of May, 1869, to the Superintendent of Public Instruction; and when said report shall be made as required by law, the Superintendent of Public Instruction will transmit a copy of the same to the Auditor, whereupon the Auditor shall draw his warrant upon the Treasurer in favor of the school commissioner of Lawrence county for the amount due district No. 13, for the year 1867, as shown by the report herein authorized to be made, to be paid out of any surplus money belonging to Lawrence county; and if there be no such surplus, then to be paid out of the bond fund for Lawrence county.

§ 2. This act to take effect from its passage.

Approved February 26, 1869.

CHAPTER 1618.

AN ACT for the benefit of School District No. 20, in Simpson County.

WHEREAS, It is represented that the trustees and citizens of common school district No. 20, in the county of Simpson, were engaged in the erection of a school-house just prior to the time the common school is usually taught in said district, which improvement was essentially necessary, and that by unavoidable delays said house was not finished so that the common school could be taught therein for three months in 1868, as required by law; and whereas, it is represented that the trustees and citizens of said district are now desirous of having said school taught in said district; therefore,

Be it enacted by the General Assembly of the Commonwealth of Kentucky:

§ 1. That the Superintendent of Public Instruction, upon satisfactory proof being made to him by the first day of September, 1869, that a common school was taught in school district No. 20, in Simpson county, for three months during the year 1869 prior to the said first day of September, be, and he is hereby, directed to issue his warrant on the Auditor, in favor of the school commissioner of said county, for the sum of money to which said school would have been entitled had the school been taught during the year 1868, said sum of money to be paid to the trustees of said school district No. 20 for the use thereof.

§ 2. This act to take effect from its passage.

Approved February 26, 1869.

CHAPTER 1619.

AN ACT for the benefit of Common School District No. 63, in Lawrence County.

Be it enacted by the General Assembly of the Commonwealth of Kentucky:

§ 1. That the commissioner of common schools for Lawrence county be, and he is hereby, authorized to make his report for school district No. 63, in Lawrence county, for the year 1860, to the Superintendent of Public Instruction, and when said report shall be made as required by law, the Superintendent of Public Instruction will transmit a copy of the same to the Auditor, whereupon the Auditor shall draw his warrant upon the Treasurer, in favor of the school commissioner of Lawrence county, for the amount due district No. 63, in Lawrence county, for the year 1860, as shown by the report herein authorized to be made, to be paid out of any surplus money belonging to Lawrence county; and if there be no such surplus, then to be paid out of the bond fund for Lawrence county.

§ 2. This act to take effect from its passage.

Approved February 26, 1869.

CHAPTER 1620.

AN ACT for the benefit of Hopkins County.

Be it enacted by the General Assembly of the Commonwealth of Kentucky:

§ 1. That the acts of the court of claims for Hopkins county, at its November term, 1868, be, and the same are hereby, legalized; and the sheriff of said county is authorized and directed to collect the amount of *ad valorem* tax fixed and levied by said court for county purposes, and pay the same at the proper time and to the proper persons.

§ 2. This act to take effect from and after its passage.

Approved February 27, 1869.

CHAPTER 1621.

AN ACT to authorise the County Court of Calloway County to change the State Road leading from Canton, by way of Murray, to Hickman.

Be it enacted by the General Assembly of the Commonwealth of Kentucky:

§ 1. That the county court of Calloway county is hereby authorized and empowered to make any change or alteration in the State road leading from Canton, via Murray, to Hickman, in said county, that may be necessary and proper; such change or alteration to be made in the manner prescribed in the general law now in force and applicable to public roads in said county.

§ 2. This act to take effect from its passage.

Approved February 27, 1869.

CHAPTER 1622.

AN ACT for the benefit of Magoffin County.

WHEREAS, The county court of Magoffin county, through the disorganization of the country caused by the late war, failed, for over twelve months, to be furnished with duplicate weights, measures, and balances, as required by law; for remedy therefor,

Be it enacted by the General Assembly of the Commonwealth of Kentucky:

§ 1. That the Secretary of State shall furnish the said county of Magoffin with duplicate weights, measures, and balances, now in the custody of the Secretary of State, and as established by law; and upon the written certificate of the Secretary of State of the cost of such duplicates, the Auditor shall draw his warrant on the Treasury for the cost thereof.

§ 2. This act shall take effect from and after its passage.

Approved February 27, 1869.

CHAPTER 1623.

AN ACT amending an act authorizing County Courts to subscribe Stock in Turnpike Roads, and for the benefit of Harrison County.

WHEREAS, By virtue of an act approved March 9th, 1868, entitled "An act authorizing county courts to subscribe stock in turnpike roads," the county court of Harrison county submitted to the voters of said county the question of subscribing stock, in accordance with the provisions of said act, and the qualified voters, at the election held in August, 1868, voted against the propositions contained in said bill; and whereas, the question was resubmitted, at the November election, by the magistrates of said county, and, at this election, the qualified voters of said county voted for the subscription of stock to build turnpike roads in said county by a decided majority; and whereas, doubts are entertained as to whether, under the act aforesaid, said county court could legally order said question to be submitted a second time; therefore,

Be it enacted by the General Assembly of the Commonwealth of Kentucky:

§ 1. That said second submission, and the vote thereon, be, and is hereby, declared as valid and obligatory as though said first submission of said question had not been made by said court.

§ 2. That said county court be, and is hereby, authorized and empowered to subscribe stock in turnpike roads to be constructed in said county to the extent and in accordance with the provisions of said original act to which this is an amendment; and that said court shall levy and collect the tax necessary to pay said subscription according to the mode prescribed in said act.

§ 3. This act to be in force from and after its passage.

. Approved February 27, 1869.

CHAPTER 1624.

AN ACT to Charter the Deposit Bank of Glasgow.

Be it enacted by the General Assembly of the Commonwealth of Kentucky:

§ 1. That there is hereby established a bank of deposit in the town of Glasgow, Kentucky, with a capital of one hundred thousand dollars, in shares of twenty-five dollars each, to be subscribed and paid for as hereinafter specified; and the subscribers, their associates, successors, and assigns, shall be a body-politic and corporate, by the name and style of "The Deposit Bank of Glasgow," and shall so continue for twenty years from its organization; and shall be capable of contracting and being contracted with, of suing and being sued, of impleading and being impleaded, of answering and defending, in all courts and places whatever; it may have a common seal, and change and renew the same at pleasure.

§ 2. Said bank shall be under the control and direction of seven directors, each of whom shall be stockholders; they shall be residents of this State; and, after the first election, shall be elected annually on the first Monday in January in each year, and hold their office until their successors are elected and qualified; they shall elect one of their number president, and shall hold regular meetings at such time as may be fixed by the by-laws, and other meetings may be had whenever deemed necessary; and in case of death or resignation of any director, the vacancy shall be filled by the board of directors. The directors shall have power to receive subscriptions for so many of the shares of the stock of said company remaining unsold as they may at any time choose to sell; to declare dividends; and to appoint such officers, agents, and servants as they may deem necessary to conduct the business of the bank, and pay them such sum as wages and salaries, and take from them such bonds to secure the faithful performance of their duties, as they shall think proper and reasonable. The stock shall be deemed to be personal estate, and shall be assignable according to such rules as the directors may prescribe; but such corporation shall have a lien on the stock to secure any indebtedness of the stockholders.

§ 3. Thomas M. Dickey, P. H. Leslie, S. H. Boles, M. H. Dickinson, C. L. Hill, W. H. Botts, and Henry Munford, are hereby appointed commissioners, any two of whom may act, and open books and receive subscriptions for the capital stock; and when shares to the amount of twenty thousand dollars shall have been subscribed, it shall be their duty to give notice in one or more newspapers, and appoint a day for the election of a board of directors, who shall hold their office until the succeeding annual election. The payment for the shares subscribed shall be made as follows: One dollar on each share at the time of subscribing, and the residue in installments of twenty per cent. on the remainder: *Provided*, That when ten thousand dollars shall be paid in, the directors may, if they think proper, extend the time for paying the remainder, and may, thereupon, commence business upon the president's making affidavit that such sum has been actually paid in.

§ 4. Said bank may receive deposits of gold, silver, bank notes, and other notes which may be lawfully circulating as money, and repay the same in such manner, at such times, and with such interest, as may be agreed upon with the depositors, by special or general contract; may deal in the loaning of money, exchange, promissory notes, bonds, stocks, bills of exchange, and other evidences of debt; take personal and other securities, except real estate, for the payment thereof, and dispose of the latter as may be agreed upon, in all respects as natural persons may lawfully do; and the promissory notes or bills made negotiable and payable at its banking-house, or at any other bank or banking-house, which may be discounted by said bank, and inland bills which may be discounted by it, shall be, and they are hereby, put upon the footing of foreign bills of exchange, and like remedy may be had thereon, jointly and severally, against the drawers and indorsers.

§ 5. The said corporation may acquire, hold, possess, use, occupy, and enjoy all such real estate, goods and chattels, as may be convenient for the transaction of its business, or which may be conveyed to it as surety for any debt, or purchased in satisfaction of any debt, judgment, or decree, and sell and convey the same; and they may make all needful by-laws for the government of said bank, not inconsistent with the Constitution of the United States or of the State of Kentucky.

§ 6. It shall be the duty of the president, on the first Monday in January in each year, to pay into the Treasury of the State fifty cents on each one hundred dollars of stock held and paid for in said institution, in full and in lieu of all other taxes, to be part of the Sinking Fund.

§ 7. If the cashier, clerk, teller, or any other of the officers or agents of said bank, shall unlawfully appropriate any of the funds of said bank, or shall willfully fail to make corrrect entries, or shall make false entries on the books of said bank, they shall be deemed to be guilty of felony, and punished by confinement in the penitentiary not less than one nor more than five years.

§ 8. It shall not be lawful for said bank to issue any note or bill to be passed or used as currency.

§ 9. The Legislature reserves the right to alter, repeal, or amend this charter at its pleasure.

§ 10. This act to take effect and be in force from its passage.

Approved February 27, 1869.

CHAPTER 1625.

AN ACT to prohibit the sale of Spirituous Liquors within the Corporate Limits of the Town of Sherburn, in Fleming County.

Be it enacted by the General Assembly of the Commonwealth of Kentucky :

§ 1. That the trustees of the town of Sherburn are hereby authorized to prohibit the sale of spirituous liquors within the corporate limits of said town, a majority of said trustees concurring therein.

§ 2. A majority of the trustees of said town may grant license to retail spirituous liquors within the corporate limits of said town, upon application and the payment of a sum of not less than twenty-five nor more than one hundred dollars; and all moneys so collected shall be disbursed as said board of trustees shall direct, for the benefit of said town: *Provided, however,* Twenty-five dollars of the tax for each tavern license or privilege of selling liquor in said town so granted by said trustees shall be paid to the trustee of the jury fund for said county.

§ 3. That before said trustees shall have power to grant to any one the privilege of selling liquor in said town, the person so applying shall have first obtained a license to

keep a tavern from the county court of said county; and 1869.
the privilege of selling liquor shall not be granted to continue longer than the tavern license is in full force.

§ 4. This act shall take effect from its passage.

Approved February 27, 1869.

CHAPTER 1626.

AN ACT to regulate the sale of intoxicating spirits in the town of Clinton, Hickman County.

*Be it enacted by the General Assembly of the Commonwealth
of Kentucky:*

§ 1. That it shall not be lawful for any person to sell
spirituous, vinous, malt, or other intoxicating liquors, by
the drink, within the corporate limits of the town of
Clinton, Hickman county, until he shall first have obtained license from the Hickman county court in the manner
now prescribed by law, and shall also have paid to the
corporate authorities of said town such sum as they may,
from time to time, fix by ordinance: *Provided, however,*
said amount shall not exceed one hundred dollars per
annum.

§ 2. Any person who shall violate the provisions of this
act shall be deemed guilty of keeping a tippling-house,
and each sale shall be a separate and distinct offense.

§ 3. This act shall take effect ninety days after its passage.

Approved February 27, 1869.

CHAPTER 1627.

AN ACT for the benefit of Taylor W. Samuels, late Sheriff of Nelson
County.

*Be it enacted by the General Assembly of the Commonwealth
of Kentucky:*

§ 1. That Taylor W. Samuels, late sheriff of Nelson
county, have until the first day of October, 1869, to collect and account for the railroad tax in districts Nos. 1,
5, and 9, in the county of Nelson; and he may collect
said taxes without exacting the payment of the ten per
cent. required of delinquent tax-payers in said districts:
Provided, however, That the said Samuels shall not have
the benefit of this act unless he shall, on or before the
second Monday in April, 1869, appear in the county court
for the county of Nelson, and execute in said court a
covenant, with good and sufficient security, payable to
the Commonwealth of Kentucky, for the faithful collec-

tion and paying over to the treasurer of said railroad company said tax.

§ 2. This act shall take effect and be in force from its passage.

Approved February 27, 1869.

CHAPTER 1628.

AN ACT repealing all acts or parts of acts authorizing the Trustees of the Town of Winchester to grant Coffee-house Licenses.

Be it enacted by the General Assembly of the Commonwealth of Kentucky:

§ 1. That all acts and parts of acts authorizing the trustees of the town of Winchester to grant coffee-house licenses be, and the same are hereby, repealed.

§ 2. This act to take effect from its passage.

Approved February 27, 1869.

CHAPTER 1629.

AN ACT to provide Books for the County of Pike.

WHEREAS, There was passed at this session of the Legislature a bill to provide books for the counties of Pike and Letcher, which bill was approved on the 9th day of March, 1868, and the necessary appropriation therein being more than one hundred dollars, and at the passage of said bill the yeas and nays were not called on the same in the Senate, consequently, the same is inoperative; and whereas, from a certified copy of an order of the Pike county court there appears to be missing from the offices of the county and circuit courts and justices of the peace, the books specified in this act, the same having been lost and destroyed during the war, and not having been since supplied; therefore,

Be it enacted by the General Assembly of the Commonwealth of Kentucky:

§ 1. That the following books shall be purchased for the county of Pike, to-wit: *For the county court*—1st, 2d, 3d, and 4th volumes Bibb's Reports; 1st and 2d volumes A. K. Marshall's Reports; 1st, 2d, and 3d volumes Littell's Reports; 1st, 2d, 5th, and 7th volumes T. B. Monroe's Reports; 1st, 3d, 5th, and 7th volumes J. J. Marshall's Reports; 1st, 2d, and 5th volumes Dana's Reports; 1st, 2d, 3d, 4th, 5th, 6th, 7th, 8th, 9th, 10th, 12th, 13th, and 15th volumes B. Monroe's Reports; 1st volume Metcalfe's Reports. *For circuit court*—1st, 2d, and 3d volumes Bibb's Reports; 1st volume A. K. Marshall's Reports; 1st, 3d, and 5th volumes Littell's Reports; 1st volume T. B. Monroe's Reports; 1st and 7th volumes J. J. Marshall's Reports; 4th, 5th, and 8th volumes Dana's Reports; 6th and 10th volumes Benj. Monroe's Reports; 1st volume Metcalfe's Reports; 1st and 2d volumes Monroe and Harlan's Digest of Kentucky Reports. *For justices of the peace*—12 copies of the Revised Statutes of Kentucky, 1st and 2d . volumes.

§ 2. It is made the duty of the State Librarian, immediately upon the passage of this bill, to purchase the books herein specified, and to deliver the same at Frankfort, Kentucky, packed ready for shipping to the Representative in the Legislature from the county of Pike, whose duty it shall be to deliver the same to the clerk of the Pike county court, and take his receipt therefor and forward it to the Librarian.

§ 3. If the above-named volumes of the Kentucky reports cannot be purchased without purchasing the entire set, the Librarian is directed to purchase two entire sets of Kentucky reports; and he will deliver the several volumes above mentioned as above directed; the remainder of the sets he will retain for the use of the State Library.

§ 4. The State Librarian will certify the amount of money necessary to make the above purchase, for packing, and for paying transportation on the same to Frankfort, to the Auditor, who will draw his warrant on the Treasurer for the amount, who is directed to pay the same out of any money in the Treasury not otherwise appropriated.

§ 5. This act shall take effect from its passage.

Approved February 27, 1869.

CHAPTER 1630.

AN ACT for the benefit of the Common Schools of the City of Newport.

Be it enacted by the General Assembly of the Commonwealth of Kentucky:

§ 1. That the city council of the city of Newport be, and are hereby, empowed to levy and collect a special tax, not to exceed five cents on the hundred dollars valuation of the taxable property of the city, for the sole and exclusive benefit of the common schools of said city; said tax shall be levied and collected at the same time, and in the same manner, that the annual revenue taxes of the city are levied and collected, and shall be in addition thereto; and when said tax is collected, it shall be paid over to the treasurer of the school board of said city.

§ 2. This act to take effect from its passage and continue in force for one year only.

Approved February 27, 1869.

CHAPTER 1631.

AN ACT for the benefit of the Stanford Male and Female Seminary.

Be it enacted by the General Assembly of the Commonwealth of Kentucky:

§ 1. That the board of trustees of the Stanford Male and Female Seminary, located at Stanford, Lincoln county, be, and they are hereby, granted full power and authority to apply any funds in their hands or under their control, or any part of the "Endowment Fund," belonging to said seminary, not, however, exceeding the sum of four thousand dollars, for the purpose of erecting a female seminary building at or near Stanford, Lincoln county, Kentucky; and a majority of said board, including the president, shall have power and authority to decide what amount must be raised by individual subscription, before any part of said endowment fund is applied to the erection of said building or the purchase of grounds.

§ 2. A majority of said board may, if deemed expedient by them, use of said fund the sum of four thousand dollars, for the purpose of purchasing grounds, erecting said house, and otherwise improving the property, whether any other moneys are subscribed or not.

§ 3. This act to take effect from its passage.

Approved February 27, 1869.

CHAPTER 1632.

AN ACT to amend "An act to incorporate the Bank of Russellville," approved June 2, 1865.

Be it enacted by the General Assembly of the Commonwealth of Kentucky:

§ 1. That an act, entitled "An act to incorporate the Bank of Russellville," approved June 2, 1865, be, and the same is hereby, amended, so as to allow any person to serve as director in said bank who shall own, in his own right and name, five shares of stock, instead of twenty-five, as provided in said act of incorporation.

§ 2. This act shall be in force from and after its passage.

Approved February 27, 1869.

CHAPTER 1633.

AN ACT to amend an act, entitled "An act to amend the Law in relation to the selection and pay of Jail Guards," passed the 9th of March, 1867, so far as Kenton county is concerned.

Be it enacted by the General Assembly of the Commonwealth of Kentucky:

§ 1. That an act, entitled "An act to amend the law in relation to the selection and pay of jail guards," approved March 9, 1867, be, and the same is hereby, so amended, that whenever a prisoner charged with a felony is confined in the jail at Covington, and guards are ordered, as provided in said act, approved March 9, 1867, for the safe-keeping of such prison, the city of Covington shall pay all the costs and expenses of said guards; and when a prisoner charged with a felony is confined in the jail at Independence, and guards are ordered, as provided in said act, approved March 9, 1867, for the safe-keeping of such prisoner, the county outside of the city of Covington shall pay the cost and expenses of said guards out of the county levy.

§ 2. This act to take effect from its passage.

Approved February 27, 1869.

CHAPTER 1634.

AN ACT for the benefit of the Colored School of Lebanon.

WHEREAS, Senaca Wade, John McElroy, and Allen G. Drake, men of color, trustees of the African School, at Lebanon, Kentucky, hold by deed, in trust for the benefit of the colored people of Marion county, a lot of ground in Lebanon, Kentucky; and whereas, said lot of ground was purchased and deeded in trust to said trustees for the purpose of erecting a school-house upon the same; and whereas, John Goggin has a lot of ground near the one above described, in Lebanon, Kentucky, which affords a more eligible site for building purposes, and is of equal value in all respects to the lot now held by said trustees; therefore,

Be it enacted by the General Assembly of the Commonwealth of Kentucky:

§ 1. That Senaca Wade, John McElroy, and Allen G. Drake, men of color, trustees of the African School, at Lebanon, Kentucky, be, and they are hereby, authorized to sell and convey to John Goggin the lot of land they now hold in trust for the benefit of the colored people of Marion, and to receive in exchange the lot now owned by said Goggin, subject to all the restrictions, &c., and in trust for the colored people of Marion county, Kentucky,

1869.   as they now hold the lot of land to be conveyed to Goggin.

§ 2. This act to take effect from its passage.

Approved February 27, 1869.

• CHAPTER 1635.

AN ACT to amend an act, entitled "An act to incorporate the Germans' Saving Bank, of Covington."

Be it enacted by the General Assembly of the Commonwealth of Kentucky:

§ 1. That an act, entitled "An act to incorporate the Germans' Saving Bank, of Covington," be, and the same is hereby, amended by striking out the word "twenty," in the last sentence of the third section of said act; and that in lieu thereof the word "ten" be inserted, so that the said corporation may be authorized to commence business when ten thousand dollars of capital shall have been paid in.

§ 2. This act to take effect from and after its passage.

Approved February 27, 1869.

CHAPTER 1636.

AN ACT concerning School Trustees of Paducah.

Be it enacted by the General Assembly of the Commonwealth of Kentucky:

§ 1. That hereafter there shall be two school trustees elected in each ward of the city of Paducah, at the same time, and in the same manner, and under the same qualifications, that members of the council for said city are now elected; and shall hold their offices for the same length of time as members of said city council; and the first election for said trustees under this act shall be held on the first Monday in May, 1869; and the board of trustees then elected shall, within three months after their election, divide themselves, by lot, into two classes—first class and second class—and the seats of the members of the first class shall be vacated on the first Monday in May, 1870, and the seats of the members of the second class shall be vacated on the first Monday in May, 1871; and one trustee from each ward shall be elected annually thereafter.

§ 2. That the trustees thus elected shall be the trustees of the common schools and of the male and female seminaries of Paducah; and they shall have all the rights, privileges, and powers that the trustees of said male and female seminaries now have, and shall be styled "The Trustees of the Public Schools of Paducah."

§ 3. That all acts and parts of acts in conflict herewith are hereby repealed, and this act is to be in force from and after its passage.

Approved February 27, 1869.

CHAPTER 1637.

AN ACT to amend an act, entitled "An act to establish a Police Judge for the Town of Carrollton."

Be it enacted by the General Assembly of the Commonwealth of Kentucky:

§ 1. That the act establishing a police judge for the town of Carrollton be, and is hereby, so amended as to authorize the marshal of said town, on his own view, or on reliable information of others, to arrest, without warrant, all persons charged with crime or disorderly conduct within the corporate limits of said town, and he shall safely keep said persons by confinement in the jail of Carroll county, or otherwise, until such persons can be conveniently brought before the police judge or some other magistrate for examination and trial; and for this purpose, the jailer of said county shall receive and safely keep all persons placed in his custody by said marshal.

§ 2. That upon the trial of any person or persons for criminal or penal offenses within his jurisdiction, as now established by law, before the police judge of the said town of Carrollton, the said judge may, if such person or persons be found guilty of the offense alleged against him or them, punish the defendant or defendants by fine or imprisonment, or both, at his discretion; and in case the punishment is by fine alone, and the same is not immediately paid or replevied, the said judge shall have the power to make an order committing the defendant or defendants to prison until such fine is paid or replevied; but such imprisonment shall not continue for a period longer than one day for each two dollars of said fine, exclusive of costs.

§ 3. That from and after the passage of this act, the police judge and town marshal shall be elected annually on the first Thursday in May.

§ 4. That this act shall take effect and be in force from its passage.

Approved February 27, 1869.

CHAPTER 1638.

1869.

AN ACT to amend an act, entitled "An act to authorize the County Judge of the Kenton County Court to sell the Poor-house in said County," approved February 27, 1867.

Be it enacted by the General Assembly of the Commonwealth of Kentucky:

§ 1. That an act, entitled "An act to authorize the presiding judge of Kenton county court to sell the poor-house in said county," approved February 27, 1867, be, and the same is hereby, so amended that W. L. Manson, H. H. Mullins, and Walker Wilson, be, and they are hereby, appointed commissioners, with full power and authority to collect the unpaid purchase money for which the poor-house and lands were sold, by suit or otherwise, in the name of Kenton county; and they are further authorized and empowered to collect, by suit or otherwise, in the name of Kenton county, from John P. Harrison, or any other person, so much of the purchase money as may have been paid to him, the said Harrison, or to any other person, and which he, the said Harrison, or such other person, have not paid over to the said county of Kenton; and the said commissioners are hereby authorized to reinvest the proceeds of said sale of the poor-house and land in some property suitable for a poor-house, and take the title of the property so purchased to the justices of the peace of the Kenton county court, and their successors in office forever, to be held and used by them as a poor-house and lands for said county : *Provided*, Nothing herein shall be so construed as to prevent the said commissioners from purchasing at once such property as may be suitable for poor-house purposes.

§ 2. That the sale heretofore made of the poor-house and lands belonging to Kenton county, to John A. Hall, be, and the same is hereby, declared binding upon the county of Kenton and the said Hall, and that the deed made in pursuance of said sale is also declared legal and binding, and shall have the effect to invest the title to the same in fee simple in the said Hall, his heirs and assigns.

§ 3. This act to take effect from its passage.

Approved February 27, 1869.

CHAPTER 1639.

AN ACT to empower the County Court of Bath to submit to the voters thereof a proposition to take stock in Turnpikes, and to make valid an order therefor made by said Court.

WHEREAS, The county court of the county of Bath, heretofore submitted to the voters of said county the proposition to subscribe to the capital stock of turnpikes in said county, as provided for by an act approved 9th March, 1868, entitled "An act to empower county courts to take stock in turnpike roads in this Commonwealth," which proposition was defeated and not acceded to; and whereas, said county court, at its December term, 1868, ordered that the same proposition should again be submitted to the voters of said county at the next May election; and whereas, doubts exist of the power of said court to resubmit said proposition; for remedy whereof,

Be it enacted by the General Assembly of the Commonwealth of Kentucky:

§ 1. That the said order of said court, at its last December term, resubmitting said question to a vote of the people, be, and is hereby, ratified and declared to be valid; and said court is empowered to submit to the voters of said county the proposition to take stock in turnpikes, in pursuance of said act of 9th March, 1868, as often as in its judgment shall be proper and right; and any action of said court in regard thereto shall be as binding as if the said power had been granted by said act.

§ 2. This act shall take effect from its passage.

Approved February 27, 1869.

CHAPTER 1640.

AN ACT to authorize the appointment of a Treasurer for Trimble County.

Be it enacted by the General Assembly of the Commonwealth of Kentucky:

§ 1. That the county court of Trimble county is hereby authorized to appoint a treasurer for said county, whose duty it shall be to receive and hold all moneys belonging to said county which may be ordered into his hands by said court, and to pay the same over at the proper times to such persons as may be entitled to same under the orders of said court, made in conformity with law. Said officer shall hold his said office at the discretion of said county court; and, before he enters upon this discharge of his duties, shall take the oaths prescribed by the Constitution of this Commonwealth, and shall execute bond, with good and sufficient security, to be approved and received by said court, conditioned that he will well and truly discharge

1869.   the duties of his office, and pay out such moneys as may
come to his hands to the persons entitled thereto, and such
balance as may remain in his hands, when he goes out of
office, to his successor, or to such other persons as said
county court may direct.   He shall receive for his services
a sum, to be fixed by said county court, not to exceed five
per cent. on the amount of money received and disbursed
by him.

§ 2. An action shall lie on said bond, in any court of
competent jurisdiction, in favor of the county of Trimble
and against said treasurer, for any breach of his official
duty.

§ 3. Nothing in this act shall be construed so as to give
the judge of the Trimble county court any greater power
to order the payment of claims against said county than
he now has under existing laws.

§ 4. This act to take effect from and after its passage.

Approved March 1, 1869.

CHAPTER 1642.
AN ACT to authorise the sale of part of Fairview Cemetery.

*Be it enacted by the General Assembly of the Commonwealth
of Kentucky:*

§ 1. That the trustees of the town of Bowling Green
may sell, for the use of said town, any part of Fairview
Cemetery, where there is no interment of the dead: *Provided, however*, That no such sale shall be made other than
such as they are already authorized to make, until they
shall first have submitted the question to the qualified
voters of said town, and until a majority of those voting
shall have approved it; and for this purpose they may
call an election at any time, upon first giving public notice
thereof by at least two weekly insertions in the Bowling
Green Democrat.

§ 2. This act to take effect from and after its passage.

Approved March 1, 1869.

CHAPTER 1645.
AN ACT to amend and reduce into one the acts in relation to the Town of Ashland.

*Be it enacted by the General Assembly of the Commonwealth
of Kentucky:*

§ 1. That there shall be elected in the town of Ashland,
Trustees to be   on the first Monday of June, 1869, six trustees, and annu-
elected, how &
by whom.   ally, on the first Monday in June in each year thereafter,

there shall be an election of three trustees. Of the six
first elected, three shall hold their offices for two years;
and it shall be determined by lot who shall hold for two
years, and the result entered on the minutes of the board
of directors. Ten days' notice in writing of the time and
place of each election must be set up by the clerk of the
board at five of the most public places in the town. If
two or more persons receive an equal number of votes,
the clerk shall decide who is elected. No person shall
be eligible to the office of a trustee who is not a citizen of
the town and a qualified elector of this Commonwealth.
No person shall vote at an election of trustees who has
not resided in the town where the election is held sixty
days next preceding the same, and who is not a citizen of
the State. The trustees shall appoint two discreet persons, citizens of the town and qualified voters, to act as
judges of the election. The clerk of the board shall be
clerk of the election; but if, from any cause, he should fail
to attend, the judges of the election may appoint a clerk
of the election. The judges and clerk shall be sworn before proceeding with the election faithfully to discharge
their duties; and shall make report of the result of the
election to the clerk of the county court, and also to the
trustees. If, from any cause, no election is held at the
time prescribed, the county court of the county shall appoint five trustees for such town, to act until the next
stated election. Trustees shall enter upon the duties of
their office on the Monday next succeeding their election
or appointment, and continue in office until their successors are qualified. A trustee appointed to fill a vacancy
shall enter upon the duties of his office immediately after
he qualifies as such. Every trustee and clerk of the board
of trustees shall, before he enters on the duties of his station, take the oaths prescribed in the Constitution.

§ 2. The trustees may make such rules and regulations
for the government of the town, not inconsistent with the
laws and Constitution, as they may deem necessary and
proper. They may fill vacancies in their board until the
next stated election. They must cause the streets of the
town to be kept clean and in good order. They may levy
an annual tax on the males over twenty-one years of age
residing in the town, not exceeding one dollar upon the
head, and may levy an ad valorem tax on the real estate
in the town of not exceeding one dollar on the hundred
dollars. They may appoint a clerk, assessor, town war-
den, collector, and treasurer, and take from the two latter
bond and good security for the faithful performance of
their duties. Four trustees may constitute a board to do
business.

VOL. I.—LOO. L.—35

1869.

When to en-
ter upon duties

To take oath.

May make
rules & by-laws,
&c.

Vacancies.

Keep streets
clean.
May levy taxes.

May appoint
officers.

Quorum.

§ 3. The trustees shall be a body corporate, and, by the name of the trustees of the town of Ashland, may sue and be sued, and may appoint all necessary agents and attorneys in that behalf. They may elect one of their body chairman of the board.

§ 4. They shall have power to purchase, take, and hold the title to not exceeding forty acres of land in or near the town, for a public cemetery. They shall have the power to improve such ground, and appoint a keeper thereof; to sell small parcels of the ground to individuals, for the purpose of interment; to receive and collect subscriptions to aid in purchasing, improving, taking care of, and repairing such ground.

§ 5. They shall have the power to tax any show or exhibition and bowling-alleys within the town, or within a quarter of a mile of the limits thereof, to the same amount as they may be taxed by the State.

§ 6. No stallion or jackass shall stand within the bounds of the town, without first being authorized so to do by a license from the trustees thereof, designating the place at which he is to stand. For a violation of this section, the keeper and owner of such animal shall be jointly and severally liable to a fine of five dollars for each day, to be recovered by warrant in behalf of the trustees of the town.

§ 7. The board of trustees shall keep a journal of their proceedings, and, at the request of a member, the ayes and noes on any question shall be recorded. At the next meeting, the proceedings shall be read and signed by the member who presided at the last preceding meeting. If he is not present, by the person presiding when they are read. No member shall have a vote on a subject in which he has a private interest. A meeting of the board may be called by the chairman or by two members. They shall keep an account of all moneys levied, collected, and disbursed, and keep an accurate account thereof for what objects each sum is disbursed. Their books shall at all times be open to the inspection of the citizens of the town.

§ 8. They shall, once in each year, give a full and fair statement in writing, signed by the chairman, of all sums collected and all sums disbursed the preceding year, and what for, and of all debts due them or owing by them, which shall be posted up for inspection at three of the most public places in town.

§ 9. That the trustees shall have full power and authority to cause any or all the streets, alleys, and lanes in said town to be improved, or reimproved, or repaired, in whole or in part, in any manner they may deem advisable, at the expense and cost of the owners of the property fronting the same. Said trustees shall have full power and authority to cause and procure any or all the streets, alleys, and lanes in said town, in whole or in part, to be graded, culverted, or otherwise drained, paved, and curbed, or graded, curbed, and macadamized, or graded, curbed, and graveled, or to be graded, curbed, and paved entirely across the street, or paved and curbed a portion of the distance across the street and macadamized the balance of the distance between the paved portions; or, after the grading, to put upon the same either any or all of said kinds of improvements, and to underlay either any or all of the said kinds of improvements, after the grading, with gravel, or sand, or both, and to spread upon the top of either any or all of said kinds of improvements gravel, or sand, or both; and to do, or cause to be done, either any or all of said kinds of improvements with bowlders or any other sort of stone, at the expense and cost of the owners of lots and fractions of lots fronting on such streets, alleys, or lanes; and a petition, in writing, to the said trustees of the owner or owners of the larger part of the ground, between the points to be improved, fronting on any street, alley, or lane, shall be sufficient to authorize the said trustees to contract for either any or all of the above-mentioned kinds of improvements: *Provided*, That the said trustees, not less than four concurring in the vote, may cause any street, alley, or lane, to be improved as aforesaid, at the cost and expense of the owners of the lots or parts of lots fronting the same, without petition or consent. The culverting and draining shall be included in the cost and expense as a part of the grading. And when the improvements ordered shall be completed, the said trustees shall apportion the cost and expense thereof *pro rata* among the lot-owners according to the value of their respective lots or fractions of lots; or may, in their discretion, so apportion a part of the cost and expense of such improvement upon the property fronting thereon and pay the balance out of the general revenue of the town. And a lien is hereby given on the lots or parts of lots for the same; which cost and expense may be listed and collected as other taxes, by the town collector, or by any special collector, either of whom shall have power to sell and convey the lots and parts of lots for the same, according to such by-laws and regulations as the trustees may prescribe. All sales to be at or near the premises, after having been advertised as required by law in sales of real estate under execution. Any statement made by any collector in any bond or deed selling, or conveying property sold, for the payment of any of the taxes hereby imposed, or imposed by any other part of this act, shall be *prima facie* evidence of the truth of the facts stated to have been done, but such statements may be contradicted: *Provided further,* That the owner or owners of any lot or lots, or parts of lots, sold for the cost and expense of such improvements as aforesaid, who have not consented, in writing. for that purpose, shall be allowed three years in which to redeem the same by paying to the purchaser of said lot or lots, or part of a lot, so sold as aforesaid, the purchase money, with fifteen per centum interest per annum, and all the taxes and levies that may have subsequently accrued and been paid by the purchaser, and ten per cent. thereon; and those who have consented in writing may redeem at any time within one year on like terms: *Provided further,* That infants, *femes covert,* and persons of unsound mind, shall have one year in which to redeem, on like terms, after their respective disabilities shall be removed, not exceeding, however, fifteen years from the date of sale. In the collection of any taxes imposed by this act, the town may become the purchaser at any sale made for the purpose of collecting any tax, through any person authorized to bid by the trustees.

§ 10. The trustees shall have full power and authority

May cause foot-walks to be graded, &c.

to compel the owners of lots or parts of lots to grade, curb, and pave a foot-walk in front of their lots not exceeding sixteen feet wide, with good brick, rock, or plank, in accordance to the directions of the trustees; or cause the owners of lots or parts of lots to grade, curb, and gravel a foot-walk in front of their respective lot or lots, or part of lots. They may require some portions to be done in one manner and others in another, as they may deem proper. They may require the pavements and sidewalks to be repaired from time to time, as they may deem necessary; and may, in such repairing, require a different material to be used from that of which the pavement or sidewalk is made. Where the trustees shall deem proper to order sidewalks to be made, or repairs thereto, reasonable notice shall be given to the owner or owners to make such pavement or foot-walk, or improvement. The notice shall be signed by the chairman of the board of trustees, and shall specify the time within which such improvement, pavement, foot-walk, or repairs, shall be commenced and finished. Twenty days within which to commence the work shall be deemed reasonable. If the owner of any lot or lots, or parts of lots, shall fail or refuse to begin such pavement, foot-walk, or repairs within the time prescribed; or, having commenced, shall fail to complete the same within the time prescribed, the trustees may cause the same to be made or repaired at the cost and expense of the owner or owners of the lot or lots, or fraction of lot, and shall have a lien on such lot or lots, or fraction of lot' for said cost and expense; which cost and expense shall be listed and collected as other tax, as provided in the preceding section of this act for the collection of assessments for improving streets, alleys, &c.; and the owner of lots or part of lots sold shall have the same right of redemption as the owners of property sold for improving streets, &c., have in said section, and upon the same terms and conditions. If the owner of any lot or fraction of lot, before which the trustees may desire to make, or cause to be made, the improvements provided for in this section, does not reside in the county of Boyd, then the notice required by this section shall be posted in at least two public places in said town for at least one month, and have the same effect as personal service. The lien created by this act shall attach from the time the improvement is ordered to be put under contract. They shall have power to require the owners of lots or parts of lots to fill them with earth to such grade as they may fix, and to make drains and keep them in repair. If the owner of lots or fractions shall fail, after reasonable notice, to make the fill or drain required, the trustees may cause the same to be done at the expense of the owner, and have a lien therefor, which may be enforced in the same manner as the cost of improving streets, alleys, &c., as provided in section nine of this act.

§ 11. In the collection of any tax authorized by this act, the collector shall first sell the personal property of the person owing such tax: *Provided*, That no personal property shall be sold but such as may be liable to execution under the general laws of this Commonwealth: *Provided further*, That the failure of any collecting officers to sell personal property as herein directed, shall not render invalid sales made of real estate as directed in this act.

§ 12. The trustees shall have power and authority, by by-laws, to fix fines and penalties for the violation of the rules and regulations they may adopt for the government of the town, and may alter and amend the same; may repeal and again re-enact, and from time to time fix such fines and penalties as they may deem proper, not inconsistent with the laws and Constitution: *Provided*, That no fine shall exceed twenty dollars, nor shall imprisonment extend beyond ten days. The proceedings to enforce such fines and penalties shall be in the name of the Commonwealth of Kentucky, for the use of the trustees of the town of Ashland, before the police judge of said town, or any justice of the peace residing within the town. If at any time there should be a vacancy in the office of police judge, or he absent, and no justice of the peace residing in said town, then such fines and forfeitures may be recovered before any justice of the peace for Boyd county.

1869.

What property to be sold for taxes.

May fix fines for violation of ordinances, &c.

1869.

Fines to be
paid to town
treasurer.

§ 13. All fines collected for a violation of the by-laws,
rules and regulations, of the town; all fines recovered in
any court for violations of the penal laws of the Commonwealth, for offenses committed within the boundary of said
town, shall, when collected, be paid to the treasurer of the
town, and shall form part of the revenue of the town, and
may be applied as revenue derived from the general tax
within said town.

Chapter 100,
Revised Stat-
utes to apply to
town: may im-
prove wharf.
&c.

· § 14. That article six of chapter (100) one hundred, Revised Statutes, shall apply to the town of Ashland; that
the board of trustees shall have power to make a grade
and improve the public landing at the town, and may appropriate money for this purpose from time to time, as they
may deem proper. They may pass by-laws requiring
steamboats, and other boats and water crafts, to pay
wharfage; and shall, by by-laws, regulate the amount and
the mode of collection. They shall have power to regulate and control the public landing.

May extend
streets & alleys.

§ 15. The board of trustees may extend the streets and
alleys within the town limits, and shall have power to
contract with the owners of land for such extension, and
pay such price as may be agreed upon; and in case no
agreement can be made, they may proceed to condemn
the same under the rules and regulations prescribed for
the condemnation of land for turnpike and plank roads.

May appoint
street commis-
sioners; their
powers and du-
ties.

§ 16. The board of trustees may appoint one or more
street commissioners, whose duty it shall be to keep the
streets, alleys, and lanes within said town in repair.
They shall be governed by the orders of the board of
trustees, and shall have such compensation as the board
may fix. The persons residing within the limits of said
town, liable by the general law to work on public roads,
shall work on the streets, alleys, and lanes within the
town limits, and upon the public roads for one half mile
beyond the corporate limits, under the street commissioners, but not exceeding three days in any one year. Any
person failing to work when notified, shall be liable to
pay a . fine of five dollars, unless reasonable excuse be
shown for such failure. Any person notified to work
may, in lieu of each day, pay to the town treasurer the
sum of two dollars. Persons within the town limits shall
not be required to work the roads outside of the town
beyond one half mile. The board of trustees may, at
any time, remove the street commissioners and appoint
others. The public roads for one half mile beyond the
town limits shall be under the jurisdiction and control
of the board of trustees.

May tax ven-
dors of spiritu-
ous liquors.

§ 17. That the board of trustees of said town may require of all vendors of spirituous, vinous, or malt liquors,
within the corporate limits, to pay a tax not exceeding

fifty dollars, and obtain a license. The tax to be paid to the treasurer of the town, and to be applied by the board of trustees in aid of the public schools in the town.

§ 18. That no license shall be granted by the county court of Boyd county to keep a tavern within the corporate limits of the town of Ashland, until the applicant for such license shall have first obtained the consent of the trustees of said town, and shall produce to the court the written permission of the board of trustees of the town. This shall not be construed to abridge the power of the county court in the exercise of its discretion in refusing a license to keep a tavern. The party obtaining a license to keep a tavern shall, in addition to the tax fixed by law, pay to the treasurer of the town, and to be applied in aid of the common schools of the town, a sum not less than ten nor more than fifty dollars, to be fixed by the by-laws of the town. Any person who shall violate the provisions of this or the preceding section, shall, for every offense, be liable to pay a fine of twenty dollars, which may be recovered by proceedings in the name of the Commonwealth of Kentucky, for the use of the board of trustees of the town of Ashland.

County court not to license, unless consent of trustees first obtained.

To pay town for license.

§ 19. The board of trustees shall have power to require all persons within the corporate limits of said town, engaged in selling spirituous, vinous, or malt liquors, by license or otherwise, to close their doors and not to sell, loan, barter, give away, or permit to be drank, any spirituous, vinous, or malt liquors, or the mixture of either, on an election day, or any other public day or occasion when, in the judgment of the board of trustees, the peace, quiet, and good order of the town may require it, and also on the Sabbath day; and the board of trustees are also hereby authorized to make such rules and regulations, by by-laws, as will be necessary, in their judgment, to enforce their orders. They may authorize the marshal of the town, or any peace officer, to enter any house or place where there are reasonable grounds to suspect that there is liquor being sold, drank, or otherwise disposed of, and take possession of the same, and make such other rules and by-laws as will enforce the order. May impose a fine and imprisonment, the fine not to exceed twenty dollars for each offense, and imprisonment not exceeding ten days; and in addition to such penalty the person found guilty shall forfeit his or her license, and shall not again have a license for two years.

May require houses to be closed.

§ 20. The jailer of Boyd county is hereby authorized to receive into and confine in the jail of the county, such persons as may be ordered to be confined in jail, in pursuance of the by-laws of the town.

Jailer of Boyd county to receive town prisoners.

1869.

Police court established, & officers of same, and when and how elected.

§ 21. That there is hereby established in the town of Ashland a police court, the officers of which shall be a judge and marshal, to be called the judge and marshal of the town of Ashland; that said officers shall be elected by the qualified voters residing within the limits of said town. The first election of said officers shall be on the first Monday in June, 1869, at any place in said town which may be designated by the board of trustees, and conducted by the officers that may be appointed to con-

Term of office. duct the election of trustees for said town. The said officers shall hold their offices for the term of two years, and until their successors shall be duly qualified. The regular elections for said officers shall be held on the first Monday of June, and be conducted by the officers

To reside within town limits, &c. appointed to conduct the election of trustees; they shall reside within the limits of said town, and hold their offices therein. Contested elections shall be determined in the same way that contested elections for county judges are; and in case of a tie between two or more candidates, the officers who conduct the election shall choose between those having the highest equal vote, by lot. Vacancies shall be filled by an election to be ordered by the board of trustees, who shall appoint the officers to conduct the election, of which ten days' notice shall be given. The officers of the election shall give a certificate thereof to the persons elected. The Governor shall, upon information by certificate of the election, commission the judges, who shall, in the form of an affidavit, take the oath required by the Constitution, and also an oath of office, that he will discharge the duties of his office without favor or affection, and to the best of his ability, according to law. The commission of the police judge, together with the affidavit, shall be filed in the county court clerk's office, and duly recorded, for which the clerk shall receive one dollar.

Marshal to give bond. § 22. The marshal of said court, before he enters upon the duties of his office, shall execute a covenant in the Boyd county court, with good security, to be approved by the court, payable to the Commonwealth of Kentucky, conditioned that he will faithfully discharge the duties of his office according to law; he shall take the

Suit may be instituted on same. oath required by law of a constable; any person aggrieved by the acts of said marshal, may institute suit on said bond in any court having jurisdiction of the same; said

Who to keep record. bond shall be kept in the county court clerk's office as part of its records; and the clerk of said court shall be allowed the same fees as are allowed by law for taking bonds from, and administering oaths to, constables.

Qualifications of judge and marshal. § 23. The judge shall possess the qualifications of a justice of the peace, and the marshal those of constable;

and for malfeasance or misfeasance in office, on the presentment of a grand jury, they may be removed from office, but subject to an appeal to the Court of Appeals, and shall also be liable to impeachment, and the penalties arising therefrom.

§ 24. The police court of Ashland shall have concurrent jurisdiction, within the boundary of the town, of all matters, both civil and penal, of which justices of the peace have jurisdiction, with the same powers, privileges, and rights, and under the same rules and restrictions; and jurisdiction of all criminal matters, within the county of Boyd, concurrent with two justices of the peace. The marshal shall exercise the same powers, and possess the same rights, as a constable. They shall be severally entitled to charge and receive the same fees as justices of the peace and constables are, or may hereafter be entitled to receive, for like services; and such fees may be collected in the same manner as other officer's fees. The marshal may be appointed by the board of trustees collector.

§ 25. Appeals shall be allowed from the judgments of said police court in the same manner as are allowed from those of justices of the peace.

§ 26. When said officers go out of office they shall hand over to their successors all of their official records and papers, and may demand a receipt for the same: *Provided*, That the marshal shall have the same rights to wind up the business in his hands that is allowed by law to constables.

§ 27. The marshal shall execute the process of said court; but in cases of urgency, and when he cannot be procured, the judge may direct the same to any constable, or the sheriff of Boyd county, or to any private person, who shall execute the same.

§ 28. The said judge shall keep a faithful record of all his official acts, in the same manner and mode as are now required by law of justices of the peace.

§ 29. The said judge shall not enter upon the discharge of the duties of his office until he has been commissioned and qualified as herein directed; nor the marshal until he has executed the bond and taken the oaths required by this act; and should he fail to do so, within forty days after his election, the office shall be vacant, and a new election shall be ordered by the trustees, which shall be conducted as other elections provided for in this act; ten days' notice of such election shall be given by posting written notices at three public places in the town.

§ 30. The police court and marshal shall be authorized to do any act specially authorized by this act or by any general law conferring jurisdiction, powers, or duties, on police courts and marshals, in addition to the powers and duties hereinbefore named.

1869.

Jurisdiction of police court.

Fees, &c.

Appeals may be had.

On going out of office to hand over papers, &c.

Who to execute process.

Judge to keep record.

When to enter upon duties of office.

When office of marshal to be vacant.

Further powers of police court.

§ 31. The boundary of the town of Ashland shall be as follows. viz: Beginning at the Ohio river, at low water-mark, on the line dividing the land of the Kentucky Iron, Coal, and Manufacturing Company and the land of S. and E. Ward; thence with said line southerly to the top of the hill; thence southeasterly, with a line parallel to the course of Winchester street, to the land owned by Peter Smith; thence with the lines of his lands, so as to include the same, to the intersection of the lower line of Fourth street extended; thence with said line of Fourth street extended southwesterly to the south side of the Back road; thence southeasterly with said road, on the south side thereof, to its intersection of the line of Broadway street extended; thence with said line of Broadway street extended, north-easterly, to the lot of Mrs. Orra Bagby; thence southeast-erly, a line parallel to the course of Winchester street, to the intersection of the upper line of F street extended; thence with the line of F street extended, northeasterly, to the southerly side of Winchester street; thence south-easterly, with the line of Winchester street extended, to the line of I street extended; thence with the extended course of I street to the Ohio river; thence down the river, at low water, to the beginning.

§ 32. The board of trustees may, in levying any tax up-on the real estate within the boundary of the town, dis-criminate, and lay a less tax upon the lands not laid off into town lots than upon that so laid off.

§ 33. That all acts and parts of acts relating to the town of Ashland are hereby repealed.

§ 34. This act shall take effect from its passage.

Approved March 1, 1869.

CHAPTER 1647.

AN ACT to Perfect the Records of the Bullitt County Court.

WHEREAS, The orders of the Bullitt county court, from and including the 4th day of September, 1862, up to and including 20th July, 1863, were not signed by William R. Thompson, the then presiding judge of said county court, during said period; therefore,

Be it enacted by the General Assembly of the Commonwealth of Kentucky:

§ 1. That the said Wm. R. Thompson is hereby author-ized to sign the orders of the Bullitt county court unsigned from the 4th day of September, 1862, to 20th July, 1863, including both days; and said orders, when so signed, shall be held legal and valid, and their validity shall date back to the date of their respective entries.

§ 2. This act shall take effect from its passage.

1869.

Approved March 1, 1869.

CHAPTER 1648.

AN ACT in relation to the Public Square of Greenup County.

WHEREAS, The presiding judge of the Greenup county court was authorized by said act, chapter 279, to lease portions of the public square in Greenupsburg; and whereas, leases have been granted under said act to John C. Adams, Geo. E Roe, Jesse Corum, and John Seaton, which have been confirmed by the county court of said county; and whereas, it is not deemed best to further encumber the public square with more private offices; therefore,

Be it enacted by the General Assembly of the Commonwealth of Kentucky:

§ 1. That neither the presiding judge nor county court of Greenup county shall have power to grant any other leases of any portion of said public square: *Provided, however,* That said leases so granted as aforesaid shall not be invalidated, but shall remain in full force according to their terms and conditions, and for the times for which they were granted.

§ 2. All acts inconsistent with this act are hereby repealed.

§ 3. This act shall take effect from its passage.

Approved March 1, 1869.

CHAPTER 1649.

AN ACT for the benefit of School Districts Nos. 19, 38, 50, 58, 61, 18, and 26, in Lawrence County.

Be it enacted by the General Assembly of the Commonwealth of Kentucky:

§ 1. That the commissioner of common school districts for Lawrence county be, and he is hereby, allowed to make his report for school districts Nos. 38, 19, 50, 58, 61, 18, and 26, in Lawrence county, for the year 1862, to the Superintendent of Public Instruction; and when said report shall be made as required by law, the Superintendent of Public Instruction will transmit a copy of the same to the Auditor, whereupon, the Auditor shall draw his warrant upon the Treasurer, in favor of the common school commissioner of Lawrence county, for the amount due districts Nos. 38, 50, 58, 61, 18, and 26, in Lawrence county, for the year 1862, as shown by the report herein authorized to be made, to be paid out of any surplus money belonging to Lawrence county; and if there be no such surplus, then to be paid out of the bond fund for Lawrence county.

§ 2. This act to take effect from its passage.

Approved March 1, 1869.

CHAPTER 1650..

AN ACT to authorize the Town of Carlisle, in Nicholas County, to take Stock in its corporate capacity in the Maysville and Lexington Railroad Company, Northern Division.

Be it enacted by the General Assembly of the Commonwealth of Kentucky:

§ 1. That upon the petition of not less than ten tax-payers of the town of Carlisle, Nicholas county, it shall be the duty of the trustees of said town to submit to a vote of the qualified voters of said town, on a day to be designated by such trustees, not later than thirty days after the filing or presenting of such petition, the question of subscribing for and on behalf of said town the amount of stock proposed by such petition to the capital stock of the Maysville and Lexington railroad company, Northern Division, not exceeding, however, the sum of twenty thousand dollars; and if a majority of those voting shall vote in favor of making such subscription, it shall be the duty of such board of trustees to enter the result of said vote upon its record; and the president of the board of trustees of said town shall make the subscription in accordance with the vote. Said election shall be held at the place in said town and by the officer as now required by law in holding elections for officers of said town; and notice of said election shall be given by said officer, by printed advertisements posted up at (3) three or more public places in said town at least ten days before the election.

§ 2. That if said town shall subscribe to the capital stock of said railroad company under the provisions of this act, it shall be the duty of the board of trustees of said town to issue the bonds of the town, in denominations of not less than ($100) one hundred nor more than ($1,000) one thousand dollars, in payment thereof, with coupons attached. The bonds shall be signed by the president of the board of trustees and countersigned by the town clerk; and the coupons shall be signed by the clerk alone. Such bonds shall be negotiable and payable to bearer, in the town of Carlisle, at not more than (30) thirty years from their date, and shall bear interest at a rate not greater than (8) eight per cent., payable semi-annually in the town of Carlisle.

§ 3. That in case said town shall subscribe to the capital stock of said railroad company under the provisions of this act, and issue bonds for the payment of such subscription, it shall be the duty of the board of trustees of said town to cause to be levied and collected a tax, from year to year, sufficient to pay the semi annual interest, on all the real estate and personal property in said town subject to taxation under the revenue laws of the State, including the amounts owned by residents of said town which ought to be given in under the equalization laws.

§ 4. That taxes levied under the authority of this act shall be collected by the officer of said town who is by law the collector of taxes levied for the ordinary purposes of said town. But before such officer shall be authorized to collect said tax, he shall execute a bond, with such security or securities as may be approved by the trustees of said town, conditioned that said officer will promptly and faithfully collect and pay over to the proper persons, within the time prescribed by law, all taxes levied under this act which may be placed in his hands for collection.

§ 5. That the officer having in his hands for collection taxes levied under this act shall have all the powers of distraining and selling personal property which sheriffs have in the collection of the State revenue; but the owner of any real estate sold may redeem the same at any time within one year after such sale, by paying the purchase money and (10) ten per cent. per annum thereon, with all taxes paid by the purchaser thereon after his purchase, and (10) ten per cent. per annum thereon.

§ 6. That the officer selling real estate for taxes levied under this act, shall give to the purchaser a certificate of his said purchase, which shall describe the real estate, and state the amount for which it was sold, and the date of the sale, which certificate shall be lodged by the purchaser with the clerk of the county court within (60) days, who shall record the same in a book to be kept for that purpose, for which said clerk shall be entitled to charge a fee of (50) fifty cents; and if such certificate is not lodged for record as herein provided, the land may be redeemed at any time within (15) years, on paying the purchase money and (6) six per cent. per annum thereon.

§ 7. That the officer collecting taxes under this act shall receive such compensation as may be allowed him by the board of trustees of said town.

§ 8. That one half of the tax levied in any one year, shall be collected by the collecting officer and paid over to the treasurer of the town or board of trustees, within

(120) one hundred and twenty days after the same is placed in his hands, and the residue within (6) six months after the first ought to have been paid; and if the officer, whose duty it is to collect taxes levied under this act, shall fail or refuse to execute bond as required by this act, for (20) twenty days after the tax is levied, he shall forfeit his office, and the board of trustees may appoint a collector, who shall execute bond with securities, and have all the powers, and be subject to all the duties and liabilities as the collecting officer before named in collecting taxes under this act.

§ 9. That if the officer or collector, having in his hands for collection taxes levied under this act, shall fail to collect and pay over the same within the time prescribed, said officer or collector shall, with his sureties, be liable for the amount not paid as required, and (10) ten per cent. thereon, to be recovered on motion on (10) ten days' notice, in any court having jurisdiction; and any execution issued on such judgment shall not be replevied, and shall be indorsed by the officer issuing it, that no security of any kind is to be taken.

§ 10. It shall be the duty of the board of trustees of said town to see that the collecting officer or collector collects and pays over taxes placed in his hands for collection, according to law, and to institute legal proceedings against him on his failure to do so. They shall appropriate such moneys, when collected, to the payment of the interest on the bonds of their town; they shall, whenever a dividend is declared by said railroad company, cause their treasurer to receive the same, and pay the interest on their bonds out of it; and when a surplus shall remain, after paying the interest due, they shall apply such surplus to the purchase of their bonds, if they can be purchased at par or less; and if they cannot be purchased at par, they shall invest such surplus in some safe and profitable manner, and in such way that the money may be readily realized when needed to buy or pay off their bonds.

§ 11. That all dividends which shall be received upon the stock held and owned by said town under this act, shall be, and are hereby, set apart to be held sacred as a sinking fund, to be only used as provided in this act, for the payment of the principal and interest of the bonds issued under the authority of this act.

§ 12. That in case the dividends upon the stock held and owned under this act by said town, and for which bonds shall have been issued, shall not be sufficient to enable said town to pay off its bonds at maturity, it shall be the duty of said trustees, whenever said fact shall become apparent, to cause a tax to be levied from year to year, and collected on all the property in said town which, by the provisions of this act, is subject to taxation, to pay interest sufficient, with the profits which may be realized by the board on said collections, to discharge the bonds at maturity, or at any time before maturity, when they may be bought or paid at par or less: *Provided*, That any tax levied under the provisions of this section, shall be collected by the same officer or collector, under the same powers, and subject to the same responsibilities, in every respect, as provided in this act, in relation to the collection of taxes levied to pay interest.

§ 13. That dividends accruing to said town upon its stock in said company, after the discharge of its bonds, shall go into the treasury of the town, and be controlled and expended as taxes levied by said corporation are or may be authorized by law to be used.

§ 14. This act shall take effect from and after its passage.

Approved March 1, 1869.

CHAPTER 1651.

AN ACT to release to the Town of Smithland all right and·title of the State of Kentucky in and to Cumberland Hospital.

Be it enacted by the General Assembly of the Commonwealth of Kentucky:

§ 1. That the building situate in the town of Smithland, known as the Cumberland Hospital, together with all the interest owned by the State of Kentucky in and to the lands upon which the same was built, or in any lands in any way connected therewith, as well as to all furniture and other fixtures belonging thereto, and to any and all property and assets belonging to said hospital now in the hands of any party or parties, be, and the same are hereby, surrendered by the State of Kentucky to the corporate authorities of said town of Smithland, to be held and used for the sole and exclusive purpose of carrying on a high school in said town.

§ 2. Said hospital building, lands, and other property, is, for the present, to be under the control of the corporate authorities of said town; but in case at any time a high school or seminary shall be incorporated in said town, then, upon a petition signed by a majority of all the legal voters of said town, it shall be the duty of said corporate authorities to convey said buildings, lands, and other property, to the legally appointed trustees of such high school or seminary, subject to such restrictions as may be prescribed by the act of the General Assembly incorporating the same.

§ 3. This act to take effect from and after its passage.

Approved March 1, 1869.

CHAPTER 1652.

AN ACT for the benefit of School Districts Nos. 3 and 19, of Lawrence County.

Be it enacted by the General Assembly of the Commonwealth of Kentucky:

§ 1. That the commissioner of common schools for Lawrence county be, and he is hereby, allowed to make his report for school districts Nos. 3 and 19, in Lawrence county, for the year 1868, on or before the first day of May, 1869, to the Superintendent of Public Instruction; and when said report shall be made as required by law, the Superintendent of Public Instruction will transmit a copy of the same to the Auditor, whereupon the Auditor shall draw his warrant upon the treasurer, in favor of the school commissioner of Lawrence county, for the amount due school districts Nos. 3 and 19 for the year 1868, as shown by the report herein authorized to be made, to be paid out of any surplus belonging to Lawrence county; and if there be no such surplus, then to be paid out of the bond fund for Lawrence county.

§ 2. This act to take effect from its passage.

Approved March 1, 1869.

CHAPTER 1656.

AN ACT to amend the Road Laws for the Counties of Hickman, Fulton, and Ballard.

Be it enacted by the General Assembly of the Commonwealth of Kentucky:

§ 1. That the county courts of the counties of Hickman, Fulton, and Ballard, are hereby authorized and empowered, at any time they may deem proper, to lay off their respective counties into road precincts, the boundaries of which shall be distinctly defined, and the plat of said precincts, with the necessary explanations, shall be entered of record on the order books of said county courts. For each of said road precincts there shall be appointed a surveyor, whose duty shall, in all things, be the same as now prescribed by law; and he shall be subject to all the penalties prescribed by law for failure to discharge the duties imposed upon him.

§ 2. Every person subject by existing laws to work upon the public roads, who resides within the limits of said road precincts, shall be subject to the orders of the surveyors of said precincts, in the same manner as though his name was on the list of hands furnished the surveyors of the roads by the county courts in conformity with existing laws. The order of the county court appointing surveyors for said precincts shall give a full and complete description of the precinct over which he shall be appointed surveyor, which order shall be delivered to him in the manner now prescribed by law.

§ 3. The existing laws relating to roads and passways shall not be repealed or suspended to any extent in either of said counties, until the county court thereof shall comply with the conditions of this act; and each of said counties have the right to act independently of the other.

§ 4. No part of existing laws relating to roads and passways are repealed by this act, except where the same are clearly inconsistent therewith.

§ 5. This act to take effect from and after its passage.

Approved March 2, 1869.

CHAPTER 1657.

AN ACT to amend an act, entitled "An act to amend an act providing for the erection of Public Buildings in Lewis County."

Be it enacted by the General Assembly of the Commonwealth of Kentucky:

§ 1. That an act, entitled "An act to amend an act, providing for the erection of public buildings in Lewis county," approved January the 17th, 1868, is amended as follows: The tax levied by said act shall be levied, collected, and appropriated by the Lewis county court to the building of the turnpike roads named in said act, and the following additional roads: the Concord and Tollsboro, the Vanceburg, Quincy, and Springville, the Vanceburg and Kinniconick road, and any other turnpike roads now incorporated, or hereafter incorporated, and which roads shall be built in Lewis county.

§ 2. That there shall be collected a poll-tax of three dollars upon and from all male persons over twenty-one years of age, residing in Lewis county; and, after paying the annual expenses of said county, the balance shall be applied to assist in building turnpike roads in said county. That said tax shall be collected each year, whether any or all the roads named in the act to which this is an amendment commence or prosecute their work or not; and the fourth section of said act is amended to this extent: the money, when collected, shall be applied to the payment of the county bonds issued by the order of the Lewis county court, under the various acts of the Legislature, to aid in building turnpike roads in said county, always paying those bonds first falling due; and said taxes are pledged and dedicated as a fund to pay off said county bonds, and shall never be divested from that object, and this shall be construed, and is intended to include, the bonds already issued, and all bonds here- after issued by the Lewis county court to aid any turn- pike road in said county.

§ 3. That the title of the act to which this is an amend- ment shall be, and is hereby, changed to "An act au- thorizing and requiring the Lewis county court to aid in building turnpike roads in said county."

§ 4. That in order to avoid the necessity of a separate act for each turnpike road, it is hereby enacted that the Lewis county court is authorized, empowered, and re- quired to assist all turnpike roads built in Lewis county to the extent of one thousand dollars to the mile, and this assistance shall be rendered by said court issuing the bonds of said county to the road intended to be assisted, and deliver said bonds to the president or board of directors of said road; said bonds shall draw interest at a rate not exceeding six per cent. per annum, and be due within twenty years from their date; said court shall issue said bonds at the request of the president of the road desiring said bonds, upon proof that the portion of road for which the bonds are asked has been put under contract, to a responsible contractor or contract- ors; that sufficient subscriptions have been raised (by the aid of $1,000 per mile) by responsible individuals, to build that part of said road for which the bonds of the county are asked; that said road, or that part of it under contract, as the case may be, will be speedily built, and be a substantial good turnpike when finished.

§ 5. That the fifth section of said act (approved January 17th, 1868) is hereby repealed.

§ 6. This act shall be in force from its passage.

Approved March 2, 1869.

CHAPTER 1661.

AN ACT to provide a Mechanics' Lien Law for the City of Louisville and County of Jefferson.

Be it enacted by the General Assembly of the Commonwealth of Kentucky:

§ 1. That all persons who shall perform labor, or furnish materials, fixtures, or machinery for constructing, finish-

ing, altering, adding to, or repairing any house, building,   1869.
mill, manufactory, or other structure, within the city of
Louisville or county of Jefferson, by or under any employment or contract, express or implied, shall and may have
a joint lien upon such house, building, mill, manufactory,
or other structure, and upon the interest of the employer
in the parcel of land on which such structure may be situated, and in the previous structure added to, altered, or
repaired, to secure the payment of their several demands,
which lien shall be prior and superior to all other liens or
encumbrances on any such house, building, mill, manufactory, or other structure, and the fixtures and machinery
so constructed, when the structure is wholly new; and
upon any machinery or fixtures, alterations, additions, or
repairs to a previous building, which are capable of being
severed or removed from such previous building without
material injury thereto, and shall be prior and superior to
all other liens or encumbrances upon the interest of the
employer in the lot or parcel of land built upon, and upon
any previous structure so altered, repaired, or added to, created after the commencement of constructing the house,
building, mill, manufactory, or other structure, or adding
to, altering, or repairing a previous structure: *Provided*,
That no lien shall so attach for any sum amounting to less
than ten dollars.

§ 2. That any person or persons, having a lien under
this act, may enforce the same by petition in equity in the
Louisville chancery court, or in any court of similar jurisdiction which may hereafter be established or exist in said
county and city: *Provided*, Such petition be filed within
one year from the completion of the work or furnishing
the materials. All the persons having a lien may join in
the petition, or one or more may file a petition against the
employer, and the other persons, or any of them, having
a lien. Any person having a lien, not a party to the case,
may, on his motion, be made a party defendant; and all
defendants having liens may set up their respective claims
by answer, without the necessity of making the same a
cross-petition. It shall be the duty of the owner or employer to make distinct answer to each claim set up in
petition or answer, without other service of process, except the summons on original petition. In all respects,
other than as herein provided, the case shall proceed and
be conducted according to equity law and practice, and the
rules of the court in which the same may be prosecuted.
No lien shall exist in favor of any person or persons, by
virtue of this act, who shall not have proceeded within
the time aforesaid to enforce the same; and the *lis pendens*
shall be construed to commence as to the several demands
from the time of filing the petition or answer asserting or

setting up the same; and any party in interest other than the employer, may, by motion of record previous to judgment, without answer, require any claimant, or all claimants, to prove their demands as if controverted by general denial; and the plaintiff, on service of summons, and each defendant, on filing his answer and claim, may proceed to take evidence to prove the same.

§ 3. That any journeyman, laborer, mechanic, artisan, lumber merchant, brick-maker, or other person performing labor or furnishing materials for any of the purposes described in the first section of this act, not under contract or employment of the owner, but as sub-contractor, may avail himself of this act by giving notice in writing to the owner or employer, before payment is made to the contractor or building mechanic, that he looks to the property for the payment of what may be due to him for such labor done or materials furnished; whereupon, he shall have and acquire a lien as valid, and to be enforced in the same way, as if he had contracted with or furnished to the owner or employer: *Provided*, That the lien or liens so acquired by sub-contractors shall not swell the aggregate payments or indebtedness of the owner or employer beyond what he would be bound for by contract, where the work has been done on contract, or in other cases beyond what he would be lawfully bound for upon the *quantum meruit*, after giving credit for payments made before notice by sub-contractors; and it is further provided, that the demands of sub-contractors shall be severally paid out of what may be due to the contractor or building mechanic under whom they claim, if so much be due to him, after giving credit to the employer as to each demand of sub-contractors for payments made to the contractor or building mechanic, prior to notice as above provided; and no sub-contractor shall be prejudiced on account of any payment made by the employer to the contractor or building mechanic, after notice as aforesaid by such sub-contractor; and if payments are made by the employer after notice by one or more sub-contractors, and prior to notice by another or others, such notice or notices so given, prior to such payments, shall have preference to the extent of such payments; and in such cases the sub-contractors shall be classified; and under these regulations the court shall distribute the fund amongst the parties according to their respective rights and equities.

§ 4. It shall and may be lawful for any such owner or employer, upon receiving notice from any sub-contractor as provided in the third section, to assume the amount justly due to such sub-contractor, and thereupon at once become entitled to credit therefor as a payment as between himself and the contractor: *Provided*, That this be not done to the prejudice of any sub-contractor who may have given previous notice of his claim and lien.

§ 5. Any sub-contractor may, before furnishing any materials or performing any labor as aforesaid, give notice to the owner or employer of his intention to furnish or perform the same, and the contract price or probable value thereof, and that he looks to the property for payment; and if, within the next day after receiving such notice, the owner or employer does not warn or notify such sub-contractor not to furnish such materials or perform such labor on the credit of the property, and the sub contractor goes on to furnish the materials or perform the labor, he shall have a lien, as in the first section provided, for the sum justly due to him, not exceeding that named in the notice, not to be scaled or lessened on account of any payments made by the owner or employer to the contractor or building mechanic, whether before or after such notice; and after doing work or furnishing materials, either without notice or under notice as aforesaid, the sub-contractor may give like notice, and do or furnish other work or materials with like effect and upon like conditions, as above herein provided.

§ 6. The liens herein provided shall be enforced by appropriate orders, judgments, or decrees, for the sale of the property on which the lien exists, according to equity usage; and if it shall appear that the employer did not own or had no right to bind the land for a sufficient estate to satisfy the liens, then the court may provide for the sale and removal of the house, building, mill, manufactory, or other structure, where it is wholly a new structure, or of the fixtures, machinery, alterations, additions, or repairs, upon which the lien exists, so far as the same may or can be removed without material injury to the former structure not owned by the employer, or to rent the same for the benefit of lien claimants, if it shall appear the rents will pay the lien claims in a reasonable time, in cases where the owner of the land or former structure consents to the renting, on election given.

§ 7. And if the land upon which any such structure is erected, or the land and structure upon which any such alterations and repairs are made, shall be owned by or held for any infant or cestui que trust, or as the separate estate of a married woman, without power of sale or encumbrance, and the court shall be of opinion that the contract or employment was not such as to bind the land, or any interest therein, sufficient to raise the amount necessary to satisfy the liens, then it may and shall be competent for the guardian of such infant, or the trustee or married woman. to exhibit his, her, or their petition, or, by answer to any petition pending under this act, to allege and prove to the satisfaction of the court that it would redound to the interest of the infant or *cestui que trust*, or married woman, to cause said property so built upon or improved to be either sold or leased or rented out, to pay the lien claims established, rather than remove the structure or improvements, or to ascertain the comparative value of the property independent of the improvements, and of the improvements, and to have the whole, or so much thereof as may be necessary, sold, and the lien claims paid, or the proceeds distributed between the married woman, infant, or *cestui que trust*, and the lien claimants, the court making proper orders for the safe-keeping, or the reinvestment of the portion going to such infant or *cestui que trust* or married woman.

§ 8. If the interest of the employer in the land on which the work or materials were done or furnished is that of a lessee for years, or other interest less than a fee simple, the court may either sell the house or other improvements, with the privilege to the purchaser or his assigns to enter and remove it; or may sell the interest of the employer during his term, with privilege of removal of the house or other improvement; or may sell the land, subject to the contingency affecting the title; or may order the property to be rented, whichever may seem best for the interest of all parties consistent with the liens and equities herein created.

§ 9. In case any lumber merchant, brick-maker, or other material man, shall have furnished or sold materials to any contractor or building mechanic, who shall be engaged in building more than one structure at the same time, and it shall be beyond the power of such material man to make it appear in proof how much of his materials went into any one structure, the court may permit his lien claim to be proved and established against any and all such structures, and the interest in the land, as herein provided: *Provided*, That no valid lien of any other mechanic or material man is lessened or impaired by any such allowance beyond the amount actually proved as to each structure: *And provided also*, That the rights by this section provided shall take effect only from the date of its being claimed by suit, and subject to prior conveyances and equities.

§ 10. Any notice provided for in this act may be served by the sheriff or any constable of said city or county, by delivering a true copy thereof, and whose return thereon shall be received in evidence without further proof, or the service of the notice may be proved by a disinterested witness, or as provided by existing laws as to notices generally.

§ 11. The act providing a general mechanics' lien law for certain cities and counties, approved February 17, 1858, so far as it is inconsistent with this act, and only as to the city of Louisville and county of Jefferson, be repealed; but, as to the matters provided for by amendment, approved June 3d, 1865, as to the said city and county, and in all respects as to the other cities and counties to which those acts extend, they shall continue in force.

Approved March 2, 1869.

CHAPTER 1662.
AN ACT to protect small Birds and Game in Lewis County.

Be it enacted by the General Assembly of the Commonwealth of Kentucky:

§ 1. That it shall be unlawful to pursue, hunt, kill, or in any manner injure any of the birds commonly known as the blue bird, swallow, martin, robin, wren, or any other bird whatsoever, smaller than the quail, including the quail and dove, in Lewis county, at any season of the year, or at any time or under any circumstances, without the consent of the owners of said lands.

§ 2. That it shall be unlawful, on the lands of another person or on another's premises, without his, her, or their permission, at any time to hunt, pursue, catch, kill, or in any manner destroy or injure, any quail, partridge, pheasant, wild goose, wood duck, teal, or other wild duck, woodcock, or to have in possession, or expose for sale, any of the game mentioned in this act, taken from the premises or lands of another. In like manner it shall be unlawful for any person to hunt, kill, or injure any deer on the land or premises of another, without the proprietor's consent; and any person violating any of the provisions of this act shall, upon conviction thereof before a justice of the peace, be liable to a fine of not less than one nor more than fifteen dollars and costs of suit.

§ 3. This act shall be in force from its passage.

Approved March 2, 1869.

CHAPTER 1663.
AN ACT to amend an act, entitled "An act to establish the Deposit Bank of Princeton, Kentucky."

Be it enacted by the General Assembly of the Commonwealth of Kentucky:

§ 1. That there is hereby established a savings and deposit bank in the town of Princeton, Kentucky, with a capital of fifty thousand dollars, in shares of one hun-

1869. dred dollars each, to be subscribed and paid for as hereinafter specified; and the subscribers, their associates,
successors, and assigns, shall be a body-politic and incorporate, by the name and style of the "Deposit Bank
of Princeton," and shall so continue for twenty-five
years from its organization; and shall have all the rights
and privileges of a natural person in contracting and
being contracted with, in suing and being sued, and of
impleading, answering, and defending, in all courts and
places whatever; said bank may have and use a common seal, and change the same at pleasure.

§ 2. Said bank shall be under the control and management of three directors, who shall be stockholders residing in this State; they shall hold their office until their
successors are elected and qualified; and after the first
election, shall be elected the first Monday in July in
each year, or as soon thereafter as practicably convenient; and in case of vacancy, the remaining directors
shall have power to appoint a successor; they may elect
one of their number president, who shall preside at their
meetings, and shall perform such other duties as may be
assigned by this charter or their by-laws; they shall have
power to sell any of the stock remaining unsold; to declare dividends of the profits arising out of the business
of the bank; to appoint such officers, agents, and employes, as they may deem necessary to conduct the business of the bank, and pay them for their services; to
take from the president, cashier, and other employes,
such bond as they may deem proper and reasonable, to
secure the faithful performance of their respective duties;
and to make such by-laws as they may deem necessary
for the proper management of the affairs of the bank:
Provided, The same be not contrary to the Constitution
and laws of this State and of the United States. The
stock shall be deemed personal property, and shall be
transferable only on the books of the bank by the stockholder or his attorney, under such rules and regulations
as the directors shall, from time to time, establish; but
the corporation shall have a lien on the stock to secure
any indebtedness to the bank by the stockholders.

§ 3. That T. L. McNary, R. B. Ratliff, and Hugh F.
McNary, are hereby appointed commissioners, any two
of whom, after giving notice to the others, may open
books in the town of Princeton, and receive subscriptions for the capital stock of said bank; and whenever
fifteen thousand dollars of said stock shall have been
subscribed for, it shall be their duty to give notice to
the stockholders, and appoint a day for the election of
a board of directors, who shall hold their office until
the ensuing annual election. The payments for the

shares shall be as follows, viz: Five dollars on each share at the time of subscribing, and ten dollars within thirty days after the election of the first board of directors, and the remainder in such amounts, and at such times, as the directors may require: *Provided*, That no one call shall be for a larger amount than ten dollars per share, and at shorter notice than thirty days; and furthermore, that nothing contained herein shall be construed so as to prevent any stockholder from making payments on his stock in advance of the calls made by the directors; said corporation may commence business so soon as one third the amount subscribed shall have been paid in as capital.

§ 4. Said bank may receive deposits of gold and silver, bank notes, and other notes which may be lawfully circulating as money, and repay the same in such manner, at such times, and with such rate of interest, as may be agreed upon with the depositors by special or general contract; may deal in the loaning of money; may buy and sell bills of exchange, promissory notes, uncurrent money, stocks, bonds, mortgages, and other evidences of debt; take personal and other securities for the payment of the same, and dispose of the latter, except real estate, as may be agreed upon between the parties in writing, and pass a valid title to the same; all promissory notes and inland bills of exchange, which may be discounted and owned by said bank, shall be, and are hereby, put upon the same footing of foreign bills of exchange, and like remedy may be had thereon, jointly and severally, against the drawers and indorsers.

§ 5. This act to take effect from its passage.

Approved March 2, 1869.

CHAPTER 1664.

AN ACT incorporating the Deposit Bank of Cynthiana.

Be it enacted by the General Assembly of the Commonwealth of Kentucky:

§ 1. That there is hereby created and established in Cynthiana, Kentucky, a deposit bank, which shall be a body-politic and corporate, by the name of the Deposit Bank of Cynthiana; and shall have power and authority in that name to contract and be contracted with, sue and be sued, plead and be impleaded, answer and defend, in all courts and places as a natural person; and may have and use a common seal, and alter and change the same at will.

1869.   § 2. The property, business, and affairs of said bank shall be under the management, government, and control of a board of seven directors, one of whom shall be elected president of the board, and T. J. Megibben, C. B. Cook, T. A. Frazier, Thos. V. Ashbrook, H. W. Shawhan, Ruddel Sharp, and I. T. Martin, are hereby constituted and appointed a board of directors for said bank, to serve as such until others are duly elected and qualified; and should any of the persons above named fail or refuse to qualify and serve as directors, his or their place or places may be declared and treated as vacant, and the vacancy may be filled by the remainder; and all vacancies accruing in the board of directors may be filled by the other directors, who shall provide for an election of directors by the stockholders, within one year from the organization of the company, and every year thereafter at the office of said bank, in the city of Cynthiana, notice of which shall be given in one or more papers published in Cynthiana; and said election shall be held by three stockholders appointed by the board of directors, who shall certify the result for record on the books of the bank; those having the highest number of votes shall be declared duly elected; each stockholder to have one vote for each share of stock he or she may own, and may cast the same in person or by proxy. The board may regulate the form of proxy in casting the vote.

§ 3. The capital stock of said bank shall be five hundred shares, of the par value of one hundred dollars each; but may be increased, from time to time, to one thousand shares, as the board of directors may deem advisable and proper; and whenever as many as two hundred and fifty shares of said stock shall have been subscribed and paid in, or secured to be paid in, in accordance with the terms and conditions upon which the same were subscribed, and an affidavit to that effect has been made by the president before the clerk of the Harrison county court, said bank may proceed to transact a general banking and financial business, and may loan money, discount promissory notes, buy and sell exchange, stocks, bonds, and other securities and things; and the promissory notes made payable at its banking house, which may be discounted by said bank, and inland bills of exchange, which may be discounted or purchased by it, shall be, and they are hereby, put upon the footing of foreign bills of exchange, and like remedy may be had thereon, jointly and severally, against the makers, drawers, indorsers, or other parties thereto.

§ 4. The said bank may acquire and hold, possess and use, occupy and enjoy, all such real and personal property, goods, chattels, or other things, as may be convenient for the transaction of its business, or which may be pledged or conveyed to it as security for any debts or purchase in satisfaction of any debts, judgments, or decree, and sell and convey or otherwise dispose of the same, except real estate, as a natural person; and it shall be the duty of the president or cashier of said bank, during the first week in each year, to pay into the Treasury of this Commonwealth fifty cents on each hundred dollars of capital stock held and paid for in said bank, which shall be in full of all tax or bonus, and be a part of the common school fund of this Commonwealth.

§ 5 The said bank shall have power to make advances on approved securities of any kind, and it may receive stocks, bonds, and other things, in pledge for the security of loaned or debts owing, and sell the same on the non-payment of the debts or demand at the stipulated time of payment, according to any agreement made between the parties in writing at the time of loan or renewal thereof, and pass a good title to the purchaser; and any power given for that purpose shall be irrevocable, until the debt or demand is paid or duly tendered. Said bank may receive deposits of gold, silver, bank notes, United States Treasury notes, or other currency, and pay the same in kind, or as may be agreed upon by special or general contract, and may allow interest on deposits, not to exceed the rates allowed by the laws of this Commonwealth. It may issue certificates of credit, payable throughout the United States and elsewhere, for the convenience of merchants and travelers, but shall not issue any notes or bills to circulate as money.

§ 6. The board of directors of said bank are hereby authorized and empowered to enact and put in force such rules, by-laws, and regulations, for the management, government, and control of its property, business, and affairs, as they may deem expedient, and alter, amend, and repeal the same at will; and shall specify therein the number of directors necessary to constitute a quorum for the transaction of business. They may appoint such officers, agents, and servants as they may deem necessary to conduct the business of the bank, and pay them such sums for their services, and take from them bonds in such penalties to secure the faithful performance of their duties, as they may think reasonable and proper; and upon any bonds thus taken, recovery may be had for breaches of the contract thereof. If any officer of the bank shall appropriate any funds of said bank to his own use, or shall willfully fail to make correct returns, or knowingly make false ones, on the books of said bank, with the intent to cheat or defraud the corporation or other person, such officer shall be deemed guilty of felony, and shall, upon conviction thereof,

1869.   be sentenced to confinement in the jail or penitentiary of this Commonwealth for a period of not less than two nor more than twenty years.

§ 7. The stock of said bank shall be deemed personal property, and shall only be assigned in accordance with such rules as the board of directors shall from time to time prescribe; and said bank shall hold a lien on the shares of any stockholder who may be indebted to it, and such shares shall not be assignable or transferred until the debt shall be paid or discharged.

§ 8. This act shall take effect from its passage and remain in force for twenty-one years from the first organization of the said institution, provided it is organized within three years from its passage.

§ 9. The General Assembly shall have the right to examine into the affairs of said corporation, by any committee they may appoint for that purpose.

Approved March 2, 1869.

CHAPTER 1665.

AN ACT to amend the Charter of the Louisville Turnpike Company.

Be it enacted by the General Assembly of the Commonwealth of Kentucky:

§ 1. That the Louisville turnpike company shall have the right, with the consent of a majority in stock of the stockholders in said road, to contract with, sell and convey, to the city of Louisville, all that portion of their road lying and being within the corporate [limits] of said city.

§ 2. That the said turnpike road company shall have the right to reduce their capital stock in proportion as the length of road sold bears to the whole length of said road.

§ 3. That the said Louisville turnpike company, with the consent of a majority in stock of the stockholders in said road, shall have the right to subscribe for stock in any connecting road, to an amount not exceeding ten thousand dollars; and to the extent of any such subscription she may add to her capital stock.

§ 4. This act to take effect from and after its passage.

Approved March 3, 1869.

CHAPTER 1666.

AN ACT to incorporate the Frankfort Lumber, Brick and Implement Manufacturing Company.

Be it enacted by the General Assembly of the Commonwealth of Kentucky:

§ 1. That Lewis E. Harvie, Philip Swigert, Hugh Rodman, R. C. Steele, W. J. Chinn, George W. Craddock, and John S. Harvie, and their associates, be, and are hereby, constituted and created a corporation, by the name of the Frankfort Lumber, Brick, and Implement Manufacturing Company. It shall be capable of contracting and being contracted with, suing and being sued, pleading and being impleaded, purchasing, holding, and selling property; and shall have all the rights, immunities, and powers that may be necessary and proper for the management and prosecuting of its business, which shall be the manufacturing and vending of lumber, farming implements and utensils of any and all sorts, fire-brick, tile, and retorts. It may purchase and hold real estate to any amount not exceeding one hundred thousand dollars, or may lease the same; and may at any time sell any real estate so purchased, and convey title to the same.

§ 2. The capital stock shall not exceed two hundred and fifty thousand dollars, divided into shares of one hundred dollars each. The board of managers may, at their discretion, receive subscriptions of stock up to the limit above fixed. The subscriptions of stock shall be payable in such calls as the board of managers may, from time to time, make upon the shareholders, and the payment thereof may be enforced by suit in the name of the company. The corporation may forfeit and sell delinquent shares; declare and pay dividends in such manner as the by-laws may direct.

§ 3. The affairs of the company shall be conducted, after its regular organization as hereinafter provided, by a board of five managers, one of whom shall be chosen president, and all of whom shall be stockholders. They shall conduct and manage all business, and may exercise all or any of the corporate powers of the company, except those herein granted expressly to the stockholders, in accordance with any resolutions or by-laws prescribed by the stockholders: *Provided*, Such resolutions or by-laws do not conflict with the laws of this State or the United States. They shall have power to fill all vacancies that may arise in their own body until the next annual election of managers; and they, or any of them, may be removed at the pleasure of a majority in interest of the stockholders.

§ 4. The individuals above named shall constitute the first board of managers; they shall call together the shareholders at some convenient day after this act takes

effect, for the purpose of organizing the company and
electing a board of managers, to hold until the next
annual election. The president and managers, after
those herein named, shall hold their offices for one
year, or until their successors are elected and qualified.

§ 5. There shall be an annual meeting of the stockholders on the first Tuesday in May, or such other day as the
stockholders may appoint by by-law, for the election of
the board of managers, and the transaction of any other
business of the corporation which may come before them;
and at every such meeting, the board of managers shall
lay before them a full statement of the business, condition, and accounts of the corporation. Stockholders'
meetings may be called at other times by the board of
managers, or by the majority in interest of the stockholders, of which at least one week's notice shall be
given in a Frankfort newspaper. Each stockholder shall
have one vote for every share of stock owned by him,
and may vote in person or by proxy, in writing.

§ 6. The president and managers may appoint a superintendent or superintendents, and such other agents as
may be necessary and proper to manage the affairs of
the corporation, and may prescribe their duties respectively, and may allow them such salaries as may be
deemed just; and may take from any of them bond for
the faithful performance of their duties.

§ 7. The shares of said corporation shall be personal
estate, and shall be transferable on the books of the
company, according to its by-laws; but the corporation
may hold a lien on the shares of any stockholder who
may be indebted to it, and such shares shall not be transferred without the consent of the president and managers,
until such debt shall be paid or discharged.

§ 8. That said corporation shall have power to build or
construct any wagon road or railroad from any of its lands,
mines or quarries, to the Kentucky river, and from said
river to its place of manufacture; and shall have power
to appropriate the necessary lands for the right of way
therefor, upon paying the owner or owners of such lands
a just compensation for the same; and if the price therefor cannot be agreed upon and determined by and between the parties, then the company may apply to the
county court of the county in which the same is situated
for the appointment of proper viewers, &c.; and the court
shall be governed by the general laws now in force in this
State in assessing damages under writs of *ad quod damnum* ·
for lands taken for turnpikes.

§ 9. Said company may borrow money, from time to
time, and pledge the property, or any part thereof, of the
company, if necessary, to secure the payment of the

same, and may sell or issue their notes or bonds as evidence of such debt; but shall not borrow or sell their bonds or notes to an amount exceeding the true valuation of their stock subscribed, or a fair estimated worth of their lands, buildings, and other property. It shall have a common seal, which they may alter and change at pleasure, if the president and managers deem it proper to purchase such seal; but if they do not, then all writings made in the name of the corporation, and approved by the managers, and signed by the president, with his name as president, shall be binding on the corporation as much as if done under the seal of the corporation. The stockholders, after they have paid the full amount of stock subscribed by them, shall not be liable for any debt or obligation or contract entered into by the corporation.

§ 10. The stockholders may dissolve the corporation whenever experience proves that it cannot carry on a profitable business; and upon such dissolution, the corporate powers of the president and managers shall continue for five years thereafter; and the power to sue and be sued, in the name of the corporation, shall continue for the same length of time, with a view to wind up and close the business and affairs of the company, and to sell their property, and collect the proceeds and pay their debts, and divide the residue among the shareholders, if any.

§ 11. This act shall take effect from its passage.

Approved March 3, 1869.

CHAPTER 1667.

AN ACT to incorporate the Winchester Fuel Company.

Be it enacted by the General Assembly of the Commonwealth of Kentucky:

§ 1. That there is hereby created a body-politic and corporate, by the name of the "Winchester Fuel Company," with perpetual succession, and full power to contract and be contracted with, to sue and be sued, and to have and possess all the powers necessary and proper to the carrying out of the purposes for which said corporation is created; and may have and use a common seal.

§ 2. That said corporation is created for the purpose of furnishing and supplying the stockholders and other citizens of Clarke county with wood, coal, and other fuel; and to that end said company is hereby authorized to buy, sell, and deal in wood, coal, and other fuel, and may acquire by purchase any real and personal property necessary in the prosecution of said business. The capital stock of the said company shall not exceed seventy-five thousand dollars,

1869. which shall be divided into shares of twenty-five dollars each.

§ 3. That John Catherwood, B. F. Buckner, Wm. W. Beckour, W. E. Reese, T. F. Phillips, and R. H. C. Bush, or such of them as shall act, are hereby appointed commissioners to effect an organization of said company. They shall have power to open books and receive subscriptions of stock, and may, in their discretion, require an installment of not more than ten dollars on each share, to be paid at the time of subscription, and shall have power to receive and receipt for the same in the name of the company. When, in the opinion of the commissioners herein named, or such of them as shall act under the authority of this act, a sufficiency of stock shall be subscribed to justify it, they shall proceed to call a meeting of the stockholders, who shall elect five directors, who shall hold their offices for one year and until their successors are duly elected. The board of directors shall choose one of their number president, another secretary and treasurer, who shall execute to the board covenants, with good security, bound therein for the faithful performance of the duties of their respective offices. None but stockholders shall be eligible to the office of director. The board of directors shall have power to fill any vacancies in the board of directors resulting from death, resignation, sale of stock, or removal from the county. The company may, in the course of business, buy and sell any personal or real property which may be deemed advisable by the board of directors: *Provided, however,* That the company shall not at any one time own more than fifteen thousand dollars' worth of real estate. The stock of the company shall be personal estate and descend as such, and shall be transferable alone on the books of the company. At all elections held under the authority of this act, each stockholder shall be entitled to one vote for each share of stock owned by him, and the stockholders may vote at elections in person or by proxy.

§ 4. The board of directors shall have power to adopt by-laws for the management of the company, provided the same shall not contain any provision repugnant to the Constitution and laws of the United States or of this State. They shall keep a record of their proceedings, and shall have power to execute all such deeds, mortgages, and other conveyances, as may be necessary in the prosecution of the business of the company. All such deeds, mortgages, and other conveyances, shall be executed by the president and secretary, under the seal of the corporation, and shall recite the order of the board authorizing their execution.

§ 5. The Legislature reserves the right to alter, amend, or repeal this charter.

§ 6. This act shall take effect from its passage.

Approved March 3, 1869.

CHAPTER 1668.

AN ACT to amend the Charter of the Owensboro Gas-light Company.

Be it enacted by the General Assembly of the Commonwealth of Kentucky:

§ 1. That the city council of the city of Owensboro may select the mayor of said city, or some member of the city council, who, so long as he shall continue in office, or until his power is revoked by the council, represent the said city in all meetings of the directors of the Owensboro Gas-light Company, and cast all votes that said city of Owensboro may be entitled to cast at all meetings of its directors and in all affairs of said company.

§ 2. This act shall be in force from its passage.

Approved March 3, 1869.

CHAPTER 1669.

AN ACT to incorporate the Kentucky Cheese Company.

Be it enacted by the General Assembly of the Commonwealth of Kentucky:

§ 1. That there shall be, and hereby is, established in the county of Clark, a corporation by the name of the Kentucky Cheese Company, with a capital stock of fifteen thousand dollars, to be divided into shares of one hundred dollars each, and subscribed and paid for by individuals, companies, or corporations, in the manner hereinafter prescribed; and said corporation, by the name and style aforesaid, shall have power and authority to sue and be sued, to contract and be contracted with, to plead and be impleaded, answer and defend, in all courts and places, and in all matters whatsoever, as natural persons may do, with full power to acquire, hold, use, enjoy, and lease, and the same to sell, convey, dispose of, and release, all such real estate, chattels, goods and effects, as may be necessary or convenient for the transaction of its business, or which may be acquired as security for or in payment of a debt or demand; and may have and use a common seal, and alter, change, or renew the same at pleasure; and may make and establish all necessary rules, regulations, and by-laws for the efficient management of its affairs and conduct of its business, not inconsistent with the provisions of this act or the laws of this Commonwealth.

§ 2. The business of said corporation shall be the manufacturing of cheese and butter, in any and all the departments thereof, and to buy or sell, in or out of this State, such stock and materials as may be necessary to the successful carrying on of said business.

§ 3. That J. L. Wheeler, J. V. Grigsby, James H. Holloway, Silas Barkley, W. D. Sutherland, Leeland Hathaway, George Stapleton, and H. McCoy, be, and they are hereby, appointed commissioners, whose duty it shall be to open books for subscription of stock in said corporation, and at such times and at such places in Clark county as they or any three of them may deem expedient; and when not less than two thousand dollars of said stock are subscribed for, then said commissioners, or any three of them, may, by publication of not less than five days in any newspaper of said county, call a meeting of the stockholders for the election of five directors, who, when elected, shall complete the organization of the corporation by electing one of its number president, and also by creating such offices and electing such persons to fill the same as they may deem necessary for the efficient carrying on of the said business. After such organization, the president and board of directors shall have control of the business and affairs of the corporation, and may keep the books open for the further subscription to stock until the whole amount is subscribed for.

§ 4. That, after the first election, the stockholders shall annually, on the second Monday of March, in each year, elect the same number of five directors, who shall hold their offices for one year, or until their successors are duly elected and qualified; and each board, when elected, shall appoint one of its number president, and choose such other officers as may be provided for by its own regulations or by-laws.

§ 5 At all stockholders' meetings, each stockholder shall cast one vote for each share of stock held by him; and votes may be cast by proxy, upon written authority from the stockholder, signed by him.

§ 6. The stock in the corporation shall be deemed personal property, and shall be assignable according to such rules as the board of directors shall, from time to time, establish; but said corporation shall have a lien on the stock to secure any indebtedness by the stockholder.

§ 7. The board of directors shall have power to fill any vacancies that may occur between the times of holding the regular elections.

§ 8. The stockholders, after they have paid up their stock subscriptions, shall not be individually liable for any debt, obligation, contract, or other liability contracted by, entered into, or incurred in any way by said corporation.

§ 9. This act shall take effect from its passage.

Approved March 3, 1869.

1869.

CHAPTER 1671.

AN ACT to amend the Charter of the City of Covington.

Be it enacted by the General Assembly of the Commonwealth of Kentucky:

§ 1. That the boundary of the city of Covington shall include all the territory embraced within the limits of said city by the provisions of an act, entitled "An act to amend and reduce into one the several acts concerning the city of Covington," approved March 2, 1850, and another act, entitled "An act to amend the charter of the city of Covington," approved March 1st, 1860, and all the real estate within said boundary shall be subject to taxation for municipal purposes.

§ 2. That this act shall take effect from and after its passage.

Approved March 3, 1869.

CHAPTER 1672.

AN ACT to amend the Town Charter of the Town of Morganfield.

Be it enacted by the General Assembly of the Commonwealth of Kentucky:

§ 1. That the trustees of the town of Morganfield be, and they are hereby, authorized and empowered to grant coffee-house licenses within the limits of said town.

§ 2. Before granting such license, the trustees shall require of the applicant satisfactory proof of his good moral character, and require him to take an oath and execute a bond to the Commonwealth, with approved sureties, in the penalty of five hundred dollars, to the effect that he will keep an orderly house; will vend good, wholesome liquors; that he will not sell liquor to a minor without the written consent of his parent or guardian, nor to persons in anywise intoxicated; that he will not suffer or permit any gambling in his house; and that he will in all things conform to the laws governing coffee-houses and taverns in this State, so far as the same are applicable.

1869.

§ 3. That any clerk, salesman, or assistant, such coffee-house keeper may have in his employ, shall take the oath aforesaid.

§ 4. Before obtaining such license, the applicant shall, in addition to the State tax, pay such town tax to the treasurer of the board of trustees of said town as the trustees may impose upon coffee-houses.

§ 5. For any breach of the bond herein required to be executed, the same proceedings shall be had, and the same penalties imposed, as are by law had and imposed for breaches of the bonds of tavern-keepers: *Provided, however,* the penalty of no one act or omission shall exceed five hundred dollars.

§ 6. The trustees of said town shall have the same power and duties in regard to suspending and suppressing the license of coffee-houses granted by them as judges of the county courts now have with regard to tavern licenses; and the proceedings for such suspension or suppression shall be the same as in like cases of tavern licenses.

§ 7. This act to take effect from and after its passage.

Approved March 3, 1869.

CHAPTER 1673.

AN ACT to incorporate the Kentucky and Ohio Bridge Company.

Be it enacted by the General Assembly of the Commonwealth of Kentucky:

§ 1. That David Sinton, S. S. L'Hommedieu, Wm. A. Dudley, Geo. H. Pendleton, H. C. Lord, Q. M. St. John, Lewis Worthington, Jay Gould, John King, jr., Wm. Ernst, and Washington McLean, and their associates, be, and they are hereby, created a body corporate and politic, under the name of the Kentucky and Ohio Bridge Company; and under that name they, their associates and successors, shall have perpetual succession, with power to contract, sue, plead, and answer, in all courts of justice; and to make and use a common seal.

Corporators' names, and corporate powers.

§ 2. The said corporation is hereby authorized to erect a bridge over and across the Ohio river, from the city of Covington, Kentucky, to the city of Cincinnati, Ohio, at any point between the eastern line of Washington street, extended, in the city of Covington, and the western boundary of the city of Covington, and to renew and rebuild said bridge when necessary or proper, and to keep the same in repair.

Where may erect bridge.

§ 3. The said corporation is hereby authorized to purchase and hold so much real estate as shall be necessary for the site of said bridge, or of the piers, abutments, and

May purchase and hold real estate, &c.

toll-houses pertaining thereto, and for suitable avenues leading to the same; and if it cannot obtain the title to such real estate in Kenton county, Kentucky, by contract with the owner, it is hereby authorized to apply to and to have from the county court of Kenton county, Kentucky, the writ of *ad quod damnum,* for the purpose of having such real estate condemned to its use for the purposes aforesaid; and the proceedings under said writ shall conform to like proceedings as prescribed in chapter one hundred and three of the Revised Statutes of Kentucky, except that the jury shall find the value of such real estate in gold, and the same shall be paid for by said company before it takes possession thereof, in gold coin.

§ 4. The said corporation may lay down railway tracks upon its said bridge, of such breadth of gauge as it may deem expedient and proper, and may permit locomotives and railroad cars, singly or in trains, to pass over said bridge; and may also permit street railway cars to pass over its bridge, and also vehicles, passengers, and stock of all descriptions; and it is at liberty to construct a bridge for a part or all of the purposes aforesaid.

May lay railway track on bridge.

§ 5. But the said bridge shall not be of less than ninety (90) feet in the clear above the low water-mark of said river; and if constructed upon piers, the span over the main channel of said river shall not be of less than three hundred and fifty feet in width in the clear, or such width as Congress has or may prescribe.

Construction of bridge.

§ 6. The capital stock of said corporation shall be one million dollars, to be increased to five million dollars by vote of the stockholders, and divided into ten thousand shares, of one hundred dollars each, to be subscribed and paid in the manner hereinafter indicated, for which the subscribers shall receive certificates, when the same is fully paid; and the said stock shall be transferable in the manner to be prescribed by the by-laws of said corporation.

Capital stock.

§ 7. For the purpose of organizing said corporation, the persons named in the first section of this act, or a majority of them, shall, within sixty days after the passage of this act, hold a meeting at some place in the city of Cincinnati or Covington aforesaid, and shall elect a chairman and secretary; at which a committee or committees shall be appointed, who shall advertise the time and place of opening books of subscription to the stock of said company, which books shall be kept open by said committee for the purpose of receiving subscriptions to the said capital stock, not less than fifteen days nor more than twelve months; the time to be fixed by a vote at said meeting may be extended by it at any adjourned or called meeting,

Organization of company. books to be opened for subscription of stock, &c.

1869. held at any time before the full amount of said stock has been subscribed. If, at the time of closing said subscription, it shall be found that more than the whole amount of the said capital stock has been subscribed, the same shall be reduced to the proper amount by rejecting the shares in excess.

§ 8. Whenever the said stock shall have been subscribed, the said committee shall give at least fifteen days' notice of the time and place of a meeting of said subscribers, which notice shall be published in one or more newspapers of general circulation in the city of Cincinnati and vicinity, and shall specify that the object of said meeting is the organization of said corporation by the election of a president and board of directors.

Meeting of stockholders to organize.

§ 9. At said meeting, and at all subsequent meetings of the stockholders of said corporation, each share of stock shall entitle the holder to one vote up to the number of fifteen shares, and to one vote for every five shares exceeding fifteen up to fifty shares, and to one vote for every ten shares exceeding fifty; and the shares in said company may be voted by proxies authorized by writing, to be satisfactorily proved at the time of voting.

How stock voted.

§ 10. At the meeting of said subscribers mentioned in section eight, and at every annual meeting of the stockholders thereafter held, there shall be elected a president and nine directors of said company, who shall be stockholders therein, and who shall hold their offices until their successors are elected and accept their election; and if any officer to be elected by said stockholders shall decline to act, resign, or die pending the time for which he was elected, the board of directors shall elect another to supply his place.

President and directors to be elected.

§ 11. The annual meetings of said stockholders shall be held in the city of Covington, on the first Wednesday of March in each year, of the time and place of which meetings the secretary of the board shall give at least fifteen days' notice in one or more papers published in Cincinnati and Covington; and at such annual meetings, a statement of the affairs of said company, made out by the president and directors, shall be presented to the stockholders; and such dividends of the profits shall be declared and paid as shall be deemed advisable by the directors. The stockholders shall, at their annual meetings, fix the salaries to be paid to the president and board of directors.

Annual meetings.

§ 12. The board of directors shall make such by-laws and regulations as shall be necessary for the government of the corporation, not in conflict with this charter or the laws of the land.

May make by-laws, &c.

§ 13. They shall elect a secretary and treasurer, and such other officers and agents as shall be necessary for

Secretary and treasurer to be appointed.

the management of the affairs of said corporation, and **1869.**
may require from any of said officers bond and surety
for the faithful discharge of their duties, and shall allow
and pay such agents and officers such sums as they may
agree upon.

§ 14. The board of directors shall have the general *Who to man-*
management, control, and supervision of the business of *age affairs of company.*
said company in erecting said bridge, and in the man-
agement of it and the affairs of said company after it is
erected; they shall hold meetings at stated intervals, and
shall preserve a fair record of all their proceedings at
such meetings.

§ 15. The president and four directors shall constitute a *Quorum.*
quorum for the transaction of business; and in the absence
of the president, five directors shall constitute a quorum,
who shall elect one of their number president *pro tem.*

§ 16. The president and directors may make such assess- *Calls on stock.*
ments on the shares of stock subscribed in said company,
payable at such times as they may deem advisable, with
such conditions of forfeiture for non-payment, not exceeding the amount of stock delinquent, as may be deemed
proper; and where any share of stock shall be forfeited to
the company, the directors shall resell the same : *Provided,*
No share shall be sold for less than its nominal or par
value.

§ 17. The board of directors shall fix the rates of toll *Rates of toll.*
for passing over said bridge, and provide for its collection
from all and every person or corporation passing over the
same with their cars, carriages, animals, and stock of
every description; and may make any contract or arrangement with any railroad company for the passage of their
cars and trains over said bridge, which they may deem
proper and just to said corporation: *Provided,* That said
bridge company shall not discriminate in its tolls, or in
the facilities granted by it to any corporation or individual as against any other corporation or individual ; but
shall permit the use of its bridge upon the same terms
and conditions by all; and the General Assembly hereby
reserves the right to regulate the tolls on said bridge.

§ 18. That copies of all papers and records belonging to *Copies of pa-*
the office of said company, certified by its secretary, shall *pers evidence.*
be *prima facie* evidence in all courts of the existence and
contents of the original, and shall be received where the
originals would be competent.

§ 19. The said corporation may borrow money not ex- *May borrow*
ceeding the amount of its capital stock, and at any rate of *money.*
interest not exceeding ten per cent. per annum, which the
board of directors may agree upon, and may secure the
same by mortgage upon the property and franchises of the
company.

1869.   § 20. That this act shall take effect from and after its passage.

Approved March 3, 1869.

CHAPTER 1674.

AN ACT to incorporate the Shepherdsville, Bardstown Junction, and Pitt's Point Turnpike Road Company.

Be it enacted by the General Assembly of the Commonwealth of Kentucky:

Company formed, name and style, &c.

§ 1. That a company shall be, and the same is hereby, incorporated, for the purpose of building a turnpike road from Shepherdsville to Pitt's Point, by way of Bardstown Junction, upon the nearest and most practicable route between said points named above, under the name and style of the "Shepherdsville, Bardstown Junction, and Pitt's Point turnpike company;" and by that name and style may sue and be sued, contract and be contracted with, plead and be impleaded; and use and have a common seal, and alter or amend the same at pleasure.

Capital stock.

§ 2. The capital stock of said company shall be sixteen thousand dollars, to be increased or diminished at the pleasure of the company, and to be divided into shares of one hundred dollars each.

Commissioners to open books.

§ 3. Books of subscription of stock shall be opened by Robert Greenwell, William Dawson, Leander Lee, J. P. McAfee, A. H. Bowman, J. F. Smith, and Henry Trunnell, who are hereby appointed commissioners for that purpose, at such time and place as they may deem proper. They shall insert in said subscription book an

Obligation of subscribers.

obligation as follows, viz: We, whose names are hereunto subscribed, severally promise to pay to the president and directors of the Shepherdsville, Bardstown Junction, and Pitt's Point turnpike road company, the sum of one hundred dollars for every share of stock set oposite our names, in such manner and at such times as shall be by them required under the law incorporating said company, to be collected as other debts: *Provided, however,* That the sum of said stock, or any part thereof, may be paid in work on said road, subject to such regulations as the board of directors may deem proper.

When president and directors to be elected.

§ 4. When the sum of seven thousand dollars shall have been subscribed to the capital stock, it shall be the duty of the commissioners named to give notice, in such manner and at such time as they may think proper, of a meeting of the stockholders, at such time and place as the notice may designate, for the purpose of electing a

president and five directors; one vote shall be allowed
for each share of stock; and the president and directors
shall continue in office for one year, and until their successors are qualified; the time and place of election after
the first shall be fixed by the president and directors; a
majority of the board shall be competent to do business.

§5. That no person shall be eligible as president or
director who is not the owner, in his own name, of one
or more shares of stock in said road.

§ 6. Said corporation shall fix and regulate the grade of
said road, and its covering with stone or gravel; may
designate the place of toll gates, fix the rates of toll, and
regulate and change the same; but such rates shall not
exceed those prescribed by general law. They shall have
power, after two miles and a half of the road is completed,
to erect a gate and collect tolls, and apply the same to the
completion of the road.

§ 7. It shall be lawful for the officers and employes of
the company, with their tools and appliances, to enter
upon the lands over and contiguous to which the intended
road shall pass, having first given notice to the owners or
occupants thereof. They shall have the right to take and
receive the right of way over and through the lands where
said road shall be located. If, in any instance, they cannot procure the right of way, and cannot agree with the
owner or owners of lands through which said road is to
pass, as to the damages which said owner will sustain by
reason thereof, then the president shall apply to the county
court of the county wherein the land is located for a writ
of *ad quod damnum* to assess the damages which may be
sustained; and, upon the payment or the tender of the
damages assessed, it shall be lawful for the company to
open and make said road, and do all the work pertaining
thereto.

§ 8. The president and directors shall give notice, as
they may deem proper, of the amount of call on each
share of stock, and the time and place of its payment.

§ 9. The president and directors may appoint annually
such officers as they deem necessary, with such compensation as they may deem just, among whom the treasurer
shall give bond and security, in such sum as they deem
discreet, conditioned to pay over all sums in his hands to
the order of the board.

§ 10. When the stockholder shall have made full payment of his stock, it shall be the duty of the president,
over his signature, to issue certificates of stock to all persons entitled to the same, attested by the secretary of said
company.

§ 11. The provisions of the most favored charter shall
apply to this charter in the same manner and to the same
extent as if embraced herein.

1869.

Eligibility of
president and
directors.

Grade of road,
gates, rate of
toll, &c.

May enter
upon lands.

May receive
right of way.

Writ of ad
quod damnum.

Calls on stock.

May appoint
officers.

Certificates of
stock.

Other provi-
sions to apply.

§ 12. That the president and directors may put any part or parts of said road under contract, whenever eight thousand dollars of the capital stock shall be taken, and the remainder whenever they shall think a sufficient amount of stock is taken to complete said road.

When may put a part under contract.

§ 13. It shall be the duty of the president and directors to keep a record of their proceedings in a well-bound book, and the same shall be open to inspection by the stockholders in said road at all times.

To keep a record.

§ 14. This act shall take effect from its passage.

Approved March 3, 1869.

———

CHAPTER 1675.

AN ACT to amend the Charter of the City of Paducah.

Be it enacted by the General Assembly of the Commonwealth of Kentucky:

§ 1. That an act, entitled "An act to incorporate the city of Paducah," approved March 10, 1856, be amended as follows: If, after election, any member of the city council ceases to be a *bona fide* freeholder within said city, his seat shall thereby be vacated, and the vacancy shall be filled as directed by charter.

§ 2. The mayor shall receive a salary of not less than five hundred nor more than two thousand dollars per annum, to be fixed by ordinance.

§ 3. The council shall, at such times as may be fixed by ordinance, elect one person as treasurer, and as many collectors of taxes as they may deem necessary, not exceeding one for each ward. All of the officers so chosen shall, before entering upon the duties of their office, take such oaths or affirmations, and enter into such bonds, with conditions and sureties, as may be prescribed by the charter or ordinances. And the council shall, by ordinance, fix their compensation and term of office, and prescribe their duties and the manner of discharging them.

§ 4. That all moneys authorized to be collected by statute from shows, concerts, lectures, theatres, or other exhibitions (except circuses), given within the city limits, at which an entrance fee is charged, shall be paid into the city treasury for the use and benefit of the city.

§ 5. That the said council may pass ordinances to procure the grading, paving, guttering, and curbing of sidewalks on any of the squares within the city limits. When the street has been graded and paved, or graded and otherwise improved, for more than one year, said work to be at the cost of the owner or owners of lots or parts of lots fronting on such sidewalks, and to be apportioned accord-

ing to the amount of work actually done in front of such
lots or parts of lots, and for such costs a lien is hereby
created against such lots or parts of lots: *Provided, however,* That no such ordinance shall be enforced until an
advertisement has been published at least ten days, in one
or more of the newspapers published in Paducah, describing the square or squares, or part of square or squares, in
which the sidewalks are situated which it is proposed to
pave, grade, gutter, and curb, and giving the name or
names, or the owner-or owners, when known, fronting the
proposed paving, grading, guttering, and curbing, and notifying the owner or owners that if the work is not done
within thirty days from the first publication of the advertisement, the ordinance will be enforced.

§ 6. The council shall have power, by ordinance, to have
such sidewalks as in their opinion require it, recurbed, re-
paved, reguttered, and repaired, at the cost of the owner
or owners of lots fronting on such sidewalks, and to be
apportioned according to the amount of work actually done
in front of such lots or parts of lots; and for such costs a
lien is hereby created against such lots or parts of lots.

§ 7. That all of section eleven (11) and section twelve
(12), article fourth (4th), except that part of section twelve
relating to interpreter of the city court, and so much
of sections four (4), sixteen (16), and twenty (20), article
fifth (5th), as relates to slaves, be, and the same is hereby,
repealed.

§ 8. That hereafter there shall be two school trustees
elected in each ward of the city of Paducah, at the same
time and in the same manner that members of the council
are now elected, and shall possess the same qualifications,
and hold their offices for the same length of time, as members of said city council; and the first election for said trustees
under this act shall be held on the first Monday in May,
1869; and the board of trustees then elected shall, within
three months after their election, divide themselves by lot
into two classes, first and second class; and the seats of
the members of the first class shall be vacated on the first
Monday in May, 1870, and the seats of the members of the
second class shall be vacated on the first Monday in May,
1871; and one trustee from each ward shall be elected annually thereafter.

§ 9. That the trustees thus elected shall be the trustees
of the common schools, male and female seminaries, of the
city of Paducah; and they shall have all the rights, privileges, and powers, that the trustees of said male and female seminaries now have, and shall be styled the trustees
of the public schools of the city of Paducah.

§ 10. That all acts and parts of acts in conflict herewith,
relative to the election of trustees for the public schools,

male and female seminaries, of the city of Paducah, be, and the same are hereby, repealed.

§ 11. That all acts or parts of acts, either in the **original** charter or amended charter of the city of Paducah, in conflict with the preceding amendments, be, and the same **are** hereby, repealed.

§ 12. This act to take effect from the date of its **passage.**

Approved March 3, 1869.

CHAPTER 1676.

AN ACT to incorporate a Board of Trustees of the Bishops' Fund of the Protestant Episcopal Church in the Diocese of Kentucky.

Be it enacted by the General Assembly of the Commonwealth of Kentucky:

§ 1. That the Rev. O. B. Thayer, the Rev. G. M. Everhart, R. A. Robinson, Thomas S. Kennedy, and Jas. Bridgeford, are hereby incorporated into a Board of Trustees for the Bishops' Fund of the Protestant Episcopal Church in the Diocese of Kentucky, and shall continue in office until their successors are elected and qualified.

§ 2. That the Diocesan Convention of the said Protestant Episcopal Church shall have power, in perpetuity, **to** elect, from time to time, members of the board of trustees; limit their term of office; provide for creating and for filling vacancies in said board; may hold them to a strict accountability, and may require of them, or either **of** them, bond and security, with penalties attached, for the faithful performance of their duties, and for the proper use of the funds and property intrusted to their control.

§ 3. The said board of trustees, and their successors in office, are hereby empowered to elect from their number such executive officers as may be deemed necessary, and to define the duties of the same; to adopt and amend by-laws and rules for their own guidance; to make and break at pleasure a corporate seal; to sue and be sued, contract and be contracted with; to receive, hold, loan, assign, buy, sell and convey, any estate, real or personal, moneys, stocks, bonds, mortgages, public or private securities, **or** other obligations or evidences of debt that may come into their possession, or be due to them, as trustees of said Bishops' Fund; and to exercise in their corporate capacity any other rights and privileges pertaining to this trust and necessary to the proper discharge thereof, not inconsistent with the laws of this Commonwealth and of the United States.

§ 4. The said board of trustees are hereby authorized and empowered to receive, recover, hold, invest, sell, con-

vey, assign, transfer, and reinvest all and any voluntary
donations, contributions, subscriptions, and bequests, of
any kind whatever, that may be given, subscribed, devised, or conveyed for the object or purpose of creating,
increasing, or endowing the said Bishops' Fund; the principal and interest of which shall be exclusively used and
applied to the maintenance and for the support of the
Bishop and the Assistant Bishop, if there be one, of the
said Protestant Episcopal Church in the Diocese of Kentucky, including the purchase, if deemed advisable, of
residences for either or both the said Bishop and Assistant Bishop. The Diocesan Convention of the said Protestant Episcopal Church shall fix and determine the
annual proportion which shall be paid for the support
of the Bishop and for the support of the Assistant Bishop,
by the board of trustees, out of the Bishops' Fund, or the
proceeds thereof, or out of the income of the same.

§ 5. No member or officer of the board of trustees shall
receive any compensation out of the Bishops' Fund, or the
product thereof, for his services; nor shall either or any of
the said trustees ever be interested, either directly or indirectly, whether as principal, surety, or agent, in any
loan or other transaction involving the use, benefit, or
appropriation of said fund, or any portion thereof; nor
shall the principal, at its current assessed value of said
fund, ever exceed at any time the sum of one hundred
thousand dollars, without the consent of the General
Assembly of this Commonwealth, authorizing the increase of the fund over and above the said limitation.

§ 6. All acts or parts of acts heretofore passed, inconsistent with the provisions of this act, are hereby repealed.

§ 7. This act shall take effect and be in force from and
after its passage.

Approved March 3, 1869.

CHAPTER 1677.

AN ACT to amend the Charter of the Little Flat Creek Turnpike Road Company.

*Be it enacted by the General Assembly of the Commonwealth
of Kentucky:*

§ 1. That the charter of the Little Flat Creek turnpike
road company be so amended so as to authorize said
company to extend and make said road from the town
of Bethel to the mouth of Bald Eagle creek, in Bath
county, or to some point near the mouth of said creek;
and in the making of said extension, said company shall

have all the powers and privileges, and be under the
same restrictions, as are provided for in the original
charter.

§ 2. This act shall take effect from and after its passage.

Approved March 3, 1869.

CHAPTER 1678.

AN ACT to incorporate the Lebanon and Calvary Turnpike Road Company.

*Be it enacted by the General Assembly of the Commonwealth
of Kentucky:*

§ 1. That a company shall be formed, under the name
and style of the Lebanon and Calvary Turnpike Road
Company, for the purpose of constructing an artificial
road from Calvary to intersect the turnpike road from
Lebanon to Bradfordsville, at some point near Lebanon.

§ 2. The capital stock of said company shall be eight
thousand dollars, to be divided into shares of fifty dollars
each; and if it shall be ascertained that the amount of
capital stock is not sufficient to accomplish the object of
this act, then the president and directors may enlarge it to
such amount as they may deem necessary, and open subscription therefor in such manner as they may think
proper.

§ 3. Books for the subscription of stock in said company
shall be opened the first Monday in March next, or as soon
thereafter as will be convenient, at Lebanon, Kentucky,
under the direction of L. A. Spalding, Ben. Luckett, Jas.
Calwell, J. D. Fogle, and Celestus Abell, or some two or
more of them, who may be appointed commissioners.
The said commissioners shall get a book or books, and
the subscribers to the stock in said company shall enter
into the following obligation, viz: We, whose names are
hereunto subscribed, promise to pay to the president and
directors of Lebanon and Calvary turnpike road company
the sum of fifty dollars for every share of stock so subscribed, agreeable to an act of the General Assembly
of Kentucky incorporating said company. Witness our
hands and seals this — day of ———, 18—.

§ 4. All the provisions of an act, entitled "An act to
incorporate the Texas, Maxville, and Riley's Station
turnpike road company," and an act, entitled "An act to
incorporate the Danville and Hustonville turnpike road
company," except so far as already provided for in this
act, or may come in collusion with the same, and so far as
the same are applicable to the objects and intent hereof,
be, and the same are hereby, incorporated and made part

of the charter hereby granted the president and directors of the Lebanon and Calvary turnpike road company, with all the rights, powers, privileges, and immunities therein contained, so far as applicable.

§ 5. That the width of said road shall be graded not less than sixteen feet, and covered with stone or gravel, as the company may elect, to a width of not less than ten feet on the side or middle, as the company may direct, with whatever degree of elevation or depression, either in width or length, the company may determine.

§ 6. That the number and place of locating gates be determined by the company; and although the road may not be over four miles, that the company have the right to charge toll as though the road was five miles in length.

§ 7. That the Marion county court, a majority of the justices being present, may subscribe five hundred dollars per mile in stock in said road; and the county court of said county is hereby authorized to levy a tax of —— dollars on the assessed value of the property in said county to pay said sum.

Approved March 3, 1869.

CHAPTER 1679.

AN ACT to amend the Charter of the Covington and Lexington Turnpike Road Company.

Be it enacted by the General Assembly of the Commonwealth of Kentucky:

§ 1. That the charter of the Covington and Lexington turnpike road company be so amended as to authorize the president and directors of said company to construct a side road sixteen feet wide alongside of their road for the first five miles, commencing at the town of Lewisburg.

§ 2. That the president and directors of said company be, and they are hereby, authorized to build a substantial fence upon the lower side of said road, at any point or points on said road between the town of Lewisburg and the first toll-gate.

§ 3. That the president and directors of said company shall have power and authority to straighten their said road, whenever they deem it expedient, at any point or points between Lewisburg and the first toll-gate; and for that purpose, shall have the same power and authority to condemn land and material as is now provided by law in such cases, and may sell and convey any part of the old road-bed vacated by any change of location provided for in this section.

§ 4. That the president and directors of said company be, and the same are hereby, authorized to use all or so much of the earnings of said road as may be necessary to make the improvements provided for by this act.

§ 5. This act to take effect from and after its passage.

Approved March 3, 1869.

CHAPTER 1680.

AN ACT, entitled "An act to charter the Mercer County Line and Cove Spring Turnpike Road Company."

Be it enacted by the General Assembly of the Commonwealth of Kentucky:

§ 1. That the charter for a turnpike road leading from Pleasant Hill to Boyle county line shall be extended through the northwest corner of Boyle county to a point on the Harrodsburg and Danville turnpike road, near Cove Spring.

§ 2. Said road to have all the rights and privileges, and to be in conjunction with the Pleasant Hill and Mercer County Line road.

§ 3. The following named persons to act as corporators: Joseph Faulkner, A. W. Eastland, Joseph McDowel, and J. B. Tilford.

§ 4. Said company or board shall have the right to collect tolls according to the length of its line.

§ 5. This act to take effect from and after its passage.

Approved March 3, 1869.

CHAPTER 1681.

AN ACT to amend the Charter of the Union and Richwood Turnpike Road Company.

Be it enacted by the General Assembly of the Commonwealth of Kentucky:

§ 1. That the charter of the Union and Richwood turnpike road company be, and the same is hereby, so amended as to authorize said company to erect, on the line of said road, a toll-gate before the completion of said road, at which gate the company may charge and collect the same rates of toll, in proportion to the length of road completed and traveled, as is now allowed by the charter and amendments thereto of the Covington and Lexington turnpike road company.

§ 2. This act to take effect from and after its passage.

Approved March 3, 1869.

CHAPTER 1682.

AN ACT for the benefit of George Wills, of Henry County.

WHEREAS, The general appropriation bill for work and labor done on Green, Barren, and Kentucky rivers, omitted to mention all the claims of George Wills, of Henry county, and to make an appropriation to him therefor; therefore,

Be it enacted by the General Assembly of the Commonwealth of Kentucky:

§ 1. That the Auditor of Public Accounts be, and he is hereby, directed to draw his warrant on the State Treasury for one hundred and fifty dollars, out of any moneys in the Treasury not otherwise appropriated, in favor of George Wills, for money advanced by order of Samuel Steele, former superintendent of the Kentucky river navigation, to Robert Williams, contractor, to repair dam at lock No. 3, on said river, in August, 1867.

§ 2. This act to take effect from its passage.

Approved March 3, 1869.

CHAPTER 1683.

AN ACT to provide certain Books for the County of Metcalfe.

Be it enacted by the General Assembly of the Commonwealth of Kentucky:

§ 1. That the Secretary of State be, and he is hereby, directed to furnish to the circuit court clerk of Metcalfe county, for the use of said county, Stanton's Revised Statutes, and the Supplement thereto by Myers; Myers' Code of Practice; Monroe and Harlan's Digest; Cofer's Digest; a complete set of the Reports of the Kentucky Court of Appeals up to Bush, and the public and private acts of the Legislature, for the years 1860 to 1866-7, inclusive, and forward the same by express or otherwise to said clerk.

§ 2. That if any of the foregoing books cannot be supplied by the State, it shall be the duty of said Secretary to purchase the same on the best possible terms, and certify the amount thereof to the Auditor, who shall draw his warrant therefor on the Treasurer.

§ 3. This act to take effect from its passage.

Approved March 3, 1869.

1869.   CHAPTER 1684.
AN ACT for the benefit of Breathitt and Morgan Counties.

Be it enacted by the General Assembly of the Commonwealth of Kentucky:

§ 1. That the Secretary of State is hereby empowered and directed to furnish the county courts, circuit courts, and magistrates of Breathitt and Morgan counties, with such books as by law they are entitled to, according to the provisions of chapter sixty-one of the Revised Statutes, and the several acts amending the same and supplementary thereto; and which books are missing from their offices, having been lost or destroyed. When a certified copy of an order of the county courts of said counties is filed in the office of said Secretary of State, specifying what books are missing from the offices in said counties, and if it is necessary to purchase said books, the Secretary of State shall purchase them, and report the same to the Auditor, who shall draw his warrant upon the Treasurer for the payment of the same, and the Treasurer shall pay for the same out of any money in the Treasury not otherwise appropriated.

§ 2. This act to take effect from its passage.

Approved March 3, 1869.

CHAPTER 1686.
AN ACT, entitled "An act for the benefit of E. D. Morgan."

WHEREAS, It appearing to the satisfaction of the General Assembly, that a claim against the Board of Internal Improvement of the State of Kentucky, for the sum of seven hundred and twelve dollars and thirty-eight cents, held and owned by E. D. Morgan as assignor of J. H. Dennis, as evidenced by the voucher held by said Morgan, was, by accident or unintentional omission, left out of an act, approved January 19, 1869, appropriating money to pay claims against the Kentucky river improvement; and for remedy whereof,

Be it enacted by the General Assembly of the Commonwealth of Kentucky:

§ 1. That the sum of seven hundred and twelve dollars and thirty-eight cents be, and is hereby, appropriated to E. D. Morgan, out of any money in the Treasury not otherwise appropriated, in full liquidation of said claim.

§ 2. This act shall take effect from its passage.

Approved March 3, 1869.

CHAPTER 1687.

AN ACT for the benefit of John French, late Sheriff of Powell County.

WHEREAS, John French, sheriff of Powell county for the year 1863, was unable to collect the revenue in a portion of the county, on account of the then disturbed condition of the country; and whereas, the court-house and all the public records of said county, including the sheriff's books and papers, and the said sheriff's delinquent list for said year, was destroyed by fire, and said sheriff has been compelled to pay the whole revenue of said county, with cost, interest, and damage, and without having the benefit of a delinquent list; now, therefore,

Be it enacted by the General Assembly of the Commonwealth of Kentucky:

§ 1. That the Auditor of Public Accounts is directed to draw his warrant on the Treasurer, in favor of said John French, for the sum of fifty-seven dollars and fifty-two cents damages, and eighty-seven dollars and eleven cents for delinquent list, to be paid out of any money not otherwise appropriated.

§ 2. This act to be in full force from its passage.

Approved March 3, 1869.

CHAPTER 1688.

AN ACT to amend an act to incorporate the Lexington, Chilesburg, and Winchester Turnpike Road Company.

Be it enacted by the General Assembly of the Commonwealth of Kentucky:

§ 1. That the company owning the turnpike road running from the city of Lexington to the town of Winchester, shall be hereafter known as "The Lexington and Winchester turnpike road company;" and under that name and style shall do all the acts which it is now authorized by law to do, and exercise all the powers granted it in the original charter and the subsequent amendments thereto.

§ 2. That said company shall have power, and is hereby authorized, to remove the toll-gate on said road nearest to the town of Winchester, to some point east of its present location, not nearer than three fourths of a mile to the court-house in said town, to be determined on by the board of directors, and to collect tolls thereat, as it is now authorized by law to do.

§ 3. This act shall be in force from and after its passage.

Approved March 3, 1869.

CHAPTER 1689.

AN ACT to repeal an act authorizing the Sardis Company to subscribe
stock in the Sardis and Mount Olivet Turnpike Road.

*Be it enacted by the General Assembly of the Commonwealth
of Kentucky:*

§ 1. That an act authorizing the directors of the Sardis
turnpike road company to subscribe stock to aid in constructing a road from Sardis, in Mason county, to Mount
Olivet, in Robertson county, approved February 21, 1868,
be, and the same is hereby, repealed.

§ 2. That any subscription of stock (not exceeding in
amount one thousand dollars) made by the directors of
the Sardis company to said road, under and in accordance with the above act, shall not be rendered invalid
by the passage of this act.

§ 3. This act shall take effect from and after its passage.

Approved March 3, 1869.

CHAPTER 1690.

AN ACT to change the time of holding the Quarterly Courts in Christian
County.

*Be it enacted by the General Assembly of the Commonwealth
of Kentucky:*

§ 1. That the times of holding the March and September term of the Christian quarterly courts, be so changed
that they shall be respectively commenced on the last
Mondays in February and August.

§ 2. This act shall take effect from its passage.

Approved March 3, 1869.

CHAPTER 1691.

AN ACT to Charter the Lexington and Carter County Mining Company.

*Be it enacted by the General Assembly of the Commonwealth
of Kentucky:*

§ 1. That Evan T. Warner, Dr. George S. Savage,
Thomas Henson, J. M. Hocker, A. Dodge, Wm. J. Lard,
Dr. J. W. Bright, and John C. Hansbro, their associates,
successors, and assigns, be, and are hereby constituted, a
body corporate and politic, by the name and style of the
"Lexington and Carter County Mining Company;" and
by that name and style shall have perpetual succession,
with power to contract and be contracted with, to own
property, both real and personal, and to sue and be sued,

in all courts and places; to have a common seal; to engage in mining for coal, iron, and other minerals, and in preparing them for market, and transporting and selling the same within or without the State; and in sawing of lumber; and to do other acts, and to have all other powers needful for the successful prosecution of their business, and for the execution of the powers herein granted.

§ 2. That said corporators may organize said company by the election of a president, and such other officers and managers as they may deem necessary, at such time and place as they may designate, by notice previously given; and when thus organized, the said company shall have power to make such by-laws, rules and regulations, as they may deem necessary, from time to time, for the government and prosecution of the business of said corporation, not inconsistent with the Constitution and laws of the United States and of this State.

§ 3. The capital stock of said company shall not exceed three hundred thousand dollars, to be divided into three thousand shares, of one hundred dollars for each share.

§ 4. The said company may buy, lease, or rent any suitable lands, mines, mining privileges, or products, rights of way, and other property and rights necessary for their business, and may dispose of the same, or any portion of the same, by sale or otherwise; they may receive real estate, leasehold, mining rights, and rights of way, in payment of such part of subscriptions as they may deem advisable: *Provided*, That nothing herein contained shall be so construed as to confer upon the said company any lottery privileges, or authority to dispose of any property, real, or personal, except by sale, mortgage, or hypothecation.

§ 5. Said company may erect and build on any of their lands such buildings, furnaces, engines, machinery and fixtures, as may be deemed convenient and proper for establishing and conducting the business of said corporation.

§ 6. That this act shall take effect from and after its passage; but such purchases and acts as have already been made and done by the company and in its corporate name, shall be held as valid and binding as if done or performed after the passage of this act; and the right to repeal, alter, or amend this charter is reserved to the General Assembly.

Approved March 3, 1869.

CHAPTER 1692.

AN ACT to Charter the Richmond and Boone's Gap Turnpike Road Company, in Madison County.

Be it enacted by the General Assembly of the Commonwealth of Kentucky:

§ 1. That a company is hereby created, under the name and style of the Richmond and Boone's Gap turnpike road company, for the purpose of making an artificial road from a point at or near Harris' scales, on the Richmond and Lancaster pike, or from a point on the Richmond and Big Hill pike at or near the scales of R. J. White; thence by Duncannon depot, on the Richmond Branch railroad, to Hart's Fork of Silver creek; thence on a line of survey for a railroad from Cincinnati to Charleston by way of Boone's Gap, as made by McKee and Memminger, some years ago, to Boone's Gap. The following persons are appointed commissioners to receive subscriptions of stock, viz: John A. Duncan, James Ballard, and Madison Todd.

§ 2. The capital stock of said company, and the shares into which such capital stock shall be divided, shall be regulated by the commissioners named above, and may be diminished or enlarged by the president and directors, from time to time, as the exigencies of the case may require.

§ 3. That the books for subscription of stock in said company shall be opened at such times and places, under the direction of the commissioners above named, as they may deem proper, due notice thereof having been given in any paper published in Richmond, Kentucky, and by written notices posted up in various public places in Madison county.

§ 4. That so soon as a sufficient amount of stock shall be subscribed to justify a commencement of said road, the commissioners of said company, or such of them as may act, shall, at such time and place as they may appoint, call a meeting of the stockholders and hold an election for president and four directors, who shall hold their offices for one year, and until their successors are elected and qualified. That upon the election and qualification of the president and directors of said company, they shall be a body-politic and corporate, by the name and style aforesaid; and by said name shall have perpetual succession, and all the privileges and franchises incident to a corporation.

§ 5. That all the provisions of an act, entitled "An act to incorporate the Danville and Hustonville turnpike road company," approved March 1, 1844, except so far as they may be local in their application or come in collision with the provisions of this act, be, and the same are hereby,

made part of this act, and shall have the same force and 1869.
effect as if enacted at length.

§ 6. This act to take effect from its passage.

Approved March 3, 1869.

CHAPTER 1693.

AN ACT to amend the several acts relating to the town of Greenville.

Be it enacted by the General Assembly of the Commonwealth of Kentucky:

§ 1. That the several acts in relation to the town of *May levy and collect taxes.* Greenville be so amended, that hereafter it shall be lawful for the trustees of said town to levy and collect an ad valorem tax of not exceeding one dollar upon each one hundred dollars' worth of taxable property of said town, and a capitation tax of not exceeding two dollars and fifty cents upon every male person residing in said town over twenty-one years of age.

§ 2. That the trustees of said town. upon the petition of a majority of the voters thereof, may direct the *May cause streets & alleys to be graded & paved.* streets and alleys to be graded and paved in any manner by the owners of the adjacent property; but this shall not be done unless all the streets and alleys of said town are improved in the manner directed by the owners of the adjacent property; and the trustees shall not have the power to order any improvement to be made in this manner, unless it be upon the petition of a majority of the property-owners, as well as a majority of the voters thereof. If the streets and alleys should be improved, as contemplated by this section, then a capitation tax of not more than five dollars may be collected of the male residents of said town, not the owners of real property, over twenty-one years of age, for the purpose of grading and paving the crossings of the streets and alleys of said town.

§ 3. An assessment of the property of the citizens and *Annual assessment.* residents of said town shall be made annually by an assessor, to be appointed by the trustees of said town, in the same manner and under the same restrictions as required of assessors for the county.

§ 4. The town marshal for said town shall collect the *Who to collect taxes.* taxes due said town in the same manner, and have the same powers to distrain, that the sheriffs have for county and State taxes; and the same penalties shall attach to him and his acts for an illegal distress or distraint, as would to the sheriff of the county in making an illegal distress or distraint.

1869.

Jurisdiction of police judge.

§ 5. That the police judge of said town shall have exclusive jurisdiction over the county judge and justices of said county for the trial of all penal offenses occurring within the corporate limits of said town, over which he now has jurisdiction; and all fines and forfeitures for offenses committed in said town, when collected, shall be paid to the treasurer of said board of trustees of said town, to be by them used in the improvement of the streets of said town.

Town attorney may be employed.

§ 6. The trustees of said town may employ an attorney for said town, whose duty it shall be to prosecute all infractions of the penal laws of this State and the by-laws of said town; and said attorney shall receive as part compensation for his services thirty per cent. of all fines and forfeitures wherein he appears and prosecutes for the Commonwealth or town.

May collect tavern license.

§ 7. That the trustees of said town shall have the power to collect from each tavern-keeper of said town, who vends spirituous liquors in connection with his or their tavern, a tax not exceeding fifty dollars, before such person shall be licensed as a tavern-keeper by the county court of Muhlenburg county, which tax shall be equal and uniform; and the rate to be charged shall be fixed at the meeting of said board in the month of June, and shall not be increased for twelve months from that meeting.

May license coffee-houses.

§ 8. That the trustees of said town shall have the power to license coffee-houses in said town where spirituous liquors may be sold, and shall have the power to collect from any person or persons to whom they have granted such privileges, an annual tax not exceeding two hundred and fifty dollars, which may be paid by such person or persons annually, semi-annually, or quarterly, as may be prescribed by the trustees of said town; but the tax shall always be paid in advance. The trustees shall have power to prescribe rules for the government of such saloons or coffee-houses, and may, at any time, for a violation of the rules, suspend such person from the right to sell or vend spirituous liquors.

May license ale and beer saloons.

§ 9. That the trustees of said town shall have the right to license ale and beer saloons in said town, and may collect a tax not exceeding one hundred dollars from such saloon-keeper; and shall have the same powers and privileges conferred upon them as is conferred by the ninth section of this act.

Printed copy of rules to be stuck up.

§ 10. The owners of saloons, wherein spirituous liquors, ale, beer, porter, or wine is permitted to be sold, shall, at all times, keep a printed copy of the rules prescribed by the trustees for the government of saloons, posted in some conspicuous place in the room where such sale is made.

§ 11. Any tavern-keeper, or any person having a license from the trustees of said town, as authorized by sections eight and nine of this act, in addition to being suspended from their privileges, may be fined in any sum not exceeding one hundred dollars, for a violation of the State law or the laws governing said town, or for a violation of the rules prescribed for the government of such taverns or saloons: *Provided,* That no person shall be fined but once for each offense, to be recovered before the police judge of said town, unless for some cause he cannot legally try such person, then to be tried before the county judge of said county.

§ 12. That the trustees shall have the power to impose a tax upon any merchant or trader doing business in said town not exceeding twenty dollars per annum; and any person attempting to sell goods, as a grocer or merchant, without having paid the tax fixed by the trustees of said town, shall forfeit and pay the sum of twenty-five dollars in addition to the tax thus imposed.

§ 13. That the trustees of said town shall have power to fix and collect such tax as they may deem proper for peddlers and auctioneers doing business in said town; except master commissioners, sheriffs, constables, and other officers, as well as executors and administrators, when in the discharge of their duties, shall not be required to pay any tax to said town.

§ 14. That if any person shall leave any wagon, box, wood, or other thing in the streets, or upon the sidewalks of said town, for more than twenty-four hours, that is calculated to obstruct the free and uninterrupted passage of any part of the streets or sidewalks, he shall be fined in a sum not less than ten dollars and not more than twenty-five dollars for each day such obstruction remains upon the said streets or sidewalks. But the trustees may grant to any person erecting or repairing any building in said town the right to place any material on said streets or sidewalks for a reasonable time, and may, from time to time, extend said privilege for good cause.

§ 15. It shall be the duty of the trustees of said town, annually, to prepare sanitary rules for the government of said town, which shall be enforced by the enactment of suitable by-laws.

§ 16. That the penalties now fixed by law for all infractions of the penal laws of this Commonwealth shall be doubled for all offenses committed within the corporate limits of said town, when any part of the penalty is a fine; but if it be for imprisonment, that part of the penalty shall not be increased.

§ 17. That an election shall be holden in said town on the first Saturday in May, in each year, for the election

1869.

of trustees, after said election shall be advertised for ten days at the court-house door, and three other public places in said town, at which time five white persons, citizens of the town, shall be elected to serve as trustees of said town, three at least of whom shall be owners of real estate in said town. Said trustees shall qualify on or before the third Saturday in May, and shall hold their office until the qualification of their successor in office.

May cause streets & alleys to be opened.

§ 18. That it shall be the duty of the trustees of said town to cause all the streets and alleys of said town to be opened, and be kept open; and they shall have no power to permit any person to close any street or alley in said town; but shall have authority to change the location of any street or alley, upon the application of the owners of the adjacent property and, the owners of property over whose lots said change may be made.

May appoint special police.

§ 19. That the trustees of said town shall have the power, when in their opinion the necessity demands it, to appoint one or more sober, discreet men, as a special police, to assist the town marshal in executing the law, and aid in preserving order in said town. Such person shall not act as a policeman until after he has received a copy of the order appointing him to the position, designating the length of time he is to hold his position, and duty required to be performed. Whilst holding such position, he shall have all the ministerial powers of the town marshal for said town in making arrests for breaches of the penal laws of this Commonwealth, and for violations of the laws and by-laws governing said town; and the said town shall be responsible for any illegal conduct of said officer; and any person aggrieved by the act or acts of such person whilst holding a certificate of appointment from the trustees of said town, may institute his suit in any court of said county having jurisdiction thereof, for the recovery of any damages such person may have sustained at the hands of such officer; and if such person should recover a judgment, it shall be the duty of the trustees to pay said judgment; but nothing in this act shall be construed to prevent either party from appealing from the judgment of any court, in the same manner, and under the same limitations and restrictions, as is now provided by law.

In relation to ten-pin alleys, &c.

§ 20. That the trustees shall have power to grant to any person the right to erect ten-pin alleys in said town, upon their paying a tax of twenty-five dollars annually to the treasurer of said town; but if the owner or keeper shall permit any money or other thing to be bet, won, or lost in said alleys upon the result of any game, his license shall be immediately revoked by the trustees of said town, and he shall be fined in a sum of not less than two hundred dollars and not more than five hundred dollars; and if, upon the rendition of judgment, such person fails immediately to replevy or pay such fine, he shall be committed to jail until said fine is replevied or paid; such fine to be recovered upon indictment of the grand jury of Muhlenburg county. It shall be the duty of the trustees to prescribe rules for the government of such ten-pin alleys as is prescribed in sections eight and nine of this act.

§ 21. That the trustees shall have power to impose a tax, not exceeding twenty-five dollars, upon each billiard-table in said town.

May tax billiard tables.

§ 22. It shall be the duty of the trustees of said town to prescribe the places and manner in which powder, benzine, and coal oils shall be stored and sold; also, to see that all chimneys and flues are kept in good order, and require the owners thereof to repair such flue, stove, or chimney; and upon his or her failure to do so, in ten days after notice, to cause said repairs to be made at the costs of the owner; and for this purpose, they shall have ingress and egress to all buildings, the flues, stoves, or chimneys of which have been ordered to be repaired.

In relation to powder, &c.

§ 23. That all acts and parts of acts inconsistent with this act, so far as the same applies to the town of Greenville, are hereby repealed.

§ 24. This act to take effect thirty days after its passage.

Approved March 4, 1869.

CHAPTER 1694.

AN ACT for the benefit of the Mechanics of Hopkins County.

Be it enacted by the General Assembly of the Commonwealth of Kentucky:

§ 1. That the provisions of an act, entitled "An act for the benefit of the mechanics of Union county," approved January the 22d, 1849, be, and the same are, applied to Hopkins county, with this exception, that the lowest sum for which a lien may attach shall be ten dollars, instead of twenty dollars, as therein provided.

§ 2. This act to be in force from and after its passage.

Approved March 4, 1869.

CHAPTER 1696.

AN ACT to incorporate the Newport and Dayton Turnpike Road Company.

Be it enacted by the General Assembly of the Commonwealth of Kentucky:

§ 1. That Henry Weavering, James B. Chadwick, Geo. Nolte, II. D. Helm, Antvn Link, Charles Kuhlman, and George E. Currie, and their associates and successors, shall be, and they are hereby, incorporated, under the name and style of the Newport and Dayton turnpike road company; and shall have and exercise, by that name, the powers and privileges usual and necessary to their existence as a body-politic and corporate.

§ 2 Said company are hereby authorized to construct and maintain a turnpike or gravel road, from a point at the east line of the city of Newport, near Taylor's creek, to the west line of the city of Dayton, to run with and along the present county road leading from Newport to Dayton, and as a part of said turnpike road; may also build a toll-bridge across Taylor's creek, at the point where said turnpike may cross said creek.

§ 3. Said company may charge for the passage of persons, animals, and vehicles, over said road and bridge, any sums not exceeding the following rates, to-wit: For horses, mules, and cattle passing over said bridge, two (2) cents each; for light-wheeled vehicles passing over said bridge, one (1) cent per wheel of such vehicle; for heavy-wheeled vehicles passing over said bridge, two (2) cents per wheel of such vehicles; and for passing over said road horses, mules, and cattle may be charged tolls at the rate of one cent per mile for each mile traveled by them; and light-wheeled vehicles, one cent per mile for each wheel of such vehicle for each mile traveled; and heavy-wheeled vehicles, one cent and a half per mile for each wheel of such vehicle for every mile traveled; hogs and sheep shall not be charged over one fifth the rates fixed for horses and cattle; said company may erect a toll-gate at the bridge, and commence charging tolls at the rates herein fixed, whenever said bridge is completed, so as to be ready for the safe passage of persons, vehicles, and animals.

§ 4. The corporators named in the first section shall constitute the board of directors for one year after the organization of the company, and until their successors are elected and qualified. The stockholders shall meet at the city of Dayton, in Campbell county, on the first Monday in June of each following year, for the election of five directors; the directors may elect such officers and agents, and may make such rules and by-laws for the government of said company, as they may deem proper, not violating therein the provisions of this act or the laws of this Commonwealth.

§ 5. The capital stock of said company shall be ten thousand dollars, to be divided into shares of ten dollars each; but the capital stock may be increased by resolution of the board of directors to such sum as may be necessary to build said bridge and turnpike; said company may begin operations as soon as twenty-five hundred dollars shall have been subscribed to the stock.

§ 6. Said company shall have all the rights and powers usually granted turnpike companies, and necessary to obtain or condemn rights of way, take and use earth, stone, or timber, and such other rights, powers and privileges, as shall authorize, empower, and enable said corporation to lay out, construct, maintain, and repair their said turnpike or gravel road and toll-bridge on said route, and over such land as a majority of the board of directors may elect, and shall have power to condemn, take and use earth, stone, or timber necessary therefor.

§ 7. The stockholders of said company shall meet annually in the city of Dayton, in Campbell county, on the first Monday in June, and may hold such other meetings as may be called by the board of directors, or a majority in interest of the stockholders; and at such meeting, each stockholder may cast one vote for each share held in said company, to the number of five, and for every five shares thereafter shall be entitled to one vote, and may cast such vote in person or by proxy, duly authorized in writing; and a majority of the directors shall constitute a quorum to transact business.

§ 8. Said corporation may receive subscriptions to its capital stock by the city of Newport and city of Dayton, or either of them; and any such subscription by either or both of said cities, duly authorized by the city council of said cities, shall be held legal and binding on either of said cities so subscribing.

§ 9. This act to take effect from its passage.

Approved March 4, 1869.

CHAPTER 1697.

AN ACT to create a Mechanics' Lien Law for Marshall County.

Be it enacted by the General Assembly of the Commonwealth of Kentucky:

§ 1. That the carpenters, joiners, brick-masons, stone-masons, plasterers, tinners, painters, brick-makers, lumber-merchants, or millers, and all other persons performing labor or furnishing material for the construction or repair of any building within Marshall county (journeymen excepted), shall have a lien, to the extent of their respective interests, upon the building they may construct or repair, or towards the construction or repairing of which they may have furnished material or performed labor, and also upon the lot or tract of land on which such building is situated; which lien shall extend to the interest of the employer, and to such building and lot or land.

§ 2. That if such employer holds or claims by executory contract, and for any cause whatever such executory contract shall be set aside or rescinded, the lien herein given shall continue, so far as the person to whom the estate may come or with him so may remain, by reason of such rescission or setting aside, shall be made richer by such building, repairing, or materials furnished.

§ 3. That where the employer shall be directed by the judgment of a court of competent jurisdiction, and shall by law be entitled to compensation from the successful claimant for improvements made on the premises, the persons who, under the provisions of this act, have liens as against such employer, shall, to the extent of their liens respectively, be substituted for the person evicted, and recover compensation from the successful claimant, so far as by law such claimant is bound to make compensation to the evicted person.

§ 4. That the lien declared shall exist against private corporations, private *quasi* corporations, and societies, or trustees holding estates for charitable uses, whether the building, repairing, or furnishing of materials shall be done or furnished at the request of such corporation, *quasi* corporation, society, or trustee, or by their servants or agents authorized by parol or otherwise.

§ 5. That all and every person claiming a lien in virtue of this act shall, within six months after the cessation of work thereon by order of the party, or his or its agent, against whom the lien is sought to be enforced, and shall file in the clerk's office of the Marshall county court his claim or account specifying the lien claimed by him, which shall operate as a notice to the world of such lien; and no lien shall exist in favor of any person, in virtue of this act, who has not filed his accounts in the time aforesaid, or proceed by suit to enforce said lien; in which latter case the *lis pendens* shall be construed to commence from the time of filing the suit.

§ 6. That the rules of equity for the enforcement of liens and settling of priorities shall govern proceedings arising under this act, as well as liens under this act, and other liens upon the same property.

§ 7. This act shall take effect from its passage.

Approved March 4, 1869.

CHAPTER 1698.

AN ACT for the benefit of Jane E. Farris and her Children.

WHEREAS, Dabney Farrar, of Muhlenburg county, Virginia, by his last will, bequeathed certain of his estate to his wife "during life or widowhood," and, after her death, the same to go into the hands of William Farris, of Lincoln county, Kentucky, as trustee, for the support and maintenance of Jane E. Farris, wife of Henry W. Farris, and her children; and, after her death, to be equally divided between "the lawful issue of her body," &c.; and whereas, the widow of said testator has departed this life, and also William Farris, the trustee appointed by said will; and whereas, the proceeds of the real estate bequeathed are now ready to be paid over to a trustee; therefore,

Be it enacted by the General Assembly of the Commonwealth of Kentucky:

§ 1. That upon the application of Jane E. Farris, wife of Henry W. Farris, now of Jefferson county, Kentucky, the presiding judge of the Jefferson county court be, and he is hereby, authorized and empowered to appoint a trustee to receive and execute the trust created by said will; and said judge will take from the trustee appointed by him bond, with approved security, payable to the Commonwealth of Kentucky, for the use and benefit of Jane E. Farris and her children, conditioned for the faithful performance and discharge of the said trust, upon which an action may be maintained by any of said beneficiaries for each and every breach of said trust.

§ 2. This act to take effect from and after its passage.

Approved March 4, 1869.

CHAPTER 1699.

AN ACT to incorporate the Louisville Agricultural Works.

Be it enacted by the General Assembly of the Commonwealth of Kentucky:

§ 1. That R. A. Robinson, John B. Smith, George W. Anderson, Wm. L. McCampbell, and S. W. Pope, their associates and assigns, be, and are hereby, created a body-politic and corporate, under the name and style of the "Louisville Agricultural Works," with perpetual succession; and by that name may contract and be contracted with, sue and be sued, plead and be impleaded, in all courts and places whatsoever; may have a common seal, and alter, make, and renew the same at pleasure; may buy, hold, sell and convey, all kinds of estate, real, personal, and mixed, necessary for the prosecution of its business.

§ 2. The business of said company shall be the manufacture and sale of reapers and mowers, threshers, horsepowers, plows, cultivators, and other agricultural implements and machinery. Its office and place of business may be in the city of Louisville, or in any other place in the State of Kentucky.

§ 3. The capital stock of the company shall be one hundred thousand dollars, divided into shares of one hundred dollars each, which shall be deemed personal estate, and transferable on the books of the company in such manner as may be prescribed in the by-laws. The stock shall be paid in such installments and at such times as the board of directors may determine; and for default of payment, the by-laws may authorize a forfeiture of the stock, and the company shall be entitled to a prior lien upon all the stock of any stockholder indebted to the company, to the full extent of his indebtedness. The said company shall have power to increase its capital stock, not to exceed two hundred and fifty thousand dollars, by a vote of the majority of all the stock represented.

§ 4. The affairs of said company shall be conducted by a board of directors of not less than three nor more than seven, to be fixed by the stockholders, one of whom shall be elected president; and they shall hold their offices for one year, and until their successors are elected, and each one of whom shall own at least five shares of the said capital stock. The said board of directors shall have power to make all by-laws, and alter the same at pleasure, which may be necessary to carry out the powers herein expressly granted, not inconsistent with the Constitution of the United States or the Constitution and laws of this State; and to prescribe by said by-laws the manner and times of the election of officers; to employ any and all agents necessary or proper to carry on the business; to require bonds of its employes and officers; and to do all things necessary or proper to the successful prosecution of the said business.

§ 5. The above named corporators shall be commissioners to open books of subscription; and when twenty-five thousand dollars shall have been subscribed, the said company may commence business; and the above named corporators shall have power to elect the first board of directors.

§ 6. Every stockholder shall be entitled to one vote for each share of the said stock which he may own at the election of officers, and in all stockholders' meetings; and he may vote either in person or by written proxy, signed by himself.

§ 7. There shall be annual meetings of the stockholders, and special meetings may be called by the directors, or by any number of stockholders representing a majority of the votes, under such regulations as the by-laws may prescribe, and at such meetings, the officers of the company shall, if required, submit a full statement of its affairs, business, and accounts.

§ 8. No banking privileges are conferred by this charter.

§ 9. This act shall be in force from its passage.

Approved March 4, 1869.

CHAPTER 1700.

AN ACT to amend an act, entitled "An act to amend the Charter of the Town of Cadiz," approved April 4, 1861.

Be it enacted by the General Assembly of the Commonwealth of Kentucky:

§ 1. That an act, entitled "An act to amend the charter of the town of Cadiz," approved April 4, 1861, be, and is hereby, amended, by adding thereto the following as an additional section: And when any person is tried and fined for any of the aforesaid offenses, and fails to pay or replevy such fine; or, if any one should be tried and sentenced to jail by said police court, instead of sending such person to jail, the party so convicted may elect to work upon the streets of the town of Cadiz; and if such election is made, the court shall enter the same upon the records of his court, and direct the party thus electing to be delivered into the custody of the trustees of said town, who shall require him to work upon the streets for the same number of days such person would have been confined in jail, and no longer, at which time he shall be discharged; and it shall be the duty of said police judge to made an entry upon the records of his court discharging him from further liability; and the trustees shall, from any moneys belonging to said town, pay the officers their fees, provided the party works upon the streets after thus electing; and the trustees shall have power to appoint some one to superintend those who elect to work as herein provided. Should any person thus electing refuse to work, then the police judge may have said person confined, as provided in the original act. The trustees shall have power to employ an attorney for said town, and contract with him for his services; such attorney shall receive, in addition to any salary paid him by said town, thirty per cent. of all fines and forfeitures in cases tried before said police judge for violations of the penal laws

1869.

of this State, or the by-laws of said town, in which such attorney appears and prosecutes such offenders.

§ 2. This act to take effect upon its passage.

Approved March 4, 1869.

CHAPTER 1701.

AN ACT to amend an act, entitled "An act to establish the County of Josh Bell," approved February 28, 1867.

Be it enacted by the General Assembly of the Commonwealth of Kentucky:

§ 1. That so much of the fifth section of an act, entitled "An act to establish the county of Josh Bell," approved 28th February, 1867, as appoints Isaac Dean a commissioner to run and mark the boundary line of said county of Josh Bell, agreeably to the boundary designated in said act, be, and the same is hereby, repealed.

§ 2. That Wm. F. Westerfield be, and is, appointed a commissioner, in conjunction with Robert Howard and Wm. North, and such assistants as they may employ, to do and perform all the duties required by the act to which this is an amendment, so far as the running and marking of the said boundary line is concerned.

§ 3. This act to take effect from its passage.

Approved March 4, 1869.

CHAPTER 1702.

AN ACT to prevent the sale of ardent spirits in and near Bohontown.

Be it enacted by the General Assembly of the Commonwealth of Kentucky:

§ 1. That no liquor, or distilled spirits that will produce intoxication, shall be sold within an area of two miles from the village of Bohontown, in Mercer county; and the county judge of said county is hereby prohibited from granting license to sell liquor or distilled spirits within the precincts of said boundary.

§ 2. This act to be a law from its passage.

Approved March 4, 1869.

CHAPTER 1704.

AN ACT to amend an act, entitled "An act to punish certain trespasses in Jefferson and other Counties," passed the 23d of December, 1861, so as to apply its provisions and the amendment thereto, passed the 8th of March, 1862, to the County of Grant.

Be it enacted by the General Assembly of the Commonwealth of Kentucky:

§ 1. That an act, entitled "An act to punish certain trespasses in Jefferson and other counties," passed the 23d of December, 1861, and the amendment thereto, passed the 8th of March, 1862, be, and the same are, so amended as to apply all the provisions of said original act, and the amendment thereto, to the county of Grant.

§ 2. This act shall take effect from its passage.

Approved March 4, 1869.

CHAPTER 1705.

AN ACT to amend the Charter of the Iron Hill Railway Company, and the title thereof.

Be it enacted by the General Assembly of the Commonwealth of Kentucky:

§ 1. That the title of the Iron Hill railway company be so amended that hereafter it shall read "Iron Hill Railway, Mining, and Manufacturing Company."

§ 2. That said company shall have full power to mine coal, iron ore, and all other kinds of ores, and to manufacture the same in any way they may think proper; and all the rights and privileges in their said charter shall extend and apply to the mining and manufacturing business, as well as railway business.

§ 3. This act to take effect from its passage.

Approved March 4, 1869.

CHAPTER 1706.

AN ACT to repeal an act, entitled "An act to incorporate the town of Consolation, in Shelby County."

Be it enacted by the General Assembly of the Commonwealth of Kentucky:

§ 1. That an act, entitled "An act to incorporate the town of Consolation, in Shelby county," approved February 22, 1860, be, and the same is hereby, repealed.

§ 2. That this act take effect from its passage.

Approved March 4, 1869.

CHAPTER 1707.

AN ACT to amend the Charter of the Lexington, Harrodsburg, and Perryville Turnpike Road Company.

*Be it enacted by the General Assembly of the Commonwealth
of Kentucky:*

§ 1. That any person or persons traveling or driving
stock upon the Lexington, Harrodsburg, and Perryville
turnpike road, who shall turn off the road within a short
distance of a toll gate (say two or three hundred yards),
and return upon the road on the other side of the toll-gate
within the like distance of it, shall be liable to pay toll as
though they had passed through the toll-gate.

§ 2. This act to take effect from its passage.

Approved March 4, 1869.

CHAPTER 1708.

AN ACT to amend the Charter of the City of Augusta.

*Be it enacted by the General Assembly of the Commonwealth
of Kentucky:*

§ 1. That the mayor and common council of the city of
Augusta, in Bracken county, be, and they are hereby,
authorized and empowered to erect, or cause to be erected
and kept, on any of the public grounds, streets, or alleys
of said city, scales for the weighing of coal, hay, and
other products; but such scales shall not be so located as
to obstruct or interfere with the travel along or over any
street or alley.

§ 2. That this act shall take effect from and after its
passage.

Approved March 4, 1869.

CHAPTER 1709.

AN ACT to incorporate Venus Lodge, No. 154, Independent Order of Odd
Fellows, at Florence, in Boone County.

*Be it enacted by the General Assembly of the Commonwealth
of Kentucky:*

§ 1. That J. A. Corey, Benjamin Stephens, and their
associates, be, and they are hereby, created a body corporate, by the name and style of Venus Lodge, No. 154, of
the Independent Order of Odd Fellows; and they and their
associates and successors shall so continue and have perpetual succession, and by that name are made capable in
law, as natural persons, to sue and be sued, plead and be
impleaded, contract and be contracted with, answer and
be answered, in all courts of law and equity in this Com-

monwealth ; to make, have, and use a common seal, and the same to break, alter, or amend at pleasure. They may make and ordain regulations and by-laws for their government, and those now in force in said lodge to alter when deemed proper, and may change and renew the same at pleasure, provided they be not in contravention of the constitution, laws and regulations, of the Grand Lodge of the Independent Order of Odd Fellows, incorporated by an act approved February 16, 1838, nor in contravention of the Constitution and laws of the United States or of this State.

§ 2. That the said corporation shall have power and authority to acquire and hold real estate, not exceeding in value twenty thousand dollars, and from time to time, if deemed expedient, sell and convey the same, or any part thereof, and to reinvest and dispose of the proceeds.

§ 3. That the right to alter, amend, or repeal this act is hereby reserved to the General Assembly.

§ 4. This act to take effect from and after its passage.

Approved March 4, 1869.

——

CHAPTER 1710.

AN ACT for the benefit of the Town of Greensburg.

Be it enacted by the General Assembly of the Commonwealth of Kentucky:

§ 1. That the third section of the act, entitled "An act to amend an act, entitled 'An act to incorporate the town of Greensburg,'" approved February 21, 1849, be, and the same is hereby, repealed.

§ 2. That this act shall take effect and be in force from and after its passage.

Approved March 4, 1869.

——

CHAPTER 1711.

AN ACT to amend the Charter of the Southern Mutual Life Insurance Company of Kentucky.

Be it enacted by the General Assembly of the Commonwealth of Kentucky:

§ 1. That so much of the eighteenth section of the act incorporating the Southern Mutual Life Insurance Company of Kentucky, approved February 7, 1866, as provides for the payment in scrip or otherwise, of twenty (20) per cent. of the net profits of said company to the stockholders thereof, be, and the same is hereby, repealed.

1869.

§ 2. That the whole amount of the net profits or surplus of said company, to be ascertained in the manner prescribed in the seventeenth and eighteenth sections of said act of incorporation, shall be applied in the form of dividends to the policy-holders of said company, and each insured member who may be entitled to share in the profits of the company, and whose policy may not have become forfeited, shall be entitled to be credited on the books of the company, or on premium notes, for such proportional part of such surplus as the sum of the annual premiums, paid by said member, shall bear to the aggregate of the surplus to be divided.

§ 3. This act shall be in force from its passage.

Approved March 4, 1869.

CHAPTER 1712.

AN ACT to incorporate Warsaw Royal Arch Chapter, No. 97.

Be it enacted by the General Assembly of the Commonwealth of Kentucky:

§ 1. That J. W. Ellis, R. R. Russell, Dr. J. T. Robinson, and their associates and successors, are hereby created a body corporate, under the name and style of Warsaw Royal Arch Chapter, No. 97, Ancient York Masons, in the town of Warsaw, Gallatin county; and by the name and style aforesaid they are hereby made capable in law to sue and be sued, plead and be impleaded, to contract and be contracted with; to make, have, and use a seal, and the same to alter at pleasure.

§ 2. The said corporation shall have the right to take and hold, by purchase, gift or devise, real and personal estate, not to exceed the sum of ten thousand dollars, to dispose of and convey the same at their pleasure, with, and by the consent of a majority of the members of said chapter.

§ 3. That the business of said chapter or corporation shall be under the management of the principal officers, to be elected at the regular annual election by the members of said chapter.

§ 4. This act to take effect from its passage.

Approved March 4, 1869.

CHAPTER 1713.

AN ACT to incorporate the Odd Fellows' Temple Association, of Lexington.

Be it enacted by the General Assembly of the Commonwealth of Kentucky:

§ 1. That A. Gilmore, James Chrystal, Isaiah King, Z. Gibbons, J. D. Trapp, Thos. W. Foster, and D. A. King, and their associates, be, and they are hereby, created a body corporate, by the name and style of "The Odd Fellows' Temple Association," and they and their associates and successors shall so continue and have perpetual succession; and by that name are made capable in law as natural persons to sue and be sued, plead and be impleaded, contract and be contracted with, answer and be answered, in all courts of law and equity in this Commonwealth; to make, have, and use a common seal, and the same to break, alter, or amend at pleasure; they may make and ordain regulations and by-laws for their government, and those now in force in said association to alter when deemed proper, and may change and renew the same at pleasure: *Provided*, They be not in contravention of the Constitution and laws of the United States or of this State. The said corporation shall have power and authority to acquire and hold real and personal estate, not exceeding fifty thousand dollars in value, and, from time to time, if deemed expedient, sell and convey the same, or any part thereof, and to reinvest and dispose of the proceeds. The right to alter, amend, or repeal this act is hereby reserved to the General Assembly.

§ 2. This act shall take effect from its passage.

Approved March 4, 1869.

CHAPTER 1714.

AN ACT to incorporate the St. Louis Bertrand Society of Louisville.

Be it enacted by the General Assembly of the Commonwealth of Kentucky:

§ 1. That the Revs. Dennis J. Meagher, William D. O'Carroll, Vincent J. Daley, Peter C. Coll, Hugh Lilly, and Alphonsus Daley, and their successors, be, and are hereby, created a body-politic and corporate, under the name of the "Saint Louis Bertrand Literary Society;" and by that name shall have perpetual succession and corporate existence, with full power to contract and be contracted with, sue and be sued; to have a corporate seal, and the same to alter or renew at pleasure; and to ordain and put into execution such by-laws, rules and regulations, for the government of said society, and for the prudent and efficient management of its affairs, as may be deemed expedient and proper by them : *Provided,* The same are not inconsistent with the laws of this State or the United States.

§ 2 Said society is hereby authorized and empowered to acquire and hold by purchase, devise, bequest, gift, grant, or otherwise, real estate to the value of not more than two hundred and fifty thousand dollars, and personal property to the value of not more than one hundred thousand dollars; and may sell and convey, by the deed of its president or chief officer, under the corporate seal, all or any of its real estate at any time, and acquire other not in excess of the limitation above fixed; and may sell and dispose of its personal property at pleasure.

§ 3. The corporators herein named, and their successors under said corporate name, shall hold all the property vested in this corporation in trust for the use of said society, subject to the power of sale above provided for, and to be under the control of the council of said society as now organized, or as it may be hereafter organized; and vacancies by death, removal, resignation, or otherwise, in said board of corporators, shall be filled by election of said council under the by-laws and constitution of said society.

§ 4. The Rev. Dennis J. Meagher is hereby declared president and chief officer of this corporation until his successor, as prior of said society, is duly elected, when such successor shall, *ex-officio,* be president of this corporation during his term as prior, and so on, perpetually, the prior shall be president until otherwise provided for in the by-laws and constitution of the society.

§ 5. This act to take effect from and after its passage.

Approved March 4, 1869.

CHAPTER 1716.

AN ACT to amend the Charter of the Town of Brooksville, in Bracken County.

Be it enacted by the General Assembly of the Commonwealth of Kentucky:

§ 1. That the various acts of the General Assembly incorporating the town of Brooksville, in Bracken county, be so amended, that it shall be the duty of the officers holding the annual election now authorized to be held on the first Monday in April in each year, for the election of police judge, trustees, and marshal, to open a poll for and against license, in which all the legal voters in said town may vote.

§ 2. That if, at the said annual election, there shall be a majority of the votes cast in favor of granting license, then the trustees of said town shall be authorized to grant license under the provisions and restrictions of an act amending the charter of said town, approved February 25, 1860.

§ 3. That if, at said annual election, there shall not be a majority of votes cast in favor of granting license, then the trustees of said town shall have no power to grant license to any tavern-keeper, merchant, or other person to sell any spirituous, vinous, or malt liquors in the corporate limits of said town, until at a subsequent annual election a different result shall occur in the vote upon the question of license.

§ 4. That it shall be the duty of the clerk of the annual election of the officers of said town, to certify the vote taken upon the question of license to the presiding judge. of the county court, who shall have the same filed in the clerk's office thereof; and if the vote is in favor of license, he may grant license as now provided by law; and if the vote is not in favor of license, he shall not grant any license to sell spirituous, vinous, or malt liquors within said town, or within one mile of the corporate limits thereof.

§ 5. That all acts conflicting with this act be, and the same are hereby, repealed.

§ 6. That this act shall take effect from and after its passage.

Approved March 4, 1869.

CHAPTER 1717.

AN ACT to amend the Charter of the City of Augusta, in Bracken County.

Be it enacted by the General Assembly of the Commonwealth of Kentucky:

§ 1. That the exclusive right to grant license to vend spirituous, vinous, and malt liquors within the corporate limits of the city of Augusta, is hereby conferred upon the mayor and council of said city.

§ 2. That merchant's license to sell spirituous liquors within the corporate limits of the city of Augusta shall not be granted by the county court of Bracken county, but the same may be granted by the mayor and council of said city alone, upon such terms as they may deem proper: *Provided, however*, Before any person shall be permitted to exercise any of the privileges that may be granted them by the mayor and council of said city of Augusta, under the provisions of this act, he shall present to the county court of said county his license from the mayor and council of Augusta, execute bond, take the oath, and

1869.   pay the State tax, as is now required by law in such cases.

§ 3. This act to take effect from its passage.

Approved March 4, 1869.

CHAPTER 1718.

AN ACT to amend an act, entitled "An act to incorporate the Ursuline Society and Academy of Education," approved January 8, 1864.

Be it enacted by the General Assembly of the Commonwealth of Kentucky:

§ 1. That the Ursuline Society and Academy of Education, shall have power to receive from the county court of Jefferson county, the city court of Louisville, or from individuals or parents, such child or children as the said courts, individuals, or parents may desire, and have power to bind out; and the indentures so made shall be binding on the parties to the same extent as though said courts or parents should make indenture. to an individual.

§ 2. This amendment to take effect from and after its passage.

Approved March 4, 1869.

CHAPTER 1719.

AN ACT to incorporate the Cynthiana Malt and Brewing Company.

Be it enacted by the General Assembly of the Commonwealth of Kentucky:

§ 1. That T. J. McGibben, C. B. Cook, H. E. Shawhan, T. V. Ashbrook, and G. W. Taylor, and their associates, successors, and assigns, be, and they are hereby, created a body-politic and corporate, under the name and style of the Cynthiana Malt and Brewing Company; and by that name shall have power to contract and be contracted with, sue and be sued, plead and be impleaded; and the said corporation shall have power to adopt a common seal, and to alter or change the same at pleasure; and to make such regulations, rules and by-laws, as may be deemed necessary, not inconsistent with the laws of this State or the United States.

§ 2. The capital stock of said company shall not exceed fifty thousand dollars, to be divided into shares of one hundred dollars each, and to be subscribed and paid for as the board of directors of said company shall prescribe. The corporators herein named shall constitute the board of directors of said company for one year, at the end of which time, and annually thereafter, the stockholders shall elect a board, consisting of five members.

§ 3. That said company shall have power to purchase, hold, and sell and dispose of, all such real and personal property as may be deemed necessary for the convenient transaction of its business; and it shall have power to make malt, and to manufacture, transport, and vend all kinds of malt liquors. The principal office and place or places of business of said company shall be located at or near the town of Cynthiana, in Harrison county.

§ 4. That this act shall take effect from and after its passage.

Approved March 4, 1869.

CHAPTER 1720.

AN ACT to amend act, entitled "An act to incorporate the Ashland Library Company," approved March 9th, 1868.

Be it enacted by the General Assembly of the Commonwealth of Kentucky:

§ 1. That the act, entitled "An act to incorporate the Ashland Library Company," approved March 9th, 1868, be amended as follows, viz: That the shares of stock shall be five dollars. The company may organize when there shall have been subscribed two hundred and fifty dollars to the capital stock.

§ 2. This act shall take effect from its passage.

Approved March 4, 1869.

CHAPTER 1721.

AN ACT to incorporate the town of Moscow, Hickman County.

Be it enacted by the General Assembly of the Commonwealth of Kentucky:

§ 1. That the corporate limits of the town of Moscow, Kentucky, be, and the same are, declared to exist as prescribed by previous acts relating to said town, and also to embrace the following territory: Beginning at the northeast corner of the present corporate limits of said town, and running due east far enough to include the present residence of A. M. Furgeson; thence due south to a point parallel with the present western boundary of said town, so as to include the property owned and now occupied by H. I. Thorne; thence west to the present southwest corner of the present corporate limits of said town.

§ 2. That an act, entitled "An act to amend and reduce into one all previous acts incorporating the town of Clin-

ton, Hickman county," approved February 13th, 1866, be,
and the same is hereby, applied to said town of Moscow;
and all previous acts relating to said town, inconsistent
with the provisions of said act, be, and the same are hereby, repealed.

§ 3. That the first election for the town officers provided
for by this act shall be held on the first day of May, 1869;
and that J. H. Cayce. John Watkins, J. W. Lawrence, J.
R. Humphreys, and J. H. Smith, or any two of them, be,
and they are hereby, authorized to hold said election.

§ 4. This act to take effect from and after its passage.

Approved March 4, 1869.

CHAPTER 1722.

AN ACT to include George Field in the Town of Shepherdsville.

Be it enacted by the General Assembly of the Commonwealth
of Kentucky:

§ 1. That the boundary lines of Shepherdsville be so
changed as to include within the town limits the residence
and lot of ground now owned by George Field, a man of
color.

§ 2. This act shall take effect from its passage.

Approved March 4, 1869.

CHAPTER 1723.

AN ACT to amend an act, approved February 16, 1866, entitled "An act to
amend and reduce into one the several acts in relation to the Town of
Greenupsburg, and also of the several acts amendatory thereof."

Be it enacted by the General Assembly of the Commonwealth
of Kentucky:

§ 1. That in case the clerk of the board of trustees shall
fail to give the notice and hold the election, as he is required to do, annually, by the first section of article two,
chapter one hundred, Revised Statutes, he shall be fined in
any sum, in the discretion of a jury, not exceeding twenty-
five dollars, to be recovered by action at the suit of any
one, or on indictment of a grand jury; and the board of
trustees then in office shall not, under any state of case,
hold their office longer than twenty days after the first day
of June of each year.

§ 2. In case an election for trustees of said town is failed
to be held annually, on the first Monday of June, then the
county judge of Greenup county, or any justice of the
peace, may, and it shall be their duty, on the written request of any two voters of said town, to authorize the elec-

tion to take place at any day thereafter within four months thereafter; and said officer ordering said election shall conduct it in the same manner as the clerk of the board is required to do, and shall have the same power and authority as is given to him.

§ 3. No *ad valorem* tax, under the authority of said trustees, shall be collected on any other property than the real estate within the corporate limits; and no such tax for all purposes, or any assessment under their authority, shall exceed, for any one year, one dollar on one hundred dollars of such valuation.

§ 4. The one half of the costs of paving, grading, opening, and improving the streets, alleys, and lanes of said town, shall be paid out of the town treasury, and the other half by the proprietors of lots and lands adjoining them, in proportion to the extent of said lots on them.

§ 5. The trustees shall not create any debt on said town by borrowing money, or otherwise, which shall not be paid out of the funds of the town within said year, nor pay on any debt a greater interest than six per cent.; and for all debts so created by them, by borrowing money contrary to this section, said trustees shall be personally liable.

§ 6. That it shall be the duty of the sheriff of Greenup county to open a poll and hold an election at the courthouse in the town of Greenupsburg, between the hours of eight o'clock A. M. and five o'clock P. M., on the first Monday in June next, at which election none but the qualified voters residing in the limits of said town shall be entitled to vote; and he shall submit this act to said voters for their approval or rejection. The poll-book shall be compared by the same board now established by law to compare poll-books of general elections; and if a majority of the votes are cast in favor of this act, it shall thenceforth be in full force; but if a majority of said votes are cast against it, then it shall be declared rejected and of no binding force whatsoever.

§ 7. Said sheriff shall give at least ten days' notice, by written notices posted at public places in said town.

Approved March 4, 1869.

CHAPTER 1724.

AN ACT to incorporate the Greenupsburg Academy Company.

Be it enacted by the General Assembly of the Commonwealth of Kentucky:

§ 1. That the persons who subscribed and paid stock towards the purchase of lots, and the erection thereon of an academy, in the town of Greenupsburg, and those who subsequently advanced money to discharge the lien upon the house, are hereby incorporated as a body-politic, under the name and style of the "Greenupsburg Academy Company;" and by that name may sue and be sued, contract and be contracted with.

§ 2. The affairs, management, and prudential concerns of the corporation shall be under the control of three directors, to be chosen by the stockholders. The shares of stock shall be as fixed in the articles of association originally entered into; and, in the election of directors, each stockholder shall have one vote for every share of stock he may have subscribed and paid. The first election of directors shall be held at the academy building, on the first Saturday in May, 1869. Notice thereof shall be given by posting written advertisements at three or more public places in the town. The election shall take place between the hours of nine o'clock, A. M., and three o'clock, P. M., of said day. The stockholders present shall appoint a secretary to conduct the election. The result of the election shall be entered in a book and signed by the secretary. The directors elected shall choose one of their number to act as chairman of the board. They shall hold their offices until their successors are elected and qualified. An annual election of directors shall be held on the first Saturday of May in each year. If, from any cause, an election should not be held, the board of directors, or any two of them, shall order an election, upon the application of any two or more of the stockholders, and fix the day of election, of which notice shall be given for at least ten days, by posting written notices in three or more public places in the town.

§ 3. The corporation may take and hold real and personal estate, not exceeding fifty thousand dollars, which they may deem necessary for the purposes of the company in establishing an academy for educational purposes.

§ 4. The board of directors may pass by-laws for the protection and preservation of their property; and for this purpose, may impose fines not exceeding ten dollars for each offense, and imprisonment not exceeding five days; and such fines and penalties may be enforced by proceedings before any judge or justice of the peace having jurisdiction thereof, in the name of the Commonwealth of Kentucky, for the use of the board of trustees.

§ 5. The board of trustees may lease the academy and grounds to the board of trustees of the town of Greenupsburg, to be used for educational purposes, for such length of time and upon such terms as may be agreed upon.

§ 6. This act shall take effect from its passage.

Approved March 4, 1869.

CHAPTER 1725.

AN ACT to incorporate the Cabin Creek Turnpike Road Company, and to levy a tax to aid in building said road.

Be it enacted by the General Assembly of the Commonwealth of Kentucky:

§ 1. That a body corporate and politic be, and hereby is, created and authorized to be formed and organized, under the name and style of the Cabin Creek turnpike road company; and under that name and style it shall have perpetual succession; may have a common seal; may contract and be contracted with, sue and be sued, in all courts of this Commonwealth.

Name and style of company.

§ 2. The object and business of said corporation shall be to construct, keep up, and maintain a turnpike road from some point on the Concord and Tollsboro turnpike road, down Cabin creek, crossing the line between Mason and Lewis counties, and joining some turnpike in Mason county, leading to Maysville; said company shall also have power and are hereby invested with authority to construct, keep up, and maintain a turnpike road from their road on Cabin creek, the most practicable route to the Ohio river, opposite the town of Manchester, Ohio, and may extend their road and unite with any other turnpike road or roads in Lewis, Mason, or Fleming counties.

Object and powers of company.

§ 3. The capital stock of said company shall not exceed one hundred thousand dollars, to be divided into shares of twenty-five dollars each.

Capital stock.

§ 4. That books for the subscription of stock in said company may be opened at any time at the houses of Asa McNeil, David M. Dunbar, Thomas Henderson, or at any other place or places, under the supervision of Asa McNeil. David M. Dunbar, Thomas Henderson, Geo. W. Rowland, John H. Regnistine, Alex. McKenzie, A. J. Hendrickson, John D. Tully, and Wm. Fenwick, or any one or more of said persons, who are hereby appointed commissioners for that purpose. The subscribers for stock in said company shall sign the following obligation, to-wit: "We, whose names are hereunto subscribed, hereby obligate ourselves to pay to the president and directors of the Cabin Creek turnpike road company twenty-five dollars for each share of stock in said company hereby subscribed by us placed opposite our names;" and said subscription shall be made in a book in which said obligation shall be written. The said company, after it is organized, may receive subscriptions of stock to said company in real estate, rock, lumber, or other property, or payable in labor in whole, or part in labor and part payable in money, which subscriptions shall be valid and binding, and the amount in value of such subscriptions shall be expressed in the respective subscriptions; and if

Books for subscription of stock to be opened.

Obligation of subscribers.

May receive subscriptions in real estate &c.

1869. the property is not paid or surrendered and delivered, **or** the labor performed on the demand of the said company or its agent, the value thereof in money, as expressed in the subscription, may be collected of the subscriber.

§ 5. As soon as five thousand dollars is subscribed **to** the stock of said company, it may be organized; and **to** this end, the commissioners who act, or some one or more of them, shall give notice to the subscribers of stock, two weeks before the election, of the time and place of electing officers of said company, which officers shall be five directors and one president. Each stockholder shall be entitled to one vote for each share of stock owned by him or her, which vote may be cast in person or by proxy. No one but a stockholder shall be a president or director of said company. The first election shall be held under the supervision of the commissioners, or of one or more of them. The president and directors shall each take an oath faithfully to perform their duties as such, which shall be certified by the officer administering it, and filed with the papers of the company; and said officers shall serve until their successors are elected and qualified. If any vacancy occurs during the year, by death, resignation, or removal from the State, the remainder of the directors may, if they deem it necessary, fill the vacancy.

When company may organize, how stock voted, &c.

Eligibility of officers, first election, &c.

President and directors to take oath.

§ 6. The said company, after it is organized, may keep open the books for additional subscriptions of stock in said company. The Lewis county court may subscribe stock in said company to an amount not exceeding one thousand dollars per mile of said road completed within the limits of Lewis county, payable in the bonds of said county on the completion of each mile.

Books may be kept open.
Lewis county court may subscribe stock.

§ 7. The president and directors may appoint a treasurer and clerk, and prescribe their duties, fix their compensation, and may remove them at pleasure. Said treasurer and clerk shall give bond, with good security, honestly to account for all moneys that may come into their hands, and for the faithful performance of their duties; and shall also take an oath faithfully to perform their duties, which bond and the certificate of such oath shall be filed and kept with the papers of said company. The said president and directors may appoint a superintendent or agent to superintend the construction of said road, and its maintenance afterwards, and gate-keepers, and such other employes as they may deem necessary.

Treasurer, clerk, &c., may be appointed.
Treasurer and clerk shall give bond.

§ 8. The said president and directors shall have power to pass any by-laws, rules and regulations, for their own government, and the government and conduct of said company, its officers and affairs, that they may deem necessary, not inconsistent with this act, or with the Constitution of this State or the United States.

May make by-laws, &c.

§ 9. The said president and directors may let out for construction any portion of said road, as soon as five thousand dollars is subscribed, and may continue to let out other portions of said road, whenever additional subscriptions are made to pay for such portions let, first determining before commencing work the point where said road shall join the Concord and Tollsboro road, and also the point at which said road shall reach the line between Lewis and Mason counties, and so in regard to that part of said road from Cabin creek to a point on the Ohio river, opposite Manchester, whenever said company shall decide to build the last named part of said road. When they get ready to commence on that part of said road leading to Manchester, said company shall have separate subscription books; and as soon as two and a half miles of said road are completed, they may erect a toll-gate and collect toll for that portion of said road. The charges for toll on said road shall be in conformity with the general law of this State regulating tolls on turnpikes; and they shall only be authorized to charge toll on said road in proportion to the distance traveled, and only for so much of said road as shall be completed and in good repair for traveling.

§ 10. The said company may receive releases of right of way for said road and ground for rock quarries, stone, material, toll-houses, by consent or purchase; and, if they deem it necessary, they may, by proceeding instituted in conformity with the existing laws of this State on the subject of turnpikes and plank roads (Revised Statutes, chapter 103), condemn land for right of way over which said road may be located, and ground for toll-houses, and toll-gates, and rock quarries, just compensation being paid to the owners thereof, to be assessed by a jury empanneled for such purpose, according to law as aforesaid.

§ 11. The said road shall be not less than twenty-five feet nor more than fifty feet wide. Any person who shall unlawfully obstruct said road shall be subject to a fine of not less than five nor more than fifty dollars therefor, which shall, when collected, be for the use of said company, and shall be recoverable as other fines are recoverable by law. Said president and directors may pass by-laws fixing fines for failure to pay toll, or for the evasion of toll, on said road, which may be recovered as other fines of similar amount are recovered under the laws of this Commonwealth, and be for the use of said company.

§ 12. Said directors and president shall prescribe in what installments the subscriptions of stock shall be paid. They may borrow money for the use of said company, not exceeding ten thousand dollars, and give personal security

1869.

May let out road, &c.

When may erect gates.

Right of way how obtained.

Width and grade of road, obstruction to same, &c.

How stock may be paid, may borrow money, &c.

1869.

therefor, or a mortgage on said road and its franchises, which may be enforced and foreclosed.

§ 13. That to enable said company to build their road as speedily as possible, and equalize the burthens thereof, there is hereby levied on all property within one mile of that part of said road situated in Lewis county (as the same shall be located), an ad valorem tax of one dollar on each one hundred dollars' worth subject to taxation for State revenue. Said tax shall be levied and collected each year after they commence work on said road, until that part of said road in Lewis county is finished and paid for: but the taxes collected on that part of said road from where the same intersects the Concord and Tollsboro road, down Cabin creek to the Mason county line, shall be laid out and expended on that part of said road; and when that part of said road is finished and paid for, then the local tax of one dollar on each one hundred dollars' worth of property within one mile of that part of said road shall cease to be levied or collected, and the tax on that part of said road from Cabin creek to the Ohio river, opposite Manchester, shall only be collected after said company lays out and commences work on that part of said road; and said taxes shall be expended in building that part of said road, and shall cease when that part of said road is finished and paid for.

Tax may be levied to build road, &c.

§ 14. The president and directors shall have power to appoint a person, and fix his compensation, to assess and take in a list of the property liable to said tax; and, when thus assessed, they may list said taxes with the sheriff of Lewis county for collection, who shall have the same power to levy and distrain for said taxes as he now has, by law, to levy and distrain for the State revenue. Said sheriff shall account for and pay said taxes over to the president of said company on or before the first day of December in each year. For any default of said sheriff under this act, he shall be liable to suit or suits on his official bond as sheriff. Said suits shall be brought and prosecuted in the Lewis circuit court, in the name of the president of said road. Said company shall recover in such actions the amount of taxes collected by said sheriff and not paid over, or which he might have collected by due diligence, with the same interest, costs, and damages now allowed by law against sheriffs for failing to collect and pay over the county levy.

Assessor to be appointed; his powers and duties.

§ 15. The tax-payers who pay taxes under this act shall be stockholders in said road for the amount of taxes paid by them; and the taxes collected shall in all cases be expended by said company in building said road and equipping the same, paying its debts, &c.

Tax-payers stockholders.

§ 16. No property shall be taxed double by reason of being within the prescribed distance of two roads; but in such cases the distance shall be equally divided between said two roads, and the taxes paid to the road nearest the tax-payer.

1869.

Property not to be taxed double.

§ 17. This act shall be in force from its passage.

Approved March 4, 1869.

CHAPTER 1726.

AN ACT to amend an act, entitled "An act to incorporate the Lewis and Mason County Turnpike Road Company."

Be it enacted by the General Assembly of the Commonwealth of Kentucky:

§ 1. That an act to incorporate the Lewis and Mason County turnpike road company, approved March 7, 1868, is amended as follows: Said company is hereby authorized and empowered to extend their road, on the end in Lewis county, beyond Equalization to Kinniconick creek, and may connect their road with any other road or roads they may deem expedient, in Lewis or Fleming county.

§ 2. That to enable said company the more speedily to build their road, and to equalize as near as possible the burthens of building said road, there is hereby levied, and shall be collected, on all property and money, &c., taxed under the laws of the State for State revenue, on each one hundred dollars' worth, situated on each side of said road, as the same may be or has been located, and within one and a half miles of the same, one dollar per year from the time that part of said road, in Lewis county, or some portion of the same, not less than four miles, shall be located and put under contract to be built; said tax shall continue to be levied and collected until said road is finished and paid for; said road shall be divided into sections of from two to four miles; and the local tax levied by this act shall be appropriated, by the president and directors of said company, to building that section of said road in which the taxable property is situated; and when any one section is finished and paid for, then the local tax in that section shall cease. This tax shall be collected only on property in Lewis county, and shall not be construed to extend to property in Mason or Fleming county; the several tax-payers shall become stockholders in said company for the amount of tax they pay. The county court of Lewis shall, upon being requested so to do, appoint two discreet persons to assess and fix a value upon the property liable to the tax levied under this act; said persons shall make out a list of all property on each side of said road within one and a half miles of the same, in Lewis county, with a description of the same, its value and owner's name, and return said list to the Lewis county court, at its May or June term, in each year; said court shall list said taxes with the sheriff of Lewis county for collection; and it is hereby made the duty of said sheriff to receive, collect, and pay over to the president of said company, the amount of taxes collected on said list and assessment; said money must be paid over on or before the 25th day of December in each year; and for any default of said sheriff under this act, he and his sureties shall be liable on his official bond as sheriff; he shall be entitled to the same compensation for collecting and paying over said taxes, as now allowed by law for collecting the State revenue; the money thus collected shall be expended on that part of said road in Lewis county alone. Where property is located within the prescribed distance of two turnpike roads, and might be subject to two local taxes under the law, the distance shall be equally divided between the two roads, and the tax collected and paid over to that road (in Lewis county) nearest the tax-payer, so that no property or person shall be taxed, at the same time, to help build two roads, under any law or laws levying a local tax to aid in building turnpikes.

§ 3 This company shall be entitled to the same aid (of $1,000 per mile) as the Vanceburg, Salt Lick, Tollsboro, and Maysville turnpike, and on the same terms and conditions, from Lewis county; and the Lewis county court is hereby required to assist said road (that part in Lewis county) to the amount of $1,000 per mile, it being the intention to put all turnpike roads in Lewis county on the same footing in regard to the assistance from the county court.

§ 4. This act shall take effect from and after its passage.

Approved March 4, 1869.

CHAPTER 1727.

An ACT for the benefit of John and Mary E. Seaton, of Greenup County.

Be it enacted by the General Assembly of the Commonwealth of Kentucky:

§ 1. That no part of the lands now owned and occupied by John and Mary E. Seaton, as their residence, shall be included within the corporation or town boundary of the town of Greenupsburg, nor shall it be subject to the jurisdiction or control of the trustees or other officers of said town, either for the purpose of taxation or for any other purpose whatever, but shall be excluded therefrom: *Provided, however,* That said land shall be subject to the juris-

diction of the county and State for all purposes, the same 1869.
as though this act had not been passed.

§ 2. All acts or parts of acts inconsistent with this act
are hereby repealed.

§ 3. This act shall be in force from its passage.

Approved March 4, 1869.

———

CHAPTER 1728.

AN ACT incorporating the Franklin Manufacturing Company.

Be it enacted by the General Assembly of the Commonwealth
of Kentucky:

§ 1. That W. F. Collier, R. D. Solmonds, W. W. Evans,
W. W. Howell, J. B. Lewis, D. McVow, and J. B. Harris,
and their successors, are hereby created a body-politic and
corporate, in the name and style of the Franklin Manufacturing Company, and by that name have perpetual succession; may contract and be contracted with, sue and be
sued, plead and be impleaded, in all courts and places;
have a common seal, and break or alter the same at
pleasure; and may have all necessary or convenient by-
aws, rules and regulations, for the government of said
company, and the management of said business, not inconsistent with the State or Federal Constitutions.

§ 2. That said company shall have power and authority
to appoint any one or more of its members, or other person
or persons, to manage, control, and direct the business
thereof according to the by-laws, rules and regulations,
which may, from time to time, be adopted by said company for its government and the transaction of its business; and said company may be organized by the aforesaid
corporators, or a majority thereof, at such time and place
as they may appoint.

§ 3. That the capital stock of said company shall not
exceed five hundred thousand dollars, divided into shares
of one hundred dollars each, which shall be subscribed in
such manner, and paid in at such times and in such installments, as may be prescribed by said company in its
by-laws, which by-laws may provide, upon the non-payment of such assessment, or any part thereof, within the
time fixed for their payment, that the appropriate officer
or agent of the company may proceed in the manner prescribed by the by-laws of the corporation to advertise and
sell such delinquent shares, or so many of them as may
be necessary to pay the sums due thereon, with incidental
charges.

§ 4. The said company shall have power to hold such
estate, real, personal, or mixed, in Kentucky, by purchase,

lease, or otherwise, as it may deem necessary and proper for carrying on a foundry and general manufacturing business, the conversion of timber into lumber, the manufacture of iron of all sorts, and the building of houses, machinery, and other thing which may be necessary for manufacturing as aforesaid, and the transportation of coal, iron, or lumber, and all other things, with power to sell and convey all such products, material, and estate at pleasure; and to some one or more or all of the purposes and objects aforesaid the business of said company shall be confined: *Provided, however,* That whatever may be necessary and expedient as incidental to said business is not excluded from the power of said company.

§ 5. The said company may borrow money on such terms, and secure the same in such way, as may be prescribed by the by-laws or determined on by the stockholders; but no banking privileges are granted to said company.

§ 6. This act shall take effect from and after its passage.

Approved March 4, 1869.

————

CHAPTER 1729.

AN ACT to amend the Charter of Jefferson Seminary, in Barren County.

WHEREAS, On the 30th day of January, 1828, a charter was granted by the Kentucky Legislature incorporating Jefferson Seminary, in Barren county, in which act Robert Ferguson and others were named as trustees, who afterwards organized as such under said charter, took possession of the buildings and property of said seminary, and conducted its affairs through a long series of years, during which time various ones of the trustees died and others were selected and qualified in their stead; but it is now represented that all the trustees named in said charter, and all who have been selected and qualified in their places, are dead, except John B. Wilson; therefore,

Be it enacted by the General Assembly of the Commonwealth of Kentucky:

§ 1. That Tho. W. Bibb, Henry H. Burks, and Nathan Burks, are hereby appointed trustees, with said John B. Wilson, of said seminary; and they, with him, are declared to be vested with all the powers, rights and privileges, which, by said act, were conferred upon the said Ferguson and others named in said act.

§ 2. This act to take effect from its passage.

Approved March 4, 1869.

CHAPTER 1730.

AN ACT to incorporate the Germania Market Company, of Louisville.

Be it enacted by the General Assembly of the Commonwealth of Kentucky:

§ 1. That John Engeln, Francis Reidhar, Jacob Schmidt, Philip Winkler, Michael Billing, George P. Doern, Julius Von Borries, and James R. Delvecchio, their associates and successors, be, and they are hereby, created a body corporate and politic, by the name of the "Germania Market Company," for and during the term of thirty years, with all the powers and authority incident to corporations, for the purposes hereinafter mentioned.

§ 2. The said corporation may erect buildings, purchase, have, hold, retain, enjoy, sell, lease, and 'convey the necessary real and personal estate to carry on the business of a market for the sale and purchase of meats, vegetables, fruits, wares and merchandise, anywhere within the city of Louisville; and may rent stalls or apartments to any other person or persons.

§ 3. The capital stock of said corporation shall not be less than one hundred thousand dollars nor more than three hundred thousand dollars, divided into shares of one hundred dollars each, which shall be personal estate, and transferable on the books of the corporation in such manner as shall be prescribed by the by-laws.

§ 4. The business of said corporation shall be managed and conducted by not less than three nor more than seven directors, one of whom shall be chosen president, and all of whom shall be stockholders, and hold their offices for one year or until their successors are elected and qualified. The directors shall make all by-laws necessary or proper for the management of the business; may appoint and employ all agents and servants they may deem necessary or proper, and do all things expedient for the successful prosecution of the said business.

§ 5. The above-named corporators, or such of them as a majority shall appoint, may open books of subscription to the capital stock of said corporation, on such terms and conditions as they may prescribe; and when one hundred thousand dollars shall be subscribed, the said corporation may commence business.

§ 6. At all meetings of the stockholders, each share of capital stock shall be entitled to one vote. The by-laws shall prescribe the time and manner of the election of directors, and the number of stockholders or directors necessary to constitute a quorum for the transaction of business.

§ 7. The said corporation may borrow money on such terms and conditions, and at such rates of interest, as may be agreed on, and secure the same by mortgage

1869.   upon the whole or any part of its franchises and property; and may issue and sell its bonds, bearing such rate
of interest as may be prescribed, not exceeding ten per
cent. per annum, and secure said bonds by mortgage
upon the whole or any part of its franchises or property:
Provided, however, That the sum or sums so borrowed,
and the bonds so issued, shall not, at any one time, exceed the capital stock subscribed.

§ 8. The said corporation may contract or be contracted
with, sue and be sued, defend and be defended, in all courts
and places whatsoever by its said corporate name; and
may have and use a common seal, and the same may
break, alter, or renew at pleasure; but the failure to use
a common seal shall not invalidate any of its contracts.

§ 9. The above-named corporators, or such of them as
the majority shall select, shall be the first board of directors of said corporation, and shall hold their offices for one
year, or until their successors are elected and qualified.

§ 10. This act shall take effect from and after its passage.

Approved March 4, 1869.

CHAPTER 1731.

AN ACT to incorporate the United Circle, Daughters of Rebecca.

*Be it enacted by the General Assembly of the Commonwealth
of Kentucky:*

§ 1. That Susannah Fink, Philipina Deuser, Anna
Kirsch, Maria Braun, and Sophia Schiller, with their
associates, successors, and assigns, be, and are hereby,
created a corporation and body-politic, with perpetual
succession, by the name, style, and title of United Circle,
Daughters of Rebecca, of Louisville, Kentucky, for the
purpose of mutual relief and assistance in sickness and
distress; and in that name are hereby made as capable
in law as natural persons to contract and be contracted
with, to sue and be sued, to answer and be answered, in
any court of law and equity in this Commonwealth; and
to make, have, and use a common seal, the same to alter
or exchange at pleasure. Said corporators shall have the
power to prescribe the necessary qualifications of members, and establish the admission fee to be paid by each
person, and prescribe such other rules and regulations as
they may deem necessary for the control and government
of their association:

§ 2. The fund accumulated from admission fees, dues,
donations, &c., may be invested in stocks, bonds, mortgages or real estate, as the association may select.

§ 3. This act shall take effect and be in force from and after its passage.

Approved March 4, 1869.

CHAPTER 1732.

AN ACT to amend the Charter and to extend the Corporation of the Town of Independence.

Be it enacted by the General Assembly of the Commonwealth of Kentucky:

§ 1. That so much of an act, entitled "An act to reduce into one the several acts in regard to the town of Lancaster, and for other purposes," approved March 9th, 1867, and made applicable to the town of Independence, and the police judge and the police court of Independence, as requires four trustees to make their acts binding, shall, wherever four occur in said act, be legal if done by a majority of their body; and that the 29th section of said act be made to read, "fines and costs owing said town," instead of "fines owing said town;" and where the same reads, "two dollars per day," the same shall be made to read, "not less than one nor more than two dollars per day;" and that the conclusion of the 21st section of said act, where it reads, "the town of Lancaster," the same shall read, "the county of Kenton;" and in all other places in said act, "Independence" shall take the place of "Lancaster," and "Kenton" for "Garrard," wherever the same occurs.

§ 2. That the corporation of the town of Independence be extended by continuing the north and south lines of the same a due west course, sufficiently far, so that a parallel line to the original line of said corporation will inclose the residence of G. W. Carlisle: *Provided,* That the land of said Carlisle shall not be taxed for town purposes until the same shall be laid out into town lots. That the said north and south lines extend east twenty poles by parallel lines to the original corporate line: *Provided also,* That the land included thereby, belonging to E. J. McCollum, shall not be taxed for town purposes until the same be laid out in town lots. That the east and west lines, as here described, extend north twenty rods from the original corporate line, and so far as will make a line running due east and west intersect the same on the west line.

§ 3. That this act shall take effect from its passage.

Approved March 4, 1869.

CHAPTER 1733.

AN ACT to Charter the Glasgow Manufacturing Company.

Be it enacted by the General Assembly of the Commonwealth of Kentucky:

§ 1. That a corporation is hereby created, by the name and style of the Glasgow Manufacturing Company, to be located in Barren county, Kentucky. Said corporation shall be capable of contracting and being contracted with, suing and being sued, pleading and being impleaded, and shall have all the rights, immunities, and powers that may be necessary and proper for the management and prosecuting of its business, which shall be the manufacturing of wool, cotton, flax, hemp, and tow into rolls, batting, thread, yarn, cloth, or other things into which said articles can be manufactured; and the manufacturing of grain into meal, flour, and other articles, and the manufacturing of lumber; also the sale of the same. The corporation may purchase and hold real estate to the value of one hundred thousand dollars, or may lease the same, in or out of the State; and may purchase and sell such machinery, buildings, or personal property, and convey the same, as they may deem necessary, from time to time.

§ 2. The capital stock of the company shall not exceed one hundred thousand dollars, in shares of fifty dollars each. Subscriptions of stock shall be made by persons signing their names to an agreement to take the number of shares placed opposite their names, and obligating themselves to pay the Glasgow Manufacturing Company the amount thereof. J. W. Dickey, J. N. Locke, Meredith Reynolds, P. H. Leslie, John Lewis, T. M. Dickey, M. M. Winlock, and Amasa P. Childress, or any three of them, may open a book or books for subscription to such an agreement; and whenever the sum of ten thousand dollars is subscribed, they may call together the subscribers, who may organize the corporation by electing a president and four managers.

§ 3. The president and managers shall hold their offices for one year, and until their successors are elected and qualified; and shall conduct and manage the affairs of the corporation in such manner as the stockholders, by their by-laws, shall direct.

§ 4. There shall be an annual meeting of the stockholders, and oftener if called by the president and managers, or a majority of the stockholders in interest. At every such meeting, the president and managers shall submit a full statement of the affairs, business, and accounts of said corporation; and additional stock may be subscribed until the whole amount authorized by this act is taken.

§ 5. Each stockholder shall be entitled to one vote for every share of stock owned by him, and to vote in person or by proxy, at every regular or called meeting. The president and managers may, from time to time, as they see fit, make calls on the shareholders not exceeding twenty per cent. at any one time.

§ 6. The president and managers may appoint a superintendent, and such other officers as may be necessary or proper to manage its affairs, and prescribe their duties.

§ 7. The stockholders may dissolve the corporation when they think proper to do so; and, upon such dissolution, the corporate powers of the president and managers shall continue for five years thereafter; and the power to sue and be sued in the name of the corporation shall continue for the same length of time, to allow the managers to sell property and wind up the business of the corporation.

§ 8. The stockholders, after they have paid the full amount of stock subscribed by them, shall not be liable for any debt or obligation or contract entered into or contracted by the corporation, and at no time for a greater amount than that subscribed by them.

§ 9. This act to take effect from its passage.

Approved March 4, 1869.

CHAPTER 1734.

AN ACT to establish the Southwest Kentucky Mutual Aid and Benevolent Life Insurance Company.

Be it enacted by the General Assembly of the Commonwealth of Kentucky:

§ 1. That Edward J. Bullock, Milton H. Wright, of Hickman county; Samuel H. Jenkins, John R. Kemp, of Ballard county; Irvin Anderson and John Eaker, of Graves county; Peter Boaz, Joel W. Ferguson, of Calloway county; Jesse C. Gilbert and John Dycus, of Marshall county; L. D. Husbands, J. Q. A. King, T. S. McGuire, R. M. Harding, and A. Heimeberger, of McCracken county, be, and they are hereby, constituted and created a body corporate and politic, by the name and style of the "Southwest Kentucky Mutual Aid and Benevolent Life Insurance Company;" and by that name they are empowered to sue and be sued, plead and be impleaded, and shall have the right to make contracts; to own, purchase, and receive by donation, and to sell and convey property, real or personal; to deal in bills of exchange and negotiable notes.

§ 2. The object of this corporation shall be to contract for the assurance of life, to issue policies for life insurance, and to do all acts relative to that kind of insurance, in accordance with the terms and provisions hereinafter specified; and this company shall have the right to reinsure in other companies if desirable, but at its own costs and expense, and for its own benefit.

§ 3. All administrative powers shall be vested in fifteen directors, of whom five shall form a quorum, and such other officers and clerks as they may appoint. The directors shall hold their office for the term of two years from the date of their appointment or election. The persons above named shall constitute the first board of directors, and shall hold office for the term of two years from the day of their first convening. In the event of a vacancy of the board of directors, occasioned by the decease or resignation of a member or otherwise, before the expiration of the term of his appointment, such vacancy shall be supplied by the election of a fit and proper person by the remainder of the board. The board of directors shall, at their first meeting, elect a president, a vice president, a secretary, and a treasurer, and such other officers as may be necessary to carry on the business of the association, which last may be elected, from time to time, as required. No one shall be a director who is not a member of this company. The president shall be a member of the board of directors, and preside at all meetings of the board and at the meetings of the policy-holders, and shall conduct the business of the company generally under the supervision of the board of directors. The vice president shall be a member of the board of directors, and shall preside at the meetings aforesaid in the absence of the president, and, in his absence, sign the policies of insurance. The secretary and treasurer, and such employes as the president may appoint, shall, before entering upon the discharge of their duties, give bond, with security, approved by the board of directors, conditioned for the faithful discharge of their duties.

§ 4. Each person admitted a member of this company shall pay into the treasury, if between the ages of sixteen (16) and thirty (30) years, inclusive, the sum of ten dollars; between the ages of thirty-one (31) and forty (40) years, inclusive, fifteen dollars; between the ages of forty-one (41) and fifty (50) years, inclusive, twenty dollars, and between the ages of fifty-one (51) and sixty (60) years, inclusive, twenty-five dollars, which sum shall entitle the party who has paid it to a life insurance policy, which shall entitle the policy-holder to a sum equal to one dollar for each enrolled member on the books of the company at the date of his or her death, payable to his or her representative or assigns, within sixty days after the receipt of a certified evidence of the death of the policy-holder; but in no case shall the amount paid on said policy exceed three thousand dollars. Whenever the number of members shall exceed three thousand, contribution of all the members, exceeding three thousand dollars, shall be set apart as a separate fund, and on the decease of any policy-holder thereafter, and so long as said contribution exceeds three thousand dollars, the excess shall be appropriated *pro rata*, for the purpose of diminishing said contribution or assessment. The said diminution shall be the same for each and every member of the company.

§ 5 On the notification of the death of any policy-holder to the officers of the company, accompanied with a certificate fully setting forth the facts, and indorsed by the attending physician or jury of inquest, an assessment shall be made upon each policy-holder for a sum not to exceed one dollar and twenty-five cents, which is payable at the office of the company within thirty days after notification. The failure to pay this assessment within the above-stated time, on the part of any policy-holder, shall operate a forfeiture of his or her policy, and the name of such delinquent shall be erased from the books of the company, unless sufficient reasons are given, to be submitted to and determined upon by the board of directors within a reasonable time thereafter, and the assessment paid into the treasury. Any policy-holder who has forfeited his policy, from neglect to pay the regular assessment on the decease of a member, shall be debarred from all benefit arising from the previous subscriptions; but he shall not be prevented from applying for a new policy by a subscription as a new member. All application for membership, or to become a policy-holder in this company, must be made in writing to the board of directors, stating the name, age, residence, and occupation of the applicant; and any false statement that shall become apparent to the board of directors after the issue of the policy shall annul said policy. No application shall be received unless accompanied with certificate from a respectable physician, or the company's physician, that the applicant is in good health, and free from pulmonary or other constitutional disease; the company reserving the right to have any applicant, upon his certificate from any other than the company's physician, examined by the company's physician; and in all cases when he makes an examination, he shall be allowed a fee of one dollar, to be paid by the applicant. All transfers of policies shall be made upon the books of the company.

§ 6. Upon the death of a member, the secretary shall immediately notify the policy-holders of the fact, and call for the contribution specified in section four, by causing said notification to be published in five consecutive issues of that newspaper which has the largest circulation in the city of Paducah, and by letter addressed to the nearest post-office to those who live at a greater distance than forty miles from Paducah; and such publication or letter so addressed shall be due notice to each policy-holder; and on failure to comply within the time and in the manner specified in said section four, he or she shall forfeit his or her policy as policy-holders in said company: *Provided*, That any policy-holder who shall deposit in the treasury an amount to cover any specified number, as assessments paid in advance, and required to be paid by section four, and at the same time furnish the secretary, in writing, with name of the post-office nearest his residence, the policy of such policy-holder shall not be declared forfeited until after said amount deposited shall have been exhausted, and such policy-holder notified thereof, and the failure thereafter of said policy-holder to comply with section four respecting assessments.

§ 7. Before the term of office of the incumbent directors shall expire, the president shall appoint three discreet policy-holders, who shall be judges of election. They shall cause the policy-holders to be notified of the time and place of election of new directors, by publication for one month in some newspaper published in Paducah.

§ 8. The principal office of business of this company shall be in the city of Paducah, and the enrollment book of the company shall be open to access, at all times, to policy-holders.

§ 9. Should the net earnings of the company exceed sixty thousand dollars, the board of directors shall have the right to distribute such excess, from time to time, to the policy-holders, *per capita*, as dividends on the profits of the company: *Provided*, That no member shall be entitled to such dividends who has not been a member for twelve months next preceding the day said dividends shall be declared.

§ 10. No person shall be admitted as a member of this company except those between the ages of sixteen and sixty years.

§ 11. No member of this company shall be liable for any of the obligations of the company, beyond the sum or sums which may be due by such member in virtue of the requirements specified in section four.

Approved March 4, 1869.

CHAPTER 1735.

AN ACT to fix the corporate boundary of Cave City, in Barren County.

Be it enacted by the General Assembly of the Commonwealth of Kentucky:

§ 1. That an act, entitled "An act to incorporate the 'town of Cave City, in Barren county," approved February 2, 1866, be, and the same is hereby, repealed; and that the same is incorporated with the following boundary, to-wit: Beginning at a stone on the east side of the Louisville and Nashville turnpike, forty yards above Geo. T. Middleton's old dwelling; thence north 60, west 80 poles, to the Louisville and Nashville railroad track; thence north 60, west 400 yards, to a stone; thence southwest, on a parallel line with the Louisville and Nashville railroad, to the line between the Duke and Owen lands, to a stone; thence with said line south, 45 east, to a stone in the west side of the Louisville and Nashville pike, J. N. T. Rodgers' corner; thence south 45, east 84 poles, to 4 stones planted on the land of B. D. Curd; thence north 44, east 199 poles, with Curd's line, to Mr. L. Fisher's or A. Duke's corner-stone; thence with Duke's line north 41, west 43½ poles, to a stone at Duke's original corner; thence north 60, west 63 poles, with Middleton's (Duke's old) line, to a stone planted in the southeast side of the Louisville and Nashville pike; thence north 25, east 46 poles and 20 chains, to the beginning. The boundary herein shall be known by the name and style of the town of Cave City; and E. M. Hatcher, John N. T. Rodgers, Louis Viol, Geo. W. Poynter, and Samuel J. Preston, the present board of trustees, are hereby reappointed a board of trustees of said town of Cave City, who shall continue in office until the first Saturday in May, 1869, and until their successors are duly elected and qualified; they and their successors, before entering upon the duties of their office shall, in addition to the oath prescribed by the Constitution, take an oath before some justice of the peace, notary public, or other judge for Barren county, that they will faithfully and without partiality, favor, or affection to any one, discharge the duties of trustees of the town of Cave City, during their continuance in office; they shall record a plat of the survey of said town, which shall form part of their record.

§ 2. That hereafter the prudential, fiscal, and municipal concerns of Cave City shall be vested in the five trustees appointed by this act, and their successors, who shall be elected annually on the first Saturday in May, by the qualified voters resident in said town; said trustees, when elected, shall hold their office for the term of one year, and until their successors are elected and duly

Boundary of town.

Name & style of town, and first board of trustees, &c.

In whom fiscal and municipal concerns vested, & when trustees elected.

1869.

Vacancies in
board, and cor-
porate powers.

qualified; and when a vacancy may occur from any cause, the board of trustees shall have power to fill the same until the next annual election; that the board of trustees appointed by this act, and their successors, shall be a body-politic and corporate, and shall be known by the name and style of the board of trustees of the town of Cave City; and by that name shall be capable in law of contracting and being contracted with, of suing and being sued, pleading and being impleaded, answering and being answered, and in all courts and places, and in all matters and things whatsoever, and do all acts, matters and things, which a body-politic or corporate having perpetual succession can lawfully and regularly do; and may have and use a corporate seal, and change, alter, and renew the same at pleasure.

Chairman of
board, his pow-
ers and duties.

§ 3. That said trustees, after their qualification, shall elect one of their number chairman, who shall preside over the deliberations of said board when convened, and have power to convene the same, when, in his opinion, the interest of the town demands it. It shall be his duty to see that all the ordinances and by-laws of said town are duly executed; he shall have power to issue warrants in the absence of the police judge hereafter provided for, and to administer oaths, which shall, in every particular, be as valid as if done by said judge. They

Clerk.

shall elect one of their number clerk, who shall keep a fair record of all the proceedings of the board, which shall be open for inspection of any person desirous of seeing the same, and do and perform such services as

Treasurer.

the board may require; they shall elect one of their number treasurer, who shall receive all moneys collected, and pay the same to the order of the board. It shall be the duty of the treasurer to render to said board an account of all moneys received and paid out by him whenever required so to do; said treasurer shall execute bond with approved security, for the faithful performance of his duty, payable to the board of trustees of the town of Cave City, and their successors in office, in such penalty as said board may direct; they shall elect one of

Assessor.

their number assessor, who shall take a list of all the taxable inhabitants and owners of property in said town, and affix against each separately the amount of his, her, or their whole estate within said town, subject to taxation under the laws of this Commonwealth, or any ordinance of said town, which list shall be taken in the same manner that the revenue lists are now or may hereafter be taken, and return or deliver the same to the clerk of the board of trustees, whose duty it shall be to make out and deliver a fair copy of the same to the collector hereinafter provided for, and take his receipt therefor; and the trustees shall, by their warrant, authorize and direct the collector to collect the same; and shall make said clerk, assessor, collector, and other town officers, such compensation as they may deem proper. The regular meetings of said board shall be on the first Thursday in each month, when a majority shall constitute a quorum for the transaction of business; all business transacted at a called meeting shall be as valid as though transacted at a regular meeting: *Provided*, That four trustees are present.

§ 4. That said trustees, or a majority of them, shall have power to make or receive all necessary conveyances in relation to said town. They shall have power to open streets, alleys, and passways in said town, and have power over the same; and may, by an ordinance passed by said board of trustees, require the owners of lots to make sidewalks or pavements of stone or brick, not exceeding ten feet wide, in front of their respective lots, when in their judgment the interest of the town demands it. They shall have power to levy and collect an ad valorem tax on the property in said town, not exceeding ten cents on each one hundred dollars in any one year, and a poll-tax on each male person over the age of twenty-one years, not exceeding one dollar. They shall have power to tax auctions, sales, shows and exhibitions for money or profit, such sums as they may deem proper and just, or as may be, from time to time, provided in their ordinances or by-laws. They shall have the power to suppress all tippling and gambling-houses, and to fine all those who may violate their by-laws and ordinances any sum not exceeding twenty-five dollars. They shall have the right to tax and the right to license all coffee-houses, victualers, confectioneries, restaurants, and fix the tax thereon in any sum not exceeding two hundred dollars per annum, and to discontinue any of said licenses at pleasure: *Provided*, The treasurer of the board of trustees shall pay to the trustee of the jury fund for Barren county the sum that is now or may be required by the laws of this Commonwealth for each license in said town each year. Any law giving the county court of Barren county authority to license merchants and druggists to sell spirituous liquors in said town or corporation is hereby repealed; but the license which any merchant, druggist, or coffee-house keeper has obtained shall be good until the time shall have expired for which it was obtained.

§ 5. That there is hereby created and established in said town a police court, to be known and styled Cave City police court, the officers of which shall consist of a judge and marshal. R. C. Hayslip, the present police judge of said town, is hereby appointed judge of said court, who

1869.

Meetings.

May make conveyances.

May levy and collect tax.

May tax auctions.

Police court established.

1869.

shall continue in office until the first Saturday in May, 1869, and until his successor shall be duly elected and qualified. W. H. Pace, the present marshal for said town, is hereby appointed marshal of said court, who shall continue in office until the first Saturday in May, 1869, and until his successor shall be duly elected and qualified. The successor of said judge shall be commissioned by the Governor; and, before entering upon the duties of his office, in addition to the oath prescribed by the Constitution, take an oath before some justice of the peace, police or other judge, or notary public for Barren county, that he will, to the best of his ability, faithfully, and without partiality, favor or affection to any one, discharge the duties of judge of Cave City police court during his continuance in office. The successor of said marshal, before entering upon the duties of his office, in

Additional oath of marshal

addition to the oath prescribed by the Constitution, take an oath before the judge of said police court to faithfully and impartially, without favor or affection to any one, discharge the duties of marshal of Cave City police court during his continuance in office; and shall execute a bond, with one or more good and sufficient securities, to be approved by the judge of said court, in the same penalty, payable to the Commonwealth of Kentucky, and with the same conditions of a constable's bond; and the same may be put in suit for a failure to perform the conditions of said bond by any one injured, in the same manner suits are now authorized to be brought on a constable's bond; and said marshal and his securities shall also be subject to motions against them before said police court or other tribunals having jurisdiction for a failure of duty or to pay over money to the persons entitled to receive the same, under the same rules, regulations and restrictions, as motions are authorized to be made against constables. That said judge, so soon as said bond is executed, shall attest the same, and deliver it to the clerk of the Barren county court, who shall carefully preserve and file it in his office, and shall give attested copies, when required so to do by any person, which shall have the same force and credit in all courts of justice as other records from said office are entitled to under existing laws. Said clerk shall receive therefor such fees as are allowed by law for similar services.

Judge to be elected. Term of office.

§ 6. That the persons entitled to vote for trustees of said town shall, at the time and place of the election of trustees in 1869, and every two years thereafter, elect a judge of Cave City police court, who shall hold his office for the term of two years, and until his successor is duly elected and qualified; and when a vacancy occurs in said office, by death or otherwise, it shall be filled by an election for the remainder of the term, upon ten days' notice being given, in three or more public places in said town, of the time and place of said election, by the board of trustees, or any two of them. The judge appointed by this act, and his successors, when elected, commissioned, and qualified, shall be a conservator of the peace throughout Barren county. His jurisdiction, both civil and criminal, shall be the same as that which now is, or may hereafter be, conferred by law on justices of the peace, except as a court of inquiry in criminal cases, in which he shall have the jurisdiction of two justices of the peace, and shall proceed in like manner. He shall have jurisdiction of all offenses arising under the ordinances and by-laws of said town; and shall have power and authority to compel witnesses to attend and give evidence in cases pending before him, or to give their deposition, and to enter judgment and award execution accordingly, and to fine for contempt, provided the fine in no case shall exceed ten dollars. He shall have jurisdiction of all cases of motions and suits against the treasurer, marshal, or other officers of said town, for all sums of money or other thing which may be due from them or either of them. He shall have power to take depositions, keep his own records, and shall be subject to the same penalties imposed on justices of the peace for violation of duty. He shall keep a docket of cases in the order in which they are tried, showing the various steps taken therein, the judgment issued, and the return of execution; and shall safely keep all papers in every case tried by him, and make and keep a complete index to his records and execution book. He shall be allowed the same fees in civil and penal cases that justices of the peace are now or may hereafter be allowed for similar services. He shall have power to issue fee bills, and collect them, in the same manner as justices of the peace. He may direct any or all process to the marshal of Cave City police court, the sheriff, or any constable of Barren county. He shall hold a court for the trial of civil causes on the first Saturday in each of the months of February, May, August, and November.

His powers and duties.

§ 7. Appeals may be taken from the judgment of said court in the same manner, and under like regulations, as are taken from judgments of justices of the peace and the courts having like jurisdiction of them.

Appeals may be had.

§ 8. The certified copies of the official acts, records, and proceedings of said court, shall be evidence and have the same effect as records of justices of the peace.

§ 9. That the judge of said court shall be removable in the same manner and for the causes that justices of the peace are now or may hereafter be removable.

Judge may be removed.

§ 10. That the persons entitled to vote for trustees of said town shall, at the time and place of the election of trustees

Marshal to be elected, his powers & duties.

1869.

in 1869, and every two years thereafter, elect a marshal of
Cave City police court, who shall hold his office for the
term of two years, and until his successor is duly elected
and qualified; and if a vacancy occurs in said office from
any cause, it shall be filled by the judge of said court, as
vacancies in the office of constable are now filled by the
judge of the county court. The marshal appointed by this
act, and his successor, when elected and qualified, shall be
conservators of the peace throughout Barren county. He
shall have the same power and authority to execute all
original, mesne, and final process issued by the judge of
said police court, or other tribunal or officer, as constables
may now or hereafter have; in doing which, he may go to
any portion of the county, and shall be governed in the
service and execution of process by the same rules, regulations and laws, that now is or may hereafter govern them
in the service and execution of process; and shall be alike
liable for property held by virtue of a process, or for money
collected by him. It shall be his duty to serve all process
and precepts to him directed from the said police judge,
and make due return thereof; collect all taxes of said town,
executions, and other demands, which may be put into his
hands to collect, and account for and pay over the same to
whosoever may be entitled thereto, under the same rules
and regulations required of sheriffs in the collection of the
taxes, and of constables in the collection of executions or
other demands. He shall have the same power and be
entitled to the same fees for collecting the town taxes and
levy that sheriffs have for collecting the State tax and
county levy, and in all other cases the same fees allowed
constables in similar cases. He shall be vested with all
powers and authority which is given constables in all cases
cognizable before said police judge, a justice of the peace,
or other tribunal. He shall have power, if need be, to summon the aid of the county in executing any process to him
directed; and any person failing or refusing to aid him
when so summoned, may be fined by said police judge not
exceeding ten dollars.

§ 11. That each successive marshal elected as herein

Marshal to
deliver papers
to his success-
or.

directed, when he goes out of office, shall deliver to his
successor such papers as may need further official action.

Who to con-
duct elections.

§ 12. That all elections authorized by this act shall be
held by the board of trustees of said town, or any two of
them, who shall preside as judge, and shall have power to
appoint a clerk, to all of whom an oath shall first be administered by some justice of the peace, police or other
judge, or notary public for Barren county, faithfully and
impartially to discharge the duties of judges and clerk of
said election according to law.

§ 13. That any of said trustees, holding election as judges thereof, shall have power and authority to administer an oath to any one offering to vote; and for false swearing or illegal voting, the offender shall be liable and subject to the same penalties and the same punishment, and be proceeded against in the same manner, as are prescribed by the general laws of this Commonwealth for like offenses.

§ 14. That the officers holding said election shall make out and sign a certificate showing the result, and hand the same to the clerk of the Barren county court, who shall immediately record the same in a book to be by him procured and kept for that purpose; and said clerk shall receive such compensation therefor as is now allowed by law for similar services, to be paid out of the corporation funds of said town.

§ 15. That the clerk of said county court, so soon as he receives said certificate, shall forward by mail an attested copy of the same to the Governor of this Commonwealth, so far as the election of police judge is concerned, who shall, thereupon, issue a commission to the person thus returned elected as police judge of said town, and forward the same to his address: *Provided*, That this act shall not be so construed as to require R. C Hayslip, the present judge, and W. H. Pace, the present marshal of the Cave City police court, to again qualify under this act; but that their bonds now on file in the clerk's office of the Barren county court as police judge and marshal of said Cave City police court be continued in force the same as if this act had not been passed.

§ 16. That this act shall not be construed to impair any contract or invalidate any act or proceeding whatever, done by authority of the charter or act for which this is a substitute, or the by-laws made in conformity therewith.

§ 17. That all moneys for fines, forfeitures, taxes, licenses, &c., shall be paid to the treasurer of the board of trustees, to be by said board disposed of for the improvement and best interest of said town: *Provided*, That this section shall not be so construed as to exempt the treasurer of the board of trustees from paying to the trustee of the jury fund the taxes required by the fourth section of this act.

Approved March 4, 1869.

1869.

Judges of elections may administer oaths.

Result of election to be certified.

Police judge to be commissioned.

Fines, &c., to be paid to town treasurer.

CHAPTER 1736.

AN ACT for the benefit of the Citizens of Barbourville, in Knox County.

Be it enacted by the General Assembly of the Commonwealth of Kentucky:

§ 1. That the sheriff of Knox county cause an election to be held at the court-house, in the town of Barbourville, on the first Monday in May, 1869, and shall cause a poll to be opened in favor of prohibiting the sale of spirituous liquors by retail within two miles of said town, also, a poll against said prohibition; and he will, as sheriff, conduct said election.

§ 2. That all persons living within two miles of the court-house in said town, who are qualified under the laws of the State to vote at any State election, shall have the right to vote at said election.

§ 3. That William Mathews and Thomas J. Pitzer are hereby authorized and constituted judges at said election, and R. P. Stickley is appointed clerk; but before they act, they shall take an oath before some justice of the peace or county judge, that they will faithfully and impartially discharge the duties of judges and clerk respectively; and in case any of the officers fail to act, the other officers, after they have been sworn, shall appoint; and after the person appointed shall have been sworn, he shall act; or should all refuse, the county judge shall appoint the officers, who shall in like manner act, when sworn as before stated.

§ 4. That said election shall be in every respect conducted as other elections authorized by law, and shall be published by written notice on the court-house door, and three other public places in the town of Barbourville, for at least ten days before the election; and if, at said election, a majority of the citizens living within two miles of the town vote in favor of the prohibition of the sale of ardent spirits within the limits aforesaid, the judges and clerk of the election shall certify the same to the county judge, who shall cause said certificate to be entered of record in his office, and shall cause a copy thereof to be posted upon the court-house door, and upon the front door of each tavern within the limits aforesaid, together with notice to cease the sale of spirituous liquors. After the same has been done, he shall enter an order on his record that this act has been complied with, at which time this act shall be in force; and it shall be unlawful for any person to sell or vend ardent spirits, directly or indirectly, within two miles of the court-house in the town of Barbourville; and any person violating this statute shall be dealt with as now provided by law to prevent the illegal sale of spirituous liquors. But this act shall not be so construed as to prohibit any druggist, physician, or merchant from keeping pure spirits, which may be sold in case of sickness for medical purposes, when prescribed by any practicing physician, he certifying that such spirits are necessary: *Provided, however*, That nothing in this act contained shall be so construed as to prohibit any person from selling spirituous liquors within said boundary until the expiration of any license which may have been granted him prior to the passage of this act.

§ 5. This act shall take effect from its passage.

Approved ·March 4, 1869.

CHAPTER 1737.

AN ACT to amend an act, entitled "An act to incorporate the Town of Mayslick," approved February 1, 1837.

Be it enacted by the General Assembly of the Commonwealth of Kentucky:

§ 1. That an act to incorporate the town of Mayslick, approved February 1, 1837, be, and the same is hereby, so amended as to authorize and empower the trustees of the town to extend the limits of the town so as to take in and embrace the residence of George Myall or the property of Miss Lizzie Mathews, the residence lately owned by R. D. Chinn, and the dwelling situated upon the seminary lot.

§ 2. That it shall be lawful, at any election of trustees for said town, to elect a police judge and town marshal for the term of two years, whose qualifications shall be the same as are required under the act of incorporation for trustees of the town; and the police judge shall have, within the limits of the town, and for a distance of one half mile outside of the limits, the same jurisdiction over penal and criminal cases as justices of the peace now have under existing laws. He shall be a conservator of the peace, and have jurisdiction over affrays, assaults and batteries, riots, breaches of the peace, unlawful assemblies, all cases of indecent or immoral behavior or conduct, calculated to disturb the peace or dignity of the town; over all cases of drunkenness, Sabbath-breaking, running horses, firing guns or pistols, making reports by burning powder or fire-works, blowing horns, hallooing aloud by day or night, and other riotous and disorderly conduct within the limits of the town, all of which are hereby declared to be misdemeanors; and all fines imposed by the police judge of the town of Mayslick for any of the above-named misdemeanors shall, when collected, be paid into the treasury of the town. He shall have power to impose fines in all cases of misdemeanors to the amount of ten dollars, without the intervention of a jury, and shall have the right to imprison the person so fined in the county jail until the same is paid, by imprisonment at the rate of two dollars per day, in default of payment. He shall have power to issue subpœnas for witnesses in cases pending before him, and upon their failure to attend, may award compulsory process to compel their attendance. He shall have power to fine and imprison for contempt of court: *Provided*, The fine does not exceed ten dollars, nor the imprisonment twelve hours. That upon all judgments rendered by the said police judge, either party shall have the right of appeal from said judgments, in the same manner that appeals are taken from judgments of justices of the peace. The fees of police judge shall be the same as allowed justices in similar cases.

§ 3. The marshal shall see that the ordinances of the said town are carried into execution, and shall collect and pay over all fines imposed by the police judge for misdemeanors, &c. He shall serve or execute all processes issued by the police judge. He shall give bond for the faithful performance of his duties, in such sum as the trustees of the town may think proper, and take an oath to discharge faithfully his duties as marshal. He shall, within the limits allowed the police judge, have concurrent jurisdiction with the constables in penal and criminal cases, and his fees shall be the same as allowed to constables in similar cases.

§ 4. All vacancies that may occur after an election of either trustee, police judge, or town marshal, shall be filled by appointment by a majority of the trustees in office, until the next regular election.

§ 5. This act shall take effect from its passage.

Approved March 4, 1869.

CHAPTER 1738.

AN ACT to Charter the Wood House Company.

Be it enacted by the General Assembly of the Commonwealth of Kentucky:

§ 1. That William H. Sasseen, Robert J. Marten, John P. Glass, Hiram A. Phelps, John McGowan, and Joseph K. Gant, their associates and successors, be, and they are hereby, created a body-politic and corporate, by the name of "The Wood House Company;" and by that name shall have perpetual succession, may contract and be contracted with, sue and be sued, implead and defend, in all courts and places whatsoever, as if a natural person. The said company shall have power to acquire and hold, by purchase, gift, devise, or otherwise, in fee or for a term of years, such real estate and buildings in the city of Hopkinsville, Kentucky, as may be deemed necessary or expedient for a large and convenient hotel.

§ 2. The said company shall have power to keep, manage, and conduct a hotel in Hopkinsville; to purchase, from time to time, all necessary furniture, equipments, goods, and supplies; to employ clerks, servants, and other agents necessary or expedient for the keeping and management of its affairs. The said company may, if it should be deemed expedient, lease the said hotel, with or without furniture, for a term or term of years. It may erect and build all storehouses and other buildings deemed necessary or expedient for the successful keeping and conduct of said hotel; and lease or rent the same, or any part thereof, as may be deemed advisable.

§ 3. The capital stock of said company shall be fifty thousand dollars, divided into shares of one hundred dollars each; which shares shall be personal estate, and transferable on the books of the company in such manner as may be prescribed by its by-laws. Each share shall entitle the holder to one vote at all elections of directors and at all meetings of stockholders.

§ 4. The business of said company shall be conducted by a board of directors of not less than five nor more than seven, all of whom shall be the owners of at least five shares of its capital stock, and who shall hold their offices for one year, or until their successors are elected and qualified. The said directors shall choose one of their number president of the board; and the president and directors shall make by-laws prescribing the time and manner for holding annual elections of directors, the manner of filling vacancies caused by death, resignation, or otherwise; the number of directors necessary to make a quorum for the transaction of its business; and may also require bonds from the officers, agents, and servants of said company, and prescribe the manner and amount of said bonds; and may make all other regulations and by-laws, not inconsistent with the laws of the United States or of this State, necessary for its business.

§ 5. The persons hereinbefore named, or such of them as a majority shall appoint, shall be commissioners to open books of subscription, and prescribe the terms and manner of subscription for the capital stock of said company; and when not less than twenty thousand dollars of said capital stock of said company shall have been subscribed for in accordance with the terms and manner prescribed by said commissioners, the said company may organize and proceed to business; and the persons named in the first section of this act shall be the board of directors of said company, and hold their offices for one year, and until their successors are elected and qualified.

§ 6. The said company shall have power to borrow money, not exceeding fifty thousand dollars, at any rate of interest not exceeding eight per centum per annum, and issue its bonds therefor, for sums of one hundred dollars each, payable at any time not exceeding twenty years, with interest payable semi-annually, and secure the payment of said bonds by a mortgage or mortgages on any part or the whole of its property, real or personal.

§ 7. The said company may at any time sell and convey, or otherwise dispose of, the whole or any part of its property, real or personal, by the assent of three fifths of its directors.

§ 8. This act shall take effect from and after its passage.

Approved March 4, 1869.

CHAPTER 1739.

AN ACT to amend an act, entitled "An act to incorporate the Capital Mutual Life Insurance Company," approved February 17th, 1866.

Be it enacted by the General Assembly of the Commonwealth of Kentucky:

§ 1. That the name of the Capital Mutual Life Insurance Company shall be, and is hereby, changed to the "Capital Life Insurance Company, of Kentucky;" and in and by this name shall have and enjoy all the rights and franchises conferred by the act to which this is an amendment.

§ 2. That section four of the said act to which this is amended be, and the same is hereby, repealed; and in lieu thereof it is hereby enacted, that the corporate powers of the company shall be invested in and exercised by a board of directors, of not less than thirteen nor more than one hundred persons, and such officers and agents as the board of directors, or a majority of a quorum thereof, may appoint and empower. At least thirteen of the directors shall reside in the city of Frankfort or county of Franklin, and a majority of them shall constitute a quorum to do and transact the business of the corporation.

§ 3. That in addition to the persons named in the first section of the act to which this is an amendment, the following persons shall be incorporators, viz: Alvin Duvall, George W. Craddock, R. H Crittenden, J. S. Price, H. I. Todd, E. H. Taylor, jr., D. Howard Smith, A. G. Hodges, J. T. Gray, J. T. Boyle, W. A. Dudley, R. J. Browne, James W. Tate, W. A. Gaines, James Saffell, J. M. Todd, P. P. Oldershaw, W. R. Thompson, W. T. Scott, Charles

Bridges, G. Spratt, J. F. Speed, Grant Green, and T. A. Matthews, and together with those named in the first section of the act to which this is an amendment, shall be the first board of directors of the Capital Life Insurance Company, of Kentucky, and shall continue as directors until the first Tuesday in July, 1869, or until their successors are elected. The said directors, or thirteen of their number, or a majority of them, shall elect one of their number president; and a quorum of the board of directors may appoint, or authorize their president to appoint, a secretary, treasurer, general agent, and other agents and officers; but no person shall be president or director who is not a stockholder in the said company. The incorporators and directors hereinbefore named shall have authority and power to increase the number of the board of directors to a number not exceeding one hundred, who may reside in any counties of the State, excepting the thirteen required to be residents of Franklin county.

§ 4. That the Capital Life Insurance Company, of Kentucky, incorporated by this and the act to which this is an amendment, are hereby invested with authority to conduct insurance as a stock as well as a mutual insurance company; and to do and perform all other things relative to the objects of this incorporation, which now is or shall be lawful for any other life insurance company or corporation to do under the laws of the State of Kentucky, and shall be subject to any and all general insurance laws which are or may be hereafter in force in this State; and the said Capital Life Insurance Company, of Kentucky, may invest their capital and funds in United States, State, county, city, and railroad mortgage bonds, bank stock, and other stocks and securities, deemed safe and satisfactory by the board of directors, or such executive or financial committee as the board of directors may appoint.

§ 5. That any one or more of the persons herein named, or of those named in the act to which this is an amendment, may act as commissioners, and open books of subscription to the capital stock of the company at any time and place, with or without notice; and the said books shall be kept open until one hundred thousand dollars shall be subscribed; and at the time of subscription there shall be paid ten dollars on each share subscribed to the commissioner receiving subscription. The said company shall not commence business until one hundred thousand dollars are subscribed, and at least fifty thousand dollars shall be paid in, and be held in cash or invested before the said company shall commence business of insurance.

§ 6. That the last clause of section twenty-two of the act to which this is an amendment, limiting the duration of the company to thirty years, is hereby repealed, and the said company invested with perpetual succession of numbers.

§ 7. That sections eighteen and nineteen of the act to which this is an amendment are hereby repealed.

§ 8. That the capital stock of said company shall be divided into shares of fifty dollars each, instead of one hundred dollars each, as provided in act of incorporation.

§ 9. That this act shall be in force from and after its passage.

Approved March 4, 1869.

———

CHAPTER 1740.

AN ACT to extend the Limits of the City of Newport.

Be it enacted by the General Assembly of the Commonwealth of Kentucky:

That the following described tract of land, the property of James Taylor, is hereby added to and made part of the city of Newport, subject, however, to certain restrictions, conditions and limitations, as hereinafter set forth: Beginning at the corner of said Taylor's tract, where the north line of Eglantine street, if extended, would intersect the east line of East Row; thence with said Taylor's land north 38 east, to a point where the west line of said Taylor's lane, extended straight, would intersect the same; thence with the line of said Taylor's lane south 51 east, to a point on the Covert Run turnpike; thence south 39¼ east, to said Taylor's post-and-rail fence at the foot of the hill; thence south 30¼ west, to a point in East Row; thence with the same to Harris street; thence binding on James Taylor's East Row addition laid out last year and recorded, to the corner of East Row and Jefferson streets; thence with East Row to the place of beginning, containing seventy-five acres, more or less: *Provided, however,* That the city of Newport shall not be allowed to levy any tax or assessments of any kind on said above described tract of land while owned by him for the period of four years from the passage of this act: *And provided also,* That said Taylor reserves to himself and his heirs and legal representatives the right to control the way and manner of laying off said tract of land as additions to the said city of Newport: *And provided also,* That if, at the end of the four years, any part of said tract of land shall not be laid off by him into lots, but used by him for agricultural purposes, that the same shall be taxed at a fair rate as such, by the acre, and not as town lots.

Approved March 4, 1869.

CHAPTER 1741.

AN ACT to extend the corporate limits of Newport.

Be it enacted by the General Assembly of the Commonwealth of Kentucky:

That the following tracts of land are hereby added to and made part of the city of Newport, by James Taylor, subject to all the laws and regulations relating to said city as now established: Beginning in the easterly line of East Row, where the southerly line of Jefferson street, extended, intersects said East Row: thence with Jefferson street, extended, north 50½. east 220 feet; thence parallel with East Row north, 39¼ east, to the south line of Harris street; thence with Harris street to East Row; thence with East Row to the place of beginning, containing seven and fifty-seven hundredths acres. Also the following tract of land: Beginning in the southerly line of Williamson street, where the easterly line of Saratoga street intersects the same; thence with the southerly line of Williamson street to the east line of East Row; thence with East Row south, 39 east, seventy-four and forty-five hundredths feet; thence south 30¼ west, to a point where the easterly line of Saratoga street, extended, intersects the same; thence with Saratoga street to the place of beginning—said two tracts having been sub-divided into lots and plats, recorded in the county court clerk's office, in Campbell county, Kentucky, reference being had to the same will fully appear.

Approved March 4, 1869.

CHAPTER 1742.

AN ACT to re-enact and amend the Town Charter of the Town of Dixon, in Webster County.

Be it enacted by the General Assembly of the Commonwealth of Kentucky:

§ 1. That the charter of the town of Dixon, in Webster county, Kentucky, approved the 6th February, 1861, be, and the same is hereby, re-enacted, and, so far as not inconsistent with the provisions of this act, is hereby declared to be in full force and virtue.

§ 2. That James M. Dixon, Dr. Geo. P. Cosby, P. H. Jones, George W. Soverin, and M. C. Doris, be, and they are hereby, appointed trustees of said town, to act as such until the regular election as hereinafter prescribed.

§ 3. That the boundary of said town shall be the same as fixed in the said act of the 6th of February, 1861, chartering said town.

1869.   § 4. That the officers of said town shall consist of a
police judge, town marshal, assessor, and five trustees,
all of whom shall be residents of said town, and white
men over twenty-one years old; and the police judge
and marshal shall respectively have the same qualifications as are required of county court judges and sheriffs.

§ 5. That a police judge of said town shall be elected
by the qualified voters thereof on the first Monday in
August, 1869, and every four years thereafter, whose
term of office shall be four years, and until his successor
is duly elected and qualified; that he shall have concurrent jurisdiction with the justices of the peace for Webster county in all matters of a civil character, and exclusive jurisdiction of all criminal and penal actions
arising in the boundary of said town, of which justices
of the peace by law have jurisdiction; and shall be entitled to the same fees as are, from time to time, allowed
justices of the peace for similar services; that said police
judge shall keep a docket book, order book, and execution book, in which to make all necessary entries; and
that all process, warrants and executions, issued by him
or from his office, shall be, when executed, returned to
his said office for trial, judgment, or other proper steps
to be taken thereon; that said police judge shall be a
conservator of the peace, and shall, before he enters
upon the discharge of the duties of his said office, take
the several oaths and execute the bonds prescribed by
the Constitution and laws of the State of Kentucky, as
are now or may hereafter be required of the justices of
the peace of this Commonwealth; that vacancies in said
office of police judge in said town shall be filled by
appointment by the trustees of said town, until the next
regular election next thereafter; that said police judge
shall be commissioned by the Governor of this State,
and shall hold his regular terms of court on the second
Mondays in March, June, September, and December in
each year.

§ 6. That a marshal for said town shall be elected by
the qualified voters of said town on the first Monday in
August, 1869, and every two years thereafter, whose term
of office shall be two years, and until his successor shall
be duly elected and qualified. That said marshal shall
have concurrent jurisdiction with constables of Webster
county, and he shall execute and return all process, warrants, executions, &c., that may be issued from the office
of the police judge of said town. That said marshal shall
be entitled to the same fees and commissions in all cases
that constables are now or may hereafter be entitled to;
that he collect all taxes, fines, and other dues that may
hereafter be due the town of Dixon or its legally consti-

tuted authorities, and pay the same (less ten per cent for collecting) over to the chairman of the board of trustees of said town, and take his receipt for the same; that he collect the tax of said town, and pay the same over, as above specified, within one month after the list thereof shall be furnished him by the proper officer, under pain of ten per cent. damages on the amount uncollected and paid over as above specified, to be recovered off of him and his securities in his official bond by the chairman of the trustees of said town, by motion before the police judge of said town, after having been first duly notified by written notice at least five days next before the rendition of the judgment; that said marshal be, and he is hereby, held responsible on his official bond to any and all parties for whom he may collect money and fail to pay over the same according to law, or for any malfeasance, misfeasance, or nonfeasance in office, to the same extent and in the same manner that constables are now or may hereafter be liable on their official bonds; and for the remedy whereof, the party or parties aggrieved shall have redress against the said marshal and his securities on his official bond, by motion before the police judge of said town, by giving written notice thereof for at least five days next before the day of judgment thereon; that vacancies in the office of marshal of said town shall be filled by appointment by the police judge thereof, until the next regular election next thereafter; that the marshal of said town, before he enters upon the discharge of the duties of his office, shall, before the police judge of said town, execute bond, with good and approved security, to be worth not less than ten thousand dollars, conditioned as constables' bonds are; which bond shall be attested by the police judge of said town, and by him entered of record in his order book, and filed and safely kept in his office; upon which bond suit or motion may be instituted, from time to time, as above specified.

§ 7. That an assessor for said town shall be elected by the qualified voters thereof on the first Monday in August in the year 1869, and every four years thereafter, whose term of office shall be the same as that of the police judge of said town, whose duty shall be to take a full and fair list of all the tithes and taxable property of said town, at such times and in such manner as may be prescribed by the board of trustees of said town, and return a full and complete copy thereof to said board within such time as they may require. That said assessor, before he enters upon the discharge of the duties of his office, shall take all the oaths prescribed by the Constitution and laws of Kentucky for assessors of counties, and execute bond, with approved security, before the police judge of said town, in the penalty of one thousand dollars, for the faithful discharge of all the duties of his said office. That said police judge attest said bond and enter the same of record in his order book, and file the same in his office for safe-keeping: upon which bond suit or motion in the police court of said town may be, from time to time, instituted by the trustees of said town for any breach thereof. That said assessor shall be liable on his said bond for any malfeasance, misfeasance, or nonfeasance in office, to the same extent that county assessors are liable on their official bonds; and he shall receive such compensation for his said services as the trustees of said town may, by an order entered on their books, allow him from time to time. That vacancies in the office of assessor of said town shall be filled by appointment by the police judge thereof, until the next regular election.

§ 8. That there shall be five trustees for said town, elected by the qualified voters thereof, on the first Monday in August, in the year 1869, and every two years thereafter, whose term of office shall be two years, and until their successors are duly elected and qualified. That said trustees shall, immediately after their election, meet and organize by electing one of their body chairman, who shall be styled the chairman of the board of trustees of the town of Dixon, and by electing one of their said body clerk, who shall be styled the clerk of the board of trustees of the town of Dixon. That the chairman of the board of said trustees shall have power to call a meeting of the trustees of said town, at any and all times that he shall see proper, for the transaction of business pertaining to their said office. That said chairman shall preside over all the meetings and deliberations of said board of trustees, and preserve good order and decorum, and sign all minutes, orders, drafts, &c., entered of record by said trustees. That he receive all taxes and other dues coming to said town or its legally constituted authorities, and receipt therefor, and disburse the same according to the order of the said board of trustees. That he make settlements of his official fiduciary transactions quarter-yearly with the police judge of said town; that said settlements shall show his debits and credits; and said settlements shall be entered of record by the police judge on his order-book, and filed in his office. That said chairman, before he enters upon the discharge of the duties of his office, shall take the oaths prescribed by the Constitution and laws of Kentucky for chairmen of boards of trustees of towns, and execute bond, with good security, to be approved by the police judge of said town, in the penalty of one thousand dollars, for the faithful performance of all the duties of his office, which bond shall be attested by said police judge, and by him entered of

1869.

record on his order-book, and filed in his office for safe-keeping, upon which bond suit or motion may be, from time to time, instituted in the police court of said town by any one aggrieved, for any mal, non, or misfeasance committed by the said chairman in his official transactions, by giving five days' written notice thereof before the day of judgment or trial thereon. That the clerk of the said board of trustees shall keep a book in which he shall make an entry of all the meetings of said board of trustees, and enter therein all the proceedings of said meetings, and keep and preserve the same, and give attested copies thereof when required. That the trustees of said town are hereby empowered to assess and collect, as hereinbefore stipulated, annually, taxes for the purposes of said town, not exceeding twenty-five cents on each one hundred dollars of taxable property in said town, and a tax not exceeding two dollars on each tithe, annually, in said town. That said trustees shall see to and keep all the streets and cross-streets, alleys and sidewalks, in said town clean and in good repair all the time; and they shall have power to compel the owners of real estate in said town, on Main and main cross-streets, to pave or cause to be paved and curbed in front of their said property, the curbing to be of good material; the pavement to be of brick, six feet wide, and to see that the same be kept clean and in good repair all the time; and in case the owners of said property fail or refuse to curb, pave, &c., as herein provided, the said trustees are hereby empowered to have the same done, by advertising and letting out the same to the lowest bidder; and the said property thus curbed and paved shall, in every instance, be bound to him who does the curbing and paving thereof until the price therefor shall be fully paid him by the owner thereof, his agent or attorney; and the said lien thus created may be enforced by the contractor by action in the circuit court, and the property sold in satisfaction of said lien. That said trustees shall have power to pass all needful rules, regulations and by-laws, for the proper government of the said town and its citizens, and the property therein contained, that they may, from time to time, see fit, under circumstances pointing to the ends of civil and moral justice, not inconsistent with the Constitution and laws of the State of Kentucky. That all vacancies in the office of trustee in said town shall be filled by the police judge thereof, by appointment, until the next regular election. That said trustees shall be liable to presentment by the grand jury, and prosecuted for any and all misfeasance, nonfeasance, or malfeasance in office, as provided by the laws of this State. That said trustees

1869.   shall have power to employ an attorney at law to prosecute all actions in behalf of said town, both criminal,
penal, and civil, and pay him such fees as they may agree
upon.

§ 9. That all fines, forfeitures, and taxes arising in said
town shall be, when collected, paid to the chairman of the
board of trustees of said town, and by him disbursed for
the benefit of the streets, alleys, and other public property
of said town, as may be, from time to time, ordered by the
said board of trustees.

§ 10. That H. H. Smith be, and he is hereby, appointed
police judge of said town of Dixon, to act as such until
the regular election, as hereinbefore prescribed. And that
Henry Brewer be, and he is hereby, appointed town marshal in and for the town of Dixon, to act as such until the
regular election, as hereinbefore mentioned; and that C.
S. Cobb be, and he is hereby, appointed assessor in and
for the town of Dixon, to act as such until the regular
election aforesaid.

§ 11. That all acts and parts of acts inconsistent with
this act are hereby repealed; and this act to take effect
and be in force from and after its passage.

                                   Approved March 4, 1869.

CHAPTER 1743.

AN ACT to amend an act, entitled "An act to incorporate the Town of
New Concord, in Calloway County."

WHEREAS, The election mentioned in section five of an
act, entitled "An act to incorporate the town of New Concord, in Calloway county," was not held at the time prescribed therein; therefore,

*Be it enacted by the General Assembly of the Commonwealth
of Kentucky:*

§ 1. That it shall be lawful for the first election of trustees of the town of New Concord, in Calloway county, to
be held on the first Monday in April, 1869, at which time
there shall be elected a police judge, marshal, and treasurer. The said election is hereby authorized to be held
by Cyrus Owen, P. A. Stilley, and C. D. Boaz, or any two
of them, who shall return the poll-books to the county
clerk's office of said county, there to be kept and used, and
in the manner as prescribed by law; and their certificates
of election shall be given to each of the officers named in
this election.

§ 2. This act to take effect from its passage.

                                   Approved March 5, 1869.

INDEX TO LOCAL AND PRIVATE ACTS.